The Practice of Theology

The
Practice of
Theology

A Reader

edited by

Colin E. Gunton, Stephen R. Holmes
and Murray A. Rae

scm press

. © SCM Press 2001

British Library Cataloguing in Publication data

A catalogue record for this book is available
from the British Library

0 334 02816 7

First published in 2001 by SCM Press
9–17 St Albans Place, London N1 0NX

SCM Press is a division of
SCM-Canterbury Press Ltd

Typeset by Rowland Phototypesetting Ltd,
Bury St Edmunds, Suffolk
and printed in Great Britain by
Biddles Ltd, Guildford and King's Lynn

CONTENTS

I.5 Reflecting on experience of God

PART II:
THE NATURE OF THEOLOGICAL CLAIMS

II.1 Can we know anything about God anyway?

C *Modern attempts at recovery*

II.2 How do we know what we know?

II.3 The nature of religious language

II.4 Neutral and committed knowledge

PART III:
DOING THEOLOGY TODAY

III.1 Modernity and postmodernity

III.2 The rise of local theologies

A Liberation theology

B Feminist theology

III.3 Christian theology in a multi-faith world

PART IV

Doing Theology in the University Today:
   ## Colin Gunton

For Brian Horne

PREFACE

'There are a hundred faults in this thing, and a hundred things might be said to prove them beauties.' So began the advertisement for Oliver Goldsmith's masterpiece, *The Vicar of Wakefield*. No doubt the same is true of every book, and no doubt Goldsmith's refusal to anticipate and answer his critics was wise. Nonetheless, it is perhaps worth saying one or two things here about the conception of this reader.

We are conscious that we have told the story of the development of Christian theology from a particular perspective, and that other perspectives could have been chosen. The grand narrative here runs from the Fathers, through Aquinas and Calvin, to Schleiermacher and Barth, although many texts point to alternative developments. In part, this is simply an expression of context: in other places, it would have made more sense to follow the Greek, rather than Latin, development, in which case the Palamite – one of our more embarrassing omissions – would have become central. Again, we might at the Reformation have chosen to follow a Roman (Cajetan and Suarez are both missing) or Lutheran (there is nothing here by Quenstedt) trail. The broadly Reformed path we have in fact chosen, however, seems to us to be more relevant to at least those British and American university introductory theology courses of which we are aware. Again, an alternative turn would have been possible after Schleiermacher, focusing on those writers who followed, rather than opposed, his re-orientation of theological method; this is not so much a question of context, as a judgement that the 'conservative' route we in fact chose seemed to us to be simply more intellectually interesting and likely to be more nearly correct in the long run: where in that liberal tradition, after all, is there a theologian even half as creative, as convincing, or as academically powerful, as Barth?

Amongst the modern writers represented, our choices are not a reflection of the esteem in which we hold particular theologians so much as the texts which we felt best summarized important positions. There are theologians of great eminence and ability not found here, simply because they have not focused their attention on particular questions of method. At certain points our choices were also dictated by academically indefensible, but practically unavoidable, issues of copyright. We are as aware of the omissions and gaps as any reader will be – more so, inasmuch as we struggled over what to leave out in order to meet the word limit, or worked unsuccessfully to obtain permission to use an important text. Nonetheless, we believe that what is here meets our aim of providing an overview of what Christian theology is and how it is practised.

Finally, we should perhaps note that we have allowed the extracts to retain their own stylistic integrity, so texts which originally italicized foreign phrases, adopted American English spelling, or capitalized pronouns referring to God, have been left in this state.

It is a pleasure as well as a duty to record our gratitude to Alex Wright and, particularly, Anna Hardman of SCM Press. With constant good humour and patience, they have bent rules and stretched deadlines to enable us to produce the book we wanted to produce; this reader would be a less satisfactory work, and certainly would have appeared later (if at all), were it not for them.

Goldsmith entitled chapter XX of *The Vicar of Wakefield* 'The History of a philosophical Vagabond, pursuing Novelty, but losing Content'. In it, George Primrose recalls that he 'resolved to write a book that was wholly new', but could find nothing of any value left to say: 'The jewels of truth have been so often imported by others, that nothing was left for me to import'. We do not find the situation so desperate, by any means, but equally make no apology for re-importing these 'jewels of truth', and for arranging them in such a way that we hope their varied beauties will be more easily discovered and grasped by others.

It so happens that the impending changes to the theology courses at King's College London which provided the initial inspiration for this reader coincide with the retirement of our colleague, Dr Brian Horne. He will be missed for many reasons, not least of which is his record over many years of being a truly outstanding teacher of theology. Every student who was fortunate enough to come into contact with him will testify to his warmth, patience, inspiration, encouragement and clarity. For this reason it seems particularly appropriate to dedicate a textbook such as this to Brian.

CEG, SRH and MAR
Pentecost 2001

ACKNOWLEDGEMENTS

Full bibliographic details may be found at the foot of each extract, but here we wish to record our gratitude to all those who have permitted us to use copyrighted material:

To Augsburg Fortress for the material in extracts I.1.4 (reprinted from *Luther's Works, Vol 35*, edited by E. Theodore Bachman, copyright © 1960 Fortress Press. Used by permission of Augsburg Fortress.); 1.2.12 (reprinted from *The Word of God and Tradition* by Gerhard Ebeling, translation copyright © 1968 Fortress Press. Used by permission of Augsburg Fortress); and I.3.8 (reprinted from *Luther's Works, Vol 34*, edited by Lewis W. Spitz, copyright © 1960 Fortress Press. Used by permission of Augsburg Fortress.)

To Beacon Press for extract III.2.4 (reproduced from *Beyond God the Father* by Mary Daly, copyright © 1973 by Mary Daly. Reprinted by permission of Beacon Press, Boston.)

To Blackwell Publishers Ltd for extract III.2.6

To Cambridge University Press for extracts III.1.6 and III.3.9

To the Christian Century Foundation for extract I.3.12 (copyright 1951 Christian Century Foundation. Reprinted with permission from the Dec. 19, 1957 issue of the *Christian Century*. Subscriptions: $42/yr (36 issues), from P.O. Box 378, Mt Morris, IL 61054.)

To T&T Clark Ltd for extracts I.5.4, II.1.7, II.1.8, II.1.9, II.2.7, II.3.4, II.3.9, II.4.7, II.4.8 and III.3.5

To Continuum for extracts I.1.8, I.4.3, II.1.5, II.1.6, II.2.1, II.2.2, II.2.6, II.4.4 and III.2.1

To CTBI for extract 1.3.6

To Darton, Longman and Todd for extracts I.3.11, I.5.6 (taken from *Foundations Of Christian Faith* by Karl Rahner, published and copyright 1978 by Darton, Longman and Todd Ltd, and used by permission of the publishers.); III.3.6 (taken from *Theological Investigations Vol V* by Karl Rahner, published and copyright 1966 by Darton, Longman and Todd Ltd, and used by permission of the publishers.)

To Wm. B. Eerdmans Publishing Co. for extracts I.1.11, I.2.9 and III.3.8

To the Edwin Mellen Press for the material in extract I.1.5

To HarperCollins for extracts I.2.12 and III.3.2

To Hodder and Stoughton Ltd for extract I.3.10

To *The Journal of Theology for Southern Africa* for extract I.3.9

To *Louvain Studies* for extract I.2.11

To the Methodist Publishing House for extract II.1.1 (*The Letters of St Athanasius Concerning the Holy Spirit* copyright © Epworth Press and used by permission of Methodist Publishing House.)

To the *New Left Review* for extract III.1.1

To Oxford University Press for extracts I.4.9, II.4.9, III.1.4 and III.1.5 (reprinted by permission of Oxford University Press, Inc.) and I.5.5 and II.3.8 (reprinted by permission of Oxford University Press.)

To Paulist Press for extract I.2.4 (excerpted from *Prosper of Aquitaine* translated by P. De Letter, SJ, copyright © 1963 Newman Press. Used with permission of Paulist Press www.paulistpress.com.)

To Peeters for extract II.2.8

To Penguin Putnam Inc. for extract III.1.2 ('The Gay Science', from *The Portable Nietzsche* by Friedrich Nietzsche, edited by Walter Kaufmann, copyright 1954 by The Viking Press, renewed copyright © 1982 by Viking Penguin Inc. Used by permission of Viking Penguin, a division of Penguin Putnam Inc.)

To P&R Publishing for extracts I.1.10 and I.4.5

To Princeton University Press for extract I.4.7

To the Scottish Academic Press for extract II.3.6

To SPCK for the material in extracts I.1.2, I.3.2, II.1.3 and II.3.7

To the University of Chicago Press for extract I.5.8, (copyright © The University of Chicago, 1951.)

To Westminster John Knox Press for extracts I.1.7, I.2.5, II.2.3 and II.4.5 (reproduced from *Calvin: Institutes of The Christian Religion*, Library of Christian Classics, edited by John T. McNeill.) Used by permission of Westminster John Knox Press.); I.3.7 (reproduced from *Calvin: Theological Treatises*, Library of Christian Classics, edited by J. K. S. Reid. Used by permission of Westminster John Knox Press.); and III.2.7 (reproduced from *An Introduction to Christian Theology*, edited by Roger A. Badham copyright © 1998 Westminster John Knox Press. Used by permission of Westminster John Knox Press.)

To Alan Wolter for extract II.3.2.

Every effort has been made to identify and acknowledge the copyright holders for the various materials included here, but if there are any inadvertent errors or omissions, we apologise and will undertake to rectify the situation in any future edition.

In addition we would like to record our gratitude to Dr Mike Higton, Dr Stuart Murray-Williams and Kelly Kapic for their advice on various points.

GENERAL INTRODUCTION

I

This reader is designed to be used as a sourcebook for an introductory course exploring two questions: what systematic theology is and how it should be done. The various excerpts included are attempts to demonstrate something of the range of available positions on these issues, both through history and in theological work today. Of course the range presented is not exhaustive (More than once the last text to be reluctantly excluded from this or that section was one representing a minor, but in our view interesting, position that was not otherwise hinted at. One or two of these 'survived' as asides in the section introductions, if nowhere else) and the length of excerpts prohibits any serious presentation of the various cases made by the writers included, but an attentive reader of this selection of material should still gain some sense of the shape of the discipline of theology.

By 'theology' we mean, as a first approximation, the intellectual discipline of asking who God is and what the world is like in the light of the gospel of Jesus Christ, and consequently how we should live before God in the world. Theology is the hard intellectual work of asking what it means to believe that in Jesus Christ God the Son walked among us as one of us, died for our sins, rose again on the third day, ascended to the right hand of the Father, sent the Spirit upon the church, and will return one day to bring in his kingdom. If this story is true then it changes everything. Theology is the task of exploring that change.

Theology as here considered is a specifically Christian discipline: saying this is not to imply that other religious and philosophical traditions cannot or do not engage in rational discourse about the divine, but to recognize that there is something methodologically distinctive about such discourse in a Christian context (as we presume there is about such discourse in a Jewish, Islamic, Buddhist, or indeed any other, context). In part this is for historical reasons: the early and definitive work of Christian theology was affected decisively by the intellectual climate in which it was performed, and so the particular respect for rationality and careful statement that marked Greek philosophy was inherited by Christian theology and has remained influential, despite the demands that it cease to be made by some voices represented in this reader.

The distinctiveness goes much further than this, however: every rational discourse is necessarily shaped by its object, and so different religious descriptions of who God is (or the gods are) will give rise to different discourses. To take merely one example, central to a Christian account of God is the incarnation, the assertion that God made himself available to us in a radical way, completely bridging the gulf that separates the divine from the human by being 'made man' and living as man, as one particular Jewish man, with us. One result of this is that it has been characteristic of Christian theology to be rather bold in speaking about God's nature and purposes, because God has made such knowledge available. What the great twentieth-century theologian Karl Barth referred to as 'the humanity of God', the fact that God is God toward us, for us, amongst us even, makes an enormous difference to the work of Christian theology. It is noticeable that the intellectually serious discourse of other religious traditions is often called 'philosophy' rather than 'theology' by its practitioners: from most points of view, to claim to be able to talk meaningfully about God (*theos*) would be the height of arrogance; rather, one patiently explores wisdom (*sophia*). For Christians, however, God has given himself to be known, and so we may dare to speak about who he is.

(A similar argument defended the visual theology of icons in the Eastern Orthodox tradition of Christian theology. The practice grew up very early in the Eastern tradition of using pictures of Christ and the Saints as aids to prayer, but the propriety of this practice was disputed on the basis of the appeal, still so decisive for some other religious traditions, that God who is spirit could not be represented visually without falling into idolatry. This was met with an argument based on Christology: in Christ we have seen God face to face, and so God's face may be drawn. Likewise, Christian theology begins with the belief that human beings have looked God full in the face, so to speak, and so presumes to speak with familiarity about God.)

II

The reader is divided into four parts. Part I, on sources, considers where theological claims may be grounded: if we are to speak of God's nature and purposes, we must find some place or practice which offers trustworthy data about who God is and what he is about. In a theological argument, where two people have different views on who God is, they need a common point of reference to appeal to, a locus of authority from which they can seek to convince each other. Various locations are commonly appealed to in theological work: Scripture; the teaching of the Christian tradition; certain documents which enshrine doctrinal norms; rational proofs; or direct experience of God. As will be clear from the texts, these are not necessarily exclusive options, and the question is not so much which to choose as how to relate and balance them all, and hence how to deal with apparent differences.

There are also questions about the nature of these authorities, and the proper way to appeal to them: How is Scripture to be read? If the historic Christian tradition has authority, then in a divided church, which part of that tradition is to be listened to? Again, does authority exist in the church as a whole, or in a particular ecclesiastical hierarchy or teaching office within the church? Similar questions may be and have been asked of each of the proposed sources discussed in the first part, and the extracts seek to represent something of the range of answers that have been given. The challenge in each case is the necessarily utterly serious nature of whatever authority is accorded to these sources: something St Ignatius Loyola, the founder of the Jesuit order, understood well when he asserted that if only the church were to teach that black is white, he would believe it.

In Part II, we turn to questions about what a theological assertion, a claim about who God is, might mean. The statement that 'this chair is wooden' remains rather easy to interpret (despite the attempts of some philosophy to complicate matters!). 'God is good' might be more difficult, however: 'God' is a more difficult concept to think about than 'this chair', and so our confidence that we mean the same thing when we use the word must be reduced. Further problems occur when we take biblical and traditional Christian language such as 'God is a rock'. Clearly, the meaning here is not literal, but does that mean that the language is 'poetic' and so not 'true'? In which case is all our language about God not true, or at least not as true as our language about chairs? One section in Part II, 'The nature of religious language', picks up directly on these questions, exploring key theological discussions around apophaticism (the idea that we speak about God best by speaking negatively, i.e. saying what he is not rather than what he is), analogy, metaphor and symbol in order to make sense of precisely what is being said when a theological claim is made.

It is tempting just to accept that theological language is necessarily untrue, and so deny that we can ever actually know anything about

God. The modern form of this is a religious relativism: spirituality is a good thing in a person, and those spiritual practices which help you are to be welcomed and commended, but any suggestion that there is any actual knowledge about spiritual things – including God – is simply excluded, and so any suggestion that particular practices and beliefs might be 'false' or 'wrong' is to be resisted. Such ideas are not only currently fashionable, but have a long history. Christian theologians have rarely found them convincing, and the various responses that have been made are explored in the first section of Part II, 'Can we know anything about God anyway?'.

The second section, 'How do we know what we know?', assumes that these arguments succeed (the study of theology would be fairly pointless if they do not, after all) and asks how we know what we in fact do know about God. The separation is fairly artificial, of course, and it may be that the best response to the first question is to ask the second: it is intrinsic to Christian theology to claim that knowledge of God is in fact received in the gospel of Jesus Christ; the only interesting question is how it is received. A variety of answers follow, many of them suggesting that models of personal relationship are most appropriate: we come to know God in an analogous way to that in which we come to know other human beings, by committing ourselves to a relationship with him.

One consequence of such an account is the suggestion that only someone who has made such a commitment can actually have knowledge of God, that there is a knowledge effectively internal to Christian commitment which those outside the faith may overhear but will never understand. Such suggestions are explored in the fourth section of Part II, on 'Neutral and committed knowledge'. The idea might be like the relationship of a tone-deaf person to music: he or she may, with sufficient study, understand musical theory far better than most of the population, but their knowledge will be in some sense of the wrong sort; there is an importance sense in which that person will have less appreciation for a fine performance of a Bach 'cello suite than an untutored person with an ear for music. Just so, it has regularly been asserted throughout the Christian tradition that one who approaches theology without Christian commitment can become proficient in the arguments but still never grasp what is really going on in theological discourse. As Samuel Taylor Coleridge was in the habit of saying of those who were not living the Christian life, 'They must become better before they become wiser.'

Part III turns to a cluster of questions that are related only in being significant issues in theological work currently. We begin with a discussion of 'Modernity and postmodernity'. 'Postmodern' has become a very fashionable term in many areas of discourse, but the particular issue here is the way the philosophical questions raised affect Christian theology. The move from a 'pre-modern' era which has been accused of simple credulity in its allegedly uncritical and unreflective acceptance of the truth and explanatory power of the Christian narrative, to a 'modern' world-view which demanded very particular forms of evidence before any assertion could be believed, and then to 'postmodernity' and a rising dissatisfaction with the limitations and the pretensions of the modernist accounts all force theologians to examine carefully the basis on which they seek to build their theology.

The second section picks up a recent move in theology which might be regarded as evidence of the coming of postmodernity, the rise of what have been called 'local theologies'. These are theological systems which are self-consciously located in particular cultural, social, economic or even geographical contexts, and which proceed by examining the particular challenges and comforts brought by the gospel to those contexts. Such theological work is hotly disputed for a variety of reasons, and we have sought in the space available to represent the main contours of that dispute.

The third section of Part III, 'Christian theology in a multi-faith world', reflects a growing realization that has taken place in Christian theology in the past century or two. It is difficult now to imagine never having met a person from a different faith tradition, or even anyone who themselves has never met such a person, but it is not unlikely that many Christian believers were in that situation for much of the history of the church. The increasing awareness of other religious traditions has led to a variety of responses, which the later extracts in this section illustrate. We begin, however, with several texts indicating the problem is not a new one: the church began, after all, in a religiously plural situation in the Roman empire, and a refusal to fall in line with the state religion was the immediate cause of most of the early Christian martyrdoms.

Part IV contains the one extended piece in the book, an essay on the practice of theology in the light of all that has come before.

III

The subjects covered here, concerning the basis, possibility and proper nature of theological claims are sometimes described as the 'prolegomena' to theology. The various questions here considered do form a connected whole, and are about issues that may well be conveniently discussed at the head of a theological system to make it clear what is being done in what comes afterwards. Thus far to describe them as 'prolegomena' is useful and not greatly objectionable. It does, however, invite one misconception that it would be as well to identify and deal with here: the writings included in this reader are, almost without exception, theological rather than pre-theological. That is, in speaking of 'prolegomena' we are not intending to describe the work of establishing the possibility of theology on some non-theological ground, rather we are describing the theological task of self-reflection, of thinking theologically about the work of the theologian.

This is necessarily the case because Christian theology must claim to be speaking at a logically basic level: if God created all that is, then there is no more basic reality we can go to in order to establish the validity of discourse about God. Rather, all discourse has its validity established by comparison to this basic ground. Just so, it would be bad theology to look elsewhere for a defence of the possibility of doing theology; this discipline can only make sense on its own terms.

All the various strategies of appealing elsewhere for evidence of the truth of Christian theology, then, are improper if they are regarded as anything more than *ad hoc* apologetics. There is, for example, nothing wrong (theologically) with seeking to convince a sceptic of the truth of Scripture by appealing to evidence derived from historical research (assuming the evidence is fairly handled, of course); but to seek to base the authority of Scripture on history, rather than a theological account of how the triune God has chosen to make himself known, would be to concede too much – everything, in fact.

So, although this reader is about how to do theology, the answers given are unashamedly and irreducibly theological. This is just as well: inasmuch as theology is a practical discipline, one which issues in changed lives, not just changed minds, then it is clearly a discipline that cannot be understood without being practised, any more than it is possible to learn how to swim by reading books about swimming. To wrestle with the extracts here, to side with one against another, or to find one's own position within their various arguments; this is to be about the business of doing theology, to take the first steps on the road to becoming a theologian.

IV

Finally in this introduction, a note about the extracts. As this is intended to be an introductory text, the 'classics' are mostly here – they are classics, after all, because they establish a point with an economy and a brilliance that are alike remarkable. There are also some more unusual texts which we found interesting, arresting or enlightening. The texts span the history of Christian theology; the reasons for that need not be spelt out in detail here, as the various texts in 1.2 are devoted to establishing why beliefs and writings from throughout the Christian tradition should be taken seriously. Suffice to say that we find such arguments wholly convincing, and part of the motivation behind the production of this work was a desire to have a text which would intro- duce our students to the high points of the theological tradition at the same time as introducing them to theology – because a student is not properly introduced to theology if he or she has no knowledge of the tradition.

Each extract comes with only as much introduction (in italicized type, above the text) as is necessary for comprehension. More general historical and biographical details of authors and texts can be found collected together at the back of the book. Unusual or technical words within the extracts are defined in the glossary, which is also found at the end.

Christian theology boasts amongst its sources some of the greatest minds in intellectual history, and some of the most powerful writers; it deals with ultimate issues of life and death, and of meaning and pur- pose; it explores and defends ideas for which in the early centuries of the church and alike today in some parts of the world women and men have been prepared to suffer great personal hardship, and even risk death, rather than disown. It may be – it often is – hard work; it may be existentially or emotionally challenging; it may demand that we change our minds and lives; at times it may enlighten or enrage in equal measure; but the rewards are still out of all proportion to the cost. These texts, so cruelly ripped from their contexts, are perhaps only snapshots in a guidebook of what may be seen and experienced by one with the discipline and commitment to scale the peaks of this mountain range, but in putting them together it is our hope and our prayer that some at least who read them will glimpse the beauties of theology and be inspired to climb as high and to range as far as they are able to go. The task of exploring how God's all-sufficient gift of himself in Jesus Christ is sufficient in each particular circumstance will remain an urgent one until the Lord returns; if this reader should play a part in encouraging some to take up that task, our work will have been more than worthwhile.

PART I: SOURCES FOR THEOLOGY

I.1 Scripture as the source of Christian theology:

Introductory essay

The title, first: 'the source of Christian theology'? It is, I think, correct. The definite article in English may convey a range of meanings, after all. If it were being used here to indicate uniqueness, that Scripture is the only source from which theological claims may draw support or validation, then it would indicate a defensible position, one that is represented in the pages that follow (notice particularly the regular theme in the following sections asserting the relative authority of tradition, creeds, councils and the like: they are important only in so far as they correctly codify the teaching of Scripture), and one for which I have much sympathy. It would, however, not be universally accepted (see, for instance, the comments of Basil of Caesarea in I.2.2), and it is not what is being indicated by this title. The definite article may also convey pre-eminence, one item amongst others to be sure, but one that stands out sufficiently to claim first place. It would be fair to assert that there can be no properly Christian theology that does not give at least such a place to Scripture.

Christian theology, after all, must speak centrally about Jesus Christ, and about all other realities as they are known in and through him. Trivially, Jesus Christ is known only, finally, through Scripture. There are, to be sure, occasional references elsewhere: that a Jewish man of this name lived, and preached, and claimed to work miracles, and was executed, and left followers: this much we might know. To do theology we need more, however: to know his teaching; the relationship he claimed with the God of Israel; the interpretation he, and those who reflected afterwards, put on his shameful death, and on his resurrection; and enough of the religious history of the people of Israel to make sense of all this. We need, in short, to know those things that the church has found in the Scriptures, and that is why Scripture is 'the' source of Christian theology.

Which only raises more questions, of course: Which books, and on what grounds? How do we interpret the books? Can anyone understand them, or must we rely on specialists? These questions, in various forms, occur again and again in the texts that follow. One example might be the question of who can claim the authority of the Bible. Tertullian (I.1.1) in the second century claimed that only the church, defined by those who held to a particular doctrinal tradition, could understand the Scriptures; the heretics quoted texts to no avail. A millennium and more later, the Roman Catholic Church used the same argument against those who protested and sought reform, who countered with an assertion that the plain teaching of Scripture could not be denied by anyone (see the Decree of the Council of Trent, I.1.6). Today, a debate may be found between a guild of academic biblical specialists and certain theologians as to whether the Bible is most properly read by the academy or the church.

A second perennial problem can be traced through the texts in this chapter: How does Scripture, the Old Testament in particular, speak about Jesus Christ? In amongst these ancient Hebrew law codes, collections of proverbial wisdom, poems and prayers, prophetic condemnations, histories of clans and kings, and even a faintly scandalous erotic poem, where do we find a witness to Jesus? A recent fashion amongst Christian theologians for referring to the Old Testament as the 'Hebrew Bible' makes the point: this is not Christian Scripture, it is Hebrew Scripture, necessary to understanding the genuinely Christian New Testament, to be sure, but not in itself a Christian book. Calling it, as the older Bibles did, 'The Old Testament of Our Lord and Saviour Jesus Christ' is simply inappropriate.

In the early church, the belief that Christ's life and work was 'according to the Scriptures [i.e., the Old Testament]' (1 Cor. 15.4) was commonplace. This is constantly assumed by the Gospels, the book of Acts, and the epistles, as again and again scriptural citations or allusions are used to explain the significance of certain actions of Jesus. These Scriptures, after all, were God's witness through his prophets to his purposes in the world, and if God had raised this man from the dead, and exalted him to be Lord, and if this man is indeed God incarnate, then it was only natural to assume that these books would speak often about this man. Besides which, Jesus himself appeared to regard the Scriptures as speaking with God's authority, and his opinion carried weight. To begin with, Christian appeals to the Jewish Scriptures presumably took a fairly *ad hoc* form, as people noticed resonances between a particular text and a particular event in the life of Jesus. We can trace, however, some of the development towards a theological assertion, for instance in Tertullian's *Prescription against Heretics* (I.1.1), or Justin Martyr's *Dialogue with Trypho the Jew* (not included here).

To assert theologically that these books witness to Jesus, however, is to raise the question of interpretation in an acute form: how so? This, theological, background is necessary to understand the interpretative methods that have been common through much of the history of the church, witnessed to here by Origen (I.1.2) and John Cassian (I.1.3). Origen argues that the literal sense cannot be the essence of the meaning of Scripture, and Cassian offers the earliest codification of what was to become the standard Western position throughout the Middle Ages, that alongside the literal sense there are three 'spiritual' senses: the allegorical (a devotional, christological, or theological meaning); the anagogical (an eschatological meaning, referring to future things such as final judgment and consummation); and the tropological (a moral meaning, using the text to speak of ways in which we should live). These complex methods of interpretation never ignored the literal sense, as they have sometimes been accused of doing, but neither were they prepared to be restricted to the literal sense, seeking deeper readings which would speak more clearly of the life and atoning death of Jesus Christ, of the coming consummation of all things in him and of the ways in which we should live in the light of these truths.

The Reformers have sometimes been held up as the forerunners of the modern practice of non-theological, 'literal', reading. Whilst they certainly did object to the multiple senses and the profusion of imaginative readings, each claiming the authority of Scripture, that were present in their day, they did not do so in the name of any straightforwardly historical reading. Luther's *Brief Instruction* (I.1.4) or Hubmaier's *Christian Catechism* (I.1.5) show clearly the concern that the Bible should be about Jesus Christ and his gospel only. Calvin, again, sees the problem as how those who lived before Christ's day could have the saving knowledge of God as redeemer which their writings communicate (I.1.7). In calling for a return to the 'literal' sense of Scripture, it never occurred to these theologians that Scripture was not literally about Jesus Christ.

Two related developments in the centuries since the Reformation shape the last four extracts in this chapter: the rise of historical criticism and questions about inspiration. A new 'scientific' approach to history led to the Scriptures being treated as historical artefacts, written by people who were assumed to be primitive, and witnessing to the pressing issues of the time of their composition. Variously, then, the Old Testament could not be about Jesus Christ, but must be about the particular challenges facing the Israelites through their own history; the gospels should not be read as straightforward accounts of Christ's life, but as documents shaped by particular needs and factions in the early church; Paul's epistles were not attempts to apply a universal gospel to particular situations, but a series of witnesses to power struggles in the early Christian movement; and, most universally and fundamentally, each text meant what its original author meant, and nothing else. At the same time, treating the books of the Bible as a collection of historical artefacts enabled their own history to be examined, resulting in the suggestion of some complicated pre-histories, with more-or-less clumsy editors (or 'redactors') stitching together selections from earlier documents to suit their own purposes, thus leaving a complex text which had no unitary meaning but a surface intent (the redactor's) and a number of hidden, but discernible, positions belonging to the authors of the earlier texts. In the face of all this, finally, what could it possibly mean to say that God had 'inspired' these texts, and so that they were in some way authoritative?

It is probably safe to say that there is considerably less confidence about many of 'the assured results of modern criticism' than there was when that phrase was current, a century or so ago. What is of interest in the context of this Reader, however, is the theological implications of it all. One very positive aspect, for instance, has been the bringing to the fore of the fact that the Bible is a collection of human writings. Too often in history, particularly under the influence of the elaborate medieval interpretative strategies, Scripture has been treated as if it came into being in a similar way to the Qu'ran, according to devout Muslims, or the Torah, according to orthodox Jews: every word, every choice of synonym, every grammatical peculiarity was directly dictated and intended by God. Almost all Christian theologians would accept now that, whatever it means to say that God inspired Paul to write Romans, it does not mean that Paul's part in the process was no more than that of my computer's part in bringing this essay into being: a convenient method for getting the real author's thoughts on to paper. Paul's own personality, his commitments, his historical situation, all do affect and shape what he has to say.

This recognition is the content of Lessing's *On the Proof of the Spirit and of Power* (I.1.8), and is seen by Coleridge (I.1.9) as something to be positively celebrated, as enabling Scripture to speak much more powerfully. Warfield (I.1.10) is less happy with the consequences of this, and not without reason, given its effect on many Christian believers in the nineteenth century. Finally, Karl Barth (I.1.11) represents what might be the majority opinion amongst systematic theologians today, although with a subtlety and eloquence that is much less common: these men and women, precisely as the men and women they were, were enabled to speak words that are able to convey the truth of God.

Without the Bible there would be no Christian theology, and these texts still occupy a place of authority and pre-eminence in the discipline. Arguments may, and should, be had over what is meant when we say that 'God inspired Scripture'; and we may, and should, increasingly recognize the complexity and richness of the biblical witness. Neither of these, however, should detract from the fundamental point: the claim 'It is written', if backed up by correct exegesis and appreciation of the context of a text, should always be enough to settle any theological argument.

SRH

A. Rightly interpreting Scripture: early discussions

I.1.1 Tertullian, from *The Prescription against Heretics*

Tertullian outlines the Rule of Faith (see I.3), and argues that only the church, which holds to this rule, is able to interpret the Scriptures.

XII. Now, with regard to this rule of faith – that we may from this point acknowledge what it is which we defend – it is, you must know, that which prescribes the belief that there is one only God, and that He is none other than the Creator of the world, who produced all things out of nothing through His own Word, first of all sent forth; that this Word is called His Son, and, under the name of God, was seen 'in diverse manners' by the patriarchs, heard at all times in the prophets, at last brought down by the Spirit and Power of the Father into the Virgin Mary, was made flesh in her womb, and, being born of her, went forth as Jesus Christ; thenceforth He preached the new law and the new promise of the kingdom of heaven, worked miracles; having been crucified, He rose again the third day; (then) having ascended into the heavens, He sat at the right hand of the Father; sent instead of Himself the Power of the Holy Ghost to lead such as believe; will come with glory to take the saints to the enjoyment of everlasting life and of the heavenly promises, and to condemn the wicked to everlasting fire, after the resurrection of both these classes shall have happened, together with the restoration of their flesh. This rule, as it will be proved, was taught by Christ, and raises amongst ourselves no other questions than those which heresies introduce, and which make men heretics.

XIV. So long, however, as its form exists in its proper order, you may seek and discuss as much as you please, and give full rein to your curiosity, in whatever seems to you to hang in doubt, or to be shrouded in obscurity. You have at hand, no doubt, some learned brother gifted with the grace of knowledge, some one of the experienced class, some one of your close acquaintance who is curious like yourself; although with yourself, a seeker he will, after all, be quite aware that it is better for you to remain in ignorance, lest you should come to know what you ought not, because you have acquired the knowledge of what you ought to know. 'Thy faith,' He says, 'hath saved thee' not observe your skill in the Scriptures. Now, faith has been deposited in the rule; it has a law, and (in the observance thereof) salvation. Skill, however, consists in curious art, having for its glory simply the readiness that comes from knack. Let such curious art give place to faith; let such glory yield to salvation. At any rate, let them either relinquish their noisiness, or else be quiet. To know nothing in opposition to the rule (of faith), is to know all things. (Suppose) that heretics were not enemies to the truth, so that we were not forewarned to avoid them, what sort of conduct would it be to agree with men who do themselves confess that they are still seeking? ... But when, for the sake of deceiving us, they pretend that they are still seeking, in order that they may palm their essays upon us ... What sort of truth is that which they patronize, when they commend it to us with a lie? Well, but they actually treat of the Scriptures and recommend (their opinions) out of the Scriptures! To be sure they do. From what other source could they derive arguments concerning the things of the faith, except from the records of the faith?

XV. We are therefore come to (the gist of) our position; for at this point we were aiming, and for this we were preparing in the preamble of our address (which we have just completed), – so that we may now join issue on the contention to which our adversaries challenge us. They put forward the Scriptures, and by this insolence of theirs they at once influence some ... Accordingly, we oppose to them this step above all others, of not admitting them to any discussion of the Scriptures. If in these lie their resources, before they can use them, it ought to be clearly seen to whom belongs the possession of the Scriptures, that none may be admitted to the use thereof who has no title at all to the privilege.

XIX. Our appeal, therefore, must not be made to the Scriptures; nor must controversy be admitted on points in which victory will either be impossible, or uncertain, or not certain enough. But even if a discussion from the Scriptures should not turn out in such a way as to place both sides on a par, (yet) the natural order of things would require that this point should be first proposed, which is now the only one which we must discuss: 'With whom lies that very faith to which the Scriptures belong. From what and through whom, and when, and to whom, has been handed down that rule, by which men become Christians?' For wherever it shall be manifest that the true Christian rule and faith shall be, there will likewise be the true Scriptures and expositions thereof, and all the Christian traditions.

XXI. From this, therefore, do we draw up our rule. Since the Lord Jesus Christ sent the apostles to preach, (our rule is) that no others ought to be received as preachers than those whom Christ appointed; for 'no man knoweth the Father save the Son, and he to whomsoever the Son will reveal Him.' Nor does the Son seem to have revealed Him to any other than the apostles, whom He sent forth to preach – that, of course, which He revealed to them. Now, what that was which they preached – in other words, what it was which Christ revealed to them – can, as I must here likewise prescribe, properly be proved in no other way than by those very churches which the apostles rounded in person, by declaring the gospel to them directly themselves, both *viva voce*, as the phrase is, and subsequently by their epistles. If, then, these things are so, it is in the same degree manifest that all doctrine which agrees with the apostolic churches – those moulds and original sources of the faith must be reckoned for truth, as undoubtedly containing that which the (said) churches received from the apostles, the apostles from Christ, Christ from God. Whereas all doctrine must be prejudged as false which savours of contrariety to the truth of the churches and apostles of Christ and God. It remains, then, that we demonstrate whether this doctrine of ours, of which we have now given the rule, has its origin in the tradition of the apostles, and whether all other doctrines do not ipso facto proceed from falsehood. We hold communion with the apostolic churches because our doctrine is in no respect different from theirs. This is our witness of truth.

(Taken from the Ante-Nicene Fathers vol. III, ed. A. Roberts and J. Donaldson, trans. Peter Holmes.)

I.1.2 Origen, from *On First Principles*

Origen argues that it is impossible to take many passages of Scripture literally, and so the meaning of Scripture must be the 'spiritual' meaning, found by allegorizing.

CHAPTER III

1. Now what man of intelligence will believe that the first and the second and the third day, and the evening and the morning existed without the sun and moon and stars? And that the first day, if we may so call it, was even without a heaven? And who is so silly as to believe that God, after the manner of a farmer, 'planted a paradise eastward in Eden', and set in it a visible and palpable 'tree of life', of such a sort that anyone who tasted its fruit with his bodily teeth would gain life; and again that one could partake of 'good and evil' by masticating the fruit taken from the tree of that name? And when God is said to 'walk in the paradise in the cool of the day' and Adam to hide himself behind a tree, I do not think anyone will doubt that these are figurative expressions which indicate certain mysteries through a semblance of history and not through actual events.
. . .

Even the gospels are full of passages of this kind, as when the devil takes Jesus up into a 'high mountain' in order to show him from thence 'the kingdoms of the whole world and the glory of them'. For what man who does not read such passages carelessly would fail to condemn those who believe that with the eye of the flesh, which requires a great height to enable us to perceive what is below and at our feet, the kingdoms of the Persians, Scythians, Indians and Parthians were seen, and the manner in which their rulers are glorified by men? And the careful reader will detect thousands of other passages like this in the gospels, which will convince him that events which did not take place at all are woven into the records of what literally did happen.

2. And to come to the Mosaic legislation, many of the laws, so far as their literal observance is concerned, are clearly irrational, while others are impossible. An example of irrationality is the prohibition to eat vultures, seeing that nobody even in the worst famine was ever driven by want to the extremity of eating these creatures.
. . .

3. If now we approach the gospel in search of similar instances, what can be more irrational than the command: 'Salute no man by the way', which simple people believe that the Saviour enjoined upon the apostles? And it is impossible to accept the precept from the gospel about the 'right eye that offends'; for granting the possibility of a person being 'offended' through

his sense of sight, how can the blame be attributed to the right eye, when there are two eyes that see? And what man, even supposing he accuses himself of 'looking on a woman to lust after her' and attributes the blame to his right eye alone, would act rationally if he were to cast this eye away?
. . .

4. We have mentioned all these instances with the object of showing that the aim of the divine power which bestowed on us the holy scriptures is not that we should accept only what is found in the letter; for occasionally the records taken in a literal sense are not true, but actually absurd and imposs-ible, and even with the history that actually happened and the legislation that is in its literal sense useful there are other matters interwoven.

But someone may suppose that the former statement refers to all the scrip-tures, and may suspect us of saying that because some of the history did not happen, therefore none of it happened; and because a certain law is irrational or impossible when taken literally, therefore no laws ought to be kept to the letter; or that the records of the Saviour's life are not true in a physical sense; or that no law or commandment of his ought to be obeyed. We must assert, therefore, that in regard to some things we are clearly aware that the historical fact is true
. . .

For the passages which are historically true are far more numerous than those which are composed with purely spiritual meanings.
. . .

When, therefore, as will be clear to those who read, the passage as a connected whole is literally impossible, whereas the outstanding part of it is not impossible but even true, the reader must endeavour to grasp the entire meaning, connecting by an intellectual process the account of what is literally impossible with the parts that are not impossible but are historically true, these being interpreted allegorically in common with the parts which, so far as the letter goes, did not happen at all. For our contention with regard to the whole of divine scripture is, that it all has a spiritual meaning, but not all a bodily meaning; for the bodily meaning is often proved to be an impossibility. Consequently the man who reads the divine books reverently, believing them to be divine writings, must exercise great care.

(Taken from G. W. Butterworth's translation (of the Greek text), London: SPCK 1936.)

I.1.3 John Cassian, from *The Conferences*

Cassian describes the classic 'fourfold' interpretation of Scripture, whereby each text yields a literal sense, and three spiritual senses: allegorical, analogical (i.e. eschatological) and tropological (i.e. moral).

The First Conference of Abbot Nesteros: On Spiritual Knowledge

Chapter 1: The words of Abbot Nesteros on the knowledge of the religious
The order of our promise and course demands that there should follow the instruction of Abbot Nesteros, a man of excellence in all points and of the greatest knowledge: who when he had seen that we had committed some parts of Holy Scripture to memory and desired to understand them, addressed us in these words. There are indeed many different kinds of knowledge in this world, since there is as great a variety of them as there is of the arts and sciences. But, while all are either utterly useless or only useful for the good of this present life, there is yet none which has not its own system and method for learning it, by which it can be grasped by those who seek it. If then those arts are guided by certain special rules for their publication, how much more does the system and expression of our religion, which tends to the contemplation of the secrets of invisible mysteries, and seeks no present gain but the reward of an eternal recompense, depend on a fixed order and scheme. And the knowledge of this is twofold: first practical, which is brought about by an improvement of morals and purification from faults: secondly, theoretical, which consists in the contemplation of things Divine and the knowledge of most sacred thoughts.

Chapter 2: On grasping the knowledge of spiritual things
Whoever then would arrive at this theoretical knowledge must first pursue practical knowledge with all his might and main. For this practical knowledge can be acquired without theoretical, but theoretical cannot possibly be gained without practical. For there are certain stages, so distinct, and arranged in such a way that man's humility may be able to mount on high; and if these follow each other in turn in the order of which we have spoken, man can attain to a height to which he could not fly, if the first step were wanting. In vain then does one strive for the vision of God, who does not shun the stains of sins: 'For the spirit of God hates deception, and dwells not in a body subject to sins.'

Chapter 8: Of spiritual knowledge
Thus, as we said above, practical knowledge is distributed among many subjects and interests, but theoretical is divided into two parts, i.e., the historical interpretation and the spiritual sense. Whence also Solomon when he had

summed up the manifold grace of the Church, added: 'for all who are with her are clothed with double garments.' But of spiritual knowledge there are three kinds, tropological, allegorical, anagogical, of which we read as follows in Proverbs: 'But do you describe these things to yourself in three ways according to the largeness of your heart.' And so the history embraces the knowledge of things past and visible, as it is repeated in this way by the Apostle: 'For it is written that Abraham had two sons, the one by a bond-woman, the other by a free: but he who was of the bondwoman was born after the flesh, but he who was of the free was by promise.' But to the allegory belongs what follows, for what actually happened is said to have prefigured the form of some mystery 'For these,' says he, 'are the two covenants the one from Mount Sinai, which gendereth into bondage, which is Hagar. For Sinai is a mountain in Arabia, which is compared to Jerusalem which now is, and is in bondage with her children.' But the anagogical sense rises from spiritual mysteries even to still more sublime and sacred secrets of heaven, and is subjoined by the Apostle in these words: 'But Jerusalem which is above is free, which is the mother of us. For it is written, Rejoice, thou barren that bearest not, break forth and cry, thou that travailest not, for many are the children of the desolate more than of her that hath an husband.' The tropological sense is the moral explanation which has to do with improvement of life and practical teaching, as if we were to understand by these two covenants practical and theoretical instruction, or at any rate as if we were to want to take Jerusalem or Sion as the soul of man, according to this: 'Praise the Lord, O Jerusalem: praise thy God, O Sion.' And so these four previously mentioned figures coalesce, if we desire, in one subject, so that one and the same Jerusalem can be taken in four senses: historically as the city of the Jews; allegorically as the Church of Christ, anagogically as the heavenly city of God 'which is the mother of us all,' tropologically, as the soul of man, which is frequently subject to praise or blame from the Lord under this title. Of these four kinds of interpretation the blessed Apostle speaks as follows: 'But now, brethren, if I come to you speaking with tongues what shall I profit you unless I speak to you either by revelation or by knowledge or by prophecy or by doctrine?' For 'revelation' belongs to allegory whereby what is concealed under the historical narrative is revealed in its spiritual sense and interpretation, as for instance if we tried to expound how 'all our fathers were under the cloud and were all baptized unto Moses in the cloud and in the sea,' and how they 'all ate the same spiritual meat and drank the same spiritual drink from the rock that followed them. But the rock was Christ.' And this explanation where there is a comparison of the figure of the body and blood of Christ which we receive daily, contains the allegorical sense. But the knowledge, which is in the same way mentioned by the Apostle, is tropological, as by it we can by a careful study see of all things that have to do with practical discernment whether they are useful and good, as in this case, when we are told to judge of our own selves 'whether it is fitting for a woman to pray to God with her head uncovered.' And this system, as has been said, contains the moral meaning. So 'prophecy' which the Apostle puts in the third place, alludes to the anagogical sense by which the words are applied to things future and invisible, as here: 'But we would not have you ignorant, brethren, concerning those that sleep: that ye be not sorry as others also who have no hope. For if we believe that Christ died and rose again, even so them also which sleep in Jesus will God bring with Him. For this we say to you by the word of God, that we which are alive at the coming of the Lord shall not prevent those that sleep in Christ, for the Lord Himself shall descend from heaven with a shout, with the voice of the archangel and with the trump of God; and the dead in Christ shall rise first.' In which kind of exhortation the figure of anagoge is brought forward. But 'doctrine' unfolds the simple course of historical exposition, under which is contained no more secret sense, but what is declared by the very words: as in this passage: 'For I delivered unto you first of all what I also received, how that Christ died for our sins according to the Scriptures, and that He was buried, and that He rose again on the third day, and that he was seen of Cephas;' and: 'God sent His Son, made of a woman, made under the law, to redeem them that were under the law;' or this: 'Hear, O Israel, the Lord the God is one Lord.'

(Taken from the Nicene and Post-Nicene Fathers, second series, vol. XI, ed. Philip Schaff, trans. Edgar C. S. Gibson, Book XIV.)

B. The Reformation debate

1.1.4 Martin Luther, from 'A Brief Instruction on What to Look for and Expect in the Gospels'

Luther argues that we should consider every book of Scripture a 'gospel', because a gospel is nothing more than a book which tells us about Christ, and all of Scripture tells us about Christ. We should understand, from every part of Scripture, that Christ comes to us as a gift before he comes as an example, and so that grace always precedes law.

It is a common practice to number the gospels and to name them by books and say that there are four gospels. From this practice stems the fact that no one knows what St. Paul and St. Peter are saying in their epistles, and their teaching is regarded as an addition to the teaching of the gospels. There is, besides, the still worse practice of regarding the gospels and epistles as law books in which is supposed to be taught what we are to do and in which the works of Christ are pictured to us as nothing but examples. Now where these two erroneous notions remain in the heart, there neither the gospels nor the epistles may be read in a profitable or Christian manner, and [people] remain as pagan as ever.

One should thus realize that there is only one gospel, but that it is described by many apostles. Every single epistle of Paul and of Peter, as well as the Acts of the Apostles by Luke, is a gospel, even though they do not record all the works and words of Christ, but one is shorter and includes less than another. There is not one of the four major gospels anyway that includes all the words and works of Christ; nor is this necessary. Gospel is and should be nothing else than a discourse or story about Christ, just as happens among men when one writes a book about a king or a prince, telling what he did, said, and suffered in his day. Such a story can be told in various ways; one spins it out, and the other is brief. Thus the gospel is and should be nothing else than a chronicle, a story, a narrative about Christ, telling who he is, what he did, said, and suffered – a subject which one describes briefly, another more fully, one this way, another that way.

For at its briefest, the gospel is a discourse about Christ, that he is the Son of God and became man for us, that he died and was raised, that he has been established as a Lord over all things. This much St. Paul takes in hand and spins out in his epistles. He bypasses all the miracles and incidents [in Christ's ministry] which are set forth in the four gospels, yet he includes the whole gospel adequately and abundantly. This may be seen clearly and well in his greeting to the Romans [1:1–4], where he says what the gospel is, and declares, 'Paul, a servant of Jesus Christ, called to be an apostle, set apart for the gospel of God which he promised beforehand through his prophets in the holy scriptures, the gospel concerning his Son, who was descended from David according to the flesh and designated Son of God in power according to the Spirit of holiness by his resurrection from the dead, Jesus Christ our Lord,' etc.

There you have it. The gospel is a story about Christ, God's and David's Son, who died and was raised and is established as Lord. This is the gospel in a nutshell. Just as there is no more than one Christ, so there is and may be no more than one gospel. Since Paul and Peter too teach nothing but Christ, in the way we have just described, so their epistles can be nothing but the gospel.

Yes even the teaching of the prophets, in those places where they speak of Christ, is nothing but the true, pure, and proper gospel – just as if Luke or Matthew had described it. For the prophets have proclaimed the gospel and spoken of Christ, as St. Paul here [Rom. 1:2] reports and as everyone indeed knows. Thus when Isaiah in chapter fifty-three says how Christ should die for us and bear our sins, he has written the pure gospel. And I assure you, if a person fails to grasp this understanding of the gospel, he will never be able to be illuminated in the Scripture nor will he receive the right foundation.

Be sure, moreover, that you do not make Christ into a Moses, as if Christ did nothing more than teach and provide examples as the other saints do, as if the gospel were simply a textbook of teachings or laws. Therefore you should grasp Christ, his words, works, and sufferings, in a twofold manner. First as an example that is presented to you, which you should follow and imitate. As St. Peter says in I Peter 4, 'Christ suffered for us, thereby leaving us an example.' Thus when you see how he prays, fasts, helps people, and shows them love, so also you should do, both for yourself and for your neighbor. However this is the smallest part of the gospel, on the basis of which it cannot yet even be called gospel. For on this level Christ is of no more help to you than some other saint. His life remains his own and does not as yet contribute anything to you. In short this mode [of understanding Christ as simply an example] does not make Christians but only hypocrites. You must grasp Christ at a much higher level. Even though this higher level has for a long time been the very best, the preaching of it has been something rare. The chief article and foundation of the gospel is that before you take Christ as an example, you accept and recognize him as a gift, as a present that God has given you and that is your own. This means that when you see or hear of Christ doing or suffering something, you do not doubt that Christ himself, with his deeds and suffering, belongs to you. On this you may depend as surely as if you had done it yourself; indeed as if you were Christ himself. See, this is what it means to have a proper grasp of the gospel, that is, of the overwhelming goodness of God, which neither prophet, nor apostle, nor angel was ever able fully to express, and which no heart could adequately fathom or marvel at. This is the great fire of the love of God for us, whereby the heart and conscience become happy, secure, and content. This is what preaching the Christian faith means. This is why such preaching is called gospel, which in German means a joyful, good, and comforting 'message'; and this is why the apostles are called the 'twelve messengers.'

Concerning this Isaiah 9[:6] says, 'To us a child is born, to us a son is given.' If he is given to us, then he must be ours; and so we must also receive him as belonging to us. And Romans 8[:32], 'How should [God] not give us all things with his Son?' See, when you lay hold of Christ as a gift which is given you for your very own and have no doubt about it, you are a Christian. Faith redeems you from sin, death, and hell and enables you to overcome all things. O no one can speak enough about this. It is a pity that this kind of preaching has been silenced in the world, and yet boast is made daily of the gospel.

Now when you have Christ as the foundation and chief blessing of your salvation, then the other part follows: that you take him as your example, giving yourself in service to your neighbor just as you see that Christ has given himself for you. See, there faith and love move forward, God's commandment is fulfilled, and a person is happy and fearless to do and to suffer all things. Therefore make note of this, that Christ as a gift nourishes your faith and makes you a Christian. But Christ as an example exercises your works. These do not make you a Christian. Actually they come forth from you because you have already been made a Christian. As widely as a gift differs from an example, so widely does faith differ from works, for faith possesses nothing of its own, only the deeds and life of Christ. Works have something of your own in them, yet they should not belong to you but to your neighbor.

So you see that the gospel is really not a book of laws and commandments which requires deeds of us, but a book of divine promises in which God promises, offers, and gives us all his possessions and benefits in Christ. The fact that Christ and the apostles provide much good teaching and explain the law is to be counted a benefit just like any other work of Christ. For to teach aright is not the least sort of benefit. We see too that unlike Moses in his book, and contrary to the nature of a commandment, Christ does not horribly force and drive us. Rather he teaches us in a loving and friendly way. He simply tells us what we are to do and what to avoid, what will happen to those who do evil and to those who do well. Christ drives and compels no one. Indeed he teaches so gently that he entices rather than commands. He begins by saying, 'Blessed are the poor, Blessed are the meek,' and so on [Matt. 5:3, 5]. And the apostles commonly use the expression, 'I admonish, I request, I beseech,' and so on. But Moses says, 'I command, I forbid,' threatening and frightening everyone with horrible punishments and penalties. With this sort of instruction you can now read and hear the gospels profitably.

When you open the book containing the gospels and read or hear how Christ comes here or there, or how someone is brought to him, you should therein perceive the sermon or the gospel through which he is coming to you, or you are being brought to him. For the preaching of the gospel is nothing else than Christ coming to us, or we being brought to him. When you see how he works, however, and how he helps everyone to whom he comes or who is brought to him, then rest assured that faith is accomplishing this in you and that he is offering your soul exactly the same sort of help and favor through the gospel. If you pause here and let him do you good, that is, if you believe that he benefits and helps you, then you really have it. Then Christ is yours, presented to you as a gift.

After that it is necessary that you turn this into an example and deal with your neighbor in the very same way, be given also to him as a gift and an example. Isaiah 40[:1, 2] speaks of that, 'Be comforted, be comforted my dear people, says your Lord God. Say to the heart of Jerusalem, and cry to her, that her sin is forgiven, that her iniquity is ended, that she has received from the hand of God a double kindness for all her sin,' and so forth. This double kindness is the twofold aspect of Christ: gift and example. These two are also signified by the double portion of the inheritance which the law of Moses [Deut. 21:17] assigns to the eldest son and by many other figures.

What a sin and shame it is that we Christians have come to be so neglectful of the gospel that we not only fail to understand it, but even have to be shown by other books and commentaries what to look for and what to expect in it. Now the gospels and epistles of the apostles were written for this very purpose. They want themselves to be our guides, to direct us to the writings of the prophets and of Moses in the Old Testament so that we might there read and see for ourselves how Christ is wrapped in swaddling cloths and laid in the manger [Luke 2:7], that is, how he is comprehended [*Vorfassett*] in the writings of the prophets. It is there that people like us should read and study, drill ourselves, and see what Christ is, for what purpose he has been given, how he was promised, and how all Scripture tends toward him. For he himself says in John 5 [:46], 'If you believed Moses, you would also believe me, for he wrote of me.' Again [John 5:39], 'Search and look up the Scriptures, for it is they that bear witness to me.'

This is what St. Paul means in Romans 1[:1, 2], where in the beginning he says in his greeting, 'The gospel was promised by God through the prophets in the Holy Scriptures.' This is why the evangelists and apostles always direct us to the Scriptures and say, 'Thus it is written,' and again, 'This has taken place in order that the writing of the prophets might be fulfilled,' and so forth. In Acts 17 [:11], when the Thessalonians heard the gospel with all eagerness, Luke says that they studied and examined the Scriptures day and night in order to see if these things were so. Thus when St. Peter wrote his epistle, right at the beginning [I Pet. 1:10–12] he says, 'The prophets who prophesied of the grace that was to be yours searched and inquired about this salvation; they inquired what person or time was indicated by the Spirit of Christ within them; and he bore witness through them to the sufferings that were to come upon Christ and the ensuing glory. It was revealed to them that they were serving not themselves but us, in the things which have now been preached among you through the Holy Spirit sent from heaven, things which also the angels long to behold.' What else does St. Peter here desire than to lead us into the Scriptures? It is as if he should be saying, 'We preach and open the Scriptures to you through the Holy Spirit, so that you yourselves may read and see what is in them and know of the time about which the prophets were writing.' For he says as much in Acts 4[3:24], 'All the prophets who ever prophesied, from Samuel on, have spoken concerning these days.'

Therefore also Luke, in his last chapter [24:45], says that Christ opened the minds of the apostles to understand the Scriptures. And Christ, in John 10 [:9, 3], declares that he is the door by which one must enter, and whoever enters by him, to him the gatekeeper (the Holy Spirit) opens in order that he might find pasture and blessedness. Thus it is ultimately true that the gospel itself is our guide and instructor in the Scriptures, just as with this foreword I would gladly give instruction and point you to the gospel.

But what a fine lot of tender and pious children we are! In order that we might not have to study in the Scriptures and learn Christ there, we simply regard the entire Old Testament as of no account, as done for and no longer valid. Yet it alone bears the name of Holy Scripture. And the gospel should really not be something written, but a spoken word which brought forth the Scriptures, as Christ and the apostles have done. This is why Christ himself did not write anything but only spoke. He called his teaching not Scripture but gospel, meaning good news or a proclamation that is spread not by pen but by word of mouth. So we go on and make the gospel into a law book, a teaching of commandments, changing Christ into a Moses, the One who would help us into simply an instructor.

What punishment ought God to inflict upon such stupid and perverse people! Since we abandoned his Scriptures, it is not surprising that he has abandoned us to the teaching of the pope and to the lies of men. Instead of Holy Scripture we have had to learn the *Decretales* of a deceitful fool and an evil rogue. O would to God that among Christians the pure gospel were known and that most speedily there would be neither use nor need for this work of mine. Then there would surely be hope that the Holy Scriptures too would come forth again in their worthiness. Let this suffice as a very brief foreword and instruction. In the exposition we will say more about this matter. Amen.

(Taken from **Luther's Works** *vol. 35, ed. E. Theodore Bachmann, Philadelphia, PA: Fortress Press, 1960, pp. 117–24.)*

I.1.5 Balthasar Hubmaier, The Dedicatory Epistle to 'A Christian Catechism'

Hubmaier here represents the most radical wing of the Reformation, completely repudiating the Catholic tradition, he opposes Scripture to the tradition, almost suggesting that one may read Aquinas or Paul, but not both. His verbal assaults on the Roman Catholic Church of the day add little to the argument, but do convey rather well a sense of the sort of invective that was not uncommon in Reformation debate.

To the esteemed Lord Martin, heretofore Bishop of Nikopolis, but now legitimate member of the Christian congregation at Nikolsburg, your gracious sir:

Grace and peace in Christ Jesus our only Savior, to whom be praise, thanks, honor, and glory forever. For on behalf of us poor, wretched and powerless men, he has so graciously and without any of our merits boarded the trembling little vessel; through his healing, living and eternal word he has encouraged, instructed and so thoroughly taught us that we now truly know how we are to navigate by the shining star of his holy word alone; and we know how we are to cast our nets in the water in his name, so that we might fish profitably and prosperously, catching the souls of men with the hook of his divine teaching, and pulling them out of the salty, tumultuous Syrian Sea of this world. But all such things are futile, even if we work through the whole night, unless they are done in his name.

Gracious sir and brother. For some time it has been clear to us that the Christian life must begin with the doctrine out of which faith flows; and according to this doctrine there then follows the baptism of water in conformity with the institution of Christ; through this baptism for the forgiveness of sins the person, in open confession of his faith, makes his first entry and beginning in the holy, catholic, Christian Church (outside of which there is no salvation); and by virtue of the first key which Christ promised and gave to his Church (Matt. 16:19, 18:18, John 20:23), he is at that time admitted and accepted into the community of the saints. But since your grace recognizes and is aware that it is not enough to know *that* one should be taught and instructed before the reception of baptism by water, but rather that it is also necessary to say *what* a person should first learn and know – therefore, your grace, as a true, diligent and conscientious shepherd and bishop, has earnestly encouraged, exhorted and required me to write a catechism or text book of the articles which one should make known first. With this the youth (for whom we are truly to a large extent responsible) will be instructed correctly and in an orderly way, and will be fed, given to drink and elevated with the teaching of Christ from childhood on. Yet we still clearly recognize that the divine word can have so little effect because of that which is antiquated and frozen in the mud holes and cesspools of human dogmas, and that it has so little effect on the attitudes of persons with old customs and long-held habits because of their lack of faith, and that the divine word is presented so miserably that it is an affront before God.

Although, gracious sir, I would have liked to conveniently excuse myself on the grounds of my ignorance and for other reasons, yet since this exhortation is so honorable, profitable and Christian, I have no right to refuse such a salutary request. Accordingly, with the grace of God's Holy Ghost, I must and will heartily and glady accede to your grace. I do this not only for the sake of helping the inexperienced youth but also because, until recently, we both lay in many errors, hypocrisies and vile abominations which we planted and nurtured with great diligence (although in ignorance we knew no better at the time.) Yes, and we expended great effort, until with doctrine, persuassion, cowls, tonsures, and with oil and chrism we had made priests or monks. But the almighty and good God, by his divine grace, has so graciously opened our eyes, that we both see, recognize and acknowledge the guilt of our errors, so that we have renounced them, and so that we have determined in the power of our Lord Jesus Christ to live henceforth according to his rule. We also know with certainty that he forgives us our sins. To him be praise in eternity. Therefore, in writing, teaching and deed, our earnest and heartfelt desire is to give all those who through us have fallen into the same darkness and pit reason to open their eyes, to cry to God for enlightenment, to arise from their fallen state, and to better their lives. The power of God help them to do this. Amen.

Although as examiners, questioners and assessors we have made quite a few priests and monks, out of all of these, none knew in the least how to translate the Epistles of Paul into German, nor how to read them correctly. Still it is said that 'all those who are worthy are righteous', that is, that they are all supposed to be pious, worthy and qualified priests. O the great lie and folly! Indeed, what the popes, bishops, provosts, abbots and also the secular kaisers, kings, princes and lords have forced upon us through their bulls and decrees for naive shepherds and pastors is in many cases obvious: they are really benefice hunters, ass strokers, whores, adulterers, pimps, gamblers, drunkards and buffoons whom we certainly would not have trusted to take care of sows and nanny goats; so neither did we have to accept them as shepherds of our souls. Out of them has come nothing but thieves and murderers since they have not entered the Christian calling by the right door (John 10:9). But that I may testify to my ignorance with my own blushing, so I say frankly, and God knows that I do not lie, that I too became a Doctor of Sacred Scripture (as sophistry was then called) and still did not understand these Christian articles contained in this little book. Indeed I had at that time not read any Gospel or Epistle of Paul from beginning to end. What holy word then could I teach to others or preach to them? In fact, only Thomas, Scotus, Gabriel [Biel], Occam, decrees, decretals, legends of the saints and the other high-thinkers [scholastics]. These have formerly been our hellish scriptures.

However, gracious sir, so that no one is too amazed at our blindness and folly, it is necessary to realize that the pure, unalloyed and genuine word of God has, from the beginning until now, never reached our German nation in its seven times purged and uncorrupted form; rather the pastors and bishops have tended their flock in accordance with what they were then and always have been from the beginning. But right from the start they have been papists. According to all the chronicles, monks and priests were sent by the papists in Rome, Scotland and England into the fields of Christ to sow their weeds, tricks, law and teaching. The people slept and did not test or judge their teaching by the guiding principle of the Bible. In them, such weeds have taken root, grown up and on the whole taken over that one cannot entirely root them out until the harvest time, till the Lord himself comes. Still some naive idolaters and mass-priests fill their mouths and cry: 'We have then and always heard, learned, and ourselves preached the gospel.' I answer: Dear friend. I allow you to speak and cry, but what you say is not true. Because even if one of you has drawn out some fragments and patch-work of the gospel for us, still he has so mixed it with the chaff and bran of human glosses and additions, that we have not experienced the sweetness of the true wheat and kernel. And we have also been misled so far from the source of the living well that we have drunken nothing but muddy, dirty and poisoned cistern water, fouled by human feet. How then can health and salvation come from this? All who have read the historians on how the German nation is supposed to have come to the Christian faith confirm me on this. But since we now also say such things and warn the people about such empty chaff and filthy cesspools, just as Augustine, Jerome and the papists even themselves do, so we must now be heretics, blasphemers, rebels, perjurers, insurgents and seducers. Still, we should not let this cause us to waver, but rather we should be joyful that God has made us worthy to suffer disgrace, shame, mockery and harm, ostracism, poverty, misery, imprison-ment, martyrdom and all kinds of tribulation for the sake of his holy word. He alone gives us patience to willingly and joyfully take on and bear all these things. For it is exactly this which is the right path leading to eternal life. Christ himself had to go through just this path to enter into his glory. Whoever looks for another path through temporal honor, sensual pleasure, worldly joys, or through the devilish goods and money which is a root of all our blindness, he will fall short of the heavenly gates.

So in order that I might reach the shore, gracious sir, I have on your grace's Christian desire recently composed a dialogue or conversation, in which I introduce two persons, namely Leonharten and Johannsen, who in a brotherly way converse with one another on the articles concerning a Christian life. The special affection and zeal which we both have for the honorable and Christian men, remarkable lovers of the holy gospel, Mr. Leonharten and

Mr. Hansen of Leichtenstein at Nikolsburg, has moved me, my gracious sir, to use these two names here to stand for others. May the merciful and benevolent God keep them in his protection, in his shelter, and in an upright, uncorrupted and Christian faith against all offense of sin, the world, the devil and hell until they reach their end. May Jesus Christ our Savior, who for our salvation died and rose again, grant this to you and to all of us. With this, your grace, live happily in the Lord, together with your Christian wife. Given at Nikolsburg on the tenth day of December, in the year 1526.

Your Grace's,
Balthasar Hubmaier
of Freiburg

(Taken from Denis Janz, Three Reformation Catechisms: Catholic, Anabaptist, Lutheran, *Lewiston NY: Edwin Mellen Press 1982, pp. 133–40.)*

I.1.6 The Council of Trent, from the 'Decree concerning the Canonical Scriptures'

In response to the attempts of the Reformers to demonstrate that certain Roman Catholic practices and doctrines were not in accord with Scripture, the Council insisted on three points: (a) that only the Church can interpret Scripture; (b) that there is an unwritten tradition besides Scripture, which is equally authoritative; (c) that the only acceptable text of Scripture is the Latin Vulgate.

The sacred and holy, œcumenical and general Synod of Trent, lawfully assembled in the Holy Ghost, the same three legates of the Apostolic See presiding therein, – keeping this always in view, that, errors being removed, the purity itself of the Gospel be preserved in the Church; which [Gospel], before promised through the prophets in the holy Scriptures, our Lord Jesus Christ, the Son of God, first promulgated with His own mouth, and then commanded to be preached by His apostles to every creature, as the fountain both of every saving truth, and discipline of morals; and perceiving that this truth and discipline are contained in the written books, and the unwritten traditions which, received by the apostles from the mouth of Christ himself, or from the apostles themselves, the Holy Ghost dictating, have come down even unto us, transmitted as it were from hand to hand; [the synod] following the examples of the orthodox fathers, receives and venerates with equal affection of piety, and reverence, all the books both of the Old and of the New Testament, – seeing that one God is the author of both, as also the said traditions, as well those appertaining to faith as to morals, as having been dictated, either by Christ's own word of mouth, or by the Holy Ghost, and preserved by a continuous succession in the Catholic Church. And it has thought it meet that a catalogue of the sacred books be inserted in this decree, lest doubt arise in any one's mind as to which, are the books that are received by this synod ... But if any one receive not, as sacred and canonical, these same books entire with all their parts, as they have been used to be read in the Catholic Church, and as they are contained in the old Latin vulgate edition; and knowingly and deliberately despise the traditions aforesaid; let him be anathema. Let all, therefore, understand, in what order, and in what manner, this said synod, after having laid the foundation of the confession of faith, will proceed, and what testimonies and defences it will mainly use in confirming dogmas, and in restoring morals in the Church.

DECREE CONCERNING THE EDITION AND THE USE OF THE SACRED BOOKS

Moreover, the same sacred and holy synod, considering that no little utility may accrue to the Church of God, if, out of all the Latin editions now in circulation of the sacred books, it be known which is to be held as authentic, ordains and declares, that the said old and vulgate edition, which, by the long usage of so many ages, has been approved in the Church, be, in public lectures, disputations, preachings, and expositions, held as authentic; and that no one is to dare, or presume to reject it under any pretext soever.

Furthermore, in order to restrain petulant spirits, It decrees, that no one, relying on his own skill, shall, in matters of faith, and of morals pertaining to the edification of Christian doctrine, wresting the sacred Scripture to his own senses, dare to interpret the said sacred Scripture contrary to that sense which holy mother Church, whose it is to judge of the true sense and interpretation of the holy Scriptures, hath held and doth hold, or even contrary to the unanimous consent of the Fathers; even though suchlike interpretations were never [intended] to be at any time published. They who shall contravene shall be made known by their ordinaries, and be published, and be punished with the penalties by law established.

[this synod] ordains and decrees, that, henceforth, the sacred Scripture, and especially the aforesaid old and vulgate edition, be printed in the most correct manner possible; and that it shall not be lawful for any one to print, or cause to be printed, any books whatever, on sacred matters, without the name of the author; nor to sell them in future, or even to keep them by them, unless they shall have been first examined, and approved of; under pain of the anathema and fine imposed in a canon of the last Council of Lateran. But as to those who lend, or circulate them in manuscript, without their having been first examined and approved, they shall be subjected to the same penalties as the printers. And they who shall have them in their possession, or shall read them, shall, unless they discover the authors, be themselves regarded as the authors. And this approbation of books of this kind shall be given in writing; and to this end it shall appear authentically at the beginning of the book, whether the book be written or printed; and all this, that is, both the approbation and the examination, shall be done gratis, so that things to be approved, may be approved, and things to be condemned, condemned.

After these matters, wishing to repress that temerity, by which the words and sentences of sacred Scripture are turned and twisted to all manner of profane uses, to wit, to things scurrilous, fabulous, vain, to flatteries, detractions, superstitions, impious and diabolical incantations, divinations, casting of lots, nay, even hereafter defamatory libels; [the synod] commands and enjoins, for the doing away with this kind of irreverence and contempt, and that no one may hereafter dare in any manner to apply the words of sacred

Scripture to these and such like purposes; that all men of this description, profaners and violators of the word of God, be restrained by the bishops by the penalties of law and of their own appointment.

(Taken from Theodore A. Buckley's translation, The Canons and Decrees of the Council of Trent, *London: George Routledge 1851, pp.17–21.)*

I.1.7 John Calvin, from *The Institutes of the Christian Religion*

Calvin here first simply asserts the high place given to Scripture by the Reformers, and then goes on to argue that Scripture does not depend on the church for its validity, but on God; indeed, the church depends on Scripture. Finally, in response to the implied question of what validates Scripture, if not the church, Calvin appeals to the testimony of the Holy Spirit.

CHAPTER VI

2. The Word of God as Holy Scripture

But whether God became known to the patriarchs through oracles and visions or by the work and ministry of men, he put into their minds what they should then hand down to their posterity. At any rate, there is no doubt that firm certainty of doctrine was engraved in their hearts, so that they were convinced and understood that what they had learned proceeded from God. For by his Word, God rendered faith unambiguous forever, a faith that should be superior to all opinion. Finally, in order that truth might abide forever in the world with a continuing succession of teaching and survive through all ages, the same oracles he had given to the patriarchs it was his pleasure to have recorded, as, it were, on public tablets. With this intent the law was published, and the prophets afterward added as its interpreters. For even though the use of the law was manifold, as will be seen more clearly in its place, it was especially committed to Moses and all the prophets to teach the way of reconciliation between God and men, whence also Paul calls 'Christ the end of the law' [Rom. 10:4]. Yet I repeat once more: besides the specific doctrine of faith and repentance that sets forth Christ as Mediator, Scripture adorns with unmistakable marks and tokens the one true God, in that he has created and governs the universe, in order that he may not be mixed up with the throng of false gods. Therefore, however fitting it may be for man seriously to turn his eyes to contemplate God's works, since he has been placed in this most glorious theater to be a spectator of them, it is fitting that he prick up his ears to the Word, the better to profit. And it is therefore no wonder that those who were born in darkness become more and more hardened in their insensibility; for there are very few who, to contain themselves within bounds, apply themselves teachably to God's Word, but they rather exult in their own vanity. Now, in order that true religion may shine upon us, we ought to hold that it must take its beginning from heavenly doctrine and that no one can get even the slightest taste of right and sound doctrine unless he be a pupil of

Scripture. Hence, there also emerges the beginning of true understanding when we reverently embrace what it pleases God there to witness of himself. But not only faith, perfect and in every way complete, but all right knowledge of God is born of obedience. And surely in this respect God has, by his singular providence, taken thought for mortals through all ages.

3. Without Scripture we fall into error

Suppose we ponder how slippery is the fall of the human mind into forgetfulness of God, how great the tendency to every kind of error, how great the lust to fashion constantly new and artificial religions. Then we may perceive how necessary was such written proof of the heavenly doctrine, that it should neither perish through forgetfulness nor vanish through error nor be corrupted by the audacity of men. It is therefore clear that God has provided the assistance of the Word for the sake of all those to whom he has been pleased to give useful instruction because he foresaw that his likeness imprinted upon the most beautiful form of the universe would be insufficiently effective. Hence, we must strive onward by this straight path if we seriously aspire to the pure contemplation of God. We must come, I say, to the Word, where God is truly and vividly described to us from his works, while these very works are appraised not by our depraved judgment but by the rule of eternal truth. If we turn aside from the Word, as I have just now said, though we may strive with strenuous haste, yet, since we have got off the track, we shall never reach the goal. For we should so reason that the splendor of the divine countenance, which even the apostle calls 'unapproachable' [I Tim. 6:16], is for us like an inexplicable labyrinth unless we are conducted into it by the thread of the Word; so that it is better to limp along this path than to dash with all speed outside it. David very often, therefore, teaching that we ought to banish superstitions from the earth so that pure religion may flourish, represented God as regnant [Ps. 93:1; 96:10; 97:1; 99:1; and the like]. Now he means by the word 'regnant' not the power with which he is endowed, and which he exercises in governing the whole of nature, but the doctrine by which he asserts his lawful sovereignty. For errors can never be uprooted from human hearts until true knowledge of God is planted therein.
. . .

CHAPTER VII

1. Scripture has its authority from God, not from the church

Before I go any farther, it is worth-while to say something about the authority of Scripture, not only to prepare our hearts to reverence it, but to banish all doubt. When that which is set forth is acknowledged to be the Word of God, there is no one so deplorably insolent – unless devoid also both of common sense and of humanity itself – as to dare impugn the credibility of Him who speaks. Now daily oracles are not sent from heaven, for it pleased the Lord to hallow his truth to everlasting remembrance in the Scriptures alone [cf. John 5:39]. Hence the Scriptures obtain full authority among believers only when men regard them as having sprung from heaven, as if there the living words of God were heard . . .

But a most pernicious error widely prevails that Scripture has only so much weight as is conceded to it by the consent of the church. As if the eternal and inviolable truth of God depended upon the decision of men! For they mock the Holy Spirit when they ask: Who can convince us that these writings came from God? Who can assure us that Scripture has come down whole and intact even to our very day? Who can persuade us to receive one book in reverence but to exclude another, unless the church prescribe a sure rule for all these matters? What reverence is due Scripture and what books ought to be reckoned within its canon depend, they say, upon the determination of the church. Thus these sacrilegious men, wishing to impose an unbridled tyranny under the cover of the church, do not care with what absurdities they ensnare themselves and others, provided they can force this one idea upon the simple-minded: that the church has authority in all things. . . .

2. The church is itself grounded upon Scripture

But such wranglers are neatly refuted by just one word of the apostle. He testifies that the church is 'built upon the foundation of the prophets and apostles' [Eph. 2:20]. If the teaching of the prophets and apostles is the foundation, this must have had authority before the church began to exist. Groundless, too, is their subtle objection that, although the church took its beginning here, the writings to be attributed to the prophets and apostles nevertheless remain in doubt until decided by the church. For if the Christian church was from the beginning founded upon the writings of the prophets and the preaching of the apostles, wherever this doctrine is found, the acceptance of it – without which the church itself would never have existed – must certainly have preceded the church. It is utterly vain, then, to pretend that the power of judging Scripture so lies with the church that its certainty depends upon churchly assent. Thus, while the church receives and gives its seal of approval to the Scriptures, it does not thereby render authentic what is otherwise doubtful or controversial. But because the church recognizes Scripture to be the truth of its own God, as a pious duty it unhesitatingly venerates Scripture. As to their question – How can we be assured that this has sprung from God unless we have recourse to the decree of the church? – it is as if someone asked: Whence will we learn to distinguish light from darkness, white from black, sweet from bitter? Indeed, Scripture exhibits fully as clear evidence of its own truth as white and black things do of their color, or sweet and bitter things do of their taste.

. . .

4. The witness of the Holy Spirit: this is stronger than all proof

We ought to remember what I said a bit ago: credibility of doctrine is not established until we are persuaded beyond doubt that God is its Author. Thus, the highest proof of Scripture derives in general from the fact that God in person speaks in it. The prophets and apostles do not boast either of their keenness or of anything that obtains credit for them as they speak; nor do they dwell upon rational proofs. Rather, they bring forward God's holy name, that by it the whole world may be brought into obedience to him. Now we ought to see how apparent it is not only by plausible opinion but by clear truth that they do not call upon God's name heedlessly or falsely. If we desire to provide in the best way for our consciences – that they may not be perpetually beset by the instability of doubt or vacillation, and that they may not also boggle at the smallest quibbles – we ought to seek our conviction in a higher place than human reasons, judgments, or conjectures, that is, in the secret testimony of the Spirit. True, if we wished to proceed by arguments, we might advance many things that would easily prove – if there is any god in heaven – that the law, the prophets, and the gospel come from him. . . . Yes, if we turn pure eyes and upright senses toward it, the majesty of God will immediately come to view, subdue our bold rejection, and compel us to obey.

Yet they who strive to build up firm faith in Scripture through disputation are doing things backwards. For my part, although I do not excel either in great dexterity or eloquence, if I were struggling against the most crafty sort of despisers of God, who seek to appear shrewd and witty in disparaging Scripture, I am confident it would not be difficult for me to silence their clamorous voices. And if it were a useful labor to refute their cavils, I would with no great trouble shatter the boasts they mutter in their lurking places. But even if anyone clears God's Sacred Word from man's evil speaking, he will not at once imprint upon their hearts that certainty which piety requires. Since for unbelieving men religion seems to stand by opinion alone, they, in order not to believe anything foolishly or lightly, both wish and demand rational proof that Moses and the prophets spoke divinely. But I reply: the testimony of the Spirit is more excellent than all reason. For as God alone is a fit witness of himself in his Word, so also the Word will not find acceptance in men's hearts before it is sealed by the inward testimony of the Spirit. The same Spirit, therefore, who has spoken through the mouths of the prophets must penetrate into our hearts to persuade us that they faithfully proclaimed what had been divinely commanded. . . . Some good folk are annoyed that a clear proof is not ready at hand when the impious, unpunished, murmur against God's Word. As if the Spirit were not called both 'seal' and 'guarantee' [II Cor. 1:22] for confirming the faith of the godly; because until he illumines their minds, they ever waver among many doubts!

5. Scripture bears its own authentication

Let this point therefore stand: that those whom the Holy Spirit has inwardly taught truly rest upon Scripture, and that Scripture indeed is self-authenticated; hence, it is not right to subject it to proof and reasoning. And the certainty it deserves with us, it attains by the testimony of the Spirit. For even if it wins reverence for itself by its own majesty, it seriously affects us only when it is sealed upon our hearts through the Spirit. Therefore, illumined by his power, we believe neither by our own nor by anyone else's judgment that Scripture is from God; but above human judgment we affirm with utter certainty (just as if we were gazing upon the majesty of God himself) that it has flowed to us from the very mouth of God by the ministry of men. We seek no proofs, no marks of genuineness upon which our judgment may lean; but we subject our judgment and wit to it as to a thing far beyond any guesswork! This we do, not as persons accustomed to seize upon some unknown thing, which, under closer scrutiny, displeases them, but fully conscious that we hold the unassailable truth! Nor do we do this as those miserable men who habitually bind over their minds to the thralldom of superstition; but we feel that the undoubted power of his divine majesty lives and breathes there. By this power we are drawn and inflamed, knowingly and willingly, to obey him, yet also more vitally and more effectively than by mere human willing or knowing!

God, therefore, very rightly proclaims through Isaiah that the prophets together with the whole people are witnesses to him; for they, instructed by prophecies, unhesitatingly held that God has spoken without deceit or ambiguity [Isa. 43:10]. Such, then, is a conviction that requires no reasons; such, a knowledge with which the best reason agrees – in which the mind truly reposes more securely and constantly than in any reasons; such, finally, a feeling that can be born only of heavenly revelation. I speak of nothing other than what each believer experiences within himself – though my words fall far beneath a just explanation of the matter.
. . .

(Taken from The Institutes of the Christian Religion *ed.* John T. McNeil, *trans.* Ford Lewis Battles, The Library of Christian Classics, *vol XX, Philadelphia, PA: Westminister Press 1960, I.vi–vii.)*

C. Responses to biblical criticism

I.1.8 Gotthold Ephraim Lessing, from *On the Proof of the Spirit and of Power*

Lessing here is engaged in arguing that historical events can never prove eternal verities, and so that the life of Jesus cannot be the decisive witness for the nature of God. In the course of this argument, he draws a sharp distinction between seeing miracles and merely reading reports, however trustworthy, of the miraculous. His protestations that his faith in the truth of the Gospels is unwavering are probably disingenuous, but the argument presented serves to undermine the credibility of the Scriptures regardless.

Fulfilled prophecies, which I myself experience, are one thing; fulfilled prophecies, of which I know only from history that others say they have experienced them, are another.

Miracles, which I see with my own eyes, and which I have the opportunity to verify for myself, are one thing; miracles, of which I know only from history that others say they have seen them and verified them, are another.

That surely, is beyond controversy? Surely there is no objection to be made against that?

If I had lived at the time of Christ, then of course the prophecies fulfilled in his person would have made me pay great attention to him. If I had actually seen him do miracles; if I had had no cause to doubt that these were true miracles; then in a worker of miracles who had been marked out so long before, I would have gained so much confidence that I would willingly have submitted my intellect to his, and I would have believed him in all things in which equally indisputable experiences did not tell against him.

Or: if I even now experienced that prophecies referring to Christ or the Christian religion, of whose priority in time I have long been certain, were fulfilled in a manner admitting no dispute; if even now miracles were done by believing Christians which I had to recognize as true miracles: what could prevent me from accepting this proof of the spirit and of power, as the apostle calls it?

In the last instance Origen was quite right in saying that in this proof of the spirit and of power the Christian religion was able to provide a proof of its own more divine than all Greek dialectic. For in his time there was still 'the power to do miraculous things which still continued' among those who lived after Christ's precept; and if he had undoubted examples of this, then if he was not to deny his own senses he had of necessity to recognize that proof of the spirit and of power.

But I am no longer in Origen's position; I live in the eighteenth century, in which miracles no longer happen. If I even now hesitate to believe anything on the proof of the spirit and of power, which I can believe on other arguments more appropriate to my age: what is the problem?

The problem is that this proof of the spirit and of power no longer has any spirit or power, but has sunk to the level of human testimonies of spirit and power.

The problem is that reports of fulfilled prophecies are not fulfilled prophecies; that reports of miracles are not miracles. These, the prophecies fulfilled before my eyes, the miracles that occur before my eyes, are immediate in their effect. But those – the reports of fulfilled prophecies and miracles, have to work through a medium which takes away all their force.

If then this proof of the proof has now entirely lapsed; if then all historical certainty is much too weak to replace this apparent proof of the proof which has lapsed: how is it to be expected of me that the same inconceivable truths which sixteen to eighteen hundred years ago people believed on the strongest inducement, should be believed by me to be equally valid on an infinitely lesser inducement?

Or is it invariably the case, that what I read in reputable historians is just as certain for me as what I myself experience?

I do not know that anyone has ever asserted this. What is asserted is only that the reports which we have of these prophecies and miracles are as reliable as historical truths ever can be. And then it is added that historical truths cannot be demonstrated: nevertheless we must believe them as firmly as truths that have been demonstrated.

To this I answer: *First,* who will deny (not I) that the reports of these miracles and prophecies are as reliable as historical truths ever can be? But if they are only as reliable as this, why are they treated as if they were infinitely more reliable?

And in what way? In this way, that something quite different and much greater is founded upon them than it is legitimate to found upon truths historically proved.

If no historical truth can be demonstrated, then nothing can be demonstrated by means of historical truths.

That is: *accidental truths of history can never become the proof of necessary truths of reason.*

I do not for one moment deny that in Christ prophecies were fulfilled; I do not for one moment deny that Christ performed miracles. But since the truth of these miracles has completely ceased to be demonstrable by miracles still happening at the present time, since they are no more than reports of miracles (however incontroverted and incontrovertible they may be), I deny that they can and should bind me in the least to a faith in the other teachings of Christ. These other teachings I accept on other grounds.

Then *secondly:* What does it mean to accept an historical proposition as true? to believe an historical truth? Does it mean anything other than this: to accept this proposition, this truth as valid? to accept that there is no objection to be brought against it? to accept that one historical proposition is built on one thing, another on another, that from one historical truth another follows? to reserve to oneself the right to estimate other historical things accordingly? Does it mean anything other than this? Anything more? Examine carefully.

We all believe that an Alexander lived who in a short time conquered almost all Asia. But who, on the basis of this belief, would risk anything of great, permanent worth, the loss of which would be irreparable? Who, in consequence of this belief, would forswear for ever all knowledge that conflicted with this belief? Certainly not I. Now I have no objection to raise against Alexander and his victory: but it might still be possible that the story was founded on a mere poem of Choerilus just as the ten-year siege of Troy depends on no better authority than Homer's poetry.

If on historical grounds I have no objection to the statement that Christ raised to life a dead man; must I therefore accept it as true that God has a Son who is of the same essence as himself? What is the connection between my inability to raise any significant objection to the evidence of the former and my obligation to believe something against which my reason rebels?

If on historical grounds I have no objection to the statement that this Christ himself rose from the dead, must I therefore accept it as true that this risen Christ was the Son of God?

That the Christ, against whose resurrection I can raise no important historical objection, therefore declared himself to be the Son of God; that his disciples therefore believed him to be such; this I gladly believe from my heart. For these truths, as truths of one and the same class, follow quite naturally on one another.

But to jump with that historical truth to a quite different class of truths, and to demand of me that I should form all my metaphysical and moral ideas accordingly; to expect me to alter all my fundamental ideas of the nature of the Godhead because I cannot set any credible testimony against the resurrection of Christ: if that is not a μετάβασις εἰς ἄλλο γένος, then I do not know what Aristotle meant by this phrase.

It is said: 'The Christ of whom on historical grounds you must allow that he raised the dead, that he himself rose from the dead, said himself that God had a Son of the same essence as himself and that he is this Son.' This would be quite excellent! if only it were not the case that it is not more than historically certain that Christ said this.

If you press me still further and say: 'Oh yes! this is more than historically certain. For it is asserted by inspired historians who cannot make a mistake.'

But, unfortunately, that also is only historically certain, that these historians were inspired and could not err.

That, then, is the ugly, broad ditch which I cannot get across, however often and however earnestly I have tried to make the leap. If anyone can help me over it, let him do it, I beg him, I adjure him. He will deserve a divine reward from me.

(Taken from Henry Chadwick, Lessing's Theological Writings, *London: A&C Black 1956, pp. 51–6.)*

I.1.9 Samuel Taylor Coleridge, from the *Confessions of an Enquiring Spirit*

Coleridge begins by asking two questions: Is conviction of the truth of the Scriptures a necessary condition for Christian faith, or may one come to believe, and then gradually grow more convinced as one sees the truth of the Scriptures proved again and again? The text seems to address a slightly different question: In speaking of inspiration, must one believe the Scriptures to be divinely dictated, or is there a more supple account of the work of the Spirit preserving the various human characters of the authors? He speaks movingly of the spiritual power of Scripture, and then suggests that the idea that these writings were dictated by God completely destroys this power.

Seven Letters to a friend concerning the bounds between the right, and the superstitious, use and estimation of the Sacred Canon; in which the Writer submissively discloses his own private judgment on the following Questions: —

I. Is it necessary, or expedient, to insist on the belief of the divine origin and authority of all, and every part of the Canonical Books as the condition, or first principle, of Christian Faith?

II. Or, may not the due appreciation of the Scriptures collectively be more safely relied on as the result and consequence of the belief in Christ; the gradual increase – in respect of particular passages – of our spiritual discernment of their truth and authority supplying a test and measure of our own growth and progress as individual believers, without the servile fear that prevents or overclouds the free honour which cometh from love? 1 *John*, iv. 18.

LETTER I

V. But there is a Book, of two parts, – each part consisting of several books. The first part – (I speak in the character of an uninterested critic or philologist) – contains the reliques of the literature of the Hebrew people, while the Hebrew was still the living language. The second part comprises the writings, and, with one or two inconsiderable and doubtful exceptions, all the writings of the followers of Christ within the space of ninety years from the date of the Resurrection. I do not myself think that any of these writings were composed as late as A.D. 120; but I wish to preclude all dispute. This Book I resume, as read, and yet unread. I take up this work with the purpose to read it for the first time as I should read any other work, – as far at least as I can or dare. For I neither can, nor dare, throw off a strong and awful prepossession in its favour – certain as I am that a large part of the light and life, in and by which I see, love, and embrace the truths and the strengths co-organised into a living body of faith and knowledge in the four preceding classes, has been directly, or indirectly derived to me from this sacred volume, – and unable to determine what I do not owe to its influences. But even on this account, and because it has these inalienable claims on my reverence and gratitude, I will not leave it in the power of unbelievers to say that the Bible is for me only what the Koran is for the deaf Turk, and the Vedas for the feeble and acquiescent Hindoo. No; I will retire *up into the mountain*, and hold secret commune with my Bible above the contagious blastments of prejudice, and the fog-blight of selfish superstition. *For fear hath torment*. And what though *my* reason be to the power and splendour of the Scriptures but as the reflected and secondary shine of the moon compared with the solar radiance; – yet the sun endures the occasional co-presence of the unsteady orb, and leaving it visible seems to sanction the comparison. There is a Light higher than all, even *the Word that was in the beginning*; – the Light, of which light itself is but the *shechinah* and cloudy tabernacle; the Word that is light for every man, and life for as many as give heed to it. If between this Word and the written Letter I shall anywhere seem to myself to find a discrepance, I will not conclude that such there actually is; nor on the other hand will I fall under the condemnation of them that would *lie for God*, but seek as I may, be thankful for what I have – and wait.

With such purposes, with such feelings, have I perused the books of the Old and New Testaments, – each book as a whole, and also as an integral part. And need I say that I have met everywhere more or less copious sources of truth, and power, and purifying impulses; – that I have found words for my inmost thoughts, songs for my joy, utterances for my hidden griefs, and pleadings for my shame and my feebleness? In short whatever *finds* me, bears witness for itself that it has proceeded from a Holy Spirit, even from the same Spirit, *which remaining in itself, yet regenerateth all other powers, and in all ages entering into holy souls maketh them friends of God, and prophets*. (Wisd. vii.) And here, perhaps, I might have been content to rest if I had not learned that, as a Christian, I cannot, – must not – stand alone; or if I had not known that more than this was holden and required by the Fathers of the Reformation, and by the Churches collectively, since the Council of Nice at latest. This somewhat more, in which Jerome, Augustine, Luther, and Hooker, were of one and the same judgment, and less than which not one of them would have tolerated – would it fall within the scope of my present doubts and objections? I hope it would not. Let only their general expressions be interpreted by their treatment of the Scriptures in detail, and I dare confidently trust that it would not. For I can no more reconcile the Doctrine which startles my belief with the practice and particular declarations of these great men, than with the convictions of my own understanding and conscience. At all events – and I cannot too early or too earnestly guard against any misapprehension of my meaning and purpose – let it be distinctly understood that my arguments and objections apply exclusively to the following Doctrine or Dogma.

LETTER II

IN my last Letter I said that in the Bible there is more that *finds* me than I have experienced in all other books put together; that the words of the Bible find me at greater depths of my being; and that whatever finds me brings with it an irresistible evidence of its having proceeded from the Holy Spirit. But the doctrine in question requires me to believe, that not only what finds me, but that all that exists in the sacred volume, and which I am bound to find therein, was – not alone inspired by, that is, composed by men under the actuating influence of the Holy Spirit, but likewise – dictated by an Infallible Intelligence; – that the writers, each and all, were divinely informed as well as inspired. Now here all evasion, all excuse, is cut off . . .

LETTER III

But, lastly, you object, that – even granting that no coercive, positive reasons for the belief – no direct and not inferred assertions, – of the plenary inspiration of the Old and New Testament, in the generally received import of the term, could be adduced, yet, in behalf of a doctrine so catholic, and during so long a succession of ages affirmed and acted on by Jew and Christian, Greek, Romish, and Protestant, you need no other answer than – 'Tell me, first, why it should not be received! Why should I not believe the Scriptures throughout dictated, in word and thought, by an infallible Intelligence?' – I admit the fairness of the retort; and eagerly and earnestly do I answer: For every reason that makes me prize and revere these Scriptures; – prize them, love them, revere them, beyond all other books! *Why* should I not? Because the Doctrine in question petrifies at once the whole body of Holy Writ with all its harmonies and symmetrical gradations, – the flexile and the rigid, – the supporting hard and the clothing soft, – the blood *which is the life*, – the intelligencing nerves, and the rudely woven, but soft and springy, cellular substance, in which all are embedded and lightly bound together. This breathing organism, this glorious *panharmonicon*, which I had seen stand on its feet as a man, and with a man's voice given to it, the Doctrine in question turns at once into a colossal Memnon's head, a hollow passage for a voice, a voice that mocks the voices of many men, and speaks in their names, and yet is but one voice and the same; – and no man uttered it, and never in a human heart was it conceived. *Why* should I not? – Because the Doctrine evacuates of all sense and efficacy the sure and constant tradition, that all the several books bound up together in our precious family Bibles were composed in different and widely distant ages, under the greatest diversity of circumstances, and degrees of light and information, and yet that the composers, whether as uttering or as record-ing what was uttered and what was done, were all actuated by a pure and holy Spirit, one and the same – (for is there any spirit pure and holy, and yet not proceeding from God – and yet not proceeding in and with the Holy Spirit?) – one Spirit, working diversly, now awakening strength, and now glorifying itself in weakness, now giving power and direction to knowledge, and now taking away the sting from error!

But let me once be persuaded that all these heart-awakening utterances of human hearts – of men of like faculties and passions with myself, mourning, rejoicing, suffering, triumphing – are but as a *Divina Commedia* of a super-human – Oh bear with me, if I say – Ventriloquist; – that the royal Harper, to whom I have so often submitted myself as a *many-stringed instrument* for his fire-tipt fingers to traverse, while every several nerve of emotion, passion, thought, that thrids the flesh-and-blood of our common humanity, responded to the touch, – that this *sweet Psalmist of Israel* was himself as mere an instru-ment as his harp, an *automaton* poet, mourner, and supplicant; – all is gone, – all sympathy, at least, and all example. I listen in awe and fear, but likewise in perplexity and confusion of spirit.

Yet one other instance, and let this be the crucial test of the Doctrine. Say that the Book of Job throughout was dictated by an infallible Intelligence. Then re-peruse the book, and still, as you proceed, try to apply the tenet: try if you can even attach any sense or semblance of meaning to the speeches which you are reading. What! were the hollow truisms, the unsufficing half-truths, the false assumptions and malignant insinuations of the supercilious bigots, who corruptly defended the truth: – were the impressive facts, the piercing outcries, the pathetic appeals, and the close and powerful reasoning with which the poor sufferer – smarting at once from his wounds, and from the oil of vitriol which the orthodox *liars for God* were dropping into them – impatiently, but uprightly and holily, controverted this truth, while in will and in spirit he clung to it; – were both dictated by an infallible Intelligence?

(Taken from the third edition, ed. H. N. Coleridge, London: Moxon 1853.)

I.1.10 Benjamin Breckinridge Warfield, from 'The Church Doctrine of Inspiration'

Warfield saw the questions asked by those like Lessing, and the doubts and accommodations of Coleridge and others, as utterly destructive of Christian faith. In this extract he argues that the straightforward position that what the Bible says, God says has been the testimony of the church throughout the ages.

It is upon this fact that we need first of all to fix our attention. It is not of the variegated hypotheses of his fellow-theorizers, but of some high doctrine of inspiration, the common object of attack of them all, that each new theorizer on the subject of inspiration is especially conscious, as standing over against him, with reference to which he is to orient himself, and against the claims of which he is to defend his new hypothesis. Thus they themselves introduce us to the fact that over against the numberless discordant theories of inspiration which vex our time, there stands a well-defined church-doctrine of inspiration. This church-doctrine of inspiration differs from the theories that would fain supplant it, in that it is not the invention nor the property of an individual, but the settled faith of the universal church of God; in that it is not the growth of yesterday, but the assured persuasion of the people of God from the first planting of the church until to-day; in that it is not a protean shape, varying its affirmations to fit every new change in the ever-shifting thought of men, but from the beginning has been the church's constant and abiding conviction as to the divinity of the Scriptures committed to her keeping. It is certainly a most impressive fact, – this well-defined, aboriginal, stable doctrine of the church as to the nature and trustworthiness of the Scriptures of God, which confronts with its gentle but steady persistence of affirmation all the theories of inspiration which the restless energy of unbelieving and half-believing speculation has been able to invent in this agitated nineteenth century of ours. Surely the seeker after the truth in the matter of the inspiration of the Bible may well take this church-doctrine as his starting-point.

What this church-doctrine is, it is scarcely necessary minutely to describe. It will suffice to remind ourselves that it looks upon the Bible as an oracular book, – as the Word of God in such a sense that whatever it says God says, – not a book, then, in which one may, by searching, find some word of God, but a book which may be frankly appealed to at any point with the assurance that whatever it may be found to say, that is the Word of God. We are all of us members in particular of the body of Christ which we call the church: and the life of the church, and the faith of the church, and the thought of the church are our natural heritage. We know how, as Christian men, we approach this Holy Book, – how unquestioningly we receive its statements of fact, bow before its enunciations of duty, tremble before its threatenings, and rest upon its promises. Or, if the subtle spirit of modern doubt has seeped somewhat into our hearts, our memory will easily recall those happier days when we stood a child at our Christian mother's knee, with lisping lips following the words which her slow finger traced upon this open page, – words which were her support in every trial and, as she fondly trusted, were to be our guide throughout life. Mother church was speaking to us in that maternal voice, commending to us her vital faith in the Word of God. How often since then has it been our own lot, in our turn, to speak to others all the words of this life! As we sit in the midst of our pupils in the Sabbath-school, or in the centre of our circle at home, or perchance at some bedside of sickness or of death; or as we meet our fellow-man amid the busy work of the world, hemmed in by temptation or weighed down with care, and would fain put beneath him some firm support and stay: in what spirit do we turn to this Bible then? with what confidence do we commend its every word to those whom we would make partakers of its comfort or of its strength? In such scenes as these is revealed the vital faith of the people of God in the surety and trustworthiness of the Word of God.

Nor do we need to do more than remind ourselves that this attitude of entire trust in every word of the Scriptures has been characteristic of the people of God from the very foundation of the church. Christendom has always reposed upon the belief that the utterances of this book are properly oracles of God. The whole body of Christian literature bears witness to this fact. We may trace its stream to its source, and everywhere it is vocal with a living faith in the divine trustworthiness of the Scriptures of God in every one of their affirmations. This is the murmur of the little rills of Christian speech which find their tenuous way through the parched heathen land of the early second century. And this is the mighty voice of the great river of Christian thought which sweeps through the ages, freighted with blessings for men.

If we would estimate at its full meaning the depth of this trust in the Scripture word, we should observe Christian men at work upon the text of Scripture. There is but one view-point which will account for or justify the minute and loving pains which have been expended upon the text of Scripture, by the long line of commentators that has extended unbrokenly from the first Christian ages to our own. The allegorical interpretation which rioted in the early days of the church was the daughter of reverence for the biblical word; a spurious daughter you may think, but none the less undeniably a direct offspring of the awe with which the sacred text was regarded as the utterances of God, and, as such, pregnant with inexhaustible significance. The patient and anxious care with which the Bible text is scrutinized today by scholars, of a different spirit no doubt from those old allegorizers, but of equal reverence for the text of Scripture, betrays the same fundamental view-point, – to which the Bible is the Word of God, every detail of the meaning of which is of inestimable preciousness.

Of course the church has not failed to bring this, her vital faith in the divine trustworthiness of the Scripture word, to formal expression in her solemn creeds. The simple faith of the Christian people is also the confessional doctrine of the Christian churches. The assumption of the divine authority of the scriptural teaching underlies all the credal statements of the church; all of which are formally based upon the Scriptures. And from the beginning, it finds more or less full expression in them. Already, in some of the formulas of faith which underlie the Apostles' Creed itself, we meet with the phrase 'according to the Scriptures' as validating the items of belief; while in the Niceno-Constantinopolitan Creed, amid the meagre clauses outlining only what is essential to the doctrine of the Holy Spirit, place is given to the declaration that He is to be found speaking in the prophets – 'who spake by the prophets.'

Thus, in every way possible, the church has borne her testimony from the beginning, and still in our day, to her faith in the divine trustworthiness of her Scriptures, in all their affirmations of whatever kind. At no age has it been possible for men to express without rebuke the faintest doubt as to the absolute trustworthiness of their least declaration. Tertullian, writing at the opening of the third century, suggests, with evident hesitation and timidity, that Paul's language in the seventh chapter of First Corinthians may be intended to distinguish, in his remarks on marriage and divorce, between matters of divine commandment and of human arrangement. Dr. Sanday is obliged to comment on his language: 'Any seeming depreciation of Scripture was as unpopular even then as it is now.' The church has always believed her Scriptures to be the book of God, of which God was in such a sense the author that every one of its affirmations of whatever kind is to be esteemed as the utterance of God, of infallible truth and authority.

In the whole history of the church there have been but two movements of thought, tending to a lower conception of the inspiration and authority of Scripture, which have attained sufficient proportions to bring them into view in an historical sketch.

(1) The first of these may be called the Rationalistic view. Its characteristic feature is an effort to distinguish between inspired and uninspired elements within the Scriptures. . . .

In the nineteenth century it has retained a strong hold, especially upon apologetical writers, chiefly in the three forms which affirm respectively that only the *mysteries* of the faith are inspired, i.e. things undiscoverable by unaided reason, – that the Bible is inspired only in *matters of faith and practice*, – and that the Bible is inspired only in its *thoughts or concepts*, not in its words. But although this legacy from the rationalism of an evil time still makes its appearance in the pages of many theological writers, and has no doubt affected the faith of a considerable number of Christians, it has failed to supplant in either the creeds of the church or the hearts of the people the church-doctrine of the plenary inspiration of the Bible, i.e. the doctrine that the Bible is inspired not *in part* but *fully*, in all its elements alike, – things discoverable by reason as well as mysteries, matters of history and science as well as of faith and practice, words as well as thoughts.

(2) The second of the lowered views of inspiration may be called the Mystical view. Its characteristic conception is that the Christian man has something within himself, – call it enlightened reason, spiritual insight, the Christian consciousness, the witness of the Spirit, or call it what you will, – to the test of which every 'external revelation' is to be subjected, and according to the decision of which are the contents of the Bible to be valued.

Despite these attempts to introduce lowered conceptions, the doctrine of the plenary inspiration of the Scriptures, which looks upon them as an oracular book, in all its parts and elements, alike, of God, trustworthy in all its affirmations of every kind, remains to-day, as it has always been, the vital faith of the people of God, and the formal teaching of the organized church.

The more we contemplate this church-doctrine, the more pressing becomes the question of what account we are to give of it, – its origin and persistence. How shall we account for the immediate adoption of so developed a doctrine of inspiration in the very infancy of the church, and for the tenacious hold which the church has kept upon it through so many ages? The account is simple enough, and capable of inclusion in a single sentence: this is the doctrine of inspiration which was held by the writers of the New Testament and by Jesus as reported in the Gospels. It is this simple fact that has commended it to the church of all ages as the true doctrine; and in it we may surely recognize an even more impressive fact than that of the existence of a stable, abiding church-doctrine standing over against the many theories of the day, – the fact, namely, that this church-doctrine of inspiration was the Bible doctrine before it was the church-doctrine, and is the church-doctrine only because it is the Bible doctrine.

(Taken from B. B. Warfield, The Inspiration and Authority of the Bible, ed. Samuel G. Craig, Phillipsburg, NJ: Presbyterian & Reformed Publishing Co. 1948, pp. 105–14.)

I.1.11 Karl Barth, from *Evangelical Theology*

The story of Karl Barth's discovery of 'the strange new world of the Bible', of the Word of God that speaks judgment and grace to us from without, is fast becoming a part of theological folklore. This text, from towards the end of his life, attempts to define how the task of theology is related to the scriptural witness to the Word of God. Theology's task, according to Barth, is to hear and repeat what is said in the Scriptures.

We shall now attempt to clarify how evangelical theology is related to this biblical witness to the Word of God.

First of all, theology shares with the biblical prophecy and apostolate a common concern for human response to the divine Word. The witnesses of the Old and New Testaments were men like all others, men who had heard the Word and witnessed to it in a human way – in speech, vision, and thought that were human and conditioned by time and space. They were *theologians*; yet, in spite of having an identical orientation to an identical object, as theologians they differed widely from one another. Anything other than *their* intention, anything more or less than that, cannot be the substance of evangelical theology. In its study of the two Testaments, what theology has to learn as much as anything else is the method of a *human* thought and speech as they are oriented to the Word of God.

All the same, in the second place, theology is neither prophecy nor apostolate. Its relationship to God's Word cannot be compared to the position of the biblical witnesses because it can know the Word of God only at second hand, only in the mirror and echo of the biblical witness. The place of theology is *not* to be located on the same or a similar plane with those first witnesses. Since the human reply to the Word will in practice always consist partially in a basic question, theology cannot and dare not presume that its human response stands in some immediate relationship to the Word spoken by God himself. At that moment when everything depended on being present, scientific theology, as defined earlier in these lectures, is completely absent.

The position of theology, thirdly, can in no wise be exalted *above* that of the biblical witnesses. The post-Biblical theologian may, no doubt, possess a better astronomy, geography, zoology, psychology, physiology, and so on than these biblical witnesses possessed; but as for the Word of God, he is not justified in comporting himself in relationship to those witnesses as though he knew more about the Word than they. He is neither a president of a seminary, nor the Chairman of the Board of some Christian Institute of Advanced Theological Studies, who might claim some authority over the prophets and apostles. He cannot grant or refuse them a hearing as though they were colleagues on the faculty. Still less is he a high-school teacher authorized to look over their shoulder benevolently or crossly, to correct their notebooks, or to give them good, average, or bad marks. Even the smallest, strangest, simplest, or obscurest among the biblical witnesses has an incomparable advantage over even the most pious, scholarly, and sagacious latter-day theologian. From his special point of view and in his special fashion, the witness has thought, spoken, and written about the revelatory Word and act in direct confrontation with it. All subsequent theology, as well as the whole of the community that comes after the event, will never find itself in the same immediate confrontation.

Once and for all, theology has, fourthly, its position *beneath* that of the biblical scriptures. While it is aware of all their human and conditioned character, it still knows and considers that the writings with which it deals are *holy* writings. These writings are selected and separated; they deserve and demand respect and attention of an extraordinary order, since they have a direct relationship to God's work and word. If theology seeks to learn of prophecy and the apostolate, it can only and ever learn from the prophetic and apostolic witnesses. It must learn not this or that important truth but the one thing that is necessary – and with respect to this one thing on which all else depends, the biblical witnesses are better informed than are the theologians. For this reason theology must agree to let *them* look over its shoulder and correct its notebooks.

In the fifth place, the peg on which all theology hangs is acquaintance with the God of the Gospel. This acquaintance is never to be taken for granted; it is never immediately available; it can never be carried about by the theologian in some intellectual or spiritual pillbox or briefcase. The knowledge of Immanuel, the God of man and for man, includes acquaintance with the man of God. That he is Abraham's God, Israel's God, man's God – this is Yahweh's marvelous distinction from the gods of all other theologies. Theology has Immanuel – true God, true man – as its object when it comes from the Holy Scriptures and returns to them. 'It is they that bear witness to me.' Theology becomes evangelical theology only when the God of the Gospel encounters it in the mirror and echo of the prophetic and apostolic word. It must also grasp God's work and word as the theme and problem of *its* thinking and speaking, in the same way that the Yahwist and Elohist, Isaiah and Jeremiah, Matthew, Paul, and John saw and heard this Word. Many other things, much that is interesting, beautiful, good, and true, could also be communicated and disclosed to theology by all sorts of old and new literature of other kinds. But with respect to the theme and problem that make it theological science, it will, for better or for worse, have to stick to this literature, the Holy Scriptures.

Nevertheless, in the sixth place, theology confronts in Holy Scriptures an extremely polyphonic, not a monotonous, testimony to the work and word of God. Everything that can be heard there is differentiated – not only the voices of the Old and New Testaments as such, but also the many voices that reverberate throughout both. It should be noted that the primary and real basis of this differentiation does not lie in the various psychological, sociological, and cultural conditions which existed for each witness. There is, of course, such a preliminary basis for differentiation in the profusion of biblical witnesses, in the various factors influencing their purposes and points of view, in the variety of their languages and the special theology of each. The primary basis, however, lies in the objective multiplicity and inner contrasts sustained within the motion of the history of the covenant which they recount and affirm. This motion is all-inclusive; it encompasses even its smallest elements, reflecting the interplay of unity and disunity between God and man as the witnesses disclose them. Therefore, although theology is certainly confronted with the one God, he is One in the fullness of his existence, action, and revelation. In the school of the witnesses theology can in no way become monolithic, monomanic, monotonous, and infallibly boring. In no way can it bind or limit itself to one special subject or another. In this school theology will be oriented to the unceasing succession of different loci of the divine work and word, and in this way theological understanding, thought, and speech will receive their definite place. In the school of these witnesses theology inevitably begins to wander, though always with the same goal in mind. It migrates from the Old Testament to the New and returns again, from the Yahwist to the priestly codex, from the psalms of David to the proverbs of Solomon, from the Gospel of John to the synoptic gospels, from the Letter to the Galatians to the so-called 'straw' epistle of James, and so on continually. Within all of these writings the pilgrimage leads from one level of tradition to another, taking into account every stage of tradition that may be present or surmised. In this respect the work of theology might be compared to the task of circling a high mountain which, although it is one and the same mountain, exists and manifests itself in very different shapes. The eternally rich God is the content of the knowledge of evangelical theology. His unique mystery is known only in the overflowing fullness of his counsels, ways, and judgments.

Theology responds to the Logos of God, in the seventh place, when it endeavors to hear and speak of him always anew on the basis of his self-disclosure in the Scriptures. Its searching of the Scriptures consists in asking the texts whether and to what extent they might witness to him; however, whether and to what extent they reflect and echo, in their complete humanity, the Word of God is completely unknown beforehand. This possibility must be seen and heard again and again, and this knowledge must be won from it and illuminated repeatedly. The open, candid question *about this Word* is what theology brings to the Bible. All other questions are only conjoined and subordinated to this question; they can present only technical aids to its solution. Nowadays, of course, the 'exegetical-theological' task is often said to consist in the translation of biblical assertions out of the speech of a past time into the language of modern man. The remarkable assumption behind this project, however, seems to be that the content, meaning, and point of biblical assertions are relatively easy to ascertain and may afterward be presupposed as self-evident. The main task would be then simply to render these assertions understandable and relevant to the modern world by means of some sort of linguistic key. The message is all very well, it is said, but 'how do you tell it to the man on the street?' The truth of the matter, however, is that the central affirmations of the Bible are not self-evident; the Word of God itself, as witnessed to in the Bible, is not immediately obvious in any of its chapters or verses. On the contrary, the truth of the Word must be *sought* precisely, in order to be understood in its deep simplicity. Every possible means must be used: philological and historical criticism and analysis, careful consideration of the nearer and the more remote textual relationships, and not least, the enlistment of every device of the conjectural imagination that is available.

The question *about the Word* and this question alone fulfills and does justice to the intention of the biblical authors and their writings. And in passing, might not this question also do justice to modern man? If modern man is earnestly interested in the Bible, he certainly does not wish for its translation into his transitory jargon. Instead, he himself would like to participate in the effort to draw nearer to what stands *there*. This effort is what theology owes to modern man and, above all, to the Bible itself. 'What stands there,' in the pages of the Bible, is the witness to the *Word of God*, the Word of God in this testimony of the Bible. Just how far it stands there, however, is a fact that demands unceasing discovery, interpretation, and recognition. It demands untiring effort – effort, moreover, which is not unaccompanied by blood and tears. The biblical witnesses and the Holy Scriptures confront theology as the object of this effort.

(Taken from Karl Barth, Evangelical Theology: An Introduction *Trans. Grover Foley, London: Weidenfeld & Nicolson 1963, pp 30–6.)*

I.2 The authority of the Christian tradition

Introductory essay

Despite the position advanced in the previous section, rather obviously not all theological arguments turn on straightforward appeals to Scripture. The second major source for theological work is the Christian tradition: that 'the church has taught' a particular position, or that 'many theologians have believed' it, or that 'it has been universally held that' this thing is true, is regarded as in itself an argument in favour of the position in most, if not all, theological work. 'Tradition' comes from the Latin *traditio*, meaning simply 'a handing over' (the English word 'trade' captures another facet of the same general idea). In commending the proper practice of the eucharist to the Corinthian church, Paul speaks of 'that which was handed over to him by the Lord' which he has in turn 'handed over'. The Christian tradition is this living process whereby each generation within the church receives practices and teachings from the one before and hands them on, perhaps slightly altered, to the next. Historical writings are, in a sense, the 'fossil record' of this process of tradition, and enable us to demonstrate that what we received was no invention of those who came just before, but has long and deep roots.

A theological appeal to tradition can be variously constructed, and variously related to the authority of Scripture. In the texts below a sample of this variety will be found. In the earliest period, we find Irenaeus sketching an account of the faith of the church, which is to be held to in the face of novel teachings being put forward by a variety of groups that he characterizes as heretical, as teaching something other than the faith of the church (I.2.1). For Irenaeus the traditional beliefs of the church, as codified in the 'rule of faith' (see I.3), provide a theological pattern into which scriptural teaching should be placed; those who seek to read the Bible as upholding something other than this basic faith must be reading wrongly. Two centuries later, Basil of Caesarea invokes tradition derived from the apostles in a different way in the course of defending Trinitarian orthodoxy; he suggests that there is an unwritten teaching alongside the written teaching, preserved in the liturgical life of the church, which is just as apostolic and so just as authoritative (I.2.2). This position remains standard today in Eastern Orthodoxy.

Vincent of Lérins and Prosper of Aquitaine provide alternative, but equally influential, definitions of what makes a traditional teaching authoritative. For Vincent, again writing against a variety of heretical teachings, that which has been believed 'everywhere, by all people, always' (within the churches) is just so shown to be true (I.2.3). Vincent does not indicate how this relates to the authority of Scripture, to which he would have been committed, but it is not difficult to sketch an account: wise and respected Christian leaders across the world and across the generations have read the Scriptures this way, and so this reading is privileged by its traditional employment; we cannot suppose that we have such insight that we can see something which all who came before could not see. Prosper, by contrast, alongside ascribing authority to popes ('the apostolic see' of the title) and councils, invokes the liturgical tradition of the churches: *lex orandi lex credendi* is his slogan; roughly, belief should follow prayer, and ways in which we have been taught to pray (by liturgical tradition) form an unshakeable rule for theology (I.2.4). (At another point in his defence of the Spirit's place within the Godhead, Basil invokes a similar argument: we pray to the Spirit, which would be improper if he were not God; the way we pray is not improper, because many great saints and martyrs taught us to pray this way; so the Spirit must be God.)

These sorts of argument were highly influential whilst the church appeared to be undivided: that which the church held to and had always held to simply must be right. The high point of this respect for tradition comes in medieval scholastic theology, where the words of patristic writers were held in such esteem that much effort was expended on apparent contradictions, in order to demonstrate that although (say) Augustine and John of Damascus appeared to disagree, in fact they could both be right if only they were read in a certain way. This respect for tradition formed a significant problem for the early Reformation theologians, who wanted to argue precisely that the Roman Catholic Church had gone badly wrong at some point, and so were forced to come up with a different account of tradition.

The most radical Reformation position is not represented here for reasons of space, but may be found in certain Anabaptist writings, for instance. In these there is a simple denial that there is any

Christian tradition. The Roman Catholic Church is apostate and in no sense Christian, and there is a need to found a new church of Jesus Christ because none has existed for centuries (hints of this position may be found in the text from Balthasar Hubmaier in the previous chapter, I.1.5). The mainstream reformers were not so extreme, and indeed expended considerable energy in trying to demonstrate that they were upholding classical Christianity against recent innovations (Calvin's *Institutes*, for example, contain nearly 500 citations from Augustine). They were forced to deny, however, that there was any independent authority attached to tradition, and so Calvin argues that tradition only has authority if the teachings of Scripture are upheld (I.2.5). The Anglican *Thirty-Nine Articles* (I.2.6), still the doctrinal standard of the Church of England and other Anglican churches, assert something of a mediating position: only what is in Scripture can be thought to be 'necessary to salvation' (Art. VI), and even the Catholic creeds are to be believed only because 'they may be proved by most certain warrants of holy Scripture' (Art. VIII). The ancient churches have erred (Art. XIX), and Councils may err (Art. XXI), but even so the 'Church hath power' to order liturgy and to rule on matters of faith, so long as nothing is ordained that is contrary to Scripture.

The response to these points included here is not from the Counter-Reformation, the Roman Catholic response to the Reformation (but see the comments about unwritten tradition in the Decree of the Council of Trent, I.1.6 above), but from Eastern Orthodoxy. The *Confession of Dositheus*, which despite its name consists of the pronouncements of a synod or council, asserts that the continuity of the apostolic church is seen in the unbroken succession of bishops going back to the apostles, who have all spoken with one voice on all doctrinal issues, and so to be orthodox is to be aligned with this tradition (I.2.7). Scripture is the touchstone, but the tradition offers the only authorized interpretation of Scripture.

In the modern period the fault lines largely remain those drawn at the Reformation. John Henry Newman was one of the founders of the Oxford Movement, which gave vigour to the more Catholic tradition of the Church of England in the first half of the nineteenth century; he finally became Roman Catholic and died a cardinal. His *Essay on the Development of Doctrine* (I.2.8) is mostly concerned with arguing for the various controversial Roman positions, but the earlier chapters, excerpted here, discuss the concept of development more generally. For Newman, not only is it natural that Christian doctrine, like any system of ideas, should grow and develop through time, in this particular case we also have good reason to suppose that there will be an authoritative guide and judge of this development provided by God, which Newman identifies with the Roman Catholic Church. Thus, church tradition is an infallible guide to correct Christian doctrine. *Dei Verbum* (I.2.10), a document of the Second Vatican Council, witnesses to the same general position, seeking to link tradition to Scripture as interpreted by the teaching office of the church in a unitary revelation from God.

On the Reformed wing of the church, Karl Barth (I.2.9) thinks rather differently. The task of the theologian is to listen to the Scripture, to become a student of the Word of God. Listening to the tradition is to acknowledge that in the good providence of God one does not have to do this alone, but rather that there is a 'great cloud' of fellow-students, today and through the ages, whose own listening and conversation can and must guide and aid ours. Similarly, Gerhard Ebeling (I.2.12) argues that the principle of *sola scriptura* ('Scripture alone') demands a theological account of tradition, because the Scriptures have not come to us pristine from heaven, but through a series of hands. What is 'handed on', Ebeling insists, is however not any law or custom or teaching, but Jesus Christ himself. It is the knowledge of the gospel that we have received from those who were before, and which we are required to hand on to the future.

Finally, we have a discussion of the origins of the Christian tradition from one of the leading Greek Orthodox theologians of today, John Zizioulas (I.2.11). He examines early records of how the process of handing on from one bishop to the next was understood in the early period. The church has a history, from the first coming of Jesus to the second, and the 'handing on' of apostolicity is essentially an insertion into this history, made sense of not just by the past, but by the future. Although Zizioulas focuses on ordination, this eschatological note in the account of tradition is interesting and suggestive, and may have much wider ramifications.

As creatures with our own location in history, we need tradition. None of us saw Jesus walking the streets of Jerusalem, and so we can only know him by listening to what others tell us of him. Within that, the testimonies of those who did see him, the apostles, have a central place, and so the Scriptures stand alone at the head of the tradition, but we cannot pretend that we can ignore the centuries God has been pleased to put between us and them, and have unmediated access through them to Jesus. We need some account of how we relate to others who have struggled to take the apostolic witness seriously, and be faithful to Jesus Christ.

SRH

A. Patristic appeals to tradition

I.2.1 St Irenaeus of Lyons, from *Against the Heresies*

In this extract Irenaeus asserts the unity of the faith of the church across the world, which was received from the apostles.

The Church, though dispersed through the whole world, even to the ends of the earth, has received from the apostles and their disciples this faith: [she believes] in one God, the Father Almighty, Maker of heaven, and earth, and the sea, and all things that are in them; and in one Christ Jesus, the Son of God, who became incarnate for our salvation; and in the Holy Spirit, who proclaimed through the prophets the dispensations of God, and the advents, and the birth from a virgin, and the passion, and the resurrection from the dead, and the ascension into heaven in the flesh of the beloved Christ Jesus, our Lord, and his [future] manifestation from heaven in the glory of the Father 'to gather all things in one,' and to raise up anew all flesh of the whole human race, in order that to Christ Jesus, our Lord, and God, and Saviour, and King, according to the will of the invisible Father, 'every knee should bow, of things in heaven, and things in earth, and things under the earth, and that every tongue should confess' to him, and that he should execute just judgement towards all; that he may send 'spiritual wickednesses,' and the angels who transgressed and became apostates, together with the ungodly, and unrighteous, and wicked, and profane among men, into ever-lasting fire; but may, in the exercise of his grace, confer immortality on the righteous, and holy, and those who have kept his commandments, and have persevered in his love, some from the beginning, and others from their repent-ance, and may surround them with everlasting glory.

As I have already observed, the Church, having received this preaching and this faith, although scattered throughout the whole world, yet, as if occupying but one house, carefully preserves it. She also believes these points just as if she had but one soul, and one and the same heart, and she proclaims them, and teaches them, and hands them down, with perfect harmony, as if she possessed only one mouth. For, although the languages of the world are dissimilar, yet the import of the tradition is one and the same. For the Churches which have been planted in Germany do not believe or hand down anything different, nor do those in Spain, nor those in Gaul, nor those in the East, nor those in Egypt, nor those in Libya, nor those which have been established in the central regions of the world. But as the sun, that creature of God, is one and the same throughout the whole world, so also the preach-ing of the truth shineth everywhere, and enlightens all men that are willing to come to a knowledge of the truth. Nor will any one of the rulers in the

Churches, however highly gifted he may be in point of eloquence, teach doctrines different from these (for no one is greater than the Master); nor, on the other hand, will he who is deficient in power of expression inflict injury on the tradition. For the faith being ever one and the same, neither does one who is able at great length to discourse regarding it, make any addition to it, nor does one, who can say but little diminish it.

(Taken from the Ante-Nicene Fathers vol. III. trans. and ed. A. Roberts and J. Donaldson, I.10.)

I.2.2 St Basil of Caesarea, from *On the Holy Spirit*

Basil asserts that there is a verbal tradition handed down from the apostles alongside the written Scripture, which is reflected in various practices of the churches. He explains the significance of some of these practices, and ends by defending a doxology (which he has been attacked for using) as apostolic, although unbiblical.

66. Of the beliefs and practices whether generally accepted or publicly enjoined which are preserved in the Church some we possess derived from written teaching; others we have received delivered to us 'in a mystery' by the tradition of the apostles; and both of these in relation to true religion have the same force. And these no one will gainsay; – no one, at all events, who is even moderately versed in the institutions of the Church. For were we to attempt to reject such customs as have no written authority, on the ground that the importance they possess is small, we should unintentionally injure the Gospel in its very vitals; or, rather, should make our public defi- nition a mere phrase and nothing more. For instance, to take the first and most general example, who is it who has taught us in writing to sign with the sign of the cross those who have trusted in the name of our Lord Jesus Christ? What writing has taught us to turn to the East at the prayer? Which of the saints has left us in writing the words of the invocation at the displaying of the bread of the Eucharist and the cup of blessing? For we are not, as is well known, content with what the apostle or the Gospel has recorded, but both in preface and conclusion we add other words as being of great impor- tance to the validity of the ministry, and these we derive from unwritten teaching.

Moreover we bless the water of baptism and the oil of the chrism, and besides this the catechumen who is being baptized. On what written authority do we do this? Is not our authority silent and mystical tradition? Nay, by what written word is the anointing of oil itself taught? And whence comes the custom of baptizing thrice? And as to the other customs of baptism from what Scripture do we derive the renunciation of Satan and his angels? Does not this come from that unpublished and secret teaching which our fathers guarded in a silence out of the reach of curious meddling and inquisitive investigation? Well had they learnt the lesson that the awful dignity of the mysteries is best preserved by silence. What the uninitiated are not even allowed to look at was hardly likely to be publicly paraded about in written documents. What was the meaning of the mighty Moses in not making all the parts of the tabernacle open to every one? The profane he stationed without the sacred barriers; the first courts he conceded to the purer; the Levites alone he judged worthy of being servants of the Deity; sacrifices and burnt offerings and the rest of the priestly functions he allotted to the priests; one chosen out of all he admitted to the shrine, and even this one not always but on only one day in the year, and of this one day a time was fixed for his entry so that he might gaze on the Holy of Holies amazed at the strangeness and novelty of the sight. Moses was wise enough to know that contempt stretches to the trite and to the obvious, while a keen interest is naturally associated with the unusual and the unfamiliar. In the same manner the Apostles and Fathers who laid down laws for the Church from the beginning thus guarded the awful dignity of the mysteries in secrecy and silence, for what is bruited abroad at random among the common folk is no mystery at all. This is the reason for our tradition of unwritten precepts and practices, that the knowledge of our dogmas may not become neglected and contemned by the multitude through familiarity. 'Dogma' and 'Kerygma' are two distinct things; the former is observed in silence; the latter is proclaimed to all the world. One form of this silence is the obscurity employed in Scripture, which makes the meaning of 'dogmas' difficult to be understood for the very advantage of the reader: Thus we all look to the East at our prayers, but few of us know that we are seeking our own old country, Paradise, which God planted in Eden in the East. We pray standing, on the first day of the week, but we do not all know the reason. On the day of the resurrection we remind ourselves of the grace given to us by standing at prayer, not only because we rose with Christ, and are bound to 'seek those things which are above,' but because the day seems to us to be in some sense an image of the age which we expect it . . . Of necessity, then, the church teaches her own foster children to offer their prayers on that day standing, to the end that through continual reminder of the endless life we may not neglect to make provision for our removal thither. On this day the rules of the church have educated us to prefer the upright attitude of prayer, for by their plain reminder they, as it were, make our mind to dwell no longer in the present but in the future. Moreover every time we fall upon our knees and rise from off them we show by the very deed that by our sin we fell down to earth, and by the loving kindness of our Creator were called back to heaven.

67. Time will fail me if I attempt to recount the unwritten mysteries of the Church. Of the rest I say nothing; but of the very confession of our faith in Father, Son, and Holy Ghost, what is the written source? If it be granted that, as we are baptized, so also under the obligation to believe, we make our confession in like terms as our baptism, in accordance with the tradition of our baptism and in conformity with the principles of true religion, let our opponents grant us too the right to be as consistent in our ascription of glory as in our confession of faith. If they deprecate our doxology on the ground that it lacks written authority, let them give us the written evidence for the confession of our faith and the other matters which we have enumerated. While the unwritten traditions are so many, and their bearing on 'the mystery

of godliness' is so important, can they refuse to allow us a single word which has come down to us from the Fathers; – which we found, derived from untutored custom, abiding in unperverted churches; – a word for which the arguments are strong, and which contributes in no small degree to the completeness of the force of the mystery?

(Taken from the Nicene and Post-Nicene Fathers, second series vol. VIII, ed. Philip Schaff and Henry Wace, trans. Blomfield Jackson.)

1.2.3 Vincent of Lérins, from *The Commonitorium*

Vincent of Lérins argues that the variety of possible interpretations of Scripture makes an authoritative interpretation necessary, and suggests that the tradition of the church, defined as what has always been believed by all people, everywhere, provides such an interpretation.

[4.] I have often then inquired earnestly and attentively of very many men eminent for sanctity and learning, how and by what sure and, so to speak, universal rule I may be able to distinguish the truth of Catholic faith from the falsehood of heretical pravity; and I have always, and in almost every instance, received an answer to this effect: That whether I or any one else should wish to detect the frauds and avoid the snares of heretics as they rise, and to continue sound and complete in the Catholic faith, we must, the Lord helping, fortify our own belief in two ways; first, by the authority of the Divine Law, and then, by the Tradition of the Catholic Church.

[5.] But here some one perhaps will ask, Since the canon of Scripture is complete, and sufficient of itself for everything, and more than sufficient, what need is there to join with it the authority of the Church's interpretation? For this reason, – because, owing to the depth of Holy Scripture, all do not accept it in one and the same sense, but one understands its words in one way, another in another; so that it seems to be capable of as many interpretations as there are interpreters. For Novatian expounds it one way, Sabellius another, Donatus another, Arius, Eunomius, Macedonius, another, Photinus, Apollinarius, Priscillian, another, Iovinian, Pelagius, Celestius, another, lastly, Nestorius another. Therefore, it is very necessary, on account of so great intricacies of such various error, that the rule for the right understanding of the prophets and apostles should be framed in accordance with the standard of Ecclesiastical and Catholic interpretation.

[6.] Moreover, in the Catholic Church itself, all possible care must be taken, that we hold that faith which has been believed everywhere, always, by all. For that is truly and in the strictest sense 'Catholic,' which, as the name itself and the reason of the thing declare, comprehends all universally. This rule we shall observe if we follow universality, antiquity, consent. We shall follow universality if we confess that one faith to be true, which the whole Church throughout the world confesses; antiquity, if we in no wise depart from those interpretations which it is manifest were notoriously held by our holy ancestors and fathers; consent, in like manner, if in antiquity itself we adhere to the consentient definitions and determinations of all, or at the least of almost all priests and doctors.

. . .

[54.] But some one will say, perhaps, Shall there, then, be no progress in Christ's Church? Certainly; all possible progress. For what being is there, so envious of men, so full of hatred to God, who would seek to forbid it? Yet on condition that it be real progress, not alteration of the faith. For progress requires that the subject be enlarged in itself, alteration, that it be transformed into something else. The intelligence, then, the knowledge, the wisdom, as well of individuals as of all, as well of one man as of the whole Church, ought, in the course of ages and centuries, to increase and make much and vigorous progress; but yet only in its own kind; that is to say, in the same doctrine, in the same sense, and in the same meaning.

[55.] The growth of religion in the soul must be analogous to the growth of the body, which, though in process of years it is developed and attains its full size, yet remains still the same. There is a wide difference between the flower of youth and the maturity of age; yet they who were once young are still the same now that they have become old, insomuch that though the stature and outward form of the individual are changed, yet his nature is one and the same, his person is one and the same. An infant's limbs are small, a young man's large, yet the infant and the young man are the same. Men when full grown have the same number of joints that they had when children; and if there be any to which maturer age has given birth these were already present in embryo, so that nothing new is produced in them when old which was not already latent in them when children. This, then, is undoubtedly the true and legitimate rule of progress, this the established and most beautiful order of growth, that mature age ever develops in the man those parts and forms which the wisdom of the Creator had already framed beforehand in the infant. Whereas, if the human form were changed into some shape belonging to another kind, or at any rate, if the number of its limbs were increased or diminished, the result would be that the whole body would become either a wreck or a monster, or, at the least, would be impaired and enfeebled.

[56.] In like manner, it behoves Christian doctrine to follow the same laws of progress, so as to be consolidated by years, enlarged by time, refined by age, and yet, withal, to continue uncorrupt and unadulterate, complete and perfect in all the measurement of its parts, and, so to speak, in all its proper members and senses, admitting no change, no waste of its distinctive property, no variation in its limits.

[57.] For example: Our forefathers in the old time sowed wheat in the Church's field. It would be most unmeet and iniquitous if we, their descendants, instead of the genuine truth of corn, should reap the counterfeit error of tares. This rather should be the result, – there should be no discrepancy between the first and the last. From doctrine which was sown as wheat, we should reap, in the increase, doctrine of the same kind – wheat also; so that when in process of time any of the original seed is developed, and now flourishes under cultivation, no change may ensue in the character of the plant. There may supervene shape, form, variation in outward appearance, but the nature of each kind must remain the same. God forbid that those rose-beds of Catholic interpretation should be converted into thorns and thistles. God forbid that in that spiritual paradise from plants of cinnamon and balsam darnel and wolfsbane should of a sudden shoot forth.

Therefore, whatever has been sown by the fidelity of the Fathers in this husbandry of God's Church, the same ought to be cultivated and taken care of by the industry of their children, the same ought to flourish and ripen, the same ought to advance and go forward to perfection. For it is right that those ancient doctrines of heavenly philosophy should, as time goes on, be cared for, smoothed, polished; but not that they should be changed, not that they should be maimed, not that they should be mutilated. They may receive proof, illustration, definiteness; but they must retain withal their completeness, their integrity, their characteristic properties.

[58.] For if once this license of impious fraud be admitted, I dread to say in how great danger religion will be of being utterly destroyed and annihilated. For if any one part of Catholic truth be given up, another, and another, and another will thenceforward be given up as a matter of course, and the several individual portions having been rejected, what will follow in the end but the rejection of the whole? On the other hand, if what is new begins to be mingled with what is old, foreign with domestic, profane with sacred, the custom will of necessity creep on universally, till at last the Church will have nothing left untampered with, nothing unadulterated, nothing sound, nothing pure; but where formerly there was a sanctuary of chaste and undefiled truth, thenceforward there will be a brothel of impious and base errors. May God's mercy avert this wickedness from the minds of his servants; be it rather the frenzy of the ungodly.

[59.] But the Church of Christ, the careful and watchful guardian of the doctrines deposited in her charge, never changes anything in them, never diminishes, never adds, does not cut off what is necessary, does not add what is superfluous, does not lose her own, does not appropriate what is another's, but while dealing faithfully and judiciously with ancient doctrine, keeps this one object carefully in view, – if there be anything which antiquity has left shapeless and rudimentary, to fashion and polish it, if anything already reduced to shape and developed, to consolidate and strengthen it, if any already ratified and defined to keep and guard it. Finally, what other object have Councils ever aimed at in their decrees, than to provide that what was before believed in simplicity should in future be believed intelligently, that what was before preached coldly should in future be preached earnestly, that what was before practised negligently should thenceforward be practised with double solicitude? This, I say, is what the Catholic Church, roused by the novelties of heretics, has accomplished by the decrees of her Councils, – this, and nothing else, – she has thenceforward consigned to posterity in writing what she had received from those of olden times only by tradition, comprising a great amount of matter in a few words, and often, for the better understanding, designating an old article of the faith by the characteristic of a new name.

(Taken from the Nicene and Post-Nicene Fathers, second series, vol. XI, ed. Philip Schaff, trans. Edgar C. S. Gibson.)

I.2.4 Prosper of Aquitaine, from *The Pronouncements of the Apostolic See*

Prosper is engaged in defending St Augustine's views on free-will, predestination and divine grace. In his view, some points which have been authoritatively decided on by the church were being questioned again, so he gathered together the testimony of the authoritative pronouncements. Two interesting features appear in the text: one, an early example of the appeal to the Pope (Rome is the 'Apostolic See' of the title) as having authority to decide matters of doctrine; the other is the appeal to the tradition of worship in the church as being authoritative for belief.

There are some people who pride themselves on being Catholics, yet hang on to the condemned opinions of heretics whether in bad faith or from inexperience. They are so presumptuous as to oppose our most religious writers. Though unhesitatingly condemning Pelagius and Celestius, they yet speak against our doctors and say that these have overstepped the due limits. They profess to follow and to admit only the doctrine sanctioned and taught against the enemies of God's grace by the Holy See of the Apostle St. Peter through the ministry of its bishops. Therefore, a careful investigation was required of the pronouncements made by the rulers of the Roman Church concerning the heresy which arose in their day and concerning the doctrine which they declared should be held about the grace of God, against the dangerous extollers of free will. We should add to this also some pronouncements of the African councils which the bishops of Rome approved and made their own. Accordingly, for the better instruction of the waverers, we now publish the declarations of the holy Fathers in a brief catalogue. Anyone who is not overcritical will be able to see from it that the outcome of all that was written on grace lies in this summary of official pronouncements which we collect here, and that he can no longer have any reason to oppose the doctrine on grace if he holds the faith of Catholics and says:

ARTICLE 1

By the sin of Adam all men lost their natural ability for good and their innocence. No one can rise from the depths of this fall of his own free will unless he be raised by the grace of God's mercy. Thus, Pope Innocent of happy memory stated and wrote in his letter to the Council of Carthage: 'When Adam was tested in his free will, he used this gift inconsiderately and fell down into the abyss of sin. He could find no way of raising himself out of it. Forever deceived by his own freedom, he would have remained crushed down by this fall, had not Christ come and raised him up by His grace. By a new birth Christ washed away in baptism his every past stain.'

ARTICLE 2

No one has any goodness of himself unless he be given a share in the goodness of Him who alone is good. A pronouncement of the same Pontiff in the same letter says so in the following words: 'Could we henceforth consider as correct the opinion of men who think that they owe their goodness to themselves, who neglect to take into account Him whose grace they receive every day, who feel confident that they can attain as much without His help?'
. . .

ARTICLE 5

To God must be given the glory of all endeavor and work and merit of the saints. No one can be pleasing to God except by making use of the gifts of God. To this conclusion we are led by the authoritative pronouncement of Pope Zosimus of saintly memory, who wrote to the bishops of the entire world in these words: 'We on our part, by a divine inspiration – for every good gift must be referred to its Author – committed the whole question to the conscience of our brethren and cobishops.' The African bishops received this statement, radiant with evident sincerity and truthfulness, with such veneration as to answer the same Pontiff: 'As to what you wrote in the letter you sent to all the provinces, namely, 'We on our part, by a divine inspiration, etc.,' we understood this to signify that you, as it were, with the naked sword of truth quickly struck down the men who exalt the freedom of man's will to the detriment of God's grace. For what else did you ever do with greater freedom than to commit the whole question to the conscience of our humble selves? And in your faith and wisdom you understood that you had done so by a divine inspiration: you said so in truth and trust. Your reason for saying so was, of course, that *the will is prepared by the Lord*, and that He Himself with fatherly inspirations moves the hearts of His sons to do what is good. For *whosoever are led by the Spirit of God, they are the sons of God*. And so we are convinced that our free wills are not set aside, and yet we have no doubt that in each and every good action of our human wills His grace is the more powerful agent.'

ARTICLE 7

We also admit, as though they were the very decrees of the Apostolic See, the decisions of the Synod of Carthage; and first, the decree laid down in its third article: 'Whosoever says that the grace of God by which we are justified through Jesus Christ our Lord is apt only to forgive sins already committed, and not also to help us so as not to commit sins, let him be anathema.'

ARTICLE 8

These are the inviolable decrees of the Holy and Apostolic See by which our holy Fathers slew the pride of the baneful heresy and taught us to ascribe to the grace of Christ both the beginning of our good dispositions and the growth of our praiseworthy efforts and our final perseverance in them. Let us next look also at the sacred prayers which in keeping with the apostolic tradition our priests offer after one norm the world over in every Catholic church. Let the rule of prayer lay down the rule of faith. When the pastors of the Christian people discharge their mandate and mission, they plead the cause of the human race with the divine mercy and, in union with the supplications of the entire Church, beg and pray that faith may be given to unbelievers, idolaters freed from the errors of their ungodliness, Jews relieved of their mind's veil and shown the light of truth, schismatics given the spirit of a new charity, sinners granted salutary penance, finally catechumens led to the sacrament of regeneration and admitted into the court of divine mercy. And that all this is no pure formality and no vain prayer to the Lord, the facts themselves prove. God deigns to draw to Himself out of errors of all kinds many men whom *delivered from the power of darkness He translates into the kingdom of the Son of His love*, and whom He transforms from *vessels of wrath* into *vessels of mercy*. And the Church is so convinced that this is exclusively due to God's action that she offers perpetual thanksgivings to God as to its author and sings His praises for the light and grace bestowed on these people.

(Taken from **Prosper of Aquitaine: Defence of St Augustine,** *Ancient Christian Writers series no. 32, trans. P. de Letter, Westminster, MD: The Newman Press 1963, pp. 178–85.)*

B. The Reformation debate

I.2.5 John Calvin, from *The Institutes of the Christian Religion*

Calvin here examines the teaching authority that the biblical authors had, and claims that even they could teach nothing but what they received in the Word of God. Therefore, it is inconceivable that the church should have authority to add to or set aside the Word of God. He then examines the claims made for the Pope, and for Councils.

CHAPTER VIII

1. Task and limits of the church's doctrinal authority

There now follows the third section, on the power of the church, which resides partly in individual bishops, and partly in councils, either provincial or general. I speak only of the spiritual power, which is proper to the church. This, moreover, consists either in doctrine or in jurisdiction or in making laws. The doctrinal side has two parts: authority to lay down articles of faith, and authority to explain them.

2. The doctrinal authority of Moses and the priests

Accordingly, we must here remember that whatever authority and dignity the Spirit in Scripture accords to either priests or prophets, or apostles, or successors of apostles, it is wholly given not to the men personally, but to the ministry to which they have been appointed; or (to speak more briefly) to the Word, whose ministry is entrusted to them. For if we examine them all in order, we shall not find that they have been endowed with any authority to teach or to answer, except in the name and Word of the Lord. For, where they are called to office, it is at the same time enjoined upon them not to bring anything of themselves, but to speak from the Lord's mouth. And he himself does not bring them forth to be heard by the people before teaching them what to speak: they are to speak nothing but his Word.

3. The doctrinal authority of the prophets

Ezekiel felicitously describes the general character of the prophets' power: '"O Son of man," says the Lord, "I have appointed you as a watchman for the house of Israel; you will therefore hear a word of my mouth and will declare it to them from me"' [Ezek. 3:17]. Is not he who is bidden to hear a word from the Lord's mouth forbidden to invent anything of his own? What is it to bring tidings from the Lord? So to speak that one dare confidently boast that the word he brings is not his own, but the Lord's.

4. The doctrinal authority of the apostles

Now if you look upon the apostles, they are indeed commended with many notable titles. They are 'the light of the world' and 'the salt of the earth' [Matt. 5:13–14]; they are to be heard for Christ's sake [Luke 10:16]; whatever they 'bind or loose on earth shall be bound or loosed in heaven' [Matt. 16:19; 18:18; cf. John 20:23]. But they show by their name how much is permitted to them in their office. That is, if they are 'apostles,' they are not to prate whatever they please, but are faithfully to report the commands of Him by whom they have been sent. And Christ's words, with which he has defined their mission, are plain enough: he commanded them to go and teach all nations everything he had enjoined [Matt. 28:19–20].
. . .

7. 'The Word became flesh'

But when the Wisdom of God was at length revealed in the flesh, that Wisdom heartily declared to us all that can be comprehended and ought to be pondered concerning the Heavenly Father by the human mind. Now therefore, since Christ, the Sun of Righteousness, has shone, while before there was only dim light, we have the perfect radiance of divine truth, like the wonted brilliance of midday. For truly the apostle meant to proclaim no common thing when he wrote, 'In many and various ways God spoke of old to the fathers by the prophets; but in these last days he has begun to speak to us through his beloved Son' [Heb. 1:1–2]. For Paul means, in fact, openly declares, that God will not speak hereafter as he did before, intermittently through some and through others; nor will he add prophecies to prophecies, or revelations to revelations. Rather, he has so fulfilled all functions of teaching in his Son that we must regard this as the final and eternal testimony from him. In this way this whole New Testament time, from the point that Christ appeared to us with the preaching of his gospel even to the Day of Judgment, is designated by 'the last hour' [I John 2:18], 'the last times' [I Tim. 4:1; I Peter 1:20], 'the last days' [Acts 2:17; II Tim. 3:1; II Peter 3:3]. This is done that, content with the perfection of Christ's teaching, we may learn not to fashion anything new for ourselves beyond this or to admit anything contrived by others.

8. The apostles authorized to teach what Christ commanded

Let this be a firm principle: No other word is to be held as the Word of God, and given place as such in the church, than what is contained first in the Law and the Prophets, then in the writings of the apostles; and the only authorized way of teaching in the church is by the prescription and standard of his Word.

From this also we infer that the only thing granted to the apostles was that which the prophets had had of old. They were to expound the ancient Scripture and to show that what is taught there has been fulfilled in Christ.

9. Not even the apostles were free to go beyond the Word: much less their successors

Accordingly, Peter, who was well instructed by the Master as to how much he should do, reserves nothing else for himself or others except to impart the doctrine as it has been handed down by God. 'Let him who speaks,' he says, 'speak only the words of God' [I Peter 4:11]; that is, not hesitatingly and tremblingly as evil consciences are accustomed to speak, but with the high confidence which befits a servant of God furnished with his sure commands. What is this but to reject all inventions of the human mind (from whatever brain they have issued) in order that God's pure Word may be taught and learned in the believers' church?

Yet this, as I have said, is the difference between the apostles and their successors: the former were sure and genuine scribes of the Holy Spirit, and their writings are therefore to be considered oracles of God; but the sole office of others is to teach what is provided and sealed in the Holy Scriptures. We therefore teach that faithful ministers are now not permitted to coin any new doctrine, but that they are simply to cleave to that doctrine to which God has subjected all men without exception. When I say this, I mean to show what is permitted not only to individual men but to the whole church as well.

But someone will say, for the church universal, the case is different. My reply is that Paul also anticipates this doubt in another passage, when he says: 'Faith comes from what is heard, but what is heard comes from God's Word' [Rom. 10:17]. Well, then, if faith depends upon God's Word alone, if it applies to it and reposes in it alone, what place is now left for the word of the whole world? . . . Then here is a universal rule that we ought to heed: God deprives men of the capacity to put forth new doctrine in order that he alone may be our schoolmaster in spiritual doctrine as he alone is true [Rom. 3:4] who can neither lie nor deceive.
. . .

10. The Roman claim

But suppose we compare this power of the church, of which we have spoken, with that power by which those spiritual tyrants who have falsely called themselves bishops and prelates of religion have commended themselves now for some centuries among the people of God.

They take it for granted that a universal council is the true image of the church. Having accepted this principle, they presently conclude without hesitation that such councils are governed directly by the Holy Spirit, and therefore cannot err. But since these men rule, and even constitute, the councils, they actually claim for themselves everything they contend to be due the councils. Therefore, they would have our faith stand and fall on their decision . . .

Meanwhile, contemptuous of God's Word, they coin dogmas after their own whim, which in accordance with this rule they afterward require to be subscribed to as articles of faith. For they do not count a man a Christian unless he firmly consents to all their dogmas, whether affirmative or negative – if not with explicit faith, at least with implicit. For the church has the power to frame new articles of faith.

. . .

13. Word and Spirit belong inseparably together

That my readers may better understand the pivotal point of this question, I shall explain in a few words what our adversaries demand, and wherein we oppose them. Their statement that the church cannot err bears on this point, and this is how they interpret it – inasmuch as the church is governed by the Spirit of God, it can proceed safely without the Word; no matter where it may go, it can think or speak only what is true; accordingly, if it should ordain anything beyond or apart from God's Word, this must be taken as nothing but a sure oracle of God.

If we grant the first point, that the church cannot err in matters necessary to salvation, here is what we mean by it: The statement is true in so far as the church, having forsaken all its own wisdom, allows itself to be taught by the Holy Spirit through God's Word. This, then, is the difference. Our opponents locate the authority of the church outside God's Word; but we insist that it be attached to the Word, and do not allow it to be separated from it.

CHAPTER IX

2. *True and false councils*

Let us now speak of the matter itself. If one seeks in Scripture what the authority of councils is, there exists no clearer promise than in this statement of Christ's: 'Where two or three are gathered together in my name, there I am in the midst of them' [Matt. 18:20]. But that nonetheless refers as much to a little meeting as to a universal council. Yet the difficulty of the question does not lie in this, but in the added condition that Christ will be in the midst of a council only if it is gathered together in his name ... Let us therefore define what that means. I deny that they are gathered in his name who, casting aside God's commandment that forbids anything to be added or taken away from his Word [Deut. 4:2; cf. Deut. 12:32; Prov. 30:6; Rev. 22:18–19], ordain anything according to their own decision; who, not content with the oracles of Scripture, that is, the sole rule of perfect wisdom, concoct some novelty out of their own heads.
. . .

8. *The validity of conciliar decisions*

What then? You ask, will the councils have no determining authority? Yes, indeed; for I am not arguing here either that all councils are to be condemned or the acts of all to be rescinded, and (as the saying goes) to be canceled at one stroke. But, you will say, you degrade everything, so that every man has the right to accept or reject what the councils decide. Not at all! But whenever a decree of any council is brought forward, I should like men first of all diligently to ponder at what time it was held, on what issue, and with what intention, what sort of men were present; then to examine by the standard of Scripture what it dealt with – and to do this in such a way that the definition of the council may have its weight and be like a provisional judgment, yet not hinder the examination which I have mentioned.

Thus councils would come to have the majesty that is their due; yet in the meantime Scripture would stand out in the higher place, with everything subject to its standard. In this way, we willingly embrace and reverence as holy the early councils, such as those of Nicaea, Constantinople, Ephesus I, Chalcedon, and the like, which were concerned with refuting errors – in so far as they relate to the teachings of faith. For they contain nothing but the pure and genuine exposition of Scripture, which the holy fathers applied with spiritual prudence to crush the enemies of religion who had then arisen. In some of the later councils also we see shining forth the true zeal for piety, and clear tokens of insight, doctrine, and prudence. But as affairs usually

tend to get worse, it is to be seen from the more recent councils how much the church has degenerated from the purity of that golden age.
. . .

13. The actual significance of councils for the interpretation of Scripture

Since we have proved that the church has not been given the power to set up a new doctrine, let us now speak concerning the power which they claim for it in interpreting Scripture.

We indeed willingly concede, if any discussion arises over doctrine, that the best and surest remedy is for a synod of true bishops to be convened, where the doctrine at issue may be examined. . . . But I deny it to be always the case that an interpretation of Scripture adopted by vote of a council is true and certain.

(Taken from The Institutes of the Christian Religion *ed. John T. McNeill trans. Ford Lewis Battles, The Library of Christian Classics, vol. XXI, Philadelphia, PA: Westminister Press 1960, IV.viii–ix.)*

I.2.6 From the Thirty-Nine Articles

The Thirty-Nine Articles are among the foundational documents of the Anglican Church. Those reproduced here steer a careful middle course between ascribing independent authority to tradition and denying any worth to tradition.

VI. Of the sufficiency of the Holy Scriptures for Salvation.

Holy Scripture containeth all things necessary to salvation: so that whatsoever is not read therein, nor may be proved thereby, is not to be required of any man, that it should be believed as an article of the faith, or be thought requisite or necessary to salvation. In the name of Holy Scripture, we do understand those Canonical books of the Old and New Testament, of whose authority was never any doubt in the Church. [A list of the books of the Old Testament follows.]

And the other books (as Jerome saith) the Church doth read for example of life and instruction of manners; but yet doth it not apply them to establish any doctrine; such are these following. [A list of the Apocrypha follows.]

All the books of the New Testament, as they are commonly received, we do receive, and account them canonical.

VIII. Of the Three Creeds.

The three Creeds, Nicene Creed, Athanasius' Creed, and that which is commonly called the Apostles' Creed, ought thoroughly to be received and believed; for they may be proved by most certain warrants of Holy Scripture.

XIX. Of the Church.

The visible Church of Christ is a congregation of faithful men, in the which the pure word of God is preached and the sacraments be duly ministered according to Christ's ordinance in all those things that of necessity are requisite to the same.

As the Churches of Jerusalem, Alexandria, and Antioch have erred: so also the Church of Rome hath erred, not only in their living and manner of ceremonies, but also in matters of faith.

XX. Of the Authority of the Church.

The Church hath power to decree rites or ceremonies and authority in controversies of faith; and yet it is not lawful for the Church to ordain anything contrary to God's word written, neither may it so expound one place of

Scripture, that it be repugnant to another. Wherefore, although the Church be a witness and a keeper of Holy Writ: yet, as it ought not to decree anything against the same, so besides the same ought it not to enforce anything to be believed for necessity of salvation.

XXI. Of the authority of General Councils.

General Councils may not be gathered together without the commandment and will of princes. And when they be gathered together, forasmuch as they be an assembly of men, whereof all be not governed with the Spirit and word of God, they may err and sometime have erred, even in things pertaining to God. Wherefore things ordained by them as necessary to salvation have neither strength nor authority, unless it may be declared that they be taken out of Holy Scripture.

XXXIV. Of the Traditions of the Church.

It is not necessary that traditions and ceremonies be in all places one or utterly like; for at all times they have been diverse, and may be changed according to the diversity of countries, times, and men's manners, so that nothing be ordained against God's word. Whosoever through his private judgement willingly and purposely doth openly break the traditions and ceremonies of the Church which be not repugnant to the word of God, and be ordained and approved by common authority, ought to be rebuked openly that others may fear to do the like, as he that offendeth against common order of the Church, and hurteth the authority of the magistrate, and woundeth the conscience of the weak brethren.

Every particular or national Church hath authority to ordain, change, and abolish ceremonies or rites of the Church ordained only by man's authority, so that all things be done to edifying.

(Taken from the Book of Common Prayer.)

I.2.7 From *The Confession of Dositheus*

This confession, an Eastern Orthodox response to reports of Calvinism, asserts the unbroken continuity of the episcopal succession back to the apostles, and claims that there is also an unbroken continuity of teaching. The only proper interpretation of Scripture is the one held by this tradition.

Decree II.

We believe the Divine and Sacred Scriptures to be God-taught; and, therefore, we ought to believe the same without doubting; yet not otherwise than as the Catholic Church hath interpreted and delivered the same. For every foul heresy receiveth, indeed, the Divine Scriptures, but perversely interpreteth the same, using metaphors, and homonymies, and sophistries of man's wisdom, confounding what ought to be distinguished, and trifling with what ought not to be trifled with. For if [we were to receive the same] otherwise, each man holding every day a different sense concerning the same, the Catholic Church would not [as she doth] by the grace of Christ continue to be the Church until this day, holding the same doctrine of faith.

Wherefore, the witness also of the Catholic Church is, we believe, not of inferior authority to that of the Divine Scriptures. For one and the same Holy Spirit being the author of both, it is quite the same to be taught by the Scriptures and by the Catholic Church. Moreover, when any man speaketh from himself he is liable to err, and to deceive, and be deceived; but the Catholic Church, as never having spoken, or speaking from herself, but from the Spirit of God – who being her teacher, she is ever unfailingly rich – it is impossible for her to in any wise err, or to at all deceive, or be deceived; but like the Divine Scriptures, is infallible, and hath perpetual authority.

Decree X.

We believe that what is called, or rather is, the Holy Catholic and Apostolic Church, and in which we have been taught to believe, containeth generally all the Faithful in Christ, who, that is to say, being still on their pilgrimage, have not yet reached their home in the Fatherland.

Of which Catholic Church, since a mortal man cannot universally and perpetually be head, our Lord Jesus Christ Himself is head, and Himself holding the rudder is at the helm in the governing of the Church, through the Holy Fathers. And, therefore, over particular Churches, that are real Churches, and consist of real members [of the Catholic Church], the Holy

Spirit hath appointed Bishops as leaders and shepherds, who being not at all by abuse, but properly, authorities and heads, look unto the Author and Finisher of our Salvation, and refer to Him what they do in their capacity of heads forsooth.

But forasmuch as among their other impieties, the Calvinists have fancied this also, that the simple Priest and the High Priest are perhaps the same; and that there is no necessity for High Priests, and that the Church may be governed by some Priests; and that not a High Priest [only], but a Priest also is able to ordain a Priest, and a number of Priests to ordain a High Priest; and affirm in lofty language that the Eastern Church assenteth to this wicked notion – for which purpose the Tenth Chapter was written by Cyril – we explicitly declare according to the mind which hath obtained from the beginning in the Eastern Church: –

That the dignity of the Bishop is so necessary in the Church, that without him, neither Church nor Christian could either be or be spoken of. For he, as a successor of the Apostles, having received in continued succession by the imposition of hands and the invocation of the All-holy Spirit the grace that is given him of the Lord of binding and loosing, is a living image of God upon the earth, and by a most ample participation of the operation of the Holy Spirit, who is the chief functionary is a fountain of all the Mysteries [Sacraments] of the Catholic Church, through which we obtain salvation.

And he is, we suppose, as necessary to the Church as breath is to man, or the sun to the world. Whence it hath also been elegantly said by some in commendation of the dignity of the High Priesthood, 'What God is in the heavenly Church of the first-born, and the sun in the world, that every High Priest is in his own particular Church, as through him the flock is enlightened, and nourished, and becometh the temple of God.'

And that this great mystery and dignity of the Episcopate hath descended unto us by a continued succession is manifest. For since the Lord hath promised to be with us always, although He be with us by other means of grace and Divine operations, yet in a more eminent manner doth He, through the Bishop as chief functionary, make us His own and dwell with us, and through the divine Mysteries is united with us; of which the Bishop is the first minister, and chief functionary, through the Holy Spirit, and suffereth us not to fall into heresy.

Decree XI.

We believe to be members of the Catholic Church all the Faithful, and only the Faithful; who, forsooth, having received the blameless Faith of the Saviour Christ, from Christ Himself, and the Apostles, and the Holy Œcumenical Synods, adhere to the same without wavering; although some of them may be guilty of all manner of sins. For unless the Faithful, even when living in sin, were members of the Church, they could not be judged by the Church.

But now being judged by her, and called to repentance, and guided into the way of her salutary precepts, though they may be still defiled with sins, for this only, that they have not fallen into despair, and that they cleave to the Catholic and Orthodox faith, they are, and are regarded as, members of the Catholic Church.

Decree XII.

We believe the Catholic Church to be taught by the Holy Spirit. For he is the true Paraclete; whom Christ sendeth from the Father, to teach the truth, and to drive away darkness from the minds of the Faithful. The teaching of the Holy Spirit, however, doth not immediately, but through the holy Fathers and Leaders of the Catholic Church, illuminate the Church. For as all Scripture is, and is called, the word of the Holy Spirit; not that it was spoken immediately by Him, but that it was spoken by Him through the Apostles and Prophets; so also the Church is taught indeed by the Life-giving Spirit, but through the medium of the holy Fathers and Doctors (whose rule is acknowledged to be the Holy and Œcumenical Synods; for we shall not cease to say this ten thousand times); and, therefore, not only are we persuaded, but do profess as true and undoubtedly certain, that it is impossible for the Catholic Church to err, or at all be deceived, or ever to choose falsehood instead of truth. For the All-holy Spirit continually operating through the Holy Fathers and Leaders faithfully ministering, delivereth the Church from error of every kind.

(Taken from The acts and decrees of the Synod of Jerusalem, sometimes called the Council of Bethlehem, holden under Dositheus, Patriarch of Jerusalem in 1672: translated from the Greek with an appendix containing the confession published with the name of Cyril Lucar condemned by the Synod and with notes by J. N. W. B. Robertson, *London: Baker 1899.)*

C. Modern attempts to appeal to tradition

I.2.8 John Henry Newman, from *An Essay on the Development of Christian Doctrine*

Newman here argues that as it is natural for any set of ideas to develop, so it is natural for Christian doctrine to develop. Given this, we might suppose that God would provide an infallible guide as to which developments are acceptable and which should be repudiated.

SECTION I

DEVELOPMENTS OF DOCTRINE TO BE EXPECTED.

1

If Christianity is a fact, and impresses an idea of itself on our minds and is a subject-matter of exercises of the reason, that idea will in course of time expand into a multitude of ideas, and aspects of ideas, connected and harmonious with one another, and in themselves determinate and immutable, as is the objective fact itself which is thus represented. It is a characteristic of our minds, that they cannot take an object in, which is submitted to them simply and integrally. We conceive by means of definition or description; whole objects do not create in the intellect whole ideas, but are, to use a mathematical phrase, thrown into series, into a number of statements, strengthening, interpreting, correcting each other, and with more or less exactness approximating, as they accumulate, to a perfect image. There is no other way of learning or of teaching. We cannot teach except by aspects or views, which are not identical with the thing itself which we are teaching. Two persons may each convey the same truth to a third, yet by methods and through representations altogether different. The same person will treat the same argument differently in an essay or speech, according to the accident of the day of writing, or of the audience, yet it will be substantially the same.

And the more claim an idea has to be considered living, the more various will be its aspects; and the more social and political is its nature, the more complicated and subtle will be its issues, and the longer and more eventful will be its course. And in the number of these special ideas, which from their very depth and richness cannot be fully understood at once, but are more and more clearly expressed and taught the longer they last, – having aspects many and bearings many, mutually connected and growing one out of another, and all parts of a whole, with a sympathy and correspondence keeping pace with the ever-changing necessities of the world, multiform, prolific, and ever resourceful, – among these great doctrines surely we Christians shall not refuse a foremost place to Christianity. Such previously to the determination of the fact, must be our anticipation concerning it from a contemplation of its initial achievements.

2

It may be objected that its inspired documents at once determine the limits of its mission without further trouble; but ideas are in the writer and reader of the revelation, not the inspired text itself: and the question is whether those ideas which the letter conveys from writer to reader, reach the reader at once in their completeness and accuracy on his first perception of them, or whether they open out in his intellect and grow to perfection in the course of time. Nor could it surely be maintained without extravagance that the letter of the New Testament, or of any assignable number of books, comprises a delineation of all possible forms which a divine message will assume when submitted to a multitude of minds.

Nor is the case altered by supposing that inspiration provided in behalf of the first recipients of the Revelation, what the Divine Fiat effected for herbs and plants in the beginning, which were created in maturity. Still, the time at length came, when its recipients ceased to be inspired; and on these recipients the revealed truths would fall, as in other cases, at first vaguely and generally, though in spirit and in truth, and would afterwards be completed by developments.

Nor can it fairly be made a difficulty that thus to treat of Christianity is to level it in some sort to sects and doctrines of the world, and to impute to it the imperfections which characterize the productions of man. Certainly it is a sort of degradation of a divine work to consider it under an earthly form; but it is no irreverence, since our Lord Himself, its Author and Guardian, bore one also. Christianity differs from other religions and philosophies, in what is superadded to earth from heaven; not in kind, but in origin; not in its nature, but in its personal characteristics; being informed and quickened by what is more than intellect, by a divine spirit. It is externally what the Apostle calls an 'earthen vessel,' being the religion of men. And, considered as such, it grows 'in wisdom and stature;' but the powers which it wields, and the words which proceed out of its mouth, attest its miraculous nativity.

Unless then some special ground of exception can be assigned, it is as evident that Christianity, as a doctrine and worship, will develope in the minds of recipients, as that it conforms in other respects, in its external propagation or its political framework, to the general methods by which the course of things is carried forward.

3

Again, if Christianity be an universal religion, suited not simply to one locality or period, but to all times and places, it cannot but vary in its relations and dealings towards the world around it, that is, it will develope. Principles require a very various application according as persons and circumstances vary, and must be thrown into new shapes according to the form of society which they are to influence. Hence all bodies of Christians, orthodox or not, develope the doctrines of Scripture. Few but will grant that Luther's view of justification had never been stated in words before his time: that his phraseology and his positions were novel, whether called for by circumstances or not. It is equally certain that the doctrine of justification defined at Trent was, in some sense, new also. The refutation and remedy of errors cannot precede their rise; and thus the fact of false developments or corruptions involves the correspondent manifestation of true ones. Moreover, all parties appeal to Scripture, that is, argue from Scripture; but argument implies deduction, that is, development. Here there is no difference between early times and late, between a Pope *ex cathedra* and an individual Protestant, except that their authority is not on a par. On either side the claim of authority is the same, and the process of development.

4

And, indeed, when we turn to the consideration of particular doctrines on which Scripture lays the greatest stress, we shall see that it is absolutely impossible for them to remain in the mere letter of Scripture, if they are to be more than mere words, and to convey a definite idea to the recipient. When it is declared that 'the Word became flesh,' three wide questions open upon us on the very announcement. What is meant by 'the Word,' what by 'flesh,' what by 'became'? The answers to these involve a process of investigation, and are developments. Moreover, when they have been made, they will suggest a series of secondary questions; and thus at length a multitude of propositions is the result, which gather round the inspired sentence of which they come, giving it externally the form of a doctrine, and creating or deepening the idea of it in the mind.

5

This moreover should be considered, – that great questions exist in the subject-matter of which Scripture treats, which Scripture does not solve; questions too so real, so practical, that they must be answered, and, unless we suppose a new revelation, answered by means of the revelation which we have, that is, by development. Such is the question of the Canon of Scripture and its inspiration: that is, whether Christianity depends upon a written document as Judaism; – if so, on what writings and how many; – whether that document is self-interpreting, or requires a comment, and whether any authoritative comment or commentator is provided; – whether the revelation and the document are commensurate, or the one outruns the other; – all these questions surely find no solution on the surface of Scripture, nor indeed under the surface in the case of most men, however long and diligent might be their study of it. Nor were these difficulties settled by authority, as far as we know, at the commencement of the religion; yet surely it is quite conceivable that an Apostle might have dissipated them all in a few words, had Divine Wisdom thought fit. But in matter of fact the decision has been left to time, to the slow process of thought, to the influence of mind upon mind, the issues of controversy, and the growth of opinion.

SECTION II

AN INFALLIBLE DEVELOPING AUTHORITY TO BE EXPECTED.

It has now been made probable that developments of Christianity were but natural, as time went on, and were to be expected; and that these natural and true developments, as being natural and true, were of course contemplated and taken into account by its Author, who in designing the work designed its legitimate results. These, whatever they turn out to be, may be called absolutely 'the developments' of Christianity. That, beyond reasonable doubt, there are such is surely a great step gained in the inquiry; it is a momentous fact. The next question is, *What* are they? and to a theologian, who could take a general view, and also possessed an intimate and minute knowledge, of its history, they would doubtless on the whole be easily distinguishable by their own characters, and require no foreign aid to point them out, no external authority to ratify them. But it is difficult to say who is exactly in this position. Considering that Christians, from the nature of the case, live under the bias of the doctrines, and in the very midst of the facts, and during the process of the controversies, which are to be the subject of criticism, since they are exposed to the prejudices of birth, education, place, personal attachment, engagements, and party, it can hardly be maintained that in matter of fact a true development carries with it always its own certainty even to the learned, or that history, past or present, is secure from the possibility of a variety of interpretations.

2

If this be true, certainly some rule is necessary for arranging and authenticating these various expressions and results of Christian, doctrine. No one will maintain that all points of belief are of equal importance. 'There are what may be called minor points, which we may hold to be true without imposing them as necessary;' 'there are greater truths and lesser truths, points which it is necessary, and points which it is pious to believe.' The simple question is, How are we to discriminate the greater from the less, the true from the false.

3

This need of an authoritative sanction is increased by considering, after M. Guizot's suggestion, that Christianity, though represented in prophecy as a kingdom, came into the world as an idea rather than an institution, and has had to wrap itself in clothing and fit itself with armour of its own providing, and to form the instruments and methods of its prosperity and warfare. If the developments, which have above been called *moral*, are to take place to any great extent, and without them it is difficult to see how Christianity can exist at all, if only its relations towards civil government have to be ascertained, or the qualifications for the profession of it have to be defined, surely an authority is necessary to impart decision to what is vague, and confidence to what is empirical, to ratify the successive steps of so elaborate a process, and to secure the validity of inferences which are to be made the premises of more remote investigations.

4

Reasons shall be given in this Section for concluding that, in proportion to the probability of true developments of doctrine and practice in the Divine Scheme, so is the probability also of the appointment in that scheme of an external authority to decide upon them, thereby separating them from the mass of mere human speculation, extravagance, corruption, and error, in and out of which they grow. This is the doctrine of the infallibility of the Church; for by infallibility I suppose is meant the power deciding whether this, that, and a third, and any number of theological or ethical statements are true.

5

Let the state of the case be carefully considered. If the Christian doctrine, as originally taught, admits of true and important developments, as was argued in the foregoing Section, this is a strong antecedent argument in favour of a provision in the Dispensation for putting a seal of authority upon those developments. The probability of their being known to be true varies with that of their truth. The two ideas indeed are quite distinct, I grant, of revealing and of guaranteeing a truth, and they are often distinct in fact. There are various revelations all over the earth which do not carry with them the

evidence of their divinity. Such are the inward suggestions and secret illumi-
nations granted to so many individuals; such are the traditionary doctrines
which are found among the heathen, that 'vague and unconnected family of
religious truths, originally from God, but sojourning, without the sanction
of miracle or a definite home, as pilgrims up and down the world, and
discernible and separable from the corrupt legends with which they are
mixed, by the spiritual mind alone.' There is nothing impossible in the notion
of a revelation occurring without evidences that it is a revelation; just as
human sciences are a divine gift, yet are reached by our ordinary powers
and have no claim on our faith. But Christianity is not of this nature: it is a
revelation which comes to us as a revelation, as a whole, objectively, and
with a profession of infallibility; and the only question to be determined
relates to the matter of the revelation. If then there are certain great truths, or
duties, or observances, naturally and legitimately resulting from the doctrines
originally professed, it is but reasonable to include these true results in the
idea of the revelation itself, to consider them parts of it, and if the revelation
be not only true, but guaranteed as true, to anticipate that they too will come
under the privilege of that guarantee. Christianity, unlike other revelations
of God's will, except the Jewish, of which it is a continuation, is an objective
religion, or a revelation with credentials; it is natural, I say, to view it wholly
as such, and not partly *sui generis,* partly like others. Such as it begins, such
let it be considered to continue; granting that certain large developments of
it are true, they must surely be accredited as true.

*(Taken from the seventh edition, London: Longmans, Green & Co 1890,
pp. 55–98.)*

I.2.9 Karl Barth, from *Evangelical Theology*

Barth here describes the work of the student of theology as listening to the witness of the Scriptures, and also conversing with others who have also listened. The tradition, then, is not composed of teachers, but of fellow students.

Theological study is the contact (whether it be direct or literary) and meaningful union of pupils with their teachers – teachers who, for their part, were pupils of their own teachers. Such a regressive sequence continues until one reaches those teachers whose only chance and desire was to be the pupils of the immediate witnesses to the history of Jesus Christ which brought the history of Israel to its fulfillment. Theological study consists, therefore, in active participation in the work of that comprehensive community of teachers and learners which is found in the school of the immediate witnesses to the work and word of God.

The instruction which someone today receives from lectures, seminars, or books can be only a first and preliminary step. Such instruction can be merely an admission to the school where the theological student now hears and reads and in which, before him, his own teachers have listened, spoken, and written, gaining their knowledge, exchanging it with one another, transmitting and receiving it from one another. Ultimately and in its most decisive aspect, today's instruction is but an introduction to the source and norm of all theology: namely, the testimony of the Scriptures. Every predecessor of today's student has already attempted to understand and explain the Scriptures – in his own period, in his own way, and with his own limitations. To study theology means not so much to examine exhaustively the work of earlier students of theology as to become *their* fellow student. It means to become and to remain receptive, for they still speak, even though they may have died long ago. Serious study means to permit oneself to be stimulated by the views and insights they achieved and proclaimed, and to be guided – by their encouraging or frightening example – toward a perspective, thought, and speech which are responsible to God and man. But above all, theological study means to follow in their footsteps and to turn to the source from which they themselves were nourished, to the norm to which they had already, properly, and unqualifiedly subjected themselves. It means to hear the original testimony which made teachers out of pupils. It was to this norm that one's predecessors in theological study subordinated and directed themselves, so far as they were able.

In the light of the foregoing, theological study will have to be divided into two parts. We call them a primary and a secondary conversation. In the first conversation the student, whether he be young or old, will (like all students who preceded him) have to inquire *directly* into what the prophets of the Old Testament and the apostles of the New Testament have to say to the world, to the community of the present day, and to himself as a member of the community. In the secondary conversation the student must permit himself indirectly to be given the necessary directions and admonitions for the journey toward the answer which he seeks. Such secondary instructions are gained from theologians of the past, the recent past, and from his immediate antecedents – through examination of their biblical exegesis and dogmatics and their historical and practical inquiries. Even though he may be the most recent student of theology, he must follow in this path, for he is not the first, but, for the time being, the most contemporary of all students. No one, however, should ever confuse this secondary conversation with the primary one, lest he lose the forest for the trees. In such an eventuality, he would no longer be able to hear the echo of divine revelation in the Scriptures, for the sheer volume of patristic, scholastic, reformation, and, above all, modern academic voices would drown it out. On the other hand, no one should imagine himself so inspired or otherwise clever and wise that he can conduct the primary discussion by his own powers, dispensing with all secondary discussion with the fathers and brothers of the Church.

It scarcely needs to be added that theological study requires in this matter extraordinarily alert and circumspect attention. Theological study must always engage simultaneously in both the primary and secondary conversation. It must constantly distinguish both of these properly, but it must also properly combine them. Certainly an entire lifetime is not too long to gain and to apply some measure of this necessary attention and circumspection.

(Taken from Karl Barth, Evangelical Theology: An Introduction, *trans. Grover Foley, London: Weidenfeld & Nicolson 1963, pp. 172–5.)*

I.2.10 The Second Vatican Council, from *Dei Verbum*

Here, the Council teaches about the relationship between Scripture, the role of the church in interpreting Scripture, and the developing tradition of the church. All three are established and intended by God that the truth of Christ may be known and proclaimed.

Chapter II: Handing On Divine Revelation

7. In his gracious goodness, God has seen to it that what he had revealed for the salvation of all nations would abide perpetually in its full integrity and be handed on to all generations. Therefore Christ the Lord in whom the full revelation of the supreme God is brought to completion (see II Cor. 1:30; 3:15; 4:6), commissioned the Apostles to preach to all men that Gospel which is the source of all saving truth and moral teaching, and to impart to them heavenly gifts. This Gospel had been promised in former times through the prophets, and Christ himself had fulfilled it and promulgated it with his lips. This commission was faithfully fulfilled by the Apostles who, by their oral preaching, by example, and by observances handed on what they had received from the lips of Christ, from living with him, and from what he did, or what they had learned through the prompting of the Holy Spirit. The commission was fulfilled, too, by those Apostles and apostolic men who under the inspiration of the same Holy Spirit committed the message of salvation to writing.

But in order to keep the Gospel forever whole and alive within the Church, the Apostles left bishops as their successors, 'handing over' to them 'the authority to teach in their own place'. This sacred tradition, therefore, and Sacred Scripture of both the Old and New Testaments are like a mirror in which the pilgrim Church on earth looks at God, from whom she has received everything, until she is brought finally to see him as he is, face to face (see 1 John 3:2).

8. And so the apostolic preaching, which is expressed in a special way in the inspired books, was to be preserved by an unending succession of preachers until the end of time. Therefore the Apostles, handing on what they themselves had received, warn the faithful to hold fast to the traditions which they have learned either by word of mouth or by letter (see II Thess. 2:15), and to fight in defence of the faith handed on once and for all (see Jude 3). Now what was handed on by the Apostles includes everything which contributes toward the holiness of life and increase in faith of the People of God; and hands on to all generations all that she herself is, all that she believes.

This tradition which comes from the Apostles develops in the Church with the help of the Holy Spirit. For there is a growth in the understanding of the realities and the words which have been made by believers, who treasure these things in their hearts (see Luke 2:19, 51), through a penetrating understanding of the spiritual realities which they experience, and through the preaching of those who have received through episcopal succession the sure gift of truth. For as the centuries succeed one another, the Church constantly moves forward toward the fullness of divine truth until the words of God reach their complete fulfilment in her.

The words of the holy Fathers witness to the presence of this living tradition, whose wealth is poured into the practice and life of the believing and praying Church. Through the same tradition the Church's full canon of the sacred books is known, and the sacred writings themselves are more profoundly understood and unceasingly made active in her; and thus God, who spoke of old, uninterruptedly converses with the bride of his beloved Son; and the Holy Spirit, through whom the living voice of the Gospel resounds in the Church, and through her, in the world leads unto all truth those who believe and makes the Word of Christ dwell abundantly in them (see Col. 3:16).

9. Hence there exists a close connection and communication between sacred tradition and sacred Scripture. For both of them, flowing from the same divine wellspring, in a certain way merge into a unity and tend toward the same end. For sacred Scripture is the Word of God inasmuch as it is consigned to writing under the inspiration of the divine Spirit, while sacred tradition takes the Word of God entrusted by Christ the Lord and the Holy Spirit to the Apostles, and hands it on to their successors in its full purity, so that led by the light of the Spirit of truth, they may in proclaiming it preserve this Word of God faithfully, explain it, and make it more widely known. Consequently it is not from sacred Scripture alone that the Church draws her certainty about everything which has been revealed. Therefore both sacred tradition and sacred Scripture are to be accepted and venerated with the same sense of loyalty and reverence.

10. Sacred tradition and sacred Scripture form one sacred deposit of the Word of God, committed to the Church. Holding fast to this deposit the entire holy people united with their shepherds remain always steadfast in the teaching of the Apostles, in the common life, in the breaking of the bread and in prayers (see Acts 8:42), so that holding to, practising and professing the heritage of the faith, it becomes on the part of the bishops and faithful a single common effort.

But the task of authentically interpreting the word of God, whether written or handed on, has been entrusted exclusively to the living teaching office of the Church, whose authority is exercised in the name of Jesus Christ. This teaching office is not above the Word of God, but serves it, teaching only what has been handed on, listening to it devoutly, guarding it scrupulously and explaining it faithfully in accord with a divine commission and with the help of the Holy Spirit; it draws from this one deposit of faith everything which it presents for belief as divinely revealed.

It is clear, therefore, that sacred tradition, sacred Scripture and the teaching authority of the Church, in accord with God's most wise design, are so linked and joined together that one cannot stand without the others, and that all together and each in its own way under the action of the one Holy Spirit contribute effectively to the salvation of souls.

(Taken from the authorized Vatican translation.)

I.2.11 John Zizioulas, from 'Apostolic Continuity of the Church'

This is the 'Conclusion' to a survey of ideas of episcopal succession in the early church, which leads Zizioulas to discover an eschatological component of tradition.

We have tried in this brief presentation to outline the main ideas concerning apostolic continuity and succession in the first four centuries of the Church. This brief sketch of the historical evidence has shown that in the early Church the question we are considering here was a complex one. In speaking of continuity and succession we normally have in mind *a linear historical sequence* coming to us from the past to the present and involving the psychology of a retrospective *anamnesis*. This is in line with our typical cultural formation influenced as it is by Greek, especial Platonic, thought in which remembrance or 'anamnesis' cannot but refer to the past. It is different, however, with Biblical thought, which is conditioned by a culture different from that of the Greeks. As all Biblical scholars know the anamnesis of which the Bible speaks, above all in relation to the Eucharist, is not only an anamnesis of the past but also, if not mainly, the remembrance of the future, of the last days of the eschatological state of the Church and the world.

This dual sense of anamnesis seems to be at work in the case of apostolic continuity and succession in the early Church. On the one hand there is evidence, particularly in the West, of an understanding of succession in strictly historical terms. This we encounter mainly in *I Clement*, to some extent in Hippolytus and again in St. Cyprian. It marks Western theology ever since leading up to the present time when academic theology, in both West and East, limits its view of succession to the establishment of factual historical evidence of an uninterrupted chain of episcopal ordinations.

Yet, on the other hand there seems to have been in the early Church a strong tradition, represented mainly in Syria and Palestine of a view of continuity and succession that does not involve historicity in the usual sense but is interested mainly in securing a continuity of identity of each local Church with the eschatological community as it was originally expected in and through the original church of Jerusalem and as it is, ever since the destruction and dispersion of this community, experienced in the New Jerusalem coming down from heaven, in the community of the Eucharist. Faithfulness to this eschatological community was in this case the main requirement in the search for apostolic continuity and succession.

It is mainly this second view that accounts for the fact that apostolic continuity came to be expressed exclusively as *episcopal* succession. If we miss this we are in danger of misunderstanding what episcopal succession is about. This misunderstanding has in fact occurred when the first of these two views, namely the linear historical one, won the day in the Church. It became sufficient to speak of a continuous chain of episcopal ordinations in order to establish apostolic succession, as if it were a matter of some sort of mechanical activity. It became also a matter of transmission of power and authority from one individual to another. It also led to an understanding of the apostolic college as something standing outside and above the communities of the Church and transmitting prerogatives of a self-perpetuating cast. It led to the appearance of titular and assistant bishops in a massive way as something normal ecclesiologically, and in brief it removed succession from its natural place which is *the community* of the Church.

All this has been the result of the loss of the Christo-centric and eschatological approach to apostolic continuity and a replacement of it by the solely historical view. We need, therefore, to work out a *synthesis* of the two approaches, more or less in the sense in which we find it in St. Hippolytus of Rome or even in the New Testament itself. Such a synthesis would amount to the following points:

1. A 'holistic' way of treating succession. We cannot isolate apostolic succession from apostolic continuity in general, i.e. from the rest of the Church's life as she carries over throughout history the Gospel preached by the Apostles. This 'holistic' approach would mean that faith as well as sacramental life and ministry all form part of what is received and transmitted in and by the Church. We cannot, for example, expect to have true apostolic succession if the historic chain of ordinations is maintained, but there is deviation from the right faith. And we cannot speak of apostolic succession when there is only episcopal succession while the rest of the ministries, including the laity, are not participating in it.

2. This means that ordination as a sign and visible means of apostolic succession must be an *insertion* into the life of the community. When this happens the ordained bishop *both gives and receives* apostolicity from the community into which he is inserted. Apostolic continuity cannot be created *ex nihilo* through episcopal ordination unless it is somehow already there. And, equally, it cannot be taken for granted unless it is somehow affirmed, sealed and proclaimed through episcopal ordination. There is a reciprocal relationship between bishop and community in the realization of apostolic continuity through succession, which is analogous and equivalent to the mutual dependence between the historical and the eschatological views of continuity.

3. There is, therefore, no apostolic succession which could be limited to the episcopal college as such or to some form of apostolic collegiality. The late Cardinal Yves Congar rightly rejected such a view of episcopal collegiality and asked for its revision. Every bishop participates in the episcopal college *via his community*, not directly. Apostolic succession is a succession of apostolic communities via their heads, i.e. the bishops.

4. If we take seriously into account the view expressed by St. Cyprian and implied in the Syro-Palestinian tradition we examined here, by understanding apostolic succession as succession of communities rather than individuals (or a college existing above or outside the communities) we implicitly raise the question of the special role in apostolic succession of particular apostolic sees. In the second century and on the occasion of the Paschal controversy Rome claimed special authority because of its relationship with Saints Peter and Paul. Equally the churches of Asia Minor reacted by saying that there, too, important apostles had died (a reference to St. John). If the historical view of succession is not conditioned by the dimension that we have called the eschatological one this kind of argument acquires predominance. It was under the impact of such a historical approach to apostolic succession that Constantinople later on tried to show that it draws its apostolicity from St. Andrew. This kind of argument, however, loses a great deal of its strength if the historical view of succession is conditioned by the eschatological one. In this case every local Church is equally apostolic by virtue of the fact that it is the image of the eschatological community, especially when it celebrates the Eucharist. St. Cyprian's view that each episcopal throne is a *cathedra Petri* does not in this respect differ from Ignatius' vision of every bishop 'sitting in the place of God.' Cyprian's approach is more historical whereas Ignatius' is more eschatological. Both of them, however, see apostolic succession as a reality passing through the local Church wherever this may happen to dwell.

5. Having said this we must not exclude the possibility that a particular local Church and its bishop may have a special function in the realization of apostolic continuity through each local community. Apostolic continuity is not something that concerns a particular local Church taken in itself; it is a matter concerning all the local Churches at a regional or even a universal level. Such a ministry, however, cannot be exercised by an individual but by *a local Church*. Apostolic continuity and succession, once again, have to pass through the community even if they are applied to a broader level. This is a demand stemming from the synthesis of the historical with the eschatological approach to apostolic continuity.

6. We have been speaking here of a *synthesis* of the historical with the eschatological, for we believe that both aspects are essential to apostolic succession. The Church is an entity that receives and re-receives what her history transmits to her, but this transmission is never a purely historical affair; it takes place *sacramentally* or, if you prefer, *eucharistically*, i.e. it is experienced as a gift coming from the last days, from what God has promised and prepared for us in His Kingdom. This passage of the historical tradition through the eschaton is what the Holy Spirit does in apostolic succession, since the Spirit brings about the last days into history (see Acts 2:17), wherever He blows. Apostolic Tradition ceases to be a gift of the Spirit if it is simply a matter of historical continuity.

7. These remarks relate to our ecumenical situation in a direct way. Some

Churches seem to put the accent on historical succession whereas others have tended to regard that as secondary or even unnecessary. In the synthesis we are proposing both are essential. The Church cannot live without memory just as she cannot live without expectation and vision of her final destiny. It is the latter that gives meaning to the former and makes succession relevant to the Church's mission in the world.

Having said this we must raise the question: what about those who for some reason or other lack the historical form of apostolic succession? Here we must distinguish between those who reject historical succession out of theological conviction and those who, for accidental historical reasons (e.g. today's Orthodox Church of Albania) have interrupted their historical continuity. There is no particular difficulty with the latter, if there is the will to be re-inserted in historical succession.

With regard to those, on the other hand, who reject historical succession out of theological conviction the ecumenical dialogue demands that we raise the question why and how they have arrived at this rejection. I venture to suggest that behind this rejection probably lies a denial of historical succession as it developed after the fourth century independently of what we have called here the eschatological and community aspect of apostolicity stemming from a Christo-centric and pneumatological view of continuity. A succession of individuals or of a 'college' of individuals transmitting grace and authority from one another independently of the ecclesial community represents a kind of historical succession which does raise difficulties to anyone operating with a Biblical or Patristic ecclesiology. If, however, historical succession is purified from excesses and deviations owing to its detachment from the synthesis of the historical with the eschatological approach to apostolic continuity which we have been discussing here, we may reach a consensus on this thorny matter. Certainly, the way historical succession has come to be understood and practiced since the Middle Ages needs reconsideration. It must be conditioned by a theology of communion and transformed accordingly. This may make it more acceptable to those who have historically rejected it.

(Taken from John Zizioulas, 'Apostolic Continuity of the Church and Apostolic Succession in the First Five Centuries', Louvain Studies 21, 1996, pp. 153–68.)

I.2.12 Gerhard Ebeling, from *The Word of God and Tradition*

Ebeling here argues that even if we remain committed to the sole authority of Scripture, then we still need an account of tradition, because somehow the Scripture has been passed down to us. He further suggests that the content of tradition, that which is handed on, is not in fact Scripture, or any teachings or practices, but Jesus Christ himself.

Since the truth of *sola scriptura* depends on the reliable transmission of the Gospel, the Scripture-principle necessarily involves a doctrine of tradition. Its exposition represents a comprehensive task, calling for the hermeneutic consideration of the content of the Christian faith with regard to historicity, and including the questions of canon law and responsible activity in the world. For the present we must leave this subject on one side, and turn our attention to the theological position.

The warnings implicit in the language and thought of the reformers against surrender to the concept of Tradition should not be disregarded. As is well known, the Reformation only described *traditio* in negative theological terms drawn from the New Testament polemic against the Jewish conception of 'Scripture and Tradition', since, in the New Testament itself the noun 'Tradition' occurs in a generally critical sense as applied to the *traditiones humanae* in opposition to the *verbum Dei*. The Catholic use of the term *traditio*, which at that time was not yet fully developed – if we connect it with the correspondence, elsewhere pointed out, between the New Testament criticism of Judaism and the Reformers' criticism of Roman Catholicism – suggests that the Catholic concept of Tradition is derived from the late Jewish conception, both with regard to its supplementary character in relation to Scriptural Tradition, and to the character of these *traditiones* as single legal *tradita*. Against this view the biblical use of παραδιδόναι and παράδοσις in a positive sense was not able to get established, the more so since the prevailing use of the term *traditio* was limited to those individual traditions which were supplementary to Scripture. Hence, in the Reformers' thinking the danger developed of failing to recognize the theological importance of the problem of Tradition, although this was far from being a necessary consequence of the Reformation's understanding of the theological situation. In any case the negative emphasis was intensified through the unexampled historical break with a mass of traditions which had occurred in the Reformation, although the actual purpose of the Reformation was to guard or restore the authentic Tradition. Nevertheless it must at once be added that there was obviously no question of an archaizing restoration of specific early Christian traditions; on factual grounds, however, it is understandable that there should have been protests against the exaggerated theological importance attached to the concept of Tradition. For it was necessary to be constantly on guard against the danger that the Gospel might be confused with, or overlaid by, legal traditions, and that, coming to be regarded as law, or even as 'mere Tradition', it might consequently be abandoned.

If we wish to do justice from the theological point of view to the extraordinary ramifications of the problem of Tradition, we shall be justified in turning to those of its aspects which were neglected by the Reformation, and in pursuit of the Reformers' meaning of *sola scriptura*, enquire carefully into the nature of the *traditum tradendum*. When we consider Scripture from the point of view of historical criticism, it seems to add to our difficulties that the one *traditum tradendum* should have reached us only in the form of various oral and doctrinal traditions, from which no single one can be marked out as *the traditum tradendum*; but it is this that points to the decisive fact that the content of the *traditum tradendum* is not a doctrinal statement, nor a law, nor a book of Revelation, but the very Person of Jesus himself as the incarnate Word of God, giving its authority to the Gospel and to the event of the authoritative Word of faith; and correspondingly we have the Holy Spirit as God's Presence in the faith-creating Word of preaching. Theology can only speak of 'Tradition' in the true sense when it holds to this fundamental point of departure, and lets it have full play, in sharp contrast to all that is otherwise regarded as Tradition. In the Christian understanding of the term, the *traditum tradendum* is not law, but Gospel, hence contained in one Name, attested, not by the formation of a special tradition, but by the extension to all mankind of the saving eschatological message, not attained by works, but by faith alone. It is only the realization of the essential difference between the 'handing down' of the Gospel, and all historical traditions – which are both helpful and dangerous to mankind, and in spite of their universal claim always end in the formation of a particular tradition – that makes it possible to understand why the Gospel has and gives free access to a multiplicity of traditions, without having to be confused with any one of them. This unique situation, in which the *traditio* of that one *traditum tradendum* has only taken shape in the multiplicity of traditions, must and can fulfil its mission as Tradition wherever historical traditions exist; it is, in the last resort, identical with the essence of the Gospel itself as the eschatological fulfilment of what is necessarily still lacking in history.

From this point of view the Gospel is revealed not only as freedom *from* the false use of traditions, but also and especially as freedom *to* use them rightly. For the Gospel makes use of Tradition in many ways: the various forms of Christian witness and Christian preaching; the *verbum visibile* of sacramental ritual; the kerygmatic patterns; the orders and services of the [church]; the authoritative texts; the tradition of theological interpretation; Christian ethics; it permeates the whole breadth of life in ethics, culture, and history. Nevertheless the real *traditio* of the Holy Spirit only finds its fulfilment in all these forms of tradition when they are brought into the service of the Word of faith, through which Jesus is transmitted to men, and men are committed to Jesus. The Christian Tradition is always in danger of becoming a legal tradition, and being false to the transmission of the Gospel. Doing justice to the Tradition does not consist in the preservation and handing on of its contents and forms, but in its rightful use as ways and means of the Gospel. And it is this correct use of traditions which *sola scriptura* serves, not as a legal prescription of traditions, but as the source of the one Tradition, the giving of free play to which is the standard by which all traditions must be judged.

Thus we have indicated the point of view from which, starting from *sola scriptura*, the problem of Tradition in its manifold concrete forms should be discussed: in its relation to the theological relevance of Church history; to the hermeneutic of the Confessional discussion and the ecumenical dialogue; to the problem of the language of preaching, of Church doctrine and canon law, as well as the responsibility of Christendom for the preservation, restoration, and creation of sound, world-regarding traditions in a world threatened with the loss of Tradition.

(Taken from Gerhard Ebeling, The Word of God and Tradition: Historical Studies Interpreting the Divisions of Christianity, *trans. S. H. Hooke, London: Collins 1968, pp 144–7.)*

I.3. Creeds and confessions

Introductory essay

The Christian faith was credal from the very beginning, for the early church consisted of scattered communities which expressed their beliefs in the form of summary confessions of faith (I.3.1). Although Christianity took rather different form from what later developed into the faith we know as Judaism, these confessions have their root in the Old Testament. While it is not a credal faith in the way Christianity was to became, the fundamental conviction of Jewish belief is that expressed in Deut. 6.4: 'The Lord our God, the Lord is one.' Christianity has remained a strictly monotheistic faith, but it is a monotheism modified by the apparently disturbing addition of belief in Jesus. It is likely that 'Jesus is Lord' was the first Christian credal confession, and it uses of Jesus the Greek word used to translate the Hebrew for God, thus identifying him with the one Lord of the Old Testament. Perhaps surprisingly, this appears to have caused no difficulty for the first Christians, who were almost certainly all Jewish. They did not renounce their inherited monotheism, but believed that when they confessed Jesus in such terms they were worshipping the same God.

A review of Paul's arguments in 1 Cor. 8 will show the kind of development that this involved. After quoting Deut. 6.4, Paul then modifies it. 'There is one God the Father, from whom all things came . . . and one Lord Jesus Christ, through whom all things came'. A confession of Jesus Christ is incorporated into a confession of belief in God in such a way that the two are now inseparable. To be a Christian believer is to confess a monotheistic belief through a belief in Jesus Christ. It is important to notice that these are confessions – affirmations of faith – and therefore perform two functions. They are neither simply merely intellectual in form, summarizing teaching – though they are that – nor merely forms of words through which God was worshipped, though they are that too. They are expressions of worship and praise to God which also involve claims to be true.

This leads us to a further important feature of credal belief. It is not the same as a philosophy. A philosophy is a teaching which seeks to incorporate the truth of the world in it – what in modern times has come to be called a world-view, a teaching which gives an insight into the meaning of the totality of things. A philosophy, we might say, is an attempt to create a map of the whole of reality. A confession is rather different, for it cannot be demonstrated to be true in the way in which a philosophy can. Creeds involve a personal commitment that can be defended by argument, but which cannot be demonstrated to be true. What is confessed is often first of all an action: something that God has done, is doing and will do. Like a philosophy, it gives a view of the whole of things, not, however, in a comprehensive teaching but by pointing beyond the words to the God who made, upholds and redeems the world he has created. The things that creeds claim to be true are not therefore discovered by free thought and argument, but result from thinking through the meaning of the belief that in Jesus Christ God has acted, is acting and will act for the good of the world he made.

That is why the first formal creeds take the form that they do. What is called the rule of faith or rule of truth – and it can be read below (I.3.2) in the form reported by Origen of Alexandria – is a summary of the past, present and future acts of God. It seeks to summarize what Irenaeus called the economy of God's actions; literally, of the way God organizes his household, which is the whole of creation. There are generally three sections, concerning creation in the beginning, salvation in Christ in the middle, so to speak, and life in the church as the outcome of the first two. The part played by Jesus Christ is central, for an account of his significance includes the life, death, resurrection and ascension to the right hand of God the Father in glory, from where he is to come to judge the world. By the late second century AD, Irenaeus was claiming that the rule of faith was universal in the church, which had now spread widely across the ancient world. There is not yet however a fixed form of words, and he summarizes it slightly differently in different places.

The creeds developed into formal statements of belief whose acceptance determined whether someone was a member of the church. This happened as the result of the struggles about heresy, which is a teaching which is apparently Christian in form but is judged to falsify the faith in some central way. Gnosticism is the heresy which denies God's universal creatorhood, while Arianism denied the full divinity of Jesus Christ. The creeds of Nicaea and Constantinople represent two stages on the way to a teaching that God is a Trinity. Nicaea (I.3.3) confirms the full divinity of the eternal Son of God against any teaching that would make him less than divine, while Constantinople (I.3.4) follows a period of debate after which the divinity of the Holy Spirit is likewise affirmed. Thereafter, confession of the Trinity becomes a criterion of Christian belief. That by no means settled everything christological or trinitarian, however. Alongside the divinity of God the Son, his full humanity within the unity of one person waited until Chalcedon in 451 to be credally defined (I.3.5) while to this day differences remain between East and West about the way in which the Sprit is related to the Father and the Son, after the West's unilateral addition to the creed of the *Filioque* ('and from the Son') (see I.3.6). Two other creeds are worth mentioning, though they are not printed here. The so-called Athanasian Creed is a version of the Nicene-Constantinopolitan Creed to which the *Filioque* was added in 589, while the 'Apostles' Creed', which remains for many people the most familiar summary of the faith, took its present form in the sixth or seventh century, although its origin was possibly as early as the second century. There were both gains and losses in the later developments, for alongside the gain in precision there went a tendency to understand the creeds as legal formularies – a process sometimes attributed to the legally trained theologian Tertullian – to the loss of their original purpose as confessions of faith and worship. Their imposition before the modern age by force of law is one reason why today some churches remain reluctant to incorporate them into formal public worship.

The split between East and West was succeeded in the sixteenth century by a further schism within the Western churches at the Reformation. Though divided by their difference over the Spirit, East and West both enjoyed a long period of credal stability, and this was not fundamentally upset by the Reformation, none of whose main streams denied the creeds. The Reformation was rather an era of new confessions as the churches sought to do two things within the structure of the ancient creeds. First, they established the distinctive theological bases of the new bodies which were formed when subjects of the former Holy Roman Empire split into nation states with varying convictions about the church and its relation to the state. Second, they needed to define the places at which they differed from Rome, and this often centred on the central matter of dispute in the Reformation, over justification (how God made the believer to be righteous). Below are printed three typical confessions from the Reformation tradition. The *Genevan Confession of Faith* (I.3.7) formed the basis for the arrangement of church and state which defined the Swiss city's formal divorce from Rome. By contrast, Lutheranism, which was largely the achievement of one man, is represented by excerpts from Luther's own meditations on the Western forms of the creed and the *Te Deum* (I.3.8). The modern age is represented by the Barmen Declaration (I.3.9) which was a reaffirmation of credal beliefs about Jesus Christ by those German churches which refused to accept the corruption of the faith under the impact of Nazism in Germany. This is a good illustration of the fact that new confessions generally have their place in an emergency, when the integrity of the faith is imperilled.

The third group of writings contains accounts of the purposes of creeds and confessions by three influential modern theologians, from the Reformed, Roman Catholic and Eastern Orthodox churches. Barth (I.3.10) shares the belief of Calvin that creeds and confessions have a subordinate authority and must always be tested against the witness of Scripture, which provides their norm. He writes in awareness of the long tradition of confessions which followed the Reformation and were directed to the particular needs of the time. They represent, like the ancient creeds, the confession of the whole church and have their basis in an act of faith in which the reality of God is recognized: 'Dogmatics is the Credo speaking here and today.' In turn the confessions operate as foundations for the dogmatic work of theologians, who are servants of the church in expounding her message.

Karl Rahner's account (I.3.11) of the interest the creeds serve is rather idiosyncratic, especially in light of more recent official Roman Catholic pronouncements. Creeds – and he takes the Apostles' Creed as his model – are needed for rather individualistic reasons, to show the lay person what are the essentials of the faith and to make the faith intelligible in the modern world. The assumptions of the Apostles' Creed render it unsuitable for the modern apologetic task in view of widespread modern scepticism about the existence of God. This makes Rahner pessimistic about the possibility of a universal new creed that is suitable for modern conditions. There could scarcely be a greater contrast with Barth, for whom the task of creeds and confessions is to proclaim the reality of God, if necessary in face of modern doubt.

George Florovsky's contribution (I.3.12) comes from a church whose fundamental structures of belief and authority are claimed to come unchanged from the first five or six centuries of the church's life. Barth's idea that theology should ask about the possibility of new confessions of faith would be something he would almost certainly not even envisage as a possibility. While this author is aware that modern movements of thought have affected the way the church thinks, he gives modern movements far less weight than his Catholic contemporary. For the Orthodox churches, Scripture and tradition especially as they reach us through the creeds and the writings of the Fathers represent a totality which cannot be broken up after the manner of Western thought. Creeds do not convey metaphysical 'facts', but are confessions: intellectual contours 'of the mystery which is apprehended by faith'.

CEG

A. The development of the catholic creeds

I.3.1 Proto-creeds in the New Testament

New Testament scholarship has uncovered a number of places, particularly in the epistles, where the writer appears to be quoting liturgical or credal material that he expects to be familiar to his readers. Various criteria are used to identify these passages (e.g., the use of vocabulary unusual to that writer; introductory formulae ('handed on'); etc.). It is widely believed that these are fragments of baptismal confessions: formal summaries of the Christian faith to be recited by candidates as they come to baptism. The identifications cannot be certain, of course, but in many cases there is widespread agreement. Some of these are reproduced below.

The most basic Christian confession was the simple assertion 'Jesus is Lord':
. . . no one can say 'Jesus is Lord' except by the Holy Spirit. (1. Cor. 12.3)
. . . if you confess with your lips that 'Jesus is Lord' . . . you will be saved (Rom. 10.9)

Other simple christological claims can also be discerned:
Who is the liar but the one who denies that 'Jesus is the Christ'? This is the antichrist (1 John 2.22)
Everyone who believes that 'Jesus is the Christ' has been born of God . . . (1 John 5.1)
God abides in those who confess that 'Jesus is the Son of God' . . . (1 John 4.15)

Elsewhere, longer and fuller statements of who Christ is and what he has done seem to appear:
. . . the gospel concerning his Son, who 'was descended from David according to the flesh and was declared to be the Son of God with power according to the Spirit of holiness by resurrection from the dead' (Rom. 1.3–4)
    For I handed on to you as of first importance what I in turn had received: 'that Christ died for our sins in accordance with the scriptures, and that he was buried, and that he was raised on the third day in accordance with the scriptures, and that he appeared to Cephas, then to the twelve' . . . (1 Cor. 15.3–5)

There are also what appear to be proto-trinitarian creeds, often binitarian in form:

... Yet for us 'there is one God, the Father, from whom are all things and for whom we exist, and one Lord, Jesus Christ, through whom are all things and through whom we exist.'(1 Cor. 8.6)

For 'there is one God; there is also one mediator between God and human-kind, Christ Jesus, himself human, who gave his life as a ransom for all.' (1 Tim. 2.5–6)

(Quotations taken from the New Revised Standard Version.)

I.3.2 Origen, from *On First Principles*

Origen gives an account of the 'rule of faith', the early summary of Christian teaching that, although not presented in a fixed form of words, is nonetheless cited in broadly similar forms by many of the Fathers.

2. Many of those, however, who profess to believe in Christ, hold conflicting opinions not only on small and trivial questions but also on some that are great and important; on the nature, for instance, of God or of the Lord Jesus Christ or of the Holy Spirit, and in addition on the natures of those created beings, the dominions and the holy powers. In view of this it seems necessary first to lay down a definite line and unmistakable rule in regard to each of these, and to postpone the inquiry into other matters until afterwards. For just as there are many among Greeks and barbarians alike who promise us the truth, and yet we gave up seeking for it from all who claimed it for false opinions after we had come to believe that Christ was the Son of God and had become convinced that we must learn the truth from him; in the same way when we find many who think they hold the doctrine of Christ, some of them differing in their beliefs from the Christians of earlier times, and yet the teaching of the church, handed down in unbroken succession from the apostles, is still preserved and continues to exist in the churches up to the present day, we maintain that that only is to be believed as the truth which in no way conflicts with the tradition of the church and the apostles.

3. But the following fact should be understood. The holy apostles, when preaching the faith of Christ, took certain doctrines, those namely which they believed to be necessary ones, and delivered them in the plainest terms to all believers, even to such as appeared to be somewhat dull in the investigation of divine knowledge. The grounds of their statements they left to be investigated by such as should merit the higher gifts of the Spirit and in particular by such as should afterwards receive through the Holy Spirit himself the graces of language, wisdom and knowledge. There were other doctrines, however, about which the apostles simply said that things were so, keeping silence as to the how or why; their intention undoubtedly being to supply the more diligent of those who came after them, such as should prove to be lovers of wisdom, with an exercise on which to display the fruit of their ability. The men I refer to are those who train themselves to become worthy and capable of receiving wisdom.

4. The kind of doctrines which are believed in plain terms through the apostolic teaching are the following: –

First, that God is one, who created and set in order all things, and who, when nothing existed, caused the universe to be. He is God from the first creation and foundation of the world, the God of all righteous men, of Adam,

Abel, Seth, Enos, Enoch, Noah, Shem, Abraham, Isaac, Jacob, of the twelve patriarchs, of Moses and the prophets. This God, in these last days, according to the previous announcements made through his prophets, sent the Lord Jesus Christ, first for the purpose of calling Israel, and secondly, after the unbelief of the people of Israel, of calling the Gentiles also. This just and good God, the Father of our Lord Jesus Christ, himself gave the law, the prophets and the gospels, and he is God both of the apostles and also of the Old and New Testaments.

Then again: Christ Jesus, he who came to earth, was begotten of the Father before every created thing. And after he had ministered to the Father in the foundation of all things, for, 'all things were made through him', in these last times he emptied himself and was made man, was made flesh, although he was God, and being made man, he still remained what he was, namely, God. He took to himself a body like our body, differing in this alone, that it was born of a virgin and of the Holy Spirit. And this Jesus Christ was born and suffered in truth and not merely in appearance, and truly died our common death. Moreover he truly rose from the dead, and after the resurrection companied with his disciples and was then taken up into heaven.

Then again, the apostles delivered this doctrine, that the Holy Spirit is united in honour and dignity with the Father and the Son. In regard to him it is not yet clearly known whether he is to be thought of as begotten or unbegotten, or as being himself also a Son of God or not; but these are matters which we must investigate to the best of our power from holy scripture, inquiring with wisdom and diligence. It is, however, certainly taught with the utmost clearness in the Church, that this Spirit inspired each one of the saints, both the prophets and the apostles, and that there was not one Spirit in the men of old and another in those who were inspired at the coming of Christ.

5. Next after this the apostles taught that the soul, having a substance and life of its own, will be rewarded according to its deserts after its departure from this world; for it will either obtain an inheritance of eternal life and blessedness, if its deeds shall warrant this, or it must be given over to eternal fire and torments, if the guilt of its crimes shall so determine. Further, there will be a time for the resurrection of the dead, when this body, which is now 'sown in corruption', shall 'rise in incorruption', and that which is 'sown in dishonour' shall 'rise in glory'.

This also is laid down in the Church's teaching, that every rational soul is possessed of free will and choice; and also, that it is engaged in a struggle against the devil and his angels and the opposing powers; for these strive to weigh the soul down with sins, whereas we, if we lead a wise and upright life, endeavour to free ourselves from such a burden. There follows from this the conviction that we are not subject to necessity, so as to be compelled by every means, even against our will, to do either good or evil. For if we are possessed of free will, some spiritual powers may very likely be able to urge us on to sin and others to assist us to salvation; we are not, however, compelled by necessity to act either rightly or wrongly, as is thought to be the case by those who say that human events are due to the course and motion of the stars, not only those events which fall outside the sphere of our freedom of will but even those that lie within our own power.

In regard to the soul, whether it takes its rise from the transference of the seed, in such a way that the principle or substance of the soul may be regarded as inherent in the seminal particles of the body itself; or whether it has some other beginning, and whether this beginning is begotten or unbegotten, or at any rate whether it is imparted to the body from without or no; all this is not very clearly defined in the teaching.

6. Further, in regard to the devil and his angels and the opposing spiritual powers, the Church teaching lays it down that these beings exist, but what they are or how they exist it has not explained very clearly. Among most Christians, however, the following opinion is held, that this devil was formerly an angel, but became an apostate and persuaded as many angels as he could to fall away with him; and these are even now called his angels.

7. The Church teaching also includes the doctrine that this world was made and began to exist at a definite time and that by reason of its corruptible nature it must suffer dissolution. But what existed before this world, or what will exist after it, has not yet been made known openly to the many, for no clear statement on the point is set forth in the Church teaching.

8. Then there is the doctrine that the scriptures were composed through the Spirit of God and that they have not only that meaning which is obvious, but also another which is hidden from the majority of readers. For the contents of scripture are the outward forms of certain mysteries and the images of divine things. On this point the entire Church is unanimous, that while the whole law is spiritual, the inspired meaning is not recognised by all, but only by those who are gifted with the grace of the Holy Spirit in the word of wisdom and knowledge.

10. This also is contained in the church teaching, that there exist certain angels of God and good powers, who minister to him in bringing about the salvation of men; but when these were created, and what they are like, or how they exist, is not very clearly defined. And as for the sun, moon and stars, the tradition does not clearly say whether they are living beings or without life.

Everyone therefore who is desirous of constructing out of the foregoing a connected body of doctrine must use points like these as elementary and foundation principles, in accordance with the commandment which says, 'Enlighten yourselves with the light of knowledge'. Thus by clear and cogent arguments he will discover the truth about each particular point and so will produce, as we have said, a single body of doctrine, with the aid of such illustrations and declarations as he shall find in the holy scriptures and of such conclusions as he shall ascertain to follow logically from them when rightly understood.

(Taken from G. W. Butterworth's translation (of the Latin text), London: SPCK 1936.)

I.3.3 The First Council of Nicaea

The first ecumenical council, held in AD 325, was largely concerned with the question of Arianism, the denial that Jesus Christ was truly divine. The balance of the creed (now usually known as the Creed of Nicaea), and the content of the anathemas reflect that.

The Creed and Anathemas:

We believe in one God, the Father Almighty, maker of all things visible and invisible;

And in one Lord Jesus Christ, the Son of God, the only-begotten of his Father, of the substance of the Father, God of God, Light of Light, very God of very God, begotten, not made, being of one substance with the Father. By whom all things were made, both which be in heaven and in earth. Who for us men and for our salvation came down [from heaven] and was incarnate and was made man. He suffered and the third day he rose again, and ascended into heaven. And he shall come again to judge both the quick and the dead.

And in the Holy Ghost.

And whosoever shall say that there was a time when the Son of God was not, or that before he was begotten he was not, or that he was made of things that were not, or that he is of a different substance or essence [from the Father] or that he is a creature, or subject to change or conversion – all that so say, the Catholic and Apostolic Church anathematizes them.

(Taken from the Nicene and Post-Nicene Fathers, second series, vol. XIV, ed. Henry R. Percival.)

I.3.4 The First Council of Constantinople

At Constantinople, the divinity of Christ was re-affirmed and the question of the status of the Spirit was addressed. Amongst the heretics condemned in the first Canon are the Pneumatomachoi, who denied the deity of the Spirit, and the Apollinarians, who denied the true humanity of Christ. The creed promulgated by the Council, known properly as the Nicene-Constantinopolitan Creed, but more usually as the Nicene Creed, is one of the key ecumenical documents. The version here lacks the later addition of the filioque.

The Creed:

We believe in one God, the Father Almighty, maker of heaven and earth and of all things visible and invisible.

And in one Lord Jesus Christ, the only begotten Son of God, begotten of his Father before all worlds, Light of Light, very God of very God, begotten not made, being of one substance with the Father, by whom all things were made. Who for us men and for our salvation came down from heaven and was incarnate by the Holy Ghost and the Virgin Mary, and was made man, and was crucified also for us under Pontius Pilate. He suffered and was buried, and the third day he rose again according to the Scriptures, and ascended into heaven, and sitteth at the Right Hand of the Father. And he shall come again with glory to judge both the quick and the dead. Whose kingdom shall have no end.

And in the Holy Ghost, the Lord and Giver-of-Life, who proceedeth from the Father, who with the Father and the Son together is worshipped and glorified, who spake by the prophets.

And in one, holy, Catholic and Apostolic Church. We acknowledge one Baptism for the remission of sins, [and] we look for the resurrection of the dead and the life of the world to come. Amen.

The Canons of the 150 Fathers who Assembled at Constantinople during the Consulate of those illustrious men, Flavius Eucherius and Flavius Evagrius on the 7th of the Ides of July.

The bishops out of different provinces assembled by the grace of God in Constantinople, on the summons of the most religious Emperor Theodosius, have decreed as follows:

Canon 1. The Faith of the Three Hundred and Eighteen Fathers assembled at Nice in Bithynia shall not be set aside, but shall remain firm. And every heresy shall be anathematized, particularly that of the Eunomians or [Anomoeans, the Arians or] Eudoxians, and that of the Semi-Arians or Pneumatomachi, and that of the Sabellians, and that of the Marcellians, and that of the Photinians, and that of the Apollinarians . . .

(Taken from the Nicene and Post-Nicene Fathers, second series, vol. XIV, ed. Henry R. Percival.)

I.3.5 The Definition of Faith of The Council of Chalcedon

This Council, held in AD 451, was mostly concerned with establishing the orthodox doctrine in the area of Christology. The Extract from the Acts of the Council below records the acceptance of the earlier creeds, and then the Council's own definition.

The most glorious judges and great Senate said: 'Let there be read the expositions of the 318 fathers gathered together at Nicea.'
Eunomius, the most reverend bishop of Nicomedia read from a book [the Exposition of faith of the 318 fathers.]
The Exposition of faith of the Council held at Nice:

> 'In the consulate of Paul and Julian' etc.
> 'We believe in one God,' etc.
> 'But those who say,' etc.

The most reverend bishops cried out, 'This is the orthodox faith; this we all believe: into this we were baptized; into this we baptize . . .'

The most glorious judges and great senate said, 'Let there be read what was set forth by the 150 holy fathers.'
Aetius, the reverend deacon of Constantinople read from a book [the creed of the 150 fathers.]
The holy faith which the 150 fathers set forth as consonant to the holy and great Synod of Nicea:
'We believe in one God,' etc. [The Nicene Creed, defined at Constantinople]
All the most reverend bishops cried out, 'This is the faith of all of us: we all so believe.'

The Definition of Faith of The Council of Chalcedon
The holy, great, and ecumenical synod, assembled by the grace of God and the command of our most religious and Christian Emperors, Marcian and Valentinan, Augusti, at Chalcedon, the metropolis of the Bithynian Province, in the martyry of the holy and victorious martyr Euphemia, has decreed as follows:
    Our Lord and Saviour Jesus Christ, when strengthening the knowledge of the Faith in his disciples, to the end that no one might disagree with his neighbour concerning the doctrines of religion, and that the proclamation of the truth might be set forth equally to all men, said, 'My peace I leave with you, my peace I give unto you.' But, since the evil one does not desist from sowing tares among the seeds of godliness, but ever invents some new device against the truth; therefore the Lord, providing, as he ever does, for the

human race, has raised up this pious, faithful, and zealous Sovereign, and has called together unto him from all parts the chief rulers of the priesthood; so that, the grace of Christ our common Lord inspiring us, we may cast off every plague of falsehood from the sheep of Christ, and feed them with the tender leaves of truth. And this have we done with one unanimous consent, driving away erroneous doctrines and renewing the unerring faith of the Fathers, publishing to all men the Creed of the Three Hundred and Eighteen, and to their number adding, as their peers, the Fathers who have received the same summary of religion. Such are the One Hundred and Fifty holy Fathers who afterwards assembled in the great Constantinople and ratified the same faith. Moreover, observing the order and every form relating to the faith, which was observed by the holy synod formerly held in Ephesus, of which Celestine of Rome and Cyril of Alexandria, of holy memory, were the leaders, we do declare that the exposition of the right and blameless faith made by the Three Hundred and Eighteen holy and blessed Fathers, assembled at Nicea in the reign of Constantine of pious memory, shall be pre-eminent: and that those things shall be of force also, which were decreed by the One Hundred and Fifty holy Fathers at Constantinople, for the uprooting of the heresies which had then sprung up, and for the confirmation of the same Catholic and Apostolic Faith of ours.

The Creed of the three hundred and eighteen Fathers at Nicea.
　We believe in one God, etc.

The Creed of the one hundred and fifty holy Fathers who were assembled at Constantinople:
　We believe in one God, etc.

This wise and salutary formula of divine grace sufficed for the perfect knowledge and confirmation of religion; for it teaches the perfect [doctrine] concerning Father, Son, and Holy Ghost, and sets forth the Incarnation of the Lord to them that faithfully receive it. But, forasmuch as persons undertaking to make void the preaching of the truth have through their individual heresies given rise to empty babblings; some of them daring to corrupt the mystery of the Lord's incarnation for us and refusing [to use] the name Mother of God [*Theotokos*] in reference to the Virgin, while others, bringing in a confusion and mixture, and idly conceiving that the nature of the flesh and of the Godhead is all one, maintaining that the divine Nature of the Only Begotten is, by mixture, capable of suffering; therefore this present holy, great, and ecumenical synod, desiring to exclude every device against the Truth, and teaching that which is unchanged from the beginning, has at the very outset decreed that the faith of the Three Hundred and Eighteen Fathers shall be preserved inviolate. And on account of them that contend against the Holy Ghost, it confirms the doctrine afterwards delivered concerning the substance of the

Spirit by the One Hundred and Fifty holy Fathers who assembled in the imperial City; which doctrine they declared unto all men, not as though they were introducing anything that had been lacking in their predecessors, but in order to explain through written documents their faith concerning the Holy Ghost against those who were seeking to destroy his sovereignty. And, on account of those who have taken in hand to corrupt the mystery of the dispensation [i.e. the Incarnation] and who shamelessly pretend that he who was born of the holy Virgin Mary was a mere man, it receives the synodical letters of the Blessed Cyril, Pastor of the Church of Alexandria, addressed to Nestorius and the Easterns, judging them suitable, for the refutation of the frenzied folly of Nestorius, and for the instruction of those who long with holy ardour for a knowledge of the saving symbol. And, for the confirmation of the orthodox doctrines, it has rightly added to these the letter of the President of the great and old Rome, the most blessed and holy Archbishop Leo, which was addressed to Archbishop Flavian of blessed memory, for the removal of the false doctrines of Eutyches, judging them to be agreeable to the confession of the great Peter, and as it were a common pillar against misbelievers. For it opposes those who would rend the mystery of the dispensation into a Duad of Sons; it repels from the sacred assembly those who dare to say that the Godhead of the Only Begotten is capable of suffering; it resists those who imagine a mixture or confusion of the two natures of Christ; it drives away those who fancy his form of a servant is of an heavenly or some substance other than that which was taken of us, and it anathematizes those who foolishly talk of two natures of our Lord before the union, conceiving that after the union there was only one.

Following the holy Fathers we teach with one voice that the Son [of God] and our Lord Jesus Christ is to be confessed as one and the same [Person], that he is perfect in Godhead and perfect in manhood, very God and very man, of a reasonable soul and [human] body consisting, consubstantial with the Father as touching his Godhead, and consubstantial with us as touching his manhood; made in all things like unto us, sin only excepted; begotten of his Father before the worlds according to his Godhead; but in these last days for us men and for our salvation born [into the world] of the Virgin Mary, the Mother of God according to his manhood. This one and the same Jesus Christ, the only-begotten Son [of God] must be confessed to be in two natures, unconfusedly, immutably, indivisibly, inseparably [united], and that without the distinction of natures being taken away by such union, but rather the peculiar property of each nature being preserved and being united in one Person and subsistence, not separated or divided into two persons, but one and the same Son and only-begotten, God the Word, our Lord Jesus Christ, as the Prophets of old time have spoken concerning him, and as the Lord Jesus Christ hath taught us, and as the Creed of the Fathers hath delivered to us.

These things, therefore, having been expressed by us with the greatest accuracy and attention, the holy Ecumenical Synod defines that no one shall be suffered to bring forward a different faith (*heteran pistin*), nor to write, nor to put together, nor to excogitate, nor to teach it to others. But such as dare either to put together another faith, or to bring forward or to teach or to deliver a different Creed (*heteron symbolon*) to such as wish to be converted to the knowledge of the truth from the Gentiles, or Jews or any heresy whatever, if they be Bishops or clerics let them be deposed, the Bishops from the Episcopate, and the clerics from the clergy; but if they be monks or laics: let them be anathematized.

(After the reading of the definition, all the most religious Bishops cried out, 'This is the faith of the fathers: let the metropolitans forthwith subscribe it: let them forthwith, in the presence of the judges, subscribe it: let that which has been well defined have no delay: this is the faith of the Apostles: by this we all stand: thus we all believe.')

(Taken from the Nicene and Post-Nicene Fathers, second series, volume XIV, ed. Henry R. Percival.)

I.3.6 Costa Carras, 'A Brief History of the *Filioque* Dispute'

This was originally an appendix to a British Council of Churches study guide entitled The Forgotten Trinity.

Historical and theological disputes are notoriously difficult to write about objectively because inevitably differing sides to disputes have differing interpretations of events. Nevertheless, we thought it important that we at least try to describe the salient facts of the division between Eastern and Western churches. It may very well be that B.C.C. member churches will be indifferent to the issues, or they may decide that one side was right and another wrong. Whatever the case our brief history demonstrates that there was never a great formal break between East and West on a single issue. Nor can it be said that the date of 1054, which many textbooks cite as the date of the schism between East and West, is more than one point in a long historical development.

The Creed of the Council of Nicaea (325), as amended by the Council of Constantinople (381), proclaims:

'And in the Holy Spirit, the Lord, the giver of life, who proceeds from the Father, who with the Father and the Son together is worshipped and glorified, who spake by the Prophets'.

The view that the Holy Spirit proceeds from the Father *and* the Son (*Filioque*) existed before St. Augustine (354-430) but it is his theology of the Trinity that has been most frequently used to support this position. By contrast the Trinitarian theology of the Fathers who wrote in Cappadocia in the second half of the fourth century – St. Basil, St. Gregory Nazianzen, and St. Gregory of Nyssa – has been most frequently used to oppose it.

Acceptance of the *Filioque* as correct doctrine did not imply its inclusion in the Nicene-Constantinopolitan Creed (commonly called 'Nicene' for brevity). Indeed a great deal of generally accepted theology was never incorporated into the Nicene Creed, which is without doubt the greatest single credal statement of united Christendom.

On the other hand the 'Athanasian' creed, which has no connection with the historical St. Athanasius (d. 373), but was drawn up in the West under Augustinian influence, did contain the *Filioque*. In 589, when the Visigothic kingdom of Spain officially abandoned Arianism at the Council of Toledo the *Filioque* seems to have been included in the Spanish version of the Nicene Creed.

From Spain the insertion of the *Filioque* spread to the Frankish Empire (today's France and Germany). Under Charlemagne it was openly argued, as for instance at the Council of Frankfurt in 794, that the East was in error in not including it. The large majority of the Western Church accepted the Augustinian theology of the *Filioque*, as did Pope Leo III (795-816).

However he urged the Franks to remove the word from the Creed; and to emphasise his support for the original Nicene Creed he had two silver shields engraved with the original words in both Greek and Latin which he prominently displayed in St. Peter's Rome.

The *Filioque* issue surfaced again when Bulgaria accepted Christianity (864). Both East and West competed for her jurisdictional allegiance. This led to a period of intense controversy during which Patriarch Photius of Constantinople, basing himself on the Greek Fathers, argued not only against the insertion of the *Filioque* into the Creed, but also against the truth of this doctrine itself.

Peace was achieved at the Council of 879-880, which was held at Constantinople, with the participation of legates from Pope John VIII. On the Pope's behalf they signed an agreement that declared that the Creed 'cannot be substracted from, added to, altered, or distorted in any way'. This settlement lasted until the early eleventh century, by which time influence on Rome from across the Alps had increased greatly.

The last Pope commemorated in Constantinople was John XVIII (1003-1009). In an age of poor communications and with as many political and ecclesiastical disputes as in our own day, there could be many explanations as to why the Popes were no longer commemorated. It seems safe to say, however, that as Benedict VIII (1012-1024) allowed the *Filioque* to be included in the Creed sung at an Imperial coronation in Rome, his credal statement (and those of his successors who followed this innovation) would have been unacceptable in Constantinople.

The non-commemoration of Popes in Constantinople was a very serious matter and evidence of tension and bad feeling between the two ancient sees. But in itself it did not amount to a formal schism between East and West. For one thing there had been serious schisms before between Popes and Patriarchs which had been healed. For another, the other remaining Patriarchates of Alexandria, Antioch, and Jerusalem did not automatically follow Constantinople. Finally, to the degree that there was tension between East and West, other issues were also important. Some of these were political, some jurisdictional, some canonical (the West, unlike the East, increasingly expected celibacy from all their clergy), some liturgical (the West used unleavened, the East leavened bread at the Eucharist). In fact a sense of the continual unity of Christendom survived, despite the widening gaps, throughout the eleventh and twelfth centuries. During this period, for example, there was non-polemical theological discussion of the *Filioque* between Easterners and Westerners.

Gradually, however, this dispute and the Papacy's increasing desire for universal jurisdiction (for example, in the appointment of bishops) estranged the East, with its long tradition of Cappadocian theology, particularly in the doctrine of the Trinity, and its background of collegiate and synodical government. The long-standing dispute between Rome and Constantinople spread to the other Patriarchates. There was, for example, schism at Antioch from 1100, when shortly after the Crusaders' arrival a Latin Patriarch was installed there whilst the Greek Patriarch and his successors lived in exile. Evidence of the growth in hostility can be seen by the late twelfth century when a Patriarch of Constantinople, Michael Anchialus (1169-1177) could argue that political subjection to Muslims was preferable to accepting the faith of the West.

The Fourth Crusade's capture and sack of Constantinople in 1204, followed by the continuing attacks made on Russian lands from the Baltic regions of the Teutonic Knights, under the patronage of Rome, crystallised the already deep division between East and West. From this time onwards there was a seemingly insuperable barrier of popular hostility between the two halves of Christendom.

In the centuries that followed there were many attempts to find a road back to reunion between East and West (and there were instances of intercommunion up to the eighteenth century). There was, however, no longer a dialogue of equality between the two halves of Christendom. The East, now much weakened by wars with Islam, was requesting help against Muslim powers or was even subjected to them, and it is even harder than before to distinguish theological and political motivations in this period.

In the middle ages some Westerners suggested that the *Filioque* could be seen as being equivalent to *per filium*, or *through the Son* (this phrase, though not the argument that it was equivalent to the *Filioque*, goes back to the third century theologian Tertullian). Some Easterners approved such a formulation in respect of the Holy Spirit's mission, or of the Spirit's eternal manifestation, but never of the procession, that is of the Spirit's mode of being itself. Neither side wanted the phrase *through the Son* in the Creed. Instead at the Councils of Lyons in 1274 and Ferrara-Florence in 1438–1439, the West with some Eastern bishops declared that a satisfactory basis for reunion had been found in acceptance of the *Filioque* in the Nicene creed. But this was rejected by the vast majority of Eastern clergy and laity who would accept neither the *Filioque* nor the idea of universal papal jurisdiction (which was part of the conditions of reunion).

Rome was prepared to recognise the validity of the Eastern churches' liturgical traditions, as well as their right to a married clergy. It was even prepared to allow them to continue using the Creed in its original form. However, it insisted that the East recognise the addition of the *Filioque* to the Creed as theologically and canonically justified. The Orthodox would agree with neither of these however. It would be true to say that in the Orthodox church today, with its great emphasis on patristic theology, the *Filioque* dispute has become more rather than less important.

It is unwise to underestimate the importance of political and cultural differences that divided East and West. Nevertheless it remains true that the *Filioque* – which was inherited by the Protestant Reformers by default as it were

– has remained one of the major issues that continues to separate Eastern from Western Christendom.

(Taken from The Forgotten Trinity, *London: British Council of Churches 1989, pp. 37–40.)*

B. The use of confessions

I.3.7 The Genevan Confession of 1536

Many confessions outlining particular positions were produced around the time of the Reformation, and afterwards. This is a brief example of the genre, here reproduced in full. This confession was traditionally ascribed to John Calvin, but is now generally regarded as being by William Farel. Whoever the author was, it exemplifies the twin aims of all confessions: aligning the sponsoring group with orthodox opinion on such points as Trinity and Christology, and announcing the position adhered to on such points of controversy as the sacraments and the authority of the church.

1. THE WORD OF GOD

First we affirm that we desire to follow Scripture alone as rule of faith and religion, without mixing with it any other thing which might be devised by the opinion of men apart from the Word of God, and without wishing to accept for our spiritual government any other doctrine than what is conveyed to us by the same Word without addition or diminution, according to the command of our Lord.

2. ONE ONLY GOD

Following, then, the lines laid down in the Holy Scriptures, we acknowledge that there is one only God, whom we are both to worship and serve, and in whom we are to put all our confidence and hope: having this assurance, that in him alone is contained all wisdom, power, justice, goodness and pity. And since he is spirit, he is to be served in spirit and in truth. Therefore we think it an abomination to put our confidence or hope in any created thing, to worship anything else than him, whether angels or any other creatures, and to recognize any other Saviour of our souls than him alone, whether saints or men living upon earth; and likewise to offer the service, which ought to be rendered to him, in external ceremonies or carnal observances, as if he took pleasure in such things, or to make an image to represent his divinity or any other image for adoration.

3. THE LAW OF GOD ALIKE FOR ALL

Because there is one only Lord and Master who has dominion over our consciences, and because his will is the only principle of all justice, we confess all our life ought to be ruled in accordance with the commandments of his holy law in which is contained all perfection of justice, and that we ought to have no other rule of good and just living, nor invent other good works to supplement it than those which are there contained, as follows: Exodus 20: 'I am the Lord thy God, who brought thee,' and so on.

4. NATURAL MAN

We acknowledge man by nature to be blind, darkened in understanding, and full of corruption and perversity of heart, so that of himself he has no power to be able to comprehend the true knowledge of God as is proper, nor to apply himself to good works. But on the contrary, if he is left by God to what he is by nature, he is only able to live in ignorance and to be abandoned to all iniquity. Hence he has need to be illumined by God, so that he come to the right knowledge of his salvation, and thus to be redirected in his affections and reformed to the obedience of the righteousness of God.

5. MAN BY HIMSELF LOST

Since man is naturally (as has been said) deprived and destitute in himself of all the light of God, and of all righteousness, we acknowledge that by himself he can only expect the wrath and malediction of God, and hence that he must look outside himself for the means of his salvation.

6. SALVATION IN JESUS

We confess then that it is Jesus Christ who is given to us by the Father, in order that in him we should recover all of which in ourselves we are deficient. Now all that Jesus Christ has done and suffered for our redemption, we veritably hold without any doubt, as it is contained in the Creed, which is recited in the Church, that is to say: I believe in God the Father Almighty, and so on.

7. RIGHTEOUSNESS IN JESUS

Therefore we acknowledge the things which are consequently given to us by God in Jesus Christ: first, that being in our own nature enemies of God and subjects of his wrath and judgment, we are reconciled with him and received again in grace through the intercession of Jesus Christ, so that by his righteousness and guiltlessness we have remission of our sins, and by the shedding of his blood we are cleansed and purified from all our stains.

8. REGENERATION IN JESUS

Second, we acknowledge that by his Spirit we are regenerated into a new spiritual nature. That is to say that the evil desires of our flesh are mortified by grace, so that they rule us no longer. On the contrary, our will is rendered conformable to God's will, to follow in his way and to seek what is pleasing to him. Therefore we are by him delivered from the servitude of sin, under whose power we were of ourselves held captive, and by this deliverance we are made capable and able to do good works and not otherwise.

9. REMISSION OF SINS ALWAYS NECESSARY FOR THE FAITHFUL

Finally, we acknowledge that this regeneration is so effected in us that, until we slough off this mortal body, there remains always in us much imperfection and infirmity, so that we always remain poor and wretched sinners in the presence of God. And, however much we ought day by day to increase and grow in God's righteousness, there will never be plenitude or perfection while we live here. Thus we always have need of the mercy of God to obtain the remission of our faults and offences. And so we ought always to look for our righteousness in Jesus Christ and not at all in ourselves, and in him be confident and assured, putting no faith in our works.

10. ALL OUR GOOD IN THE GRACE OF GOD

In order that all glory and praise be rendered to God (as is his due), and that we be able to have true peace and rest of conscience, we understand and confess that we receive all benefits from God, as said above, by his clemency and pity, without any consideration of of our worthiness or the merit of our works, to which is due no other retribution than eternal confusion. None the less our Saviour in his goodness, having received us into the communion of his son Jesus, regards the works that we have done in faith as pleasing and agreeable; not that they merit it at all, but because, not imputing any of the imperfection that is there, he acknowledges in them nothing but what proceeds from his Spirit.

11. FAITH

We confess that the entrance which we have to the great treasures and riches of the goodness of God that is vouchsafed to us is by faith; inasmuch as, in certain confidence and assurance of heart, we believe in the promises of the

Gospel, and receive Jesus Christ as he is offered to us by the Father and described to us by the Word of God.

12. INVOCATION OF GOD ONLY AND INTERCESSION OF CHRIST

As we have declared that we have confidence and hope for salvation and all good only in God through Jesus Christ, so we confess that we ought to invoke him in all necessities in the name of Jesus Christ, who is our Mediator and Advocate with him and has access to him. Likewise we ought to acknowledge that all good things come from him alone, and to give thanks to him for them. On the other hand, we reject the intercession of the saints as a superstition invented by men contrary to Scripture, for the reason that it proceeds from mistrust of the sufficiency of the intercession of Jesus Christ.

13. PRAYER INTELLIGIBLE

Moreover since prayer is nothing but hypocrisy and fantasy unless it proceed from the interior affections of the heart, we believe that all prayers ought to be made with clear understanding. And for this reason, we hold the prayer of our Lord to show fittingly what we ought to ask of him: Our Father which art in heaven, . . . but deliver us from evil. Amen.

14. SACRAMENTS

We believe that the sacraments which our Lord has ordained in his Church are to be regarded as exercises of faith for us, both for fortifying and confirming it in the promises of God and for witnessing before men. Of them there are in the Christian Church only two which are instituted by the authority of our Saviour: Baptism and the Supper of our Lord; for what is held within the realm of the pope concerning seven sacraments, we condemn as fable and lie.

15. BAPTISM

Baptism is an external sign by which our Lord testifies that he desires to receive us for his children, as members of his Son Jesus. Hence in it there is represented to us the cleansing from sin which we have in the blood of Jesus Christ, the mortification of our flesh which we have by his death that we may live in him by his Spirit. Now since our children belong to such an alliance with our Lord, we are certain that the external sign is rightly applied to them.

16. THE HOLY SUPPER

The Supper of our Lord is a sign by which under bread and wine he represents the true spiritual communion which we have in his body and blood. And we acknowledge that according to his ordinance it ought to be distributed in the company of the faithful, in order that all those who wish to have Jesus for their life be partakers of it. In as much as the mass of the pope was a reprobate and diabolical ordinance subverting the mystery of the Holy Supper, we declare that it is execrable to us, an idolatry condemned by God; for so much is it itself regarded as a sacrifice for the redemption of souls that the bread is in it taken and adored as God. Besides there are other execrable blasphemies and superstitions implied here, and the abuse of the Word of God which is taken in vain without profit or edification.

17. HUMAN TRADITIONS

The ordinances that are necessary for the internal discipline of the Church, and belong solely to the maintenance of peace, honesty and good order in the assembly of Christians, we do not hold to be human traditions at all, in as much as they are comprised under the general command of Paul, where he desires that all be done among them decently and in order. But all laws and regulations made binding on conscience which oblige the faithful to things not commanded by God, or establish another service of God than that which he demands, thus tending to destroy Christian liberty, we condemn as perverse doctrines of Satan, in view of our Lord's declaration that he is honoured in vain by doctrines that are the commandment of men. It is in this estimation that we hold pilgrimages, monasteries, distinctions of foods, prohibition of marriage, confessions and other like things.

18. THE CHURCH

While there is one only Church of Jesus Christ, we always acknowledge that necessity requires companies of the faithful to be distributed in different places. Of these assemblies each one is called Church. But in as much as all companies do not assemble in the name of our Lord, but rather to blaspheme and pollute him by their sacrilegious deeds, we believe that the proper mark by which rightly to discern the Church of Jesus Christ is that his holy gospel be purely and faithfully preached, proclaimed, heard, and kept, that his sacraments be properly administered, even if there be some imperfections and faults, as there always will be among men. On the other hand, where the Gospel is not declared, heard, and received, there we do not acknowledge the form of the Church. Hence the churches governed by the ordinances of the pope are rather synagogues of the devil than Christian churches.

19. EXCOMMUNICATION

Because there are always some who hold God and his Word in contempt, who take account of neither injunction, exhortation nor remonstrance, thus requiring greater chastisement, we hold the discipline of excommunication to be a thing holy and salutary among the faithful, since truly it was instituted by our Lord with good reason. This is in order that the wicked should not by their damnable conduct corrupt the good and dishonour our Lord, and that though proud they may turn to penitence. Therefore we believe that it is expedient according to the ordinance of God that all manifest idolaters, blasphemers, murderers, thieves, lewd persons, false witnesses, sedition-mongers, quarrellers, those guilty of defamation or assault, drunkards, dissolute livers, when they have been duly admonished and if they do not make amendment, be separated from the communion of the faithful until their repentance is known.

20. MINISTERS OF THE WORD

We recognize no other pastors in the Church than faithful pastors of the Word of God, feeding the sheep of Jesus Christ on the one hand with instruction, admonition, consolation, exhortation, deprecation; and on the other resisting all false doctrines and deceptions of the devil, without mixing with the pure doctrine of the Scriptures their dreams or their foolish imaginings. To these we accord no other power or authority but to conduct, rule, and govern the people of God committed to them by the same Word, in which they have power to command, defend, promise, and warn, and without which they neither can nor ought to attempt anything. As we receive the true ministers of the Word of God as messengers and ambassadors of God, it is necessary to listen to them as to him himself, and we hold their ministry to be a commission from God necessary in the Church. On the other hand we hold that all seductive and false prophets, who abandon the purity of the Gospel and deviate to their own inventions, ought not at all to be suffered or maintained, who are not the pastors they pretend, but rather, like ravening wolves, ought to be hunted and ejected from the people of God.

21. MAGISTRATES

We hold the supremacy and dominion of kings and princes as also of other magistrates and officers, to be a holy thing and a good ordinance of God. And since in performing their office they serve God and follow a Christian vocation, whether in defending the afflicted and innocent, or in correcting and punishing the malice of the perverse, we on our part also ought to accord them honour and reverence, to render respect and subservience, to execute their commands, to bear the charges they impose on us, so far as we are able without offence to God. In sum, we ought to regard them as vicars and lieutenants of God, whom one cannot resist without resisting God himself; and their office as a sacred commission from God which has been given them so that they may rule and govern us. Hence we hold that all Christians are bound to pray God for the prosperity of the superiors and lords of the country where they live, to obey the statutes and ordinances which do not contravene the commandments of God, to promote welfare, peace and public good, endeavouring to sustain the honour of those over them and the peace of the people, without contriving or attempting anything to inspire trouble or dissension. On the other hand we declare that all those who conduct themselves unfaithfully towards their superiors, and have not a right concern for the public good of the country where they live, demonstrate thereby their infidelity towards God.

(Taken from Calvin: Theological Treaties, *trans. J. K. S. Reid, The Library of Christian Classics, vol. XXII, Philadelphia, PA: Westminster Press 1954, pp. 26–33.)*

I.3.8 Martin Luther, from *The Three Symbols or Creeds of the Christian Faith*

The three texts Luther has in mind are the Apostles' Creed, the Athanasian Creed (which, despite Luther's acceptance of the legend, is not by St Athanasius) and the hymn Te Deum Laudamus (which again probably has no connection with St Ambrose and St Augustine). Luther suggests they all turn on right belief in Christ, and discusses some ways in which this right belief is attacked.

Although I have already taught and written a great deal about faith – what it is, what it does – and although I have also published my confession of what I believe and where I intend to stand, still the devil keeps hatching new plots against me. Therefore I have decided in addition to publish the three symbols (as they are called) or creeds together, in German, the ones which hitherto have been kept, read, and sung in the whole church, so that I may again bear witness that I hold to the real Christian Church, which up until now has preserved these symbols or creeds, and not to that false, arrogant church which is indeed the worst enemy of the real church. That one has set much idolatry next to these beautiful creeds, just as in ancient times the people of Israel set up many idols in valleys, on hills, under trees, next to the beautiful divine service instituted by God, and the temple – and nevertheless claimed to be the real people of God and, using that excuse, persecuted and slew all the prophets, and finally the Lord Christ himself also.

The first symbol, that of the apostles, is truly the finest of all. Briefly, correctly, and in a splendid way it summarizes the articles of faith, and it can easily be learned by children and simple people. The second, that of St. Athanasius, is longer and for the benefit of the Arians. It expands more amply the one article, namely, how Jesus Christ is God's own Son and our Lord, in whom we believe with the same faith with which we believe in the Father, as the text reads in the first symbol, 'I believe in God,' etc., 'and in Jesus,' etc. For if he were not very God, he would not have to be honored with the same faith as the Father. This is what St. Athanasius argues and emphasizes in his symbol, which is, as it were, a symbol in defense of the first symbol. The third symbol is said to be of SS. Augustine and Ambrose, and is supposed to have been sung at the baptism of St. Augustine. Whether that is true or not – and it does no harm whether one believes it or not – it is nevertheless a fine symbol or creed (whoever the author) composed in the form of a chant, not only for the purpose of confessing the true faith, but also for praising and thanking God.

I have perceived and noted in all histories of all of Christendom that all those who have correctly had and kept the chief article of Jesus Christ have remained safe and secure in the right Christian faith. Although they may have sinned or erred in other matters, they have nevertheless been preserved at the last. For whoever stands correctly and firmly in the belief that Jesus Christ is true God and man, that he died and has risen again for us, such a person has all other articles added to him and they firmly stand by him. Therefore, what St. Paul says is quite certain, that Christ is 'capital wealth,' base, ground, and the whole sum, around and under which everything is gathered and found, and in him are hidden all the treasures of wisdom and understanding [Col. 2:3]. Christ also says himself, 'He who abides in me, he it is that bears much fruit' [John 15:5]; 'he who is not with me is against me, and he who does not gather with me scatters,' etc. [Luke 11:23].

For thus it is decided (so speaks St. Paul) that in Jesus Christ the whole fulness of deity dwells bodily [Col. 2:9] or personally, in such manner that whoever does not find or receive God in Christ shall nevermore and nowhere have or find God outside of Christ, even though he should go beyond heaven, below hell, or outside of the world. For here I will dwell (says God), in this humanity, born of Mary the virgin, etc. If you believe this, then good for you; if not, then have your own way, but your lack of belief will change nothing herein. And Christ will indeed remain in spite of you, together with all his believers, as he has remained heretofore, against all the power of the devil and the world.

On the other hand, I have also noticed that all error, heresy, idolatry, offense, misuse, and evil in the church originally came from despising or losing sight of this article of faith in Jesus Christ. And if one looks at it correctly and clearly, all heresies do contend against this dear article of Jesus Christ, as Simeon says of him, that he is 'set for the fall and rising of many in Israel, and for a sign that is spoken against' [Luke 2:34]. And Isaiah [8:14] long before proclaimed him a stone of offense and a rock of stumbling. For whatsoever stumbles, certainly stumbles on this stone, which lies in everyone's way and is rejected by the builders, as he himself shows in the one hundred eighteenth Psalm. In his epistle, St. John also gives no other or more certain sign for recognizing false and anti-Christian spirits than their denial of Jesus Christ [II John 7]. They have all wanted to reap honor at his expense and have instead garnered shame from it.

Some have attacked his deity, doing this in various ways. It is said by one group that he is nothing more than any other man and not God at all. Some say that he is one Person with the Father, and that the Father suffered for us. Others, however, say that he is a creature above all angels and is to be called a kind of God through whom all other creatures are created, but that he is not real, genuine, eternal God with the Father. It is a marvel, a marvel, to see how discerning minds have fairly writhed here in their attempt to avoid believing in Christ as a real, true God! They have always wanted to measure, grasp, and master this article and the Scriptures with their reason. But it has stood firm, and they have all passed away, although the devil has continued to sow his seed in the hearts of his children, the unbelievers, and finally Mohammed came and nearly led the whole world in the East astray and away from Christ.

Some have attacked Christ's humanity, and how strange their antics have been! The Manichaeans said he was a specter or a shadow who had passed through Mary like a phantom having neither a real body nor soul. Others said that he had no soul, and that the deity ruled his body in place of a soul. Others said that he was not Mary's real, natural son. The Jews consider themselves very clever people because they can say that he was conceived by Joseph. And some among them have said such infamous things that they do not bear repeating. But they have hit the mark unusually well in contriving how there cannot be three Persons in the Godhead, saying that these cannot be brothers or relatives, and what other way would there be of reckoning how the three Persons are equal? O clever people, who judge God's unsearchable, eternal substance in the manner of mortal human beings – or of dogs! To sum up: the devil has not been able to find any peace where our dear Christ is preached according to the first symbol, i.e., that he is God and man, who died and rose again for us. This is the woman's seed, who crushes his head and whose heel he bites [Gen. 3:15]. Therefore the enmity will not cease until the last day.

And what have *we* done, who are the latest, greatest saints of the papacy? We have confessed that he is God and man. But, that he is our Savior, who died and rose again for us, etc. – this we have denied and persecuted with all our might, and still do not cease. Some have taught that he died only for original sin, and that we ourselves must make satisfaction for the rest. Others, however, have taught that if we sin after our baptism, then Christ is no longer of use to us. Then saint worship came into being, and pilgrimages, and purgatory, and masses, and cloisters, and more such verminous nonsense without end and number, by means of which we have tried to propitiate Christ himself, as if he were not our advocate, but on the contrary our judge, before God. Even now, there are still those who claim to be the best Christians and who boast of the holy church while they burn other men at the stake and bathe in innocent blood. These, too, consider the best doctrine to be this, that we attain grace and salvation through our works. The only honor left to Christ is that he has begun the work; but we are the heroes who complete it with merits. For us, Christ must mean his dying at the beginning and also the forgiveness of sins; but we are able to attain salvation with works.

Thus the devil has work to do and attacks Christ in three lines of battle. One will not let him be God, another will not let him be man, and the third will not let him do what he has done. Each of the three wants to reduce Christ to nothing.

(Taken from Luther's Works *vol 34, ed. Lewis W. Spitz, Philadelphia, PA: Muhlenberg Press 1960, pp. 201–10.)*

I.3.9 The Barmen Theological Declaration

This text is an outstanding example of a modern Confession. At the end of May 1934, a synod of German theologians and church leaders met at Barmen to organize the churches' opposition to Hitler. There, this statement was adopted as the confession of what was to be called the Confessing Church. It was produced two weeks earlier, when a triumvirate came together to prepare it, but Karl Barth claims to have written most of the text alone, 'fortified by strong coffee and one or two Brazilian cigars', whilst the other two slept.

In view of the errors of the 'German Christians' and of the present Reich Church Administration, which are ravaging the Church and at the same time also shattering the unity of the German Evangelical Church, we confess the following evangelical truths:

1.'I am the Way and the Truth and the Life; no one comes to the Father except through me.' (Jn. 14:6)

Truly, truly I say to you, he who does not enter the sheepfold through the door but climbs in somewhere else, he is a thief and a robber. I am the Door; if anyone enters through me, he will be saved.' (Jn. 10:1,9)

Jesus Christ, as he is attested to us in Holy Scripture, is the one Word of God which we have to hear, and which we have to trust and obey in life and in death.

We reject the false doctrine that the Church could and should recognise as a source of its proclamation, beyond and besides this one Word of God, yet other events, powers, historic figures and truths as God's revelation

2. 'Jesus Christ has been made wisdom and righteousness and sanctification and redemption for us by God.' (1 Cor. 1:30).

As Jesus Christ is God's comforting pronouncement of the forgiveness of all our sins, so, and with equal seriousness, he is also God's vigorous announcement of his claim upon our whole life. Through him there comes to us joyful liberation from the godless ties of this world for free, grateful service to his creatures.

We reject the false doctrine that there could be areas of our life in which we would belong not to Jesus Christ but to other lords, areas in which we would not need justification and sanctification through him.

3. 'Let us, however, speak the truth in love, and in every respect grow into him who is the head, into Christ, from whom the whole body is joined together.' (Eph. 4:15–16)

The Christian Church is the community of brethren in which, in Word and sacrament, through the Holy Spirit, Jesus Christ acts in the present as Lord. With both its faith and its obedience, with both its message and its

order, it has to testify in the midst of the sinful world, as the Church of pardoned sinners, that it belongs to him alone and lives and may live by his comfort and under his direction alone, in expectation of his appearing.

We reject the false doctrine that the Church could have permission to hand over the form of its message and of its order to whatever it itself might wish or to the vicissitudes of the prevailing ideological and political convictions of the day.

4. 'You know that the rule of the Gentiles exercise authority over them and those in high position lord it over them. So shall it not be among you; but if anyone would have authority among you, let him be your servant.' (Matt. 20:25–26)

The various offices in the Church do not provide a basis for some to exercise authority over others but for the ministry with which the whole community has been entrusted and charged to be carried out.

We reject the false doctrine that, apart from this ministry, the Church could, and could have permission to, give itself or allow itself to be given special leaders (*Fuhrer*) vested with ruling authority.

5. 'Fear God, honour the King!' (I Pet. 2:17)

Scripture tells us that by divine appointment the State, in this still unredeemed world in which also the Church is situated, has the task of maintaining justice and peace, so far as human discernment and human ability make this possible, by means of the threat and use of force. The Church acknowledges with gratitude and reverence toward God the benefit of this, his appointment. It draws attention to God's Kingdom (*Reich*), God's commandment and justice, and with these the responsibility of those who rule and those who are ruled. It trusts and obeys the power of the Word, by which God upholds all things.

We reject the false doctrine that beyond its special commission the State should and could become the sole and total order of human life and so fulfil the vocation of the Church as well.

We reject the false doctrine that beyond its special commission the Church should and could take on the nature, tasks and dignity which belong to the State and thus become itself an organ of the State.

6. 'See, I am with you always, to the end of the age.' (Matt. 28:20)

'God's Word is not fettered.' (II Tim. 2:9)

The Church's commission, which is the foundation of its freedom, consists in this: in Christ's stead, and so in the service of his own Word and work, to deliver to all people, through preaching and sacrament, the message of the free grace of God.

We reject the false doctrine that with human vainglory the Church could place the Word and work of the Lord in the service of self-chosen desires, purposes and plans. The Confessional Synod of the German Evangelical Church declares that it sees in the acknowledgement of these truths and in the rejection of these errors the indispensable theological basis of the German

Evangelical Church as a confederation of Confessional Churches. It calls upon all who can stand in solidarity with its Declaration to be mindful of these theological findings in all their decisions concerning Church and State. It appeals to all concerned to return to unity in faith, hope and love.

Verbum Dei manet in aeternum.

(Taken from Douglas S. Bax, 'The Barmen Theological Declaration: A New Translation,' Journal of Theology for Southern Africa *47, 1984.)*

C. Recent reflection on the authority of creeds and confessions

I.3.10 Karl Barth, from *Credo*

Here Barth discusses the relationship between the practice of theology and the Apostles' Creed.

The Credo is fitted to be the basis of a discussion of the chief problems of Dogmatics not only because it furnishes, as it were, a ground-plan of Dogmatics but above all because the meaning, aim and essence of *Dogmatics* and the meaning, aim and essence of the *Credo*, if they are not identical, yet stand in the closest connection. In this first lecture we attempt to refer from the *conception of Credo*, as it stands at the head of the symbol (at once as beginning and title) to the *conception* in which we are interested, that *of Dogmatics*.

1. Like the corresponding Greek πιστεύω, *Credo* at the head of the symbol means first of all quite simply the act of recognition – in the shape of definite cognitions won from God's revelation – of the reality of God in its bearing upon man. Faith therefore is a decision – the exclusion of unbelief in, the overcoming of opposition to, this reality, the affirmation of its existence and validity. *Man* believes. And therefore: man makes this decision, *credo*. But what gives faith its seriousness and power is not that man makes a decision, nor even the way in which he makes it, his feelings, the movement of his will, the existential emotion generated. On the contrary, faith lives by its *object*. It lives by the call to which it responds. It lives by that, because and in so far as that is the call of *God: credo in unum Deum . . . et in Jesum Christum . . . et in Spiritum sanctum*. The seriousness and the power of faith are the seriousness and power of the *truth*, which is identical with God Himself, and which the believer has heard and received in the form of definite truths, in the form of articles of faith. And even the *disclosure* of this truth is a free gift that positively comes to meet the believing man. It is God's own revelation. In believing, man obeys by his decision the decision of God.

All this holds for Dogmatics also. It, too, is human recognition of the reality of God as it is revealed. It, too, lives by the truth that comes to man – as obedience to a decision of God over which man has no power. It, too, is carried out concretely – in the affirmation of definite truths, and in this process the truth of God becomes concretely man's own. Dogmatics, too, is in its substance an act of faith. But the *special characteristic* of Dogmatics is that it wants to *understand* and *explain* itself. Dogmatics endeavours to take what is first said to it in the revelation of God's reality, and to think it over again in human thoughts and to say it over again in human speech. To that end Dogmatics *unfolds* and *displays* those truths in which the truth of God concretely meets us. It articulates again the articles of faith; it attempts to see them and to make them plain in their interconnection and context; where necessary it inquires after new articles of faith, i.e. articles that have not up to now been known and acknowledged. In all this, it would like to make clear and intelligible the fact that in faith we are concerned with the austere, yet healing sovereignty of the truth and to what extent this is so. Dogmatics is the act of the Credo determined by the scientific method appropriate to it – *credo, ut intelligam.*

2. Credo at the head of the symbol does not signify the act of faith of a well-disposed or gifted or even an especially enlightened individual as such. The act of the Credo is the act of *confession.* But the subject of confession is the *Church* and therefore not the individual as such nor in virtue of any human or even divine mark of individuality, but the individual solely in virtue of his bearing the mark of membership of the Church. When God's reality, as it affects man, is recognised by the Church in the form of definite cognitions won from God's revelation, then there comes into existence in this *eo ipso* public and responsible recognition a confession, a symbol, a dogma, a catechism; then there come into existence articles of faith. When the individual says in the sense of the symbol, *credo,* he does not do that as an individual, but he *confesses,* and that means – he includes himself in the *public* and *responsible* recognition made by the *Church.*

Dogmatics belongs entirely to the same sphere. It is indeed not itself confession; but it is *allied with* it as the action of definite individual members of the confessing Church; it is the elucidation of the current confession and the preparation of a new one. Because the Church must again and again understand its Confession anew and because it is again and again confronted with the necessity of confessing anew, it requires Dogmatics alongside of the Confession. There is no other justification for Dogmatics. An individual can be its subject only as commissioned 'teacher of the Church,' i.e. as teacher *in* the Church *from* the Church *for* the Church, not as savant, but as one who has a vocation to teach. The private character of the professor of Theology, his views and insights as such are matters of no interest. And the same is to be said of his hearers and readers as the future preachers. Lecturing on and study of Dogmatics are a *public* and *responsible* action inasmuch as only the Church – in Dogmatics just in the same way as in the Confession – can seriously speak and seriously hear.

3. The problem of the Credo as the Church Confession arises in the problem of the Church's *proclamation.* The good news of the reality of God as it affects man is entrusted to the Church. That is, entrusted to its *faith.* This, however, means among other things – entrusted to the *work* of its faith which is from the beginning tentative and fallible, entrusted to the human, the all too human, understanding and misunderstanding of the divine judgment, entrusted to the conflict and contradiction of human opinions and convictions. What becomes of the *purity* of that which has been entrusted to the hands of the

pardoned, who always were and will be nothing else than pardoned sinners? The answer can be, and indeed must be: even in impure hands God can and God will keep it pure. But that does not exonerate us from concern for the purity of our hands or from searching after the *true* and *proper* proclamation. From this concern and this searching springs the Church's Confession. Confession is always the result of an effort motivated by this concern and searching, is always an attempt to protect divine truth from human error and to place it on the candlestick. Confession is always concrete, historical decision, a *battle action* of the *Church*, which thinks that it hears, in various convictions and doctrines cropping up within its pale, the voice of unbelief, false belief or superstition, and feels compelled, along with the 'Yes' of faith, to oppose to it the necessary 'No': for the purpose of purifying the human hands in face of the purity of the message entrusted to them in order that its proclamation may be a proper proclamation.

It is in this connection that Dogmatics gets its meaning and its task. It is no idle intellectual game. Nor is it research for research's sake. In explaining the Confession and preparing a new confession it performs that watchman's office that is indispensable for the Church's proclamation. In face of the errors of the time it enters the breach where the old confession is no more regarded or no more understood and a new confession is not yet in existence. Certainly it cannot speak with the authority of the Church's Confession, but instead of that it can, as living science, act with greater mobility and adaptability in relation to the situation of the moment, with greater accuracy and point in the particular investigation. Certainly like the Church's proclamation itself it can deteriorate and run wild. It can very well be that, with regard to the Confession with which it is allied, it strays and leads astray. It can actually be that, instead of calling to order, Dogmatics has to be called to order and corrected by the Church's proclamation that has kept to better ways. Dogmatics is no more able than the Confession to be a mechanically effective safeguard of the good news in the Church. Yet a Church that is conscious of its responsibility towards what has been entrusted to it will always be mindful of these safeguards. What men do in Church can from beginning to end of the line be nothing else than *service*. He who acts in it is the Lord, He Himself and He alone. But just as along the whole line of Church service the function of the Confession is necessary, so also this function is necessary: the scientific examination of the Church's proclamation with regard to its genuineness. The existence of Dogmatics is the Church's admission that in its service it has cause to be humble, circumspect and careful.

6. What has been said would not be complete if finally we did not also remember the *limits* of the Credo and so also of Dogmatics. The life of the Church is not exhausted by its confessing its faith. The Credo as such and Dogmatics as such can by no means guarantee that proper proclamation with which they are connected. They are only a proposal and attempt in that direction. And even proper proclamation, secured not only on the human

side by the Credo and Dogmatics, but really and decisively secured by God's grace, has in the life of the Church three inevitable *frontiers:*

The first is the *Sacrament*, through which the Church is reminded that all its words, even those blessed and authenticated by God's Word and Spirit, can do no more than aim at that event itself, in which God in His reality has to do with man. Just these visible signs of Baptism and Holy Communion have manifestly, in the life of the Church, the important function of making visible the bounds between what can be said, understood and to that extent comprehended of God by man – and the incomprehensibility in which God in Himself and for us really *is* Who He is.

The second frontier of the Credo and Dogmatics is very simply our actual *human life*, in its weakness and strength, in its confusion and clarity, in its sinfulness and hope, that human life of which all the Church's words certainly *do* speak, without as words reaching and touching it, even where God Himself bears His witness to them. Much criticism and depreciation of Dogma and Dogmatics would remain unuttered if it were only clearly understood that human words as such *must* indeed serve the end, but can do no more than *serve* the end that our actual life be placed under God's judgment and grace.

The third frontier is the frontier which separates *eternity* from time, the coming Kingdom of God from the present age, the *eschaton* from the *hic et nunc*. Credo and Dogmatics without doubt stand together under the word of Paul (I Cor. xiii. 8 f.) according to which our gnosis and our prophecy are in like manner in part and will be done away, childish speech that will have to be put away when manhood is reached, a seeing in the dark mirror, not yet a seeing face to face. Meaning, essence and task of the Credo and of Dogmatics are based on conditions which, when God is all in all, will undoubtedly no longer prevail.

The existence of these three frontiers or limits might well be named at the outset *the* chief problem of Dogmatics. In any case we must never for a moment forget them. All that was said at the beginning holds good within these limits. And rightly understood, the very existence of these limits will no doubt give to what has been said a peculiar importance. Where you have limit, there you have also relationship and contact. Credo and Dogmatics stand facing the Sacrament, facing human life, facing the coming age, *distinguished* from them, but *facing* them! Perhaps in the way in which Moses in his death faced the land of Canaan, perhaps as John the Baptist faced Jesus Christ. Could anything more significant be said of them than this, their limitation?

(Taken from Karl Barth, Credo, *trans. J. Strathearn McNab, London: Hodder & Stoughton 1936, pp. 1–10.)*

I.3.11 Karl Rahner, from *Foundations of Christian Faith*

Rahner discusses the importance of, and the possibility for, brief 'creed-like' statements in the modern world.

THE NEED FOR BRIEF CREEDAL STATEMENTS OF CHRISTIAN FAITH

For some years now there has been a discussion in Catholic theology about the need today for brief and new basic creeds in which the Christian profession of faith is expressed in a way which corresponds to our present cultural situation.

Attention has been called to the fact that the Apostles' Creed had this kind of a function, especially as a baptismal profession in adult baptisms, and in fact these very brief formulations of the faith are already found in the New Testament. It has been emphasized that, even presupposing basic and extensive religious instructions, this kind of a creedal statement is necessary today for retaining what has been learned in instructions for catechumens, and also for seeing a clear structure in the 'hierarchy of truths' (*Unitatis redintegratio*, art. 11). Without this kind of a creed the fullness of Christian faith very quickly becomes amorphous, or a believer very easily places too much value in his religious practice on things which are only secondary. It has been said, and rightly so, that a Christian lay person, who does not have to be an expert in theology but does nevertheless have to take responsibility for his faith in his non-Christian milieu, must have at his disposal this kind of a brief formulation of his profession of faith which is orientated towards the essentials of this faith.

This also brings out another aspect of the question: the effective mission of the church in the face of modern disbelief likewise requires a testimony to the Christian message in which this message really becomes intelligible for people today. This too presupposes a separation of what is essential from everything which is of secondary importance. For otherwise a modern 'pagan' cannot distinguish the essence of Christianity from the often not very inviting and even repelling appearance and image of the church which he gets from sermons, religious practices, social relationships, and so on. Then he transfers his partially justified resistance against Christians onto Christianity itself. Hence the Christian message has to exist in such a way that it can offer a clear critique of Christians and of concrete Christianity itself. This message has to be able to express the essentials *briefly* for busy people today, and to express it again and again. This kind of a repetition is not boring if it really focuses on what is decisive and what is essential. A person will not experience this as an 'ideology' which is just imposed on him from without, and which changes nothing about the 'facts' of his life, but rather he will experience it as the reality of his very own life as he has experienced it and as he has suffered it.

In all of these reflections, of course, we are proceeding from the presupposition that however ancient and venerable the Apostles' Creed is, however important is the fact that it is used in all of the Christian churches, and however much it will always be a permanent and binding norm of faith, nevertheless it cannot simply perform the function of a basic summary of the faith today in an adequate way because it does not appeal directly enough to our contemporary intellectual and spiritual situation. This is shown especially by the fact that in it the existence of a God who transcends the world, or at least the meaning of the word 'God,' is presupposed or can be presupposed as something to be taken for granted. This is obviously impossible in an age of anti-metaphysical pragmatism and of worldwide atheism. It is for these reasons that the desire for a new creedal statement or for new creedal statements is being expressed.

THE MULTIPLICITY OF POSSIBLE CREEDAL STATEMENTS

Can we reckon with the possibility that a single basic creed can be formulated at least for the whole of Catholic Christianity, and perhaps even one which would have an official doctrinal character like the Apostles' Creed, and hence could replace this creed in religious practice and in the liturgy? Or is something like this no longer conceivable to begin with? I think that we have to answer this question with the second and negative alternative.

There will no longer be any single and universal basic creed of the Christian faith which will be prescribed as authoritative and binding for the whole church. In this sense the Apostles' Creed will not have any successor and hence it will survive.

In order to show the impossibility of a single, new, basic and universal creedal statement we may perhaps call attention first of all to the fact that attempts to create a common and universally valid world catechism and to introduce it officially have collapsed, and have met with the unambiguous resistance of both preachers and catechists. In view of these attempts it has been pointed out again and again, and rightly so, that because of the very different mentalities of the listeners, the concrete situation in which the faith is preached among individual peoples and in different cultures and social milieus is too heterogeneous to allow the same monotone and uniform catechism to be taught everywhere in these different situations. But the same thing is true then of these basic creedal statements because of their brevity.

In spite of its brevity this kind of basic creed should be as immediately intelligible as possible to the listeners without a great deal of commentary, and should be able to 'reach' them. But given the extremely great differences in people's horizons of understanding, it is quite impossible that a basic creed with the characteristics we have indicated would be the same everywhere in the world. Great differences are already manifest among the basic creedal statements which are found in the New Testament. Just think of the different titles of exaltation in which the reality of Jesus and his salvific significance for us are expressed.

In addition to this thesis that *different* basic creeds are necessary in the church because of the various situations in which the gospel has to be preached, other considerations have to be taken into account today. Our reflections so far would have required that these basic creeds should have been reformulated the moment that Christianity left the homogeneous world of Hellenistic, Roman and western culture. Hence the brief creedal statements of the faith which were appropriate for the western situation should not merely have been 'exported.' The fact that they were can very likely be explained completely only by taking into account the strange feeling of superiority which characterized European colonialism and imperialism. Now the moment that this theological European imperialism no longer possessed its obviousness and its power, and the moment that the once homogeneous West itself disintegrated into a very deep spiritual and cultural pluralism, it became clear first of all that, in spite of one and the same church and one and the same profession of faith in this church, we can no longer count on one and the same homogeneous theology today.

We can say, therefore, that we may try to formulate many of these basic creedal statements of the faith. They can vary not only according to the differences of the nations, of the cultural and historical areas, and of the world religions which co-determine a particular situation. They can also vary according to the social level, the age, and so on, of those to whom the basic creedal statement is directed.

These different basic creeds will vary especially according to what knowledge can be presupposed, and what new and unknown matter they will contain. For the differences in the situations of the listeners to which the various creeds have to be adapted are especially important when it comes to the question of what the listeners in a particular situation take for granted, and hence what can be used as a presupposition and as a point of departure for understanding the *new* matter. If, then, a basic creed appears more or less unintelligible in a milieu other than the one for which it has been formulated, this circumstance does not speak against the creed, but on the contrary it speaks for it.

REQUIREMENTS FOR A BASIC CREEDAL STATEMENT

Among the fundamental questions which have to be asked about basic creedal statements belongs of course the question what really has to be expressed in this kind of a creed and what can be left out. It is perhaps clear that these basic creeds may not be brief summaries of systematic or dogmatic theology. It cannot express at the same time everything which makes up the church's consciousness of the faith. None of the earlier creeds before Trent expressed everything which belongs to Christian faith. The Second Vatican Council's teaching about the 'hierarchy of truths' says that not everything which is true must for this reason be equally significant. A basic creed would only have to contain what is of fundamental importance and what provides a basic starting point for reaching the whole of the faith. If in addition to this we consider that we can legitimately distinguish between an objective hierarchy of truths and an existentiell and situational hierarchy of truths, and that a basic creed which is only intended to be one among many may place the emphasis on expressing an approach to and a point of departure for the whole content of faith which are correct and effective from an existentiell and situational point of view, then it becomes clear that these basic creeds can also vary a great deal in their content. It also becomes clear that this content should consist primarily and especially in what constitutes for the listeners in question an initial and hopefully success-ful point of departure for reaching an understanding of the whole of Christian faith.

A further question would be what the scope of a basic creed should be in a purely quantitative sense. On this point very considerable differences are conceivable, beginning with a basic creed in a few phrases, as in the Apostles' Creed, and extending to a creed which runs for several pages. The three brief creedal statements to be offered in what follows will aim for extreme brevity. But presumably the various possible basic or brief creedal statements of Christian faith do not have to be equal in this respect.

We must mention one further question about these basic creeds in general. For this kind of a creed really to be a Christian profession of faith, it has to give expression to our faith in the historical Jesus as our Lord and as the absolute saviour, and it has to be related to this historical facticity. There is indeed something like an anonymous Christianity in which grace, the forgiveness of sin, justification and salvation take place without the person in question being related explicitly in his objectified consciousness to the historical event of Jesus of Nazareth. Moreover, a great deal can be said about the most central reality of Christian faith without this being seen in an immediate connection with Jesus Christ. This is true especially because not every explicit relationship to the historical Jesus is already a relationship of faith, and hence the specific theological nature of this relationship itself has to be explained. In certain circumstances it can be explained in the light of other fundamental faith statements which in the first instance and *quoad nos* can be made without being explicitly related to Jesus Christ. An example of this would be the first article of the Apostles' Creed. But it is to be taken for granted that even a merely *basic creedal statement* of explicit Christian faith has to express explicitly the relationship of the other elements expressed to

Christ, or the relationship of Jesus to these other elements, and hence it has to have an explicit Christological structure in its profession.

(Taken from Karl Rahner, Foundations of Christian Faith: An Introduction to the Idea of Christianity, *trans. William V. Dych, London: Darton, Longman & Todd 1978, pp. 448–54.)*

I.3.12 Georges Florovsky, from *Bible, Church and Tradition*

Florovsky was an Eastern Orthodox scholar. In this extract he suggests that the best way to communicate the truth of Jesus to people today is to return to the language of the creeds.

What, then, are we going to preach? What would I preach to my contemporaries 'in a time such as this'? There is no room for hesitation: I am going to preach Jesus, and him crucified and risen. I am going to preach and to commend to all whom I may be called to address the message of salvation, as it has been handed down to me by an uninterrupted tradition of the Church Universal. I would not isolate myself in my own age. In other words, I am going to preach the 'doctrines of the creed.'

I am fully aware that creeds are a stumbling block for many in our own generation. 'The creeds are venerable symbols, like the tattered flags upon the walls of national churches; but for the present warfare of the church in Asia, in Africa, in Europe and America the creeds, when they are understood, are about as serviceable as a battle-ax or an arquebus in the hands of a modern soldier.' This was written some years ago by a prominent British scholar who is a devout minister too. Possibly he would not write them today. But there are still many who would wholeheartedly make this vigorous statement their own. Let us remember, however, that the early creeds were deliberately scriptural, and it is precisely their scriptural phraseology that makes them difficult for the modern man.

Thus we face the same problem again: What can we offer instead of Holy Scripture? I would prefer the language of the Tradition, not because of a lazy and credulous 'conservatism' or a blind 'obedience' to some external 'authorities,' but simply because I cannot find any better phraseology. I am prepared to expose myself to the inevitable charge of being 'antiquarian' and 'fundamentalist.' And I would protest that such a charge is gratuitous and wrong. I do keep and hold the 'doctrines of the creed,' conscientiously and wholeheartedly, because I apprehend by faith their perennial adequacy and relevance to all ages and to all situations, including 'a time such as this.' And I believe it is precisely the 'doctrines of the creed' that can enable a desperate generation like ours to regain Christian courage and vision.

The Tradition Lives

'The church is neither a museum of dead deposits nor a society of research.' The deposits are alive – *depositum juvenescens*, to use the phrase of St. Irenaeus. The creed is not a relic of the past, but rather the 'sword of the Spirit.'

What Chalcedon Meant

'And was made man.' What is the ultimate connotation of this creedal state-ment? Or, in other words, *who* was Jesus, the Christ and the Lord? What does it mean, in the language of the Council of Chalcedon, that the same Jesus was 'perfect man' and 'perfect God,' yet a single and unique personal-ity? 'Modern man' is usually very critical of that definition of Chalcedon. It fails to convey any meaning to him. The 'imagery' of the creed is for him nothing more than a piece of poetry, if anything at all. The whole approach, I think, is wrong. The 'definition' of Chalcedon is not a metaphysical state-ment, and was never meant to be treated as such. Nor was the mystery of the Incarnation just a 'metaphysical miracle.' The formula of Chalcedon was a statement of faith, and therefore cannot be understood when taken out of the total experience of the church. In fact, it is an 'existential statement.'

Chalcedon's formula is, as it were, an intellectual contour of the mystery which is apprehended by faith. Our Redeemer is *not* a man, but God *himself*. Here lies the existential emphasis of the statement. Our Redeemer is one who 'came down' and who, by 'being made man,' identified himself with men in the fellowship of a truly human life and nature. Not only the initiative was divine, but the Captain of Salvation was a divine Person. The fullness of the human nature of Christ means simply the adequacy and truth of this redeeming identification. God enters human history and becomes a historical person.

This sounds paradoxical. Indeed there is a mystery: 'And without contro-versy great is the mystery of godliness; God was manifested in the flesh.' But this mystery was a revelation; the true character of God had been disclosed in the Incarnation. God was so much and so intimately concerned with the destiny of man (and precisely with the destiny of every one of 'the little ones') as to intervene *in person* in the chaos and misery of the lost life. The divine providence therefore is not merely an omnipotent ruling of the uni-verse from an august distance by the divine majesty, but a kenosis, a 'self-humiliation' of the God of glory. There is a *personal* relationship between God and man.

Tragedy in a New Light

The whole of the human tragedy appears therefore in a new light. The mystery of the Incarnation was a mystery of the love divine, of the divine identification with lost man. And the climax of Incarnation was the cross. It is the turning point of human destiny. But the awful mystery of the cross is comprehensible only in the wider perspective of an integral Christology; that is, only if we believe that the Crucified was in very truth 'the Son of the living God.' The death of Christ was God's entrance into the misery of human death (again *in person*), a descent into Hades, and this meant the end of death and the inauguration of life everlasting for man.

There is an amazing coherence in the body of the traditional doctrine. But it can be apprehended and understood only in the living context of faith, by which I mean in a personal communion with the personal God. Faith alone makes formulas convincing; faith alone makes formulas live. 'It seems paradoxical, yet it is the experience of all observers of spiritual things: no one profits by the Gospels unless he be first in love with Christ.' For Christ is not a text but a living Person, and he abides in his body, the church.

In the early church the preaching was emphatically theological. It was not a vain speculation. The New Testament itself is a theological book. Neglect of theology in the instruction given to laity in modern times is responsible both for the decay of personal religion and for that sense of frustration which dominates the modern mood. What we need in Christendom 'in a time such as this' is precisely a sound and existential theology. In fact, both clergy and the laity are hungry for theology. And because no theology is usually preached, they adopt some 'strange ideologies' and combine them with the fragments of traditional beliefs. The whole appeal of the 'rival gospels' in our days is that they offer some sort of pseudo theology, a system of pseudo dogmas. They are gladly accepted by those who cannot find any theology in the reduced Christianity of 'modern' style. That existential alternative which many face in our days has been aptly formulated by an English theologian, 'Dogma or ... death.' The age of a-dogmatism and pragmatism has closed. And therefore the ministers of the church have to preach again doctrines and dogmas – the Word of God.

The Modern Crisis

The first task of the contemporary preacher is the 'reconstruction of belief.' It is by no means an intellectual endeavor. Belief is just the map of the true world, and should not be mistaken for reality. Modern man has been too much concerned with his own ideas and convictions, his own attitudes and reactions. The modern crisis precipitated by humanism (an undeniable fact) has been brought about by the rediscovery of the real world, in which we do believe. The rediscovery of the church is the most decisive aspect of this new spiritual realism. Reality is no more screened from us by the wall of our own ideas. It is again accessible. It is again realized that the church is not just a company of believers, but the 'Body of Christ.' This is a rediscovery of a new dimension, a rediscovery of the continuing presence of the divine Redeemer in the midst of his faithful flock. This discovery throws a new flood of light on the misery of our disintegrated existence in a world thoroughly secularized. It is already recognized by many that the true solution of all social problems lies somehow in the reconstruction of the church. 'In a time such as this' one has to preach the 'whole Christ,' Christ and the church – *totus Christus, caput et corpus*, to use the famous phrase of St. Augustine. Possibly this preaching is still unusual, but it seems to be the only way to preach the Word of God efficiently in a period of doom and despair like ours.

The Relevance of the Fathers

I have often a strange feeling. When I read the ancient classics of Christian theology, the fathers of the church, I find them more relevant to the troubles and problems of my own time than the production of modern theologians. The fathers were wrestling with existential problems, with those revelations of the eternal issues which were described and recorded in Holy Scripture. I would risk a suggestion that St. Athanasius and St. Augustine are much more up to date than many of our theological contemporaries. The reason is very simple: they were dealing with things and not with the maps, they were concerned not so much with what man can believe as with what God had done for man. We have, 'in a time such as this,' to enlarge our perspective, to acknowledge the masters of old, and to attempt for our own age an existential synthesis of Christian experience.

(Taken from Georges Florovsky, Bible, Church and Tradition: An Eastern Ortho-dox View, *Belmont, MA: Nordland 1972, chapter 1;* © *The Christian Century Foundation.)*

I.4 The place of reason in theology

Introductory essay

Although it was claimed in the introduction to the previous section that the Christian faith is not a philosophy, there have always been those who have claimed that it is one, and indeed the only true one. The early 'Apologist' for the faith, Justin Martyr, is said to have decided, after trying various philosophical schools, to adopt the Christian faith because after pondering the words of Christ, 'I found this philosophy alone to be safe and profitable. Thus, and for this reason, I am a philosopher.'[1] Justin's legacy to theology is indicated in the passage printed from the work of Clement of Alexandria (I.4.1). Drawing on and treating philosophically the description of Christ as the Logos or Word in John's Gospel, Justin tended to understand it to mean reason or rationality. He thus made links with Greek ideas of Logos as the rational structure of the universe, drawing on both Platonism and Stoicism, while at the same time attacking their inadequacies. He also introduced a principle, now little used, that Plato had stolen many of his best ideas from Moses and the Old Testament.

The development of these ideas in Alexandria, a centre of platonic philosophy, has exercised deep influence on Christian theology and ensured that a high value has been given in parts of the Christian tradition to human rational powers. Clement makes links between Old Testament wisdom and philosophical wisdom, claiming that in certain respects they are essentially the same: 'for philosophy is the study of wisdom, and wisdom is the knowledge of things divine and human . . .'. He generally believes that the Greek philosophers are on the right track so long as they do not deny divine providence, and that provides him with a general criterion of philosophical respectability. On the central question, however, he is rather ambiguous, as we see from the final sentence of our extract, where he speaks of 'the true philosophy, which the initiated possess, having found it, or rather received it . . .'. Is it

---

[1] Justin, *Dialogue with Trypho*, 8.

discovered by us or given to us? Is the gospel a form of wisdom, available to 'initiated' people, and can any aspect of it be discovered by the unaided human mind?

In his famous setting of Jerusalem and Athens in opposition to one another, Tertullian (I.4.2) represents the other side of the debate. For him, unaided philosophical enquiry, indeed, almost any philosophical enquiry, is the source of error and heresy. It is not that Tertullian did not employ reason; indeed, he is a formidable master of argument. It is rather that he understands the Christian faith to be a gift to the simple in heart in no way discoverable because it has to be received from the scriptures of the Old and New Testaments. In this, he puts his finger on one essential characteristic of the Christian faith, that it is freely available to all, whether or not they are clever, cultured and educated. That is not to deny that its truth can be defended by argument or that philosophical concepts can be avoided in theology, but to claim that if its acceptance becomes dependent upon intellectual grasp alone, it is no longer the Christian gospel.

An attempt was made in the Middle Ages to come to an arrangement whereby both sides of the tradition could be held together. Indeed, it has been claimed that the attempt to combine faith and reason is the chief feature of the medieval theological enterprise. This is often described as the 'medieval synthesis' because it sought to bring together the philosophical traditions of Greece and Rome and the biblical inheritance of the church. In so doing, it developed a conception of reason as essentially religious, in that it was at one with faith in being a distinct but parallel source for knowledge of the one truth, which was divine truth. This is often described as the 'two source' theory of knowledge. It is like later conceptions of reason in that it is relatively optimistic about human capacity to discover divine truth for itself, albeit to a limited degree. Aquinas (I.4.3) famously taught that by reason we can know that God exists and is one; faith is necessary for such truths as the Trinity and the incarnation of Christ. Unlike some modern conceptions of reason, this is a capacity which operates on the basis of belief in God. Aquinas also believed that reason operates in the service of faith in addition to providing a philosophical foundation for theology. Its function is to penetrate into the meaning of the articles of faith taught by the church in order to show how they should be understood.

There were radical criticisms of this view by later medieval philosophers – especially William of Ockham and his successors – and by the Reformers, Luther and Calvin. Luther believed that over-dependence on Aristotle's philosophy was one of the roots of the corruption he claimed to discern in the Roman Catholic Church, while Calvin, rather like Tertullian though in more moderate form, saw unaided reason as a factory of idolatry. Yet something like the traditional view continued to operate in some theological circles. Joseph Butler (I.4.4) represents a moderate Anglican view of the matter. He is aware of the challenge presented by mechanistic science, yet refuses to accept its denial that divine purpose operates in the world. Science presupposes that there is purpose in nature and therefore has much in common with theology, which, therefore can draw parallels between natural laws and God's religious purposes. Despite its distinctive form, this also harks back to the Alexandrian view that philosophical learning at its best offers a world parallel with that of the gospel, a world which can be explored in defence of the Christian dispensation.

The so-called Protestant Scholasticism, represented here by Turretin (I.4.5), is sometimes charged with a merely backwards move to a medieval Aristotelianism which had been rejected by the Reformers themselves. It seems unlikely however, that any school of theology could exist for long without thinking through the method of reason it deploys, and there are in any case considerable differences between the Protestants and their medieval predecessors. In the first place, they tended to operate with a more radical doctrine of the human fall. Many medievals taught that while the human will was indeed fallen, the intellect remained relatively undamaged, and they therefore held to a relatively optimistic view of human rational possibilities. That derived from the Greek side of their twofold inheritance. Thinkers in the Reformed tradition, especially as they distinguished themselves from their rationalist opponents like Socinus, stressed with Calvin and Luther the fallenness of the whole human being, and the necessity of revelation for both redemption and the knowledge of God which flowed from it. This meant that they were more sceptical about allowing reason any even relatively independent role.

Turretin seeks a middle way between an excessive confidence in reason and a denial of its uses, which he sees to be manifold. He objects to treating reason as 'a principle and rule in whose scale the greatest mysteries of religion should be weighed'. Turretin does not wish to treat reason merely as an instrument in the obtaining of faith – that would make him too like Tertullian – but is willing also to see it as the 'medium through which we are drawn to faith'. What he resists is the treatment of reason as a principle or foundation, the latter term being one which has caused much debate in recent theology. 'Foundationalism' is the doctrine which holds that faith must be founded in some rational principle or demonstration that is prior to it. In the modern world, this tends to involve the defence of faith in terms of considerations drawn from outside the sphere of faith, and it is this which has recently come to be held in suspicion.

Foundationalism has had a long and influential career, and in Britain its founding father is John Locke (I.4.6). Turretin, a slightly older contemporary, saw the way that the wind was blowing when he denied a view of reason according to which 'nothing can be held which is not agreeable to it'. In so doing he was already attacking the view that Locke was later to adopt. This English philosopher's view of the relation between reason and faith is parallel to that of Aquinas, but the similarities are superficial. For him reason does demonstrate the existence and unity of God, and it is followed by those things which belong to the realm of faith, but there are three main differences from Aquinas' view. First, the God demonstrated by Locke is the rationalist God of deism, who was to dominate the stage later as the clockmaker deity, one who created the world but thereafter left it to its own devices. Correspondingly, second, the content of what is believed by faith is remarkably thin, being mainly that which can be demonstrated by the fulfilment of prophecy and the miracles of Jesus. Third, reason comes fully into its own as a principle that has the last word.

A little more than a century later the rationalism espoused by Locke became, at least in the eyes of Kierkegaard (I.4.7), the enterprise wherein his opponent Hegel reduced the historic Christian faith to a rational system. In order to resist this, Kierkegaard returns to what is essentially the approach of Tertullian, some of whose famous sayings he draws upon. He attacks the platonic view that knowledge is recollection; that is, the theory that by virtue of our reason we already know what is our relation to the eternal world, so that to be taught the truth of our life and destiny we have but to be reminded of something which, though buried deep within us, is there all the time. For Kierkegaard, this is to abolish Christianity, which involves a *movement* to faith not only from ignorance but from sin, and this can be achieved only by Christ, who is both teacher and redeemer. That movement involves crossing a barrier which is absolute, and therefore beyond the capacity of the rational human being. It is not that Christian truth is irrational, but that it is beyond human rational capacity because it is a truth involving a relation to eternity, a realm entirely different from that of finitude and time. Any theology which is authentically Christian will never, therefore, be able successfully to think together eternity and time, but must rather accept the logic of the matter, which is that Christian truth will always be paradoxical in form. This does not mean that it will be contradictory, but that it will always transcend the human capacity to understand and express it satisfactorily.

The nineteenth-century Roman Catholic Church faced the challenge of modern rationalism in a different way, by seeking to return to an essentially medieval concept of reason. Appealing to the thought of Thomas Aquinas (I.4.8), it drew a distinction, which has been developed in the writings of Pope John Paul II, between proper and improper uses of reason. The first is in the interest of a holistic religious vision of things; the second, a view of reason which denies or misuses its capacity either to deny the existence of God or to develop a view of things in contradiction to the Christian one. A modern Lutheran approach to the use of reason is that of the American theologian, Robert Jenson (I.4.9), who goes some way to meet the Catholic position. His approach also reveals the influence of Karl Barth's essentially anti-foundationalist view of the theological task. Reviewing the tradition, and especially modern rationalism's corruption of the theological tradition, he seeks to return to what he sees to be the view of the Church Fathers, that, although there can be no foundation for theology that is not theological, that does not involve a refusal to learn from other traditions of thought than the Christian.

CEG

A. Faith and philosophy

I.4.1 Clement of Alexandria, from *The Stromata*

In this extract Clement offers an allegorical reading of the story of Abraham, Sarah and Hagar to describe philosophy as the 'handmaid' to theology. Philosophy, or rational thought, he suggests, was given by God to the Greeks to prepare them for the coming of Christ, just as the Law was given to the Jews. The readings might appear rather fanciful today, but the position espoused is interesting.

I:V Philosophy the Handmaid of Theology

Accordingly, before the advent of the Lord, philosophy was necessary to the Greeks for righteousness. And now it becomes conducive to piety; being a kind of preparatory training to those who attain to faith through demonstration. 'For thy foot,' it is said, 'will not stumble,' if thou refer what is good, whether belonging to the Greeks or to us, to Providence. For God is the cause of all good things; but of some primarily, as of the Old and the New Testament; and of others by consequence, as philosophy. Perchance, too, philosophy was given to the Greeks directly and primarily, till the Lord should call the Greeks. For this was a schoolmaster to bring 'the Hellenic mind,' as the law [was for] the Hebrews, 'to Christ.' Philosophy, therefore, was a preparation, paving the way for him who is perfected in Christ.

'Now,' says Solomon, 'defend wisdom, and it will exalt thee, and it will shield thee with a crown of pleasure.' For when thou hast strengthened wisdom with a cope by philosophy, and with right expenditure, thou wilt preserve it unassailable by sophists. The way of truth is therefore one. But into it, as into a perennial river, streams flow from all sides. It has been therefore said by inspiration: 'Hear, my son, and receive my words; that thine may be the many ways of life. For I teach thee the ways of wisdom; that the fountains fail thee not,' which gush forth from the earth itself. Not only did he enumerate several ways of salvation for any one righteous man, but he added many other ways of many righteous, speaking thus: 'The paths of the righteous shine like the light.' The commandments and the modes of preparatory training are to be regarded as the ways and appliances of life.

'Jerusalem, Jerusalem, how often would I have gathered thy children, as a hen her chickens!' And Jerusalem is, when interpreted, 'a vision of peace.' He therefore shows prophetically, that those who peacefully contemplate sacred things are in manifold ways trained to their calling. What then? He 'would,' and could not. How often, and where? Twice; by the prophets, and by the advent. The expression, then, 'How often,' shows wisdom to be manifold; and every mode of quantity and quality, it by all means saves some, both in time and in eternity. 'For the Spirit of the Lord fills the earth.' And if any should violently say that the reference is to the Hellenic culture, when it is said, 'Give not heed to an evil woman; for honey drops from the lips of a harlot,' let him hear what follows: 'who lubricates thy throat for the time.' But philosophy does not flatter. Who, then, does he allude to as having committed fornication? He adds expressly, 'For the feet of folly lead those who use her, after death, to Hades. But her steps are not supported.' Therefore remove thy way far from silly pleasure. 'Stand not at the doors of her house, that thou yield not thy life to others.' And he testifies, 'Then shalt thou repent in old age, when the flesh of thy body is consumed.' For this is the end of foolish pleasure. Such, indeed, is the case. And when he says, 'Be not much with a strange woman,' he admonishes us to use indeed, but not to linger and spend time with, secular culture. For what was bestowed on each generation advantageously, and at seasonable times, is a preliminary training for the word of the Lord. 'For already some men, ensnared by the charms of hand-maidens, have despised their consort philosophy, and have grown old, some of them in music, some in geometry, others in grammar, the most in rhetoric.' 'But as the encyclical branches of study contribute to philosophy, which is their mistress; so also philosophy itself co-operates for the acquisition of wisdom. For philosophy is the study of wisdom, and wisdom is the know-ledge of things divine and human; and their causes.' Wisdom is therefore queen of philosophy, as philosophy is of preparatory culture. For if philos-ophy 'professes control of the tongue, and the belly, and the parts below the belly, it is to be chosen on its own account. But it appears more worthy of respect and pre-eminence, if cultivated for the honour and knowledge of God.' And Scripture will afford a testimony to what has been said in what follows. Sarah was at one time barren, being Abraham's wife. Sarah having no child, assigned her maid, by name Hagar, the Egyptian, to Abraham, in order to get children. Wisdom, therefore, who dwells with the man of faith (and Abraham was reckoned faithful and righteous), was still barren and without child in that generation, not having brought forth to Abraham aught allied to virtue. And she, as was proper, thought that he, being now in the time of progress, should have intercourse with secular culture first (by Egyp-tian the world is designated figuratively); and afterwards should approach to her according to divine providence, and beget Isaac.

And Philo interprets Hagar to mean 'sojourning.' For it is said in connection with this, 'Be not much with a strange woman.' Sarah he interprets to mean 'my princedom.' He, then, who has received previous training is at liberty to approach to wisdom, which is supreme, from which grows up the race of Israel. These things show that that wisdom can be acquired through instruction, to which Abraham attained, passing from the contemplation of heavenly things to the faith and righteousness which are according to God. And Isaac is shown to mean 'self-taught;' wherefore also he is discovered to be a type of Christ. He was the husband of one wife Rebecca, which they translate 'Patience.' And Jacob is said to have consorted with several, his name being interpreted 'Exerciser.' And exercises are engaged in by means of many and various dogmas. Whence, also, he who is really 'endowed with the power of seeing' is called Israel, having much experience, and being fit for exercise.

Something else may also have been shown by the three patriarchs, namely, that the sure seal of knowledge is composed of nature, of education, and exercise.

You may have also another image of what has been said, in Tamar sitting by the way, and presenting the appearance of a harlot, on whom the studious Judas (whose name is interpreted 'powerful'), who left nothing unexamined and uninvestigated, looked; and turned aside to her, preserving his profession towards God. Wherefore also, when Sarah was jealous at Hagar being preferred to her, Abraham, as choosing only what was profitable in secular philosophy, said, 'Behold, thy maid is in thine hands: deal with her as it pleases thee;' manifestly meaning, 'I embrace secular culture as youthful, and a handmaid; but thy knowledge I honour and reverence as true wife.' And Sarah afflicted her; which is equivalent to corrected and admonished her. It has therefore been well said, 'My son, despise not thou the correction of God; nor faint when thou art rebuked of him. For whom the Lord loveth He chasteneth, and scourgeth every son whom He receiveth.' And the foresaid Scriptures, when examined in other places, will be seen to exhibit other mysteries. We merely therefore assert here, that philosophy is characterized by investigation into truth and the nature of things (this is the truth of which the Lord himself said, 'I am the truth', and that, again, the preparatory training for rest in Christ exercises the mind, rouses the intelligence, and begets an inquiring shrewdness, by means of the true philosophy, which the initiated possess, having found it, or rather received it, from the truth itself.

(Taken from the Ante-Nicene Fathers, vol. II, trans. A. Cleveland Coxe.)

I.4.2 Tertullian, from *The Prescription against Heretics*

Tertullian's estimate of Greek philosophy is rather less positive than Clement's. He regards it all as the teachings of demons, designed to confuse and to conceal the truth and believes that all heresies are results of accommodations to philosophy.

VII. These are 'the doctrines' of men and 'of demons' produced for itching ears of the spirit of this world's wisdom: this the Lord called 'foolishness,' and 'chose the foolish things of the world' to confound even philosophy itself. For (philosophy) it is which is the material of the world's wisdom, the rash interpreter of the nature and the dispensation of God. Indeed heresies are themselves instigated by philosophy. From this source came the Aeons, and I know not what infinite forms, and the trinity of man in the system of Valentinus, who was of Plato's school. From the same source came Marcion's better god, with all his tranquillity; he came of the Stoics. Then, again, the opinion that the soul dies is held by the Epicureans; while the denial of the restoration of the body is taken from the aggregate school of all the philosophers; also, when matter is made equal to God, then you have the teaching of Zeno; and when any doctrine is alleged touching a god of fire, then Heraclitus comes in. The same subject-matter is discussed over and over again by the heretics and the philosophers; the same arguments are involved. Whence comes evil? Why is it permitted? What is the origin of man? and in what way does he come? Besides the question which Valentinus has very lately proposed – Whence comes God? Which he settles with the answer: From *enthymesis* and *ectroma*. Unhappy Aristotle! who invented for these men dialectics, the art of building up and pulling down; an art so evasive in its propositions, so far-fetched in its conjectures, so harsh, in its arguments, so productive of contentions – embarrassing even to itself, retracting everything, and really treating of nothing! Whence spring those 'fables and endless genealogies,' and 'unprofitable questions,' and 'words which spread like a cancer?' From all these, when the apostle would restrain us, he expressly names philosophy as that which he would have us be on our guard against. Writing to the Colossians, he says, 'See that no one beguile you through philosophy and vain deceit, after the tradition of men, and contrary to the wisdom of the Holy Ghost.' He had been at Athens, and had in his interviews (with its philosophers) become acquainted with that human wisdom which pretends to know the truth, whilst it only corrupts it, and is itself divided into its own manifold heresies, by the variety of its mutually repugnant sects. What indeed has Athens to do with Jerusalem? What concord is there between the Academy and the Church? what between heretics and Christians? Our instruction comes from 'the porch of Solomon,' who had himself taught that 'the Lord should be sought in simplicity of heart.' Away with all attempts to produce a mottled Christianity of Stoic, Platonic, and dialectic composition! We want no curious disputation after possessing Christ Jesus, no inquisition after enjoying the gospel! With our faith, we desire no further belief. For this is our palmary faith, that there is nothing which we ought to believe besides.

(Taken from the Ante-Nicene Fathers vol. III, ed. A. Roberts and J. Donaldson, trans. Peter Holmes.)

B. Reason in the service of faith

I.4.3 St Thomas Aquinas, from the *Summa contra Gentiles*

Aquinas argues for a continuity between faith and reason, asserting that there is no opposition between them. However, there are some truths only available to faith, as they are simply above reason.

CHAPTER IV

THAT THE TRUTH ABOUT DIVINE THINGS WHICH IS ATTAINABLE BY REASON IS FITTINGLY PROPOSED TO MAN AS AN OBJECT OF BELIEF

While then the truth of the intelligible things of God is twofold, one to which the inquiry of reason can attain, the other which surpasses the whole range of human reason, both are fittingly proposed by God to man as an object of belief. We must first show this with regard to that truth which is attainable by the inquiry of reason, lest it appears to some, that since it can be attained by reason, it was useless to make it an object of faith by supernatural inspiration. Now three disadvantages would result if this truth were left solely to the inquiry of reason. One is that few men would have knowledge of God: because very many are hindered from gathering the fruit of diligent inquiry, which is the discovery of truth, for three reasons. Some indeed on account of an indisposition of temperament, by reason of which many are naturally indisposed to knowledge: so that no efforts of theirs would enable them to reach to the attainment of the highest degree of human knowledge, which consists in knowing God. Some are hindered by the needs of household affairs. For there must needs be among men some that devote themselves to the conduct of temporal affairs, who would be unable to devote so much time to the leisure of contemplative research as to reach the summit of human inquiry, namely the knowledge of God. And some are hindered by laziness. For in order to acquire the knowledge of God in those things which reason is able to investigate, it is necessary to have a previous knowledge of many things: since almost the entire consideration of philosophy is directed to the knowledge of God: for which reason metaphysics, which is about divine things, is the last of the parts of philosophy to be studied. Wherefore it is not possible to arrive at the inquiry about the aforesaid truth except after a most laborious study: and few are willing to take upon themselves this labour for the love of a knowledge, the natural desire for which has nevertheless been instilled into the mind of man by God.

The second disadvantage is that those who would arrive at the discovery of the aforesaid truth would scarcely succeed in doing so after a long time. First, because this truth is so profound, that it is only after long practice that the human intellect is enabled to grasp it by means of reason. Secondly, because many things are required beforehand, as stated above. Thirdly, because at the time of youth, the mind, when tossed about by the various movements of the passions, is not fit for the knowledge of so sublime a truth, whereas *calm gives prudence and knowledge,* as stated in 7 *Phys.* Hence mankind would remain in the deepest darkness of ignorance, if the path of reason were the only available way to the knowledge of God: because the knowledge of God which especially makes men perfect and good, would be acquired only by the few, and by these only after a long time.

The third disadvantage is that much falsehood is mingled with the investigations of human reason, on account of the weakness of our intellect in forming its judgments, and by reason of the admixture of phantasms. Consequently many would remain in doubt about those things even which are most truly demonstrated, through ignoring the force of the demonstration: especially when they perceive that different things are taught by the various men who are called wise. Moreover among the many demonstrated truths, there is sometimes a mixture of falsehood that is not demonstrated, but assumed for some probable or sophistical reason which at times is mistaken for a demonstration. Therefore it was necessary that definite certainty and pure truth about divine things should be offered to man by the way of faith.

Accordingly the divine clemency has made this salutary commandment, that even some things which reason is able to investigate must be held by faith: so that all may share in the knowledge of God easily, and without doubt or error.

Hence it is written (Eph. iv. 17, 18): That *henceforward you walk not as also the Gentiles walk in the vanity of their mind, having their understanding darkened:* and (Isa. liv. 13): *All thy children shall be taught of the Lord.*

CHAPTER VI

THAT IT IS NOT A MARK OF LEVITY TO ASSENT TO THE THINGS THAT ARE OF FAITH, ALTHOUGH THEY ARE ABOVE REASON

Now those who believe this truth, of *which reason affords a proof,* believe not lightly, as though *following foolish fables* (2 Pet. i. 16). For divine Wisdom Himself, Who knows all things most fully, deigned to reveal to man *the secrets of God's wisdom:* and by suitable arguments proves His presence, and the truth of His doctrine and inspiration, by performing works surpassing the capability of the whole of nature, namely, the wondrous healing of the sick, the raising of the dead to life, a marvellous control over the heavenly bodies, and what excites yet more wonder, the inspiration of human minds, so that unlettered and simple persons are filled with the Holy Ghost, and in one instant are endowed with the most sublime wisdom and eloquence. And after considering these arguments, convinced by the strength of the proof, and not by the force of arms, nor by the promise of delights, but – and this is the greatest marvel of all – amidst the tyranny of persecutions, a countless crowd of not only simple but also of the wisest men, embraced the Christian faith, which inculcates things surpassing all human understanding, curbs the pleasures of the flesh, and teaches contempt of all worldly things. That the minds of mortal beings should assent to such things, is both the greatest of miracles, and the evident work of divine inspiration, seeing that they despise visible things and desire only those that are invisible. And that this happened not suddenly nor by chance, but by the disposition of God, is shown by the fact that God foretold that He would do so by the manifold oracles of the prophets, whose books we hold in veneration as bearing witness to our faith. This particular kind of proof is alluded to in the words of Heb. ii. 3, 4: *Which,* namely the salvation of mankind, *having begun to be declared by the Lord, was confirmed with us by them that heard Him, God also bearing witness by signs and wonders, and divers . . . distributions of the Holy Ghost.*

Now such a wondrous conversion of the world to the Christian faith is a most indubitable proof that such signs did take place, so that there is no need to repeat them, seeing that there is evidence of them in their result. For it would be the most wondrous sign of all if without any wondrous signs the world were persuaded by simple and lowly men to believe things so arduous, to accomplish things so difficult, and to hope for things so sublime. Although God ceases not even in our time to work miracles through His saints in confirmation of the faith.

CHAPTER VII

THAT THE TRUTH OF REASON IS NOT IN OPPOSITION TO THE TRUTH OF THE CHRISTIAN FAITH

Now though the aforesaid truth of the Christian faith surpasses the ability of human reason, nevertheless those things which are naturally instilled in human reason cannot be opposed to this truth. For it is clear that those things which are implanted in reason by nature, are most true, so much so that it is impossible to think them to be false. Nor is it lawful to deem false that which is held by faith, since it is so evidently confirmed by God. Seeing then that the false alone is opposed to the true, as evidently appears if we examine their definitions, it is impossible for the aforesaid truth of faith to be contrary to those principles which reason knows naturally.

Again. The same thing which the disciple's mind receives from its teacher is contained in the knowledge of the teacher, unless he teach insincerely, which it were wicked to say of God. Now the knowledge of naturally known principles is instilled into us by God, since God Himself is the author of our nature. Therefore the divine Wisdom also contains these principles. Consequently whatever is contrary to these principles, is contrary to the divine Wisdom; wherefore it cannot be from God. Therefore those things which are received by faith from divine revelation cannot be contrary to our natural knowledge.

Moreover. Our intellect is stayed by contrary arguments, so that it cannot advance to the knowledge of truth. Wherefore if conflicting knowledges were instilled into us by God, our intellect would thereby be hindered from knowing the truth. And this cannot be ascribed to God.

Furthermore. Things that are natural are unchangeable so long as nature remains. Now contrary opinions cannot be together in the same subject. Therefore God does not instil into man any opinion or belief contrary to natural knowledge.

Hence the Apostle says (Rom. x. 8): *The word is nigh thee even in thy heart and in thy mouth. This is the word of faith which we preach.* Yet because it surpasses reason some look upon it as though it were contrary thereto; which is impossible.

This is confirmed also by the authority of Augustine who says (*Gen. ad lit.* ii): *That which truth shall make known can nowise be in opposition to the holy books whether of the Old or of the New Testament.*

From this we may evidently conclude that whatever arguments are alleged against the teachings of faith, they do not rightly proceed from the first self-evident principles instilled by nature. Wherefore they lack the force of demonstration, and are either probable or sophistical arguments, and consequently it is possible to solve them.

(Taken from the Fathers of the English Dominican Province translation, London: Burns, Oates & Washbourne 1924, Book I:iv–vii.)

I.4.4 Joseph Butler, from *The Analogy of Religion*

Butler here sketches the argument of his book, which suggests that Christian religion accords well enough with the observed course of nature as to offer probable, if not certain, evidence for the truth of that religious scheme.

PROBABLE evidence is essentially distinguished from demonstrative by this, that it admits of degrees; and of all variety of them, from the highest moral certainty to the very lowest presumption. We cannot indeed say a thing is probably true upon one very slight presumption for it; because, as there may be probabilities on both sides of a question, there may be some against it: and though there be not, yet a slight presumption does not beget that degree of conviction, which is implied in saying a thing is probably true. But that the slightest possible presumption is of the nature of a probability appears from hence, that such low presumption, often repeated, will amount even to moral certainty. Thus a man's having observed the ebb and flow of the tide to-day, affords some sort of presumption, though the lowest imaginable, that it may happen again to-morrow: but the observation of this event for so many days, and months, and ages together, as it has been observed by mankind, gives us a full assurance that it will.
. . .

Probable evidence, in its very nature, affords but an imperfect kind of information; and is to be considered as relative only to beings of limited capacities. For nothing which is the possible object of knowledge, whether past, present, or future, can be probable to an infinite Intelligence; since it cannot but be discerned absolutely as it is in itself, certainly true, or certainly false. But to *us*, probability is the very guide of life.
. . .

The analogy here proposed to be considered is of a pretty large extent, and consists of several parts, in some, more, in others, less, exact. In some few instances perhaps it may amount to a real practical proof; in others not so. Yet in these it is a confirmation of what is proved other ways. It will undeniably show, what too many want to have shown them, that the system of Religion, both natural and revealed, considered only as a system, and prior to the proof of it, is not a subject of ridicule, unless that of Nature be so too. And it will afford an answer to almost all objections against the system both of natural and revealed Religion; though not perhaps an answer in so great a degree, yet in a very considerable degree an answer to the objections against the evidence of it: for objections against a proof, and objections against what is said to be proved, the reader will observe are different things.

Now the Divine government of the world, implied in the notion of religion in general and of Christianity, contains in it; that mankind is appointed to live in a future state; that there every one shall be rewarded or punished; rewarded or punished respectively for all that behaviour here, which we comprehend under the words, virtuous or vicious, morally good or evil: that our present life is a probation, a state of trial, and of discipline, for that future one; notwithstanding the objections, which men may fancy they have, from notions of necessity, against there being any such moral plan as this at all, and whatever objections may appear to lie against the wisdom and goodness of it, as it stands so imperfectly made known to us at present: that this world being in a state of apostasy and wickedness, and consequently of ruin, and the sense both of their condition and duty being greatly corrupted amongst men, this gave occasion for an additional dispensation of providence; of the utmost importance, proved by miracles; but containing in it many things appearing to us strange, and not to have been expected, a dispensation of providence, which is a scheme or system of things; carried on by mediation of a Divine person, the Messiah, in order to the recovery of the world; yet not revealed to all men, nor proved with the strongest possible evidence of all those to whom it is revealed; but only to such a part of mankind, and with such particular evidence as the wisdom of God thought fit. The design then of the following treatise will be to show, that the several parts principally objected against in this moral and Christian dispensation, including its scheme, its publication, and the proof which God has afforded us of its truth; that the particular parts principally objected against in this whole dispensation, are analogous to what is experienced in the constitution and course of Nature, or Providence; that the chief objections themselves which are alleged against the former, are no other than what may be alleged with like justness against the latter, where they are found in fact to be inconclusive; and that this argument from analogy is in general unanswerable, and undoubtedly of weight on the side of religion, notwithstanding the objections which may seem to lie against it, and the real ground which there may be for difference of opinion, as to the particular degree of weight which is to be laid upon it. This is the general account of what may be looked for in the following Treatise. And I shall begin it with that which is the foundation of all our hopes and of all our fears; all our hopes and fears, which are of any consideration; I mean in a future life.

(Taken from the 'Introduction' to Joseph Butler, The Analogy of Religion to the Constitution and Course of Nature: also Fifteen Sermons *(with a life of the author, etc. by Joseph Angus), London: Religious Tract Society, n.d.)*

I.4.5 Francis Turretin, from *The Institutes of Elenctic Theology*

Turretin seeks to find a middle way in the controversies of the centuries following the Reformation, both denying that reason is the sole judge of matters of faith, and at the same time insisting that it has a role.

EIGHTH QUESTION
Is human reason the principle and rule by which the doctrines of the Christian religion and theology (which are the objects of faith) ought to be measured? We deny against the Socinians.

II. In this controversy, there is an error on both extremes. They err in excess who attribute to reason in matters of faith more than its due (as the Socinians). They err in defect who underrate it (as the Anabaptists, Lutherans and papists). Here we dispute against the first; afterwards we will engage the others.

III. The question is not whether reason has any use in theology. For we confess that its use is manifold both for illustration; for comparison; for inference; and for argumentation. But the question is simply whether it bears the relation of a principle and rule in whose scale the greatest mysteries of religion should be weighed, so that nothing should be held which is not agreeable to it, which is not founded upon and cannot be elicited from reason. This we deny against the Socinians who, the more easily to reject the mysteries of the Trinity, incarnation and the satisfaction of Chirst, contend that reason is the rule of religion of things to be believed, and that those things are not to be believed which seem to the mind to be impossible ... Rather the question is whether it is the first principle from which the doctrines of faith are proved; or the foundation upon which they are built, so that we must hold to be false in things of faith what the natural light or human reason cannot comprehend. This we deny.

V. The reasons are: (1) The reason of an unregenerate man is blinded with respect to the law (Eph. 4:17, 18; Rom. 1:27, 28; 8:7). With respect to the gospel, it is evidently blind and mere darkness (Eph. 5:8; 1 Cor. 2:14). Therefore, it must be taken captive that it may be subjected to faith, not exalted that it may rule it (2 Cor. 10:3–5). (2) The mysteries of faith are beyond the sphere of reason to which the unregenerate man cannot rise; and, as the senses do not attempt to judge of those things which are out of their sphere, so neither does reason in those things which are above it and supernatural. (3) Faith is not referred ultimately to reason, so that I ought to believe because I so understand and comprehend; but to the word because God so speaks in the Scriptures. (4) The Holy Spirit directs us to the word alone (Dt. 4:1; Is. 8:20; Jn. 5:39; 2 Tim. 3:15, 16; 2 Pet. 1:19). (5) If reason is the principle of faith, then first it would follow that all religion is natural and demonstrable by natural reason and natural light. Thus nature and grace, natural and super-natural revelation would be confounded. Second, it would follow that reason is nowhere to be made captive and to be denied, against the express passages of Scripture; and that those possessed of a more ready mind and a more cultivated genius can better perceive and judge the mysteries of faith against universal experience (1 Cor. 1:19, 20; Mt. 11:25). (6) Reason cannot be the rule of religion; neither as corrupted because it is not only below faith, but also opposed to it (Rom. 8:7; 1 Cor. 2:14; Mt. 16:17); nor as sound because this is not found in corrupt man, nor in an uncontaminated man could it be the rule of supernatural mysteries. Nor now when it is corrected by the Spirit must it be judged according to itself, but according to the first principle which illuminated reason now admits (viz., the Scriptures).

VI. A ministerial and organic relation is quite different from a principal and despotic. Reason holds the former relation to theology, not the latter. It is the Hagar (the bondmaid which should be in subjection to Scripture); not the Sarah (the mistress which presides over Scripture). It ought to compare the things proposed to be believed with the sacred Scriptures, the inflexible rule of truth. As when we refer the things we wish to measure to the public standard with the hand and eye. But reason itself neither can nor ought to be constituted the rule of belief.

X. There is a difference between deriving a doctrine from nature, and illustrating in a certain manner a doctrine already known; or to seize from nature the opportunity of teaching. The latter we recognize in the parables of our Lord, but not the former. For he did not expressly prove his mysteries by parables, but only illustrated them that under these representations they might be more easily understood.

XIII. In matters of faith reason stands not only in the relation of an instrument by which, but also sometimes from a means and argument from which the theologian argues (viz., when from his own treasury he draws arguments for the faith; or contends for principles by showing their credibility to those who do not acknowledge it; or treats from principles by drawing arguments from nature either to prove or confirm theological conclusion). Hence the same conclusion may be of faith (inasmuch as it is proved from Scripture) and of knowledge (inasmuch as it is demonstrated by reason). Yet we must not from this infer that reason is the principle and rule by which doctrines of faith should be measured.

XVII. Reason is taken either materially for the kind of doctrine derived from the light of reason, or formally for the manner of delivering it which is commonly called the mode of instruction. But in neither sense can it be called the principle of theology; not in the former sense because theology is neither built upon reason nor resolvable into it; not in the latter sense because although it is in this sense an instrument (as has been said), yet it cannot be considered as the principle.

XVIII. For a thing to be contrary to reason is different from its being above and beyond it; to be overthrown by reason and to be unknown to it. The mysteries of faith are indeed contrary to corrupt reason and are assailed by it, but they are only above and beyond right reason and are not taught by it. So in neither of these senses can it be called their principle.

XX. The proper rule of things to be believed and disbelieved is not the apprehension of their possibility or impossibility, but the word of God. Nor are those things only possible to God which seem so to men, for he can do above all that we can think (Eph. 3:20; Mt. 19:26), and it would be impious for a finite mind to circumscribe within narrow limits the infinite power of God.

XXI. Although light is not contrary to light, and natural and revealed truths are not at variance with each other, yet natural truth itself is often not what human reason dictates, which is often mistaken by an abuse of natural and revealed light. Therefore revealed truth can be opposed to ratiocination and human conceptions, although it may agree with natural truth which reason often does not see or apprehend. Thus here the first principles of nature (known of themselves) must be distinguished from the conclusions and conceptions of reason which are deduced from those principles. The former are true and sure; the latter obscure, often erroneous and fallible.

XXII. A small and a great light may differ in degree and species: in degree, as to a natural object; in species, as to a supernatural. Reason may be a small light; but in things civil and natural, not in things supernatural.

XXIII. Although reason is not the principle of faith, it does not follow that atheists cannot be converted. The manner of dealing with them can be either theological (by arguments founded on Scripture) or philosophical, so that by the principles of reason the prejudices against the Christian religion drawn from corrupt reason may be removed.

NINTH QUESTION

Does any judgment belong to reason in matters of faith? Or is there no use at all for it?

I. We must avoid two extremes here: the one of those who sin in excess attributing too much to reason, and regarding it as the rule of religion and faith (which the Socinians do against whom we argued in the preceding question); the other of those who err in defect, who (lest they might appear to consider reason as the rule of faith) attribute little or nothing to it. Of this way of thinking are not only the Anabaptists and Weigelians, but also the Lutherans and papists. These hold that the testimony of reason is not to be heard when it judges of certain mysteries of faith. For example, when it refuses to admit the doctrine of transubstantiation or ubiquity because it is repugnant to the light of right reason. And because we do not repudiate entirely the use of reason, they write about us as if we made ourselves the judges and final arbiters in matters of faith, and thus deceive the world by a fair pretence, while we glory in acknowledging Scripture as the only judge.

III. Having established this point, I say that to reason belongs the judgment of discretion in matters of faith, both subjectively (because it belongs to the intellect alone to know and distinguish these matters of faith) and normally; and indeed with respect to the truth of conclusions in all propositions (whether known by nature or by revelation), but with respect to the truth of propositions only in those known by nature and even then with this threefold caution. (1) That the judgment of reason not be considered as necessary, as if theology could not do without it. (2) That the word of God (where also these truths are revealed) be considered always as the primary rule and reason as the secondary. (3) That when the word adds something unknown to nature to a thing known by nature, then we should not judge of it by nature or reason, but by the word (not that the word and reason are at variance, but because reason is perfected by the word). But in things known only by revelation (as the mystery of the Trinity, of the incarnation, etc.), the only rule is the word of God, beyond or above which we must not be wise.

IV. The question is not whether the mysteries of faith are above reason or whether reason can reach them. For we readily grant that there are things which far surpass the comprehension not only of men, but even of angels, the disclosure of which was a work of supernatural revelation. We also grant that reason is not only incapable of discovering them without a revelation; not only weak in comprehending them after being revealed; but also slippery and fallible (readily pursuing falsehood for truth and truth for falsehood), and never believing the word of God and its mysteries unless enlightened by the grace of the Spirit. Rather the question is – Is there no use at all for it, and should we entirely reject the testimony of reason, as often as the truth or falsity of any doctrine is to be judged? This our opponents hold and we deny.

VI. Reason cannot and should not draw mysteries from its own treasury. The word of God alone has this right. Unless derived from this source, they are on that very account to be discarded (Gal. 1:8). (2) Reason must not be listened to when it complains of not being able to comprehend the mysteries of faith. For how can the infinite be comprehended by the finite? Therefore the wish to reject mysteries because they cannot be comprehended by reason is a sin not only against faith but also against reason which acknowledges itself to be finite and far inferior to those sublime mysteries. (3) It must not be heard when it wishes, by overturning the questionable truth of the first principles of natural religion, to establish its own errors under the pretext of their being mysteries of faith (either as to things merely natural or supernatural or mixed) which grace borrows from nature for its own use. Hence right reason ought to reject these fictions as incompatible with the indubitable first principles of natural religion.

VIII. There is a difference between knowing the meaning of a proposition and knowing its truth. In the former manner, the gospel is regarded simply as the word, but in the latter, as the divine and infallible word. Reason is occupied with the former, but faith alone with the latter.

IX. An incomprehensible thing (which cannot be grasped) is different from an incompossible (which cannot be conceived). The mysteries of the Trinity, incarnation and predestination are incomprehensible, as we have only an obscure and imperfect knowledge of them. But the fiction of transubstantiation or of ubiquity cannot be conceived, on account of the natural repugnance of our intellect to the conception of a thing altogether impossible.

X. Reason as corrupt and in the concrete may be at variance with theology, but not reason as sound and in the abstract (which possibly may be ignorant of mysteries and may not teach them, but must not therefore be considered as denying them). As you would improperly gather that the physician is at variance with the lawyer because he does not quote laws, so neither does the philosopher contradict the theologian, although he does not treat of his mysteries, and acknowledges them to be out of his sphere.

XIII. Because the mysteries of faith surpass the comprehension of reason, it follows that it should not be used as the first principle and foundation for exhibiting the truth of axioms of faith. But it does not follow that it cannot be used to exhibit the truth or falsity of conclusions in controversies of faith. For the truth of conclusions is perpetual in the nature of things and can be learned in those schools also which are out of the church, as Augustine frequently tells us (CI 2.31.49 [FC 2:104]).

XIV. When we allow a certain judgment to reason in things of faith, we do not mean reason as blind and corrupted by sin (in which sense we confess the natural man cannot receive the things of God [1 Cor. 2:14] and that 'the carnal mind [*phronēma*] is enmity against God,' Rom. 8:7), but we speak of reason as sound and healed by grace (in which sense 'the spiritual man is said to judge all things' [1 Cor. 2:15], and Paul often appeals to the judgment of believers, 1 Cor. 10:15; 11:13; Heb. 5:13, 14).

XVII. Although we use reason and its principles in theological controversies, it does not follow that we make a mixture of philosophy with theology and of human with divine things. They are not used as the foundation and principle of faith (from which we prove these mysteries), but only as instruments of knowledge (as when with the eye of the body and the light of the sun we see any visible object, there is no mixture of the eye with the sun because they do not concur in the same, but in a different manner).

(Taken from George Musgrave Giger's translation, ed. James T. Dennison, Phillipsburg, NJ: P&R Publishing 1992, I.viii–ix.)

C. Reason against faith – and some responses

I.4.6 John Locke, from *The Essay Concerning Human Understanding*

Locke here argues that reason is the primary judge in all matters of knowledge.

Of Faith and Reason, and their Distinct Provinces:

1. *Necessary to know their boundaries.* . . . I think we may come to lay down *the measures and boundaries between faith and reason*: the want whereof may possibly have been the cause, if not of great disorders, yet at least of great disputes, and perhaps mistakes in the world. For till it be resolved how far we are to be guided by reason, and how far by faith, we shall in vain dispute, and endeavour to convince one another in matters of religion.

2. *Faith and reason, what, as contradistinguished.* . . . *Reason*, therefore, here, as contradistinguished to *faith*, I take to be the discovery of the certainty or probability of such propositions or truths which the mind arrives at by deduction made from such ideas, which it has got by the use of its natural faculties; *viz.* by sensation or reflection.

Faith, on the other side, is the assent to any proposition, not thus made out by the deductions of reason, but upon the credit of the proposer, as coming from God, in some extraordinary way of communication. This way of discovering truths to men, we call *revelation*.

3. *No new simple idea can be conveyed by traditional revelation.* First, Then I say, *that no man inspired by God can by any revelation communicate to others any new simple ideas which they had not before from sensation or reflection.* For, whatsoever impressions he himself may have from the immediate hand of God, this revelation, if it be of new simple ideas, cannot be conveyed to another, either by words or any other signs. Because words, by their immediate operation on us, cause no other ideas but of their natural sounds: and it is by the custom of using them for signs, that they excite and revive in our minds latent ideas; but yet only such ideas as were there before. For words, seen or heard, recall to our thoughts those ideas only which to us they have been wont to be signs of, but cannot introduce any perfectly new and formerly unknown simple ideas. The same holds in all other signs; which cannot signify to us things of which we have before never had any idea at all.

Thus whatever things were discovered to St. Paul, when he was rapt up into the third heaven; whatever new ideas his mind there received, all the description he can make to others of that place, is only this, That there are such things, 'as eye hath not seen, nor ear heard, nor hath it entered into the heart of man to conceive.' And supposing God should discover to any one, supernaturally, a species of creatures inhabiting, for example, Jupiter or Saturn, (for that it is possible there may be such, nobody can deny,) which had six senses; and imprint on his mind the ideas conveyed to theirs by that sixth sense: he could no more, by words, produce in the minds of other men those ideas imprinted by that sixth sense, than one of us could convey the idea of any colour, by the sound of words, into a man who, having the other four senses perfect, had always totally wanted the fifth, of seeing. For our simple ideas, then, which are the foundation, and sole matter of all our notions and knowledge, we must depend wholly on our reason, I mean our natural faculties; and can by no means receive them, or any of them, from traditional revelation. I say, *traditional revelation*, in distinction to *original revelation*. By the one, I mean that first impression which is made immediately by God on the mind of any man, to which we cannot set any bounds; and by the other, those impressions delivered over to others in words, and the ordinary ways of conveying our conceptions one to another.

4. *Traditional revelation may make us know propositions knowable also by reason, but not with the same certainty that reason doth. Secondly, I say that the same truths may be discovered, and conveyed down from revelation, which are discoverable to us by reason, and by those ideas we naturally may have* . . . For whatsoever truth we come to the clear discovery of, from the knowledge and contemplation of our own ideas, will always be certainer to us than those which are conveyed to us by *traditional revelation*. For the knowledge we have that this revelation came at first from God can never be so sure as the knowledge we have from the clear and distinct perception of the agreement or disagreement of our own ideas: if it were revealed some ages since, that the three angles of a triangle were equal to two right ones, I might assent to the truth of that proposition, upon the credit of the tradition, that it was revealed: but that would never amount to so great a certainty as the knowledge of it, upon the comparing and measuring my own ideas of two right angles, and the three angles of a triangle. The like holds in matter of fact knowable by our senses; the history of the deluge is conveyed to us by writings which had their original from revelation: and yet nobody, I think, will say he has as certain and clear a knowledge of the flood as Noah, that saw it; or that he himself would have had, had he then been alive and seen it . . . So that the assurance of its being a revelation is less still than the assurance of his senses.

5. *Even original revelation cannot be admitted against the clear evidence of reason.* In propositions, then, whose certainty is built upon the clear perception of the agreement or disagreement of our ideas, attained either by immediate intuition, as in self-evident propositions, or by evident deductions of reason in demonstrations we need not the assistance of revelation, as necessary to gain our assent, and introduce them into our minds. Because the natural ways of knowledge could settle them there, or had done it already; which is the greatest assurance we can possibly have of anything, unless where God immediately reveals it to us: and there too our assurance can be no

greater than our knowledge is, that it *is* a revelation from God. But yet nothing, I think, can, under that title, shake or overrule plain knowledge; or rationally prevail with any man to admit it for true, in a direct contradiction to the clear evidence of his own understanding. For, since no evidence of our faculties, by which we receive such revelations, can exceed, if equal, the certainty of our intuitive knowledge, we can never receive for a truth anything that is directly contrary to our clear and distinct knowledge ... And therefore *no proposition can be received for divine revelation, or obtain the assent due to all such, if it be contradictory to our clear intuitive knowledge.* Because this would be to subvert the principles and foundations of all knowledge, evidence, and assent whatsoever: and there would be left no difference between truth and falsehood, no measures of credible and incredible in the world, if doubtful propositions shall take place before self-evident; and what we certainly know give way to what we may possibly be mistaken in. In propositions therefore contrary to the clear perception of the agreement or disagreement of any of our ideas, it will be in vain to urge them as matters of faith. They cannot move our assent under that or any other title whatsoever. For faith can never convince us of anything that contradicts our knowledge. Because, though faith be founded on the testimony of God (who cannot lie) revealing any proposition to us: yet we cannot have an assurance of the truth of its being a divine revelation greater than our own knowledge ...

6. *Traditional revelation much less.* Thus far a man has use of reason, and ought to hearken to it, even in immediate and original revelation, where it is supposed to be made to himself. But to all those who pretend not to immediate revelation, but are required to pay obedience, and to receive the truths revealed to others, which, by the tradition of writings, or word of mouth, are conveyed down to them, reason has a great deal more to do, and is that only which can induce us to receive them. For matter of faith being only divine revelation, and nothing else, faith, as we use the word, (called commonly *divine faith*), has to do with no propositions, but those which are supposed to be divinely revealed. So that I do not see how those who make revelation alone the sole object of faith can say, that it is a matter of faith, and not of reason, to believe that such or such a proposition, to be found in such or such a book, is of divine inspiration; unless it be revealed that that proposition, or all in that book, was communicated by divine inspiration. Without such a revelation, the believing, or not believing, that proposition, or book, to be of divine authority, can never be matter of faith, but matter of reason; and such as I must come to an assent to only by the use of my reason, which can never require or enable me to believe that which is contrary to itself: it being impossible for reason ever to procure any assent to that which to itself appears unreasonable.

In all things, therefore, where we have clear evidence from our ideas, and those principles of knowledge I have above mentioned, reason is the proper judge; and revelation, though it may, in consenting with it, confirm its dictates, yet cannot in such cases invalidate its decrees: nor can we be obliged, where we have the clear and evident sentience of reason, to quit it for the contrary opinion, under a pretence that it is matter of faith: which can have no authority against the plain and clear dictates of reason.

7. *Things above reason are, when revealed, the proper matter of faith.* But, Thirdly, There being many things wherein we have very imperfect notions, or none at all; and other things, of whose past, present, or future existence, by the natural use of our faculties, we can have no knowledge at all; these, as being beyond the discovery of our natural faculties, and *above reason*, are, when revealed, the proper matter of faith. Thus, that part of the angels rebelled against God, and thereby lost their first happy state: and that the dead shall rise, and live again: these and the like, being beyond the discovery of reason, are purely matters of faith, with which reason has directly nothing to do.

8. *Or not contrary to reason, if revealed, are matter of faith; and must carry it against probable conjectures of reason.* But since God, in giving us the light of reason, has not thereby tied up his own hands from affording us, when he thinks fit, the light of revelation in any of those matters wherein our natural faculties are able to give a probable determination; *revelation*, where God has been pleased to give it, *must carry it against the probable conjectures of reason.* Because the mind not being certain of the truth of that it does not evidently know, but only yielding to the probability that appears in it, is bound to give up its assent to such a testimony which, it is satisfied, comes from one who cannot err, and will not deceive. But yet, it still belongs to reason to judge of the truth of its being a revelation, and of the signification of the words wherein it is delivered. Indeed, if anything shall be thought revelation which is contrary to the plain principles of reason, and the evident knowledge the mind has of its own clear and distinct ideas; there reason must be hearkened to, as to a matter within its province. Since a man can never have so certain a knowledge that a proposition which contradicts the clear principles and evidence of his own knowledge was divinely revealed, or that he understands the words rightly wherein it is delivered, as he has that the contrary is true, and so is bound to consider and judge of it as a matter of reason, and not swallow it, without examination, as a matter of faith.

. . .

11. *If the boundaries be not set between faith and reason, no enthusiasm or extravagancy in religion can be contradicted.* If the provinces of faith and reason are not kept distinct by these boundaries, there will, in matters of religion, be no room for reason at all; and those extravagant opinions and ceremonies that are to be found in the several religions of the world will not deserve to be blamed. For, to this crying up of faith in *opposition* to reason, we may, I think, in good measure ascribe those absurdities that fill almost all the religions which possess and divide mankind. For men having been principled with an opinion, that they must not consult reason in the things of religion, however apparently contradictory to common sense and the very principles

of all their knowledge, have let loose their fancies and natural superstition; and have been by them led into so strange opinions, and extravagant practices in religion, that a considerate man cannot but stand amazed at their follies, and judge them so far from being acceptable to the great and wise God, that he cannot avoid thinking them ridiculous and offensive to a sober good man. So that, in effect, religion, which should most distinguish us from beasts, and ought most peculiarly to elevate us, as rational creatures, above brutes, is that wherein men often appear most irrational, and more senseless than beasts themselves.

(Taken from Book IV, Chapter XVIII, fifth edition 1706.)

I.4.7 Søren Kierkegaard, from *The Philosophical Fragments*

Kierkegaard here argues that knowledge of the divine can never come through reason, but only through an encounter with God, who gives both faith and the condition for faith.

b. The Teacher

If the teacher is to be the occasion that reminds the learner, he cannot assist him to recollect that he actually does know the truth, for the learner is indeed untruth. That for which the teacher can become the occasion of his recollecting is that he is untruth. But by this calling to mind, the learner is definitely excluded from the truth, even more than when he was ignorant of being untruth. Consequently, in this way, precisely by reminding him, the teacher thrusts the learner away, except that by being turned in upon himself in this manner the learner does not discover that he previously knew the truth but discovers his untruth. To this act of consciousness, the Socratic principle applies: the teacher is only an occasion, whoever he may be, even if he is a god, because I can discover my own untruth only by myself, because only when *I* discover it is it discovered, not before, even though the whole world knew it. (Under the assumed presupposition about the moment, this becomes the one and only analogy to the Socratic.)

Now, if the learner is to obtain the truth, the teacher must bring it to him, but not only that. Along with it, he must provide him with the condition for understanding it, for if the learner were himself the condition for understanding the truth, then he merely needs to recollect, because the condition for understanding the truth is like being able to ask about it – the condition and the question contain the conditioned and the answer. (If this is not the case, then the moment is to be understood only Socratically.)

But the one who not only gives the learner the truth but provides the condition is not a teacher. Ultimately, all instruction depends upon the presence of the condition; if it is lacking, then a teacher is capable of nothing, because in the second case, the teacher, before beginning to teach, must transform, not reform, the learner. But no human being is capable of doing this; if it is to take place, it must be done by the god himself.

Now, inasmuch as the learner exists, he is indeed created, and, accordingly, God must have given him the condition for understanding the truth (for otherwise he previously would have been merely animal, and that teacher who gave him the condition along with the truth would make him a human being for the first time). But insofar as the moment is to have decisive significance (and if this is not assumed, then we do in fact remain with the Socratic), he must lack the condition, consequently be deprived of it. This cannot have been due to an act of the god (for this is a contradiction) or to an accident (for it is a contradiction that something inferior would be able to vanquish something superior); it must therefore have been due to himself. If he could have lost the condition in such a way that it was not due to himself, and if he could be in this state of loss without its being due to himself, then he would have possessed the condition only accidentally, which is a contradiction, since the condition for the truth is an essential condition. The untruth, then, is not merely outside the truth but is polemical against the truth, which is expressed by saying that he himself has forfeited and is forfeiting the condition.

The teacher, then, is the god himself, who, acting as the occasion, prompts the learner to be reminded that he is untruth and is that through his own fault. But this state – to be untruth and to be that through one's own fault – what can we call it? Let us call it *sin*.

The teacher, then, is the god, who gives the condition and gives the truth. Now, what should we call such a teacher, for we surely do agree that we have gone far beyond the definition of a teacher. Inasmuch as the learner is in untruth but is that by his own act (and, according to what has already been said, there is no other way he can be that), he might seem to be free, for to be on one's own certainly is freedom. And yet he is indeed unfree and bound and excluded, because to be free from the truth is indeed to be excluded, and to be excluded by oneself is indeed to be bound. But since he is bound by himself, can he not work himself loose or free himself, for that which binds me should also be able to set me free at will, and since that is himself, he should certainly be able to do it. But first of all he must will it. But just suppose that he was very profoundly reminded of that for which that teacher became the occasion (and this must never be forgotten) of his recollecting – just suppose that he willed it. In that case (if by willing it he could do it by himself), his having been bound would become a bygone state, one that in the moment of liberation would vanish without a trace – and the moment would not gain decisive significance. He would be unaware that he had bound himself and now set himself free.

Considered in this way, the moment acquires no decisive significance, and yet this was what we wanted to assume as the hypothesis. According to the hypothesis, then, he will not be able to set himself free. (And this is truly just the way it is, for he uses the power of freedom in the service of unfreedom, since he is indeed freely in it, and in this way the combined power of unfreedom grows and makes him the slave of sin.)

What, then, should we call such a teacher who gives him the condition again and along with it the truth? Let us call him a *savior*, for he does indeed save the learner from unfreedom, saves him from himself. Let us call him a *deliverer*, for he does indeed deliver the person who had imprisoned himself, and no one is so dreadfully imprisoned, and no captivity is so impossible to break out of as that in which the individual holds himself captive! And yet, even this does not say enough, for by his unfreedom he had indeed become guilty of something, and if that teacher gives him the condition and the truth, then he is, of course, a *reconciler* who takes away the wrath that lay over the incurred guilt.

A teacher such as that, the learner will never be able to forget, because in that very moment he would sink down into himself again, just as the person did who once possessed the condition and then, by forgetting that God is, sank into unfreedom. If they were to meet in another life, that teacher would again be able to give the condition to the person who had not received it, but he would be quite different for the person who had once received it. After all, the condition was something entrusted, and therefore the receiver was always responsible for an accounting. But a teacher such as that – what should we call him? A teacher certainly can evaluate the learner with respect to whether or not he is making progress, but he cannot pass judgment on him, for he must be Socratic enough to perceive that he cannot give the learner what is essential. That teacher, then, is actually not a teacher but is a *judge*. Even when the learner has most fully put on the condition and then, by doing so, has become immersed in the truth, he still can never forget that teacher or allow him to disappear Socratically, which still is far more profound than all unseasonable punctiliousness and deluded fanaticism – indeed, it is the highest if that other is not truth.

And, now, the moment. A moment such as this is unique. To be sure, it is short and temporal, as the moment is; it is passing, as the moment is, past, as the moment is in the next moment, and yet it is decisive, and yet it is filled with the eternal. A moment such as this must have a special name. Let us call it: *the fullness of time*.

(Taken from Philosophical Fragments and Johannes Climacus *trans. and* Howard V. Hong and Edna H. Hong, Princeton, NJ: Princeton University Press *1985, pp. 14–18.)*

I.4.8 Vatican I, from *Dei Filius*

The Council teaches that faith is not opposed to reason, but is above reason, and anathematizes a number of errors that in different ways deny this understanding.

Chapter 3. On faith

1. Since human beings are totally dependent on God as their creator and lord, and created reason is completely subject to uncreated truth, we are obliged to yield to God the revealer full submission of intellect and will by faith.

2. This faith, which is the beginning of human salvation, the catholic church professes to be a supernatural virtue, by means of which, with the grace of God inspiring and assisting us, we believe to be true what He has revealed, not because we perceive its intrinsic truth by the natural light of reason, but because of the authority of God himself, who makes the revelation and can neither deceive nor be deceived.

3. Faith, declares the Apostle, is the assurance of things hoped for, the conviction of things not seen.

4. Nevertheless, in order that the submission of our faith should be in accordance with reason, it was God's will that there should be linked to the internal assistance of the holy Spirit external indications of his revelation, that is to say divine acts, and first and foremost miracles and prophecies, which clearly demonstrating as they do the omnipotence and infinite knowledge of God, are the most certain signs of revelation and are suited to the understanding of all.

5. Hence Moses and the prophets, and especially Christ our lord himself, worked many absolutely clear miracles and delivered prophecies; while of the apostles we read: 'And they went forth and preached everywhere, while the Lord worked with them and confirmed the message by the signs that attended it.' Again it is written: 'We have the prophetic word made more sure; you will do well to pay attention to this as to a lamp shining in a dark place.'

6. Now, although the assent of faith is by no means a blind movement of the mind, yet no one can accept the gospel preaching in the way that is necessary for achieving salvation without the inspiration and illumination of the holy Spirit, who gives to all facility in accepting and believing the truth . . .

Chapter 4. On faith and reason

1. The perpetual agreement of the catholic church has maintained and maintains this too: that there is a twofold order of knowledge, distinct not only as regards its source, but also as regards its object.

2. With regard to the source, we know at the one level by natural reason, at the other level by divine faith.

3. With regard to the object, besides those things to which natural reason can attain, there are proposed for our belief mysteries hidden in God which, unless they are divinely revealed, are incapable of being known. Wherefore, when the Apostle, who witnesses that God was known to the gentiles from created things, comes to treat of the grace and truth which came by Jesus Christ, he declares: We impart a secret and hidden wisdom of God, which God decreed before the ages for our glorification. None of the rulers of this age understood this. God has revealed it to us through the Spirit. For the Spirit searches everything, even the depths of God. And the Only-begotten himself, in his confession to the Father, acknowledges that the Father has hidden these things from the wise and prudent and revealed them to the little ones.

4. Now reason, does indeed when it seeks persistently, piously and soberly, achieve by God's gift some understanding, and that most profitable, of the mysteries, whether by analogy from what it knows naturally, or from the connexion of these mysteries with one another and with the final end of humanity; but reason is never rendered capable of penetrating these mysteries in the way in which it penetrates those truths which form its proper object. For the divine mysteries, by their very nature, so far surpass the created understanding that, even when a revelation has been given and accepted by faith, they remain covered by the veil of that same faith and wrapped, as it were, in a certain obscurity, as long as in this mortal life we are away from the Lord, for we walk by faith, and not by sight.

5. Even though faith is above reason, there can never be any real disagreement between faith and reason, since it is the same God who reveals the mysteries and infuses faith, and who has endowed the human mind with the light of reason.

6. God cannot deny himself, nor can truth ever be in opposition to truth. The appearance of this kind of specious contradiction is chiefly due to the fact that either the dogmas of faith are not understood and explained in accordance with the mind of the church, or unsound views are mistaken for the conclusions of reason.

7. Therefore we define that every assertion contrary to the truth of enlightened faith is totally false.

8. Furthermore the church which, together with its apostolic office of teaching, has received the charge of preserving the deposit of faith, has by divine appointment the right and duty of condemning what wrongly passes for knowledge, lest anyone be led astray by philosophy and empty deceit.

9. Hence all faithful Christians are forbidden to defend as the legitimate conclusions of science those opinions which are known to be contrary to the doctrine of faith, particularly if they have been condemned by the church; and furthermore they are absolutely bound to hold them to be errors which wear the deceptive appearance of truth.

10. Not only can faith and reason never be at odds with one another but they mutually support each other, for on the one hand right reason established the foundations of the faith and, illuminated by its light, develops the science of divine things; on the other hand, faith delivers reason from errors and protects it and furnishes it with knowledge of many kinds.

11. Hence, so far is the church from hindering the development of human arts and studies, that in fact she assists and promotes them in many ways. For she is neither ignorant nor contemptuous of the advantages which derive from this source for human life, rather she acknowledges that those things flow from God, the lord of sciences, and, if they are properly used, lead to God by the help of his grace.

12. Nor does the church forbid these studies to employ, each within its own area, its own proper principles and method: but while she admits this just freedom, she takes particular care that they do not become infected with errors by conflicting with divine teaching, or, by going beyond their proper limits, intrude upon what belongs to faith and engender confusion.

13. For the doctrine of the faith which God has revealed is put forward not as some philosophical discovery capable of being perfected by human intelligence, but as a divine deposit committed to the spouse of Christ to be faithfully protected and infallibly promulgated.

14. Hence, too, that meaning of the sacred dogmas is ever to be maintained which has once been declared by holy mother church, and there must never be any abandonment of this sense under the pretext or in the name of a more profound understanding.

Canons:

3. On faith
1. If anyone says that human reason is so independent that faith cannot be commanded by God: let him be anathema.

4. On faith and reason
1. If anyone says that in divine revelation there are contained no true mysteries properly so-called, but that all the dogmas of the faith can be understood and demonstrated by properly trained reason from natural principles: let him be anathema.

2. If anyone says that human studies are to be treated with such a degree of liberty that their assertions may be maintained as true even when they are opposed to divine revelation, and that they may not be forbidden by the church: let him be anathema.

(Taken from the standard Vatican translation.)

I.4.9 Robert Jenson, from *Systematic Theology*

Jenson argues that the best way to understand the relationship between Christian faith and what is variously called 'philosophy' or 'reason' is as an inter-religious dialogue. Philosophy is little more than a late and intellectually sophisticated form of Greek paganism.

Theological prolegomena of an epistemologically pretentious sort are a distinctively modern phenomenon. The knowledge of God attributed to 'nature' by classic premodern Western systems occupied a location in some ways similar, but did not function systematically to enable the rest of theology. Thus, to instance *the* classic Western theologian, the entire body of Thomas Aquinas' *Summa Theologiae*, encompassing alike the propositions supposed to be available by nature to all humans and those attributed to historically specific revelation alone, is shaped as a narrative of creational-incarnational procession from and return to God. That is, all its propositions have their place within the biblical story of God and his works. And while Thomas indeed says that the axioms of theology are theorems of a prior body of knowledge, this turns out to be knowledge that only God and his perfected saints possess, to which we therefore can appeal only within the mystery of the church's anticipatory participation in the Kingdom.

These relations are exactly reflected in the subtle logic of Thomas's proofs of God's reality, with which he gets both *summae* underway. In themselves as arguments, these are conducted without reference to the church's specific message. But the conclusion of each is the reality of an anonymous metaphysical entity, for example, 'a certain primary mover.' That thereby the reality of *God* has been proven is each time established by the further observation, 'and all understand this to be God.' But who are these 'all'? They are, of course, those whom Thomas expected might read his writings: Jews, Christians, and Muslims, who all worship the biblical God. A Buddhist – except in tantric apotropaic horror – would precisely *not* worship a 'primary *mover*.' Thomas's launching analyses occur within a specifically biblical apprehension already in place.

Nevertheless, the seeds of later trouble are present in classic theology. The 'natural' knowledge encompassed in it was thought to be a body of knowledge about God and his intentions not intrinsically dependent on historically particular divine dispositions, and therefore properly the common property of humanity. In fact, however, this body of theology was as historically particular as any other set of theological proposals: it comprised a part of the theology that Greek religious thinkers, pondering the revelations claimed for Homer and Parmenides, had provided for the cults of Mediterranean antiquity as it became religiously homogeneous, the part that the church's fathers also found themselves able to affirm.

Within high medieval and later theology, the description of the shared truths as 'natural' was an explanation of how such overlap was possible: there was proposed to be a knowledge of God and his works available to human reason by virtue of what makes it human and reason, and without an intrinsic need for help from particular divine dispositions. But even if such knowledge occurs, there is no reason to suppose it covers exactly the area in which the fathers found they could agree with Platonic or Stoic or Aristotelian theology. Moreover, the interpretation of such knowledge as that appropriate to humanity's 'nature' can become a covert recommendation of this knowledge, and precisely in its distinction from that given by the gospel.

Thus it is not fundamentally the content or source of the theology labeled 'natural' that has made its role in the discourse of Christian theology problematic, but – perhaps we may say – the label itself, that is, the very notion of distinguishing 'natural' from 'revealed' or 'positive' theology, as if these lay on different levels. The problems emerged from dormancy in the seventeenth and eighteenth centuries. The event makes the break between premodern and modern theology.

Amid mutual condemnation between established churches, each claiming the true version of the faith, and their invocation by the warring forces of burgeoning nationalism, seventeenth-century Europe lost trust in the way in which the culture had previously established Christian teaching's plausibility. Catholicism met this challenge by building intellectual walls around the church, thus temporarily dropping out of the story we are here tracing. Protestantism first met it by making the doctrine of scriptural authority into an antecedent basis for theology's claims. Thus traditional natural arguments for the reliability of Scripture came to bear a new load: we may, it was said, believe Christian doctrine because it is drawn from the Bible, whose truth can be made antecedently plausible. Seventeenth-century Protestant systems' doctrine of Scripture thus already carried the modern prolegomenal burden.

The more decisive break, however, occurred in the eighteenth century. The European–North American Enlightenment applied a hermeneutic of suspicion to all received wisdom, particularly that propounded by established authorities. Needing a criterion by which to scrutinize the established churches' teaching from 'revelation,' the Lockeans of the English-speaking world and the 'Neologians' of Germany thought to find it in that other theology which Christian theology itself had acknowledged: if there is a knowledge of God natural to our being, this knowledge can be the norm of other purported theology.

What in fact happened therewith was that the West's Mediterranean-pagan religious heritage – truly no more anchored in universal humanity than any other – was elevated to be judge of its biblical heritage. It took only a few decades for this misstep to evacuate elite theology of its specifically Christian content and, indeed, to repristinate – although often in sadly enfeebled form – the theology of pagan Mediterranean antiquity.

When nineteenth-century German thinkers then undertook to restore Christian theology by 'overcoming the Enlightenment,' they supposed they should fight on the field laid out by the Enlighteners. The 'Neo-Protestantism' they thereby created, and exported to the rest of Europe and America, supposed it had to find a functional replacement for the old natural theology. And it accepted the usual supposition of the Enlightenment that the church's specific theology was a problematic enterprise dependent on prior justification by more surely founded cognition; thus the replacement was more heavily burdened than the old natural theology had been. Therewith the fully modern prolegomenal effort began.

The archetype of Neo-Protestant prolegomena was provided in 1830 by the first chapter of Friedrich Schleiermacher's *Der Christliche Glaube* together with other of his writings it invokes. Schleiermacher argued that humanity is intrinsically 'religious,' that is, dependent for authenticity on experience of the eternal; that Christian faith is a particular – in his argued judgment, supreme – mode of such experience; that the first-level discourse of Christian faith is meaningful and true as it *expresses* Christian religious experience; that this expression requires critical explication for its purity; and that once all this is established, theology can proceed in intellectual respectability as the work of such explication. Few subsequent theologians reproduced Schleiermacher's particular argument; nearly all followed its general strategy.

Prolegomena have since grown ever longer and more unwieldy, as ever more desperate means are proposed to evade the logic of the situation. The project is hypertropic because it is hopeless. If theological prolegomena lay down conceptual conditions of Christian teaching that are not themselves Christian teaching, that are more than a formal demand for coherence and argumentative responsibility, and that in the Western world are therefore theologoumena of Mediterranean paganism, the prolegomena sooner or later turn against the *legomena*.

This is not to say that Neo-Protestantism did not achieve splendid things. For a systematically central instance, Schleiermacher's pioneering analysis of 'religion' is vital for many, including the present writer, who do not use it foundationally as Schleiermacher did. It is only to say that nineteenth-century response to the Enlightenment harbored a particular flaw.

Nor should the foregoing strictures be read as rejection of Western Christianity's inheritance from pagan antiquity. Conversation with the antecedent theology of each encountered religious culture is intrinsic to the gospel's mission, and this conversation is never merely polemic. That the fathers were able to agree with 'the Greeks,' as they regularly called their counterparts, that, for example, God 'has a *Logos*,' or that the debate about God's 'being' should be pursued, was constitutive in the missionary history that leads to Western forms of Christianity, and contributes irreplaceably – at least for the West – to the church's knowledge of the gospel.

What must not continue is only the Enlightenment's elevation of the Greek element of our thinking to be unilateral judge of the whole, or a practice of theological prolegomena that consciously or unconsciously accepts that elevation. Nor may we continue the mistake that suggested these moves: the qualification of truth taught by Plato or Aristotle as more 'natural' or 'rational' than truth taught by Isaiah or Paul.

There is a particular version of these errors that must be noted. We usually refer to the work of Greece's theologians with their own name for it, 'philosophy.' We have thereupon been led to think this must be a different *kind* of intellectual activity than theology, to which theology perhaps may appeal for foundational purposes or against which theology must perhaps defend itself. But this is a historical illusion; Greek philosophy was simply the theology of the historically particular Olympian-Parmenidean religion, later shared with the wider Mediterranean cultic world.

The church fathers, in direct contact with 'the Greeks,' were usually clear about this. In the view of most of them, the doctrines of the philosophers were simply the theologoumena of a different faith, with some of which it might be possible to agree, some of which had to be rejected, and some of which offered occasion of further discussion. Thus Clement of Alexandria, in his *Exhortation to the Greeks*, after chapters of invective against the Greek-taught pagans for their worship of God's works instead of God, continues: 'I long for God, not the works of God. Now – whom from among you can I take for a co-worker in this longing? For we do not altogether despair of you. Perhaps Plato. . . .' There follows a famous passage from Plato about the unknowability of God, and a calm discussion of the issue Plato raises.

The secular mood by which some forms of 'philosophy' contrast with Christian theology and that tempts us to take them for a different kind of thinking is simply a character of Olympian religion itself, which pursued a divinity purged of mystery. Insofar as Western philosophy is not now reduced to the pure study of logic, it is still in fact theology, Christian or Olympian-Parmenidean. Theologians of Western Christianity must indeed converse with the philosophers, but only because and insofar as both are engaged in the *same* sort of enterprise.

Neither can we reject the Enlightenment as such. The Enlightenment consisted largely in awe before science's seventeenth-century achievement, and that awe was earned. The new science's achievements were metaphysically significant in ways from which theology should less have suffered and more have profited than it did; nor can the methodological lessons the Enlightenment drew from new science be dismissed. The only point here made is that the standard Enlightenment erred in its strategy over against theology as it knew it, and that we must reckon with this: among other ways, by eschewing systematically pompous prolegomena.

(Taken from Robert Jenson, Systematic Theology vol. I, Oxford: Oxford University Press, 1997, © Robert Jenson, pp. 6–11.)

I.5 Reflecting on experience of God

Introductory essay

Whatever else might be said about the content and character of Christian faith, it is true that Christian faith is bound up in some way with the experience of the individual both as an individual and as a member of that community which is called the church. Christianity concerns both the acts of God in drawing to himself a people to live in covenant relationship with him, and the call of the individual to respond in faith to the saving work of Christ. Unless these things become a matter of personal experience, transforming one's life and reshaping one's understanding of the world, the Christian gospel is but a dead letter.

Despite the importance of experience, however, the precise role that experience should play in the particular task of Christian theology requires careful consideration. It is necessary to ask, for instance, what authority experience should have? Is theology in some way answerable to the experience of the individual? Does experience constitute a starting-point and touchstone from which theology proceeds and against which it must be measured? And if experience can play such a role, whose experience is to be accorded such status? It is by no means clear, given the diversity of human experience, how experience *per se* could function as a starting-point for or criterion of theological claims.

Another way of conceiving the relationship is that Christian theology constitutes a conceptual framework within which experience itself is to be interpreted and critiqued. In this case one would argue that the biblical story of God's dealings with humankind, given conceptual expression through the tradition of theological formulation, forms a standard against which all claims to religious experience are tested. This position too, however, has some difficulties, for both the biblical story and the tradition of Christian theology, are themselves shaped by the experience of successive generations who understood that God had shown them a promised land, had led them out of slavery in Egypt, had made himself known to them in his Son, and so on. The biblical story is, in part, the story of human experience. It would seem therefore, that experience is not simply shaped and critiqued by theological truths garnered from elsewhere; the experience of the people of God has also shaped and critiqued theology.

A third possibility then, is that there is a dialectical relation between theology and experience in which the conceptual framework of theology both shapes and is shaped by the experience of faith in the community of the church. Such a relation denies to experience any claim to absolute authority and yet counts it important that there is a high degree of coherence between theology and experience. According to such a model, theology will take seriously – for it believes in a God who participates in human history and is known through human experience – but will not accept uncritically, a claim to truth which is based on experience alone. It will seek, rather, to test such a claim in the light of Jesus Christ as testified to in Scripture and in the tradition of the church.

An example of the dialectical relation between theology and experience is seen in the work of St Augustine of Hippo (I.5.1) who reflects at length upon the nature of Christian experience. The opening paragraph of Augustine's autobiographical and doxological *Confessions* includes the famous prayer, 'Thou movest us to delight in praising thee; for thou hast formed us for thyself, and our hearts are restless till they find rest in thee'. Out of concern to praise God aright, however, Augustine then questions his own experience. 'Shall I call on God so as to know him?', Augustine asks, 'or do I call on him because I know him?' Augustine thus inquires whether experience of God yields knowledge of him or whether knowledge of God leads on to experience. The *Confessions* as a whole show forth both the warmth of piety and devotion which motivates Augustine's own theological endeavours, and the serious critical reflection upon his experience through which he seeks to submit it to the greater authority of God.

The close relation between individual experience and theological inquiry is similarly apparent in the writings of the Christian mystics. An example is provided by St John of the Cross's reflections upon 'the dark night of the soul' (I.5.2). St John views this dark night positively as the experience through which one is stripped both of attachment to material things and of all dependence upon rational inquiry. In this 'darkness' one relies on faith alone, but through such mystical experience, St John argues, true knowledge of God is to be found.

Jonathan Edwards (I.5.3), by contrast, urges caution about all claims that are based on experience alone. There is, Edwards claims, an authentic form of religious experience arising from the gracious working of the Holy Spirit, but it is not the case that every religious experience is attributable to the Spirit of God. It is equally possible that religious experiences may be excited by spirits other than God. In Edwards' view, therefore, experience cannot be taken as the starting-point and authority for theology, but must be interpreted and tested within a wider framework of theological understanding.

Edwards alerts us to a problem that besets any claim to base theology upon experience. The sheer variety of religious experience demands some criteria by which we may judge any particular experience to give genuine access to theological truth. Some have responded to this challenge by attempting to identify some basic religious experience which is either universal or universally accessible.

Friedrich Schleiermacher (I.5.4) is perhaps the most profound modern advocate of such a view. Reacting against what he perceived to be the cold rationalism of his day, Schleiermacher sought a basis for Christian theology which would correspond to the warm Moravian piety of his upbringing while at the same time providing a robust intellectual account of Christian doctrine. Schleiermacher found the basis for such a theology in what he claimed to be the universal human experience of absolute dependence upon an 'Other', which is the same thing, he contends, as being in relation with God. At its root, therefore, religion is neither a *knowing* – a system of doctrine or propositional truth –, or an *acting* – a form of moral life –, but a *feeling.* According to Schleiermacher, this feeling of the absolute dependence of one's own being constitutes the unique point of reference upon which all theological claims must be based.

Schleiermacher's theme is taken up, with some modifications, by Rudolf Otto (I.5.5) whose work constitutes one of the most influential attempts in twentieth-century theology to analyse the religious experience corresponding to and undergirding Christian theological discourse. Like Schleiermacher, Otto argues that there is a fundamental and universally accessible form of religious experience, but against Schleiermacher, Otto wants to make apparent that the basic fact of religious experience is not a fact about one's own experience, but about that which is experienced, about the transcendent. Otto designates the basic religious experience as 'the sense of the holy' and coins the term the *numinous* to signify the mysterious, awe-inspiring and fearful reality of God. Otto thus proposes that religion is founded upon a specific form of experience and cannot be reduced either to an ethic or to the formulations of dogma and creed.

While not disparaging of the role of reason in theology, Otto argues nevertheless that the sense of the numinous lies outside and beyond the scope of reason. The experience of the *mysterium tremendum et fascinans*, the mystery at once terrifying and fascinating, is to be combined with the rational elements of religion in order to gain assurance of the character of God.

The theology of Karl Rahner (I.5.6) is another approach owing much to Schleiermacher. Like Schleiermacher, Rahner claims to find the basis for theology in a fact of self-awareness. For Rahner this fact is the individual's experience of self as 'a being with an infinite horizon'. In the act of enquiring after a reality beyond themselves, Rahner contends, human beings reach beyond their own finitude and thus experience themselves as transcendent beings or as beings open to the beyond. It is thus an anthropological fact which lies at the basis of the theological endeavour although, again like Schleiermacher, Rahner insists that the existence of this fact can only be accounted for by the existence of a transcendent being. It 'must be understood as due to the working of that to which man is open'. In this way Rahner moves from the apprehension of a fact of human experience to a claim about the act and being of God. For Schleiermacher and Rahner alike, however, the fact of God's existence derives from, as the necessary condition of, the fact of human religious experience.

This point reveals the Achilles heel of all experience-based theologies. In finding a basis for theology in a fact of experience Schleiermacher, Rahner and Otto are all vulnerable to the critique of Ludwig Feuerbach. Feuerbach (I.5.7) contends that theological claims have no external reference but are simply a human construction, a matter of wishful thinking that is widespread amongst human beings simply because we refuse to accept the boundaries of our finite and ultimately meaningless existence. 'The true sense of theology', Feuerbach famously alleged, 'is anthropology'. The utterances of faith reveal only 'the mysteries of human nature'. Whether or not one agrees with Feuerbach's conclusion that the claims of religious experience have no external reference, his critique does call into question all attempts to ground theological truth upon human experience alone.

An attempt to avoid this problem is shown in the work of Paul Tillich. Describing his approach as a method of correlation, Tillich (I.5.8) understands theology as the attempt to bring to bear upon the questions arising out of our human situation the resources of the Christian gospel. Theology is the coming together of divine revelation and human experience – of the transcendent with the ultimate concerns of our own lives. Two things require emphasis here. First, we must note Tillich's insistence that the object of theology *concerns us*. Theology is always a matter of existential urgency, of infinite passion and inwardness (Kierkegaard). The second point is that only God is worthy of our ultimate concern. 'Nothing can be of ultimate concern for us', Tillich argues, 'which does not have the power of threatening and saving our being.' Christian faith is thus set forth as the solution to the questions surrounding our own being. The anxiety arising from the vulnerability of our own being can be met only by engagement with the 'ground of all being', an abstract signifier, for Tillich, of the reality of God. Such engagement becomes possible, Tillich further contends, through the divine act of revelation which is the incarnation of the Word of God. The encounter with Jesus becomes intelligible as an experience of God, however, only in so far as it gives an answer to the questions arising out of our own existence. This last point indicates a degree of ambiguity in Tillich's proposals. Does the coming together of divine revelation and human experience in Tillich's method allow us to make claims about who Jesus is in himself, or simply about the impact we allow him to have upon us?

This is the difficulty that attends all attempts to base theological claims upon the experience of the individual. How are we to be sure that we are speaking of God and not just about ourselves? Without discounting the evidence of experience, it would seem that other criteria too must be brought to bear in pursuing the theological task.

MAR

A. Pre-modern accounts of religious experience

I.5.1 St Augustine of Hippo, from *The Confessions*

Augustine here explores the relationship between experience of God in worship and knowledge of God, and recalls his own conversion.

Book I

1. Great art thou, O Lord, and greatly to be praised; great is thy power, and of thy wisdom there is no end. And man, being a part of thy creation, desires to praise thee, man, who bears about with him his mortality, the witness of his sin, even the witness that thou 'resistest the proud,' – yet man, this part of thy creation, desires to praise thee. Thou movest us to delight in praising thee; for thou hast formed us for thyself, and our hearts are restless till they find rest in thee. Lord, teach me to know and understand which of these should be first, to call on thee, or to praise thee; and likewise to know thee, or to call upon thee. But who is there that calls upon thee without knowing thee? For he that knows thee not may call upon thee as other than thou art. Or perhaps we call on thee that we may know thee. 'But how shall they call on Him in whom they have not believed? or how shall they believe without a preacher?' And those who seek the Lord shall praise him. For those who seek shall find him, and those who find him shall praise him. Let me seek thee, Lord, in calling on thee, and call on thee in believing in thee; for thou hast been preached unto us. O Lord, my faith calls on thee, – that faith which thou hast imparted to me, which thou hast breathed into me through the incarnation of thy Son, through the ministry of thy preacher.

2. And how shall I call upon my God – my God and my Lord? For when I call on him I ask him to come into me. And what place is there in me into which my God can come – into which God can come, even he who made heaven and earth? Is there anything in me, O Lord my God, that can contain thee? Do indeed the very heaven and the earth, which thou hast made, and in which thou hast made me, contain thee? Or, as nothing could exist without thee, doth whatever exists contain thee? Why, then, do I ask thee to come into me, since I indeed exist, and could not exist if thou wert not in me? Because I am not yet in hell, though thou art even there; for 'if I go down into hell thou art there.' I could not therefore exist, could not exist at all, O my God, unless thou wert in me. Or should I not rather say, that I could not exist unless I were in thee from whom are all things, by whom are all things, in whom are all things? Even so, Lord; even so. Where do I call thee to, since thou art in me, or whence canst thou come into me? For where outside

heaven and earth can I go that from thence my God may come into me who has said, 'I fill heaven and earth'?

3. Since, then, thou fillest heaven and earth, do they contain thee? Or, as they contain thee not, dost thou fill them, and yet there remains something over? And where dost thou pour forth that which remaineth of thee when the heaven and earth are filled? Or, indeed, is there no need that thou who containest all things shouldest be contained of any, since those things which thou fillest thou fillest by containing them? For the vessels which thou fillest do not sustain thee, since should they even be broken thou wilt not be poured forth. And when thou art poured forth on us, thou art not cast down, but we are uplifted; nor art thou dissipated, but we are drawn together. But, as thou fillest all things, dost thou fill them with thy whole self, or, as even all things cannot altogether contain thee, do they contain a part, and do all at once contain the same part? Or has each its own proper part – the greater more, the smaller less? Is, then, one part of thee greater, another less? Or is it that thou art wholly everywhere whilst nothing altogether contains thee?

Book VIII

28. But when a profound reflection had, from the secret depths of my soul, drawn together and heaped up all my misery before the sight of my heart, there arose a mighty storm, accompanied by as mighty a shower of tears. Which, that I might pour forth fully, with its natural expressions, I stole away from Alypius; for it suggested itself to me that solitude was fitter for the business of weeping. So I retired to such a distance that even his presence could not be oppressive to me. Thus was it with me at that time, and he perceived it; for something, I believe, I had spoken, wherein the sound of my voice appeared choked with weeping, and in that state had I risen up. He then remained where we had been sitting, most completely astonished. I flung myself down, how, I know not, under a certain fig-tree, giving free course to my tears, and the streams of mine eyes gushed out, an acceptable sacrifice unto thee. And, not indeed in these words, yet to this effect, spake I much unto thee, – 'But thou, O Lord, how long?' 'How long, Lord? Wilt thou be angry for ever? Oh, remember not against us former iniquities;' for I felt that I was enthralled by them. I sent up these sorrowful cries, – 'how long, how long? Tomorrow, and tomorrow? Why not now? Why is there not this hour an end to my uncleanness?'

29. I was saying these things and weeping in the most bitter contrition of my heart, when, lo, I heard the voice as of a boy or girl, I know not which, coming from a neighboring house, chanting, and oft repeating, 'Take up and read; take up and read.' Immediately my countenance was changed, and I began most earnestly to consider whether it was usual for children in any kind of game to sing such words; nor could I remember ever to have heard the like. So, restraining the torrent of my tears, I rose up, interpreting it no

other way than as a command to me from Heaven to open the book, and to read the first chapter I should light upon. For I had heard of Antony, that, accidentally coming in whilst the gospel was being read, he received the admonition as if what was read were addressed to him, 'Go and sell that thou hast, and give to the poor, and thou shalt have treasure in heaven; and come and follow me.' And by such oracle was he forthwith converted unto thee. So quickly I returned to the place where Alypius was sitting; for there had I put down the volume of the apostles, when I rose thence. I grasped, opened, and in silence read that paragraph on which my eyes first fell, – 'Not in rioting and drunkenness, not in chambering and wantonness, not in strife and envying; but put ye on the Lord Jesus Christ, and make not provision for the flesh, to fulfill the lusts thereof.' No further would I read, nor did I need; for instantly, as the sentence ended, – by a light, as it were, of security infused into my heart, – all the gloom of doubt vanished away.

(Taken from the Nicene and Post-Nicene Fathers, series I, vol I, ed. Philip Schaff, trans. J. G. Pilkington.)

I.5.2 St John of the Cross, from the *Ascent of Mt Carmel*

St John describes the work of faith when in 'the dark night of the soul', the experience where all things are stripped away by God.

Book II Chapter III

1. Faith, say the theologians, is a habit of the soul, certain and obscure. And the reason for its being an obscure habit is that it makes us believe truths revealed by God Himself, which transcend all natural light, and exceed all human understanding, beyond all proportion. Hence it follows that, for the soul, this excessive light of faith which is given to it is thick darkness, for it overwhelms greater things and does away with small things, even as the light of the sun overwhelms all other lights whatsoever, so that when it shines and disables our visual faculty they appear not to be lights at all. So that it blinds it and deprives it of the sight that has been given to it, inasmuch as its light is great beyond all proportion and transcends the faculty of vision. Even so the light of faith, by its excessive greatness, oppresses and disables that of the understanding; for the latter, of its own power, extends only to natural knowledge, although it has a faculty for the supernatural, whenever Our Lord is pleased to give it supernatural activity.

2. Wherefore a man can know nothing by himself, save after a natural manner, which is only that which he attains by means of the senses. For this cause he must have the phantasms and the forms of objects present in themselves and in their likenesses; otherwise it cannot be, for, as philosophers say: Ab objecto et potentia paritur notitia. That is: From the object that is present and from the faculty, knowledge is born in the soul. Wherefore, if one should speak to a man of things which he has never been able to understand, and whose likeness he has never seen, he would have no more illumination from them whatever than if naught had been said of them to him. I take an example. If one should say to a man that on a certain island there is an animal which he has never seen, and give him no idea of the likeness of that animal, that he may compare it with others that he has seen, he will have no more knowledge of it, or idea of its form, than he had before, however much is being said to him about it. And this will be better understood by another and a more apt example. If one should describe to a man that was born blind, and has never seen any colour, what is meant by a white colour or by a yellow, he would understand it but indifferently, however fully one might describe it to him; for, as he has never seen such colours or anything like them by which he may judge them, only their names would remain with him; for these he would be able to comprehend through the ear, but not their forms or figures, since he has never seen them.

3. Even so is faith with respect to the soul; it tells us of things which we

have never seen or understood, nor have we seen or understood aught that resembles them, since there is naught that resembles them at all. And thus we have no light of natural knowledge concerning them, since that which we are told of them bears no relation to any sense of ours; we know it by the ear alone, believing that which we are taught, bringing our natural light into subjection and treating it as if it were not. For, as Saint Paul says, Fides ex auditu. As though he were to say: Faith is not knowledge which enters by any of the senses, but is only the consent given by the soul to that which enters through the ear.

4. And faith far transcends even that which is indicated by the examples given above. For not only does it give no information and knowledge, but, as we have said, it deprives us of all other information and knowledge, and blinds us to them, so that they cannot judge it well. For other knowledge can be acquired by the light of the understanding; but the knowledge that is of faith is acquired without the illumination of the understanding, which is rejected for faith; and in its own light, if that light be not darkened, it is lost. Wherefore Isaias said: Si non credideritis, non intelligetis. That is: If ye believe not, ye shall not understand. It is clear, then, that faith is dark night for the soul, and it is in this way that it gives it light; and the more the soul is darkened, the greater is the light that comes to it. For it is by blinding that it gives light, according to this saying of Isaias. For if ye believe not, ye shall not (he says) have light. And thus faith was foreshadowed by that cloud which divided the children of Israel and the Egyptians when the former were about to enter the Red Sea, whereof Scripture says: Erat nubes tenebrosa, et illuminans noctem. This is to say that that cloud was full of darkness and gave light to the night.

5. A wondrous thing it is that, though it was dark, it should give light to the night. This was said to show that faith, which is a black and dark cloud to the soul (and likewise is night, since in the presence of faith the soul is deprived of its natural light and is blinded), can with its darkness give light and illumination to the darkness of the soul, for it was fitting that the disciples should thus be like the master. For man, who is in darkness, could not fittingly be enlightened save by other darkness, even as David teaches us, saying: Dies diei eructat verbum et nox nocti indicat scientiam. Which signifies: Day unto day uttereth and aboundeth in speech, and night unto night showeth knowledge. Which, to speak more clearly, signifies: The day, which is God in bliss, where it is day to the blessed angels and souls who are now day, communicates and reveals to them the Word, which is His Son, that they may know Him and enjoy Him. And the night, which is faith in the Church Militant, where it is still night, shows knowledge is night to the Church, and consequently to every soul, which knowledge is night to it, since it is without clear beatific wisdom; and, in the presence of faith, it is blind as to its natural light.

6. So that which is to be inferred from this that faith, because it is dark

night, gives light to the soul, which is in darkness, that there may come to be fulfilled that which David likewise says to this purpose, in these works: *Et nox illuminatio mea in deliciis meis.* Which signifies: the night will be illumination in my delights. Which is as much as to say: In the delights of my pure contemplation and union with God, the night of faith shall be my guide. Wherein he gives it clearly to be understood that the soul must be in darkness in order to have light for this road.

(*Taken from* **The Complete Works of John of the Cross,** *trans.* **E. A. Peers, London: Burns & Oates 1934.**)

I.5.3 Jonathan Edwards, from *A Treatise Concerning the Religious Affections*

Edwards here argues that the presence of 'religious affections', that is moving experiences that seem to come from God, in a person's life is no sign that they do indeed come from God.

Part II

VI. It is no sign that affections are gracious, or that they are otherwise, that persons did not make them themselves, or excite them of their own contrivance and by their own strength.

There are many in these days, that condemn all affections which are excited in a way that the subjects of them can give no account of, as not seeming to be the fruit of any of their own endeavors, or the natural consequence of the faculties and principles of human nature, in such circumstances, and under such means; but to be from the influence of some extrinsic and supernatural power upon their minds. How greatly has the doctrine of the inward experience, or sensible perceiving of the immediate power and operation of the Spirit of God, been reproached and ridiculed by many of late! They say, the manner of the Spirit of God is to co-operate in a silent, secret, and undiscernable way with the use of means, and our own endeavors; so that there is no distinguishing by sense, between the influences of the Spirit of God, and the natural operations of the faculties of our own minds.

And it is true, that for any to expect to receive the saving influences of the Spirit of God, while they neglect a diligent improvement of the appointed means of grace, is unreasonable presumption. And to expect that the Spirit of God will savingly operate upon their minds, without the Spirit's making use of means, as subservient to the effect, is enthusiastical. It is also undoubtedly true, that the Spirit of God is very various in the manner and circumstances of his operations, and that sometimes he operates in a way more secret and gradual, and from smaller beginnings, than at others.

But if there be indeed a power, entirely different from, and beyond our power, or the power of all means and instruments, and above the power of nature, which is requisite in order to the production of saving grace in the heart, according to the general profession of the country; then, certainly it is in no wise unreasonable to suppose, that this effect should very frequently be produced after such a manner, as to make it very manifest, apparent, and sensible that it is so. If grace be indeed owing to the powerful and efficacious operation of an extrinsic agent, or divine efficient out of ourselves, why is it unreasonable to suppose it should seem to be so to them who are the subjects of it? Is it a strange thing, that it should seem to be as it is? When grace in the heart indeed is not produced by our strength, nor is the effect of the natural power of our own faculties, or any means or instruments, but is properly the workmanship and production of the Spirit of the Almighty, is it a strange and unaccountable thing, that it should seem to them who are subjects of it, agreeable to truth, and not right contrary to truth; so that if persons tell of effects that they are conscious to in their own minds, that seem to them not to be from the natural power or operation of their minds, but from the supernatural power of some other agent, it should at once be looked upon as a sure evidence of their being under a delusion, because things seem to them to be as they are? For this is the objection which is made: it is looked upon as a clear evidence, that the apprehensions and affections that many persons have, are not really from such a cause, because they seem to them to be from that cause: they declare that what they are conscious of, seems to them evidently not to be from themselves, but from the mighty power of the Spirit of God; and others from hence condemn them, and determine what they experience is not from the Spirit of God, but from themselves, or from the devil. Thus unreasonably are multitudes treated at this day by their neighbors.

If it be indeed so, as the Scripture abundantly teaches, that grace in the soul is so the effect of God's power, that it is fitly compared to those effects which are farthest from being owing to any strength in the subject, such as a generation, or a being begotten, and resurrection, or a being raised from the dead, and creation, or a being brought out of nothing into being, and that it is an effect wherein the mighty power of God is greatly glorified, and the exceeding greatness of his power is manifested; then what account can be given of it, that the Almighty, in so great a work of his power, should so carefully hide his power, that the subjects of it should be able to discern nothing of it? Or what reason or revelation have any to determine that he does so? If we may judge by the Scripture this is not agreeable to God's manner, in his operations and dispensations; but on the contrary, it is God's manner, in the great works of his power and mercy which he works for his people, to order things so as to make his hand visible, and his power conspicuous, and men's dependence on him most evident, that no flesh should glory in his presence, that God alone might be exalted, and that the excellency of the power might be of God and not of man, and that Christ's power might be manifested in our weakness, and none might say mine own hand hath saved me. So it was in most of those temporal salvations which God wrought for Israel of old, which were types of the salvation of God's people from their spiritual enemies. So it was in the redemption of Israel from their Egyptian bondage; he redeemed them with a strong hand, and an outstretched arm; and that his power might be the more conspicuous, he suffered Israel first to be brought into the most helpless and forlorn circumstances. So it was in the great redemption by Gideon; God would have his army diminished to a handful, and they without any other arms than trumpets and lamps, and earthen pitchers. So it was in the deliverance of Israel from Goliath, by a stripling with a sling and a stone. So it was in that great work of God, his calling the Gentiles, and converting the Heathen world, after Christ's ascension, after that the world by wisdom knew not God, and all the endeavors of philosophers had proved in vain, for many ages, to reform the world, and it was by everything become abundantly evident, that the world was utterly helpless, by anything else but the mighty power of God. And so it was in most of the conversions of particular persons, we have an account of in the history of the New Testament: they were not wrought on in that silent, secret, gradual, and insensible manner, which is now insisted on; but with those manifest evidences of a supernatural power, wonderfully and suddenly causing a great change, which in these days are looked upon as certain signs of delusion and enthusiasm.

The Apostle, in Ephesians 1:18, 19, speaks of God's enlightening the minds of Christians, and so bringing them to believe in Christ, to the end that they might know the exceeding greatness of his power to them who believe. The words are, 'The eyes of our understanding being enlightened; that ye may know what is the hope of his calling, and what the riches of the glory of his inheritance in the saints, and what is the exceeding greatness of his power to ward us who believe, according to the working of his mighty power,' etc. Now when the apostle speaks of their being thus the subjects of his power, in their enlightening and effectual calling, to the end that they might know what his mighty power was to them who believe, he can mean nothing else than, 'that they might know by experience.' But if the saints know this power by experience, then they feel it and discern it, and are conscious of it; as sensibly distinguishable from the natural operations of their own minds, which is not agreeable to a motion of God's operating so secretly, and undiscernably, that it cannot be known that they are the subjects of the influence of any extrinsic power at all, any otherwise than as they may argue it from Scripture assertions; which is a different thing from knowing it by experience.

So that it is very unreasonable and unscriptural to determine that affections are not from the gracious operations of God's Spirit, because they are sensibly not from the persons themselves that are the subjects of them.

On the other hand, it is no evidence that affections are gracious, that they are not properly produced by those who are the subjects of them, or that they arise in their minds in a manner they cannot account for.

There are some who make this an argument in their own favor; when speaking of what they have experienced, they say, 'I am sure I did not make it myself; it was a fruit of no contrivance or endeavor of mine; it came when I thought nothing of it; if I might have the world for it, I cannot make it again when I please.' And hence they determine that what they have experienced, must be from the mighty influence of the Spirit of God, and is of a saving nature; but very ignorantly, and without grounds. What they have been the subjects of, may indeed not be from themselves directly, but may be from the operation of an invisible agent, some spirit besides their own:

but it does not thence follow, that it was from the Spirit of God. There are other spirits who have influence on the minds of men, besides the Holy Ghost. We are directed not to believe every spirit, but to try the spirits, whether they be of God. There are many false spirits, exceeding busy with men, who often transform themselves into angels of light, and do in many wonderful ways, with great subtlety and power, mimic the operations of the Spirit of God. And there are many of Satan's operations which are very distinguishable from the voluntary exercises of men's own minds. They are so, in those dreadful and horrid suggestions, and blasphemous injections with which he follows many persons; and in vain and fruitless frights and terrors, which he is the author of. And the power of Satan may be as immediate, and as evident in false comforts and joys, as in terrors and horrid suggestions; and oftentimes is so in fact. It is not in men's power to put themselves in such raptures, as the Anabaptists in Germany, and many other raving enthusiasts like them, have been the subjects of.

And besides, it is to be considered that persons may have those impressions on their minds, which may not be of their own producing, nor from an evil spirit, but from the Spirit of God, and yet not be from any saving, but a common influence of the Spirit of God; and the subjects of such impressions may be of the number of those we read of, Hebrews 6:4, 5, 'that are once enlightened, and taste of the heavenly gift, and are made partakers of the Holy Ghost, and taste the good word of God, and the power of the world to come;' and yet may be wholly unacquainted with those 'better things that accompany salvations'.

And where neither a good nor evil spirit have any immediate hand, persons, especially such as are of a weak and vapory habit of body, and the brain weak and easily susceptive of impressions, may have strange apprehensions and imaginations, and strong affections attending them, unaccountably arising, which are not voluntarily produced by themselves. We see that such persons are liable to such impressions about temporal things; and there is equal reason, why they should about spiritual things. As a person who is asleep has dreams that he is not the voluntary author of; so may such persons, in like manner, be the subjects of involuntary impressions, when they are awake.

(Taken from The Works of Jonathan Edwards, with a Memoir by Sereno E. Dwight, *revised and corrected by Edward Hickman 1834, repr. Edinburgh: Banner of Truth 1974.)*

B. The modern attempts to found religion on experience

I.5.4 Friedrich Schleiermacher, from *The Christian Faith*

Schleiermacher here describes the nature of the piety which he regards as the essence of all religious experience. It is, famously, 'a feeling of absolute dependence'.

§ 3. *The piety which forms the basis of all ecclesiastical communions is, considered purely in itself, neither a Knowing nor a Doing, but a modification of Feeling, or of immediate self-consciousness.*

1. That a Church is nothing but a communion or association relating to religion or piety, is beyond all doubt for us Evangelical (Protestant) Christians, since we regard it as equivalent to degeneration in a Church when it begins to occupy itself with other matters as well, whether the affairs of science or of outward organization; just as we also always oppose any attempt on the part of the leaders of State or of science, as such, to order the affairs of religion.
. . .

2. When Feeling and Self-consciousness are here put side by side as equivalent, it is by no means intended to introduce generally a manner of speech in which the two expressions would be simply synonymous. The term 'feeling' has in the language of common life been long current in this religious connexion; but for scientific usage it needs to be more precisely defined; and it is to do this that the other word is added. So that if anyone takes the word 'feeling' in a sense so wide as to include unconscious states, he will by the other word be reminded that such is not the usage we are here maintaining. Again, to the term 'self-consciousness' is added the determining epithet 'immediate,' lest anyone should think of a kind of self-consciousness which is not feeling at all . . . It may rather be presumed that in this respect everyone has a twofold experience. In the first place, it is everybody's experience that there are moments in which all thinking and willing retreat behind a self-consciousness of one form or another; but, in the second place, that at times this same form of self-consciousness persists unaltered during a series of diverse acts of thinking and willing, taking up no relation to these, and thus not being in the proper sense even an accompaniment of them. Thus joy and sorrow – those mental phases which are always so important in the realm of religion – are genuine states of feeling, in the proper sense explained above; whereas self-approval and self-reproach, apart from their subsequently passing into joy and sorrow, belong in themselves rather to the objective consciousness of self, as results of an analytic contemplation.
. . .

4. But now (these three, Feeling, Knowing, and Doing being granted) while we here set forth once more the oft-asserted view that, of the three, Feeling is the one to which piety belongs, it is not in any wise meant, as indeed the above discussion shows, that piety is excluded from all connexion with Knowing and Doing. For, indeed, it is the case in general that the immediate self-consciousness is always the mediating link in the transition between moments in which Knowing predominates and those in which Doing predominates, so that a different Doing may proceed from the same Knowing in different people according as a different determination of self-consciousness enters in. And thus it will fall to piety to stimulate Knowing and Doing, and every moment in which piety has a predominant place will contain within itself one or both of these in germ. But just this is the very truth represented by our proposition, and is in no wise an objection to it; for were it otherwise the religious moments could not combine with the others to form a single life, but piety would be something isolated and without any influence upon the other mental functions of our lives. However, in representing this truth, and thus securing to piety its own peculiar province in its connexion with all other provinces, our proposition is opposing the assertions from other quarters that piety is a Knowing, or a Doing, or both, or a state made up of Feeling, Knowing, and Doing; and in this polemical connexion our proposition must now be still more closely considered.

§ 4. *The common element in all howsoever diverse expressions of piety, by which these are conjointly distinguished from all other feelings, or, in other words, the self-identical essence of piety, is this: the consciousness of being absolutely dependent, or, which is the same thing, of being in relation with God.*

1. In any actual state of consciousness, no matter whether it merely accompanies a thought or action or occupies a moment for itself, we are never simply conscious of our Selves in their unchanging identity, but are always at the same time conscious of a changing determination of them. The Ego in itself can be represented objectively; but every consciousness of self is at the same time the consciousness of a variable state of being. But in this distinction of the latter from the former, it is implied that the variable does not proceed purely from the self-identical, for in that case it could not be distinguished from it. Thus in every self-consciousness there are two elements, which we might call respectively a self-caused element and a non-self-caused element; or a Being and a Having-by-some-means-come-to-be.
. . .

In self-consciousness there are only two elements: the one expresses the existence of the subject for itself, the other its co-existence with an Other.

Now to these two elements, as they exist together in the temporal self-consciousness, correspond in the subject its *Receptivity* and its (spontaneous) *Activity* . . . To these propositions assent can be unconditionally demanded;

and no one will deny them who is capable of a little introspection and can find interest in the real subject of our present inquiries.

2. The common element in all those determinations of self-consciousness which predominantly express a receptivity affected from some outside quarter is the *feeling of Dependence*. On the other hand, the common element in all those determinations which predominantly express spontaneous movement and activity is the *feeling of Freedom*. The former is the case not only because it is by an influence from some other quarter that we have come to such a state, but particularly because we *could* not so become except by means of an Other. The latter is the case because in these instances an Other is determined by us, and without our spontaneous activity could not be so determined.

. . .

Let us now think of the feeling of dependence and the feeling of freedom as *one*, in the sense that not only the subject but the corresponding Other is the same for both. Then the total self-consciousness made up of both together is one of *Reciprocity* between the subject and the corresponding Other. Now let us suppose the totality of all moments of feeling, of both kinds, as one whole: then the corresponding Other is also to be supposed as a totality or as one, and then that term 'reciprocity' is the right one for our self-consciousness in general, inasmuch as it expresses our connexion with everything which either appeals to our receptivity or is subjected to our activity. And this is true not only when we particularize this Other and ascribe to each of its elements a different degree of relation to the twofold consciousness within us, but also when we think of the total 'outside' as one, and moreover (since it contains other receptivities and activities to which we have a relation) as one together with ourselves, that is, as a *World*.

. . .

4. As regards the identification of absolute dependence with 'relation to God' in our proposition: this is to be understood in the sense that the *Whence* of our receptive and active existence, as implied in this self-consciousness, is to be designated by the word 'God,' and that this is for us the really original signification of that word. In this connexion we have first of all to remind ourselves that, as we have seen in the foregoing discussion, this 'Whence' is not the world, in the sense of the totality of temporal existence, and still less is it any single part of the world.

(Taken from F. D. E. Schleiermacher. The Christian Faith, *ed. H. R. Mackintosh and J. S. Stewart, Edinburgh: T&T Clark 1999, §§3–4.)*

I.5.5 Rudolph Otto, from *The Idea of the Holy*

Otto here offers his account of the universal religious experience of human beings, as a 'mysterium tremendum', and analyses this concept.

'Holiness' – 'the holy' – is a category of interpretation and valuation peculiar to the sphere of religion. It is, indeed, applied by transference to another sphere – that of ethics – but it is not itself derived from this. While it is complex, it contains a quite specific element or 'moment', which sets it apart from 'the rational' in the meaning we gave to that word above, and which remains inexpressible – an ἄρρητον or *ineffabile* – in the sense that it completely eludes apprehension in terms of concepts. The same thing is true (to take a quite different region of experience) of the category of the beautiful.

It will be our endeavour to suggest that unnamed Something to the reader as far as we may, so that he may himself feel it. There is no religion in which it does not live as the real innermost core, and without it no religion would be worthy of the name. It is pre-eminently a living force in the Semitic religions, and of these again in none has it such vigour as in that of the Bible. Here, too, it has a name of its own, viz. the Hebrew *qādôsh*, to which the Greek ἅγιος and the Latin *sanctus*, and, more accurately still, *sacer*, are the corresponding terms. It is not, of course, disputed that these terms in all three languages connote, as part of their meaning, *good, absolute goodness*, when, that is, the notion has ripened and reached the highest stage in its development. And we then use the word 'holy' to translate them. But this 'holy' then represents the gradual shaping and filling in with ethical meaning, or what we shall call the 'schematization', of what was a unique original feeling-response, which can be in itself ethically neutral and claims consideration in its own right. And when this moment or element first emerges and begins its long development, all those expressions (*qādôsh*, ἅγιος, *sacer*, etc.) mean beyond all question something quite other than 'the good'. This is universally agreed by contemporary criticism, which rightly explains the rendering of *qādôsh* by 'good' as a mistranslation and unwarranted 'rationalization' or 'moralization' of the term.

Accordingly, it is worth while, as we have said, to find a word to stand for this element in isolation, this 'extra' in the meaning of 'holy' above and beyond the meaning of goodness. By means of a special term we shall the better be able, first, to keep the meaning clearly apart and distinct, and second, to apprehend and classify connectedly whatever subordinate forms or stages of development it may show. For this purpose I adopt a word coined from the Latin *numen*. *Omen* has given us 'ominous', and there is no reason why from *numen* we should not similarly form a word 'numinous'. I shall speak, then of a unique 'numinous' category of value and of a definitely 'numinous' state of mind, which is always found wherever the category is applied. This mental state is perfectly *sui generis* and irreducible to any other; and therefore, like every absolutely primary and elementary datum, while it admits of being discussed, it cannot be strictly defined. There is only one way to help another to an understanding of it. He must be guided and led on by consideration and discussion of the matter through the ways of his own mind, until he reach the point at which 'the numinous' in him perforce begins to stir, to start into life and into consciousness. We can cooperate in this process by bringing before his notice all that can be found in other regions of the mind, already known and familiar, to resemble, or again to afford some special contrast to, the particular experience we wish to elucidate. Then we must add: 'This X of ours is not precisely *this* experience, but akin to this one and the opposite of that other. Cannot you now realize for yourself what it is?' In other words our X cannot, strictly speaking, be taught, it can only be evoked, awakened in the mind; as everything that comes 'of the spirit' must be awakened.

Let us consider the deepest and most fundamental element in all strong and sincerely felt religious emotion. Faith unto salvation, trust, love – all these are there. But over and above these is an element which may also on occasion, quite apart from them, profoundly affect us and occupy the mind with a wellnigh bewildering strength. Let us follow it up with every effort of sympathy and imaginative intuition wherever it is to be found, in the lives of those around us, in sudden, strong ebullitions of personal piety and the frames of mind such ebullitions evince, in the fixed and ordered solemnities of rites and liturgies, and again in the atmosphere that clings to old religious monuments and buildings, to temples and to churches. If we do so we shall find we are dealing with something for which there is only one appropriate expression, '*mysterium tremendum*'.

The Element of Awfulness

To get light upon the positive '*quale*' of the object of these feelings, we must analyse more closely our phrase *mysterium tremendum*, and we will begin first with the adjective.

Tremor is in itself merely the perfectly familiar and 'natural' emotion of *fear*. But here the term is taken, aptly enough but still only by analogy, to denote a quite specific kind of emotional response, wholly distinct from that of being afraid, though it so far resembles it that the analogy of fear may be used to throw light upon its nature. There are in some languages special expressions which denote, either exclusively or in the first instance, this 'fear' that is more than fear proper. The Hebrew *hiqdīsh* (hallow) is an example. To 'keep a thing holy in the heart' means to mark it off by a feeling of peculiar dread, not to be mistaken for any ordinary dread, that is, to appraise it by the category of the numinous.

The Element of 'Overpoweringness' ('majestas')

We have been attempting to unfold the implications of that aspect of the *mysterium tremendum* indicated by the adjective, and the result so far may be summarized in two words, constituting, as before, what may be called an 'ideogram', rather than a concept proper, viz. 'absolute unapproachability'.

It will be felt at once that there is yet a further element which must be added, that, namely, of 'might', 'power', 'absolute overpoweringness'. We will take to represent this the term *majestas*, majesty – the more readily because anyone with a feeling for language must detect a last faint trace of the numinous still clinging to the word. The *tremendum* may then be rendered more adequately *tremenda majestas*, or 'aweful majesty'. This second element of majesty may continue to be vividly preserved, where the first, that of unapproachability, recedes and dies away, as may be seen, for example, in mysticism. It is especially in relation to this element of majesty or absolute overpoweringness that the creature-consciousness, of which we have already spoken, comes upon the scene, as a sort of shadow or subjective reflection of it. Thus, in contrast to 'the overpowering' of which we are conscious as an object over against the self, there is the feeling of one's own submergence, of being but 'dust and ashes' and nothingness. And this forms the numinous raw material for the feeling of religious humility

Here we must revert once again to Schleiermacher's expression for what we call 'creature-feeling', viz. the 'feeling of dependence'. We found fault with this phrase before on the ground that Schleiermacher thereby takes as basis and point of departure what is merely a secondary effect; that he sets out to teach a consciousness of the religious *object* only by way of an inference from the shadow it casts upon *self*-consciousness. We have now a further criticism to bring against it, and it is this. By 'feeling of dependence' Schleiermacher means consciousness of *being conditioned* (as effect by cause), and so he develops the implications of this logically enough in his sections upon Creation and Preservation. On the side of the deity the correlate to 'dependence' would thus be 'causality', i.e. God's character as all-causing and all-conditioning. But a sense of this does not enter at all into that immediate and first-hand religious emotion which we have in the moment of worship, and which we can recover in a measure for analysis; it belongs on the contrary decidedly to the *rational* side of the idea of God; its implications admit of precise conceptual determination; and it springs from quite a distinct source. The difference between the 'feeling of dependence' of Schleiermacher and that which finds typical utterance in the words of Abraham already cited might be expressed as that between the consciousness of *createdness* and the consciousness of *creaturehood*. In the one case you have the creature as the work of the divine creative act; in the other, impotence and general nothingness as against overpowering might, dust and ashes as against 'majesty'

The Element of 'Energy' or Urgency

There is, finally, a third element comprised in those of *tremendum* and *majestas*, awefulness and majesty, and this I venture to call the 'urgency' or 'energy' of the numinous object.

We gave to the object to which the numinous consciousness is directed the name *mysterium tremendum*, and we then set ourselves first to determine the meaning of the adjective *tremendum* – which we found to be itself only justified by analogy – because it is more easily analysed than the substantive idea *mysterium*. We have now to turn to this, and try, as best we may, by hint and suggestion, to get to a clearer apprehension of what it implies.

The 'Wholly Other'

We need an expression for the mental reaction peculiar to it; and here, too, only one word seems appropriate though, as it is strictly applicable only to a 'natural' state of mind, it has here meaning only by analogy: it is the word 'stupor'. *Stupor* is plainly a different thing from *tremor*; it signifies blank wonder, an astonishment that strikes us dumb amazement absolute.

The Element of Fascination

The qualitative *content* of the numinous experience, to which 'the mysterious' stands as *form*, is in one of its aspects the element of daunting 'awefulness' and 'majesty', which has already been dealt with in detail; but it is clear that it has at the same time another aspect, in which it shows itself as something uniquely attractive and *fascinating*.

These two qualities, the daunting and the fascinating, now combine in a strange harmony of contrasts, and the resultant dual character of the numinous consciousness, to which the entire religious development bears witness, at any rate from the level of the 'daemonic dread' onwards, is at once the strangest and most noteworthy phenomenon in the whole history of religion. The daemonic-divine object may appear to the mind an object of horror and dread, but at the same time it is no less something that allures with a potent charm, and the creature, who trembles before it, utterly cowed and cast down, has always at the same time the impulse to turn to it, nay even to make it somehow his own. The 'mystery' is for him not merely something to be wondered at but something that entrances him; and beside that in it which bewilders and confounds, he feels a something that captivates and transports him with a strange ravishment, rising often enough to the pitch of dizzy intoxication; it is the Dionysiac-element in the numen.

(Taken from Rudolph Otto, The Idea of the Holy, trans. John W. Harvey, Oxford: Oxford University Press 1923, chapters 2 and 3.)

I.5.6 Karl Rahner, from *Foundations of Christian Faith*

Rahner's account of the universal religious experience concerns 'subjectivity', or 'self-awareness'.

PERSONHOOD AS PRESUPPOSITION OF THE CHRISTIAN MESSAGE

With regard to the presuppositions of the revealed message of Christianity, the first thing to be said about man is that he is person and subject.

There is no need to explain in any great detail that a notion of person and subject is of fundamental importance for the possibility of Christian revelation and the self-understanding of Christianity. A personal relationship to God, a genuinely dialogical history of salvation between God and man, the acceptance of one's own, unique, eternal salvation, the notion of responsibility before God and his judgment, all of these assertions of Christianity, however they are to be explained more precisely, imply that man is what we want to say here: person and subject. The same thing is true when we speak of a verbal revelation in Christianity, when we say that God has spoken to man, has called him into his presence, that in prayer man can and should speak with God. All of these assertions are terribly obscure and difficult, but they make up the concrete reality of Christianity. And none of this would be intelligible unless we include in our understanding of Christianity explicitly or implicitly what we mean here by 'person' and 'subject.'

What is meant more precisely by the subjectivity which man experiences becomes clearer when we say that man is a transcendent being.

THE TRANSCENDENT STRUCTURE OF KNOWLEDGE

In spite of the finiteness of his system man is always present to himself in his entirety. He can place everything in question. In his openness to everything and anything, whatever can come to expression can be at least a question for him. In the fact that he affirms the possibility of a merely *finite* horizon of questioning, this possibility is already surpassed, and man shows himself to be a being with an *infinite* horizon. In the fact that he experiences his finiteness radically, he reaches beyond this finiteness and experiences himself as a transcendent being, as spirit. The infinite horizon of human questioning is experienced as an horizon which recedes further and further the more answers man can discover.

Man can try to evade the mysterious infinity which opens up before him in his questions. Out of fear of the mysterious he can take flight to the familiar and the everyday. But the infinity which he experiences himself exposed to also permeates his everyday activities. Basically he is always still on the way. Every goal that he can point to in knowledge and in action is always relativized, is always a provisional step. Every answer is always just the beginning of a new question. Man experiences himself as infinite possibility because in practice and in theory he necessarily places every sought-after result in question. He always situates it in a broader horizon which looms before him in its vastness. He is the spirit who experiences himself as spirit in that he does not experience himself as *pure* spirit. Man is not the unquestioning and unquestioned infinity of reality. He is the question which rises up before him, empty, but really and inescapably, and which can never be settled and never adequately answered by him.

THE POSSIBILITY OF EVADING THE EXPERIENCE OF TRANSCENDENCE

A person can, of course, shrug his shoulders and ignore this experience of transcendence. He can devote himself to his concrete world, his work, his activity in the categorical realm of time and space, to the service of his system at certain points which are the focal points of reality for him. That is possible in three ways:

1. Most people will do this in a naive way. They live at a distance from themselves in that concrete part of their lives and of the world around them which can be manipulated and controlled. They have enough to do there, and it is very interesting and important. And if they ever reflect at all on anything which goes beyond all this, they can always say that it is more sensible not to break one's head over it.

2. Such an evasion of this question and of accepting human transcendence can also take place along with the resolve to accept categorical existence and its tasks, recognizing and accepting the fact that everything is encompassed by an ultimate question. This question is perhaps left as a question. One believes that it can be postponed in silence and in a perhaps sensible scepticism. But when one explains that it cannot be answered, he is admitting that in the final analysis such a question cannot be evaded.

3. There is also a perhaps despairing involvement in the categorical realm of human existence. One goes about his business, he reads, he gets angry, he does his work, he does research, he achieves something, he earns money. And in a final, perhaps unadmitted despair he says to himself that the whole as a whole makes no sense, and that one does well to suppress the question about the meaning of it all and to reject it as an unanswerable and hence meaningless question.

We can never know unambiguously which of these three possibilities is the case in any given person.

THE PRE-APPREHENSION OF BEING

Man is a transcendent being insofar as all of his knowledge and all of his conscious activity is grounded in a pre-apprehension (*Vorgriff*) of 'being' as such, in an unthematic but ever-present knowledge of the infinity of reality (as we can put it provisionally and somewhat boldly). We are presupposing that this infinite pre-apprehension is not grounded by the fact that it can apprehend nothingness as such. We must make this presupposition because nothingness grounds nothing. Nothingness cannot be the term of this pre-apprehension, cannot be what draws and moves and sets in motion that reality which man experiences as his real life and not as nothingness. To be sure, a person also has the experience of emptiness, of inner fragility, and, if we want to call it so lest we make it innocuous, of the absurdity of what confronts him. But he also experiences hope, the movement towards liberating freedom, and the responsibility which imposes upon him real burdens and also blesses them.

But if a person experiences *both* things and nevertheless his experience is *one*, and in it all the individual movements and experiences are borne by an ultimate and primordial movement, and if he cannot be a gnostic who either recognizes two primordial realities or accepts a dualism in the ultimate and primordial ground of being, if he cannot accept this because it contradicts the unity of his experience, then only *one* possibility is left: a person can understand that absolute being establishes limits and boundaries outside of itself, and that it could will something that is limited. But logically and existentielly he cannot think that the movements of hope and the desire to reach out that he really experiences are only a charming and foolish illusion. He cannot think that the ultimate ground of everything is empty nothingness, provided he gives the term 'nothingness' any meaning at all, and does not simply use it to signal that real and genuine existentiell anxiety that he actually experiences.

Hence what grounds man's openness and his reaching out in the unlimited expanse of his transcendence cannot be nothingness, an absolutely empty void. For to assert that of a void would make absolutely no sense. But since on the other hand this pre-apprehension as merely a question is not self-explanatory, it must be understood as due to the working of that to which man is open, namely, being in an absolute sense. But the movement of transcendence is not the subject creating its own unlimited space as though it had absolute power over being, but it is the infinite horizon of being making itself manifest. Whenever man in his transcendence experiences himself as questioning, as disquieted by the appearance of being, as open to something ineffable, he cannot understand himself as subject in the sense of an *absolute* subject, but only in the sense of one who receives being, ultimately only in the sense of grace. In this context 'grace' means the freedom of the ground of being which gives being to man, a freedom which man experiences in his finiteness and contingency, and means as well what we call 'grace' in a more strictly theological sense.

THE PRE-APPREHENSION AS CONSTITUTIVE OF PERSON

Insofar as man is a transcendent being, he is confronted by himself, is responsible for himself, and hence is person and subject. For it is only in the presence of the infinity of being, as both revealed and concealed, that an existent is in a position and has a standpoint from out of which he can assume responsibility for himself. A finite system as such can experience itself as finite only if in its origins it has its own existence by the fact that, as this conscious subject, it comes from something else which is not itself and which is not just an individual system, but is the original unity which anticipates and is the fullness of every conceivable system and of every individual and distinct subject. We shall show later how it is from this that we can acquire an original, transcendental insight into what we call creatureliness.

It is self-evident that this transcendental experience of human transcendence is not the experience of some definite, particular objective thing which is experienced alongside of other objects. It is rather a basic mode of being which is prior to and permeates every objective experience. We must emphasize again and again that the transcendence meant here is not the thematically conceptualized 'concept' of transcendence in which transcendence is reflected upon objectively. It is rather the a priori openness of the subject to being as such, which is present precisely when a person experiences himself as involved in the multiplicity of cares and concerns and fears and hopes of his everyday world. Real transcendence is always in the background, so to speak, in those origins of human life and human knowledge over which we have no control. This real transcendence is never captured by metaphysical reflection, and in its purity, that is, as not mediated objectively, it can be approached asymptotically at most, if at all, in mystical experience and perhaps in the experience of final loneliness in the face of death. Such an original experience of transcendence is something different from philosophical discussion about it, and precisely because it can usually be present only through the mediation of the categorical objectivity of man or of the world around him, this transcendental experience can easily be overlooked. It is present only as a secret ingredient, so to speak. But man is and remains a transcendent being, that is, he is that existent to whom the silent and uncontrollable infinity of reality is always present as mystery. This makes man totally open to this mystery and precisely in this way he becomes conscious of himself as person and as subject.

(*Taken from Karl Rahner,* Foundations of Christian Faith: An Introduction to the Idea of Christianity, *trans. William V. Dych, London: Darton, Longman & Todd 1978, pp. 26–35.*)

I.5.7 Ludwig Feuerbach, from *The Essence of Christianity*

Feuerbach argues that belief in God is merely wish-fulfilment: we would like there to be a God, because we do experience the world in ways that would make this an encouragement and a help, and so we invent a God to meet our needs.

Man has his highest being, his God, in himself; not in himself as an individual, but in his essential nature, his species. No individual is an adequate representation of his species, but only the human individual is conscious of the distinction between the species and the individual; in the sense of this distinction lies the root of religion. The yearning of man after something above himself is nothing else than the longing after the perfect type of his nature, the yearning to be free from himself, *i.e.*, from the limits and defects of his individuality. Individuality is the self-conditionating, the self-limitation of the species. Thus man has cognisance of nothing above himself, of nothing beyond the nature of humanity; but to the individual man this nature presents itself under the form of an individual man. Thus, for example, the child sees the nature of man *above itself* in the form of its parents, the pupil in the form of his tutor. But all feelings which man experiences towards a superior man, nay, in general, all moral feelings which man has towards man, are of a religious nature. *Man feels nothing towards God which he does not also feel towards man. Homo homini deus est.* Want teaches prayer; but in misfortune, in sorrow, man kneels to entreat help of man also. Feeling makes God a man, but for the same reason it makes man a God. How often in deep emotion, which alone speaks genuine truth, man exclaims to man: Thou art, thou hast been my redeemer, my saviour, my protecting spirit, my God! We feel awe, reverence, humility, devout admiration, in thinking of a truly great, noble man; we feel ourselves worthless, we sink into nothing, even in the presence of human greatness. The purely, truly human emotions are religious; but for that reason the religious emotions are purely human: the only difference is, that the religious emotions are vague, indefinite; but even this is only the case when the object of them is indefinite. Where God is positively defined, is the object of positive religion, there God is also the object of positive, definite human feelings, the object of fear and love, and therefore he is a positively human being; for there is nothing more in God than what lies in feeling. If in the heart there is fear and terror, in God there is anger; if in the heart there is joy, hope, confidence, in God there is love. Fear makes itself objective in anger; joy in love, in mercy. 'As it is with me in my heart, so is it with God.' 'As my heart is, so is God.' – Luther. But a merciful and angry God – *Deus vere irascitur* (Melancthon) – is a God no longer distinguishable from the human feelings and nature. Thus even in religion man bows before the nature of man under the form of a personal human being; religion itself expressly declares – and all anthropomorphisms declare this in opposition to Pantheism, – *quod supra nos nihil ad nos*; that is, a God who inspires us with no human emotions, who does not reflect our own emotions, in a word, who is not a man, – such a God is nothing to us, has no interest for us, does not concern us.

Religion has thus no dispositions and emotions which are peculiar to itself; what it claims as belonging exclusively to its object, are simply the same dispositions and emotions that man experiences either in relation to himself (as, for example, to his conscience), or to his fellow-man, or to Nature. You must not fear men, but God; you must not love man, – *i.e.*, not truly, for his own sake, – but God; you must not humble yourselves before human greatness, but only before the Lord; not believe and confide in man, but only in God. Hence comes the danger of worshipping false gods in distinction from the true God. Hence the 'jealousy' of God. Jealousy arises because a being preferred and loved by me directs to another the feelings and dispositions which I claim for myself. But how could I be jealous if the impressions and emotions which I excite in the beloved being were altogether peculiar and apart, were essentially different from the impressions which another can make on him? If, therefore, the emotions of religion were objectively, essentially different from those which lie out of religion, there would be no possibility of idolatry in man or of jealousy in God. As the flute has another sound to me than the trumpet, and I cannot confound the impressions produced by the former with the impressions produced by the latter; so I could not transfer to a natural or human being the emotions of religion, if the object of religion, God, were specifically different from the natural or human being, and consequently the impressions which he produced on me were specific, peculiar.

Feeling alone is the object of feeling. Feeling is sympathy; feeling arises only in the love of man to man. Sensations man has in isolation; feelings only in community. Only in sympathy does sensation rise into feeling. Feeling is aesthetic, human sensation; only what is human is the object of feeling. In feeling man is related to his fellow-man as to himself; he is alive to the sorrows, the joys of another as his own. Thus only by communication does man rise above merely egoistic sensation into feeling; – participated sensation is feeling. He who has no need of participating has no feeling. But what does the hand, the kiss, the glance, the voice, the tone, the word – as the expression of emotion – impart? Emotion. The very same thing which, pronounced or performed without the appropriate tone, without emotion, is only an object of indifferent perception, becomes, when uttered or performed with emotion, an object of feeling. To feel is to have a sense of sensations, to have emotion in the perception of emotion. Hence the brutes rise to feeling only in the sexual relation, and therefore only transiently; for here the being experiences sensation not in relation to itself taken alone, or to an object without sensation, but to a being having like emotions with itself, – not to another as a distinct object, but to an object which in species is identical. Hence Nature is an object of feeling to me only when I regard it as a being akin to me and in sympathy with me.

It is clear from what has been said, that only where in truth, if not according to the subjective conception, the distinction between the divine and human being is abolished, is the objective existence of God, the existence of God as an objective, distinct being, abolished: – only there, I say, is religion made a mere matter of feeling, or conversely, feeling the chief point in religion. The last refuge of theology therefore is feeling. God is renounced by the understanding; he has no longer the dignity of a real object, of a reality which imposes itself on the understanding; hence he is transferred to feeling; in feeling his existence is thought to be secure. And doubtless this is the safest refuge; for to make feeling the essence of religion is nothing else than to make feeling the essence of God. And as certainly as I exist, so certainly does my feeling exist; and as certainly as my feeling exists, so certainly does my God exist. The certainty of God is here nothing else than the self-certainty of human feeling, the yearning after God is the yearning after unlimited, uninterrupted, pure feeling. In life the feelings are interrupted; they collapse; they are followed by a state of void, of insensibility. The religious problem, therefore, is to give fixity to feeling in spite of the vicissitudes of life, and to separate it from repugnant disturbances and limitations: God himself is nothing else than undisturbed, uninterrupted feeling, feeling for which there exists no limits, no opposite. If God were a being distinct from thy feeling, he would be known to thee in some other way than simply in feeling; but just because thou perceivest him only by feeling, he exists only in feeling – he is himself only feeling.

God is man's highest feeling of self, freed from all contrarieties or disagreeables. God is the highest being; therefore, to feel God is the highest feeling. But is not the highest feeling also the highest feeling of self? So long as I have not had the feeling of the highest, so long I have not exhausted my capacity of feeling, so long I do not yet fully know the nature of feeling. What, then, is an object to me in my feeling of the highest being? Nothing else than the highest nature of my power of feeling. So much as a man can feel, so much is (his) God. But the highest degree of the power of feeling is also the highest degree of the feeling of self. In the feeling of the *low* I feel myself lowered, in the feeling of the *high* I feel myself exalted. The feeling of self and feeling are inseparable, otherwise feeling would not belong to myself. Thus God, as an object of feeling, or what is the same thing, the feeling of God, is nothing else than man's highest feeling of self. But God is the freest, or rather the absolutely only free being; thus God is man's highest feeling of freedom. How couldst thou be conscious of the highest being as freedom, or freedom as the highest being, if thou didst not feel thyself free? But when dost thou feel thyself free? When thou feelest God. To feel God is to feel oneself free.

For example, thou feelest desire, passion, the conditions of time and place, as limits. What thou feelest as a limit thou strugglest against, thou breakest loose from, thou deniest. The consciousness of a limit, as such, is already an anathema, a sentence of condemnation pronounced on this limit, for it is an oppressive, disagreeable, negative consciousness. Only the feeling of the good, of the positive, is itself good and positive – is joy. Joy alone is feeling in its element, its paradise, because it is unrestricted activity. The sense of pain in an organ is nothing else than the sense of a disturbed, obstructed, thwarted activity; in a word, the sense of something abnormal, anomalous. Hence thou strivest to escape from the sense of limitation into unlimited feeling. By means of the will, or the imagination, thou negativest limits, and thus obtainest the feeling of freedom. This feeling of freedom is God. God is exalted above desire and passion, above the limits of space and time. But this exaltation is thy own exaltation above that which appears to thee as a limit. Does not this exaltation of the divine being exalt thee? How could it do so, if it were external to thee? No; God is an exalted being only for him who himself has exalted thoughts and feelings. Hence the exaltation of the divine being varies according to that which different men or nations perceive as a limitation to the feeling of self, and which they consequently negative or eliminate from their ideal.

(Taken from George Eliot's translation, Appendix §§1–3.)

I.5.8 Paul Tillich, from *Systematic Theology*

Tillich's 'method of correlation' seeks to bring together the resources of the Christian gospel with our experienced needs.

We have used the term 'ultimate concern' without explanation. Ultimate concern is the abstract translation of the great commandment: 'The Lord, our God, the Lord is one; and you shall love the Lord your God with all your heart, and with all your soul and with all your mind, and with all your strength.' The religious concern is ultimate; it excludes all other concerns from ultimate significance; it makes them preliminary. The ultimate concern is unconditional, independent of any conditions of character, desire, or circumstance. The unconditional concern is total: no part of ourselves or of our world is excluded from it; there is no 'place' to flee from it. The total concern is infinite: no moment of relaxation and rest is possible in the face of a religious concern which is ultimate, unconditional, total, and infinite.

The word 'concern' points to the 'existential' character of religious experience. We cannot speak adequately of the 'object of religion' without simultaneously removing its character as an object. That which is ultimate gives itself only to the attitude of ultimate concern. It is the correlate of an unconditional concern but not a 'highest thing' called 'the absolute' or 'the unconditioned,' about which we could argue in detached objectivity. It is the object of total surrender, demanding also the surrender of our subjectivity while we look at it. It is a matter of infinite passion and interest (Kierkegaard), making us its object whenever we try to make it our object. For this reason we have avoided terms like '*the* ultimate,' '*the* unconditioned,' '*the* universal,' '*the* infinite,' and have spoken of ultimate, unconditional, total, infinite concern. Of course, in every concern there is *something* about which one is concerned; but this something should not appear as a separated object which could be known and handled without concern. This, then, is the first formal criterion of theology: *The object of theology is what concerns us ultimately. Only those propositions are theological which deal with their object in so far as it can become a matter of ultimate concern for us.*

The question now arises: What is the content of our ultimate concern? What *does* concern us unconditionally? The answer, obviously, cannot be a special object, not even God, for the first criterion of theology must remain formal and general. If more is to be said about the nature of our ultimate concern, it must be derived from an analysis of the concept 'ultimate concern.' *Our ultimate concern is that which determines our being or not-being. Only those statements are theological which deal with their object in so far as it can become a matter of being or not-being for us.* This is the second formal criterion of theology.

Nothing can be of ultimate concern for us which does not have the power of threatening and saving our being. The term 'being' in this context does not designate existence in time and space. Existence is continuously threatened and saved by things and events which have no ultimate concern for us. But the term 'being' means the whole of human reality, the structure, the meaning, and the aim of existence. All this is threatened; it can be lost or saved. Man is ultimately concerned about his being and meaning. 'To be or not to be' in *this* sense is a matter of ultimate, unconditional, total, and infinite concern. Man is infinitely concerned about the infinity to which he belongs, from which he is separated, and for which he is longing. Man is totally concerned about the totality which is his true being and which is disrupted in time and space. Man is unconditionally concerned about that which conditions his being beyond all the conditions in him and around him. Man is ultimately concerned about that which determines his ultimate destiny beyond all preliminary necessities and accidents.

The second formal criterion of theology does not point to any special content, symbol, or doctrine. It remains formal and, consequently, open for contents which are able to express 'that which determines our being or nonbeing.' At the same time it excludes contents which do not have this power from entering the theological realm. Whether it is a god who is a being beside others (even a highest being) or an angel who inhabits a celestial realm (called the realm of 'spirits') or a man who possesses supranatural powers (even if he is called a god-man) – none of these is an object of theology if it fails to withstand the criticism of the second formal criterion of theology, that is, if it is not a matter of being or nonbeing for us.

5. THEOLOGY AND CHRISTIANITY

Theology is the methodical interpretation of the contents of the Christian faith. This is implicit in the preceding statements about the theological circle and about theology as a function of the Christian church. The question now arises whether there is a theology outside Christianity and, if so, whether or not the idea of theology is fulfilled in Christian theology in a perfect and final way. Indeed, this is what Christian theology claims; but is it more than a claim, a natural expression of the fact that the theologian works within the theological circle? Has it any validity beyond the periphery of the circle? It is the task of apologetic theology to prove that the Christian claim also has validity from the point of view of those outside the theological circle. Apologetic theology must show that trends which are immanent in all religions and cultures move toward the Christian answer. This refers both to doctrines and to the theological interpretation of theology.

If taken in the broadest sense of the word, theology, the *logos* or the reasoning about *theos* (God and divine things), is as old as religion. Thinking pervades all the spiritual activities of man. Man would not be spiritual without words, thoughts, concepts. This is especially true in religion, the all-embracing function of man's spiritual life. It was a misunderstanding of Schleiermacher's definition of religion ('the feeling of absolute dependence') and a symptom of religious weakness when successors of Schleiermacher located religion in the realm of feeling as one psychological function among others. The banishment of religion into the nonrational corner of subjective emotions in order to have the realms of thought and action free from religious interference was an easy way of escaping the conflicts between religious tradition and modern thought. But this was a death sentence against religion, and religion did not and could not accept it.

Every myth contains a theological thought which can be, and often has been, made explicit. Priestly harmonizations of different myths sometimes disclose profound theological insights. Mystical speculations, as in Vedanta Hinduism, unite meditative elevation with theological penetration. Metaphysical speculations, as in classical Greek philosophy, unite rational analysis with theological vision. Ethical, legal, and ritual interpretations of the divine law create another form of theology on the soil of prophetic monotheism. All this is 'theo-logy,' *logos* of *theos*, a rational interpretation of the religious substance of rites, symbols, and myths.

Christian theology is no exception. It does the same thing, but it does it in a way which implies the claim that it is *the* theology. The basis of this claim is the Christian doctrine that the Logos became flesh, that the principle of the divine self-revelation has become manifest in the event 'Jesus as the Christ.' If this message is true, Christian theology has received a foundation which transcends the foundation of any other theology and which itself cannot be transcended. Christian theology has received something which is absolutely concrete and absolutely universal at the same time. No myth, no mystical vision, no metaphysical principle, no sacred law, has the concreteness of a personal life. In comparison with a personal life everything else is relatively abstract. And none of these relatively abstract foundations of theology has the universality of the Logos, which itself is the principle of universality. In comparison with the Logos everything else is relatively particular. Christian theology is *the* theology in so far as it is based on the tension between the absolutely concrete and the absolutely universal. Priestly and prophetic theologies can be very concrete, but they lack universality. Mystical and metaphysical theologies can be very universal, but they lack concreteness.

It seems paradoxical if one says that only that which is absolutely concrete can also be absolutely universal and vice versa, but it describes the situation adequately. Something that is merely abstract has a limited universality because it is restricted to the realities from which it is abstracted. Something that is merely particular has a limited concreteness because it must exclude other particular realities in order to maintain itself as concrete. Only that which has the power of representing everything particular is absolutely concrete. And only that which has the power of representing everything abstract is absolutely universal. This leads to a point where the absolutely concrete and the absolutely universal are identical. And this is the point at which Christian theology emerges, the point which is described as the 'Logos who has become flesh.' The Logos doctrine as the doctrine of the identity of the absolutely concrete with the absolutely universal is not one theological doctrine among others; it is the only possible foundation of a Christian theology which claims to be *the* theology. It is not necessary to call the absolutely universal the *logos*; other words, derived from other traditions, could replace it. The same is true of the term 'flesh' with its Hellenistic connotations. But it is necessary to accept the vision of early Christianity that if Jesus is called the Christ he must represent everything particular and must be the point of identity between the absolutely concrete and the absolutely universal. In so far as he is absolutely concrete, the relation to him can be a completely existential concern. In so far as he is absolutely universal, the relation to him includes potentially all possible relations and can, therefore, be unconditional and infinite. The biblical reference to the one side is found in the letters of Paul when he speaks of 'being in Christ.' We cannot be *in* anything particular because of the self-seclusion of the particular against the particular. We can be only *in* that which is absolutely concrete and absolutely universal at the same time. The biblical reference to the other side also is given in Paul's writings when he speaks of the subjection of the cosmic powers to the Christ. Only that which is absolutely universal and, at the same time, absolutely concrete can conquer cosmic pluralism.

It was not a cosmological interest (Harnack) but a matter of life and death for the early church which led to the use of the Stoic-Philonic *logos* doctrine in order to express the universal meaning of the event 'Jesus the Christ.' In so doing, the church announced its faith in the victory of the Christ over the demonic-natural powers which constitute polytheism and prevent salvation. For this reason the church fought desperately against the attempt of Arianism to make the Christ into one of the cosmic powers, although the highest, depriving him of both his absolute universality (he is less than God) and his absolute concreteness (he is more than man). The half-God Jesus of Arian theology is neither universal enough nor concrete enough to be the basis of Christian theology.

It is obvious that these arguments do not prove the assertion of faith that in Jesus Christ the Logos has become flesh. But they show that, if this assertion is accepted, Christian theology has a foundation which infinitely transcends the foundations of everything in the history of religion which could be called 'theology.'

(Taken from Paul Tillich, Systematic Theology I, *Chicago: University of Chicago Press 1951, (© University of Chicago), pp. 11–18.)*

PART II:
THE NATURE OF THEOLOGICAL CLAIMS

II.1 Can we know anything about God anyway?

Introductory essay

The teaching that God is unknowable has always been a part of orthodox Christian belief. But so has the claim that God has made himself
known, through his creation and especially through his revelation of
himself in Jesus Christ. In what way can we know an unknowable God?
Different theologians have given different answers to that question,
and in the set of extracts some of them can be explored. Here we shall
find a parallel set of concerns to that we met in section 1.4. Many
theologians combined two ways of approaching this question. First
there is to be found a strongly biblical and trinitarian conception of the
way God is and is not known, and this is often centred on biblical
claims that God the Son makes God the Father known through the
Spirit. Alongside this there often appears a more philosophical treatment based on the distinction between the known and unknown worlds
with which thought deals in general. The stress here is on thought's
incapacity to encompass the divine world. Sometimes the latter
approach seems to predominate, so that there will be found passages
in which the Son's revelation of the Father scarcely seems to shape
the teaching.

For Athanasius (II.1.1), the knowledge we have of God is primarily a
personal relation, the status of being children of God. It is the gift of
Father, Son and Spirit together, and he illustrates it mainly from sayings
from the Gospel of John. Notice that he says that it is both personal
and rational, for it is mediated 'by faith and by a pious and reverent
use of reason'. Knowledge of God cannot be abstractly philosophical,
but comes by the channel God chooses. Hilary of Poitiers (II.1.2), often
called 'the Athanasius of the West', emphasized the eternity, infinity,
invisibility and sheer unknowability of God, to whom the only
approaches can be through faith and worship: 'such acts of devotion
must stand in lieu of definition'. He holds the same to be the case with
our knowledge of the relation between the Father and Son, for we

cannot begin to comprehend the nature of the birth of the Son from the Father in eternity. Yet Hilary is also insistent that the Son, as the image of the invisible God, truly gives knowledge of the Father, with whom he is entirely one. When we come to the Pseudo-Dionysius (II.1.3), who obtained authority in the church because he was supposed to be the one mentioned in Acts 19.34, a very different atmosphere prevails. He appears to be saying some of the same things, but his doctrine of God's unknowability is derived from a confession more of human ignorance than of biblical revelation, more from the human mind's attempt to soar upwards than from the Son's descent into our world. In some contrast to Athanasius in particular, Pseudo-Dionysius speaks of the divine darkness and of God as the universal cause rather than of the eternal life of the triune God. There is little stress on revelation through the Son to balance the traditional teaching of the unknowability of God.

The Orthodox Faith of John of Damascus (II.1.4) represents the climax and summary of the Eastern Church's theology. Beginning with the by now standard account of the unknowability of God, John then treats systematically those things that can be known. His opening vision is scriptural and credal. God implants knowledge of himself in all people and is proclaimed by the creation and its providential order. He makes himself known as one being in three persons especially through the incarnation of his Son by the power of the Spirit and the subsequent series of events through which human salvation was achieved. After a brief rehearsal of the realization of this in the church's teaching, John ends our passage with a philosophical meditation on God's attributes, concluding that our knowledge is not of God's being but of the *qualities* of his being: not of *what* but of *how* God is.

Thomas Aquinas takes up the latter part of John's development, with a mainly philosophical discussion of the knowledge of God and his attributes. His treatment is dominated by something he learned from Pseudo-Dionysius, the notion of God as supreme cause. What is known as the way of causality achieves a limited knowledge of the kind of being that God is by ascending through a knowledge of the created world which is understood as his effect (II.1.5). However, just how limited this knowledge is becomes clear when Aquinas discusses the way in which we come to use language of God. His teaching (II.1.6) is that we know more clearly what God is not than what he is (the 'negative way'), while of our theological language we know only of the way in which we use it of him, not the way in which it applies. It is noteworthy that there is no direct appeal to the christological and trinitarian considerations which so mark the treatments of Athanasius, Hilary and John of Damascus, and Aquinas' largely negative approach to theology had a deep effect in later history when his theological caution was taken out of the context of Christian belief and turned into a sceptical philosophy.

The crucial intervening figure is the philosopher Immanuel Kant (1724–1804) who took the negative way to extremes. Influenced by modern mechanistic science, he held that because the natural world is closed to divine action there can be no proof of the existence of God from the natural world (no 'way of causality') and no demonstration of revelation in history. Kant left a chink open in his appeal to the structures of human moral reasoning, and it was this space that Schlei-ermacher sought to extend by appealing not merely to moral experi-ence but to a dimension of human being he called 'religion', 'piety' or 'feeling' (II.1.7). He is referring in this not to a narrow emotional side of the human being, but to the whole affective dimension of the person, those depths of our being which transcend and embrace our more restricted rational experience. He accepts Kant's view that there can be no knowledge of God which is inferred from the world, but claims that God is immediately present to the human heart and its affective dimensions. Because, however, this is a felt rather than a thought deity, there are strict limits to rational claims to knowledge. God is defined as the kind of being that he must be that he induces in us the kind of experience that he does: he is the 'Whence' of our feeling of 'absolute dependence'. Another way of putting this is to say that God is co-given with our experience, which can only be adequately understood when we realize this.

For Schleiermacher, religious experience is supra-rational or above reason, to the effect that any theological statements we make are rationalizations of an experience that is essentially beyond or above reason. This can be understood as a radical version of Aquinas' nega-tive theology for the following reasons. Just as for Aquinas God is defined as the cause of the known world, so for Schleiermacher he is understood as the cause of our religious experience, and only after that of our knowledge of the world. Just as, also, for Aquinas we can only know what God is not, so for Schleiermacher such rational expression as we can give to our theology owes more to the mode of our knowing than to some more knowledge of divinity. We can *experi-ence* God directly, but any claim to know him rationally is at best highly indirect.

Karl Barth (II.1.8) acknowledged that the whole of his theological career was in one sense attempting to out-think his great predecessor Schleiermacher. He also spent much energy on showing that Kant's view of the impossibility of the knowledge of God is simply wrong. For Barth, because there is revelation – because God truly makes himself known in Jesus Christ – then it is absurd to claim that he cannot be known. If he is known, then he can be. At the heart of his enterprise is to place Jesus Christ, God become man, where Schleiermacher placed religious experience. Because God meets us there in person, there can be real knowledge of God. Barth's argument goes somewhat as follows. First, God is in fact known in his revelation, and therefore he can be known. Second, the event of revelation in which God makes himself the object of our thought and concepts can be known as God's secondary objectivity. This is designed to indicate that God becomes, albeit according to the limits he himself sets, the object of our personal knowledge. Third, it follows that there is also a primary objectivity, in which God is intrinsically knowable in himself, as the Father and the Son know one another in the Spirit. God can in sum be known by us because he is knowable in and to himself, and because in Jesus Christ he opens up to us a share in this knowledge.

There are a number of respects in which Barth deliberately takes up a position different from that of most of the other representative figures in our collection, Athanasius being perhaps the closest to him. He believes that any attempt to establish the knowledge of God by reflection on experience of the world will in the modern world simply lead to charges that we are projecting our experience on to the world, charges made in our era by Feuerbach and his better known successors Marx and Freud. Our claims for knowledge must be based firmly on Jesus Christ, the place where God actually and personally makes himself known. It does not follow, however, that Barth has no doctrine of God's unknowability. He is here a strict follower of the Fathers, but believes that the doctrine is a revealed doctrine, and not something we infer from our ignorance or the weaknesses of our human capacity (appeals we have met in some of our texts, perhaps especially that of Pseudo-Dionysius). Rather, God's unknowability is the other side of the knowability of God made known in Christ, and a mark of God's absolute freedom to decide when and in what form to communicate knowledge of himself to us.

T. F. Torrance's achievement (II.1.9) in this realm is to have taken up certain aspects of Barth's achievement and sought to spell out their further implications. At the centre of his thought is not so much revelation as Barth conceived it – though he did not wish to deny its reality

– but the patristic notion that Jesus Christ is *homoousios* – one in being – with God the Father. Torrance also strengthens Athanasius' contribution to the modern conception. In the incarnation of his Son, God embraces our world, and that has implications not only for theological rationality but for our claims to knowledge in general. That God can be and is known in the incarnation of his Son is a demonstration that we know God and the world in similar and parallel ways. There is a parallel to be drawn between theological and scientific forms of knowledge. Just as in science we come to know the natural world in its truth, as it presents itself to us to be known, so we know God in his truth as he presents himself to us in his gracious condescension to our estate. Theology is therefore a kind of science, because 'science' refers to all the various forms of knowing, natural and theological alike, which God the creator makes possible and real in our world.

CEG

A. Patristic answers

II.1.1 St Athanasius, from *Letters to Serapion, on the Holy Spirit*

Athanasius reflects on the trinitarian structure of God's self-disclosure.

19. Since, therefore, such an attempt is futile madness, nay, more than madness!, let no one ask such questions any more, or else let him learn only that which is in the Scriptures. For the illustrations they contain which bear upon this subject are sufficient and suitable. The Father is called fountain and light: 'They have forsaken me,' it says, 'the fountain of living water'; and again in Baruch, 'Why, O Israel, art thou in the land of thine enemies? Thou hast forsaken the fountain of wisdom'; and, according to John: 'Our God is light.' But the Son, in contrast with the fountain, is called river: 'The river of God is full of water.' In contrast with the light, he is called radiance – as Paul says: 'Who, being the radiance of his glory and the image of his essence.' As then the Father is light and the Son is his radiance – we must not shrink from saying the same things about them many times – we may see in the Son the Spirit also by whom we are enlightened. 'That he may give you', it says, 'the Spirit of wisdom and revelation in the knowledge of him, having the eyes of your heart enlightened'. But when we are enlightened by the Spirit, it is Christ who in him enlightens us. For it says: 'There was the true light which lighteth every man coming into the world.' Again, as the Father is fountain and the Son is called river, we are said to drink of the Spirit. For it is written: 'We are all made to drink of one Spirit.' But when we are made to drink of the Spirit, we drink of Christ. For 'they drank of a spiritual rock that followed them, and the rock was Christ'. Again, as Christ is true Son, so we, when we receive the Spirit, are made sons. 'For you have not received', it says, 'the spirit of bondage again to fear; but you have received the Spirit of adoption.' But if by the Spirit we are made sons, it is clear that it is in Christ we are called children of God. For: 'So many as received him, to them gave he the power to become children of God.' Then, as the Father, in Paul's words, is the 'only wise', the Son is his Wisdom: 'Christ the Power of God and the Wisdom of God.' But as the Son is Wisdom, so we, receiving the Spirit of Wisdom, have the Son and are made wise in him. For thus it is written in the one hundred and forty-fifth psalm: 'The Lord looseth the prisoners, the Lord maketh wise the blind.' When the Holy Spirit is given to us ('Receive the Holy Spirit,' said the Saviour), God is in us; for so John wrote: 'If we love one another, God abideth in us; hereby know we that we abide in him and he in us, because he hath given us of his Spirit.' But when God is in us, the Son also is in us. For the Son himself said: 'The Father and

I will come and make our abode with him.' Furthermore, as the Son is life
– for he says 'I am the life' – we are said to be quickened by the Spirit. For
it says: 'He that raised up Christ Jesus from the dead shall quicken also your
mortal bodies, through his Spirit that dwelleth in you.' But when we are
quickened by the Spirit, Christ himself is said to live in us; for it says: 'I have
been crucified with Christ. I live, and yet no longer I, but Christ liveth in
me.' Again, the Son declared that the Father worked the works that he did
– for he says: 'The Father abiding in me doeth his works. Believe me, that I
am in the Father and the Father in me; or else believe me for his works'
sake.' So Paul declared that the works he worked by the power of the Spirit
were the works of Christ: 'For I will not dare to speak of any things save
those which Christ wrought through me, for the obedience of the Gentiles,
by word and deed, in the power of signs and wonders, in the power of the
Holy Spirit.'

But if there is such co-ordination and unity within the holy Triad, who
can separate either the Son from the Father, or the Spirit from the Son or
from the Father himself? Who would be so audacious as to say that the Triad
is unlike itself and diverse in nature, or that the Son is in essence foreign
from the Father, or the Spirit alien from the Son? But how are these things?
If one should make inquiry and ask again: How, when the Spirit is in us,
the Son is said to be in us? How, when the Son is in us, the Father is said
to be in us? Or how, when it is truly a Triad, the Triad is described as one?
Or why, when the One is in us, the Triad is said to be in us? – let him first
divide the radiance from the light, or wisdom from the wise, or let him tell
how these things are. But if this is not to be done, much more is it the
audacity of madmen to make such inquiries concerning God. For tradition,
as we have said, does not declare the Godhead to us by demonstration in
words, but by faith and by a pious and reverent use of reason. For if Paul
proclaimed the saving Gospel of the Cross, 'not in words of wisdom, but
in demonstration of the Spirit and of power'; and if in Paradise he heard
'unspeakable words which it is not lawful for a man to utter': who can declare
the holy Triad itself? Nevertheless, we can meet this difficulty, primarily by
faith and then by using the illustrations mentioned above, I mean the image
and the radiance, fountain and river, essence and expression. As the Son is
in the Spirit as in his own image, so also the Father is in the Son. For
divine Scripture, by way of relieving the impossibility of explaining and
apprehending these matters in words, has given us illustrations of this kind;
that it may be lawful, because of the unbelief of presumptuous men, to speak
more plainly, and to speak without danger, and to think legitimately, and
to believe that there is one sanctification, which is derived from the Father,
through the Son, in the Holy Spirit.

As the Son is an only-begotten offspring, so also the Spirit, being given
and sent from the Son, is himself one and not many, nor one from among
many, but Only Spirit. As the Son, the living Word, is one, so must the vital

activity and gift whereby he sanctifies and enlightens be one perfect and complete; which is said to proceed from the Father, because it is from the Word, who is confessed to be from the Father, that it shines forth and is sent and is given. The Son is sent from the Father; for he says, 'God so loved the world that he gave his only begotten Son.' The Son sends the Spirit; 'If I go away,' he says, 'I will send the Paraclete.' The Son glorifies the Father, saying: 'Father, I have glorified thee.' The Spirit glorifies the Son: for he says; 'He shall glorify me.' The Son says: 'The things I heard from the Father speak I unto the world.' The Spirit takes of the Son; 'He shall take of mine,' he says, 'and shall declare it unto you.' The Son came in the name of the Father. 'The Holy Spirit,' says the Son, 'whom the Father will send in my name.'

(Taken from C. R. B. Shapland, **The Letters of St Athanasius Concerning the Holy Spirit,** *translated with Introduction and Notes, London: Epworth Press 1951, I.19–20.)*

II.1.2 Hilary of Poitiers, from *On The Trinity, Book II*

Hilary here confesses that God cannot be known or grasped, but that the Son, Jesus Christ, reveals him to us. We cannot know how this happens, but we should have faith that it does.

6. It is the Father to whom all existence owes its origin. In Christ and through Christ he is the source of all. In contrast to all else he is self-existent. He does not draw his being from without, but possesses it from himself and in himself. He is infinite, for nothing contains him and he contains all things; he is eternally unconditioned by space, for he is illimitable; eternally anterior to time, for time is his creation. Let imagination range to what you may suppose is God's utmost limit, and you will find him present there; strain as you will there is always a further horizon towards which to strain. Infinity is his property, just as the power of making such effort is yours. Words will fail you, but his being will not be circumscribed. Or again, turn back the pages of history, and you will find him ever present; should numbers fail to express the antiquity to which you have penetrated, yet God's eternity is not diminished. Gird up your intellect to comprehend him as a whole; he eludes you, God, as a whole, has left something within your grasp, but this something is inextricably involved in his entirety. Thus you have missed the whole, since it is only a part which remains in your hands; nay, not even a part, for you are dealing with a whole which you have failed to divide. For a part implies division, a whole is undivided, and God is everywhere and wholly present wherever he is. Reason, therefore, cannot cope with him, since no point of contemplation can be found outside himself and since eternity is eternally his. This is a true statement of the mystery of that unfathomable nature which is expressed by the Name 'Father': God invisible, ineffable, infinite. Let us confess by our silence that words cannot describe him; let sense admit that it is foiled in the attempt to apprehend, and reason in the effort to define. Yet he has, as we said, in 'Father' a name to indicate his nature; he is a Father unconditioned. he does not, as men do, receive the power of paternity from an external source. He is unbegotten, everlasting, inherently eternal. To the Son only is he known, for no one knoweth the Father save the Son and him to whom the Son willeth to reveal him, nor yet the Son save the Father. Each has perfect and complete knowledge of the other. Therefore, since no one knoweth the Father save the Son, let our thoughts of the Father be at one with the thoughts of the Son, the only faithful Witness, who reveals him to us.

7. It is easier for me to feel this concerning the Father than to say it. I am well aware that no words are adequate to describe his attributes. We must feel that he is invisible, incomprehensible, eternal. But to say that he is self-existent and self-originating and self-sustained, that he is invisible and

incomprehensible and immortal; all this is an acknowledgement of his glory, a hint of our meaning, a sketch of our thoughts, but speech is powerless to tell us what God is, words cannot express the reality. You hear that he is self-existent; human reason cannot explain such independence. We can find objects which uphold, and objects which are upheld, but that which thus exists is obviously distinct from that which is the cause of its existence. Again, if you hear that he is self-originating, no instance can be found in which the giver of the gift of life is identical with the life that is given. If you hear that he is immortal, then there is something which does not spring from him and with which he has, by his very nature, no contact; and, indeed, death is not the only thing which this word 'immortal' claims as independent of God. If you hear that he is incomprehensible, that is as much as to say that he is non-existent, since contact with him is impossible. If you say that he is invisible, a being that does not visibly exist cannot be sure of its own existence. Thus our confession of God fails through the defects of language; the best combination of words we can devise cannot indicate the reality and the greatness of God. The perfect knowledge of God is so to know him that we are sure we must not be ignorant of him, yet cannot describe him. We must believe, must apprehend, must worship; and such acts of devotion must stand in lieu of definition.

8. We have now exchanged the perils of a harbourless coast for the storms of the open sea. We can neither safely advance nor safely retreat, yet the way that lies before us has greater hardships than that which lies behind. The Father is what he is, and as he is manifested, so we must believe. The mind shrinks in dread from treating of the Son; at every word I tremble lest I be betrayed into treason. For he is the Offspring of the Unbegotten, One from One, true from true, living from living, perfect from perfect; the Power of Power, the Wisdom of Wisdom, the Glory of Glory, the Likeness of the invisible God, the Image of the Unbegotten Father. Yet in what sense can we conceive that the Only-begotten is the Offspring of the Unbegotten? Repeatedly the Father cries from heaven, 'This is my beloved Son in whom I well pleased'. It is no rending or severance, for he that begat is without passions, and he that was born is the Image of the invisible God and bears witness, 'The Father is in me and I in the Father'. It is no mere adoption, for he is the true Son of God and cries, 'He that hath seen me hath seen the Father also'. Nor did he come into existence in obedience to a command as did created things, for he is the Only-begotten of the one God; and he has life in himself, even as he that begot him has life, for he says, 'As the Father hath life in himself, even so gave he to the Son to have life in himself'. Nor is there a portion of the Father resident in the Son, for the Son bears witness, 'All things that the Father hath are mine,' and again, 'And all things that are mine are thine, and thine are mine,' and the apostle testifies, 'For in him dwelleth all the fullness of the Godhead bodily'; and by the nature of things a portion cannot possess the whole. He is the perfect Son of the perfect

Father, for he who has all has given all to him. Yet we must not imagine that the Father did not give, because he still possesses, or that he has lost, because he gave to the Son.

9. The manner of this birth is therefore a secret confined to the two. If any one lays upon his personal incapacity his failure to solve the mystery, in spite of the certainty that Father and Son stand to each other in those relations, he will be still more pained at the ignorance to which I confess. I, too, am in the dark, yet I ask no questions. I look for comfort to the fact that archangels share my ignorance, that angels have not heard the explanation, and worlds do not contain it, that no prophet has espied it and no apostle sought for it, that the Son himself has not revealed it. Let such pitiful complaints cease. Whoever you are that search into these mysteries, I do not bid you resume your exploration of height and breadth and depth; I ask you rather to acquiesce patiently in your ignorance of the mode of divine generation . . .

10. Listen then to the Unbegotten Father, listen to the Only-begotten Son. Hear his words, 'The Father is greater than I,' and 'I and the Father are one,' and 'he that hath seen me hath seen the Father also,' and 'the Father is in me and I in the Father,' and 'I went out from the Father,' and 'who is in the bosom of the Father,' and 'whatsoever the Father hath he hath delivered to the Son,' and 'the Son hath life in himself, even as the Father hath in himself'. Hear in these words the Son, the Image, the Wisdom, the Power, the Glory of God. Next mark the Holy Ghost proclaiming 'Who shall declare his generation?' Note the Lord's assurance, 'No one knoweth the Son save the Father, neither doth any know the Father save the Son and he to whom the Son willeth to reveal him'. Penetrate into the mystery, plunge into the darkness which shrouds that birth, where you will be alone with God the Unbegotten and God the Only-begotten. Make your start, continue, persevere. I know that you will not reach the goal, but I shall rejoice at your progress. For he who devoutly treads an endless road, though he reach no conclusion, will profit by his exertions. Reason will fail for want of words, but when it comes to a stand it will be the better for the effort made.

11. The Son draws his life from that Father who truly has life; the Only begotten from the Unbegotten, Offspring from Parent, Living from Living. As the Father hath life in himself, even so gave he to the Son also to have life in himself. The Son is perfect from him that is perfect, for he is whole from him that is whole. This is no division or severance, for each is in the other, and the fullness of the Godhead is in the Son. Incomprehensible is begotten of Incomprehensible, for none else knows them, but each knows the other; Invisible is begotten of Invisible, for the Son is the Image of the invisible God, and he that has seen the Son has seen the Father also. There is a distinction, for they are Father and Son; not that their divinity is different in kind, for both are one, God of God, one God Only begotten of One God Unbegotten. They are not two Gods, but One of One; not two Unbegotten, for the Son is born of the Unborn. There is no diversity, for the life of the

living God is in the living Christ. So much I have resolved to say concerning the nature of their Divinity not imagining that I have succeeded in making a summary of the faith, but recognising that the theme is inexhaustible. So faith, you object, has no service to render, since there is nothing that it can comprehend. Not so; the proper service of faith is to grasp and confess the truth that it is incompetent to comprehend its object.

(Taken from the Nicene and Post-Nicene Fathers, series II, vol. IX, ed. Philip Schaff and Henry Wace, trans. E. W. Watson, L. Pullan et al.)

II.1.3 Pseudo-Dionysius, from *The Mystical Theology*

The Pseudo-Dionysius argues that all our knowing is inadequate, and so none of our concepts, positive or negative, are properly ascribed to God. Nonetheless, some things may and must be said, and we may find concepts which are better affirmed of God than denied, and others which are better denied.

Unto this Darkness which is beyond Light we pray that we may come, and may attain unto vision through the loss of sight and knowledge, and that in ceasing thus to see or to know we may learn to know that which is beyond all perception and understanding (for this emptying of our faculties is true sight and knowledge) and that we may offer Him that transcends all things the praises of a transcendent hymnody, which we shall do by denying or removing all things that are – like as men who, carving a statue out of marble, remove all the impediments that hinder the clear perceptive of the latent image and by this mere removal display the hidden statue itself in its hidden beauty. Now we must wholly distinguish this negative method from that of positive statements. For when we were making positive statements we began with the most universal statements, and then through intermediate terms we came at last to particular titles, but now ascending upwards from particular to universal conceptions we strip off all qualities in order that we may attain a naked knowledge of that Unknowing which in all existent things is enwrapped by all objects of knowledge, and that we may begin to see that super-essential Darkness which is hidden by all the light that is in existent things.

Now I have in my *Outlines of Divinity* set forth those conceptions which are most proper to the affirmative method, and have shown in what sense God's holy nature is called single and in what sense trinal, what is the nature of the Fatherhood and Sonship which we attribute unto It; what is meant by the articles of faith concerning the Spirit; how from the immaterial and indivisible Good the interior rays of Its goodness have their being and remain immovably in that state of rest which both within their Origin and within themselves is co-eternal with the act by which they spring from It; in what manner Jesus being above all essence has stooped to an essential state in which all the truths of human nature meet; and all the other revelations of Scripture whereof my *Outlines of Divinity* treat. And in the book of the *Divine Names* I have considered the meaning as concerning God of the titles Good, Existent, Life, Wisdom, Power and of the other titles which the understanding frames, and in my Symbolic Divinity I have considered what are the metaphorical titles drawn from the world of sense and applied to the nature of God; what are the mental or material images we form of God or the functions and instruments of activity we attribute to Him; what are the places where He dwells and the robes He is adorned with; what is meant by God's anger, grief, and indignation, or the divine inebriation and wrath; what is meant by God's oath and His malediction, by His slumber and awaking, and all the other inspired imagery of allegoric symbolism. And I doubt not that you have also observed how far more copious are the last terms than the first for the doctrines of God's Nature and the exposition of His Names could not but be briefer than the Symbolic Divinity. For the more that we soar upwards the more our language becomes restricted to the compass of purely intellectual conceptions, even as in the present instance plunging into the Darkness which is above the intellect we shall find ourselves reduced not merely to brevity of speech but even to absolute dumbness both of speech and thought. Now in the former treatises the course of the argument, as it came down from the highest to the lowest categories, embraced an ever-widening number of conceptions which increased at each stage of the descent, but in the present treatise it mounts upwards from below towards the category of transcendence, and in proportion to its ascent it contracts its terminology, and when the whole ascent is passed it will be totally dumb, being at last wholly united with Him Whom words cannot describe. But why is it, you will ask, that after beginning from the highest category when one method was affirmative we begin from the lowest category where it is negative? Because, when affirming the existence of that which transcends all affirmation, we were obliged to start from that which is most akin to It, and then to make the affirmation on which the rest depended; but when pursuing the negative method, to reach that which is beyond all negation, we must start by applying our negations to those qualities which differ most from the ultimate goal. Surely it is truer to affirm that God is life and goodness than that He is air or stone, and truer to deny that drunkenness or fury can be attributed to Him than to deny that we may apply to Him the categories of human thought.

WE therefore maintain that the universal Cause transcending all things is neither impersonal nor lifeless, nor irrational nor without understanding: in short, that it is not a material body, and therefore does not possess outward shape or intelligible form, or quality, or quantity, or solid weight; nor has It any local existence which can be perceived by sight or touch; nor has It the power of perceiving or being perceived; nor does It suffer any vexation or disorder through the disturbance of earthly passions, or any feebleness through the tyranny of material chances, or any want of light; nor any change, or decay, or division, or deprivation, or ebb and flow, or anything else which the senses can perceive. None of these things can be either identified with it or attributed unto It.

ONCE more, ascending yet higher we maintain that It is not soul, or mind, or endowed with the faculty of imagination, conjecture, reason, or understanding; nor is It any act of reason or understanding; nor can It be described by the reason or perceived by the understanding, since It is not number, or order, or greatness, or littleness, or equality, or inequality, and since It is not immovable nor in motion, or at rest, and has no power, and is not power or light, and does not live, and is not life; nor is It personal essence, or eternity, or time; nor can It be grasped by the understanding, since It is not knowledge or truth; nor is It kingship or wisdom; nor is It one, nor is It unity, nor is It Godhead or Goodness; nor is It a Spirit, as we understand the term since It is not Sonship or Fatherhood; nor is It any other thing such as we or any other being can have knowledge of; nor does It belong to the category of non-existence or to that of existence; nor do existent beings know It as it actually is, nor does It know them as they actually are; nor can the reason attain to It to name It or to know It; nor is it darkness, nor is It light, or error, or truth; nor can any affirmation or negation apply to it; for while applying affirmations or negations to those orders of being that come next to It, we apply not unto It either affirmation or negation, inasmuch as It transcends all affirmation by being the perfect and unique Cause of all things, and transcends all negation by the pre-eminence of Its simple and absolute nature – free from every limitation and beyond them all.

(Taken from C. E. Rolt's translation, Dionysius the Areopagite on the Divine Names and the Mystical Theology, *Translations of Christian Literature series, London: SPCK 1920, chapters II–V.)*

B. Systematizations

II.1.4 John of Damascus, from *The Exposition of the Orthodox Faith*

God is incomprehensible, but has revealed himself to us in various ways.

1. No one hath seen God at any time; the Only-begotten Son, which is in the bosom of the Father, he hath declared him. The Deity, therefore, is ineffable and incomprehensible. For no one knoweth the Father, save the Son, nor the Son, save the Father. And the Holy Spirit, too, so knows the things of God as the spirit of the man knows the things that are in him. Moreover, after the first and blessed nature no one, not of men only, but even of supramundane powers, and the cherubim [an order of angels], I say, and seraphim [another order of angels] themselves, has ever known God, save he to whom he revealed himself.

God, however, did not leave us in absolute ignorance. For the knowledge of God's existence has been implanted by him in all by nature. This creation, too, and its maintenance, and its government, proclaim the majesty of the divine nature. Moreover, by the Law and the Prophets in former times and afterwards by his Only-begotten Son, our Lord and God and Saviour Jesus Christ, he disclosed to us the knowledge of himself as that was possible for us. All things, therefore, that have been delivered to us by Law and Prophets and Apostles and Evangelists we receive, and know, and honour, seeking for nothing beyond these. For God, being good, is the cause of all good, subject neither to envy nor to any passion. For envy is far removed from the divine nature, which is both passionless and only good. As knowing all things, therefore, and providing for what is profitable for each, he revealed that which it was to our profit to know; but what we were unable to bear he kept secret. With these things let us be satisfied, and let us abide by them, not removing everlasting boundaries, nor overpassing the divine tradition.

2. It is necessary, therefore, that one who wishes to speak or to hear of God should understand clearly that alike in the doctrine of deity and in that of the incarnation, neither are all things unutterable nor all utterable; neither all unknowable nor all knowable. But the knowable belongs to one order, and the utterable to another; just as it is one thing to speak and another thing to know. Many of the things relating to God, therefore, that are dimly understood cannot be put into fitting terms, but on things above us we cannot do else than express ourselves according to our limited capacity; as, for instance, when we speak of God we use the terms sleep, and wrath, and regardlessness, hands, too, and feet, and such like expressions.

We, therefore, both know and confess that God is without beginning, without end, eternal and everlasting, uncreate, unchangeable, invariable, simple, uncompound, incorporeal, invisible, impalpable, uncircumscribed, infinite, incognisable, indefinable, incomprehensible, good, just, maker of all things created, almighty, all-ruling, all-surveying, of all overseer, sovereign, judge; and that God is One, that is to say, one essence; and that he is known, and has his being in three subsistences, in Father, I say, and Son and Holy Spirit; and that the Father and the Son and the Holy Spirit are one in all respects, except in that of not being begotten, that of being begotten, and that of procession; and that the Only-begotten Son and Word of God and God, in his bowels of mercy, for our salvation, by the good pleasure of God and the co-operation of the Holy Spirit, being conceived without seed, was born uncorruptedly of the Holy Virgin and Mother of God, Mary, by the Holy Spirit, and became of her perfect man; and that the same is at once perfect God and perfect man, of two natures, Godhead and manhood, and in two natures possessing intelligence, will and energy, and freedom, and, in a word, perfect according to the measure and proportion proper to each, at once to the divinity, I say, and to the humanity, yet to one composite person; and that he suffered hunger and thirst and weariness, and was crucified, and for three days submitted to the experience of death and burial, and ascended to heaven, from which also he came to us, and shall come again. And the Holy Scripture is witness to this and the whole choir of the Saints.

But neither do we know, nor can we tell, what the essence of God is, or how it is in all, or how the Only-begotten Son and God, having emptied himself, became man of virgin blood, made by another law contrary to nature, or how he walked with dry feet upon the waters. It is not within our capacity, therefore, to say anything about God or even to think of him, beyond the things which have been divinely revealed to us, whether by word or by manifestation, by the divine oracles at once of the Old Testament and of the New.

3. That there is a God, then, is no matter of doubt to those who receive the Holy Scriptures, the Old Testament, I mean, and the New; nor indeed to most of the Greeks. For, as we said, the knowledge of the existence of God is implanted in us by nature. But since the wickedness of the Evil One has prevailed so mightily against man's nature as even to drive some into denying the existence of God, that most foolish and woe-fullest pit of destruction (whose folly David, revealer of the divine meaning, exposed when he said, 'The fool said in his heart, there is no God'), so the disciples of the Lord and his apostles, made wise by the Holy Spirit and working wonders in his power and grace, took them captive in the net of miracles and drew them up out of the depths of ignorance to the light of the knowledge of God. In like manner also their successors in grace and worth, both pastors and teachers, having received the enlightening grace of the Spirit, were wont, alike by the

power of miracles and the word of grace, to enlighten those walking in darkness and to bring back the wanderers into the way. But as for us who are not recipients either of the gift of miracles or the gift of teaching (for indeed we have rendered ourselves unworthy of these by our passion for pleasure), come, let us in connection with this theme discuss a few of those things which have been delivered to us on this subject by the expounders of grace, calling on the Father, the Son, and the Holy Spirit.

All things, that exist, are either created or uncreated. If, then, things are created, it follows that they are also wholly mutable. For things, whose existence originated in change, must also be subject to change, whether it be that they perish or that they become other than they are by act of will. But if things are uncreated they must in all consistency be also wholly immutable. For things which are opposed in the nature of their existence must also be opposed in the mode of their existence, that is to say, must have opposite properties: who, then, will refuse to grant that all existing things, not only such as come within the province of the senses, but even the very angels, are subject to change and transformation and movement of various kinds? For the things appertaining to the rational world, I mean angels and spirits and demons, are subject to changes of will, whether it is a progression or a retrogression in goodness, whether a struggle or a surrender; while the others suffer changes of generation and destruction, of increase and decrease, of quality and of movement in space. Things then that are mutable are also wholly created. But things that are created must be the work of some maker, and the maker cannot have been created. For if he had been created, he also must surely have been created by some one, and so on till we arrive at something uncreated. The Creator, then, being uncreated, is also wholly immutable. And what could this be other than Deity?

And even the very continuity of the creation, and its preservation and government, teach us that there does exist a Deity, who supports and maintains and preserves and ever provides for this universe. For how could opposite natures, such as fire and water, air and earth, have combined with each other so as to form one complete world, and continue to abide in indissoluble union, were there not some omnipotent power which bound them together and always is preserving them from dissolution?

What is it that gave order to things of heaven and things of earth, and all those things that move in the air and in the water, or rather to what was in existence before these, viz., to heaven and earth and air and the elements of fire and water? What was it that mingled and distributed these? What was it that set these in motion and keeps them in their unceasing and unhindered course? Was it not the Artificer of these things, and he who hath implanted in everything the law whereby the universe is carried on and directed? Who then is the Artificer of these things? Is it not he who created them and brought them into existence. For we shall not attribute such a power to the spontaneous. For, supposing their coming into existence was due to the spontaneous; what of the power that put all in orders? And let us grant this, if you please. What of that which has preserved and kept them in harmony with the original laws of their existence? Clearly it is something quite distinct from the spontaneous. And what could this be other than Deity?

4. It is plain, then, that there is a God. But what he is in his essence and nature is absolutely incomprehensible and unknowable. For it is evident that he is incorporeal. For how could that possess body which is infinite, and boundless, and formless, and intangible and invisible, in short, simple and not compound? How could that be immutable which is circumscribed and subject to passion? And how could that be passionless which is composed of elements and is resolved again into them? For combination is the beginning of conflict, and conflict of separation, and separation of dissolution, and dissolution is altogether foreign to God.

Again, how will it also be maintained that God permeates and fills the universe? as the Scriptures say, 'Do not I fill heaven and earth, saith the Lord'? For it is an impossibility that one body should permeate other bodies without dividing and being divided, and without being enveloped and contrasted, in the same way as all fluids mix and commingle.

But if some say that the body is immaterial, in the same way as the fifth body [quintessence] of which the Greek philosophers speak (which body is an impossibility), it will be wholly subject to motion like the heaven. For that is what they mean by the fifth body. Who then is it that moves it? For everything that is moved is moved by another thing. And who again is it that moves that? and so on to infinity till we at length arrive at something motionless. For the first mover is motionless, and that is the Deity. And must not that which is moved be circumscribed in space? The Deity, then, alone is motionless, moving the universe by immobility. So then it must be assumed that the Deity is incorporeal.

But even this gives no true idea of his essence, to say that he is unbegotten, and without beginning, changeless and imperishable, and possessed of such other qualities as we are wont to ascribe to God and his environments. For these do not indicate what he is, but what he is not. But when we would explain what the essence of anything is, we must not speak only negatively. In the case of God, however, it is impossible to explain what he is in his essence, and it befits us the rather to hold discourse about his absolute separation from all things. For he does not belong to the class of existing things: not that he has no existence, but that he is above all existing things, nay even above existence itself. For if all forms of knowledge have to do with what exists, assuredly that which is above knowledge must certainly be also above essence: and, conversely, that which is above essence will also be above knowledge.

God then is infinite and incomprehensible and all that is comprehensible about him is his infinity and incomprehensibility. But all that we can affirm concerning God does not shew forth God's nature, but only the qualities of his nature. For when you speak of him as good, and just, and wise, and so forth, you do not tell God's nature but only the qualities of his nature. Further there are some affirmations which we make concerning God which have the force of absolute negation: for example, when we use the term darkness, in reference to God, we do not mean darkness itself, but that he is not light but above light: and when we speak of him as light, we mean that he is not darkness.

(Taken from the Nicene and Post-Nicene Fathers, second series, Vol. IX, ed. Philip Schaff and Henry Wace, trans. S. D. F. Salmond, Book I.1–4.)

II.1.5 St Thomas Aquinas, from the *Summa Theologica*

Aquinas asks about the nature of theological knowledge. Theology is a 'science' (i.e. rational discourse) that explores revealed truth, in contrast to philosophy, that explores natural truth.

Article 1: Whether, besides philosophy, any further doctrine is required?

Objection 1. It seems that, besides philosophical science, we have no need of any further knowledge. For man should not seek to know what is above reason: 'Seek not the things that are too high for thee' (Sirach 3:22). But whatever is not above reason is fully treated of in philosophical science. Therefore any other knowledge besides philosophical science is superfluous.

Objection 2. Further, knowledge can be concerned only with being, for nothing can be known, save what is true; and all that is, is true. But everything that is, is treated of in philosophical science – even God himself; so that there is a part of philosophy called theology, or the divine science, as Aristotle has proved (*Metaphysics* vi). Therefore, besides philosophical science, there is no need of any further knowledge.

On the contrary, It is written (II Tim. 3:16): 'All Scripture, inspired of God is profitable to teach, to reprove, to correct, to instruct in justice.' Now Scripture, inspired of God, is no part of philosophical science, which has been built up by human reason. Therefore it is useful that besides philosophical science, there should be other knowledge, i.e. inspired of God.

I answer that, It was necessary for man's salvation that there should be a knowledge revealed by God besides philosophical science built up by human reason. Firstly, indeed, because man is directed to God, as to an end that surpasses the grasp of his reason: 'The eye hath not seen, O God, besides thee, what things thou hast prepared for them that wait for thee' (Is. 66:4). But the end must first be known by men who are to direct their thoughts and actions to the end. Hence it was necessary for the salvation of man that certain truths which exceed human reason should be made known to him by divine revelation. Even as regards those truths about God which human reason could have discovered, it was necessary that man should be taught by a divine revelation; because the truth about God such as reason could discover, would only be known by a few, and that after a long time, and with the admixture of many errors. Whereas man's whole salvation, which is in God, depends upon the knowledge of this truth. Therefore, in order that the salvation of men might be brought about more fitly and more surely, it was necessary that they should be taught divine truths by divine revelation. It was therefore necessary that besides philosophical science built up by reason, there should be a sacred science learned through revelation.

Reply to Objection 1. Although those things which are beyond man's knowledge may not be sought for by man through his reason, nevertheless, once they are revealed by God, they must be accepted by faith. Hence the sacred text continues, 'For many things are shown to thee above the understanding of man' (Sirach 3:25). And in this, the sacred science consists.

Reply to Objection 2. Sciences are differentiated according to the various means through which knowledge is obtained. For the astronomer and the physicist both may prove the same conclusion: that the earth, for instance, is round: the astronomer by means of mathematics (i.e. abstracting from matter), but the physicist by means of matter itself. Hence there is no reason why those things which may be learned from philosophical science, so far as they can be known by natural reason, may not also be taught us by another science so far as they fall within revelation. Hence theology included in sacred doctrine differs in kind from that theology which is part of philosophy.

Article 2 Whether sacred doctrine is a science?

Objection 1. It seems that sacred doctrine is not a science. For every science proceeds from self-evident principles. But sacred doctrine proceeds from articles of faith which are not self-evident, since their truth is not admitted by all: 'For all men have not faith' (II Thess. 3:2). Therefore sacred doctrine is not a science.

Objection 2. Further, no science deals with individual facts. But this sacred science treats of individual facts, such as the deeds of Abraham, Isaac and Jacob and such like. Therefore sacred doctrine is not a science.

On the contrary, Augustine says (*De Trinitate* xiv, 1) 'to this science alone belongs that whereby saving faith is begotten, nourished, protected and strengthened.' But this can be said of no science except sacred doctrine. Therefore sacred doctrine is a science.

I answer that, Sacred doctrine is a science. We must bear in mind that there are two kinds of sciences. There are some which proceed from a principle known by the natural light of intelligence, such as arithmetic and geometry and the like. There are some which proceed from principles known by the light of a higher science: thus the science of perspective proceeds from principles established by geometry, and music from principles established by arithmetic. So it is that sacred doctrine is a science because it proceeds from principles established by the light of a higher science, namely, the science of God and the blessed. Hence, just as the musician accepts on authority the principles taught him by the mathematician, so sacred science is established on principles revealed by God.

Reply to Objection 1. The principles of any science are either in themselves self-evident, or reducible to the conclusions of a higher science; and such, as we have said, are the principles of sacred doctrine.

Reply to Objection 2. Individual facts are treated of in sacred doctrine, not because it is concerned with them principally, but they are introduced rather both as examples to be followed in our lives (as in moral sciences) and in order to establish the authority of those men through whom the divine revelation, on which this sacred scripture or doctrine is based, has come down to us.

(Taken from the Fathers of the English Dominican Province Translation, London: Burns, Oates & Washbourne 1924–34, Ia q.1.)

II.1.6 St Thomas Aquinas, from the *Summa Theologica*

Aquinas here explores what sort of statements may be properly made about God.

Article 12 Whether affirmative propositions can be formed about God?

Objection 1. It seems that affirmative propositions cannot be formed about God. For Dionysius says (*Celestial Hierarchy* ii) that 'negations about God are true; but affirmations are vague.'

Objection 2. Further, Boethius says (*On the Trinity* ii) that 'a simple form cannot be a subject.' But God is the most absolutely simple form, as shown: therefore he cannot be a subject. But everything about which an affirmative proposition is made is taken as a subject. Therefore an affirmative proposition cannot be formed about God.

Objection 3. Further, every intellect is false which understands a thing otherwise than as it is. But God has existence without any composition as shown above. Therefore since every affirmative intellect understands something as compound, it follows that a true affirmative proposition about God cannot be made.

On the contrary, What is of faith cannot be false. But some affirmative propositions are of faith; as that God is Three and One; and that he is omnipotent. Therefore true affirmative propositions can be formed about God.

I answer that, True affirmative propositions can be formed about God. To prove this we must know that in every true affirmative proposition the predicate and the subject signify in some way the same thing in reality, and different things in idea. And this appears to be the case both in propositions which have an accidental predicate, and in those which have an essential predicate. For it is manifest that 'man' and 'white' are the same in subject, and different in idea; for the idea of man is one thing, and that of whiteness is another. The same applies when I say, 'man is an animal'; since the same thing which is man is truly animal; for in the same 'suppositum' there is sensible nature by reason of which he is called animal, and the rational nature by reason of which he is called man; hence here again predicate and subject are the same as to 'suppositum,' but different as to idea. But in propositions where one same thing is predicated of itself, the same rule in some way applies, inasmuch as the intellect draws to the 'suppositum' what it places in the subject; and what it places in the predicate it draws to the nature of the form existing in the 'suppositum'; according to the saying that 'predicates are to be taken formally, and subjects materially.' To this diversity in idea corresponds the plurality of predicate and subject, while the intellect signifies the identity of the thing by the composition itself.

God, however, as considered in himself, is altogether one and simple, yet our intellect knows him by different conceptions because it cannot see him as he is in himself. Nevertheless, although it understands him under different conceptions, it knows that one and the same simple object corresponds to its conceptions. Therefore the plurality of predicate and subject represents the plurality of idea; and the intellect represents the unity by composition.

Reply to Objection 1. Dionysius says that the affirmations about God are vague or, according to another translation, 'incongruous,' inasmuch as no name can be applied to God according to its mode of signification.

Reply to Objection 2. Our intellect cannot comprehend simple subsisting forms, as they really are in themselves; but it apprehends them as compound things in which there is something taken as subject and something that is inherent. Therefore it apprehends the simple form as a subject, and attributes something else to it.

Reply to Objection 3. This proposition, 'The intellect understanding anything otherwise than it is, is false,' can be taken in two senses, accordingly as this adverb 'otherwise' determines the word 'understanding' on the part of the thing understood, or on the part of the one who understands. Taken as referring to the thing understood, the proposition is true, and the meaning is: Any intellect which understands that the thing is otherwise than it is, is false. But this does not hold in the present case; because our intellect, when forming a proposition about God, does not affirm that he is composite, but that he is simple. But taken as referring to the one who understands, the proposition is false. For the mode of the intellect in understanding is different from the mode of the thing in its essence. Since it is clear that our intellect understands material things below itself in an immaterial manner; not that it understands them to be immaterial things; but its manner of understanding is immaterial. Likewise, when it understands simple things above itself, it understands them according to its own mode, which is in a composite manner; yet not so as to understand them to be composite things. And thus our intellect is not false in forming composition in its ideas concerning God.

(Taken from the Fathers of the English Dominican Province Translation, London: Burns, Oates & Washbourne 1924–34, Ia q.13.)

C. Modern attempts at recovery

II.1.7 Friedrich Schleiermacher, from *The Christian Faith*

Here Schleiermacher argues that the language we use of God does not properly correspond to anything in God, but only to our 'feeling of absolute dependence' (see I.5.4).

> § 50. *All attributes which we ascribe to God are to be taken as denoting not something special in God, but only something special in the manner in which the feeling of absolute dependence is to be related to Him.*
>
> ...

History teaches us concerning speculation that, ever since it took the divine essence as an object of thought, it has always entered the same protest against all detailed description, and confined itself to representing God as the Original Being and the Absolute Good. And, indeed, it has frequently been recognized that even in these concepts (of which the first only is relevant here) there remains a certain inadequacy, in so far as they still contain an element of opposition or other analogy with finite being. This method of treatment, therefore, owes its origin first of all to religious poetry, particularly to hymns and other lyrics, and also to the more uncultured experience of common life which harmonizes with poetry and tries to vivify and establish the simple idea of the Supreme Being by the employment of expressions which we use about finite beings. Both methods proceed from religious interests, and have far more the aim of representing the immediate impression in its different forms than of establishing scientific knowledge. Therefore, just because both have been taken over from Judaism, it has been from the beginning the business of Christian Dogmatics to regulate these representations, so that the anthropomorphic element, to be found more or less in all of them, and the sensuous which is mixed in with many, may be rendered as harmless as possible, and that no retrogression towards polytheism should result. And in this direction the age of Scholasticism contributed much that was profound and excellent. But as afterwards Metaphysics came to be treated separately and apart from Christian Doctrine, in conformity with the nature of the subject, it was for long overlooked (as only too easily happens in such divisions of territory) that these representations of divine attributes are not of philosophical but of religious origin; and they were taken over into that philosophical discipline which went by the name of Natural Theology. There, however, the more science developed a purely speculative character, the more these representations, which had not arisen on the soil of speculation were bound to be treated in a merely critical or sceptical way. Dogmatic

Theology, on the other hand, tried more and more to systematize them, not, if it understood itself rightly, in order to arrive at the consciousness that they contained a complete knowledge of God, but only to assure itself that the God-consciousness which dwells in us in all its differentiations and as it realizes itself at the prompting of different elements of life, was included in them. As, however, the separation was not complete, and intercourse was always lively and manifold between the two disciplines, much has remained permanently under philosophical treatment which belonged only to the dogmatic, and *vice versa*. It is still therefore always necessary to premise that, without making any speculative demands but at the same time without bringing in any speculative aids, we keep ourselves altogether within the limits of purely dogmatic procedure, both with regard to the content of individual definitions and also as to method.

. . .

But as concerns method, in the treatment of Dogmatics up to the present a double procedure is found to predominate. First, rules are put forward as to how one can arrive at right ideas of the divine attributes, and then further, certain rubrics are given under which the various conceptions of divine attributes are to be divided. Now since both aim at systematizing these ideas, the same general assumption has to be made. If the list of these attributes be regarded as a complete summary of definitions to be related to God Himself, then a complete knowledge of God must be derivable from conceptions, and an explanation in due theoretic form would take the place of that ineffability of the Divine Being which the Scriptures – so far as they mention divine attributes – recognize so clearly on every page that we need not quote passages. We have therefore to strive after that completeness alone which guards against letting any of the different moments of the religious self-consciousness pass without asking what are the divine attributes corresponding to them. And with this procedure the classification emerges of its own accord, because in each division only the attributes belonging there can be subjects of exposition. All the more necessary is it to make clear at this point how little is lost for the real matter in hand when we set aside, as we do, the apparatus which has hitherto been employed.

Now we may remark concerning these methods that there are three accepted ways of arriving at the divine attributes – the way of removal of limits (*via eminentiæ*), the way of negation or denial (*via negationis*), and the way of causality (*via causalitatis*). Now it is self-evident that these are by no means homogeneous or coordinate. For in the first two a something apart from God must be posited as an attribute; and this, after it has been freed from all limitations, is ascribed to Him, or else its negation is ascribed to Him; while on the other hand causality stands in the closest connexion with the feeling of absolute dependence itself. And if the first two be viewed in their relation to each other, it is clear that negation by itself is no way to posit any attribute, unless something positive remains behind the negation.

In that case the negation will consist simply in the fact that the limits of the positive are denied. But in the same manner the way of the removal of limits is a negation, for something is posited of God, but the limits which elsewhere would be co-posited are not posited of God. The identity of these two methods becomes quite obvious in the idea of Infinity, which is at the same time the general form of absence of limits, for what is posited as infinite is also freed from limitation; but at the same time it shows quite generally (by the fact that it is a negation in which nothing is immediately posited but in which everything may be posited which can be thought of as either limited or unlimited), that by negation we can only posit an attribute in so far as something positive remains behind the negation. Both these methods then can only be applied either haphazard with reference to the question whether something, which as such could only be absolutely denied of God, can be conceived as unlimited and posited as a divine attribute; or if this is to be avoided, the application of these methods must be preceded by a definition as to what kind of attribute-conceptions are rightly to be ascribed to God in an unlimited fashion, and what kind simply must be denied of Him. The third method, on the contrary, is certainly an independent one. And even if we do not wish to maintain that all divine attributes corresponding to any modification of our feeling of dependence can equally be derived immediately from the idea of causality, but rather here at the start must premise for one thing that to this conception the other methods must first be applied, *i.e.* that the finitude of causality must be denied and its productivity posited as unlimited; and again, that in so far as a plurality of attributes is developed out of the idea of the divine causality, this differentiation can correspond to nothing real in God; indeed that neither in isolation nor taken together do the attributes express the Being of God in itself (for the essence of that which has been active can never be known simply from its activity alone) – yet this at least is certain, that all the divine attributes to be dealt with in Christian Dogmatics must somehow go back to the divine causality, since they are only meant to explain the feeling of absolute dependence.

. . .

From this discussion it follows: (*a*) that the presupposition on which the idea is based that those attributes which express God's relation to the world have the appearance of mere additions and accidents, *i.e.* the presupposition of a separation between what God is, in and for Himself, and what He is in relation to the world, is also the source of the idea that the purely internal (*innerlichen*) attributes can only be conceived negatively; (*b*) that the rules laid down to secure the collection of all the divine attributes in one *locus* evoke conceptions which are quite foreign to the interests of religion, and result in a confusion of what it was intended to distinguish. We may hope, therefore, to solve our problem equally well without this apparatus and apart from any such collection if only we treat each individual part of our scheme as adequately as possible. Still, we too shall be able to make use of many of these formulas in our own way.

. . .

And in considering the manifestations of the religious self-consciousness, if we find that everything which would destroy His presence in us must specially be denied of God, and everything which favours His presence in us specially be affirmed of Him, we can say in our own way that thus divine attributes are formulated by the methods of removal of limits and negation; but those which arise from present observation, and there will be such, are reached by the method of causality. Still, this diverges fairly widely from the general usage of those formulæ, which rather betrays an analogy with speculation.

(Taken from F. D. E. Schleiermacher, The Christian Faith, *ed. H. R. Mackintosh and J. S. Stewart, Edinburgh: T&T Clark 1999, §50.)*

II.1.8 Karl Barth, from the *Church Dogmatics*

Barth argues that the question of the knowability of God in the abstract is a non-question, because God is in fact known in Jesus Christ. Therefore, the only worthwhile form of the question is asking how this actual knowledge is in fact possible to understand better what we do know.

To ask about the 'knowability' of God is to ask about the possibility on the basis of which God is known. It is to look back from the knowledge of God and to ask about the presuppositions and conditions on the basis of which it comes about that God is known. Only in this way, only with this backward look, is it possible to ask about the knowability of God in the Church's doctrine of God. We come to it from 'the knowledge of God in its fulfilment.' It is from there that we go on to ask about the knowability of God. The type of thinking which wants to begin with the question of the knowability of God and then to pass on from that point to the question of the fulfilment of the knowledge of God is not grateful but grasping, not obedient but self-autonomous. It is not theological thinking. It does not arise from the Church, or rather, from the Church's basis, and it does not serve the Church. What it affirms to be knowable and then to be actually known – whatever else it may be – is certainly not God the Father, the Son and the Holy Spirit whose revelation and work is attested by the Holy Scriptures and proclaimed by the Church. If this God is God – and there is no other God – there is no way from the question of the knowability of God to that of the actual knowledge of Him. There is only the descending way in the opposite direction.

Now in relation to the question of the knowledge of God in its actual fulfilment we have already established the fact that it cannot be: 'Is God really known?' as though we had first to establish this from some other source than the real knowledge of God. In view of the fact that the knowledge of God is actually fulfilled we can only ask about its mode. On the presupposition that God is known, how and how far does this happen? But self-evidently we can ask about the knowability of God, too, only in this way and not otherwise. We cannot ask: 'Is God knowable?' For God is actually known and therefore God is obviously knowable. We cannot ask about an abstract possibility of the knowledge of God. We can ask only about its concrete possibility as definitely present already in its actual fulfilment. Our questioning can relate only to that foundation of the knowledge of God which is already laid and laid in a quite definite manner. It cannot relate to one which has still to be laid and determined in one way or another. Otherwise our question will again betray an untheological type of thinking, i.e., a thinking which derives from some other source than gratitude and obedience. When we think gratefully and obediently, we can start only with the fact that the possibility is also given on the basis of which God is known. And it is given in a quite definite way. Therefore the presuppositions and conditions of that fulfilment are firmly established in themselves, so that their reality is reality. In relation to their reality and kind they do not first have to be discovered by enquiry, far less do they have to be established or even created in their reality and kind by the various answers which we may discover. In this matter, too, we are asking about the mode, about the how and the how far.

Put in this way, the question of the knowability of God is also meaningful and necessary. It constitutes the second step on the way of the indispensable investigation of the knowledge of God, which forms the presupposition for the understanding of what is said and heard about God in the Church. This investigation as a whole is indispensable because the presupposition has to be kept in the consciousness of both the teaching and hearing Church, and therefore it has to be continually recalled to mind. There can be no right understanding and no right explanation of the revealed Word of God, attested in the Bible and proclaimed in the Church, without an understanding and explanation of the knowledge of Him whose Word is to be spoken and heard in the Church. But the investigation which this involves cannot be content merely to establish and describe the fact of this knowledge. If the knowledge of God which establishes the Church's language and hearing about God is to be understood and explained aright and therefore to be recalled critically and positively to the Church's consciousness, it is essential that, after the question as to its actuality, the question of its possibility must also be explicitly raised and answered. And this is the question of the genesis of its actuality. We are not dealing with a question which arises from an idle or even an anxious, but either way a dangerous, curiosity which has an inquisitive desire to probe back behind the only healthy and self-sufficient fact of the knowledge of God in its fulfilment in order to reassure itself from some superior position. If our present enquiry is on the right lines, this kind of curiosity will definitely not have its reward. But as we can conjecture at the outset from these preliminary remarks on the putting of the question, the result or at any rate one result of our enquiry will be that there is no such superior position in respect of this fact and therefore no reassurance to be gained from it. There is only the certainty inherent in the fact itself and as such. But we must conduct this further enquiry in such a way that it eliminates the conjecture that behind or above the fact of the real knowledge of God there is a kind of empty space which can be filled up by the assertions of an overlapping doctrine of being and knowledge in general. The temptation which necessitates this idea of an empty space must be attacked at its roots. It must be made explicit that the possibility of the knowledge of God is the possibility – and only the possibility – which is contained in the reality as we have described it in the foregoing section. Or conversely, the knowledge of God described there has its possibility, its presuppositions and its determinations in itself. Therefore the fact itself bears direct witness to its genesis. The knowability of God can be known only in the real knowledge of God. But it can really be known. It can never be superfluous to make all this explicit. As it is done, the glory of the knowledge of God becomes visible in a new dimension and therefore so much the clearer and the more to be adored. If it is not done the door will stand wide open for error in this dimension. But again, it can never be dangerous to make all this explicit. If only it is done in the right way there is no risk that we will be led away from the only healthy and self-sufficient fact of the knowledge of God in its fulfilment – indeed, we will be led all the more into the depth of its nature.

We must begin with the fact that there is a readiness of God to be known as He actually is known in the fulfilment in which the knowledge of God is a fact. In the first instance and decisively the knowability of God is this readiness of God Himself. 'God is knowable' means: 'God can be known' – He can be known of and by Himself. In His essence, as it is turned to us in His activity, He is so constituted that He can be known by us.

(Taken from Karl Barth, Church Dogmatics, *ed. G. W. Bromiley and T. F. Torrance, Edinburgh: T&T Clark 1956–77, II/1, pp. 63–5.)*

II.1.9 T. F. Torrance, from *Theological Science*

Torrance accepts Barth's formulation of the question, and explores what sort of knowledge of God we do in fact have in Jesus Christ.

The question as to the possibility of the knowledge of God has to be asked if we are to gain a full understanding of the objectivity of theological knowledge, but we have kept this question back until now, because it is only meaningful when correlated with the actual knowledge of God. Even so, the question has to be put in the right way in order to be real.

When, for example, we examine the question 'how is it possible to know God', we find that it questions the very fact that the question implies in order to be a question at all. It is not a scientific question, but a self-contradictory or empty movement of thought. Nevertheless its examination serves to show that we can begin meaningfully only with the fact of prior knowledge of God and then seek to test and clarify it. We cannot genuinely discuss the possibility of the knowledge of God outside of its own actual reality. Therefore to those who doubt the possibility of such knowledge we cannot scientifically seek a place outside the knowledge of God where its possibility can be judged before we acknowledge its reality, but we can only point to actual knowledge and seek to explicate and elucidate the possibility arising out of its actuality, and in that way bear witness to it.

But there is a genuine question here which we must seek to answer. It is the given Reality itself which poses it in its actual confrontation of us – the question as to its nature and ground. 'How do we actually know God? How is God known? How far is He knowable?' In the nature of the case this is not a question that can be put in general terms without making it unreal. Real questions must be asked in a real way, that is to say, without being removed from their proper setting and then considered in isolation in abstract or general terms. We shall return again to the place of scientific questions in theology, but here we are concerned with the inquiry into the ground, and therefore into the possibility, of our knowledge of God in order to test how far our knowledge of God really rests on God Himself, or how far it can stand up to the test of referring it to objective reality as its sole presupposition and the ultimate source of its necessity. This is particularly important because this is the kind of knowledge that has to be continually renewed and established on its proper object. It is then by raising the question as to the possibility of the knowledge of God, and by tracing its roots in the way in which God has actually objectified Himself for us and revealed Himself to us, that we can correct our thinking and make it genuinely theological. Thus whether to those outside who doubt the possibility of the knowledge of God or to those inside who seek its clarification, we have to point to the fact that God has given Himself to be known by us in Jesus Christ, and seek to elucidate the *mode* of that knowledge. God's decisive action in Jesus Christ invalidates all questions whether He might have acted otherwise.

It is thus in the historical actuality of Jesus Christ, very God and very Man, as the Creed speaks of Him, that the possibility of our knowledge of God is rooted. In Him and through Him God has actually become known by man. Now this means that in Jesus Christ God has broken into the closed circle of our inability and inadequacy, and estrangement and self-will, and within our alien condition has achieved and established real knowledge of Himself. It is in the freedom of God to do that, and in the fact that God actually has done that, that our knowledge of Him is grounded – that is, in His condescension to enter within our creaturely frailty and incompetence and so to realize knowledge of Himself from within our mode of existence, in the incarnate Son. We do not first have to achieve this knowledge, we do not even have to achieve the appropriation of it which first actualizes it within our creaturely existence, for that has already been achieved for us in Christ, and in Him we may now freely participate in the knowledge of God as an actuality already translated and made accessible for us by His grace. Thus our freedom in knowing and appropriating the truth is grounded in the objective freedom of God, and our decision for the truth is grounded in the objective and decisive act of God made on our behalf in the whole historical fact of Christ. We find and know God where He has sought us and condescended to communicate Himself, in His objectivity in Jesus Christ. We cannot seek to know Him by transcending His condescension or objectivity, or by going behind it, for that would be to go where God has not given Himself to be the object of our knowledge. We can only know God in His self-objectification for us, not by seeking non-objective knowledge of Him. This then is the given fact, the indispensable presupposition of theological knowledge, and with which Christian theology stands or falls, that God Himself, the only God, the living and true God, has condescended to enter within our creaturely and contingent existence, to objectify Himself for us there in Jesus Christ, so that Jesus Christ is the Way, the Truth, and the Life, in whom and through whom alone we go to the Father, and by reference to whom alone we have true knowledge of God.

Our understanding of the possibility of the knowledge of God can only carry us up to a penultimate, never to an ultimate, point, for it belongs to the very nature of the object we are concerned to know that we are unable to make our knowing of it fully comprehensible as *our* action, or therefore as a possibility of *ours*. In the nature of the case we are unable to think out to the end just how we think this truth that transcends us. If we could, it would not be the Truth of God. The demand that we must be able to think it out to the end, if it is real, presupposes that we can gain ascendency over it and that we are in fact transcendent over it. But that is to take the way of mythology, in which we project ourselves into the place of God and think out a god in man's image. Now it is this mythologizing process that is sharply inhibited and set aside by the doctrine of the Spirit in the concern to guard the transcendence and objectivity of the Truth of God, that is in biblical language, His *holiness*. God is present to us, and gives Himself to our knowing, only in such a way that He remains the Lord who has ascendency over us, who distinguishes Himself from us, and makes Himself known in His divine otherness even when He draws us into communion with Himself. He is present to us in such a way that He never resigns knowledge of Himself to our mastery, but remains the One who is Master over us, who resists, and objects to, every attempt on our part to subdue or redact the possibility of knowledge grounded in His divine freedom to an immanent and latent possibility which we deem ourselves to possess apart from Him in virtue of our own being. Hence we can never give an account of our knowledge of God in such a way as to reduce His Holiness, His Transcendence, His unapproachable Majesty, to a vanishing point, but only in such a way that we are thrown ultimately upon His mercy, upon His transcendent freedom to lower Himself to us and to lift us up to Him beyond anything that we can think or conceive out of ourselves. To know God in His Holiness means that our human subjectivity is opened out and up toward that which infinitely transcends it.

(Taken from Thomas F. Torrance, Theological Science, *Edinburgh: T&T Clark 1996,* © *T. F. Torrance, 1969, pp. 43–53.)*

II.2 How do we know what we know?

Introductory essay

It is incumbent upon every field of enquiry, and certainly upon every academic discipline, that it give some account of how it comes to know what it knows. We have noted already in this volume the resources that may be brought to bear upon our knowing of God. Scripture, reason, tradition and experience all play a role in theological enquiry. But we come now to consider the logic by which these sources may be said to yield knowledge of God. By what logic do theologians make the claim that X and Y are the case? Claims to theological knowledge have become particularly problematic in the modern and postmodern worlds. Both the modernist and postmodernist contend that to count as knowledge a claim must be both absolutely certain and empirically demonstrable. The modernist typically believes that the claims of reason and of scientific experiment will meet such criteria but the claims of theology will not. There has been a strong tendency in the West therefore, to relegate theology to the realm of private opinion. The postmodernist on the other hand, despairs of any claims meeting the criteria of absolute certainty and demonstrability and contends, not just for theology but across all spheres of human enquiry, that we must abandon our pretensions to know the truth and settle instead for a plurality of opinions and culture-bound perspectives.

On both these accounts, the prospects for a coherent defence of theological knowledge look bleak. But perhaps it is the case that we have got the wrong idea about what it is to know something. Why must knowledge be either absolutely certain or demonstrable? It turns out that very few claims to knowledge can meet such criteria. Those few that can are called analytic truths. The truth value of an analytic proposition can be discerned by anybody who understands the meanings of the terms employed in the proposition. Thus the proposition 'all bachelors are unmarried men' for instance, can be judged to be true by all who understand what the statement means. But most claims about the world are not so straightforward. Anything that happens in history, for example, cannot be stated in an analytical proposition. For historical truth we need what are called synthetic propositions. A synthetic proposition makes a claim about some contingent reality, about something that has happened or is the case but might have been otherwise: 'The Battle of Hastings was fought in 1066', is an example of such a claim. The truth value of that proposition cannot be ascertained just by understanding the meanings of the terms. We need to know a lot of other things about the world in order to ascertain the truth of such a statement and, crucially, we will have to trust the testimonies of others who have formed and preserved for posterity the records which enable us to know that the Battle of Hastings was fought in 1066. To the extent that we are reliant on the testimony of others, however, our knowledge is no longer empirically demonstrable, nor absolutely certain.

Some argue that even first-hand experience is open to doubt. And yet few people do doubt that we can nevertheless make legitimate claims to knowledge about synthetic truths. Common sense legitimates, in our day-to-day existence, a high degree of trust in the deliverances of our sense experience for instance, or in the testimonies of others about what is the case. To be sure, there is room for doubt, but for most of our knowledge claims we rely on our personal judgment and happily settle for something a little less than absolute certainty.

This concession to common sense is important for theology for many of the claims that Christian theologians wish to make are founded upon synthetic truths. Theologians draw upon the biblical story, upon a story of certain things that have happened in history. They speak for instance about Jesus of Nazareth who lived, died and rose again and who lived his life in professed obedience to the one who he called 'Father' and in dependence upon the Holy Spirit. Theologians, as part of the Christian church, tell this story under the conviction that through it the truth of God's purpose for creation and of human salvation is revealed. These historical events are contingent. They might have happened otherwise or not at all, and so we are reliant, at least in part, on the testimony of others for our knowledge of them. Equally important is the fact that, just as in many other knowledge claims, we must exercise personal judgment in assessing the coherency and plausibility of theological contentions. It is possible to doubt such claims. They are not empirically demonstrable, nor are they absolutely certain, but they cannot for that reason be abandoned as truths about the way the world really is.

In the case of theology, this commonsense epistemology is developed in a particularly important direction. We have noted that some of our claims to knowledge rely on the testimony of others. This is especially the case, for instance, in respect of our knowledge of other persons. To get to know another person is in large measure, a matter of allowing them to disclose themselves to us. In speaking about God, theology, similarly, claims to be dealing with a form of personal relation, a relation in which we are dependent upon God to disclose himself to us. The theological term for this self-disclosure of God is 'revelation'. It is only upon the basis of revelation, many theologians would argue, in attentiveness to the self-disclosure of God, that theology may claim to tell the truth about God. This does not remove the need for personal judgment, nor indeed for the commitment that is characteristic of all personal relations, but this Christian account of revelation does provide a plausible logic under which theological knowing may be said to take place. The selection of readings in this section provide further exploration of the way in which theological knowledge can be arrived at and sustained.

The first reading (II.2.1) is an extract from *Against the Heresies*, a very important second-century theological treatise by St Irenaeus. The work arose out of Irenaeus' encounters with Gnosticism. It is in part, therefore, an attempt to counter the view that we attain to knowledge of God through initiation into some secret community of knowledge. It was characteristic of the Gnostics to try to sidestep the synthetic truths of history, and to seek an alternate route to the understanding of God. But Irenaeus insisted that it was through history that God has made himself known and most especially through the history of Jesus of Nazareth. Irenaeus also emphasizes that knowledge of God is not something that we attain for ourselves, but something that we receive. The testimony of the Holy Spirit is crucial, on this account, to the way in which we may come to understand what has taken place in Jesus.

In the extract from Thomas Aquinas (II.2.2) the question is considered whether the proposition 'God exists' can be regarded as an analytic truth (what Aquinas calls a self-evident truth). In the form of a dialogue, or disputation, Aquinas presents arguments both for and against the idea that the existence of God is self-evident before drawing his own conclusion. Aquinas also offers a discussion of the relation between faith and reason in theological knowing. Faith, Aquinas argues, plays an important role in theological knowing but in co-operation with reason not at reason's expense. Aquinas himself provides a good example of how philosophical reasoning may be called upon to play a part in theology.

John Calvin (II.2.3) provides further elucidation of the role of faith in theological knowing as also of the way that God is involved in our knowing of him. In both aspects of the knowing process Jesus Christ is central. Faith is a form of personal relation with Christ who is himself to be understood as the one through whom God has made himself known.

The precise relationship between faith and reason, as also between theology and philosophy, has been a matter of some dispute in theological scholarship. Although these are not the only options, many theologians have tended to group themselves around the views either that faith is subject to reason, that faith is against reason, or that faith is above reason. This last position is exemplified in the work of the French mathematician and amateur theologian, Blaise Pascal. While considering there to be no conflict between faith and reason, Pascal nevertheless argues that faith, or what he sometimes calls 'the knowledge of the heart', gives access to truths not accessible to reason alone. A series of aphorisms from Pascal's *Pensées* (II.2.4) reveal his view that this 'knowledge of the heart' applies not just in theology but to a great deal of our experience.

The importance of faith in theological knowing is further explored in the extract from Karl Barth (II.2.5), who also elucidates the important theological claim that God is thought and known when in his own freedom he makes himself apprehensible to humankind. Revelation is thus argued to be the basis of all theological knowing. Barth is especially important in the development of twentieth-century theology for the centrality he gave to the doctrine of the Trinity. A trinitarian understanding of God, Barth argued, is both demanded by and renders intelligible God's self-disclosure in Jesus Christ through the power of the Holy Spirit.

An analysis of precisely what is meant by the term revelation is provided in the extract from Christoph Schwöbel (II.2.8). Of particular importance in Schwöbel's account is his clarification of the way in which the concept of revelation is to be understood in relational terms. The act of divine self-disclosure is at the same time an act of divine judgment and of reconciliation between God and humankind. Schwöbel, too, elucidates the logic of revelation in trinitarian terms.

Thomas F. Torrance (II.2.7) has been one of the key proponents in twentieth-century theology of the view that because theological knowing is grounded in the objectivity of God's own self-disclosure, theology itself may be regarded as properly scientific. That is to say, theology is a genuine uncovering of the truth of the object with which it is concerned. One of the distinctive aspects of theological science, however, is that we are dealing not with an object at our disposal, but with one who gives himself in personal encounter. Theology is thus dependent upon God's gift of his Word, and has no basis to proceed except through attentiveness to that Word.

The theme of revelation is continued in the extract from Hans Urs von Balthasar (II.2.6), one of the most prolific Roman Catholic theologians of the twentieth century. Von Balthasar developed a sophisticated theological aesthetics in which theological knowing is conceived, not merely as an affair of the intellect, but as an interpersonal encounter, characterized by love and in which one's whole being is engaged in the apprehension of the glory of God.

Although diverse in their detail, the readings present a consistent testimony both to the fundamental importance of revelation in Christian theology and to the centrality of Jesus Christ as the unique mediator of divine revelation. It is on the basis of this divine action that Christian theology claims to know the reality with which it is concerned.

MAR

II.2.1 St Irenaeus of Lyons, from *Against the Heresies*

In this extract Irenaeus assumes that true knowledge of God comes through knowing Christ, and so considers the problem of those who lived before Christ's coming. They were enabled to know God in Christ by the Holy Spirit.

1. But that it was not only the prophets and many righteous men, who, foreseeing through the Holy Spirit his advent, prayed that they might attain to that period in which they should see their Lord face to face, and hear his words, the Lord has made manifest, when he says to his disciples, 'Many prophets and righteous men have desired to see those things which ye see, and have not seen them; and to hear those things which ye hear, and have not heard them.' In what way, then, did they desire both to hear and to see, unless they had foreknowledge of his future advent? But how could they have foreknown it, unless they had previously received foreknowledge from himself? And how do the Scriptures testify of him, unless all things had ever been revealed and shown to believers by one and the same God through the Word; he at one time conferring with his creature, and at another propounding his law; at one time, again, reproving, at another exhorting, and then setting free his servant, and adopting him as a son; and, at the proper time, bestowing an incorruptible inheritance, for the purpose of bringing man to perfection? For he formed him for growth and increase, as the Scripture says: 'Increase and multiply.'

2. And in this respect God differs from man, that God indeed makes, but man is made; and truly, he who makes is always the same; but that which is made must receive both beginning, and middle, and addition, and increase. And God does indeed create after a skilful manner, while man is created skilfully. God also is truly perfect in all things, himself equal and similar to himself, as he is all light, and all mind, and all substance, and the fount of all good; but man receives advancement and increase towards God. For as God is always the same, so also man, when found in God, shall always go on towards God. For neither does God at any time cease to confer benefits upon, or to enrich man; nor does man ever cease from receiving the benefits, and being enriched by God. For the receptacle of his goodness, and the instrument of his glorification, is the man who is grateful to him that made him; and again, the receptacle of his just judgement is the ungrateful man, who both despises his Maker and is not subject to his Word; who has promised that he will give very much to those always bringing forth fruit, and more to those who have the Lord's money. 'Well done,' he says, 'good and faithful servant: because thou hast been faithful in little, I will appoint

thee over many things; enter thou into the joy of thy Lord.' The Lord himself thus promises very much.

3. As, therefore, he has promised to give very much to those who do now bring forth fruit, according to the gift of his grace, but not according to the changeableness of 'knowledge;' for the Lord remains the same, and the same Father is revealed; thus, therefore, has the one and the same Lord granted, by means of his advent, a greater gift of grace to those of a later period, than what he had granted to those under the Old Testament dispensation. For they indeed used to hear, by means of [his] servants, that the King would come, and they rejoiced to a certain extent, inasmuch as they hoped for his coming; but those who have beheld him actually present, and have obtained liberty, and been made partakers of his gifts, do possess a greater amount of grace, and a higher degree of exultation, rejoicing because of the King's arrival: as also David says, 'My soul shall rejoice in the Lord; it shall be glad in his salvation.' And for this cause, upon his entrance into Jerusalem, all those who were in the way recognised David their king in his sorrow of soul, and spread their garments for him, and ornamented the way with green boughs, crying out with great joy and gladness, 'Hosanna to the Son of David; blessed is he that cometh in the name of the Lord: hosanna in the highest.' But to the envious wicked stewards, who circumvented those under them, and ruled over those that had no great intelligence, and for this reason were unwilling that the king should come, and who said to him, 'Hearest thou what these say?' did the Lord reply, 'Have ye never read, Out of the mouths of babes and sucklings hast Thou perfected praise? – thus pointing out that what had been declared by David concerning the Son of God, was accomplished in his own person; and indicating that they were indeed ignorant of the meaning of the Scripture and the dispensation of God; but declaring that it was himself who was announced by the prophets as Christ, whose name is praised in all the earth, and who perfects praise to his Father from the mouth of babes and sucklings; wherefore also his glory has been raised above the heavens.

4. If, therefore, the self-same person is present who was announced by the prophets, our Lord Jesus Christ, and if his advent has brought in a fuller [measure of] grace and greater gifts to those who have received him, it is plain that the Father also is himself the same who was proclaimed by the prophets, and that the Son, on his coming, did not spread the knowledge of another Father, but of the same who was preached from the beginning; from whom also he has brought down liberty to those who, in a lawful manner, and with a willing mind, and with all the heart, do him service; whereas to scoffers, and to those not subject to God, but who follow outward purifications for the praise of men (which observances had been given as a type of future things, – the law typifying, as it were, certain things in a shadow,

and delineating eternal things by temporal, celestial by terrestrial), and to those who pretend that they do themselves observe more than what has been prescribed, as if preferring their own zeal to God himself, while within they are full of hypocrisy, and covetousness, and all wickedness, – [to such] has he assigned everlasting perdition by cutting them off from life.

(Taken from the Ante-Nicene Fathers vol. III, trans. and ed. A. Roberts and J. Donaldson, IV.II.)

II.2.2 St Thomas Aquinas, from the *Summa Theologica*

Aquinas here discusses whether we can know that God exists. The existence of God is not self-evident to us, because we do not understand who God is (if we did, it would be self-evident, or so Aquinas thinks), but there are five ways in which we can prove the existence of God – or at least of a being with characteristics we claim belong to God (notice the form of the proofs: having proved the existence of a first cause, Aquinas says that 'everyone calls this God').

Article 1 Whether the existence of God is self-evident?

Objection 1. It seems that the existence of God is self-evident. Now those things are said to be self-evident to us the knowledge of which is naturally implanted in us, as we can see in regard to first principles. But as Damascene [*i.e.* St John of Damascus] says (*The Orthodox Faith* i, 1,3), 'the knowledge of God is naturally implanted in all.' Therefore the existence of God is self-evident.

Objection 2. Further, those things are said to be self-evident which are known as soon as the terms are known, which the Philosopher [*i.e.* Aristotle] (I *Poster.* iii) says is true of the first principles of demonstration. Thus, when the nature of a whole and of a part is known, it is at once recognized that every whole is greater than its part. But as soon as the signification of the word 'God' is understood, it is at once seen that God exists. For by this word is signified that thing than which nothing greater can be conceived. But that which exists actually and mentally is greater than that which exists only mentally. Therefore, since as soon as the word 'God' is understood it exists mentally, it also follows that it exists actually. Therefore the proposition 'God exists' is self-evident.

Objection 3. Further, the existence of truth is self-evident. For whoever denies the existence of truth grants that truth does not exist: and, if truth does not exist, then the proposition 'Truth does not exist' is true: and if there is anything true, there must be truth. But God is truth itself: 'I am the way, the truth, and the life' (John 14:6) Therefore 'God exists' is self-evident.

On the contrary, No one can mentally admit the opposite of what is self-evident; as the Philosopher (*Metaphysics* vi) states concerning the first principles of demonstration. But the opposite of the proposition 'God is' can be mentally admitted: 'The fool said in his heart, There is no God' (Ps. 52:1). Therefore, that God exists is not self-evident.

I answer that, A thing can be self-evident in either of two ways: on the one hand, self-evident in itself, though not to us; on the other, self-evident in itself, and to us. A proposition is self-evident because the predicate is included in the essence of the subject, as 'Man is an animal,' for animal is contained in the essence of man. If, therefore the essence of the predicate and subject be known to all, the proposition will be self-evident to all; as is clear with regard to the first principles of demonstration, the terms of which are common things that no one is ignorant of, such as being and non-being, whole and part, and such like. If, however, there are some to whom the essence of the predicate and subject is unknown, the proposition will be self-evident in itself, but not to those who do not know the meaning of the predicate and subject of the proposition. Therefore, it happens, as Boethius says (*Hebdom.*, the title of which is: 'Whether all that is, is good'), 'that there are some mental concepts self-evident only to the learned, as that incorporeal substances are not in space.' Therefore I say that this proposition, 'God exists,' of itself is self-evident, for the predicate is the same as the subject, because God is his own existence as will be hereafter shown. Now because we do not know the essence of God, the proposition is not self-evident to us; but needs to be demonstrated by things that are more known to us, though less known in their nature – namely, by effects.

Reply to Objection 1. To know that God exists in a general and confused way is implanted in us by nature, inasmuch as God is man's beatitude. For man naturally desires happiness, and what is naturally desired by man must be naturally known to him. This, however, is not to know absolutely that God exists; just as to know that someone is approaching is not the same as to know that Peter is approaching, even though it is Peter who is approaching; for many there are who imagine that man's perfect good which is happiness, consists in riches, and others in pleasures, and others in something else.

Reply to Objection 2. Perhaps not everyone who hears this word 'God' understands it to signify something than which nothing greater can be thought, seeing that some have believed God to be a body. Yet, granted that everyone understands that by this word 'God' is signified something than which nothing greater can be thought, nevertheless, it does not therefore follow that he understands that what the word signifies exists actually, but only that it exists mentally. Nor can it be argued that it actually exists, unless it be admitted that there actually exists something than which nothing greater can be thought; and this precisely is not admitted by those who hold that God does not exist.

Reply to Objection 3. The existence of truth in general is self-evident but the existence of a Primal Truth is not self-evident to us.
. . .

Article 3 Whether God exists?

. . .

I answer that, The existence of God can be proved in five ways:

The first and more manifest way is the argument from motion. It is certain, and evident to our senses, that in the world some things are in motion. Now whatever is in motion is put in motion by another, for nothing can be in motion except it is in potentiality to that towards which it is in motion; whereas a thing moves inasmuch as it is in act. For motion is nothing else than the reduction of something from potentiality to actuality. But nothing can be reduced from potentiality to actuality, except by something in a state of actuality. Thus that which is actually hot, as fire, makes wood, which is potentially hot, to be actually hot, and thereby moves and changes it. Now it is not possible that the same thing should be at once in actuality and potentiality in the same respect, but only in different respects. For what is actually hot cannot simultaneously be potentially hot; but it is simultaneously potentially cold. It is therefore impossible that in the same respect and in the same way a thing should be both mover and moved, i.e. that it should move itself. Therefore, whatever is in motion must be put in motion by another. If that by which it is put in motion be itself put in motion, then this also must needs be put in motion by another, and that by another again. But this cannot go on to infinity, because then there would be no first mover, and, consequently, no other mover; seeing that subsequent movers move only inasmuch as they are put in motion by the first mover; as the staff moves only because it is put in motion by the hand. Therefore it is necessary to arrive at a first mover, put in motion by no other; and this everyone understands to be God.

The second way is from the nature of the efficient cause. In the world of sense we find there is an order of efficient causes. There is no case known (neither is it, indeed, possible) in which a thing is found to be the efficient cause of itself; for so it would be prior to itself, which is impossible. Now in efficient causes it is not possible to go on to infinity, because in all efficient causes following in order, the first is the cause of the intermediate cause, and the intermediate is the cause of the ultimate cause, whether the intermediate cause be several, or only one. Now to take away the cause is to take away the effect. Therefore, if there be no first cause among efficient causes, there will be no ultimate, nor any intermediate cause. But if in efficient causes it is possible to go on to infinity, there will be no first efficient cause, neither will there be an ultimate effect, nor any intermediate efficient causes; all of which is plainly false. Therefore it is necessary to admit a first efficient cause, to which everyone gives the name of God.

The third way is taken from possibility and necessity, and runs thus. We find in nature things that are possible to be and not to be, since they are found to be generated, and to corrupt, and consequently, they are possible to be and not to be. But it is impossible for these always to exist, for that which is possible not to be at some time is not. Therefore, if everything is possible not to be, then at one time there could have been nothing in existence. Now if this were true, even now there would be nothing in existence, because that which does not exist only begins to exist by something already existing. Therefore, if at one time nothing was in existence, it would have been impossible for anything to have begun to exist; and thus even now nothing would be in existence – which is absurd. Therefore, not all beings are merely possible, but there must exist something the existence of which is necessary. But every necessary thing either has its necessity caused by another, or not. Now it is impossible to go on to infinity in necessary things which have their necessity caused by another, as has been already proved in regard to efficient causes. Therefore we cannot but postulate the existence of some being having of itself its own necessity, and not receiving it from another, but rather causing in others their necessity. This all men speak of as God.

The fourth way is taken from the gradation to be found in things. Among beings there are some more and some less good, true, noble and the like. But 'more' and 'less' are predicated of different things, according as they resemble in their different ways something which is the maximum, as a thing is said to be hotter according as it more nearly resembles that which is hottest; so that there is something which is truest, something best, something noblest and, consequently, something which is uttermost being; for those things that are greatest in truth are greatest in being, as it is written in [Aristotle's] *Metaphysics* ii. Now the maximum in any genus is the cause of all in that genus; as fire, which is the maximum heat, is the cause of all hot things. Therefore there must also be something which is to all beings the cause of their being, goodness, and every other perfection; and this we call God.

The fifth way is taken from the governance of the world. We see that things which lack intelligence, such as natural bodies, act for an end, and this is evident from their acting always, or nearly always, in the same way, so as to obtain the best result. Hence it is plain that not fortuitously, but designedly, do they achieve their end. Now whatever lacks intelligence cannot move towards an end, unless it be directed by some being endowed with knowledge and intelligence; as the arrow is shot to its mark by the archer. Therefore some intelligent being exists by whom all natural things are directed to their end; and this being we call God.

(Taken from the Fathers of the English Dominican Province Translation, London: Burns, Oates & Washbourne 1924–34, Ia q.2.)

II.2.3 John Calvin, from *The Institutes of the Christian Religion*

Calvin here gives his definition of faith. It is 'a firm and certain knowledge of God's benevolence toward us, founded upon the truth of the freely given promise in Christ, both revealed to our minds and sealed upon our hearts by the Holy Spirit'.

6. Faith rests upon God's Word

This, then, is the true knowledge of Christ, if we receive him as he is offered by the Father: namely, clothed with his gospel. For just as he has been appointed as the goal of our faith, so we cannot take the right road to him unless the gospel goes before us. And there, surely, the treasures of grace are opened to us; for if they had been closed, Christ would have benefited us little. Thus Paul yokes faith to teaching, as an inseparable companion, with these words: 'You did not so learn Christ if indeed you were taught what is the truth in Christ' [Eph. 4:20–21].

Yet I do not so restrict faith to the gospel without confessing that what sufficed for building it up had been handed down by Moses and the prophets. But because a fuller manifestation of Christ has been revealed in the gospel, Paul justly calls it the 'doctrine of faith' [cf. I Tim. 4:6]. For this reason, he says in another passage that by the coming of faith the law was abolished [Rom. 10:4; cf. Gal. 3:25]. He understands by this term the new and extraordinary kind of teaching by which Christ, after he became our teacher, has more clearly set forth the mercy of the Father, and has more surely testified to our salvation.

Yet it will be an easier and more suitable method if we descend by degrees from general to particular. First, we must be reminded that there is a permanent relationship between faith and the Word. He could not separate one from the other any more than we could separate the rays from the sun from which they come. For this reason, God exclaims in The Book of Isaiah: 'Hear me and your soul shall live' [ch. 55:3]. And John shows this same wellspring of faith in these words: 'These things have been written that you may believe' [John 20:31]. The prophet, also, desiring to exhort the people to faith, says: 'Today if you will hear his voice' [Ps. 95:7]. 'To hear' is generally understood as meaning to believe. In short, it is not without reason that in The Book of Isaiah, God distinguishes the children of the church from outsiders by this mark: he will teach all his children [Isa. 54:13; John 6:45] that they may learn of him [cf. John 6:45]. For if benefits were indiscriminately given, why would he have directed his Word to a few? To this corresponds the fact that the Evangelists commonly use the words 'believers' and 'disciples' as synonyms.

This is especially Luke's usage in The Acts of the Apostles: indeed he extends this title even to a woman in Acts 9:36.

Therefore if faith turns away even in the slightest degree from this goal toward which it should aim, it does not keep its own nature, but becomes uncertain credulity and vague error of mind. The same Word is the basis whereby faith is supported and sustained; if it turns away from the Word, it falls. Therefore, take away the Word and no faith will then remain.

. . . In understanding faith it is not merely a question of knowing that God exists, but also – and this especially – of knowing what is his will toward us. For it is not so much our concern to know who he is in himself, as what he wills to be toward us.

Now, therefore, we hold faith to be a knowledge of God's will toward us, perceived from his Word. But the foundation of this is a preconceived conviction of God's truth. As for its certainty, so long as your mind is at war with itself, the Word will be of doubtful and weak authority, or rather of none. And it is not even enough to believe that God is trustworthy [cf. Rom. 3:3], who can neither deceive nor lie [cf. Titus 1:2], unless you hold to be beyond doubt that whatever proceeds from him is sacred and inviolable truth.

7. Faith arises from God's promise of grace in Christ

But since man's heart is not aroused to faith at every word of God, we must find out at this point what, strictly speaking, faith looks to in the Word. . . . We ask only what faith finds in the Word of the Lord upon which to lean and rest. Where our conscience sees only indignation and vengeance, how can it fail to tremble and be afraid? or to shun the God whom it dreads? Yet faith ought to seek God, not to shun him.

It is plain, then, that we do not yet have a full definition of faith, inasmuch as merely to know something of God's will is not to be accounted faith. But what if we were to substitute his benevolence or his mercy in place of his will, the tidings of which are often sad and the proclamation frightening? Thus, surely, we shall more closely approach the nature of faith; for it is after we have learned that our salvation rests with God that we are attracted to seek him. This fact is confirmed for us when he declares that our salvation is his care and concern. Accordingly, we need the promise of grace, which can testify to us that the Father is merciful; since we can approach him in no other way, and upon grace alone the heart of man can rest.
. . .

Now, the knowledge of God's goodness will not be held very important unless it makes us rely on that goodness. Consequently, understanding mixed with doubt is to be excluded, as it is not in firm agreement, but in conflict, with itself. Yet far indeed is the mind of man, blind and darkened as it is, from penetrating and attaining even to perception of the will of God! And the heart, too, wavering as it is in perpetual hesitation, is far from resting secure in that conviction! Therefore our mind must be otherwise illumined and our heart strengthened, that the Word of God may obtain full faith among us. Now we shall possess a right definition of faith if we call it a firm and certain knowledge of God's benevolence toward us, founded upon the truth of the freely given promise in Christ, both revealed to our minds and sealed upon our hearts through the Holy Spirit.

14. Faith as higher knowledge

Now let us examine anew the individual parts of the definition of faith. After we have diligently examined it no doubt, I believe, will remain. When we call faith 'knowledge' we do not mean comprehension of the sort that is commonly concerned with those things which fall under human sense perception. For faith is so far above sense that man's mind has to go beyond and rise above itself in order to attain it. Even where the mind has attained, it does not comprehend what it feels. But while it is persuaded of what it does not grasp, by the very certainty of its persuasion it understands more than if it perceived anything human by its own capacity. Paul, therefore, beautifully describes it as the power 'to comprehend . . . what is the breadth and length and depth and height, and to know the love of Christ, which surpasses knowledge' [Eph. 3:18–19]. He means that what our mind embraces by faith is in every way infinite, and that this kind of knowledge is far more lofty than all understanding. Nevertheless, the Lord has 'made manifest to his saints' the secret of his will, which had been 'hidden for ages and generations' [Col. 1:26; cf. ch. 2:2]. For very good reason, then, faith is frequently called 'recognition' [see Eph. 1:17; 4:13; Col. 1:9; 3:10; I Tim. 2:4; Titus 1:1; Philemon 6; II Peter 2:21], but by John, 'knowledge.' For he declares that believers know themselves to be God's children [I John 3:2]. And obviously they surely know this. But they are more strengthened by the persuasion of divine truth than instructed by rational proof. Paul's words also point this out: 'While dwelling in this body, we wander from the Lord, for we walk by faith, not by sight' [II Cor. 5:6–7]. By these words he shows that those things which we know through faith are nonetheless absent from us and go unseen. From this we conclude that the knowledge of faith consists in assurance rather than in comprehension.

15. Faith implies certainty

We add the words 'sure and firm' in order to express a more solid constancy of persuasion. For, as faith is not content with a doubtful and changeable opinion, so is it not content with an obscure and confused conception; but requires full and fixed certainty, such as men are wont to have from things experienced and proved. 'For unbelief is so deeply rooted in our hearts, and we are so inclined to it, that not without hard struggle is each one able to persuade himself of what all confess with the mouth: namely, that God is faithful.

. . .

33. *The Word becomes efficacious for our faith through the Holy Spirit*

And this bare and external proof of the Word of God should have been amply sufficient to engender faith, did not our blindness and perversity prevent it. But our mind has such an inclination to vanity that it can never cleave fast to the truth of God; and it has such a dullness that it is always blind to the light of God's truth. Accordingly, without the illumination of the Holy Spirit, the Word can do nothing.

. . .

(Taken from The Institutes of the Christian Religion, *ed. John T. McNeill; trans. Ford Lewis Battles, The Library of Christian Classics, vol. XXI, Philadelphia, PA: Westminister Press 1960, III.2.)*

II.2.4 Blaise Pascal, from *Pensées*

In these selections Pascal illuminates the famous comment he makes in another place in this work: 'The heart has its reasons, of which reason knows nothing.'

187

Order: Men despise religion; they hate it, and fear it is true. To remedy this, we must begin by showing that religion is not contrary to reason; that it is venerable, to inspire respect for it; then we must make it lovable, to make good men hope it is true; finally, we must prove it is true. Venerable, because it has perfect knowledge of man: lovable, because it promises the true good.

282

We know truth, not only by the reason, but also by the heart, and it is in this last way that we know first principles; and reason, which has no part in it, tries in vain to impugn them. The sceptics, who have only this for their object, labour to no purpose. We know that we do not dream, and however impossible it is for us to prove it by reason, this inability demonstrates only the weakness of our reason, but not, as they affirm, the uncertainty of all our knowledge. For the knowledge of first principles, as space, time, motion, number, is as sure as any of those which we get from reasoning.

And reason must trust these intuitions of the heart, and must base on them every argument. (We have intuitive knowledge of the tri-dimensional nature of space, and of the infinity of number, and reason then shows that there are two square numbers one of which is double of the other. Principles are intuited, propositions are inferred, all with certainty, though in different ways.) And it is as useless and absurd for reason to demand from the heart proofs of her first principles, before admitting them, as it would be for the heart to demand from reason an intuition of all demonstrated propositions before accepting them.

This inability ought, then, to serve only to humble reason, which would judge all, but not to impugn our certainty, as if only reason were capable of instructing us. Would to God, on the contrary, that we had never need of it, and that we knew everything by instinct and intuition! But nature has refused us this boon. On the contrary, she has given us but very little knowledge of this kind; and all the rest can be acquired only by reasoning.

Therefore, those to whom God has imparted religion by intuition are very fortunate, and justly convinced. But to those who do not have it, we can give it only by reasoning, waiting for God to give them spiritual insight, without which faith is only human, and useless for salvation.

278

It is the heart which experiences God, and not the reason. This, then, is faith: God felt by the heart, not by the reason.

279

Faith is a gift of God; do not believe that we said it was a gift of reasoning. Other religions do not say this of their faith. They only gave reasoning in order to arrive at it, and yet it does not bring them to it.

547

We know God only by Jesus Christ. Without this mediator all communion with God is taken away; through Jesus Christ we know God. All those who have claimed to know God, and to prove Him without Jesus Christ, have had only weak proofs. But in proof of Jesus Christ we have the prophecies, which are solid and palpable proofs. And these prophecies, being accomplished and proved true by the event, mark the certainty of these truths, and therefore the divinity of Christ. In Him then, and through Him, we know God. Apart from Him, and without the Scripture, without original sin, without a necessary Mediator promised and come, we cannot absolutely prove God, nor teach right doctrine and right morality. But through Jesus Christ, and in Jesus Christ, we prove God, and teach morality and doctrine. Jesus Christ is then the true God of men.

But we know at the same time our wretchedness; for this God is none other than the Saviour of our wretchedness. So we can only know God well by knowing our iniquities. Therefore those who have known God, without knowing their wretchedness, have not glorified Him, but have glorified themselves. Quia . . . non cognovit per sapientiam . . . placuit Deo per stultitiam praedicationis salvos facere. ['Since . . . [the world] did not know through wisdom . . . God was pleased to save through the foolishness of what was preached.' I Cor. 1:21]

245

There are three sources of belief: reason, custom, inspiration. The Christian religion, which alone has reason, does not acknowledge as her true children those who believe without inspiration. It is not that she excludes reason and custom. On the contrary, the mind must be opened to proofs, must be confirmed by custom, and offer itself in humbleness to inspirations, which alone can produce a true and saving effect. Ne evacuetur crux Christi. ['lest the cross of Christ be emptied [of power]' I Cor. 1:17]

(Taken from W. F. Trotter's translation of the text of Brunschvieg: W. F. Trotter, The Thoughts of Blaise Pascal, New York: P. F. Collier c. 1910.)

II.2.5 Karl Barth, from *Dogmatics in Outline*

Barth here argues that faith is knowledge of God, made available in God's freely given revelation of himself.

Christendom and the theological world were always ill-advised in thinking it their duty for some reason or other, either of enthusiasm or of theological conception, to betake themselves to the camp of an opposition to reason. Over the Christian Church, as the essence of revelation and of the work of God which constitutes its basis, stands the Word: 'The Word was made flesh.' The Logos became man. Church proclamation is language, and language not of an accidental, arbitrary, chaotic and incomprehensible kind, but language which comes forward with the claim to be true and to uphold itself as the truth against the lie. Do not let us be forced from the clarity of this position. In the Word which the Church has to proclaim the truth is involved, not in a provisional, secondary sense, but in the primary sense of the Word itself – the Logos is involved, and is demonstrated and revealed in the human reason, the human *nous*, as the Logos, that is, as meaning, as truth to be learned. In the word of Christian proclamation we are concerned with *ratio*, reason, in which human *ratio* may also be reflected and reproduced. Church proclamation, theology, is no talk or babbling; it is not propaganda unable to withstand the claim, Is it then true as well, this that is said? Is it really so? You have probably also suffered from a certain kind of preaching and edifying talk, from which it becomes only too clear that there is talking going on, emphatic talk with a plenteous display of rhetoric, which does not however stand up to this simple question as to the truth of what is said. The Creed of Christian faith rests upon knowledge. And where the Creed is uttered and confessed knowledge should be, is meant to be, created. Christian faith is not irrational, not anti-rational, not supra-rational, but rational in the proper sense. The Church which utters the Creed, which comes forward with the tremendous claim to preach and to proclaim the glad tidings, derives from the fact that it has apprehended something and it wishes to let what it has apprehended be apprehended again. These were always unpropitious periods in the Christian Church, when Christian histories of dogmatics and theology separated *gnosis* and *pistis*. *Pistis* rightly understood is *gnosis*; rightly understood the act of faith is also an act of knowledge. Faith means knowledge.

But once this is established, it must also be said that Christian faith is concerned with an illumination of the reason. Christian faith has to do with the object, with God the Father, the Son, and the Holy Spirit, of which the Creed speaks. Of course it is of the nature and being of this object, of God the Father, the Son, and the Holy Spirit, that He cannot be known by the powers of human knowledge, but is apprehensible and apprehended solely because of His own freedom, decision, and action. What man can know by his own power according to the measure of his natural powers, his under-standing, his feeling, will be at most something like a supreme being, an absolute nature, the idea of an utterly free power, of a being towering over everything. This absolute and supreme being, the ultimate and most pro-found, this 'thing in itself', has nothing to do with God. It is part of the intuitions and marginal possibilities of man's thinking, man's contrivance. Man is able to think this being; but he has not thereby thought God. God is thought and known when in His own freedom God makes Himself apprehen-sible. We shall have to speak later about God, His being and His nature, but we must now say that God is always the One who has made Himself known to man in His own revelation, and not the one man thinks out for himself and describes as God. There is a perfectly clear division there already, epis-temologically, between the true God and the false gods. Knowledge of God is not a possibility which is open for discussion. God is the essence of all reality, of that reality which reveals itself to us. Knowledge of God takes place where there is actual experience that God speaks, that He so represents Himself to man that he cannot fail to see and hear Him, where, in a situation which he has not brought about, in which he becomes incomprehensible to himself, man sees himself faced with the fact that he lives with God and God with him, because so it has pleased God. Knowledge of God takes place where divine revelation takes place, illumination of man by God, transmission of human knowledge, instruction of man by this incomparable Teacher.

We started from the point that Christian faith is a meeting. Christian faith and knowledge of Christian faith take place at the point where the divine reason, the divine Logos, sets up His law in the region of man's understand-ing, to which law human, creaturely reason must accommodate itself. When that happens, man comes to knowledge; for when God sets up His law in man's thought, in his seeing and hearing and feeling, the revelation of the truth is also reached about man and his reason, the revelation of man is reached, who cannot bring about of himself what is brought about simply by God Himself.

Can God be known? Yes, God can be known, since it is actually true and real that He is knowable through Himself. When that happens, man becomes free, he becomes empowered, he becomes capable – a mystery to himself – of knowing God. Knowledge of God is a knowledge completely effected and determined from the side of its object, from the side of God. But for that very reason it is genuine knowledge; for that very reason it is in the deepest sense free knowledge. Of course it remains a relative knowledge, a knowledge imprisoned within the limits of the creaturely. Of course it is especially true here that we are carrying heavenly treasures in earthen vessels. Our concepts are not adequate to grasp this treasure. Precisely where this genuine know-ledge of God takes place it will also be clear that there is no occasion for any pride. There always remains powerless man, creaturely reason with its limitations. But in this area of the creaturely, of the inadequate, it has pleased God to reveal Himself. And since man is foolish in this respect too, He will be wise; since man is petty. He will be great; since man is inadequate, God is adequate. 'Let my grace suffice for thee. For my strength is mighty in the weak' holds good also for the question of knowledge.

In the opening statement we said that Christian faith has to do with the illumination of the reason, in which men become free to live in the truth of Jesus Christ. For the understanding of Christian knowledge of faith it is essential to understand that the truth of Jesus Christ is living truth and the knowledge of it living knowledge. This does not mean that we are to revert once more to the idea that here knowledge is not basically involved at all. It is not that Christian faith is a dim sensation, an a-logical feeling, experiencing and learning. Faith is knowledge; it is related to God's Logos, and is therefore a thoroughly logical matter. The truth of Jesus Christ is also in the simplest sense a truth of facts. Its starting-point, the Resurrection of Jesus Christ from the dead, is a fact which occurred in space and time, as the New Testament describes it. The apostles were not satisfied to hold on to an inward fact; they spoke of what they saw and heard and what they touched with their hands. And the truth of Jesus Christ is also a matter of thoroughly clear and, in itself, ordered human thinking; free, precisely in its being bound. But – and the things must not be separated – what is involved is living truth. The concept of knowledge, of *scientia*, is insufficient to describe what Christian knowledge is. We must rather go back to what in the Old Testament is called wisdom, what the Greeks called *sophia* and the Latins *sapientia*, in order to grasp the knowledge of theology in its fullness. *Sapientia* is distinguished from the narrower concept of *scientia*, wisdom is distinguished from knowing, in that it not only contains knowledge in itself, but also that this concept speaks of a knowledge which is practical knowledge, embracing the entire existence of man. Wisdom is the knowledge by which we may actually and practically live; it is empiricism and it is the theory which is powerful in being directly practical, in being the knowledge which dominates our life, which is really a light upon our path. Not a light to wonder at and to observe, not a light to kindle all manner of fireworks at – not even the profoundest philosophical speculations – but the light on our road which may stand above our action and above our talk, the light on our healthy and on our sick days, in our poverty and in our wealth, the light which does not only lighten when we suppose ourselves to have moments of insight, but which accompanies us even into our folly, which is not quenched when all is quenched, when the goal of our life becomes visible in death. To live by this light, by this truth, is the meaning of Christian knowledge. Christian knowledge means living in the truth of Jesus Christ. In this light we live and move and have our being (Acts 17.28) in order that we may be of Him, and through Him and unto Him, as it says in Romans 11.36. So Christian knowledge, at its deepest, is one with what we termed man's trust in God's Word. Never yield when they try to teach you divisions and separations in this matter. There is no genuine trust, no really tenable, victorious trust in God's Word which is not founded in His truth; and on the other hand no knowledge, no theology, no confessing and no Scripture truth which does not at once possess the stamp of this living truth. The one must always be measured and tested and confirmed by the other.

And just because as Christians we may live in the truth of Jesus Christ and therefore in the light of the knowledge of God and therefore with an illumined reason, we shall also become sure of the meaning of our own existence and of the ground and goal of all that happens. Once more a quite tremendous extension of the field of vision is indicated by this; to know this object in its truth means in truth to know no more and no less than all things, even man, oneself, the cosmos, and the world. The truth of Jesus Christ is not one truth among others; it is *the* truth, the universal truth that creates all truth as surely as it is the truth of God, the *prima veritas* which is also the *ultima veritas*. For in Jesus Christ God has created all things, He has created all of us. We exist not apart from Him, but in Him, whether we are aware of it or not; and the whole cosmos exists not apart from Him, but in Him, borne by Him, the Almighty Word. To know Him is to know all. To be touched and gripped by the Spirit in this realm means being led into all truth. If a man believes and knows God, he can no longer ask, What is the meaning of my life? But by believing he actually lives the meaning of his life, the meaning of his creatureliness, of his individuality, in the limits of his creatureliness and individuality and in the fallibility of his existence, in the sin in which he is involved and of which daily and hourly he is guilty; yet he also lives it with the aid which is daily and hourly imparted to him through God's interceding for him, in spite of him and without his deserving it. He recognises the task assigned to him in this whole, and the hope vouchsafed to him in and with this task, because of the grace by which he may live and the praise of the glory promised him, by which he is even here and now secretly surrounded in all lowliness. The believer confesses this meaning of his existence. The Christian Creed speaks of God as the ground and goal of all that exists. The ground and goal of the entire cosmos means Jesus Christ. And the unheard-of thing may and must be said, that where Christian faith exists, there also exists, through God's being trusted, inmost familiarity with the ground and goal of all that happens, of all things; there man lives, in spite of all that is said to the contrary, in the peace that passeth all understanding, and which for that very reason is the light that lightens our understanding.

(Taken from Karl Barth, Dogmatics in Outline, *trans. G. T. Thomson, London: SCM Press 1949, pp. 22–7.)*

II.2.6 Hans Urs von Balthasar, from *Love Alone*

von Balthasar argues that the centre of the Christian revelation is the mystery of love.

Logos, as reason which understands, can only organize (*legein*) individual things, factual truths and 'dogmas' into an intelligible whole, by a process of selection, and by grouping them round a chosen point of reference. Where the revelation of God in Christ is concerned, the point of reference must be the same in both fundamental and dogmatic theology.

It is not to be found in cosmology (or in a religious ontology); for while philosophy and theology were in the past inextricably interrelated, the Reformation and modern times were perfectly justified in distinguishing clearly between them, although it was wrong to separate reason and faith in such a way that they ceased altogether to be related.

It cannot be found in anthropology, because man cannot be the measure of God, nor man's answer the measure of the word addressed to him.

It can only be found in revelation itself, that comes from God and provides the centre round which everything can be grouped. The ordinary run of Catholic theology places this centre on too low a plane for it to be possible to group the multiplicity of dogmas proposed to our belief effectively and convincingly round the unity of the Church's magisterium, which presents and justifies itself as founded by Christ, who for his part justifies himself as sent by the Father. The formal authority of the Church, and that of Christ, is ultimately credible only as the manifestation of the glory of God's love – this is real credibility.

The centre-point is equally put on too low a level in the alternative doctrine taught by orthodox Protestantism. In the place of the magisterium, it selects as the centre the demand for obedience from the self-authenticating, self-interpreting, word of Scripture: the Word in its twofold and existential form in the Old and New Covenants, as judgment and grace, law and gospel. This may be the formal structure of Scripture, but even as a whole it is only a witness to the concrete, incarnate God, who interprets himself as the absolute Love of God.

Liberal Protestant theology has perceived this clearly, for it presents Jesus of Nazareth, transcending the Old Testament knowledge of the two voices of God, the voice of his anger and the voice of his love, and revealing the Father's eternal love. But it goes on to make the revelation of the Cross and the Resurrection innocuous by transforming it into a banal 'teaching' or parable – instead of accepting the form itself realistically as the dramatic appearance of God's trinitarian love and as the Trinity's loving struggle for mankind. It was not a harmless 'teaching' that raised the already stinking body of the sinner from the grave that had been sealed for three days, and revived the flagging courage of the disciples, transforming them into witnesses to the Resurrection throughout the world.

The centre of reference put forward in these pages lies beyond the centres proposed by the theologies just mentioned. It is reached by gathering the *contents* of the kerygma into a single unity – neither gropingly nor vaguely, but in such a way that it has only one meaning. As can easily be seen, this centre-point embraces the other three and therefore shows itself – in this and no other way – to be the centre standing above any doctrine concerning man and the world. For, the formal authority of the Church's magisterium and of Scripture are neither of them impugned or weakened in any way by the glory of God's revealed love; on the contrary, it is the glory that finally confirms them and in theory and in practice establishes the obedience due to them on a firmer foundation. Only in the light of this twofold loving obedience to Church and to Scripture does the 'doctrine' of a loving God appear relevantly and convincingly as the mystery of love perpetuated in the here and now. What is more, no philosophical image of God is called in question; on the contrary, all our fragmentary knowledge is supplemented and completed when it is incorporated in the mystery of love. Moreover, the formal breadth of a philosophical view helps to prevent the theologian, the exegete and the ordinary believer from concentrating his attention so exclusively on the historical aspect of Christ's revelation that he ignores or forgets the action of the Holy Spirit. Finally, revelation does not disavow or denigrate our human, natural and supernatural aspirations, or disallow the fulfilment of our deepest desires, our *cor inquietum*, though it affirms that man's heart only understands itself when it has once realized that the divine love suffering for him on the Cross is turned towards him.

It is not because the spirit of man is sensual that love seems to come from 'outside', but because love can only exist between persons – a fact philosophy is inclined to forget. For us, God is the 'totally other' and appears to us in 'another': in 'the sacrament of our brother'. And it is only *as* the 'totally other' (than the world) – that he is at the same time, the 'not-other' (Nicholas of Cusa: *De non-alind*), who in his otherness transcends the differences of this world – where 'this' is not 'that'. It is only because he is transcendent and above the world that he is in it. But the fact that he transcends us does not deprive him of the right, the power and the Word with which to reveal himself to us as eternal love, and to give himself to us and make himself understandable in his very incomprehensibility.

Theology seems, for the most part, to be turning in directions very different from the one suggested here. It is making great efforts to reduce the distance between Christianity and the world, and to enter into fruitful exchange with it. Centuries of wasted opportunity are being made good; and fundamental Christian truths are being formulated, which once expressed appear so right and obvious, that it is difficult to conceive how they can have been overlooked or forgotten for so long. Bridges which should never have been severed are being re-built, and still others built, that have been needed for a long time by contemporary intellectual and moral life. Consequences that should have been drawn long ago are being drawn from premises which have always been there: for example, that if all men are called to supernatural salvation, grace must be active in them in some sense or other; that a dialogue between Christian and non-Christian is possible and necessary within that grace; that not only the historical world, but the whole biological genesis of the Cosmos belongs in God's world plan and must be created and ordered towards the *anakephalaiôsis* of all things in Christ, towards the entire Kingdom of God.

Truths such as these appear overwhelmingly great to the Christians of today – and so they are. But that they should appear *new* is, for anyone who knows the Fathers, for example, somewhat surprising; for at bottom they are not new; not at least for those who have meditated on the great figures of Christian spirituality – Irenaeus, Origen, Erigena, Nicholas of Cusa, etc. – and have not allowed themselves to be misled by some narrow interpretation (e.g. Augustine's theology of hell, and Cyprian's interpretation of *extra ecclesia nulla salus*). It is in fact time, high time, that the Church's great spiritual tradition should at long last emerge and be recognized.

As a result however, and owing to our enthusiasm at having burst open so many doors, we are in some danger of allowing these delayed victories to obscure the heart of Christianity. The cosmological and anthropological deductions drawn by the Fathers of the Church and the great spiritual teachers are disposed round that centre as though in the form of a monstrance designed to hold up the eucharistic heart to our view. They are simply functions of that one centre, and lose their significance in providing a perspective of the world the moment the scandal of the Cross is blurred in the slightest degree. They were never an alibi for the thinkers of the past and never exonerated them even momentarily from the unceasing meditation on the mysteries of Christ, the Trinity and the hidden depths of the Church. They were emanations from the realm of genuine theology, penetrating into realms which in themselves belonged to *philosophy*.

Where 'the discernment of Christianity' is concerned, it is probably best to start out from the assumption that we are (already) living in an atheistic, anthropocentric period and – as far as the Cosmos is concerned – in an evolutionary *milieu*. This world will not expect psychological or sociological or biological contributions from us Christians; it produces enough of its own. What, then, is the specifically Christian task? Not, surely, to busy oneself with peripheral questions, but with truths derived from the centre. And we cannot prepare ourselves too well, or fit ourselves too soon, to express these truths with the greatest degree of clarity at a level that is convincing.

(Taken from Hans Urs von Balthasar, Love Alone: The Way of Revelation, *ed. Alexander Dru, London: Burns & Oates 1968, pp. 119–25.)*

II.2.7 T. F. Torrance, from *Theological Science*

Torrance here examines the conditions of theological knowledge, suggesting that faith is a necessity because it depends on God's address to us from without, which must be received.

Christian theology arises out of the actual knowledge of God given in and with concrete happening in space and time. It is knowledge of the God who actively meets us and gives Himself to be known in Jesus Christ – in Israel, in history, on earth. It is essentially positive knowledge, with articulated content, mediated in concrete experience. It is concerned with fact, the fact of God's self-revelation; it is concerned with God Himself who just because He really is God always comes first. We do not therefore begin with ourselves or our questions, nor indeed can we choose where to begin; we can only begin with the facts prescribed for us by the actuality of the object positively known. Anything else would be unreal and unscientific, as well as untheological.

Here, then, our thinking is from inside the area delimited by actual knowledge of God, and does not operate at any time outside of it. It is from within this positive knowledge that theology puts its questions and seeks its answers and puts them to the test. It cannot, scientifically, put its questions from some point outside itself and then test them upon ground different from that on which actual knowledge of God arises – that would be quite artificial. Theology insists on being utterly genuine.

Two points must now be made clear.

(a) Theological knowledge pivots upon what is *given*, given from beyond it, and which does not depend upon our discovering it. It is concerned with fact that has objective ontological reality. Not all facts are of the same kind, and not all are to be observed or cognized in precisely the same way. But here we have a fact beyond the ordinary range of facts – there is only one of its kind. There is only one true God, who is not known by reference to other facts beyond or behind Him. This fact is given to us within the range of our consciousness, and never apart from a complex of experiences, but it is a primordial reality given from beyond our consciousness, and it is important that we do not confound it with our subjective states or with the complex of what is *also given* in those states. Strictly speaking, however, we mean by *the given*, not this complex of experiences but that stubborn element in them which cannot be reduced to anything else and which we cannot reproduce at will, the ultimately hard objective reality without which we would have no such knowledge and which we must distinguish from our knowing of it. Hence even though we know God in the givenness of faith, it is not faith that is the given subject-matter of theology but the God in whom we have faith.

Theological thinking is *theo*-logical, thinking not just from our own centres, but from a centre in God, from a divine ground. It is essentially *theo*-nomous thinking. It pivots upon the fact that God has made Himself known and continues to make Himself known, that He objectifies Himself for us, so that our knowledge is a fulfilled meeting with objective reality. Apart from that, theological thinking is objectless, meaningless, and, as it were, 'in the air'. Theology does not have its meaning, therefore, in its self-articulation, in its symbolism, in its form or its beauty, that is to say, in aesthetic or poetic, in emotional or even ethical overtones to real knowledge. It is itself real knowledge working with a given factual reality, and it will not concede anything as genuine knowledge that does not arise out of the given or is not bound to what is given.

(b) The given fact is *not a mute fact* – that is the kind of fact we have in the natural world, a fact that is only made to 'talk' as it comes to cognition and expression in our rational experience. Here our fact is the living God, the active, willing and loving God, who communicates Himself to us, and it is through His self-communication and self-disclosure that He gives Himself to us. In other words, the given fact is the *Word of God*, God giving Himself to us as Word and in Word, God speaking to us in person, as Calvin used to say, and sounding His word through to us by chosen instruments.

In theology we have knowledge of an objective reality in which we hear a Word, encounter a *Logos*, from beyond our subjective experience, a Word which utters itself in our listening to it and speech of it, a Word which speaks for itself in guiding us to ever deepening understanding of the objective reality, and to which we submit our subjective experience for constant criticism and control. But in theology this Logos is encountered as a Word to be heard, as Truth to be acknowledged, not just a rationality to be apprehended and interpreted, so that we have to learn how to distinguish the given *in its own self-interpretation* from the interpretative processes in which we engage in receiving and understanding it. This means that theological thinking is more like a listening than any other knowledge, a listening for and to a rational Word from beyond anything that we can tell to ourselves and distinct from our rational elaborations of it.

Unless we have a Word from God, some articulated communication from Himself to us, we are thrown back upon ourselves to authenticate His existence and to make Him talk by putting our own words into His mouth and by clothing Him with our own ideas. That kind of God is only a dumb idol which we have fashioned in our own image and into whose mouth we have projected our own soliloquies, and which we are unable to distinguish from our own processed interpretation. In other words, we have no genuine knowledge of God at all, for we are left alone with our own thoughts and self-deceptions.

Apart from a real Word of God it is impossible, we do not say to be aware of, but to distinguish the objective reality of God from the subjective states of our own consciousness and therefore impossible to have genuine and rational knowledge of Him. In a true theology God's Word is the condition and source of real knowledge, for it is in and through His speaking that I am not cast back upon my own resources to establish His existence or to devise a symbolism in order to make it meaningful. It is in and through His Word that God distinguishes Himself from our self-consciousness, for He so addresses us that, as Camfield has expressed it, He is not left to the mercy of our questions and answers, but we ourselves are questioned by a Word from beyond which draws us out of ourselves and declares to us what we are utterly incapable of learning and declaring to ourselves.

Thus, the given fact with which theology operates is God uttering His Word and uttering Himself in His Word, the speaking and acting and redeeming God, who approaches us and so communicates Himself to us that our knowing of Him is coordinated to His revealing of Himself, even though this does not happen to us except in a complex situation involving our cognition of the world around us and of ourselves along with it. It is within the area of this divine communication and revelation that theological thinking takes its rise and operates by referring itself to the given reality, that is, by the direction of all its rational attention to the communicated Word. That is the meaning of faith. Faith is the orientation of the reason toward God's self-revelation, the rational response of man to the Word of God. It is not only that, but more than that, as we shall see, but it is no less than that, i.e. than a fully rational acknowledgement of a real Word given to us by God from beyond us. In Alan Richardson's fine phrase, faith is a 'condition of rationality'.

(Taken from Thomas F. Torrance, Theological Science, *Edinburgh: T&T Clark 1996, © T. F. Torrance, 1969, pp. 43–53.)*

II.2.8 Christoph Schwöbel, from *God, Action and Revelation*

Schwöbel here explores the concept of revelation analytically, emphasizing that a relationship is at the heart of it.

The concept of revelation designates in Christian theology the event of God's self-disclosure in Jesus Christ for humanity which creates the condition for the possibility of faith in which the Christ event is acknowledged as the foundation of the true relationship of human beings to God, to the world and to themselves. The concept of revelation depicts revelation as the act of divine self-communication in which the triune God communicates himself through the medium of created reality as the ground and the author of creation, reconciliation and salvation of created being. This divine action enables human beings to respond to the prevenient relationship of God to his creation in their relationship to God, to the world and to themselves.

We can attempt to clarify the concept of revelation and the character of the disclosure event it signifies by taking a closer look at the formal structure of the concept. I want to suggest that we analyze 'revelation' as a relational concept in which the following five terms are set in relation: the author of revelation (A), the situation of revelation (B), the content of revelation (C), the recipient of revelation (D) and the result of revelation (E). The concept of revelation can consequently be construed in the following formula:

A discloses in the situation B the content C for the recipient D with the result E

[A] The *author* of revelation is interpreted as the triune God who relates in the disclosure event actively, directly and efficaciously to particular persons. The disclosure event itself is therefore understood as the result of the intentional action of God who as the sole author of revelation expresses his will and being in this event. The relation which characterizes the event of revelation is, because it has its ground in God's action, irreflexive and therefore asymmetrical. Consequently, no other reason can be given for the occurrence of the revelation than God's freedom. The revelation of God is therefore for its recipient completely contingent and cannot be derived or deduced from any antecedent conditions established in another context.

[B] The *situation of revelation* B in which A discloses the content C for D with the result E has predominantly received in Christian theology a christological description. The Christ event is seen as the paradigmatic disclosure situation in which God communicates himself to particular persons. This implies that God discloses himself in created reality, including its historical structure and its capacity for semiotic interpretation. We summarize here in the expression 'disclosure situation' what has been discussed in traditional terminology as the medium of revelation. The Christ event is therefore a complex occurrence comprising a variety of different dimensions which becomes a disclosure situation only in the connection of its constituent dimensions. This event includes, *first of all*, the historical dimension of Jesus' life, his message, his history and his fate, as well as its reception by those who followed him. Included in this historical dimension is the witness of Jesus to the coming of the Kingdom of God as the demonstration of the will of grace of God the Father for creation.

The Christ event is *secondly* characterized by the interpretation of the witness of Jesus' life by his followers as the actualisation of God's eschatological will and with that as the interpretation of Jesus of Nazareth as the Christ. The Christ event as the situation of revelation comprises therefore not only the *bruta facta* of the historical sequence of events, but also the claim coming to expression in this series of events (the words, deeds and suffering of Jesus) and the interpretation of both by Jesus' followers. The combination of both dimensions means that the self-interpretation of Jesus, as it is mediated by his message of God the Father and the present coming of the Kingdom, becomes part of the interpretation of his history and fate by his followers. Therefore the interpretation of the witness of Jesus' life by his followers not only asserts the truth of Jesus' self-interpretation, but also claims this truth as the truth for their own relationship to God, to the world and to themselves.

The *third* constitutive element for the Christ event as revelation becomes apparent where both elements, the self-interpretation of Jesus and the interpretation of Jesus by his followers are seen as enabled and validated by the action of God. The interpretation of Jesus as the Christ is seen as validated by God's action, where both the resurrection as the validation of Jesus' self-interpretation and the authorisation by the Spirit of the message of the resurrection of the one who was crucified are believed to be grounded in God's action.

Reference to God the Spirit points to the unity of the different dimensions of the Christ event as God's revelation. The Spirit who discloses God to Jesus as the Father who calls his human creatures into the community of salvation in the Kingdom of God, and the Spirit who enables the witness of Jesus' life as obedience to the Father and as *praxis* of the present coming of the Kingdom of God, is the same Spirit who discloses to Jesus' followers the witness of his life and validates it as the truth about their own lives and about all reality. The action of God the Spirit is therefore not only to be interpreted as consecutive upon the Christ event, but also as constitutive for it. Therefore God's action in the Spirit can be seen as the continuing presence of the revelation of Christ in the Christian community under the conditions of the absence of the earthly Jesus.

For the generations who no longer know Jesus 'according to the flesh' the Christ event becomes the Gospel of Christ, communicated in the word of proclamation, the word of Scripture and the visible words of the sacraments. This does not mean that the authority of revelation can be transferred to the medium of witnessing to revelation: neither the authority of Scripture, nor the authority of the church, nor the authority of the individual witness can

replace or effectively represent the authority of revelation. The message of
the Gospel of Christ, is as the paradigmatic *witness* to the revelation of God,
distinct from the self-disclosure of God. The truth claim of Christian proclamation is a truth claim which is witnessed is distinguished from the certainty
of faith as long as this truth claim is not validated for the hearers of the
Gospel of Christ by God's revelatory action. This happens where hearers of
the message of Christ become convinced, or better, are convicted of its truth
as the truth about all reality and therefore also as the truth for their own
lives. The paradigmatic disclosure situation of the Christ event becomes as
the Gospel of Christ a constitutive element in the disclosure situation by
which those who no longer know Christ 'according to the flesh' are enabled
to believe. It becomes the text whose truth is ascertained in the context of
the life of believers. The validation of the Gospel of Christ through the
testimonium internum of the Holy Spirit includes the validation of the claim
of the Christian Gospel to be the witness of the self-disclosure of God in the
Christ event.

[C] God's action in creation, reconciliation and salvation has in Protestant
theology from the Reformation onwards been described as 'self-giving'. Since
Hegel this notion has been explicitly integrated into the conception of God's
revelation as self-revelation. God does not reveal propositions about God,
God reveals himself. This interpretation of revelation must immediately be
safeguarded against a possible misunderstanding. Self-revelation of God does
not mean that God's self as it is present to God himself becomes now accessible to his creatures. Against such misinterpretations we have to hold fast to
the intention of the doctrine of the *ineffabilitas Dei* that assertions made on
the basis of God's relationship to creation can have a definite truth value,
but do not express what is said about God in the way it is present to God
himself. The concept of God's self-revelation is therefore to be interpreted
both as the condition and as a restriction of human discourse about God.

What the concept of self-revelation as interpretation of the disclosure event
is intended to express is that God discloses *who* he is, and that this self-
communication of God, Father, Son and Spirit is at the same time the authentic disclosure of *what* God is, i.e. of his being. The interpretation of the
Christ event as self-revelation claims, more precisely, that this event is, firstly,
an event of self-identification in which the author of the disclosure event
identifies himself in created reality, and that it is, secondly, an event of
self-predication in which God communicates himself as the creator, reconciler
and perfecter of the world.

[D] According to our structural formula of the disclosure event summarized in the concept of revelation D stands for the recipient of God's
self-communication in revelation. The concept of self-communication characterizes revelation as a process of communication for which a recipient is as
constitutive as an author [A], a content [C] and a disclosure situation [B].
The disclosure event is directed, asymmetrical and irreflexive, but without the

reception of God's self-communication one could not talk about revelation. 'Revelation' is in this sense a 'success word' (G.Ryle) which presupposes the reception of the communication (not, however its acknowledgement – unless one regards the grace of God as irresistible). Just as the self-disclosure of God has a particular author and content and happens in a particular disclosure situation, so it is also not directed at somebody in general and nobody in particular, but it is addressed to particular persons. The universal content of divine self-revelation (God's will of salvation for the whole creation) and the universal truth claim of the Gospel of Christ in which this content is expressed does not contradict this particularity. This content becomes effective only in such a way that its universal claim is vindicated for particular people as the truth about the personal reality of their lives and about the reality of creation as a whole. The mode of the actualisation of the universal truth of God's revelation is its personal particularization in the activity of the Holy Spirit.

The particularity of specific people as recipients of revelation is closely connected to the personal character of God's self-communication. The trinitarian self-communication of God, Father, Son and Spirit reveals his being as creator, reconciler and saviour in the mode of personal self-identification and personal self-predication. As the personal self-communication of God it addresses the recipients in their personal being in the relational constitution of human existence as a relationship to God, to the world and as a self-relationship. Human beings are personal relational beings in that their existence is passively constituted by its relatedness to God the creator, reconciler and saviour as the ground of their existence, its truth and its freedom, by its relatedness to the world as a part of creation and by their relatedness to themselves and other persons in the reflexivity and sociality of human existence as the medium of its personal constitution. The specific distinction of humans in creation which the tradition expressed in the doctrine of the *imago Dei* has to be seen in the fact that human beings can relate actively and in finite freedom to the relational constitution of their being, to the passively constituted structure of relatedness. Human personhood is realized in the mode of actively relating to God, to the world, to itself and other human persons and is therefore characterized by finite freedom. Human beings therefore are the creatures who can correspond to their creator or contradict their creator.

(Taken from Christoph Schwöbel, God, Action and Revelation *Kampen: Kok Pharos 1992, pp. 86–93.)*

II.3 The nature of theological language

Introductory essay

The word 'theology' is a combination of two Greek words *theos* (God) and *logoi* (words). Theology is simply words about God, the attempt to bear witness in language to the being and action of God. The question arises, however, what capacity does language have to do the job required of it in theology? How can mere human words even approximate to, let alone do justice, to the infinite and transcendent reality of God? Is not all human speech about God bound to distort and limit and thus misrepresent the reality with which it is concerned? Basil of Caesarea once wrote that 'the ineffable and unutterable [God] is to be honoured by silence'. This is an important observation pointing to the importance of worship as the starting-point of theology, and yet Basil himself poured forth a great many words about the 'ineffable and unutterable' God. The biblical writings too acknowledge the inadequacy of human language yet dare to speak both of God's action and of his being.

How can it be possible to use everyday language while yet safeguarding the transcendence of God? On the one hand, as Frederick Ferré observes, no statement with God as referent can mean what it would mean if it had any other referent. When we say that God is Father, for instance, this clearly cannot mean that God is just like a human father. Or again, when it is said that God is love, we do not understand the meaning of this claim just by looking around at all the instances of love we see in the world and then projecting them onto God. That would be to deny the transcendence of God. It would be to suggest that God is just like us – at our best! On the other hand, we have no other language to use but the language we also use of ourselves and of the world around us. Unless we are to confess, therefore, that God is simply unknowable, then the everyday language that is used of him must attain some success in referring to its object. How might this supposed success be accounted for?

We have already met in this volume the key theological concept of revelation. Revelation refers to the self-disclosure of God and implies that while God may indeed be transcendent and infinite and beyond our human capacity to conceive, he has nevertheless made himself known in a way that we can apprehend and speak about. If God is involved thus in our knowing of him, might it also be the case that he is involved in our speaking about him? Theologians have often argued that theological speech is enabled by the action of God. Or to put it in more familiar terms: our human words attain their adequacy as a witness to the divine only as they are inspired by the Spirit of God. There is debate, of course, about how this idea of inspiration should be understood, but it suggests, at least, that language about God is something more than the product of human initiative and prowess.

It is fair to say that this insight characterizes the mainstream of theological tradition, but there have been other voices too in the debate about what makes theological speech possible. It has been common in the modern era, particularly since Descartes, to suppose that the condition for the possibility of theological speech is located in the self. The human self discovers within itself some basic realities which themselves raise the religious question and provide a basis for theological speech. We encounter this stream of thought in Friedrich Schleiermacher, for instance, who finds warrant for God-talk in the experience of absolute dependence. Schleiermacher's theology actually represents a turn to anthropology, for theological speech becomes, in the first instance, a form of speech about ourselves. Rudolf Bultmann takes this further so that theological language is interesting for him, not because of what it manages to say about God but because of what it reveals about ourselves. Moving still further, some theologians in the latter half of the twentieth century have argued that theological speech is nothing more than the expression of our highest values and ideals. 'God' they say, is a human construct, so that our language about him, has no external referent. It is meaningless except as a cipher for what we believe in and value most highly. Here the problem of how human language may adequately speak of the transcendent is dissolved simply by denying the reality of the transcendent itself. This account of theological language, however, is less a defence of theology than a capitulation to unbelief. The readings below, in contrast, share the conviction that in one way or another human language can be the means of faithful witness to the God who is not our creation but our creator.

It is argued by some theologians that out of respect for the transcendent otherness of God, the faithful witness must take the form of negative affirmations about what God is not. This apophaticism, or the *via negativa*, is an approach to theological language that denies the adequacy of all human speech about God and so identifies the divine attributes by negating the attributes of the finite order. Where creatures are finite and mortal and mutable, for instance, God is said to be all that creatures are not, thus, infinite, immortal, immutable and so on. This approach has been encountered already in Part II.1 of this volume in the reading from Pseudo-Dionysius. The apophatic approach is notable for its stress upon the humility that must attend all human language about God.

We have suggested above that theological language cannot mean exactly the same thing when used of God as when it is used of other things; it cannot be univocal. Equally, however, it cannot mean something entirely different; it cannot be wholly equivocal. These requirements lead many to argue that theological language is, of necessity, analogical. Analogy is the form of language in which one object is said to be like another in some respects though not in all. One of the most influential accounts of analogy is found in the work of Thomas Aquinas (II.3.1) who bases his account upon the supposed correspondence between creatures and their creator. Aquinas argues that because God is the creator of the world – the unconditioned condition of all that is – the world itself bears the mark of its creator. This gives rise, Aquinas explains, to an analogy of attribution so that attributes like love, mercy, compassion and so on, evident in the world, can also be predicated of God. This does not entail that love means just the same thing when used of God as when predicated of human beings. Nor is the difference simply a matter of proportion; God does not merely love, as humans do, but is love. God is love as love itself, or God is good as goodness itself, whereas humans, by virtue of their being causally related to God their creator, merely participate in these attributes which have their ground and origin in God. This analogy of being (*analogia entis*), as it has been called, supposes that the love of God is of a unique character, thus safeguarding the transcendence of God, yet enables an analogical correlation between human love and divine love, thereby affirming the knowability of God.

Although Aquinas' own comments on analogy are quite brief, they have occasioned a great deal of subsequent debate. John Duns Scotus (II.3.2) for example, disputes Aquinas' claim that predicates applied both to God and to the world are in some degree equivocal. Scotus thinks that the analogy of being between God and the world demands that attributes be predicated univocally of both. Our language, that is, must have precisely the same sense in both cases. The question to be asked of Scotus' approach is whether he can avoid the problem of anthropomorphism, of simply projecting on to God the qualities we observe in the human sphere.

It is to this danger that Samuel Taylor Coleridge (II.3.3) directed his concern. Counselling against the view that creaturely forms could be used as 'measures of spiritual being', he argues instead that the sense of language is to be derived from the Word of God. The true sense of theological language, according to Coleridge, is learned in attentiveness to the speaking of God's own Word in revelation. Though Coleridge himself does not give an example, we might say that the true sense of the term 'Lord', for instance, is learned, not by observing the behaviour of human lords in the political sphere, but by attending to the pattern of Lordship exercised in the ministry of Jesus Christ.

We have noted above that under the influence of Schleiermacher, theology takes an anthropological turn. This is readily apparent in Schleiermacher's account of language (II.3.4) in which he argues that all doctrinal utterances are accounts of Christian religious affections, or, perhaps more clearly, they are expressions of the religious self-consciousness. Although in Schleiermacher's view all such affections are grounded in God, the primary referent of theological speech is not God but human experience. This may represent an appropriate humility before the inexpressible otherness of God, but Schleiermacher renders himself vulnerable to the critique of Feuerbach who alleged that theological speech refers to nothing more than the contents of human consciousness.

In the theology of Karl Barth we find a radical revision of the theological enterprise as it had prevailed in the hundred years since Schleiermacher. Barth considered all attempts to find the basis for theological speech in the conditions of human consciousness or experience as ill-conceived, and argued instead that the only possible basis for theology is found in the fact that God himself speaks. It is God's own self-disclosure that is both the basis for theological speech and the content with which theology is concerned. Expounding Barth, Eberhard Jüngel (II.3.6) contends that theological language gains its legitimacy as true speech about God by virtue of the fact that human language is 'commandeered' by God. Freely admitting the imperfection and inadequacy of all theological language, Jüngel nevertheless contends that, as an act of grace, God entrusts his self-communication to the flawed earthen vessels of human language and conceptuality. By God's empowering, human language really does become a means by which we may enter into a knowable and articulable relation with God.

Contemporary with Barth, Rudolf Bultmann (II.3.5) took the view that the real interest of theological language was not in what it revealed about God but in what it revealed about ourselves. For Bultmann, the real object of theological inquiry was not the *being* of God but our *speech* about God and what it reveals of the existential challenge to the individual who is confronted by the proclamation of the gospel. His account of theology, therefore, has little need for the transcendent. The language of theology is language about ourselves.

It has been common to think of language as the vehicle through which human thought and experience come to expression, but George Lindbeck (II.3.7) argues that language is rather to be thought of as constituting, along with other cultural forms, a cultural-linguistic framework which shapes and conditions all our thinking and experiencing. The particular cultural-linguistic world of which each individual is a part – a religious tradition, for example – is determinative both of the kinds of experience that the individual has, and of the thinking that he or she does. On this account, theological language, or doctrine, is like the set of rules for a game which delineate and give coherence to the actions, thoughts and experiences constituting the associated form of religious life. While certainly recognizing the degree of relativity and cultural conditioning which does attend our thinking and experience, Lindbeck's proposals yield little prospect of assessing the truth or falsity of theological utterance.

Two final readings in this section from Janet Martin Soskice (II.3.8) and Colin Gunton (II.3.9) investigate the metaphorical character of much theological language. Metaphorical language borrows terms used of one thing and applies them to another. So also in theology we use language from everyday experience to speak of the transcendent God. This linguistic transfer does not take place, however, without a degree of semantic transformation. Metaphorical speech presses words into the service of a new reality and allows their meanings to be reshaped under the impact of the new reality. When Jesus is referred to as 'king', for instance, the governance and authority suggested by that title is to be newly understood in the light of Jesus' compassionate and suffering service to his 'subjects'. What we mean by 'king' in this theological context is like but also unlike what we mean by 'king' in its political context. We thus see again that quality of theological language which renders it both univocal to some extent and yet partially equivocal.

MAR

II.3.1 St Thomas Aquinas, from the *Summa Theologica*

Aquinas here asks whether words mean the same thing (are 'univocally predicated') of God and creatures. He denies this, but argues that we can properly apply the same words to God as we do to human activities and feelings ('love', 'justice', 'wrath' . . .) because there is an analogical relationship between the divine and human.

Article 5 Whether what is said of God and of creatures is univocally predicated of them?

Objection 1. It seems that the things attributed to God and creatures are univocal. For every equivocal term is reduced to the univocal, as many are reduced to one; for if the name 'dog' be said equivocally of the barking dog, and of the dogfish, it must be said of some univocally – viz. of all barking dogs; otherwise we proceed to infinitude. Now there are some univocal agents which agree with their effects in name and definition, as man generates man; and there are some agents which are equivocal, as the sun which causes heat, although the sun is hot only in an equivocal sense. Therefore it seems that the first agent to which all other agents are reduced, is an univocal agent: and thus what is said of God and creatures, is predicated univocally.

Objection 2. Further, there is no similitude among equivocal things. Therefore as creatures have a certain likeness to God, according to the word of Genesis (Gen. 1:26), 'Let us make man to our image and likeness,' it seems that something can be said of God and creatures univocally.

Objection 3. Further, measure is homogeneous with the thing measured. But God is the first measure of all beings. Therefore God is homogeneous with creatures; and thus a word may be applied univocally to God and to creatures.

On the contrary, whatever is predicated of various things under the same name but not in the same sense, is predicated equivocally. But no name belongs to God in the same sense that it belongs to creatures; for instance, wisdom in creatures is a quality, but not in God. Now a different genus changes an essence, since the genus is part of the definition; and the same applies to other things. Therefore whatever is said of God and of creatures is predicated equivocally.

Further, God is more distant from creatures than any creatures are from each other. But the distance of some creatures makes any univocal predication of them impossible, as in the case of those things which are not in the same genus. Therefore much less can anything be predicated univocally of God and creatures; and so only equivocal predication can be applied to them.

I answer that, Univocal predication is impossible between God and creatures. The reason of this is that every effect which is not an adequate result of the power of the efficient cause, receives the similitude of the agent not in its full degree, but in a measure that falls short, so that what is divided and multiplied in the effects resides in the agent simply, and in the same manner; as for example the sun by exercise of its one power produces manifold and various forms in all inferior things. In the same way, as said in the preceding article, all perfections existing in creatures divided and multiplied, pre-exist in God unitedly. Thus when any term expressing perfection is applied to a creature, it signifies that perfection distinct in idea from other perfections; as, for instance, by the term 'wise' applied to man, we signify some perfection distinct from a man's essence, and distinct from his power and existence, and from all similar things; whereas when we apply to it God, we do not mean to signify anything distinct from his essence, or power, or existence. Thus also this term 'wise' applied to man in some degree circumscribes and comprehends the thing signified; whereas this is not the case when it is applied to God; but it leaves the thing signified as incomprehended, and as exceeding the signification of the name. Hence it is evident that this term 'wise' is not applied in the same way to God and to man. The same rule applies to other terms. Hence no name is predicated univocally of God and of creatures.

Neither, on the other hand, are names applied to God and creatures in a purely equivocal sense, as some have said. Because if that were so, it follows that from creatures nothing could be known or demonstrated about God at all; for the reasoning would always be exposed to the fallacy of equivocation. Such a view is against the philosophers, who proved many things about God, and also against what the Apostle says: 'The invisible things of God are clearly seen being understood by the things that are made' (Rom. 1:20). Therefore it must be said that these names are said of God and creatures in an analogous sense, i.e. according to proportion.

Now names are thus used in two ways: either according as many things are proportionate to one, thus for example 'healthy' predicated of urine and medicine in relation and in proportion to health of a body, of which the former is the sign and the latter the cause: or according as one thing is proportionate to another, thus 'healthy' is said of medicine and animal, since medicine is the cause of health in the animal body. And in this way some things are said of God and creatures analogically, and not in a purely equivocal nor in a purely univocal sense. For we can name God only from creatures (1). Thus whatever is said of God and creatures, is said according to the relation of a creature to God as its principle and cause, wherein all perfections of things pre-exist excellently. Now this mode of community of idea is a mean between pure equivocation and simple univocation. For in analogies the idea is not, as it is in univocals, one and the same, yet it is not totally diverse as in equivocals; but a term which is thus used in a multiple sense signifies various proportions to some one thing; thus 'healthy' applied to urine signifies the sign of animal health, and applied to medicine signifies the cause of the same health.

Reply to Objection 1. Although equivocal predications must be reduced to univocal, still in actions, the non-univocal agent must precede the univocal agent. For the non-univocal agent is the universal cause of the whole species, as for instance the sun is the cause of the generation of all men; whereas the univocal agent is not the universal efficient cause of the whole species (otherwise it would be the cause of itself, since it is contained in the species), but is a particular cause of this individual which it places under the species by way of participation. Therefore the universal cause of the whole species is not an univocal agent; and the universal cause comes before the particular cause. But this universal agent, whilst it is not univocal, nevertheless is not altogether equivocal, otherwise it could not produce its own likeness, but rather it is to be called an analogical agent, as all univocal predications are reduced to one first non-univocal analogical predication, which is being.

Reply to Objection 2. The likeness of the creature to God is imperfect, for it does not represent one and the same generic thing.

Reply to Objection 3. God is not the measure proportioned to things measured; hence it is not necessary that God and creatures should be in the same genus.

The arguments adduced in the contrary sense prove indeed that these names are not predicated univocally of God and creatures; yet they do not prove that they are predicated equivocally.

[See also II.1.6, a later article from the same question of the Summa]

(Taken from the Fathers of the English Dominican Province Translation, London: Burns, Oates & Washbourne 1923–34, Ia q.13.)

II.3.2 John Duns Scotus, from the *Oxford Commentary*

Scotus here argues first that we must be able to make positive affirmations about God, since, as he points out, a mere negation is as true of nothing as it is of God. Secondly, he suggests that in order to make positive affirmations, we must be able to speak univocally of God and creatures, i.e., find words which apply in exactly the same way to both.

In this first question there is no need to make the distinction that we cannot know what God is: we can only know what He is not. For every denial is intelligible only in terms of some affirmation. It is also clear that we can know negations of God only by means of affirmations; for if we deny anything of God, it is because we wish to do away with something inconsistent with what we have already affirmed.

Neither are negations the object of our greatest love.

Furthermore, if something is negated, either the negation is considered simply in itself or as predicated of something. If a negation, such as 'not-stone', is considered simply in itself, it is as characteristic of nothing as it is of God, for a pure negation is predicated of both what is and what is not a being. Consequently, what we know through such a negation is no more God than it is a chimera or nothing at all. If the negation is understood as modifying something, then I inquire after the underlying notion of which the negation is understood to be true. It will be either an affirmative or a negative notion. If it is affirmative, we have what we seek. If it is negative, I inquire as I did before. Either the negation is conceived simply in itself or as predicated of something.

If the first be true, then the negation applies to nothing as well as to God. If it is conceived as predicated of something, then I argue as before. And no matter how far we proceed with negations, either what we know is no more God than nothing is, or we will arrive at some affirmative concept which is the first concept of all.

Secondly, I say that God is conceived not only in a concept analogous to the concept of a creature, that is, one which is wholly other than that which is predicated of creatures, but even in some concept univocal to Himself and to a creature.

And lest there be a dispute about the name 'univocation', I designate that concept univocal which possesses sufficient unity in itself, so that to affirm and deny it of one and the same thing would be a contradiction. It also has sufficient unity to serve as the middle term of a syllogism, so that wherever two extremes are united by a middle term that is one in this way, we may conclude to the union of the two extremes among themselves. Univocation in this sense I prove by the following four arguments.

. . .

A fourth argument can also be adduced. Either some pure perfection has a common meaning as applied to God and creatures (which is our contention), or not. If not, it is either because its meaning does not apply formally to God at all (which is inadmissible), or else it has a meaning that is wholly proper to God, in which case nothing need be attributed to God because it is a pure perfection. For such an assumption is equivalent to saying that the meaning of such a perfection in so far as it applied to God, is a pure perfection and therefore is affirmed of God. But this is to bring to nought what Anselm teaches in the *Monologion*, namely that, with regard to everything except relations, whatever is unconditionally better than something which is not it, must be attributed to God, even as everything not of this kind [i.e. everything that is not better than anything positive that is incompatible with it] must be denied of Him. According to Anselm, then, we first know something to be a pure perfection and secondly we attribute this perfection to God. Therefore, it is not a pure perfection precisely in so far as it is in God.

This is also confirmed by the fact that otherwise no pure perfection would exist in creatures. The consequence is evident, for in this hypothesis only such concepts as express such pure perfections analogously can be applied to a creature. But such a notion in itself is imperfect since it is only analogous to the pure perfection. And therefore, nothing is any better for having this analogous perfection than it would be if it did not have it, for otherwise such a perfection would be affirmed of God.

This fourth reason is also confirmed as follows. Every metaphysical inquiry about God proceeds in this fashion: the formal notion of something is considered; the imperfection associated with this notion in creatures is removed, and then, retaining this same formal notion, we ascribe to it the ultimate degree of perfection and then attribute it to God. Take, for example, the formal notion of 'wisdom' or 'intellect' or 'will'. Such a notion is considered first of all simply in itself and absolutely. Because this notion includes formally no imperfection nor limitation, the imperfections associated with it in creatures are removed. Retaining this same notion of 'wisdom' and 'will', we attribute these to God – but in a most perfect degree. Consequently, every inquiry regarding God is based upon the supposition that the intellect has the same univocal concept which it obtained from creatures.

If you maintain that this is not true, but that the formal concept of what pertains to God is another notion, a disconcerting consequence ensues; namely that from the proper notion of anything found in creatures nothing at all can be inferred about God, for the notion of what is in each is wholly different. We would have no more reason to conclude that God is formally wise from the notion of wisdom derived from creatures than we would have reason to conclude that God is formally a stone. For it is possible to form another notion of a stone to which the notion of a created stone bears some relation, for instance, stone as an idea in God. And so we could say formally,

'God is a stone', according to this analogous concept, just as we say, 'He is wise', according to another analogous concept.

II.3.3 Samuel Taylor Coleridge, from *The Statesman's Manual*

Coleridge examines what he regards as the reductionist philosophy of the Enlightenment, which asserted that only sense-experience could produce facts, and so undermined any meaning ascribed to theological language. He suggests such a position totally fails to make sense of the world, and believes that this demonstrates that all language finds its meaning in theological language.

In all ages of the Christian Church, and in the later period of the Jewish there have existed individuals (Laodiceans in spirit, minims in faith, and nominalists in philosophy) who mistake outlines for substance, and distinct images for clear conceptions; with whom therefore not to be a thing is the same as not to be at all. The contempt in which such persons hold the works and doctrines of all theologians before Grotius, and of all philosophers before Locke and Hartley (at least before Bacon and Hobbes) is not accidental. It is a real instinct of self-defence acting offensively by anticipation. For the authority of all the greatest names of antiquity is full and decisive against them; and man, by the very nature of his birth and growth, is so much the creature of authority, that there is no way of effectually resisting it, but by undermining the reverence for the past *in toto*. Thus, the Jewish Prophets have, forsooth, a certain degree of antiquarian value, as being the only specimens extant of the oracles of a barbarous tribe: the Evangelists are to be interpreted with a due allowance for their superstitious prejudices concerning evil spirits, and St. Paul never suffers them to forget that he had been brought up at the feet of a Jewish Rabbi! The Greeks indeed were a fine people in works of taste; but as to their philosophers – the writings of Plato are smoke and flash from the witch's cauldron of a disturbed imagination: – Aristotle's works a quickset hedge of fruitless and thorny distinctions; and all the philosophers before Plato and Aristotle fablers and allegorisers!

But these men have had their day: and there are signs of the times clearly announcing that that day is verging to its close. Even now there are not a few, on whose convictions it will not be uninfluencive to know, that the power, by which men are led to the truth of things, instead of the appearances, was deemed and entitled the living and substantial Word of God by the soundest of the Hebrew Doctors; that the eldest and most profound of the Greek philosophers demanded assent to their doctrine, mainly as a traditionary wisdom that had its origin in inspiration

When education has disciplined the minds of our gentry for austerer study; when educated men shall be ashamed to look abroad for truths that can be only found within; within themselves they will discover, intuitively will they discover, the distinctions between *the light that lighteth every man that cometh into the world;* and the understanding, which forms the *peculium* of each man, as different in extent and value from another man's understanding, as his estate may be from his neighbour's estate. The words of St. John, i. 7–12, are in their whole extent interpretable of the understanding, which derives its rank and mode of being in the human race (that is, as far as it may be contrasted with the instinct of the dog or elephant, in all, which constitutes it human understanding) from the universal light. This light, therefore, comes as to its own. Being rejected, it leaves the understanding to a world of dreams and darkness: for in it alone is life and the *life is the light of men.* What then but apparitions can remain to a philosophy, which strikes death through all things visible and invisible; satisfies itself then only when it can explain those abstractions of the outward senses, which by an unconscious irony it names indifferently facts and *phenomena*, mechanically – that is, by the laws of death; and brands with the name of mysticism every solution grounded in life, or the powers and intuitions of life?

To discourse rationally (if we would render the discursive understanding discourse of reason) it behoves us to derive strength from that which is common to all men (*the light that lighteth every man*). For all human under-standings are nourished by the one Divine Word, whose power is commen-surate with his will, and is sufficient for all and overfloweth (*shineth in darkness, and is not contained therein, or comprehended by the darkness*).

(Taken from Appendix D of 'The Statesman's Manual'.)

II.3.4 Friedrich Schleiermacher, from *The Christian Faith*

Schleiermacher here argues that religious language does not so much describe God as our experience or apprehension of God.

§15. *Christian doctrines are accounts of the Christian religious affections set forth in speech.*

1. All religious emotions, to whatever type and level of religion they belong, have this in common with all other modifications of the affective self-consciousness, that as soon as they have reached a certain stage and a certain definiteness they manifest themselves outwardly by mimicry in the most direct and spontaneous way, by means of facial features and movements of voice and gesture, which we regard as their expression. Thus we definitely distinguish the expression of devoutness from that of a sensuous gladness or sadness, by the analogy of each man's knowledge of himself. Indeed, we can even conceive that, for the purpose of maintaining the religious affections and securing their repetition and propagation (especially if they were common to a number of people), the elements of that natural expression of them might be put together into sacred signs and symbolical acts, without the thought having perceptibly come in between at all. But we can scarcely conceive such a low development of the human spirit, such a defective culture, and such a meagre use of speech, that each person would not, according to the level of reflection on which he stands, become in his various mental states likewise an object to himself, in order to comprehend them in idea and retain them in the form of thought. Now this endeavour has always directed itself particularly to the religious emotions; and this, considered in its own inward meaning, is what our proposition means by an account of the religious affections. But while thought cannot proceed even inwardly without the use of speech, nevertheless there are, so long as it remains merely inward, fugitive elements in this procedure, which do indeed in some measure indicate the object, but not in such a way that either the formation or the synthesis of concepts (in however wide a sense we take the word 'concept') is sufficiently definite for communication. It is only when this procedure has reached such a point of cultivation as to be able to represent itself outwardly in definite speech, that it produces a real doctrine (*Glaubenssatz*), by means of which the utterances of the religious consciousness come into circulation more surely and with a wider range than is possible through the direct expression. But no matter whether the expression is natural or figurative, whether it indicates its object directly or only by comparison and delimitation, it is still a doctrine.

2. Now Christianity everywhere presupposes that consciousness has reached this stage of development. The whole work of the Redeemer Himself

was conditioned by the communicability of His self-consciousness by means of speech, and similarly Christianity has always and everywhere spread itself solely by preaching.

. . .

§16. *Dogmatic propositions are doctrines of the descriptively didactic type, in which the highest possible degree of definiteness is aimed at.*

1. The poetic expression is always based originally upon a moment of exaltation which has come purely from within, a moment of enthusiasm or inspiration; the rhetorical upon a moment whose exaltation has come from without, a moment of stimulated interest which issues in a particular definite result. The former is purely descriptive and sets up in general outlines images and forms which each hearer completes for himself in his own peculiar way. The rhetorical is purely stimulative, and has, in its nature, to do for the most part with such elements of speech as, admitting of degrees of signification, can be taken in a wider or narrower sense, content if at the decisive moment they can accomplish the highest, even though they should exhaust themselves thereby and subsequently appear to lose somewhat of their force. Thus both of these forms possess a different perfection from the logical or dialectical perfection described in our proposition. But, nevertheless, we can think of both as being primary and original in every religious communion, and thus in the Christian Church, in so far as we ascribe to everyone in it a share in the vocation of preaching. For when anyone finds himself in a state of unusually exalted religious self-consciousness, he will feel himself called to poetic description, as that which proceeds from this state most directly. And, on the other hand, when anyone finds himself particularly challenged by insistent or favourable outward circumstances to attempt an act of preaching, the rhetorical form of expression will be the most natural to him for obtaining from the given circumstances the greatest possible advantage. But let us conceive of the comprehension and appropriation of what is given in a direct way in these two forms, as being now also wedded to language and thereby made communicable: then this cannot again take the poetic form, nor yet the rhetorical; but, being independent of that which was the important element in those two forms, and expressing as it does a consciousness which remains self-identical, it becomes, less as preaching than as confession, precisely that third form – the didactic – which, with its descriptive instruction, remains distinct from the two others, and is made up of the two put together, as a derivative and secondary form.

. . .

3. As regards the poetic and rhetorical forms of expression, it follows directly from what we have said, that they may fall into apparent contradiction both with themselves and with each other, even when the self-consciousness which

is indicated by different forms of expression is in itself one and the same. And a solution will only be possible, in the first place, when it is possible in interpreting propositions that are apparently contradictory to take one's bearings from the original utterances of Christ (a thing which can in very few cases be done directly), and, in the second place, when the descriptively didactic expression, which has grown out of those three original forms put together, is entirely or largely free from those apparent contradictions. This, however, will not be possible of achievement so long as the descriptively didactic expression itself keeps vacillating between the emotional and the didactic, in its presentation to the catechumens or the community, and approaches sometimes more to the rhetorical and sometimes more to the figurative. It will only be possible in proportion as the aim indicated in our proposition underlies the further development of the expression and its more definite separation from the rhetorical and the poetic, both of which processes are essentially bound up with the need of settling the conflict. Now, of course, this demand, that the figurative expression be either exchanged for a literal one or transformed into such by being explained, and that definite limits be imposed on the corresponding element in the rhetorical expressions, is unmistakably the interest which science has in the formation of language; and it is mainly with the formation of religious language that we are here concerned. Hence dogmatic propositions develop to any considerable extent and gain recognition only in such religious communions as have reached a degree of culture in which science is organized as something distinct both from art and from business, and only in proportion as friends of science are found and have influence within the communion itself, so that the dialectical function is brought to bear on the utterances of the religious self-consciousness, and guides the expression of them. Such a union with organized knowledge has had a place in Christianity ever since the earliest ages of the Church, and therefore in no other religious communion has the form of the dogmatic proposition evolved in such strict separation from the other forms, or developed in such fulness.

Postscript. – This account of the origin of dogmatic propositions, as having arisen solely out of logically ordered reflection upon the immediate utterances of the religious self-consciousness, finds its confirmation in the whole of history.

(Taken from F. D. E. Schleiermacher, The Christian Faith, *ed. H. R. Mackintosh and J. S. Stewart, Edinburgh: T&T Clark 1999, §15–16.)*

II.3.5 Rudolf Bultmann, from 'What does it mean to Speak of God?'

Bultmann here argues that all speech about God is in fact only speech about ourselves.

If 'speaking of God' is understood as *'speaking about God'*, then such speaking has no meaning whatever, for its subject, God, is lost in the very moment it takes place. Whenever the idea, God, comes to mind, it connotes that God is the Almighty; in other words, God is the reality determining all else. But this idea is not recognized at all when I speak *about* God, i.e. when I regard God as an object of thought, about which I can inform myself if I take a standpoint where I can be neutral on the question of God and can formulate propositions dealing with the reality and nature of God, which I can reject or, if they are enlightening, accept.

Anyone who is persuaded by arguments to believe the *reality* of God can be certain that he has no comprehension whatever of the reality of *God*. And anyone who supposes that he can offer evidence for God's reality by proofs of the existence of God is arguing over a phantom. For every 'speaking *about'* presupposes a standpoint external to that which is being talked about. But there cannot be any standpoint which is external to God. Therefore it is not legitimate to speak about God in general statements, in universal truths which are valid without references to the concrete, existential position of the speaker.

To speak of God in this sense is not only error and without meaning – it is *sin*. In his interpretation of Genesis, Luther made it very clear that Adam's sin was not really the act of eating the forbidden fruit by which he disobeyed the command. His sin was that he raised the question, 'Ought God to have said?' He began to 'argue about God' and so set himself outside God and made God's claim upon men a debatable question.

It is therefore clear that if a man will speak of God, he must evidently *speak of himself*. But how? For if I speak of myself am I not speaking of man? And is it not essential to the concept of God that God is the 'Wholly Other', the annulment of man? Are we not then confronted by two negatives which make no position possible for us except resignation to silence? On the one side is the specific certainty: no speaking in which we detach ourselves from our own concrete existence is a speaking of God. It can only be a speaking about our own existence. On the other side is the equally specific certainty: no speaking of ourselves can ever be a speaking of God, because it speaks only of man.

Actually, every confession of faith, all talk of experience and of the inner life would be a man's speech. And however enthusiastic the confession of faith which another man makes to me, his confession would be of no help to me in my situation of doubt unless I were willing to deceive myself. Indeed, even my own experiences, if I tried to put my trust in them or to depend on them for support in the situation of doubt, would dissolve in my hands. For who can assure me that the experience was not an illusion? That it is not something I should leave behind? That I do not now see reality more clearly?

Or ought the claim none the less to be made that we are speaking directly *from* God when we confess our faith, when our inner life speaks, when our experience finds expression? That unquestionably can happen. But *at the very moment* when we set before ourselves *our* creed, *our* inner life, *our* experience *on the basis of which* we trust in God, or when we recommend them to others as something *on the basis of which* they can be certain of God – in that moment we are speaking *about* our existence and have detached ourselves from it.

The situation is the same when we go looking for experiences and coveting them for ourselves. We are seeking after ourselves, not after God. If, looking backward or forward, I rely on myself, then I split my personality. The relying self is my existential self; the other self on which I rely, taking it as something objective, is a phantom without existential reality. And the existential self, who looks around, who questions, is proved by this very questioning, this looking around, to be godless. So if we wish to speak of God, evidently we cannot begin by speaking of our experiences and our inner life, for both of these lose their existential character as soon as we objectify them. It is in opposition to this human nature seen as something objectively given that the statement that *'God is the Wholly Other'* is valid.

(Taken from R. Bultmann, Faith and Understanding I, *trans. L. P. Smith, London: SCM Press 1969, pp. 53–65.)*

II.3.6 Eberhard Jüngel, from *The Doctrine of the Trinity*

Jüngel is here expounding the first part volume of Karl Barth's Church
Dogmatics; *following Barth, he argues that revelation involves God's
coming to human language and making it his own.*

The problem of the *vestigium trinitatis* is posed by the history of the dogma
of the Trinity. In the Fathers, in Scholasticism, in the Reformers and in the
more recent theology, both Protestant and Catholic, attempts have been made
in an abundance of variations to exhibit a similarity between certain structures of created reality and the structure of the being of God understood
from a Trinitarian point of view. It was thought possible to discover 'an
essential trinitarian disposition supposedly immanent in some created realities quite apart from their possible conscription by God's revelation' as 'traces
of the trinitarian Creator God in being as such'. When one acknowledges
that there are such *vestigia trinitatis* and that they are recognizable as such,
then the problem arises whether these are not to be seen as the root of the
doctrine of the Trinity. This problem is 'of the greatest importance, not only
for the question of the root of the *doctrine of the Trinity*, but for that of *revelation
generally*, for that of the grounding of theology in revelation alone, and finally
even for that of the meaning and possibility of theology . . .'[14] Without doubt,
we are concerned here with a hermeneutical problem.

After his review of the 'material' which was utilized for the purpose of
defending the *vestigia trinitatis*, Barth expresses the impression that 'there
must be "something in" the connection between the Trinity and all the
"trinities" to which reference is made here. . . . The only question is what.'
This question is then discussed by him as a problem – no, as 'the problem
of *theological language*'.

If one takes seriously the assurances of the Church Fathers and Scholastics
that the real perception of *vestigia trinitatis* can take place only *trinitate posita*,
that one has not to understand God from what he has done, but the things
he has done, from God, then one will have to grant them that for all the
trouble they took to discover *vestigia trinitatis* they were 'in search of language
for the mystery of God which was known to them by revelation'. In the sense
of their search for the right language, there is 'something in' their effort. For
'theology and the Church, and even the Bible itself, speak no other language
than the language of this world' on the presupposition 'that in this language
God's revelation *might* be referred to, witness *might* be given, God's word
might be proclaimed, dogma *might* be formulated and declared'. According
to Barth, what marks out 'the discoverers of the *vestigia trinitatis*' in this their
common oneness with the Bible, the Church and every theology, is that in
that they spoke the language of this world they were seeking *in* this language
the language for the Trinitarian mystery of God. Thereby theology is con-

fronted with the question of the *capacity* of language. For the decisive question for Barth in his debate with the 'discoverers' of the *vestigia trinitatis* is whether the capacity to speak about God in the language of the world 'is to be understood as a capability *inherent* in the language and thus in the world, i.e. in man, or as an act of daring *demanded* of the language and so of the world or man, so to speak, from without'.

The question is then: what capability does language possess? Barth always presupposes here that it is a question concerning the language 'shaped in form and content by the creaturely nature of the world and also conditioned by the limitations of humanity: the language in which man as he is, as sinful and corrupt man, wrestles with the world as it encounters him and as he sees and tries to understand it'. Is this language capable of grasping revelation? The fact that revelation is spoken about in this language, and indeed appropriately spoken about, cannot be disputed. The dispute concerns the *possibility* of this fact.

In that the possibility in this sense is disputed, in that it is not only asked *how* one shall speak about God's revelation but what makes such speech about revelation possible, we pass beyond the horizon of the problem of a hermeneutic which is orientated about the relationship by which sounds, words and things are designated and which therefore is essentially a hermeneutic of signification. More is at stake when it is maintained 'not that the language could grasp the revelation but that revelation ... could grasp the language'. Thus theology moves within a sphere of problems which is hermeneutically determined by the antithesis of *analogia entis* and *analogia fidei*. At any rate this is how Barth understands it when he fears that the teaching of the *vestigia trinitatis* concerns – probably against the intention of its discoverers – 'a genuine *analogia entis*'.

It is of significance for what follows that Barth agrees with the teachers of the *vestigia trinitatis* that starting from revelation 'enough elements could be found' in the language 'to be able to speak about revelation ... but still to some extent intelligibly and perspicuously'. He perceives in the 'more or less felicitous discoveries of *vestigia' trinitatis* an 'expression ... of confidence in the *capacity of revelation over reason'*. In so far it is not a question of an '*analogia entis'* but rather of the thoroughly legitimate 'attempt to speak theological language'. The problem of making such an attempt to speak theological language consists in the fact that this language 'can only be the language of the world' which, however, 'must ... at root always speak *contrary* to the natural capacity of this language, must speak of God's revelation *in* this language as *theological* language.' Revelation cannot be brought to speech 'by a possibility of logical construction'. In Barth's sense that would be just an *analogia entis*. But the language in which the revelation shall be able to come to speech must, 'as it were, be commandeered' by revelation. Where such 'commandeering' of the language by revelation for revelation becomes event, then there is a *gain to language*. It consists in the fact that God as God comes to speech. Over against this, in the reverse case, one would have to speak of a *loss of revelation* if revelation is commandeered by language on the pattern of the *analogia entis per analogiam nominum*. This loss consists in the fact that God does not come to speech as God but as *nomen*. The antithesis of *analogia entis* and *analogia fidei* can accordingly be so characterized: *analogia entis (nominum)* leads to a loss of revelation; *analogia fidei* leads to a gain to language, to the possibility of theological speech about God.

It is a question, here and there, of an analogy. And in so far we now have to ask what guards theology in its necessary use of analogy (which in the attempt to investigate theological language seems to be clearly not only unavoidable, but even indispensable) from placing revelation and language in a false relationship and thus speaking inappropriately of revelation. According to Barth, revelation is spoken of inappropriately when the revelation is not *interpreted* but *illustrated*. For 'revelation will submit only to interpretation and not to illustration'. The appropriate relationship between revelation and language is therefore that of interpretation. It is thus clear from the foregoing discussion that the interpretation of revelation by language is an event in which language is 'commandeered' by revelation, that the interpretation of revelation is thus an act of daring which is '*demanded* of language from outside it'. At the same time, however, this demand on language will have to be understood in such a way that revelation grants *courage* to speak of God, so that interpretation is possible.

This courage which is granted to language by revelation as a demand on language is, however, to be strictly distinguished from the '*desire* to illustrate revelation'. The desire to illustrate does not spring from the demand on language but from language's own capability. Barth knows extremely well that there is 'no interpretation of revelation – not excepting the most careful dogmatics and even Church dogma itself – which does not contain elements of illustration'. Nevertheless, for him 'the *desire* to illustrate revelation, let alone the claim that illustration is *essential*, let alone the assertion that this or that *is* an illustration of revelation', is tantamount to 'a desertion of revelation' and thus 'unbelief'.

The teaching of the *vestigia trinitatis* is for Barth the illegitimate transition from the interpretation to the illustration of revelation, a transition which should 'obviously not take place in the language of theology'. Therefore he rejects 'the teaching of the *vestigia*'.

The relationship between interpretation and illustration requires further explanation. Barth's informative statement, 'Interpretation means saying *the same thing* in other words. Illustration means saying the same thing *in other words*', is certainly not exhaustive, but points in a definite direction. It is clearly a problem of the *sameness* of revelation. Interpretation protects the sameness of revelation in that it brings revelation (and only this) *as* revelation to speech. Illustration endangers the sameness of revelation in that it brings *with* revelation *also* language (*nomina*) as revelation to speech. But where also language (*nomina*) as revelation is brought to speech along with revelation, revelation is no longer protected as revelation *and* language no longer as language. *Therefore every loss of revelation is at the same time a loss of language.* When language itself aims to be revelation it loses itself as language. But where revelation commandeers language, *the word of God* takes place. The word of God *brings* language to its true essence.

If in the interpretation of the revelation there is a gain to language which itself is grounded in the event of revelation, then we shall now have to inquire after the possibility of this gain to language and also after the possibility of the interpretation of revelation. We have already seen that it is a question of the capability of revelation. Yet in what sense *can* revelation make demands on language? It can do so only because it speaks as revelation itself. 'If we know what revelation is, even in deliberately speaking about it we shall be content to let revelation speak for itself.' The revelation of God thus 'commandeers' language not as a dumb aggressor but enters into language as a movement of speech. The revelation of God is no silent demand for language but by its speaking makes demands on the language. Thus *the revelation of God itself is the enabling of the interpretation of revelation.* It is so, therefore, 'because revelation is the self-interpretation of this God'. But revelation as the *self-interpretation of God* is the root of the doctrine of the Trinity. The doctrine of the Trinity is then consequently the interpretation of revelation and therewith the interpretation of the being of God made possible by revelation as the self-interpretation of God.

(Taken from Eberhard Jüngel, The Doctrine of the Trinity: God's Being is in Becoming, *trans. Horton Harris, Edinburgh: Scottish Academic Press 1976, pp. 5–15.)*

II.3.7 George Lindbeck, from *The Nature of Doctrine*

Lindbeck has described what he regards as the predominant model of constructing theological language, one which is based on the attempt to express religious experience, and here offers his 'cultural-linguistic' alternative, whereby theological language gives shape to our experience.

The description of the cultural-linguistic alternative that I shall now sketch is shaped by the ultimately theological concerns of the present inquiry, but it is consonant, I believe, with the anthropological, sociological, and philosophical studies by which it has been for the most part inspired. In the account that I shall give, religions are seen as comprehensive interpretive schemes, usually embodied in myths or narratives and heavily ritualized, which structure human experience and understanding of self and world. Not every telling of one of these cosmic stories is religious, however. It must be told with a particular purpose or interest. It must be used, to adopt a suggestion of William Christian, with a view to identifying and describing what is taken to be 'more important than everything else in the universe,' and to organizing all of life, including both behavior and beliefs, in relation to this. If the interpretive scheme is used or the story is told without this interest in the maximally important, it ceases to function religiously. To be sure, it may continue to shape in various ways the attitudes, sentiments, and conduct of individuals and of groups. A religion, in other words, may continue to exercise immense influence on the way people experience themselves and their world even when it is no longer explicitly adhered to.

Stated more technically, a religion can be viewed as a kind of cultural and/or linguistic framework or medium that shapes the entirety of life and thought. It functions somewhat like a Kantian *a priori*, although in this case the *a priori* is a set of acquired skills that could be different. It is not primarily an array of beliefs about the true and the good (though it may involve these), or a symbolism expressive of basic attitudes, feelings, or sentiments (though these will be generated). Rather, it is similar to an idiom that makes possible the description of realities, the formulation of beliefs, and the experiencing of inner attitudes, feelings, and sentiments. Like a culture or language, it is a communal phenomenon that shapes the subjectivities of individuals rather than being primarily a manifestation of those subjectivities. It comprises a vocabulary of discursive and nondiscursive symbols together with a distinctive logic or grammar in terms of which this vocabulary can be meaningfully deployed. Lastly, just as a language (or 'language game,' to use Wittgenstein's phrase) is correlated with a form of life, and just as a culture has both cognitive and behavioral dimensions, so it is also in the case of a religious tradition. Its doctrines, cosmic stories or myths, and ethical directives are integrally related to the rituals it practices, the sentiments or experiences it evokes, the actions it recommends, and the institutional forms it develops. All this is involved in comparing a religion to a cultural-linguistic system.

Turning now in more detail to the relation of religion and experience, it may be noted that this is not unilateral but dialectical. It is simplistic to say (as I earlier did) merely that religions produce experiences, for the causality is reciprocal. Patterns of experience alien to a given religion can profoundly influence it. The warrior passions of barbarian Teutons and Japanese occasioned great changes in originally pacifistic Christianity and Buddhism. These religions were pressed into service to sanction the values of militaristic societies and were largely transformed in the process. Yet in providing new legitimations for the ancient patterns, they also altered the latter. Presumably the inner experiences as well as the code of behavior of a Zen samurai or a Christian knight are markedly different from those of their pagan or pre-Buddhist predecessors. Yet, as this illustration shows, in the interplay between 'inner' experience and 'external' religious and cultural factors, the latter can be viewed as the leading partners, and it is this option which the cultural and/or linguistic analyst favors.

Thus the linguistic-cultural model is part of an outlook that stresses the degree to which human experience is shaped, molded, and in a sense constituted by cultural and linguistic forms. There are numberless thoughts we cannot think, sentiments we cannot have, and realities we cannot perceive unless we learn to use the appropriate symbol systems. It seems, as the cases of Helen Keller and of supposed wolf children vividly illustrate, that unless we acquire language of some kind, we cannot actualize our specifically human capacities for thought, action, and feeling. Similarly, so the argument goes, to become religious involves becoming skilled in the language, the symbol system of a given religion. To become a Christian involves learning the story of Israel and of Jesus well enough to interpret and experience oneself and one's world in its terms. A religion is above all an external word, a *verbum externum*, that molds and shapes the self and its world, rather than an expression or thematization of a preexisting self or of preconceptual experience. The *verbum internum* (traditionally equated by Christians with the action of the Holy Spirit) is also crucially important, but it would be understood in a theological use of the model as a capacity for hearing and accepting the true religion, the true external word, rather than (as experiential-expressivism would have it) as a common experience diversely articulated in different religions.

This stress on the code, rather than the (e.g., propositionally) encoded, enables a cultural-linguistic approach to accommodate the experiential-expressive concern for the unreflective dimensions of human existence far better than is possible in a cognitivist outlook. Religion cannot be pictured in the cognitivist (and voluntarist) manner as primarily a matter of deliberately choosing to believe or follow explicitly known propositions or directives. Rather, to become religious – no less than to become culturally or linguistically competent – is to interiorize a set of skills by practice and training. One learns how to feel, act, and think in conformity with a religious tradition that is, in its inner structure, far richer and more subtle than can be explicitly articulated. The primary knowledge is not *about* the religion, nor *that* the religion teaches such and such, but rather *how* to be religious in such and such ways. Sometimes explicitly formulated statements of the beliefs or behavioral norms of a religion may be helpful in the learning process, but by no means always. Ritual, prayer, and example are normally much more important. Thus – insofar as the experiential-expressive contrast between experience and knowledge is comparable to that between 'knowing how' and 'knowing that' – cultural-linguistic models, no less than expressive ones, emphasize the experiential or existential side of religion, though in a different way.

As a result there is also room for the expressive aspects. The aesthetic and nondiscursively symbolic dimensions of a religion – for example, its poetry, music, art, and rituals – are not, as propositional cognitivism suggests, mere external decorations designed to make the hard core of explicitly statable beliefs and precepts more appealing to the masses. Rather, it is through these that the basic patterns of religion are interiorized, exhibited, and transmitted. The proclamation of the gospel, as a Christian would put it, may be first of all the telling of the story, but this gains power and meaning insofar as it is embodied in the total gestalt of community life and action.

Furthermore, interiorized skill, the skill of the saint, manifests itself in an ability to discriminate 'intuitively' (nondiscursively) between authentic and inauthentic, and between effective and ineffective, objectifications of the religion. Having been inwardly formed by a given tradition – by, for example, 'the mind of Christ' (I Cor. 2:16), as Paul puts it – the saint has what Thomas Aquinas calls 'connatural knowledge' and by what Newman calls 'the illative sense' in matters religious. This is quite different from the reflective and theoretical knowledge of the trained theologian, who employs publicly assessable rules and procedures in seeking to distinguish between the good and the bad, the true and the false. Rather, it is like the grammatical or rhetorical knowledge of a poet such as Homer, who could not enunciate a single rule in either discipline and yet was able to sense as could no one else what conformed or did not conform to the spirit, the unarticulated rules, of the Greek language. On this view, the way a religion functions once it is interiorized is much better described in expressivist than in cognitivist terms.

(Taken from George Lindbeck, The Nature of Doctrine, *London: SPCK 1984, pp. 32–6.)*

II.3.8 Janet Martin Soskice, from *Metaphor and Religious Language*

Soskice here explores the meaning that is conveyed by metaphorical language, arguing that metaphors do successfully convey meaning, and indeed that there are many situations where a metaphor is the only available way of conveying meaning.

Does each metaphor have two meanings?

At the level of utterance, where we should properly consider the meaning of a metaphor, we find yet another thesis about literal and metaphorical, namely that every metaphor has at the same time a literal meaning and a metaphorical one. Sometimes it is suggested that the tension that characterizes metaphor is the tension between these two readings. This 'dual meanings' thesis arises at the intuitive level because many metaphors, particularly those of the much favoured 'A is B' kind, are ambiguous out of context, and this prompts the thought that certain uses of a sentence like 'Her ears were seashells' contains two meanings – one literal (and false), the other metaphorical (and true). To show how unhelpful this 'two meanings' thesis is we need only notice that with many metaphors, indeed many of the most interesting ones, the alternative to understanding them as metaphors is not to understand them literally but to fail to make sense of them at all. Consider the passage already cited from Virginia Woolf's *To the Lighthouse*:

> Never did anyone look so sad. Bitter and black, halfway down, in the darkness, in the shaft which ran from the sunlight to the depths perhaps a tear formed; a tear fell; the waters swayed this way and that, received it, and were at rest. Never did anybody look so sad.

There are not two meanings here, one literal and one metaphorical, but one meaning; the alternative is nonsense. Either we understand this passage as a metaphor or we do not understand it.

The thesis that each metaphor has two meanings rests on a confusion between what the speaker says (the words and sentences he or she uses) and what the speaker intends by uttering them within a particular context. Usually, a speaker has one intended meaning for an utterance – otherwise speech would be impossibly ambiguous. So, given the presumed context in which the remark is appropriate, a speaker who says 'Her ears were seashells' intends a remark about his loved one's ears, and intends that this should be evident to the hearer from the context of utterance. By the time the hearer has recognized an utterance as metaphorical, he has normally grasped the speaker's intention and his (single) meaning.

In an important sense, then, the truth or falsity of the metaphorical claim can be assessed only at the level of intended meaning. Thus Aquinas has reason when he says that the literal sense (*sensus litteralis*) of Scripture is its intended sense: 'When Scripture speaks of the arm of God, the literal sense is not that he has a physical limb, but that he has what it signifies, namely the power of doing and making.' By this means Aquinas was able to argue that, despite its figurative nature, Scripture is 'literally' true since, in his terms, 'the metaphorical sense of a metaphor is then its literal sense, so also the parabolic sense of a story'. In this sense, the literal truth of Scripture would not preclude but necessitate critical exegesis and hermeneutical analysis.

The last topic we wish to consider under the heading of 'Metaphor and Words Proper' is irreducibility, in particular what have been called 'irreducible religious metaphors'. What has gone before in this chapter gives a hint as to how what is apparently the problem with these metaphors may be resolved.

It is sometimes asserted and more frequently assumed that a metaphor, to be genuinely meaningful, must be reducible without loss to a literal statement. Any metaphor which cannot be so reduced, it is argued, lacks cognitive (referential, assertive) meaning.

There is one kind of irreducibility which all metaphors share by virtue of their relational nature. No metaphor is completely reducible to a literal equivalent without consequent loss of content, not even those metaphors for which one can specify an ostensive referent. When we speak of the camel as 'the ship of the desert', the relational irreducibility of the metaphor lies in the potentially limitless suggestions that are evoked by considering the camel on the model of a ship: the implied corollaries of a swaying motion, a heavy and precious cargo, a broad wilderness, a route mapped by stars, distant ports of call, and so on. Saying merely 'camel' does not bring in these associations at all, and the difficulty with the position of those, like Hobbes, who suggest that we should replace our metaphors with 'words proper' is that the words proper do not say what we wish to say. In so far as a metaphor suggests a community of relations (and all active metaphors do), its significance is not reducible to a single atomistic predicate. This same relational irreducibility characterizes other forms of figurative speech common to religious writings and is especially noteworthy in the case of parable. Rather than irreducibility being a flaw, it is one of the marks of the particular conceptual utility of metaphor. The demand for complete redescription is, in fact, a stipulation that only those metaphors which are direct substitutes for literal descriptions (those which are the least interesting and most dispensable sorts of metaphors) have cognitive significance. But there is no particular virtue in literal language for literal language's sake; we may need to use metaphor to say what we mean and particularly so when we are seeking terminology to deal with abstract states of affairs, entities, and relations.

In understanding this one goes a long way towards understanding the irreducibility of a great many religious metaphors, especially in the language of the mystics. Despite their reputation for speaking of the trans-empirical, a good number of the mystics' figures are attempts to describe human experiences, albeit experiences of religious import. A good example of this is Teresa of Avila's descriptions of the prayer of quiet in *The Way of Perfection*:

> The soul is here like a babe at the breast of its mother, who, to please it, feeds it without its moving its lips. Thus it is now, for the soul loves without using the understanding. Our Lord wishes it to realise, without reasoning about the matter, that it is in His company.

Teresa's difficulty in giving account of the life of prayer, the main theme of *The Way of Perfection*, is not that she is talking of the transcendent God, but that she is describing human experiences which few have had and for which, consequently, there is no established set of literal terms. She is attempting to guide novices into experiences they have not yet had, by means of situations which are already familiar to them, hence her constant use of metaphor, particularly those sanctioned by biblical or mystical tradition; the life of prayer is described in terms of the flowing of rivers, rivulets, and fountains; as the return of bees to a hive; as a journey made across the sea. St Teresa's difficulty is in many respects similar to that of the ancient Greeks who made use of metaphor to chart the unexplored reaches of the mind, and in other ways her reliance on metaphor can be compared to that of the psychologist who speaks of 'streams of consciousness' or the political scientist who speaks of the 'cold war' or the wine taster trying to differentiate two clarets. There are many areas where, if we do not speak figuratively, we can say very little.

(Taken from Janet Martin Soskice, Metaphor and Religious Language, *Oxford: Clarendon Press 1985, © Janet Martin Soskice, pp. 84–96.)*

II.3.9 Colin Gunton, from *The Actuality of Atonement*

Gunton explores the nature of metaphor in connection with classic theological language about the atonement. He argues that metaphors are useful and indeed necessary ways of making sense of this central divine action.

Words and the World

Examples taken from recent writing in the philosophy of science have dominated the argument so far for obvious reasons. The sciences have become for our culture the models of reliable knowledge of our world. If metaphor is necessary there, it cannot be dismissed as an abuse of language; and if it cannot, we must consider what follows for our understanding of the way language works and of the kind of world we live in. So far as language is concerned, we are liberated from the narrow view that the only words capable of being true are those which in some way directly 'fit' the world as a mirror image fits a face; that some words – supposedly 'literal' ones – directly reflect reality while others entirely or mostly fail to do so.
. . .

On the other hand, the disappearance of the conception of language as a mirror of reality can be taken as an opportunity to develop an alternative 'realist' account to the traditional one. . . . But that is to beg the whole question of what we are to expect of our language. As finite beings, we should more modestly demand only partial and provisional success with our naming and describing: 'we know in part.' The strength of the account of metaphor being developed here is that it is consistent with that more modest requirement. Metaphor claims only an indirect purchase on reality, bringing to expression some but not all aspects and relationships of the segment of the world to which it is directed. As a very simple example of the way it works, we may take the word *muscle*, which when first used presumably drew upon some of the associations of the Latin *musculus*, 'little mouse'. No-one now thinks of those associations, but that is because it has been so successful. When it first emerged as a metaphor it succeeded precisely because in an indirect way it enabled physiologists to name and begin to understand one part of the anatomy.

The example is also useful as an introduction to another very important feature of the topic, and one which is the cause of much confusion. What is the difference between a metaphorical and a literal use of a term? As we have seen, it was once widely believed that if there is to be genuine knowledge, it must be expressed in literal terms, any metaphors having first been appropriately 'translated'. Such a doctrine presupposes something that the argument so far has been seeking to undermine, that certain privileged words directly correspond to things, while others do not. Yet if the relation between words and things is essentially indirect, part of a process of interaction between person and world, that static view has to disappear. There are no words that are 'literal' in all times and places, nor can words be neatly divided into two classes in that way. The same word can begin life as a metaphor and become a literal usage, as the example of *muscle* shows. It also shows, however, that there is a difference between the literal and the metaphorical. In process of time, the metaphoral becomes literal. What then is the difference? Not that it now mirrors its object as once it did not, but that it has come to be accepted as the primary use of the term. *The difference between literal and metaphorical is a difference between different ways of using a word in discourse.*

One implication of that claim is that there can be no absolute distinction between the literal and the metaphorical because the same word is sometimes one, sometimes the other. We can conceive of some technical terms which have lost almost all of their metaphorical characteristics – though we may still ask, for example, how far this is completely true of *field* in *magnetic field* – while others, for example *eternal generation*, retain more of them. It is always a matter of observing how a word is used in its context. Language is dynamic and protean, and words cannot be sorted into mutually exclusive classes. And so metaphors die, but may also be recalled to life, and over a period of time reveal a wide spectrum of movement to and from the metaphorical. The important point for our purposes is that the truth of a claim about the world does not depend upon whether it is expressed in literal or metaphorical terms, but upon whether language of whatever kind expresses human inter-action with reality successfully (truthfully) or not.
. . .

The key to the relation between language and world is something we have met already, its *indirectness*. The world can be known only indirectly, and therefore metaphor, being indirect, is the most appropriate form that a duly humble and listening language should take. In all this, there is a combination of openness and mystery, speech and silence, which makes the clarity and distinctness aimed at by the rationalist tradition positively hostile to the truth. Thus the tables are turned: metaphor rather than being the cinderella of cognitive language becomes the most rather than the least appropriate means of expressing the truth. If, then, we are to be true to the way things are in our world we must see metaphor as the most, not the least significant part of our language. And so it is not at all fanciful to conceive our interaction with the world as a kind of conversation, in which, as in other conversations, there can be exploitation, misunderstanding and deliberate deafness, but, equally, the excitement of successful communication and discovery. It is not, of course, a conversation between equals, and the rather anthropomorphic language should be carefully qualified.
. . .

Because the world is, so to speak, our shape and we are world-shaped, there is a readiness of the world for our language, a community of world and person which enables the world to come to speech.
. . .

Janet Martin Soskice has alluded to the fact that many theologians working in this area present a confused picture. Drawing on recent philosophy, they begin by advocating a realist use of metaphor and other symbols – in science, for example – but end by collapsing into subjectivism when they come to theology. Why should this be so? The first reason, or rather cluster of reasons, derives from theology's continuing captivity to Kantian theories of knowledge. It is widely supposed that our descriptive words speak only of the phenomenal world, the world, that is, which is presented to our senses. Anything beyond that is 'subjective.' Another way of putting it would be to say that although empiricism has been discredited in much science and philosophy, it still casts its spell upon the theologians. Both Kantianism and empiricism, however, are built upon a narrow view of the way language relates to reality; that, precisely, which modern studies of metaphor appear to have destroyed. It is not only the owl of Minerva which takes flight after dusk. But if theories which distinguish rigidly between different types of discourse continue to affect approaches to theology, it can scarcely be surprising that theological language should appear to be not about the real world, but about the human response to reality or the structures of our minds.
. . .

Theological language is not concerned to accommodate language to causal features of the world after the manner of natural science. But insofar as the first Christians can be said – metaphorically – to have found themselves, after what had happened with Jesus, to have found themselves newly accommodated to 'the causal structures of reality' – set in a different place before God and in the world – the language they used of the atonement can be understood in a similar way. The central focus of the proclamation after Easter was that the events of Jesus' history, and particularly of the Easter period, had changed the status of believers, indeed of the whole world. The metaphors of atonement are ways of expressing the significance of what had happened and was happening. They therefore enable the Christian community to speak of God as he is found in concrete personal relationship with human beings and their world. Language that is customarily used of religious, legal, commercial and military relationships is used to identify a divine action towards the world in which God is actively present remaking broken relationships. That is a causal fixing of reference in the sense that reference is made to God by means of a narration of historical happenings and their outcome.

(Taken from Colin E. Gunton, The Actuality of Atonement: A Study in Metaphor, Rationality and the Christian Tradition, *Edinburgh: T&T Clark 1988, pp. 32–46.)*

II.4 Neutral and committed knowledge

Introductory essay

This reader was conceived as a textbook for a course introducing first year university students to Christian theology within the British higher education system. In contrast to the United States where much (although certainly not all) of the best theology has traditionally been done in seminaries which are explicitly attached to particular churches, or Germany where it is not uncommon for university chairs to be tied to particular ecclesiastical traditions, in Britain theological research has usually been done in universities which are in essence secular institutions. (Although some British universities have historical connections to the established churches, whether Anglican or Church of Scotland, these links do not define the life of the institution in the way that the life of a seminary or church college is defined by its identity.) This raises a particular question for the theologian who works in a university, a question about loyalties to sometimes conflicting commitments.

The modern ideal of a university typically pictures a community committed to the dispassionate pursuit of the truth. As a member of this community one may, of course, have particular commitments (membership of a political party, for example), but these commitments will be laid aside as far as is possible whilst about the work of the university, and will certainly not so affect one's work as to determine in advance the position to be reached in a particular line of argument. Knowledge is ideologically neutral, not affected by particular personal beliefs or positions.

A theologian, however, is likely to have definite faith commitments. Many who teach theology are ordained, which is to say that they have taken solemn vows to uphold the doctrines not just of Christianity, but of a particular strand of Christianity. These and others probably recite the creed in the course of worship Sunday by Sunday, or even at more-or-less official services within the academic community. Such teachers are nonetheless required by the modern ideal to be dispassionate and fair in their presentation of arguments. Equally, although the body of students studying theology in the university may well include some who are active members of organizations committed to evangelism, these students are apparently expected to be able to consider the evidence for a view to which they have just been trying to convince their flat-mates to commit themselves in a detached way. To do otherwise, the modern ideal suggests, is to fail to meet standards for proper academic work, and so a discipline which finds such standards difficult, as theology often will, thereby excludes itself from being regarded as a properly academic subject.

The extracts in this section could be regarded as presenting the theologians' case. These are intellectually serious arguments from across the history of the church as to why Christian commitment is necessary to the practice of theology. In a sense, the case has already been made in earlier sections about theological knowledge: whether that knowledge is considered a gift from without, or a description of pious feelings from within, one who has not received the gift and/ or experienced piety lacks any real theological knowledge. Faith is a necessary prerequisite for doing theology.

This is not to say that theology is merely opaque to those who lack faith. There are important critical discussions that are a part of the theological task that rely on generic intellectual skills. The first part of this reader, on the sources of theology, will have indicated some of these: if the primary appeal is to a text, and there are rules for properly interpreting that text, the question of whether, in a particular case, those rules have been appropriately applied is a public one, answerable by anyone with sufficient expertise in judging hermeneutic practices. Again, the role of reason in theological work is no different from the role of reason elsewhere. Syllogisms in theology look no different, and the law of non-contradiction still applies. Anyone practised in logical argument may demonstrate whether a particular conclusion follows from the premises presented, regardless of their faith commitment.

So, what need is there for commitment in theology? Gregory of Nazianzus (II.4.1) and Augustine (II.4.2) both argue the need for prayer. When we consider that the aim of theology is to know a person, or rather the three-personed God, then this makes some sense: it seems unlikely that one could study the character and activity of a human subject without at least some co-operation from him or her; if Christian claims about God are true, this applies *a fortiori* to God, who searches minds and hearts. He will not let himself be known by the arrogant, but delights to reveal himself to the humble: 'I thank you Father, Lord of heaven and earth, because you have hidden these things from the wise and the intelligent and have revealed them to infants ... for such was your gracious will' (Matt. 11.25–26).

Anselm (II.4.3) makes the same point even more strongly: human beings are fallen, sinful and evil, and so we can have no hope that God will chose to be known by us. Will a king choose to consort with beggars? Nonetheless, God has made a way by which we may come to know him, the way of faith, and so we must believe first, and only afterwards seek to understand. To seek knowledge of God by any other route than that which God has made available is to court disaster: 'anyone who does not enter the sheepfold by the gate but climbs in by another way is a thief and a bandit ...' – and cannot hope that the Good Shepherd will give himself to him or her (John 10.1).

Aquinas (II.4.4) addresses a different aspect of the question in asking whether theology ('sacred doctrine') is a theoretical or practical science. A practical science is one that necessarily involves some measure of activity, as, for instance, the knowledge of how to ride a bicycle. One may know a considerable amount about the theory of cricket (including perhaps a deeper understanding of the physics of how a ball swings in the air) than many experienced bowlers, but so long as the knowledge remains on this theoretical level, one cannot claim to know 'how to bowl'. Aquinas thinks that sacred doctrine contains within it ethics, the art of living well, and so the implication is that one who is not living well cannot claim to be expert in theology. In saying this, Aquinas represents the mainstream of medieval thought, but the Reformers still believed that theology had become too theoretical, too disconnected from Christian practice, in the hands of their predecessors. That complaint is represented here by John Calvin (II.4.5), whose account of true knowledge of God demands that it includes piety, trust and reverence. Calvin thinks that it is impossible to know God, who is surpassingly gracious and majestic, without being moved to love and worship. Just so, those who do not trust and worship demonstrate by their actions that they have no real knowledge of God. Karl Barth (II.4.7) adopts a similar position to those who have come before, but gives a theological defence of it: theology, for Barth, is concerned above all with the explication of what God has done in Jesus Christ, which is to say that theology does not merely treat of divine action, but of human action as well. Thus knowledge of theology brings with it an understanding of what it is to be a human being, and how to live before God. Again, the converse point is crucial: where that is lacking, there is no true theological knowledge.

Schleiermacher (II.4.6) follows in this broad tradition when he describes theology as a 'positive science', and derives from this definition the conclusion that theologians must be involved in the ordering of the affairs of a particular Christian communion. From a rather different perspective, Robert Jenson (II.4.9) also locates the proper practice of theology within the life of the churches – or rather, as Jenson would want to insist, – the church. Recalling Prosper of Aquitaine's ancient slogan (see 1.2.4), Jenson argues that participation in the liturgical life of the church is a necessary precondition to doing worthwhile theology.

The final extract here, from Francis Watson (II.4.9), describes the field where this issue of neutral and committed knowledge is most pressing at the moment, the question of the proper way to interpret Scripture. Watson argues that what has been the predominant form of academic reading, the 'historical-critical method' (in which a text is presumed to mean what its original author intended it to mean and nothing else) is incompatible with the way these texts are in fact used in churches (and synagogues). He gives reasons to think that reading practices that are more attentive to the biblical text's communal locatedness might, in fact, be more basic than its presumed original authorship.

Theology, then, if these writers are correct, is properly done within the fellowship, life and discipline of the Christian church. Does this mean that students who have a different faith commitment, or no definite faith commitment at all, should not study theology? A distinction needs to be drawn: one may certainly study the beliefs and practices of Christians, or indeed any other community, without being a member of that community. Further, as I have already indicated in this essay, there is critical work that may be done by anybody who is schooled in the generic skills of the humanities: reading texts, constructing logical arguments, and the like. One may, then, study theology in the sense of learning about it, and examining how intellectually adequate certain presentations are. What will remain unavailable if the arguments presented here are correct is the constructive work, the practice of theology. For many years there was no good scientific explanation of why a cricket ball swung more through the air in humid weather, leading some scientists to suggest the effect was an illusion; anyone who played cricket, however, knew that it was very real indeed. Just so, the writers in this section suggest that there might be no good reason apparent from the outside as to why certain argumentative moves seem more promising theologically than others. To one within the community of faith, however, the fact is as clear as day.

SRH

II.4.1 St Gregory of Nazianzus, from the *First Theological Oration*

Gregory, in a sermon preached during the turbulent period before the Council of Constantinople, asserts that theology cannot be done by everybody, but only by those who have learnt to pray and are attaining to holiness.

III. Not to every one, my friends, does it belong to philosophize about God; not to every one; the subject is not so cheap and low; and I will add, not before every audience, nor at all times, nor on all points; but on certain occasions, and before certain persons, and within certain limits.

Not to all men, because it is permitted only to those who have been examined, and are passed masters in meditation, and who have been previously purified in soul and body, or at the very least are being purified. For the impure to touch the pure is, we may safely say, not safe, just as it is unsafe to fix weak eyes upon the sun's rays. And what is the permitted occasion? It is when we are free from all external defilement or disturbance, and when that which rules within us is not confused with vexatious or erring images; like persons mixing up good writing with bad, or filth with the sweet odours of unguents. For it is necessary to be truly at leisure to know God; and when we can get a convenient season, to discern the straight road of the things divine. And who are the permitted persons? They to whom the subject is of real concern, and not they who make it a matter of pleasant gossip, like any other thing, after the races, or the theatre, or a concert, or a dinner, or still lower employments. To such men as these, idle jests and pretty contradictions about these subjects are a part of their amusement.

IV. Next, on what subjects and to what extent may we philosophize? On matters within our reach, and to such an extent as the mental power and grasp of our audience may extend. No further, lest, as excessively loud sounds injure the hearing, or excess of food the body, or, if you will, as excessive burdens beyond the strength injure those who bear them, or excessive rains the earth; so these too, being pressed down and overweighted by the stiffness, if I may use the expression, of the arguments should suffer loss even in respect of the strength they originally possessed.

V. Now, I am not saying that it is not needful to remember God at all times; . . . I must not be misunderstood, or I shall be having these nimble and quick people down upon me again. For we ought to think of God even more often than we draw our breath; and if the expression is permissible, we ought to do nothing else. Yea, I am one of those who entirely approve that Word which bids us meditate day and night, and tell at eventide and morning and noon day, and praise the Lord at every time; or, to use Moses' words, whether a man lie down, or rise up, or walk by the way, or whatever else he be doing – and by this recollection we are to be moulded to purity. So that it is not the continual remembrance of God that I would hinder, but only the talking about God; nor even that as in itself wrong, but only when unseasonable; nor all teaching, but only want of moderation. As of even honey repletion and satiety, though it be of honey, produce vomiting; and, as Solomon says and I think, there is a time for every thing, and that which is good ceases to be good if it be not done in a good way; just as a flower is quite out of season in winter, and just as a man's dress does not become a woman, nor a woman's a man; and as geometry is out of place in mourning, or tears at a carousal; shall we in this instance alone disregard the proper time, in a matter in which most of all due season should be respected? Surely not, my friends and brethren (for I will still call you brethren, though you do not behave like brothers). Let us not think so nor yet, like hot tempered and hard mouthed horses, throwing off our rider Reason, and casting away reverence, that keeps us within due limits, run far away from the turning point? but let us philosophize within our proper bounds, and not be carried away into Egypt, nor be swept down into Assyria, nor sing the Lord's song in a strange land, by which I mean before any kind of audience, strangers or kindred, hostile or friendly, kindly or the reverse, who watch what we do with over great care, and would like the spark of what is wrong in us to become a flame, and secretly kindle and fan it and raise it to heaven with their breath and make it higher than the Babylonian flame which burnt up every thing around it. For since their strength lies not in their own dogmas, they hunt for it in our weak points. And therefore they apply themselves to our – shall I say 'misfortunes' or 'failings'? – like flies to wounds. But let us at least be no longer ignorant of ourselves, or pay too little attention to the due order in these matters. And if it be impossible to put an end to the existing hostility, let us at least agree upon this, that we will utter mysteries under our breath, and holy things in a holy manner, and we will not cast to ears profane that which may not be uttered, nor give evidence that we possess less gravity than those who worship demons, and serve shameful fables and deeds; for they would sooner give their blood to the uninitiated than certain words. But let us recognize that as in dress and diet and laughter and demeanour there is a certain decorum, so there is also in speech and silence; since among so many titles and powers of God, we pay the highest honour to The Word. Let even our disputings then be kept within bounds.

VI. Why should a man who is a hostile listener to such words be allowed to hear about the generation of God, or his creation, or how God was made out of things which had no existence, or of section and analysis and division? Why do we make our accusers judges? Why do we put swords into the hands of our enemies? How, thinkest thou, or with what temper, will the arguments about such subjects be received by one who approves of adulteries, and corruption of children, and who worships the passions and cannot conceive of aught higher than the body ... who till very lately set up gods for himself, and gods too who were noted for the vilest deeds? Will it not first be from a material standpoint, shamefully and ignorantly, and in the sense to which he has been accustomed? Will he not make thy theology a defence for his own gods and passions? For if we ourselves wantonly misuse these words, it will be a long time before we shall persuade them to accept our philosophy. And if they are in their own persons inventors of evil things, how should they refrain from grasping at such things when offered to them? Such results come to us from mutual contest. Such results follow to those who fight for the Word beyond what the Word approves; they are behaving like mad people, who set their own house on fire, or tear their own children, or disavow their own parents, taking them for strangers.

(Taken from the Nicene and Post-Nicene Fathers, series II, vol. VII, ed. Philip Schaff and Henry Wace.)

II.4.2 St Augustine of Hippo, from *On the Trinity*

Augustine examines the dangers of beginning to speak about God on the basis of reason alone, and without faith.

1. The following dissertation concerning the Trinity, as the reader ought to be informed, has been written in order to guard against the sophistries of those who disdain to begin with faith, and are deceived by a crude and perverse love of reason. Now one class of such men endeavour to transfer to things incorporeal and spiritual the ideas they have formed, whether through experience of the bodily senses, or by natural human wit and diligent quickness, or by the aid of art, from things corporeal; so as to seek to measure and conceive of the former by the latter. Others, again, frame whatever sentiments they may have concerning God according to the nature or affections of the human mind; and through this error they govern their discourse, in disputing concerning God, by distorted and fallacious rules.

While yet a third class strive indeed to transcend the whole creation, which doubtless is changeable, in order to raise their thought to the unchangeable substance, which is God; but being weighed down by the burden of mortality, whilst they both would seem to know what they do not, and cannot know what they would, preclude themselves from entering the very path of understanding, by an over-bold affirmation of their own presumptuous judgements; choosing rather not to correct their own opinion when it is perverse, than to change that which they have once defended. And, indeed, this is the common disease of all the three classes which I have mentioned, – *viz.*, both of those who frame their thoughts of God according to things corporeal, and of those who do so according to the spiritual creature, such as is the soul; and of those who neither regard the body nor the spiritual creature, and yet think falsely about God; and are indeed so much the further from the truth, that nothing can be found answering to their conceptions, either in the body, or in the made or created spirit, or in the Creator himself. For he who thinks, for instance, that God is white or red, is in error; and yet these things are found in the body. Again, he who thinks of God as now forgetting and now remembering, or anything of the same kind, is none the less in error; and yet these things are found in the mind. But he who thinks that God is of such power as to have generated himself, is so much the more in error, because not only does God not so exist, but neither does the spiritual nor the bodily creature; for there is nothing whatever that generates its own existence.

2. In order, therefore, that the human mind might be purged from falsities of this kind, Holy Scripture, which suits itself to babes has not avoided words drawn from any class of things really existing, through which, as by nourishment, our understanding might rise gradually to things divine and

transcendent. For, in speaking of God, it has both used words taken from things corporeal, as when it says, 'Hide me under the shadow of thy wings;' and it has borrowed many things from the spiritual creature, whereby to signify that which indeed is not so, but must needs so be said: as, for instance, 'I the Lord thy God am a jealous God;' and, 'It repenteth me that I have made man.' But it has drawn no words whatever, whereby to frame either figures of speech or enigmatic sayings, from things which do not exist at all. And hence it is that they who are shut out from the truth by that third kind of error are more mischievously and emptily vain than their fellows; in that they surmise respecting God, what can neither be found in himself nor in any creature. For divine Scripture is wont to frame, as it were, allurements for children from the things which are found in the creature; whereby, according to their measure, and as it were by steps, the affections of the weak may be moved to seek those things that are above, and to leave those things that are below. But the same Scripture rarely employs those things which are spoken properly of God, and are not found in any creature; as, for instance, that which was said to Moses, 'I am that I am;' and, 'I Am hath sent me to you.' For since both body and soul also are said in some sense to be, Holy Scripture certainly would not so express itself unless it meant to be understood in some special sense of the term. So, too, that which the Apostle says, 'Who only hath immortality.' Since the soul also both is said to be, and is, in a certain manner immortal. Scripture would not say 'only hath,' unless because true immortality is unchangeableness; which no creature can possess, since it belongs to the creator alone. So also James says, 'Every good gift and every perfect gift is from above, and cometh down from the Father of Lights, with whom is no variableness, neither shadow of turning.' So also David, 'Thou, shall change them, and they shall be changed; but thou art the same.'

3. Further, it is difficult to contemplate and fully know the substance of God; who fashions things changeable, yet without any change in himself, and creates things temporal, yet without any temporal movement in himself. And it is necessary, therefore, to purge our minds, in order to be able to see ineffably that which is ineffable; whereto not having yet attained, we are to be nourished by faith, and led by such ways as are more suited to our capacity, that we may be rendered apt and able to comprehend it. And hence the Apostle says, that 'in Christ indeed are hid all the treasures of wisdom and knowledge;' and yet has commended him to us, as to babes in Christ, who, although already born again by his grace, yet are still carnal and psychical, not by that divine virtue wherein he is equal to the Father, but by that human infirmity whereby he was crucified. For he says, 'I determined not to know anything among you, save Jesus Christ and him crucified;' and then he continues, 'And I was with you in weakness, and in fear, and in much trembling.' And a little after he says to them, 'And I, brethren, could not speak unto you as unto spiritual, but as unto carnal, even as unto babes in Christ. I have fed you with milk, and not with meat: for hitherto ye were

not able to bear it, neither yet now are ye able.' There are some who are angry at language of this kind, and think it is used in slight to themselves, and for the most part prefer rather to believe that they who so speak to them have nothing to say, than that they themselves cannot understand what they have said. And sometimes, indeed, we do allege to them, not certainly that account of the case which they seek in their inquiries about God, – because neither can they themselves receive it, nor can we perhaps either apprehend or express it, – but such an account of it as to demonstrate to them how incapable and utterly unfit they are to understand that which they require of us. But they, on their parts, because they do not hear what they desire, think that we are either playing them false in order to conceal our own ignorance, or speaking in malice because we grudge them knowledge; and so go away indignant and perturbed . . .

(From the Nicene and Post-Nicene Fathers, series I, vol. III, ed. Philip Schaff, Book I.)

II.4.3 St Anselm, from the *Proslogion*

Anselm addresses God, asking how he may know him, as God is so far above any human thought, and particularly human thought corrupted by sin and evil. He finally suggests that God in his graciousness may reveal himself, coming to the famous conclusion: 'I believe in order to understand'.

I. Up now, slight man! flee, for a little while, your occupations; hide yourself, for a time, from your disturbing thoughts. Cast aside, now, your burdensome cares, and put away your toilsome business. Yield room for some little time to God; and rest for a little time in him. Enter the inner chamber of your mind; shut out all thoughts save that of God, and such as can aid you in seeking him; close your door and seek him. Speak now, my whole heart! speak now to God, saying, I seek your face; your face, Lord, will I seek (Psalm 27:8). And come you now, O Lord my God, teach my heart where and how it may seek you, where and how it may find you.

Lord, if you are not here, where shall I seek you, being absent? But if you are everywhere, why do I not see you present? Truly you dwell in unapproachable light. But where is unapproachable light, or how shall I come to it? Or who shall lead me to that light and into it, that I may see you in it? Again, by what marks, under what form, shall I seek you? I have never seen you, O Lord, my God; I do not know your form. What, O most high Lord, shall this man do, an exile far from you? What shall your servant do, anxious in his love of you, and cast out afar from your face? He pants to see you, and your face is too far from him. He longs to come to you, and your dwelling-place is inaccessible. He is eager to find you, and knows not your place. He desires to seek you, and does not know your face. Lord, you are my God, and you are my Lord, and never have I seen you. It is you that hast made me, and has made me anew, and has bestowed upon me all the blessing I enjoy; and not yet do I know you. Finally, I was created to see you, and not yet have I done that for which I was made.

O wretched lot of man, when he has lost that for which he was made! O hard and terrible fate! Alas, what has he lost, and what has he found? What has departed, and what remains? He has lost the blessedness for which he was made, and has found the misery for which he was not made. That has departed without which nothing is happy, and that remains which, in itself, is only miserable. Man once did eat the bread of angels, for which he hungers now; he eateth now the bread of sorrows, of which he knew not then. Alas! for the mourning of all mankind, for the universal lamentation of the sons of Hades! He choked with satiety, we sigh with hunger. He abounded, we beg. He possessed in happiness, and miserably forsook his possession; we suffer want in unhappiness, and feel a miserable longing, and alas! we remain empty.

Why did he not keep for us, when he could so easily, that whose lack we should feel so heavily? Why did he shut us away from the light, and cover us over with darkness? With what purpose did he rob us of life, and inflict death upon us? Wretches that we are, whence have we been driven out; whither are we driven on? Whence hurled? Whither consigned to ruin? From a native country into exile, from the vision of God into our present blindness, from the joy of immortality into the bitterness and horror of death. Miserable exchange of how great a good, for how great an evil! Heavy loss, heavy grief heavy all our fate!

But alas! wretched that I am, one of the sons of Eve, far removed from God! What have I undertaken? What have I accomplished? Whither was I striving? How far have I come? To what did I aspire? Amid what thoughts am I sighing? I sought blessings, and lo! confusion. I strove toward God, and I stumbled on myself. I sought calm in privacy, and I found tribulation and grief, in my inmost thoughts. I wished to smile in the joy of my mind, and I am compelled to frown by the sorrow of my heart. Gladness was hoped for, and lo! a source of frequent sighs!

And you too, O Lord, how long? How long, O Lord, do you forget us; how long do you turn your face from us? When will you look upon us, and hear us? When will you enlighten our eyes, and show us your face? When will you restore yourself to us? Look upon us, Lord; hear us, enlighten us, reveal yourself to us. Restore yourself to us, that it may be well with us, – yourself, without whom it is so ill with us. Pity our toilings and strivings toward you since we can do nothing without you. You do invite us; do you help us. I beseech you, O Lord, that I may not lose hope in sighs, but may breathe anew in hope. Lord, my heart is made bitter by its desolation; sweeten you it, I beseech you, with your consolation. Lord, in hunger I began to seek you; I beseech you that I may not cease to hunger for you. In hunger I have come to you; let me not go unfed. I have come in poverty to the Rich, in misery to the Compassionate; let me not return empty and despised. And if, before I eat, I sigh, grant, even after sighs, that which I may eat. Lord, I am bowed down and can only look downward; raise me up that I may look upward. My iniquities have gone over my head; they overwhelm me; and, like a heavy load, they weigh me down. Free me from them; unburden me, that the pit of iniquities may not close over me.

Be it mine to look up to your light, even from afar, even from the depths. Teach me to seek you, and reveal yourself to me, when I seek you, for I cannot seek you, except you teach me, nor find you, except you reveal yourself. Let me seek you in longing, let me long for you in seeking; let me find you in love, and love you in finding. Lord, I acknowledge and I thank you that you have created me in this your image, in order that I may be mindful of you, may conceive of you, and love you; but that image has been so consumed and wasted away by vices, and obscured by the smoke of wrong-doing, that it cannot achieve that for which it was made, except you renew it, and create it anew. I do not endeavour, O Lord, to penetrate your sublimity, for in no wise do I compare my understanding with that; but I long to understand in some degree your truth, which my heart believes and loves. For I do not seek to understand that I may believe, but I believe in order to understand. For this also I believe, – that unless I believed, I should not understand.

(From St. Anselm: Proslogium; Monologium: An Appendix In Behalf Of The Fool By Gaunilo; And Cur Deus Homo, Translated From The Latin By Sidney Norton Deane, B. A. With An Introduction, Bibliography, And Reprints Of The Opinions Of Leading Philosophers And Writers On The Ontological Argument, *Chicago: The Open Court Publishing Company, 1903, reprinted 1926.)*

II.4.4 St Thomas Aquinas, from the *Summa Theologica*

Aquinas asks whether theology is a 'speculative science', a mode of knowing concerned only with right knowledge, or a 'practical science', one concerned with right action as well. He suggests that the division does not apply to theology, since God's own knowledge of himself is at the same time knowledge of who he is and what he does. True theological knowledge, then, although primarily concerned with knowledge of God, includes within it right action.

Article 4: Whether sacred doctrine is a practical science?

Objection 1. It seems that sacred doctrine is a practical science; for a practical science is that which ends in action according to the Philosopher [*i.e.* Aristotle] (*Metaphysics II*). But sacred doctrine is ordained to action: 'Be ye doers of the word, and not hearers only' (James 1:22). Therefore sacred doctrine is a practical science.

Objection 2. Further, sacred doctrine is divided into the Old and the New Law. But law implies a moral science which is a practical science. Therefore sacred doctrine is a practical science.

On the contrary, Every practical science is concerned with human operations; as moral science is concerned with human acts, and architecture with buildings. But sacred doctrine is chiefly concerned with God, whose handiwork is especially man. Therefore it is not a practical but a speculative science.

I answer that, Sacred doctrine, being one, extends to things which belong to different philosophical sciences because it considers in each the same formal aspect, namely, so far as they can be known through divine revelation. Hence, although among the philosophical sciences one is speculative and another practical, nevertheless sacred doctrine includes both; as God, by one and the same science, knows both himself and his works. Still, it is speculative rather than practical because it is more concerned with divine things than with human acts; though it does treat even of these latter, inasmuch as man is ordained by them to the perfect knowledge of God in which consists eternal bliss. This is a sufficient answer to the Objections.

(Taken from the Fathers of the English Dominican Province Translation, London: Burns, Oates & Washbourne 1924–34, Ia q.1.)

II.4.5 John Calvin, from *The Institutes of the Christian Religion*

Calvin argues that true knowledge of God includes piety, trust and reverence for God.

1. Piety is requisite for the knowledge of God

Now, the knowledge of God, as I understand it, is that by which we not only conceive that there is a God but also grasp what befits us and is proper to his glory, in fine, what is to our advantage to know of him. Indeed, we shall not say that, properly speaking, God is known where there is no religion or piety. . . .

Moreover, although our mind cannot apprehend God without rendering some honor to him, it will not suffice simply to hold that there is One whom all ought to honor and adore, unless we are also persuaded that he is the fountain of every good, and that we must seek nothing elsewhere than in him. This I take to mean that not only does he sustain this universe (as he once founded it) by his boundless might, regulate it by his wisdom, preserve it by his goodness, and especially rule mankind by his righteousness and judgment, bear with it in his mercy, watch over it by his protection; but also that no drop will be found either of wisdom and light, or of righteousness or power or rectitude, or of genuine truth, which does not flow from him, and of which he is not the cause. Thus we may learn to await and seek all these things from him, and thankfully to ascribe them, once received, to him. For this sense of the powers of God is for us a fit teacher of piety, from which religion is born. I call 'piety' that reverence joined with love of God which the knowledge of his benefits induces. For until men recognize that they owe everything to God, that they are nourished by his fatherly care, that he is the Author of their every good, that they should seek nothing beyond him – they will never yield him willing service. Nay, unless they establish their complete happiness in him, they will never give themselves truly and sincerely to him.

2. Knowledge of God involves trust and reverence

What is God? Men who pose this question are merely toying with idle speculations. It is more important for us to know of what sort he is and what is consistent with his nature. What good is it to profess with Epicurus some sort of God who has cast aside the care of the world only to amuse himself in idleness? What help is it, in short, to know a God with whom we have nothing to do? Rather, our knowledge should serve first to teach us fear and reverence; secondly, with it as our guide and teacher, we should learn to seek every good from him, and, having received it, to credit it to his account. For how can the thought of God penetrate your mind without your realizing immediately that, since you are his handiwork, you have been made over and bound to his command by right of creation, that you owe your life to him? – that whatever you undertake, whatever you do, ought to be ascribed to him? If this be so, it now assuredly follows that your life is wickedly corrupt unless it be disposed to his service, seeing that his will ought for us to be the law by which we live. Again, you cannot behold him clearly unless you acknowledge him to be the fountainhead and source of every good. From this too would arise the desire to cleave to him and trust in him, but for the fact that man's depravity seduces his mind from rightly seeking him.

For, to begin with, the pious mind does not dream up for itself any god it pleases, but contemplates the one and only true God. And it does not attach to him whatever it pleases, but is content to hold him to be as he manifests himself; furthermore, the mind always exercises the utmost diligence and care not to wander astray, or rashly and boldly to go beyond his will. It thus recognizes God because it knows that he governs all things; and trusts that he is its guide and protector, therefore giving itself over completely to trust in him. Because it understands him to be the Author of every good, if anything oppresses, if anything is lacking, immediately it betakes itself to his protection, waiting for help from him. Because it is persuaded that he is good and merciful, it reposes in him with perfect trust, and doubts not that in his loving-kindness a remedy will be provided for all its ills. Because it acknowledges him as Lord and Father, the pious mind also deems it meet and right to observe his authority in all things, reverence his majesty, take care to advance his glory, and obey his commandments. Because it sees him to be a righteous judge, armed with severity to punish wickedness, it ever holds his judgment seat before its gaze, and through fear of him restrains itself from provoking his anger. And yet it is not so terrified by the awareness of his judgment as to wish to withdraw, even if some way of escape were open. But it embraces him no less as punisher of the wicked than as benefactor of the pious. For the pious mind realizes that the punishment of the impious and wicked and the reward of life eternal for the righteous equally pertain to God's glory. Besides, this mind restrains itself from sinning, not out of dread of punishment alone; but, because it loves and reveres God as Father, it worships and adores him as Lord. Even if there were no hell, it would still shudder at offending him alone.

Here indeed is pure and real religion: faith so joined with an earnest fear of God that this fear also embraces willing reverence, and carries with it such legitimate worship as is prescribed in the law. And we ought to note this fact even more diligently: all men have a vague general veneration for God, but very few really reverence him; and wherever there is great ostentation in ceremonies, sincerity of heart is rare indeed.

(Taken from The Institutes of the Christian Religion, *ed. John T. McNeill, trans. Ford Lewis Battles, The Library of Christian Classics, vol XX, Philadelphia, PA: Westminister Press 1960, 1.2.)*

II.4.6 F. D. E. Schleiermacher, from *A Brief Outline on the Study of Theology*

Schleiermacher defines the nature of theological study.

§ 1. Theology is a positive science, whose parts join into a cohesive whole only through their common relation to a particular mode of faith, i.e., a particular way of being conscious of God. Thus, the various parts of Christian theology belong together only by virtue of their relation to 'Christianity.' This is the sense in which the word 'theology' will always be used here.

> Generally speaking, a positive science is an assemblage of scientific elements which belong together not because they form a constituent part of the organization of the sciences, as though by some necessity arising out of the notion of science itself, but only insofar as they are requisite for carrying out a practical task.
> Reference is certainly also made to the God of whom we are conscious in the case of 'rational theologies' formerly constructed within the organization of sciences. As speculative science, however, these are entirely different from the theology whose definition we are elaborating here.

§ 2. Whether any given mode of faith will give shape to a definite theology depends on the degree to which it is communicated by means of ideas rather than symbolic actions, and likewise on the degree to which it attains historical importance and autonomy. Theologies, moreover, may differ according to every particular mode of faith, in that they correspond to the distinctiveness of each both in content and in form.

> A real theology will develop only on the two conditions stated. For, in the first instance, no need for one will arise in a community of small extent; and in the second, where a preponderance of symbolic actions exists the ritual which interprets these hardly deserves to be called a science.

§ 3. Theology is not the special responsibility of everyone who belongs to a particular Church, except as they take part in the leadership of the Church. Consequently, we can say that the contrast between leaders and ordinary members and the rise to prominence of theology mutually condition each other.

> The expression 'leadership of the Church' is meant to be regarded in the broadest sense here, without restriction to any one particular form.

§ 4. The more the Church advances in its growth, and the more linguistic and cultural areas it includes, the more complicated the organization of theology becomes. Christian theology, on this account, has become the most extensively cultivated of all.

The more these two factors enter into the picture, the more numerous are the different ideas and ways of living which theology must take into account, and the more diverse are the historical data to which it must refer.

§ 5. Christian theology, accordingly, is that assemblage of scientific knowledge and practical instruction without the possession and application of which a united leadership of the Christian Church, i.e., a government of the Church in the fullest sense, is not possible.

This is precisely the relation set forth in § 1. [It is important to point out this 'positive' relation of theology,] for the Christian faith, in and of itself, does not absolutely require such an apparatus for its effectiveness either within the individual soul or within the relationships which make up the common life of a family.

§ 6. When this same knowledge is acquired and possessed without relation to the 'government' of the Church, it ceases to be theological and devolves to those sciences to which it belongs according to its varied content.

Depending on the subject matter, such knowledge would be referred to linguistic and historical studies, psychology and ethics, together with general studies on various sorts of technique and philosophy of religion – two disciplines which are based on psychology and ethics.

§ 7. By virtue of this relation, that same manifold of knowledge is as integrally related to the will to be effective in the leadership of the Church as the body is to the soul.

Without this will, the unity of theology disappears, and its parts decompose into its various elements.

§ 8. However, just as that multifarious knowledge is combined into a theological whole only in the service of a definite interest in Christianity, so this interest in Christianity can likewise only manifest itself appropriately by assimilating that knowledge.

In accordance with § 2, the function of leadership in the Church can only be adequately performed on the basis of a highly developed consciousness of history. At the same time, its true success rests upon a clear knowledge concerning the relationship of the religious aspects of man's life to all the rest.

§ 9. If one should imagine both a religious interest and a scientific spirit conjoined in the highest degree and with the finest balance for the purpose of theoretical and practical activity alike, that would be the idea of a 'prince of the Church.'

> This nomenclature for the theological ideal would, of course, be strictly applicable only when the disparity between such a person and his fellow members in the Church is very great, and where it is possible for him to influence a large part of the Church. It does seem more suitable than the term 'Church father,' which is already used for a special category of men. Furthermore, its denotation is not in the least restricted to an official position, as such.

§ 10. If one thinks of this balance as having broken down, then the one who has primarily cultivated the knowledge of Christianity is a theologian, in the narrower sense; and, on the contrary, the one who has primarily cultivated activity which pertains to Church government is a clergyman.

> This natural separation is more in evidence at certain times and places than at others. The more it prevails, however, the less can the Church subsist without a vital interchange between the two.
>   Hereafter, the term 'theologian' will normally be used in the broader sense, which comprehends both tendencies.

§ 11. Every treatment of theological subjects as such, whatever their nature, stands always within the province of Church leadership; and however the activity of Church leadership may be considered, whether in a more constructive or in a more regulative fashion, this kind of thinking likewise always belongs within the purview of theology in the narrower sense.

> Even the especially scientific work of the theologian must aim at promoting the Church's welfare, and is thereby clerical; and even those technical regulations for essentially clerical activities belong within the circle of the theological sciences.

§ 12. If, accordingly, all true theologians also participate in the leadership of the Church, and all who are active in Church government live also within the theological arena, it follows that both an ecclesial interest and a scientific spirit must be united in each person, despite any tendency to lean toward the one side or the other.

If the opposite were the case, then the scholar would no longer be a theologian; he would merely be engaged in working over various theological subjects in the spirit of whatever particular science is proper to them. Likewise, the clergyman's activity would lack both the skill and the foresight of good leadership, degenerating into a mere muddle of attempted influence.

§ 13. Everyone who finds himself called to exercise leadership in the Church discovers the function he is to perform according to the measure in which one or the other of these two elements is dominant within him.

Without such an inner calling, no one is truly either a theologian or a clergyman. Neither of these two functions, moreover, is changed one iota by the circumstance that Church government should happen to be the basis for a special civil status.

. . .

§ 17. Whether a man strives to perfect a certain discipline, and which discipline he selects, are matters determined chiefly by the peculiar nature of his own talent, but also partly by his apprehension of the current needs of the Church.

In any given period, the favorable advancement of theology as a whole largely depends upon whether outstanding talents are found to serve the most pressing needs. Those who achieve a certain balance in cultivating the largest number of disciplines, without striving for expertness in any one of them, are always in a better position to exercise the most varied influence. On the other hand, those who devote their attention wholly to one area are in a position to accomplish most in a purely scholarly way.

§ 18. The following factors, then, are indispensable for every theologian: (a) first, an adequate perspective over the ways in which the various parts of theology interrelate, and of the particular value of each for serving the overall aim of theology; (b) then, an understanding of the internal organization of each discipline, and of those principal parts which are most essential for the whole structure; (c) further, an acquaintance with aids for quickly obtaining whatever information may be required; and (d) finally, practice and confidence in applying the necessary precautions for making the best and the most apt use of what others have produced.
. . .

§ 21. Insofar as one tries to make do with a merely empirical method of interpreting Christianity, he cannot achieve a genuine knowledge of it. One's task is rather to endeavor both to understand the essence of Christianity in contradistinction to other churches and other kinds of faith, and to understand the nature of piety and of religious communities in relation to all the other activities of the human spirit.

> That the essence of Christianity is attached to a certain history merely determines more precisely what mode of understanding is required; by itself, however, this fact cannot be supposed to prejudice the task of understanding what Christianity is.

. . .

§ 25. The purpose of leadership in the Christian Church is to hold the various concerns of the Church together and to build on them further, both in a comprehensive as well as in a concentrated way. The knowledge concerning this activity forms a kind of technology which, in combining all its different branches, we designate as practical theology.

> Earlier work in this discipline too has been extremely erratic. Administrative details have been copiously discussed. What relates to the work of real leadership and planning, however, has on the whole received but scanty attention, and what systematic work has been done has treated the individual parts of this discipline in isolation from each other.

§ 26. Good leadership of the Church also requires a knowledge of the whole community which is to be led: (a) of its situation at any given time, and (b) of its past, with the realization that this community, regarded as a whole, is a historical entity, and that its present condition can be adequately grasped only when it is viewed as a product of the past. Now these two things taken together constitute historical theology, in the broader sense of the term.

> The present simply cannot be regarded as the kernel of a future which is to correspond more nearly to the full conception of the Church, or to any other notion, unless one perceives how it has developed out of the past.

§ 27. Since historical theology attempts to exhibit every point of time in its true relation to the idea of 'Christianity,' it follows that it is at once not only the foundation of practical theology but also the verification of philosophical theology.

> It will be able to fulfill both roles the more easily, of course, the greater the fund of historical developments which lies ready to hand. Thus it can be understood why Church leadership was at first rather a matter of right instinct, and why philosophical theology manifested itself only in fits and starts of little power.

§ 28. Accordingly, historical theology is the actual corpus of theological study, which is connected with science, as such, by means of philosophical theology and with the active Christian life by means of practical theology.

> Since a correct understanding of any given period must also demonstrate by what prominent ideas the Church was governed, historical theology also includes the practical aspect in its work; and on account of the connection pointed out in § 27, philosophical theology is also reflected in what historical theology does.

§ 29. If philosophical theology were adequately developed as a discipline, the whole course of theological study could begin with it. For the present, however, its individual components will only be acquired fragmentarily along with the study of historical theology, though even this is possible only when preceded by the study of ethics, which we must regard as being at the same time the science of the principles of history.

> Without constant reference to ethical principles, even the study of historical theology is reduced to a kind of haphazard calisthenics, and is bound to degenerate into a process of handing down meaningless information. The lack of such references goes a long way toward explaining the confusing state of theological disciplines which is often encountered and the total lack of trustworthiness in their application to matters of Church leadership.

§ 30. Not only can the technology regarding Church leadership which is still lacking proceed further only through the improvement of historical theology, which in turn requires the agency of philosophical theology, but even the ordinary formulation of rules for administrative duties can only have the effect of a mechanical prescription so long as it is not preceded by the study of historical theology.

> Out of a premature occupation with this technology arise a superficiality in practice and an indifference to scientific progress.

(Taken from Friedrich Schleiermacher, A Brief Outline on the Study of Theology, trans. T. N. Tice, Richmond, VA: John Knox Press 1966, pp. 19–27.)

II.4.7 Karl Barth, from the *Church Dogmatics*

Barth here argues that 'dogmatics is ethics'.

The truth of the evangelical indicative means that the full stop with which it concludes becomes an exclamation mark. It becomes itself an imperative. The concept of the covenant between God and man concluded in Jesus Christ is not exhausted in the doctrine of the divine election of grace. The election itself and as such demands that it be understood as God's command directed to man; as the sanctification or claiming which comes to elected man from the electing God in the fact that when God turns to Him and gives Himself to him He becomes his Commander.

This makes it plain that ethics belongs not only to dogmatics in general but to the doctrine of God. This is something which ought to have been apparent for some time. For who can possibly see what is meant by the knowledge of God, His divine being, His divine perfections, the election of His grace, without an awareness at every point of the demand which is put to man by the fact that this God is his God, the God of man? How can God be understood as the Lord if that does not involve the problem of human obedience? But what is implicit must now be made explicit. What is self-evident must now be brought out specifically. The doctrine of God must be expressly defined and developed and interpreted as that which it also is at every point, that is to say, *ethics*. Otherwise, human carelessness and forgetfulness may only too easily skim over the fact that it actually is this, and that all that we have so far said as the doctrine of God has also this further sense – the sense of basically ethical reflection and explanation.

If we adopt here the term ethics to describe the special task of dogmatics which the Law as the form of the Gospel has imposed on us, we do it in the freedom – which is so very necessary and is always enjoyed in dogmatics – to take such terms as are to hand, not allowing ourselves to be bound and fettered by the meaning which they may have acquired from their use elsewhere, but using them in the sense which, when they are applied to the object with which we are concerned, they must derive from this object itself. No term has as such an absolutely universal and therefore binding sense. This is equally true of 'ethics.' At any rate the dogmatics of the Christian Church cannot make use of any terms (not even those of mathematics!) without examination, without reserving the right to give them a sense of its own, and to apply them in its own way. And this is also true of the term 'ethics.' But – granted this reservation – there is no reason not to make use of the term in dogmatics. A relatively general conception of ethics which we might take as our point of departure γυμναστικῶς is as follows. The ethical question is the question as to the basis and possibility of the fact that in the multitude and multiplicity of human actions there are certain modes of action, i.e., certain constants, certain laws, rules, usages or continuities. It is the question as to the rightness of these constants, the fitness of these laws. It is the question as to the value which gives any action the claim to be the true expression of a mode of action, the fulfilment of a law – the right to be repeated and in virtue of its normative character to serve as an example for the actions of others. What is the true and genuine continuity in all the so-called continuities of human action? What is it that really gives force to all these recognised laws? What is the good in and over every so-called good of human action? This is – roughly – the ethical question, and – roughly again – the answering of it is what is generally called 'ethics.'

Our contention is, however, that the dogmatics of the Christian Church, and basically the Christian doctrine of God, is ethics. This doctrine is, therefore, the answer to the ethical question, the supremely critical question concerning the good in and over every so-called good in human actions and modes of action.

(Taken from Karl Barth, Church Dogmatics, *ed. G. W. Bromiley and T. F. Torrance, Edinburgh: T&T Clark 1956–77, II/2, pp. 512–5.)*

II.4.8 Francis Watson, from *Text, Church and World*

In this extract Watson discusses why academic biblical interpretation should be responsible to the reading of the Scriptures in faith communities.

Concrete and generalized historicity

According to the historical-critical paradigm, a text is bound in perpetuity to its historical circumstances of origin. Any subsequent life that it enjoys will entangle it in misunderstanding and misuse as circumstances change and the manner of its origin is forgotten. There is, in fact, something contrary to the nature of the text in the act of belated reading, unless one acknowledges one's belatedness by reading it as a communicative act directed towards people other than oneself – the original, intended addressees. The fact that in the church (or synagogue) context such self-abnegating reading is structurally impossible is seen as a sign of the contradictoriness of communal usage. Over against this doctrine of the concrete historicity of the text, one might, with Childs, set the equally and necessarily doctrinaire claim that it is church usage that is primary and historical-critical practice that is contradictory. The peculiar historicity of these texts is constituted not genetically but by the fact that they have been uninterruptedly read and reread as authoritative within a particular community. It is by definition the final form of these texts which equips them for and launches them into this historical role, and this final form must therefore be the primary object of investigation, rather than the historical circumstances of origin.

As one of the primary liturgical and devotional texts of the Christian and Jewish communities, the psalms offer an appropriate test-case. According to Childs, 'the crucial historical critical discovery came with the form-critical work of H. Gunkel who established conclusively that the historical settings of the psalms were not to be sought in particular historical events, but in the cultic life of the community'. The result was that 'the more sharply the lines of the original sociological context emerged within ancient Israel, the sharper became the rupture with the traditional Jewish-Christian understanding of the Psalter'. The traditional messianic psalms now seemed to be directed not towards the future but towards a reigning monarch, and to be closely linked with similar Egyptian and Babylonian texts. The Davidic psalms of book I were anchored in circumstances which included prayers for rain and the exorcism of demons. A hitherto unknown enthronement festival was postulated as the origin of the hymns. 'In the light of this development, it is hardly surprising that the traditional use of the Psalter by the synagogue and church appeared highly arbitrary and far removed from the original function within ancient Israel'. Once again we detect the presence of the evaluative schema which identifies reality with the origin and dismisses subsequent usage as unreal.

This gulf between the generalized historicity postulated by liturgical or devotional usage and the concrete historicity postulated by form-criticism is mediated, according to Childs, by the final, canonical form of the text. It is not the case that concrete historicity gives way to a generalized role only by way of a rupture with the text, for the text in its canonical form has already been structured in such a way as to prepare it for this generalized role. Thus, again proceeding descriptively, we note that the canonical collection is prefaced by a psalm in praise of meditation on the Torah, and that 'the present editing of this original Torah psalm has provided the psalm with a new function as the introduction to the whole Psalter ... As a heading to the whole Psalter, the blessing now includes the faithful meditation on the sacred writings which follow. The introduction points to these prayers as the medium through which Israel now responds to the divine word. Because Israel continues to hear God's word through the voice of the psalmist's response, these prayers now function as the divine word itself. The original cultic role of the psalms has been subsumed under a larger category of the canon ... The introduction is, therefore, the first hint that the original setting has been subordinated to a new theological function for the future generations of worshipping Israel'. The meaning of Ps. 1 is itself transformed as it is employed as the hermeneutical key to the texts that follow, now conceived not in terms of original function but as a response to God's word which is itself incorporated into that word.

At one point, however, the canonical form appears to introduce its own form of concrete (even if fictitious) historicity, in those psalm titles which associate the psalms with specific events in the life of David: for example, with the occasion 'when he feigned madness before Abimelech, so that he drove him out, and he went away' (Ps. 34), or 'when Nathan the prophet came to him, after he had gone in to Bathsheba' (Ps. 51), or 'when Doeg the Edomite came and told Saul, "David has come to the house of Ahimelech"' (Ps. 52). How are we to understand the redactors' activity here? Childs notes that 'the incidents chosen as evoking the psalms were not royal occasions or representative of the kingly office. Rather, David is pictured simply as a man, indeed chosen by God for the sake of Israel, but who displays all the strengths and weaknesses of all human beings ... The effect of this new context has wide hermeneutical implications. The psalms are transmitted as the sacred psalms of David, yet they testify to all the common troubles and joys of ordinary human life in which all persons participate ... The effect has been exactly the opposite from what one might have expected. Far from tying these hymns to the ancient past, they have been contemporized and individualized for every generation of suffering and persecuted Israel'. These psalm titles indicate that the generalized historicity for which they are preparing the texts is not without its own mode of concretion which anticipates that future readers will derive from their own experience analogies with David's experiences of danger, betrayal or guilt. This concretion operates *within* the generalized historicity of the canonical texts: other examples might be found in the historical note that prefaces most of the prophetic books and in the many contextual indications in the Pauline letters. The canonical function of these instances of concrete historicity is not, however, to legitimate a hermeneutical programme which uses them to render ineffectual the generalized historicity of communal usage. On the contrary, they operate within that broader category.

Childs' opposition to an exaggerated emphasis on concrete historicity leads him to criticize R. E. Brown's approach to the study of the Johannine epistles. Childs notes that 'Brown's exegesis of I John is made to rest completely upon his theoretical reconstruction of the opponents of the author'; everything the author says is directed against the hypothetical contrary opinions of the 'secessionists'. There are indeed instances of concrete historicity within this text – for example, in the statement about the secession in 2.19 – and yet to make these one's central exegetical principle is, in typical historical-critical fashion, to ignore the fact that the text in its present form and location is part of the canon and therefore relatively independent of its circumstances of origin. One might instead choose to emphasize that this text, generically evidently a letter, nevertheless lacks the characteristic epistolary introduction and conclusion: 'Regardless of how one is to explain the omission, the effect of the present structure of I John is to move its interpretation in exactly the opposite direction from that proposed by Brown, and to universalize its message for the whole church'.

It is, in other words, inherent in the genre of (biblical) canonical text to be transmitted in a form which has erased, to a greater or lesser extent, most of the particularities of its circumstances of origin. From the historical-critical point of view, this erasure is both lamented as the loss of the only context which could make satisfactory sense of these texts, and exploited as an invitation to remedy the damage by historical hypothesis and reconstruction. In a canonical perspective, however, the erasure is to be seen as an intentional act rather than a regrettable accident, and welcomed as such, since it subordinates a merely historical curiosity about what was really happening in, say, the Johannine community to the ability of the text to function in quite different later circumstances. The pious hope that the quest for concrete historicity would ultimately serve the contemporary actualization of the text is belied both by the realities of historical-critical practice and – the crucial theoretical point – by the fact that this practice *begins* by ignoring or destroying precisely the vehicle which mediates between situation of origin and subsequent actualization, that is, the canonical form.

(Taken from Francis Watson, Text, Church and World: Biblical Interpretation in Theological Perspective, *Edinburgh: T&T Clark 1994, pp. 37–41.)*

II.4.9 Robert Jenson, from *Systematic Theology*

Jenson discusses the responsibility of theology to the Christian community.

The church has a mission: to see to the speaking of the gospel, whether to the world as message of salvation or to God as appeal and praise. Theology is the reflection internal to the church's labor on this assignment. We are thus led to a standard prolegomenal question of classic Western theology: about theology's 'speculative' and 'practical' characters. In this terminology, a 'practical' discipline is a guide to some practice; a 'speculative' discipline is a cognitive enterprise so captivated by a determinate object that it is its own reward.

Medieval theology tended to say that theology is a 'more speculative than practical' discipline, Reformation theology the reverse. Identification of theology as thinking about how to speak the gospel – that is, how to do something – supports the Reformation answer as the first to be given. Yet we will see that the older answer is equally necessary.

Any 'practical' reflection will be in some degree a critical and self-critical activity, for there is always the possibility that the practice in question is being inappropriately pursued. Thus theology as a practical discipline must always examine the church's verbal and other practice, and its own guidance of that practice, with the question, Does this teaching or other practice further or hinder the saying of the gospel?

No community cares greatly for self-critique, nor does the church. The Reformers were theologians who in a particular moment of the church's history thought self-critique overdue in certain domains and set out to renew it – with unanticipated church-political results. The Reformers' emphasis on the practical role of theology was correlate to their demand for churchly self-critique.

Insofar, however, as Protestant theology has since often tended to forget its original position that theology is at least *also* speculative, the result has been conversely disastrous. Protestant theology has regularly slipped away from captivity to any determinate object.

What is first given to theology is the gospel itself as a communication occurring in fact in human history. The gospel, however, is an intrinsically endangered object of thought in that it is itself a discourse. It does not occur without a speaker; and theologians, who take the gospel for the object of their reflection, are normally among the speakers by whom the gospel comes to pass. Theologians are therefore vocationally tempted to take as the object of their reflection, as 'the gospel,' whatever religious propositions they find themselves being in fact moved to utter. A major and generally conservative nineteenth-century systematic theologian stated the position with all desirable clarity: 'I, the Christian, am the object of knowledge for me, the theologian.'

One way in which theology falls to this temptation is by not noticing it – by proceeding as if theologians occupied some third-person vantage from which to view and describe the affair between God and his people. But equally disastrous is the oppositely besetting sin of Protestant – and much post-Vatican II Catholic – theology that escapes control by any determinate object and makes the gospel be whatever is 'justifying' or 'healing' or 'liberating' or whatever such value the theologian finds her- or himself affirming.

Our reflective situation over against the gospel as our object can be subtle rather than merely treacherous only if we persevere in attending to one character of the gospel: that it is witness *to* something. For however odd a historical event the Resurrection may have been, either it happened or it did not, and, if it did, occurred as it did and not otherwise. As witness to the Resurrection, the gospel is a determinate object of thought. Moreover, if we remember what the word 'resurrection' must mean in the linguistic context where it comes to mean anything at all, Israel's Bible, we will understand that to attend to a putative resurrection must be to attend to a certain putative God. In Israel's Scripture, life and death are in the Lord's hands exclusively; if a death and resurrection, that is, a new ordering of life and death, is the given of theology, just so must be this God.

Israel's Scripture materially concludes with the question posed to Ezekiel: Son of a human – what do you think? Can these bones live? These bones that are the whole of my people? Can the death of my people be reversed? Perhaps there has yet been no answer to the question; Christians are those who believe Jesus' Resurrection was the Lord's answer to his own question.

If this conviction is true, then Israel's God and the 'Father' to whom this man committed his life and from whom he received it again are forever identified. To attend to the resurrection is to attend to God self-identified as 'the one who raised the Lord Jesus.' Whoever – and, indeed, whatever – did that, the church says, is the reality we mean by 'God.' To attend to the Resurrection and to attend to this particular putative God, to take either as the object of our reflection, are the same.

IV

We have with these last propositions moved far into the theological circle, using as warrants theologoumena themselves as yet unfounded. Nor can we be finished with this hasty procedure. Can the gospel's God really thus be an *object* for us, that is, something we see and hear and can intend? He can be if the voice of the gospel, which witnesses to the resurrection and which we do in fact hear, is God's own voice, and if the objects to which this voice calls us to attend – the loaf and cup, the bath, and the rest of the gospel's factual churchly embodiment – are his own objectivity. That is, the gospel's

God can be an object for us if and only if God is so identified *by* the risen Jesus and his community as to be identified *with* them.

What we have rushed into is thus the doctrine of Trinity, and our haste but reproduces that which took the church to this doctrine as her first deliberately defined dogma. The present, here much unclarified, point: to attend theologically to the Resurrection of Jesus is to attend to the triune God. To attend to the gospel in its character as witness to a determinate reality is to worship in trinitarian specificity: in petition and praise to the Father with the Son in the Spirit. It is by failure intentionally to cast its theology in the space determined by these co-ordinates that much Protestant theology slips its object.

There is an ancient catholic rule: *lex orandi lex credendi*, 'the law of praying is the law of believing.' According to this principle, there are distinguishing regularities in the church's communal life of prayer, and these must govern the church's formulation of her belief. Chief among such patterns of the church's prayer is its triune structure, and chief among historical instances of obedience to the catholic rule is the third- and fourth-century development of a conceptually elaborated doctrine of Trinity.

The Reformation in effect proposed an analogous rule. The Reformation understood theology as critical reflection interior to the church's mission of proclamation. Thus the Reformation's claim can be summarized by a parody of the catholic formula: *lex proclamandi lex credendi*, 'the law of proclaiming is the law of believing.' Theology is to take for its rule the specific character by which the gospel is the gospel and not some other sort of discourse; theology must be thinking that guards the proclamation in this authenticity.

The Reformation's doctrine of 'justification' was an attempt to state the particular character of gospel-discourse, to state its *lex*. At least since the Council of Orange, it has not in the Western church been controversial that God's gifts are gratis, given only because God freely chooses to give them. Reformation theology merely pointed to one relatively neglected aspect of the agreed situation: since God's gifts are given in and through the person Jesus, the giving itself must be a personal act. Which is to say that God's grace occurs as *word*, as the address by which one person communicates him- or herself to others.

Thus God's gifts are, said the Reformation, intrinsically *bespoken* to us, as the church speaks the word of Christ. Therefore, if those gifts are to be gratis, this speaking must itself be gratuitous in its linguistic character. The kind of speaking that bestows something gratis can be specified: it is *promising* that does so.

Thus the decisive maxim of all the Reformation's theology: God's gifts are *res promissa*, 'the stuff of promise.'

Surely *both* formulas are needed. When the Reformation's rule from proclamation is not followed, theology slips from its assignment. When the catholic rule from prayer is not followed, theology slips from its object, for it is in the church's prayer and praise, in their verbal form and in the obtrusively embodied forms called sacrifice, that the church's discourse turns and fastens itself to God as its object. And it is the ineluctably trinitarian pattern of the church's prayer, its address *to* the one Jesus called Father, *with* Jesus who thus made himself the Son, *in* their common Spirit, by which the church's discourse grasps the resurrection's particular God as the object finally given to it.

(Taken from Robert Jenson, Systematic Theology vol.I, *Oxford: Oxford University Press 1997,* © *Robert Jenson, pp. 11–14.)*

PART III: DOING THEOLOGY TODAY

III.1 Modernity and postmodernity

Introductory essay

Theologians seek to investigate the content and coherency of the Christian gospel and to do so within the cultural and intellectual context of their time. Understanding one's own culture, however, is never an easy task, especially so today when the cultural framework of 'modernity' is giving way to what has been called 'postmodernity'. What do these terms mean? To begin with, they both describe a set of assumptions, values and patterns of thought which impact upon human behaviour and generate a general public consensus about what is true and good. It is part of the task of theology to explore the ways in which such ruling presuppositions are compatible or conflict with the Christian proclamation of the gospel.

While owing a great deal to classical Greek and Roman culture, modernity refers particularly to the world-view that emerged during the Enlightenment. Whereas church and Scripture were regarded throughout the Middle Ages as the repositories and arbiters of truth, modernity urges individuals to think for themselves and to test all things against the authority of reason. Many early advocates of such an approach were in no doubt of the compatibility of reason with the truths of revelation, but as modernity took hold, appeal to revelation was viewed with increasing scepticism. The success of science encouraged people to believe that the world was governed by rational universal laws, discoverable by the human mind. Whether or not God was the author of such laws became increasingly irrelevant to their proper understanding. If everything was explicable in terms of natural laws, there was little need to refer to God at all, except in the realm of private devotion.

The discovery of such laws depended, it was thought, upon the detachment, neutrality and objectivity of the enquirer. These are the cardinal epistemic virtues for modernity. Accordingly, the intrusion of personal faith and belief into one's judgments about the world inevitably hampers the quest for truth. The high value placed on rationality and scientific experiment is accompanied in modernity by a habit of mind called reductionism, whereby a true explanation of reality is achieved by breaking it down into its smallest parts and identifying the laws by which those parts are related to each other. John Locke, for instance, accounted for society and politics in this way, Adam Smith for economics, B. F. Skinner for human behaviour, and so on. It was further thought that the cumulative identification of all the laws governing the universe would yield a grand unified theory capable of explaining everything. Representatives of this view are still be found in such contemporary writers as Stephen Hawking. These trends combine to characterize modernity as an age of immanentism. As Colin Gunton has put it, the modern world has widely accepted the belief that the world can be understood from within itself, and not from any being or principle that is supposed to operate from without. That view is reflected in the work of some theologians who attempt to account for religion purely in terms of human behaviour and aspirations and without reference to the transcendent.

The term 'postmodernity' suggests a form of culture that has left modernity behind. That is only partially true, for in some of its defining characteristics postmodernity clings tenaciously to the convictions of modernity. This is evident, for example, in the extreme individualism of postmodernity. Approving modernity's injunction to think for oneself, postmodernity contends that all individuals construct the world for themselves. Where modernity trusted in reason, however, to yield agreement between all rational individuals, postmodernity denies the prospect of any such agreement. We each see the world from our own point of view, and there simply is no truth which is true for us all. In common again with modernity, postmodernity holds the view that access to truth is denied wherever subjective and personal factors like faith, personal commitment, culture, gender and race impact upon our thinking. The difference postmodernism brings to the matter, however, is its contention that there is no escape from the constraints of such particularities. The truth is, we are told – not without irony – that all utterances of the human subject reveal only the thought world and perspective of that subject itself. Postmodernism finally extends across the whole spectrum of human culture the judgement once made by Ludwig Feuerbach upon theological propositions: Our claims to knowledge reveal only the mysteries of our own nature.

Postmodernism thus takes the world apart, in typical reductionist fashion, but denies the existence of laws enabling us to put it back together again. Reality is simply fragmentary and disconnected. Exhibiting an 'incredulity towards all meta-narratives', as Jean-

François Lyotard has famously put it, people of postmodern persuasion are suspicious of all attempts to make sense of the whole. Postmodernism thus emphasizes particularity rather than universality, celebrates individual choice, and discourages evaluative judgements about truth and falsity, right and wrong, good and evil. Construed more positively, however, it offers a legitimate critique of the tyrannies of totalitarian regimes and world-views, and encourages respect for the diversity which does indeed characterize the reality of humankind.

Despite postmodernism's embrace of modernity's individualistic and self-centred conception of the knowing process, it offers, nevertheless, a salutary critique of some of modernity's other excesses. Postmodernism is critical, for instance, of the confidence with which modernity claimed to understand and organize the world. An absolute but misplaced confidence in science, for example, is increasingly giving way to a more cautious estimation of the role science may play in the resolution of our biggest problems. The increasing awareness of the ramifications of difference in culture, in race, and in gender has caused us to repent of the imperialistic attitudes which have characterized the not so distant past. The postmodern recognition of the impact of contextuality and personal perspective on our epistemic processes has liberated us from the constricting ideal of an objectivity from which all subjectivity has been eliminated. It has helped us to see that the truth is not coterminous with the deliverances of an impassionate and detached rationality. What remains at issue, however, is whether postmodernism can offer a way forward, or whether it has already been exposed as no more than the death throes of modernity.

Modernity's reductionistic account of religion and its confidence in the rational progress of history are evident in the first reading below from Karl Marx (III.1.1). Heavily influenced by Hegel's dialectical philosophy, Marx wrote famously of the inevitable and revolutionary progress of history towards the communist state, and contended that a feature of such progress would be the eventual obsolescence of religion. Marx's celebrated but much misrepresented remark about religion being the opium of the people allows to religion the role of a palliative in the midst of unjust social and economic structures, but looks forward to the day when those structures will be transformed and religion will be needed no more.

The reading from Ludwig Feuerbach seen earlier in this volume (see I.5.7) provides a good example of the modernist assumptions with which we are concerned in this section. Like Marx, his contemporary, Feuerbach believed that Hegel's dialectic method was basically correct, but that his analysis of history was inverted. Whereas Hegel believed that reality is comprised fundamentally of a single mind or Spirit (*Geist*) whose self-unfolding gave rise to the material world and the progress of history itself, Marx and Feuerbach countered that the fundamental reality is in fact material, and that the ideas of spirit and transcendence are products of the evolving material world. It is for this reason that Feuerbach alleged, as seen earlier, that theological speech reduces under analysis to talk about our own highest values and ideals. It is not inspired by some transcendent reality but is simply the highest reach of the material world. Here we see the modern predilection for immanentist accounts of the world.

Though denying its transcendent reference, Feuerbach maintained a positive regard for religion. In his view religion had a civilizing function and contributed to the good-ordering of society. Friedrich Nietzsche (III.1.2), by contrast, while sharing Feuerbach's view that theological utterance was a mere human construction, regarded Christianity as a form of moral enslavement, a corrupting influence which belittled and destroyed humanity. Famously announcing that 'God is dead' (though he had taken the claim from Hegel), Nietzsche set forth the ideal of *Übermensch* (superman) who, freed from the shackles of Christianity and driven by the will to power, would pursue his goals without enslavement to the categories of good and evil. It is important to note that Nietzsche does not suppose that a once existent God is now dead. Rather his proclamation is designed to draw attention to the alleged fact that people of the modern world have stopped believing in God, thus renouncing, in Nietzsche's view, their allegiance to a lie. Nietzsche's contribution to the erosion of faith in God anticipates the postmodern scepticism about the category of truth. In this respect, Nietzsche was one of modernity's most ardent critics. He rejected the ideal of a rationalized account of reality and emphasized the fragmentation and disorder of the world.

In the 1960s there arose in theology an echo of Nietzsche's proclamation of the death of God. Conforming their thought to the spirit of the age, the 'death of God' theologians capitulated entirely to the view that the true story of the world could be told without reference to the transcendent. In the reading from Wolfhart Pannenberg (III.1.3), this view is sharply criticized. Pannenberg then offers his own view of how theology should respond to the modern secular world.

The reading from Alvin Plantinga (III.1.4) offers a forceful critique of the foundationalist epistemology that characterizes modernity. Foundationalism, in its modern guise, received definitive formulation in the work of René Descartes. Seeking to establish a sure basis for knowledge, Descartes began by doubting everything of which he could not be absolutely certain. From this process arose his famous proposition, 'I think, therefore I am.' This proposition cannot be doubted, Descartes argued, and so forms a foundation upon which other knowledge claims may be built. The foundationalist approach to knowledge thus insists that *claims to knowledge should either be self-evident, or they should be built upon self-evident propositions.* Plantinga, however, argues that such an epistemology will not do, not least because it is self-referentially incoherent. The proposition highlighted above is itself unable to meet the strict criteria that it describes. It cannot be derived from self-evident truths. The problems with foundationalism have led some – particularly those of postmodern persuasion – to assert that all claims to knowledge are illegitimate. For Plantinga, this is simply an overreaction. The foundationalist epistemology of modernity may have collapsed but, in Plantinga's view, that simply means that we need another account of how we know the truth.

In the final reading, Colin Gunton (III.1.5) argues that the weaknesses of modernity are largely due to the loss of a proper understanding of creation – by which Christian theology has asserted that things are the way that they are by virtue of the relation they have with their creator. This has led to serious deficiencies in thought about the practice of relationality, particularity, temporality and truth, and is accompanied at the level of society by increasing fragmentation and lack of cohesion. Where the world is thought to be comprehensible apart from its relation to God, and in disregard, therefore, of its created character, its reality is both distorted and misunderstood. Gunton's critique is applicable to modernity and postmodernity alike.

MAR

III.1.1 Karl Marx, from *Towards a Critique of Hegel's Philosophy of Right*

Marx here assumes the validity of the critique of religion, which finds all religion as only a projection of human desires onto the outside world; he looks for a time when those desires will be realized (in the communist state), and so religion will not be needed.

For Germany, the *criticism of religion* has been essentially completed, and the criticism of religion is the prerequisite of all criticism.

The *profane* existence of error is compromised as soon as its *heavenly plea on behalf of hearth and home has been refuted. Man, who has found only the reflection* of himself in the fantastic reality of heaven, where he sought a superman, will no longer feel disposed to find the mere appearance of himself, the non-man, where he seeks and must seek his true reality.

The foundation of irreligious criticism is: *Man makes religion*, religion does not make man. Religion is indeed the self-consciousness and self-esteem of man who has either not yet won through to himself or has already lost himself again. But *man* is no abstract being squatting outside the world. Man is *the world of man*, state, society. This state and this society produce religion, which is an *inverted consciousness of the world*, because they are an *inverted world*. Religion is the general theory of this world, its encyclopedic compendium, its logic in popular form, its spiritual *point d'honneur*, its enthusiasm, its moral sanction, its solemn complement and its universal basis of consolation and justification. It is the *fantastic realization* of the human essence since the human essence has not acquired any true reality. The struggle against religion is therefore indirectly the struggle against *that world*, whose spiritual *aroma* is religion.

Religious suffering is at one and the same time the *expression* of real suffering and a protest against real suffering. Religion is the sigh of the oppressed creature, the heart of a heartless world and the soul of soulless conditions. It is the *opium* of the people.

The abolition of religion as the *illusory* happiness of the people is the demand for their *real* happiness. To call on them to give up their illusions about their condition is to *call on them to give up a condition that requires illusions*. The criticism of religion is therefore in *embryo* the *criticism of that vale of tears* of which religion is the *halo*.

Criticism has plucked the imaginary flowers on the chain not in order that man shall continue to bear that chain without fantasy or consolation but so that he shall throw off the chain and pluck the living flower. The criticism of religion disillusions man, so that he will think, act and fashion his reality like a man who has discarded his illusions and regained his senses, so that he will move around himself as his own true sun. Religion is only the illusory sun which revolves around man as long as he does not revolve around himself.

It is therefore the *task of history*, once the *other-world of truth* has vanished, to establish the *truth of this world*. It is the immediate *task of philosophy*, which is in the service of history, to unmask self-estrangement in its *unholy* forms once the *holy form* of human self-estrangement has been unmasked. Thus the criticism of heaven turns into the criticism of earth, the *criticism of religion* into the *criticism of law* and the *criticism of theology* into the *criticism of politics*.

(Taken from Gregor Benton's translation in Karl Marx: Early Writings, Harmondsworth: Penguin 1975, pp. 243–5.*)*

III.1.2 Friedrich Nietzsche, from *The Gay Science*

In this text Nietzsche foresees the consequences of the loss of Christian faith from European civilization. There is 'no up or down left'; we must now 'become gods ourselves' (i.e., make our own values and morality, without reference to any other).

[125]

The Madman. Have you not heard of that madman who lit a lantern in the bright morning hours, ran to the market place, and cried incessantly, 'I seek God! I seek God!' As many of those who do not believe in God were standing around just then, he provoked much laughter. Why, did he get lost? said one. Did he lose his way like a child? said another. Or is he hiding? Is he afraid of us? Has he gone on a voyage? or emigrated? Thus they yelled and laughed. The madman jumped into their midst and pierced them with his glances.

'Whither is God' he cried. 'I shall tell you. *We have killed, him* – you and I. All of us are his murderers. But how have we done this? How were we able to drink up the sea? Who gave us the sponge to wipe away the entire horizon? What did we do when we unchained this earth from its sun? Whither is it moving now? Whither are we moving now? Away from all suns? Are we not plunging continually? Backward, sideward, forward, in all directions? Is there any up or down left? Are we not straying as through an infinite nothing? Do we not feel the breath of empty space? Has it not become colder? Is not night and more night coming on all the while? Must not lanterns be lit in the morning? Do we not hear anything yet of the noise of the gravediggers who are burying God? Do we not smell anything yet of God's decomposition? Gods too decompose. God is dead. God remains dead. And we have killed him. How shall we, the murderers of all murderers, comfort ourselves? What was holiest and most powerful of all that the world has yet owned has bled to death under our knives. Who will wipe this blood off us? What water is there for us to clean ourselves? What festivals of atonement, what sacred games shall we have to invent? Is not the greatness of this deed too great for us? Must not we ourselves become gods simply to seem worthy of it? There has never been a greater deed; and whoever will be born after us – for the sake of this deed he will be part of a higher history than all history hitherto.'

Here the madman fell silent and looked again at his listeners; and they too were silent and stared at him in astonishment. At last he threw his lantern on the ground, and it broke and went out. 'I come too early,' he said then; 'my time has not come yet. This tremendous event is still on its way, still wandering – it has not yet reached the ears of man. Lightning and thunder require time, the light of the stars requires time, deeds require time even after they are done, before they can be seen and heard. This deed is still more distant from them than the most distant stars – *and yet they have done it themselves.'*

It has been related further that on that same day the madman entered divers churches and there sang his *requiem aeternam deo.* Led out and called to account, he is said to have replied each time, 'What are these churches now if they are not the tombs and sepulchers of God?'

[343]

The background of our cheerfulness. The greatest recent event – that 'God is dead,' that the belief in the Christian God has ceased to be believable – is even now beginning to cast its first shadows over Europe. For the few, at least, whose eyes, whose suspicion in their eyes, is strong and sensitive enough for this spectacle, some sun seems to have set just now. . . . In the main, however, this may be said: the event itself is much too great, too distant, too far from the comprehension of the many even for the tidings of it to be thought of as having *arrived* yet, not to speak of the notion that many people might know what has really happened here, and what must collapse now that this belief has been undermined – all that was built upon it, leaned on it, grew into it; for example, our whole European morality. . . .

Even we born guessers of riddles who are, as it were, waiting on the mountains, put there between today and tomorrow and stretched in the contradiction between today and tomorrow, we firstlings and premature births of the coming century, to whom the shadows that must soon envelop Europe really *should* have appeared by now – why is it that even we look forward to it without any real compassion for this darkening, and above all without any worry and fear for *ourselves?* Is it perhaps that we are still too deeply impressed by the first consequences of this event – and these first consequences, the consequences for *us,* are perhaps the reverse of what one might expect: not at all sad and dark, but rather like a new, scarcely describable kind of light, happiness, relief, exhilaration, encouragement, dawn? Indeed, we philosophers and 'free spirits' feel as if a new dawn were shining on us when we receive the tidings that 'the old god is dead'; our heart overflows with gratitude, amazement, anticipation, expectation. At last the horizon appears free again to us, even granted that it is not bright; at last our ships may venture out again, venture out to face any danger; all the daring of the lover of knowledge is permitted again; the sea, *our* sea, lies open again; perhaps there has never yet been such an 'open sea.'

(Taken from Walter Kaufmann, The Portable Nietzsche, *New York: The Viking Press 1954, pp. 95–6, 447–8.)*

III.1.3 Wolfhart Pannenberg, from *Christianity in a Secularized World*

Pannenberg here criticizes what he sees as the surrender to modernist secularism in the 'Death of God' theology, which was popular in the 1960s but is almost forgotten now. He then offers an alternative programme whereby Christian theology can offer a more rational account of secular rationality.

It is difficult in secular culture to make the transition from the implicit presence of the religious theme to an explicit religious attitude because the contents of faith, particularly those of the Christian tradition, have been denied any objective binding force in the secular consciousness. Therefore faith appears as irrational commitment to a content which is regarded as 'true' only in a private perspective. Religious need can therefore easily assume the form of irrational commitment if it is recognized and affirmed as such by people. However, such a commitment can be just as binding to other contents as to that of Christianity. The fact that it is made to Christian belief is then primarily conditioned by a person's life history, say a Christian religious socialization received in childhood but later pushed into the background. At all events, in the light of secular awareness the step towards an explicit commitment in faith looks like a leap into the irrational.

So how should the churches conduct themselves in the world of a secular culture in order to make it easier for people to move from the implicit presence of the religious theme in their lives to an explicit Christian commitment of faith? What can theology contribute to this?

The possible strategies on the part of the churches and theology towards secular culture extend from the various forms of assimilation to a move in precisely the opposite direction. Both the extreme alternatives here seem to me to be false. The resolute course away from assimilation which has been attempted in Catholic integralism or traditionalism, or on the Protestant side in the theology of Karl Barth and his school, can make an impression on people and at least in passing even on the public awareness of secular culture. Particularly in times of cultural crisis like the years after the First World War and in another way also after the Second, people have been susceptible to authoritarian claims and demands because they promise firm ground in a world which at least for the moment does not provide any support. The authoritative affirmation of religious truth is imposing by virtue of the impression of self-assurance that it gives, and its message of judgment on a world which is in any case felt to be collapsing or broken is a plausible one. But the authoritarian position is very much less impressive in the face of a secular world which is still functioning more or less. For it puts the believer into an alien atmosphere which is not conveyed by the everyday world and its criteria of reality except perhaps through the demand for radical change. Moreover left-wing Barthianism, for example, derives its impressiveness from the demand for radical change, which makes the theology of diastasis and its political programme seem topical. However, its activism provides only an apparent link with reality as it is experienced, because it goes directly against the reality that is to hand, and therefore if the radical change it seeks actually came about, the results would be quite different from what its supporters expect.

The opposite strategy is that of assimilation to the secular understanding of reality. This is thought to be a possible way of bringing people who live in the modern secularized world to faith as a possibility of understanding themselves in this world without actually having the presumption to take a leap from it into a quite different world, the world of faith – a leap which can never in fact completely leave this world, so that the leap rather goes through the existence of believers themselves. The strategy of assimilation to the secular understanding of reality seeks to avoid this situation, which Hegel already described under the title of the 'unhappy consciousness'. But in so doing it risks giving up the decisive content of the tradition of faith, so that in some cases the content of faith becomes so empty that the question arises why one should still turn to religion at all. If one hears from the pulpit only what one can read in newspapers or get from psychology courses at the local college, why still go to church? Something is expected there which the secular world does not offer, namely religion. Often, however, it happens that those who have to represent the cause of religion by virtue of their office have been so unsettled by the spirit of secular culture that they think that they can serve the faith by concealing its content completely under the cloak of secularity, thus making it almost invisible. So the strategy of assimilation is largely the expression of the problems of those who hold office in the church.

I shall now go on to discuss some examples of such excessive assimilation of theology to the secularism of modern culture.

1. One such example, which is at the same time interesting because it is concerned with the theological thematization of secular culture, is the formula of the 'death of God' in this modern secular culture. This formula was introduced poetically by Jean Paul and philosophically by Hegel in 1803 as a cipher for modern secular culture. It describes the world in which the autonomous self which needs no transcendent foundation merely stands over against things as its objects, a world in which all reality is finite and the finite is absolute, and so at the same time everything is nothing, because by definition the finite ends and that is its true being. That is the world in which God is dead. In this world of nothingness God is seen to be dead because only finite realities, things and subjects are acknowledged to have reality. That is only possible if human beings, finite selves, make themselves infinite,

and thus take the place of God. So for secular culture (in the 'new time', as Hegel puts it), God is dead because human beings have taken the place of God by making the human self infinite and contrasting everything else with it as finite. That is a very profound diagnosis of the metaphysical nature of modern culture. But it is only illuminating as a statement about God if the present state of the cultural world is bound up with the being of God in such a way that it can be expressed as an event which affects God himself. This conception of the 'speculative Good Friday, which otherwise was historical' comes at least very close to a pantheistic identification of the world with the divine life. The fascination which this notion has exercised on theology is probably to be explained from the fact that it makes a description of the character of secular culture in theological language possible. In that very way, it may seem, the secularism of the secular consciousness is transcended. But the price paid for this is too high. In the case of the philosophy of the early Hegel it consists in giving up the transcendence of God over against the world. Here Hegel's view was that while God is dead in secular culture, he is experienced in the impending cultural renewal of his resurrection, namely through what Hegel in his doctrine of the infinite as the absolute idea in contrast to the finitude of human subjectivity envisaged as the justification of the religious consciousness. This expectation was no longer shared in the subsequent period. Since Feuerbach had described all the divine properties as anthropomorphic transference and thus also the idea of the divine subject itself as a mere human projection, the 'new man' in Nietzsche's *Joyful Science* (1882) asserted that God is in fact dead and remains dead, having been killed by man (Aphorism 125). That, too, is a statement about the nature of secular culture or about the fact that 'belief in the Christian God has become incredible', as Nietzsche observed by way of explanation in a later aphorism (343). Christian theology cannot allow such a statement to stand as a statement about God, but only as a statement about the nature of secular culture. If need be it can speak of an 'absence' of God from the world of this culture, but only in the sense that God is absent *for the person* who has turned away from him. The Bible also knows such an absence of God from human beings regardless of the ceaselessly efficacious presence of the creator in every breath of his creatures. If God appears to human beings to be absent, although they depend on his sustaining their life at every moment of their existence, that means that they have turned away from the divine source of their life and are close to death. For God to hide himself and leave men and women to do as they fancy is an expression of his anger (Ps.89.47). Therefore the pious man prays, 'Hide not thy face from me, that I be not like those who go down to the pit' (Ps.143.7). The experience of the absence of God announces the imminence of his judgment, for according to Paul the divine judgment consists in the fact that God leaves the sinner and the world to themselves, that he 'hands them over' to the consequences of their actions.

That is how Christian theology must speak of the phenomenon that Hegel and Nietzsche have described as the death of God in modern secular culture. However, theology should not itself take over the formula of the death of God and seek some metaphysical profundity in it, as happened among the American 'Death of God' theologians in the 1960s. That is excessive assimilation to the secularism of the modern world. It is in no way justified by the fact that the Christian message is the word of the cross. The death of Jesus on the cross is not the death of God, nor even the death of the Son in contrast to Father and Spirit. The dogmatically correct way of expressing the theological tradition is rather that the Son of God died on the cross in accordance with the human nature that he assumed. It has been rightly stressed in the most recent theological discussion that the God of Christian faith may not be thought of as untouched by the death of Jesus in his eternal Godhead, any less than the incarnation is to be imagined as an event external to the Godhead of the Son. The Godhead of God himself is at risk in the death of Jesus, the Godhead of the Son, but therefore also that of the Father, who would not be Father without the Son. However, that does not mean that God himself died on the cross, but that he has affirmed his Godhead against the death on the cross – the Godhead of the Son which is also that of the Father and the Spirit – by the resurrection of Jesus. If one wants to compare the aversion of secular culture from the Christian God with the crucifixion of Jesus, as happened in Hegel, in theological terms it has to be said that in the Easter event God already victoriously affirmed his deity, and that he will finally affirm it on the Last Day in judgment upon the world. Christian theology in the secular world must not give up central elements in God's transcendence of the world and in his salvation or allow them to fade into the background for the sake of assimilation to the secular understanding of reality. On the other hand, Christianity may not be content with just securing the existence of the dogmatic content of the tradition. That would be merely to oppose a counter-world of faith to the secular world, not to bear witness to God as the creator and reconciler of this world of ours. It is a temptation for church and theology to regard as an opportunity for faith the readiness of human beings to succumb to the irrational, to an irrationally affirmed counter-world, as a result of a feeling of alienation in the secular world of culture. Flight from the meaninglessness of the secular world into irrationality can just as well turn to other religious and ideological elements and groups as to the church. The exotic attraction of such groups – like the Hare Krishna people, the New Age movement and also anthroposophy – is greater than that of the churches, which seem conventional alongside it. A church and theology which rely on a readiness to escape into the irrational on the part of those who are homeless in the secular world could very soon prove to be the loser. Rather, the opportunity for Christianity and its theology is to integrate the reduced understanding of reality on the part of the secular culture and its picture of human nature into a greater whole, to offer the reduced rationality of secular culture a greater breadth of reason, which would also include the horizon of the bond between humankind and God. In the theology of our century this task was perceived with great mastery by Karl Rahner, who thought that we should see that which is universally human in every dogmatic theme, but also perceive human need at the same time, and the way in which human beings are directed towards the divine mystery which has been manifested in Jesus Christ. A theology like that of Rahner is not of course concerned with just any form of rationalism. Indeed Rahner used to talk of the mystery of the divine reality which everyone is confronted with in his or her personal life. But he did that in a rational way. From the beginning the link with reason has been part of the missionary dynamism of Christianity. In the Christian patristic period it characterized the claim of the gospel to universality against all the irrationalisms in which late antiquity was particularly rich. So I think that it is also important for the Christian controversy with the secular world to oppose the shortcomings of secular culture with a deeper and broader reason. By that means the apparent opposition between theonomy and autonomy will be done away with, and the great achievements of secular culture like the idea of tolerance and the rights of political freedom will be preserved. This approach will also, however, have to overcome the clashes between confessions – had these not been so irreconcilable, modern secularism would never in fact have come into being. The continuation of divisions in Christianity gives the lie both to the spirit of the love of Christ and to the capacity of Christianity to achieve a breadth of reason which would be spiritually superior to the diminutions of secular culture. Therefore the ecumenical movement of our time, the movement towards a plurality of churches which mutually recognize one another within the community of the one church of Christ, is one of the basic conditions for a credible form of Christianity generally in the face of the secular world of culture which has emerged from the division of the church.

(Taken from Wolfhart Pannenberg, Christianity in a Secularized World, New York: Crossroad 1989, pp. 44–58.)

III.1.4 Alvin Plantinga, from *Warrant: The Current Debate*

Plantinga here describes and criticizes the dominant modernist way of describing the reasons we have to believe in the truth of ('warrant for') a particular belief, foundationalism.

We form, discard, maintain, and modify beliefs. And a salient characteristic of our way of doing these things is that we sometimes do them on the basis of *evidence*. Taking the term 'evidence' in perhaps its most familiar sense (at any rate most familiar to *philosophers*), the evidence on the basis of which I form a given belief will be *some other proposition or propositions* I believe; in the preceding chapter I called such evidence 'propositional' evidence. There is, for example, the evidence for relativity theory, or for the proposition that the gospel of John was composed late in the first century A.D., or for the claim that life began on earth more than three billion years ago

Foundationalism – a family of views that has had an extraordinarily illustrious career in Western thought – takes its fundamental inspiration from the first kind of evidence, from propositional evidence. It starts from the apparent cleavage between those beliefs you accept on the evidential basis of other beliefs, and those you accept in the *basic* way – accept, but not on the evidential basis of other beliefs.

Aristotle and some of his medieval followers are classical foundationalists – *ancient* classical foundationalists, as I shall call them, to distinguish them from such modern classical foundationalists as, for example, Descartes, Malebranche, Locke, Leibniz, Berkeley, Hume, and a thousand lesser lights. Modern classical foundationalism, obviously enough, has been the dominant tradition in epistemology, in the West, since the seventeenth century.

The foundationalist, therefore – call him a *generic* foundationalist, since we are here concerned with what is common to all foundationalists – starts from the distinction between beliefs we accept in the basic way and those we accept on the evidential basis of other beliefs. Thus I believe $23 \times 48 = 1,104$ on the evidential basis of such propositions as $3 \times 8 = 24$, $3 \times 4 = 12$, $12 + 2 = 14$, and the like. His idea is that every belief is either basic or accepted on the basis of other beliefs (and given the definition of basicality I just gave, here he will encounter no disagreement); he adds that in a correct or healthy human system of beliefs, there *are* basic beliefs, and every nonbasic belief will be accepted on the basis of other beliefs that offer evidential support for it, in such a way that every belief is supported, finally, by basic beliefs, beliefs in the foundations. These beliefs, of course, are not accepted on the basis of others; the basis relation is finite and terminates in the foundations.

An immediate and important consequence of this fundamental idea is the rejection of *circular* reasoning: that is, the foundationalist finds fault with a system of beliefs in which a belief A_0 is accepted on the evidential basis of a belief A_1, which is accepted on the basis of A_2, which is accepted on the basis of $A_3, \ldots$, which is based on A_n, which is based on A_0.

Now it is often said that the central difference between foundationalism and coherentism lies just here: the coherentist does *not* object to circular reasoning, 'provided the circle is big enough.' Indeed, so the suggestion goes, the coherentist goes further; he *revels* in circular reasoning, for it is precisely in such circular chains that he sees warrant as arising. He must therefore suppose, if this characterization is correct, that the basis relation in a noetic structure does not simply *transfer* warrant: it somehow *generates* it, at least if the chain involved is sufficiently long. On this view (so the story goes) *every* belief is accepted on the basis of other beliefs; none holds the privileged position of being basic or foundational; and apart from coherence considerations, none is more warranted than any other. Suppose we begin by looking into this alleged opposition. Can it really be that the coherentist does not reject circular reasoning, instead recommending it as the path of true philosophy? And why does the foundationalist reject circular reasoning? Why do *we* reject it? And how shall we characterize foundationalism?

According to the foundationalist view some of my beliefs are basic for me: the rest, naturally enough, are nonbasic for me, held on the evidential basis of other beliefs I hold. If things are going properly, however, I will not (of course) believe a given proposition on the basis of just *any* proposition; I will instead believe A on the basis of B only if B *evidentially supports* A. Foundationalists of varying stripes, naturally enough, have made different suggestions as to the further characteristics of this relation. Descartes seemed to think that the only support worth its salt is deductive support. Locke added inductive evidence. (The facts that Feike is a seventeen-year-old Frisian and 19 out of 20 seventeen-year-old Frisians can swim evidentially support the proposition that Feike can swim.) Peirce added *abductive* evidence: the sort of evidence provided (for example) for special relativity by the null result of the Michelson-Morley experiment, muon decay phenomena, the Hafele-Keating experiment involving jet transport of cesium clocks, and so on.

Coherentism is therefore to be rejected: coherence is not the only source of warrant. But what are the other sources? According to modern classical foundationalism (an extraordinarily influential picture dominating Western epistemological thought for nearly three centuries), they are *reason* and *experience* – but then both reason and experience narrowly construed. On this view a proposition is properly basic if and only if it is either self-evident or else appropriately about one's own immediate experience – specifying how one is appeared to, for example. Any other propositions that are acceptable for you must be ones that are appropriately supported by propositions of these kinds.

Classical foundationalism has fallen on evil days; and rightly so. As Reid saw and argued, the whole development of modern philosophy from Descartes to Hume shows that classical foundationalism 'taken to its logical conclusion', as they say, yields the consequence that very little, far less than we would ordinarily think, is epistemically acceptable for us. None of the propositions we believe about ordinary material objects, or the past, or other persons – none of these propositions seems to be appropriately supported by propositions that are properly basic according to the classical foundationalist's standards for proper basicality; the latter offer precious little by way of evidence for the former. But these propositions certainly seem to be acceptable for us: why, then, should we accept classical foundationalism? If there were powerful and compelling arguments for it, then perhaps we should have to grit our teeth and accept it; but the powerful arguments are not forthcoming. So classical foundationalism has fallen into disrepute if not desuetude. I don't propose to add my voice to that of the howling mob, except to say that many forms of classical foundationalism look to be self-referentially incoherent. According to these forms, a proposition A is acceptable for me if and only if it is either properly basic or believed on the evidential basis of propositions that are (1) properly basic, and (2) support A. But this proposition itself is not properly basic by this criterion: it is neither self-evident nor appropriately about someone's immediate experience, and (subject to the indeterminateness of what is to count as support here) it is certainly hard to see that it is appropriately supported by propositions that do meet that condition.

So classical foundationalism fails. This fact has been widely celebrated (sometimes with a sort of foolish extravagance); it has also been widely hailed as requiring rejection of all of epistemology, or even all of traditional philosophy, or even the very idea of *truth* itself. In a moment of anguish, Dostoyevski blurted that if God does not exist, everything is possible. Richard Rorty and his friends go him one (or more) better and without the anguish: if classical foundationalism is wrong, there is no such thing as truth. These intemperate reactions to the demise of classical foundationalism betray agreement with it at a deep level: agreement that the only security or warrant for our beliefs must arise by way of evidential relationship to beliefs that are certain: self-evident or about our own mental states. But why think a thing like that? And why follow these enthusiasts into that grand confusion between metaphysics and epistemology, confusing truth with our access to it, announcing the demise of the latter as a consequence of the failure of classical foundationalism? Here we have confusion twice confounded: first, confusion of truth with our access to it and, second, confusion of knowledge with Cartesian certainty. But as to the first, truth owes nothing to our access to it; and as to the second, Cartesian certainty is indeed a will-o'-the-wisp, but nothing follows for knowledge.

(Taken from Alvin Plantinga, Warrant: The Current Debate, *Oxford: Oxford University Press 1993,* © Alvin Plantiga, pp. 67–85.)*

III.1.5 Colin Gunton, from *The One, The Three and The Many*

Gunton here claims that modernity is parasitic on the preceding Christ-ian thought-world, and that its basic flaw is a loss of the doctrine of creation.

What, then, in sum are we to make of the culture of modernity? First, we can say that as a historical phenomenon, modernity can be understood as the era which arises out of Christendom by making against its predecessor a charge of hypocrisy: that its freedom is a cloak for tyranny, its creed a pretext for the suppression of the authentic human quest for truth. Another way of putting the matter would be to say that it renders to Christianity account for its institutional, social and intellectual deficiencies, with interest. It is the interest that concerns us, because, if my analysis is right, modernity is parasitic upon the preceding Christendom in the sense that it takes its major orientation from its rejection of some of the latter's primary doctrines, and in particular its ontology of the transcendent basis of things. Yet, as we have also seen, the plight of the one delivered from possession by one devil is not in every respect improved.

Second, it has been argued that with respect to the content of its ideologies and assumptions, the deficiencies of the modern age are in certain respects similar to those of ancient thought and practice. Like antiquity, modernity can be understood as an era which has serious deficiencies in thought about and practice of relationality, particularity, temporality and truth, even though they are the values on whose behalf it rejected the inheritance of Christendom. In that respect, it is far less distinctive than its apologists suppose. What gives the deficiencies their distinctive unpleasantness – as well as much of their positive power – is the theological background against which they must be understood. There has been a displacement in which the characteristically monistic God of mediaeval antiquity has been displaced to the individual mind and will, producing a fragmentation that threatens the health of culture and social order. An attempt to wrest from God the prerogatives of absolute freedom and infinity leads to the inversion of Pentecost and what is in effect a new Babel. 'Postmodernism' represents that Babel perfectly, because when each speaks a language unrelated to that of the other – when language is not the basis of the communication that shapes our being – the only outcome can be fragmentation. In that sense, postmodernism is modernity come home to roost.

Third, the theological heart of the matter is to be found in the doctrine of creation. Much has been made of Václav Havel's image of the coordinates by which the relative importance of things may be judged. It has been argued that with the dismantling of the transcendent measure by which the world is understood, modernity has come to be marked by a loss of measure and balance: everything, both the good and the bad, is disproportionately magnified. But that is precisely where the doctrine of creation is so important, not simply as a teaching about the origin of things in the unconstrained freedom of God but as an articulating of the way things are by virtue of the relation they have with their creator. The deficiencies in thought about and practice of relationality, particularity, temporality and truth that have been uncovered in successive chapters derive in part from a deficiency of fundamental ontology. Parmenides and Heraclitus have called the tune and so have obliterated the trinitarian categories which enable us to think of the world – and therefore also culture and society – as both one and many, unified and diverse, particular and in relation. That is why the doctrine of creation as triune act is so important.

The question now is: what is to be done? The voices with which I began this chapter are for the most part stronger as laments for the disasters of modernity than prescriptions for its healing. So, indeed, is much of the content of the book so far. But we are only half way, and my hope in the second half will be to ask whether theology can contribute to the healing of modern fragmentation. Can there be found a vision of things which unifies without producing totalitarianism or homogeneity? Can Christianity find the means by which it can be renewed and contribute to the healing of the modern world? The lineaments of an answer to the question will be attempted in the second part of the book, where I shall hope to develop some of the concepts with the help of which new approaches can be made to the questions that have engaged our attention so far.

(Take from Colin E. Gunton, The One, The Three and The Many: God, Creation and the Culture of Modernity (the 1992 Bampton Lectures), *Cambridge: Cambridge University Press 1993, pp. 123–5.)*

III.2 The rise of local theologies

Introductory essay

'Local' here from 'locus' – place; the distinctive common feature of what have become called local theologies is their locatedness. In each case, Christian theologians who shared a particular location (social, geographical, racial, or whatever) began to question whether the inherited tradition of theology adequately addressed the needs and insights they shared with others who inhabited that location, and then sought to do theology which would. Liberation theology (III.2.1) began with an analysis of oppression, and found theological resources to understand that oppression, and theological insights that were particularly, or even only, available to those suffering oppression. Feminist theology asked whether the Christian intellectual tradition had taken the particular gifts, experiences and concerns of women seriously enough – not just over questions of church praxis, like ordination, but over basic theological issues, such as the practice of naming God using exclusively male terms, or the attempt to define what it is to be human by looking only to a man, Jesus Christ.

Local theology is a relatively recent phenomenon. The commonly-accepted starting point is the response of various Latin American theologians and Bishops to the Second Vatican Council's call for an *aggiornamento* ('updating') of the (Roman Catholic) Church. Looking at the 'base communities', small gatherings of believers who, in the absence of a local priest, would meet regularly for prayer and Bible study instead of mass, that had been growing in Brazil (particularly) and other Latin American countries, new possibilities for what the church could and should be began to be discerned, possibilities which grew out of the particular local situatedness of the church in those countries.

The key realities experienced by people in the base communities were poverty and oppression, and their central need was clearly liberation from oppression (III.2.2). As they read the Bible together, these realities became invested with theological significance, as they had to if Scripture and theology were to be at all relevant to these people's lives.[1] The poor are the 'poor and needy' who throughout the Old Testament wait with longing for the Lord's deliverance; they are the people of Israel groaning in Egypt, the exiles longing for Jerusalem, the righteous ones under oppression who cry to God for justice in the Psalms and hear God promising deliverance through the prophets. Again, they are the poor in spirit, to whom is promised the Kingdom, and amongst whom Jesus became incarnate. The poor and oppressed are still 'despised and rejected of men', still have nowhere to lay their heads; as such, they are collectively the 'disfigured Son of God', the sacrament on earth of the Nazarene, who will be the Lord and Judge of history.

Alongside those who are poor are those who have embraced the way of poverty for the sake of the gospel, the evangelically poor, who recognize the presence of Jesus with his suffering and op-pressed people and choose to side with Jesus and his people against the oppressors. God's promise is salvation, liberation: not an other-worldly deferred reward that will encourage patient endurance of oppression in this world, but a holistic vision of human flourishing, based around biblical narratives: the exodus; the return from exile; God's sponsoring of armed uprising under Judas Maccabeus. Political and economic liberation is a part of God's salvific action, and cannot be ignored by the church, particularly by the church of the poor and the oppressed.

The critique of liberation theology has been, at times, fierce; included here are some selections from a Vatican document (III.2.3) rebuking the errors of the liberation theologians. Amongst the most significant criticisms is the suggestion that the liberation theologians start their theology too late: the place from which they work, a particularly theor-ized understanding of poverty, oppression, and the necessary solution to these problems, is based on fairly straightforward economic analysis of a Marxist kind. This is not to say the analysis is wrong, of course, but Christian theology must surely claim (on the basis of doctrines of creation and providence) to speak adequately about these realities itself; it seems at least possible that if the situation is understood using a Christian analysis of human flourishing, it will look rather different. A

---

[1] The following summary owes much to Boff & Boff, *Introducing Liberation Theology* (see the extract under III.2.1 for full bibliographic details).

new wave of liberation theology has taken this criticism seriously and sought to be much more nuanced in its account of the nature of oppression.

Alongside this Latin American theology of liberation, other local theologies have grown up. Some are fairly similar; although located elsewhere geographically, they share a common sense of being the theological reflections of an oppressed community, and so a common focus on political and economic liberation as a goal. Sharing a common analysis of oppression, although in the first world, and without the post-colonial context, James Cone has pioneered black theology in the United States, starting with an analysis of what it means to be black in that context, and seeking to do theology on that basis.

The most populated local theology in the developed world, however, has been rather different. Feminist theology cannot point to the same straightforward account of poverty and political oppression as the original liberation theologians could: although women earn (on average) less than men, even in the same jobs, in all developed countries, there are still some very rich women around; universal suffrage is now common in Western societies, although it was late in coming; and again, although women are under-represented in most political structures, there is no straightforward exclusion and indeed, many Western nations (including Britain) have had a female head of government. The statistics of under-representation, lower salaries, and so on, however, do point to a need for liberation, although of a more complex social kind.

It is, I suspect (and I write as a white male British subject, and so as an overhearer of, and an outsider to, all these conversations) this complexity that has given feminism generally, and feminist theology in particular, its persistent interest in theorizing about culture. If men and women are equal in law, then why are women under-represented, under-paid, and under-valued? One persistent answer given by feminist theologians has been the centrality of male imagery in the church's depiction of who God is, a charge classically made in Mary Daly's *Beyond God the Father* (III.2.4). Given this, suddenly what might have seemed a rather abstract theological issue becomes pressing: what is the nature of this language? Is 'Father' no more than a metaphor, an attempt to describe the fundamentally indescribable reality that is God? If so, then there could, conceivably, come a point when we realize that this metaphor now obscures more than it illuminates, and so must be discarded. If, however, 'Father' is something different, more akin to a proper name perhaps, it might appear harder to leave behind. We have already addressed such questions in this reader (see section II.3), but it is important to note one reason why they matter today.

It is not just the imagery of God that is unhelpfully male, according to some feminist theologians, however. The church's understandings of sin and virtue, for example, have been seen as inadequate when viewed from the perspective of women's experience. For a woman, humility and patience might not be virtues, but instead sinful complicity in her own oppression; equally pride, self-love and anger might be appropriately liberating and so holy. Again, what are we to do with Christian understandings of what it means to be human which assert that the man Jesus Christ is the definition of true humanity? Is it the case that the Christian tradition necessarily teaches, in Dorothy Sayers' words, that women are 'the human-not-quite-human'?

Questions like these have led some feminist theologians to identify themselves as 'post-Christian', finding the Christian tradition incurably inhospitable to their religious sensibilities. Others believe that a re-configured Christian praxis which has heard the particular insights and challenges of a woman's experience can emerge. In each case, the criterion for judgment is woman's experience; it is interesting to notice in the extracts below both Rosemary Radford Ruether's defence (III.2.5) – celebration even – of this methodological move, and Linda Woodhead's criticism (III.2.6).

The great benefit of local theologies is the reminder that the gospel of Jesus Christ is not confined to any particular society or culture; tales (however apocryphal) of the early missionary movement which sought to make others European as it made them Christian indicate the necessity of this reminder, in a world where Christianity has been identified with European culture for much of the past thousand years (in the earlier centuries of the church, the great theologians, at least, came more from Asia Minor and North Africa than Europe, a fact sometimes forgotten). The process that started at Pentecost, of telling and re-telling the story of Jesus Christ in ways understandable to each culture on earth, and that will continue until the visions of Revelation, of people from every language, every ethnic group, every national identity uniting in praise, teaches us that there is indeed a proper locatedness to theology. Whether that locatedness is best dealt with by present methodologies of local theology, with their emphasis on theorized experience, must be an open question. In the meantime, the constant challenge to a theological tradition that has largely been developed by the infamous 'dead white European males' is valuable: what, here, is necessary to the gospel, and what is cultural baggage which could and should be discarded?

One of the problems with local theologies is their appeal to a located experience; just as appeals to universal experience are vulnerable to the objection 'but I don't experience the world like that' (see section I.5), so accounts which assert a particular local experience must be credible to the vast majority of people, at least, in that location before they can be accepted. One result of this in the rise of local theologies over the last thirty years or so has been fragmentation, witnessed to here by Emilie Townes (III.2.7): as a black woman, Townes does not feel that either black theology or feminist theology expresses her experience of the world, and so engages in womanist theology, located in the experience of black women. Similarly, some Hispanic-American women have found the options available unhelpful and now practise mujerista theology. Can any locus larger than a particular person (or, perhaps, local church congregation) ultimately be sustained? Only time will tell.

SRH

A. Liberation Theology

III.2.1 Boff and Boff, from *Introducing Liberation Theology*

Leonardo and Clodovis Boff here give an account of 'how liberation theology is done'.

The Preliminary Stage: Living Commitment

Before we can do theology we have to 'do' liberation. The first step for liberation theology is pre-theological. It is a matter of trying to live the commitment of faith: in our case, to participate in some way in the process of liberation, to be committed to the oppressed.

Without this specific precondition, liberation theology would be simply a matter of words. So it is not enough here only to reflect on what is being practiced. Rather we need to establish a living link with living practice. If we fail to do this, then 'poverty,' 'oppression,' 'revolution,' 'new society' are simply words that can be found in a dictionary.

The essential point is this: links with specific practice are *at the root* of liberation theology. It operates within the great dialectic of theory (faith) and practice (love).

In fact, it is *only* this effective connection with liberating practice that can give theologians a 'new spirit,' a new style, or a new way of doing theology. Being a theologian is not a matter of skillfully using methods but of being imbued with the theological spirit. Rather than introducing a new theological method, liberation theology is a new way of being a theologian. Theology is always a second step; the first is the 'faith that makes its power felt through love' (Gal. 5:6). Theology (not the theologian) comes afterward; liberating practice comes first.

So first we need to have direct knowledge of the reality of oppression/ liberation through objective engagement in solidarity with the poor. This pre-theological stage really means conversion of life, and this involves a 'class conversion,' in the sense of leading to effective solidarity with the oppressed and their liberation.

Of course the most appropriate and specific way for theologians to commit themselves to the poor and oppressed is to produce good theology. But what we want to stress here is that this is impossible without at least *some* contact with the world of the oppressed. Personal contact is necessary if one is to acquire new theological sensitivity.

Three Mediations

The elaboration of liberation theology can be divided into three basic stages, which correspond to the three traditional stages involved in pastoral work: seeing, judging, acting.

In liberation theology, we speak of three main 'mediations': socio-analytical mediation, hermeneutical mediation, and practical mediation. The term 'mediation' is used because the three stages represent means or instruments of the theological process. Briefly, these three mediations work and relate to each other as follows:

• Socio-analytical (or historico-analytical) mediation operates in the sphere of the world of the oppressed. It tries to find out why the oppressed are oppressed.

• Hermeneutical mediation operates in the sphere of God's world. It tries to discern what God's plan is for the poor.

• Practical mediation operates in the sphere of action. It tries to discover the courses of action that need to be followed so as to overcome oppression in accordance with God's plan.

Let us treat each of these mediations in more detail.

Socio-analytical Mediation

'Liberation' means liberation from oppression. Therefore, liberation theology has to begin by informing itself about the actual conditions in which the oppressed live, the various forms of oppression they may suffer.

Obviously, the prime object of theology is God. Nevertheless, before asking what oppression means in God's eyes, theologians have to ask more basic questions about the nature of actual oppression and its causes. The fact is that understanding God is not a substitute for or alternative to knowledge of the real world. As Thomas Aquinas said: 'An error about the world redounds in error about God' (*Summa contra Gentiles*, II, 3).

Furthermore, if faith is to be efficacious, in the same way as Christian love, it must have its eyes open to the historical reality on which it seeks to work.

Therefore, to know the real world of the oppressed is a (material) part of the overall theological process. Though not the whole process in itself, it is an indispensable stage or mediation in the development of further and deeper understanding, the knowledge of faith itself.

Explaining the Phenomenon of Oppression

Faced with the oppressed, the theologian's first question can only be: Why is there oppression and what are its causes?

The oppressed are to be found in many strata of society. Puebla lists them: young children, juveniles, indigenous peoples, campesinos, laborers, the underemployed and unemployed, the marginalized, persons living in over-crowded urban slums, the elderly ... (§§32–39). There is one overarching characteristic of the oppressed in the Third World: they are *poor* in socio-economic terms. They are the dispossessed masses on the peripheries of cities and in rural areas.

We need to start from here, from this 'infrastructural' oppression, if we want to understand correctly all other forms of oppression and see how they relate to each other. In effect, as we shall see in more detail later, this socio-economic form conditions all other forms.

Historical Mediation and the Struggles of the Oppressed

The socio-analytical interpretation, as presented above, leads on to a historical approach to the problem of poverty. This approach focuses on the poor not only in their present situation, but as the end-product of a long process of plunder and social marginalization. It includes a consideration of the struggles of 'the lowly' throughout their historical journey.

This shows that the situation of the oppressed is defined not only by their oppressors but also by the way in which they react to oppression, resist it, and fight to set themselves free from it. The poor cannot be understood without including their dimension as social subjects or co-agents – though submerged ones – of the historical process. This means that any analysis of the world of the poor has to take account not only of their oppressors but also of their own history and efforts at liberation, however embryonic these may be.

Relationships with Marxism

When dealing with the poor and the oppressed and seeking their liberation, how do we avoid coming into contact with Marxist groups (on the practical level) and with Marxist theory (on the academic level)?

In liberation theology, Marxism is never treated as a subject on its own but always *from and in relation to the poor*. Placing themselves firmly on the side of the poor, liberation theologians ask Marx: 'What can you tell us about the situation of poverty and ways of overcoming it?' Here Marxists are submitted to the judgment of the poor and their cause, and not the other way around.

Therefore, liberation theology uses Marxism purely as an *instrument*. It does not venerate it as it venerates the gospel. And it feels no obligation to account to social scientists for any use it may make – correct or otherwise – of Marxist terminology and ideas, though it does feel obliged to account to the poor, to their faith and hope, and to the ecclesial community, for such use. To put it in more specific terms, liberation theology freely borrows from Marxism certain 'methodological pointers' that have proved fruitful in understanding the world of the oppressed.

Enlarging on the Concept of 'the Poor'

Liberation theology is about liberation of the oppressed – in their totality as persons, body and soul ... [T]he poor are not merely human beings with needs; they are not just persons who are socially oppressed and at the same time agents of history. They are all these and more: they are also bearers of an 'evangelizing potential' and beings called to eternal life.

Hermeneutical Mediation

Once they have understood the real situation of the oppressed, theologians have to ask: What has the word of God to say about this? This is the second stage in the theological construct – a specific stage, in which discourse is *formally* theological.

It is therefore a question, at this point, of seeing the 'oppression/liberation' process 'in the light of faith.' What does this mean? The expression does not denote something vague or general; it is something that has a positive meaning in scripture, where we find that 'in the light of faith' and 'in the light of the word of God' have the same meaning.

The liberation theologian goes to the scriptures bearing the whole weight of the problems, sorrows, and hopes of the poor, seeking light and inspiration from the divine word. This is a new way of reading the Bible: the hermeneutics of liberation.

The Bible of the Poor

An examination of the whole of scripture from the viewpoint of the oppressed: this is the hermeneutics or specific interpretation (reading) used by liberation theology.

We must say straightaway that this is not the only possible and legitimate reading of the Bible. For us in the Third World today, however, it is the obvious one, the 'hermeneutics for our times.' From the heart of the great revelation in the Bible, it draws the most enlightening and eloquent themes that speak to the poor: God the father of life and advocate of the oppressed, liberation from the house of bondage, the prophecy of a new world, the kingdom given to the poor, the church as total sharing. The hermeneutics of liberation stresses these veins, but not to the exclusion of everything else. They may not be the most *important* themes in the Bible (in themselves), but they are the most *relevant* (to the poor in their situation of oppression). But then it is the order of importance that determines the order of relevance.

The Marks of a Theological-liberative Hermeneutics

The rereading of the Bible done from the basis of the poor and their liberation project has certain characteristic marks.

It is a hermeneutics that favors *application* rather than explanation. In this the theology of liberation takes up the kind of probing that has been the perennial pursuit of all true biblical reading, as can be seen, for example, in the church fathers – a pursuit that was neglected for a long time in favor of a rationalistic exegesis concerned with dragging out the meaning-in-itself.

Liberative hermeneutics reads the Bible as a book of life, not as a book of strange stories. The textual meaning is indeed sought, but only as a function of the *practical* meaning: the important thing is not so much interpreting the text of the scriptures as interpreting life 'according to the scriptures.' Ultimately, this old/new reading aims to find contemporary actualization (practicality) for the textual meaning.

Liberative hermeneutics seeks to discover and activate the *transforming energy* of biblical texts. In the end, this is a question of finding an interpretation that will lead to individual change (conversion) and change in history (revolution). This is not a reading from ideological preconceptions: biblical religion is an open and dynamic religion thanks to its messianic and eschatological character. Ernst Bloch once declared: 'It would be difficult to make a revolution without the Bible.'

Finally, without being reductionist, this theological-political rereading of the Bible stresses the *social context* of the message. It places each text in its historical context in order to construct an appropriate – not literal – translation into our own historical context. For example, liberative hermeneutics will stress (but not to the exclusion of other aspects) the social context of oppression in which Jesus lived and the markedly political context of his death on the cross. Obviously, when it is approached in this way, the biblical text takes on particular relevance in the context of the oppression now being experienced in the Third World, where liberating evangelization has immediate and serious political implications – as the growing list of martyrs in Latin America proves.

Practical Mediation

Liberation theology is far from being an inconclusive theology. It starts from action and leads to action, a journey wholly impregnated by and bound up with the atmosphere of faith. From analysis of the reality of the oppressed, it passes through the word of God to arrive finally at specific action. 'Back to action' is a characteristic call of this theology. It seeks to be a militant, committed, and liberating theology.

It is a theology that leads to practical results because today, in the world of the 'wretched of the earth,' the *true form* of faith is 'political love' or 'macro-charity.' Among the poorest of the Third World, faith is not only 'also' political, but *above all else* political.

But despite all this, faith cannot be reduced to action, however liberating it may be. It is 'always greater' and must always include moments of contemplation and of profound thanksgiving. Liberation theology also leads one up to the Temple. And from the Temple it leads back once more to the practice of history, now equipped with all the divine and divinizing powers of the Mystery of the world.

And so, yes: liberation theology leads to action: action for justice, the work of love, conversion, renewal of the church, transformation of society.

(Taken from L. Boff and C. Boff, Introducing Liberation Theology *Liberation and Theology series 1, trans. Paul Burns, Tunbridge Wells: Burns & Oates 1987, pp 22–39.)*

III.2.2 James Cone, from *God of the Oppressed*

In this extract Cone identifies black experience and Scripture as the two sources of black theology, and explores the relationship between them.

There is no truth for and about black people that does not emerge out of the context of their experience. Truth in this sense is black truth, a truth disclosed in the history and culture of black people. This means that there can be no Black Theology which does not take the black experience as a source for its starting point. Black Theology is a theology of and for black people, an examination of their stories, tales, and sayings. It is an investigation of the mind into the raw materials of our pilgrimage, telling the story of 'how we got over.' For theology to be black, it must reflect upon what it means to be black. Black Theology must uncover the structures and forms of the black experience, because the categories of interpretation must arise out of the thought forms of the black experience itself.

However, the black experience as a source of theology is more than the so-called 'church experience,' more than singing, praying, and preaching about Jesus, God, and the Holy Spirit. The other side of the black experience should not be rigidly defined as 'secular,' if by that term one means the classical Western distinction between secular and sacred, for it is not antireligious or even nonreligious. This side of the black experience is secular only to the extent that it is earthy and seldom uses God or Christianity as the chief symbols of its hopes and dreams. It is sacred because it is created out of the same historical community as the church experience and thus represents the people's attempt to shape life and to live it according to their dreams and aspirations. Included in these black expressions are animal tales, tales of folk figures, slave seculars, blues, and accounts of personal experiences.

Another important theological source of the black experience is the narratives of slaves and ex-slaves, the personal accounts of black people's triumph and defeats. Here are found many dimensions of the black experience as told by those who lived it in the midst of servitude and oppression. There are slaves who might be described as 'religious,' and others who are indifferent toward 'religion.' There are slaves who praise their masters for 'kind' treatment; and those who say: 'I had much rather starve in England, a free woman than be a slave for the best man that ever breathed upon the American continent.' This is the stuff of the black experience which makes Black Theology possible and necessary.

More recent black literature is another expression of the black experience. Particularly notable are the poets of the Harlem Renaissance (1920s and 1930s) and their successors.

The question inevitably arises. What is the relation of the black experience as a source of Black Theology to the Bible, which is traditionally identified as the source of Christian theology? The connection is this. When black people sing, preach, and tell stories about their struggle, one fact is clear: they are not dealing simply with themselves. They are talking about another reality, 'so high you can't get over him, so low you can't get under him, so wide you can't get around him.' It is this affirmation of transcendence that prevents Black Theology from being reduced merely to the cultural history of black people. For black people the transcendent reality is none other than Jesus Christ, of whom Scripture speaks. The Bible is the witness to God's self-disclosure in Jesus Christ. Thus the black experience requires that Scripture be a source of Black Theology. For it was Scripture that enabled slaves to affirm a view of God that differed radically from that of the slave masters. The slave masters' intention was to present a 'Jesus' who would make the slave obedient and docile. Jesus was supposed to make black people better slaves, that is, faithful servants of white masters. But many blacks rejected that view of Jesus not only because it contradicted their African heritage, but because it contradicted the witness of Scripture. That was why Richard Allen and his companions walked out of St. George Methodist Episcopal Church in 1787 as a prophetic protest against segregated worship. The same was true for Henry Highland Garnet. Through the reading of Scripture he concluded that liberty was a gift from God, and therefore black slaves ought to use any available means that promises success in the attainment of freedom. Throughout black history Scripture was used for a definition of God and Jesus that was consistent with the black struggle for liberation. Further examples are found in Henry M. Turner's affirmation that 'God is a Negro,' Howard Thurman's association of Jesus with the disinherited, and Martin Luther King's view that political struggle was consistent with the gospel of Jesus. Scripture established limits to white people's use of Jesus Christ as a confirmation of black oppression.

Having described the two sources of Black Theology (black experience and Scripture), it is now important to distinguish both sources from their subject or essence, which is Jesus Christ. The subject of theology is that which creates the precise character of theological language, thereby distinguishing it from other ways of speaking. By contrast, the sources of theology are the materials that make possible a valid articulation of theology's subject.

Jesus Christ is the subject of Black Theology because he is the content of the hopes and dreams of black people. He was chosen by our grandparents, who saw in his liberating presence that he had chosen them and thus became the foundation of their struggle for freedom. He was their Truth, enabling them to know that white definitions of black humanity were lies. When their way became twisted and senseless, they told Jesus about it. He lifted their burdens and eased their pain, thereby bestowing upon them a vision of freedom that transcended historical limitations.

(Taken from James H. Cone, God of the Oppressed, *New York: Seabury Press 1975, pp 16–38.)*

III.2.3 Sacred Congregation for the Doctrine of the Faith, from the 'Instruction on Certain Aspects of "Theology of Liberation"'

In this Instruction, the Vatican made clear its theological reservations concerning liberation theology. These involve a concern about the uncritical use of Marxist analysis, and a sense that vital aspects of the gospel message are being ignored, or at least under-emphasized.

. . . The Gospel of Jesus Christ is a message of freedom and a force for liberation. In recent years, this essential truth has become the object of reflection for theologians, with a new kind of attention which is itself full of promise.

Liberation is first and foremost liberation from the radical slavery of sin. Its end and its goal is the freedom of the children of God, which is the gift of grace. As a logical consequence, it calls for freedom from many different kinds of slavery in the cultural, economic, social, and political spheres, all of which derive ultimately from sin, and so often prevent people from living in a manner befitting their dignity. To discern clearly what is fundamental to this issue and what is a by-product of it, is an indispensable condition for any theological reflection on liberation.

Faced with the urgency of certain problems, some are tempted to emphasize, unilaterally, the liberation from servitude of an earthly and temporal kind. They do so in such a way that they seem to put liberation from sin in second place, and so fail to give it the primary importance it is due. Thus, their very presentation of the problems is confused and ambiguous. Others, in an effort to learn more precisely what are the causes of the slavery which they want to end, make use of different concepts without sufficient critical caution. It is difficult, and perhaps impossible, to purify these borrowed concepts of an ideological inspiration which is incompatible with Christian faith and the ethical requirements which flow from it.

The present Instruction has a much more limited and precise purpose: to draw the attention of pastors, theologians, and all the faithful to the deviations, and risks of deviation, damaging to the faith and to Christian living, that are brought about by certain forms of liberation theology which use, in an insufficiently critical manner, concepts borrowed from various currents of Marxist thought.

. . .

The yearning for justice and for the effective recognition of the dignity of every human being needs, like every deep aspiration, to be clarified and guided.

In effect, a discernment process is necessary which takes into account both the theoretical and the practical manifestations of this aspiration. For there are many political and social movements which present themselves as authentic spokesmen for the aspirations of the poor, and claim to be able, though by recourse to violent means, to bring about the radical changes which will put an end to the oppression and misery of people.

So the aspiration for justice often finds itself the captive of ideologies which hide or pervert its meaning, and which propose to people struggling for their liberation goals which are contrary to the true purpose of human life. They propose ways of action which imply the systematic recourse to violence, contrary to any ethic which is respectful of persons.

The interpretation of the signs of the times in the light of the Gospel requires, then, that we examine the meaning of this deep yearning of people for justice, but also that we study with critical discernment the theoretical and practical expressions which this aspiration has taken on.
. . .

To some it even seems that the necessary struggle for human justice and freedom in the economic and political sense constitutes the whole essence of salvation. For them, the Gospel is reduced to a purely earthly gospel.

The different theologies of liberation are situated between the preferential option for the poor . . . on the one hand, and the temptation to reduce the Gospel to an earthly gospel on the other.
. . .

Concepts uncritically borrowed from Marxist ideology and recourse to theses of a biblical hermeneutic marked by rationalism are at the basis of the new interpretation which is corrupting whatever was authentic in the generous initial commitment on behalf of the poor.
. . .

Impatience and a desire for results has led certain Christians, despairing of every other method, to turn to what they call 'marxist analysis'.

Their reasoning is this: an intolerable and explosive situation requires effective action which cannot be put off. Effective action presupposes a scientific analysis of the structural causes of poverty. Marxism now provides us with the means to make such an analysis, they say. Then one simply has to apply the analysis to the third-world situation, especially in Latin America.
. . .

Let us recall the fact that atheism and the denial of the human person, his liberty and rights, are at the core of the Marxist theory. This theory, then, contains errors which directly threaten the truths of the faith regarding the eternal destiny of individual persons. Moreover, to attempt to integrate into theology an analysis whose criterion of interpretation depends on this atheistic conception is to involve oneself in terrible contradictions. What is more, this misunderstanding of the spiritual nature of the person leads to a total subordination of the person to the collectivity, and thus to the denial of the principles of a social and political life which is in keeping with human dignity.
. . .

This all-embracing conception thus imposes its logic and leads the 'theologies of liberation' to accept a series of positions which are incompatible with the Christian vision of humanity. In fact, the ideological core borrowed from Marxism, which we are referring to, exercises the function of a determining principle.

. . .

The class struggle is presented as an objective, necessary law. Upon entering this process on behalf of the oppressed, one 'makes' truth, one acts 'scientifically'. Consequently, the conception of the truth goes hand in hand with the affirmation of necessary violence, and so, of a political amorality. Within this perspective, any reference to ethical requirements calling for courageous and radical institutional and structural reforms makes no sense.

. . .

As a result, participation in the class struggle is presented as a requirement of charity itself. The desire to love everyone here and now, despite his class, and to go out to meet him with the non-violent means of dialogue and persuasion, is denounced as counterproductive and opposed to love. If one holds that a person should not be the object of hate, it is claimed nevertheless that, if he belongs to the objective class of the rich, he is primarily a class enemy to be fought. Thus the universality of love of neighbour and brotherhood become an eschatological principle, which will only have meaning for the 'new man', who arises out of the victorious revolution.

. . .

In giving such priority to the political dimension, one is led to deny the radical newness of the New Testament and above all to misunderstand the person of Our Lord Jesus Christ, true God and true man, and thus the specific character of the salvation he gave us, that is above all liberation from sin, which is the source of all evils.

. . .

By the same token, the overthrow by means of revolutionary violence of structures which generate violence is not ipso facto the beginning of a just regime. A major fact of our time ought to evoke the reflection of all those who would sincerely work for the true liberation of their brothers: millions of our own contemporaries legitimately yearn to recover those basic freedoms of which they were deprived by totalitarian and atheistic regimes which came to power by violent and revolutionary means, precisely in the name of the liberation of the people. This shame of our time cannot be ignored: while claiming to bring them freedom, these regimes keep whole nations in conditions of servitude which are unworthy of mankind. Those who, perhaps inadvertently, make themselves accomplices of similar enslavements betray the very poor they mean to help.

The class struggle as a road toward a classless society is a myth which slows reform and aggravates poverty and injustice. Those who allow themselves to be caught up in fascination with this myth should reflect on the bitter examples history has to offer about where it leads. They would then understand that we are not talking here about abandoning an effective means of struggle on behalf of the poor for an ideal which has no practical effects. On the contrary, we are talking about freeing oneself from a delusion in order to base oneself squarely on the Gospel and its power of realization.

(Taken from the Vatican translation.)

B. Feminist Theology

III.2.4 Mary Daly, from *Beyond God the Father*

Daly regards religious symbols as human constructs that can be dis-carded when no longer liberating. She claims the symbol of 'God the Father' has reached this point.

The biblical and popular image of God as a great patriarch in heaven, rewarding and punishing according to his mysterious and seemingly arbitrary will, has dominated the imagination of millions over thousands of years. The symbol of the Father God, spawned in the human imagination and sustained as plausible by patriarchy, has in turn rendered service to this type of society by making mechanisms for the oppression of women appear right and fitting. If God in 'his' heaven is a father ruling 'his' people, then it is in the 'nature' of things and according to divine plan and the order of the universe that society be male-dominated.

Within this context a mystification of roles takes place: the husband dominating his wife represents God 'himself.' The images and values of a given society have been projected into the realm of dogmas and 'Articles of Faith,' and these in turn justify the social structures which have given rise to them and which sustain their plausibility. The belief system becomes hardened and objectified, seeming to have an unchangeable independent existence and validity of its own. It resists social change that would rob it of its plausibility. Despite the vicious circle, however, change can occur in society, and ideologies can die, though they die hard.

As the women's movement begins to have its effect upon the fabric of society, transforming it from patriarchy into something that never existed before – into a diarchal situation that is radically new – it can become the greatest single challenge to the major religions of the world, Western and Eastern. Beliefs and values that have held sway for thousands of years will be questioned as never before. This revolution may well be also the greatest single hope for survival of spiritual consciousness on this planet.

The Challenge: Emergence of Whole Human Beings

There are some who persist in claiming that the liberation of women will only mean that new characters will assume the same old roles, and that nothing will change essentially in structures, ideologies, and values. This supposition is often based on the observation that the very few women in 'masculine' occupations often behave much as men do. This kind of reasoning is not at all to the point, for it fails to take into account the fact that tokenism does not change stereotypes or social systems but works to preserve them, since it dulls the revolutionary impulse. The minute proportion of women in the United States who occupy such roles (such as senators, judges, business executives, doctors, etc.) have been trained by men in institutions defined and designed by men, and they have been pressured subtly to operate according to male rules. There are no alternate models. As sociologist Alice Rossi has suggested, this is not what the women's movement in its most revolutionary potential is all about.

What *is* to the point is an emergence of woman-consciousness such as has never before taken place. It is unimaginative and out of touch with what is happening in the women's movement to assume that the becoming of women will simply mean uncritical acceptance of structures, beliefs, symbols, norms, and patterns of behavior that have been given priority by society under male domination. Rather, this becoming will act as catalyst for radical change in our culture. It has been argued cogently by Piaget that structure is maintained by an interplay of transformation laws that never yield results beyond the system and never tend to employ elements external to the system. This is indicative of what *can* effect basic alteration in the system, that is, a potent influence *from without*. Women who reject patriarchy have this power and indeed *are* this power of transformation that is ultimately threatening to things as they are.

The roles and structures of patriarchy have been developed and sustained in accordance with an artificial polarization of human qualities into the traditional sexual stereotypes. The image of the person in authority and the accepted understanding of 'his' role has corresponded to the eternal masculine stereotype, which implies hyper-rationality (in reality, frequently reducible to pseudo-rationality), 'objectivity,' aggressivity, the possession of dominating and manipulative attitudes toward persons and the environment, and the tendency to construct boundaries between the self (and those identified with the self) and 'the Other.' The caricature of human being which is represented by this stereotype depends for its existence upon the opposite caricature – the eternal feminine. This implies hyper-emotionalism, passivity, self-abnegation, etc. By becoming whole persons women can generate a counterforce to the stereotype of the leader, challenging the artificial polarization of human characteristics into sex-role identification. There is no reason to assume that women who have the support of each other to criticize not only the feminine stereotype but the masculine stereotype as well will simply adopt the latter as a model for ourselves. On the contrary, what is happening is that women are developing a wider range of qualities and skills. This is beginning to encourage and in fact demand a comparably liberating process in men – a phenomenon which has begun in men's liberation groups and which is taking place every day within the context of personal relationships. The becoming of androgynous human persons implies a radical change in the fabric of human consciousness and in styles of human behavior.

This change is already threatening the credibility of the religious symbols of our culture. Since many of these have been used to justify oppression, such a challenge should be seen as redemptive. Religious symbols fade and die when the cultural situation that gave rise to them and supported them ceases to give them plausibility. Such an event generates anxiety, but it is part of the risk involved in a faith which accepts the relativity of all symbols and recognizes that clinging to these as fixed and ultimate is self-destructive and idolatrous.

The becoming of new symbols is not a matter that can be decided arbitrarily around a conference table. Rather, symbols grow out of a changing communal situation and experience. This does not mean that we are confined to the role of passive spectators. The experience of the becoming of women cannot be understood merely conceptually and abstractly but through active participation in the overcoming of servitude. Both activism and creative thought flow from and feed into the evolving woman-consciousness The cumulative effect is a surge of awareness beyond the symbols and doctrines of patriarchal religion.

The Inadequate God of Popular Preaching

The image of the divine Father in heaven has not always been conducive to humane behavior, as any perceptive reader of history knows. The often cruel behavior of Christians toward unbelievers and toward dissenters among themselves suggests a great deal not only about the values of the society dominated by that image, but also about how that image itself functions in relation to behavior. There has been a basic ambivalence in the image of the heavenly patriarch – a split between the God of love and the jealous God who represents the collective power of 'his' chosen people. As historian Arnold Toynbee has indicated, this has reflected and perpetuated a double standard of behavior. Without debating the details of his historical analysis, the insight is available on an experiential level. The character of Vito Corleone in *The Godfather* is a vivid illustration of the marriage of tenderness and violence so intricately blended in the patriarchal ideal. The worshippers of the loving Father may in a sense love their neighbors, but in fact the term applies only to those within a restricted and unstable circumference, and these worshippers can 'justifiably' be intolerant and fanatic persecutors of those outside the sacred circle.

Sophisticated thinkers, of course, have never intellectually identified God with a Superfather in heaven. Nevertheless it is important to recognize that even when very abstract conceptualizations of God are formulated in the mind, images survive in the imagination in such a way that a person can function on two different and even apparently contradictory levels at the same time. Thus one can speak of God as spirit and at the same time imagine 'him' as belonging to the male sex. Such primitive images can profoundly affect conceptualizations which appear to be very refined and abstract. So too the Yahweh of the future, so cherished by the theology of hope, comes through on an imaginative level as exclusively a He-God, and it is consistent with this that theologians of hope have attempted to develop a political theology which takes no explicit cognizance of the devastation wrought by sexual politics.

The widespread conception of the 'Supreme Being' as an entity distinct from this world but controlling it according to plan and keeping human beings in a state of infantile subjection has been a not too subtle mask of the divine patriarch. The Supreme Being's plausibility and that of the static worldview which accompanies this projection has of course declined, at least among the more sophisticated, as Nietzsche prophesied. This was a projection grounded in specifically patriarchal societal structures and sustained as subjectively real by the usual processes of producing plausibility such as preaching, religious indoctrination, and cult. The sustaining power of the social structure has been eroded by a number of developments in recent history, including the general trend toward democratization of society and the emergence of technology. However, it is the women's movement which appears destined to play the key role in the overthrow of such oppressive elements in traditional theism, precisely because it strikes at the source of the societal dualism that is reflected in traditional beliefs. It presents a growing threat to the plausibility of the inadequate popular 'God' not so much by attacking 'him' as by leaving 'him' behind. Few major feminists display great interest in institutional religion. Yet this disinterest can hardly be equated with lack of spiritual consciousness. Rather, in our present experience the woman-consciousness is being wrenched free to find its own religious expression.

It can legitimately be pointed out that the Judeo-Christian tradition is not entirely bereft of elements that can foster intimations of transcendence. Yet the liberating potential of these elements is choked off in the surrounding atmosphere of the images, ideas, values, and structures of patriarchy. The social change coming from radical feminism has the potential to bring about a more acute and widespread perception of qualitative differences between the conceptualizations of 'God' and of the human relationship to God which have been oppressive in their connotations, and the kind of language that is spoken from and to the rising woman-consciousness.

Castrating 'God'

I have already suggested that if God is male, then the male is God. The divine patriarch castrates women as long as he is allowed to live on in the human imagination. The process of cutting away the Supreme Phallus can hardly be a merely 'rational' affair. The problem is one of transforming the collective imagination so that this distortion of the human aspiration to transcendence loses its credibility.

(Taken from: Mary Daly, Beyond God the Father: Towards a Philosophy of Women's Liberation, *Boston: Beacon Press 1977,* © Mary Daly, pp. 13–19.)

III.2.5 Rosemary Radford Ruether, from *Sexism and God-Talk*

Ruether explores how women's experience can and should provoke a crisis in the Christian tradition.

WOMEN'S EXPERIENCE AND HISTORICAL TRADITION

It has frequently been said that feminist theology draws on women's experience as a basic source of content as well as a criterion of truth. There has been a tendency to treat this principle of 'experience' as unique to feminist theology (or, perhaps, to liberation theologies) and to see it as distant from 'objective' sources of truth of classical theologies. This seems to be a misunderstanding of the experimental base of all theological reflection. What have been called the objective sources of theology; Scripture and tradition, are themselves codified collective human experience.

Human experience is the starting point and the ending point of the hermeneutical circle. Codified tradition both reaches back to roots in experience and is constantly renewed or discarded through the test of experience. 'Experience' includes experience of the divine, experience of oneself, and experience of the community and the world, in an interacting dialectic. Received symbols, formulas, and laws are either authenticated or not through their ability to illuminate and interpret experience. Systems of authority try to reverse this relation and make received symbols dictate what can be experienced as well as the interpretation of that which is experienced. In reality, the relation is the opposite. If a symbol does not speak authentically to experience, it becomes dead or must be altered to provide a new meaning.

The uniqueness of feminist theology lies not in its use of the criterion of experience but rather in its use of *women's* experience, which has been almost entirely shut out of theological reflection in the past. The use of women's experience in feminist theology, therefore, explodes as a critical force, exposing classical theology, including its codified traditions, as based on *male* experience rather than on universal human experience. Feminist theology makes the sociology of theological knowledge visible, no longer hidden behind mystifications of objectified divine and universal authority.

The Hermeneutical Circle of Past and Present Experience

A simplified model of the Western theological tradition can illustrate this hermeneutical circle of past and present experience. We must postulate that every great religious idea begins in the revelatory experience. By *revelatory* we mean breakthrough experiences beyond ordinary fragmented consciousness that provide interpretive symbols illuminating the means of the *whole* of life. Since consciousness is ultimately individual, we postulate that revelation always starts with an individual. In earlier societies in which there was much less sense of individualism, this breakthrough experience may have been so immediately mediated through a group of interpreters to the social collective that the name of the individual is lost. Later, the creative individual stands out as Prophet, Teacher, Revealer, Savior, or Founder of the religious tradition.

However much the individual teacher is magnified, in fact, the revelatory experience becomes socially meaningful only when translated into communal consciousness.

The formative community that has appropriated the revelatory experience in turn gathers a historical community around its interpretation of the vision. This process goes through various stages during which oral and written teachings are developed. At a certain point a group consisting of teacher and leaders emerges that seeks to channel and control the process, to weed out what it regards as deviant communities and interpretations, and to impose a series of criteria to determine the correct interpretive line.

The ordinary believers now have increasingly complex formulas of faith, customs, rituals, and writings proposed to them as the basis for appropriating the original revelatory paradigm as personal redeeming experience. These individuals, in their local communities of faith, are always engaged in making their own selection from the patterns of received tradition that fit or make sense in their lives. There is always an interaction between the patterns of faith proposed by teachers to individuals and the individuals' own appropriation of these patterns as interpretations of experience. But these differences remain unarticulated, held within the dominant consensus about what the revelatory pattern 'means.'

A religious tradition remains vital so long as its revelatory pattern can be reproduced generation after generation and continues to speak to individuals in the community and provide for them the redemptive meaning of individual and collective experience. Such has been the Exodus-Passover pattern for Jews and the death-resurrection paradigm of personal conversion for Christians. The circle from experience to experience, mediated through instruments of tradition, is thus completed when the contemporary community appropriates the foundational paradigm as the continuing story of its own redemption in relation to God, self, and one another.

Crises of Tradition

Religious traditions fall into crisis when the received interpretations of the redemptive paradigms contradict experience in significant ways. The crisis may be perceived at various levels of radicalness. Exegetical criticism of received theological and Scriptural traditions can bring forth new interpretations that speak to new experiences. This kind of reform goes on in minor and major ways all the time.

A more radical break takes place when the institutional structures that transmit tradition are perceived to have become corrupt. They are perceived not as teaching truth but as teaching falsehood dictated by their own self-interest and will to power. The revelatory paradigms, the original founder, and even the early stages of the formulation of tradition are still seen as authentic. It seems necessary to go behind later historical tradition and insti-tutionalized authorities and 'return to' the original revelation. In the literal sense of the word, there is no possibility of return to some period of the tradition that predates the intervening history. So the myth of return to origins is a way of making a more radical interpretation of the revelatory paradigm to encompass contemporary experiences, while discarding insti-tutions.

A still more radical crisis of tradition occurs when the total religious herit-age appears to be corrupt. This kind of radical questioning of the meaning-fulness of the Christian religion began to occur in Western Europe during the Enlightenment. Marxism carried the Enlightenment critique of religion still further. Marxism teaches that all religion is an instrument the ruling class uses to justify its own power and to pacify the oppressed. This makes religion not the means of redemption but the means of enslavement. The very nature of religious knowledge is seen as promoting alienation rather than integration of the human person. This kind of ideological critique throws the truth content of religion into radical ethical disrepute. Such an attack on religion is considered 'true' by a growing minority of people when they perceive the dominant religious traditions as contradictory to the contempor-ary experience of meaning, truth, and justice.

Ideological criticism of the truthfulness of the religion may still allow for some residue of genuine insight into the original religious experiences and foundational teachers. The prophets of Jesus may be said to have had truthful insights into just and meaningful life, but this became corrupted and turned into its opposite by later teachers, even within Scripture. Discarding even the truthfulness of foundational teachers, the critic may turn to alternative sources of truth: to recent critical schools of thought against the religious traditions; to suppressed traditions condemned as heretical by the dominant tradition; or to pre-Christian patterns of thought. Modern rationalist, Marxist, and romantic criticism of religion have followed such alternatives in the last two hundred years.

Why seek alternative traditions at all? Why not just start with contemporary experience? Doesn't the very search for foundational tradition reveal a need for authority outside contemporary experience? It is true that the received patterns of authority create a strong need, even in those seeking radical change, to find an authoritative base of revealed truth 'in the beginning' as well as a need to justify the new by reference to recognized authority. These needs reveal a still deeper need: to situate oneself meaningfully in history.

The effort to express contemporary experience in a cultural and historical vacuum is both self-deluding and unsatisfying. It is self-deluding because to communicate at all to oneself and others, one makes use of patterns of thought, however transformed by new experience, that have a history. It is unsatisfying because, however much one discards large historical periods of dominant traditions, one still seeks to encompass this 'fallen history' within a larger context of authentic and truthful life. To look back to some original base of meaning and truth before corruption is to know that truth is more basic than falsehood and hence able, ultimately, to root out falsehood in a new future that is dawning in contemporary experience. To find glimmers of this truth in submerged and alternative traditions through history is to assure oneself that one is not mad or duped. Only by finding an alternative historical community and tradition more deeply rooted than those that have become corrupted can one feel sure that in criticizing the dominant tradition one is not just subjectively criticizing the dominant tradition but is, rather, touching a deeper bedrock of authentic Being upon which to ground the self. One cannot wield the lever of criticism without a place to stand.

The Critical Principle of Feminist Theology

The critical principle of feminist theology is the promotion of the full humanity of women. Whatever denies, diminishes, or distorts the full humanity of women is, therefore, appraised as not redemptive. Theologically speaking, whatever diminishes or denies the full humanity of women must be presumed not to reflect the divine or an authentic relation to the divine, or to reflect the authentic nature of things, or to be the message or work of an authentic redeemer or a community of redemption.

This negative principle also implies the positive principle: what does promote the full humanity of women is of the Holy, it does reflect true relation to the divine, it is the true nature of things, the authentic message of redemption and the mission of redemptive community. But the meaning of this positive principle – namely, the full humanity of women – is not fully known. It has not existed in history. What we have known is the negative principle of the denigration and marginalization of women's humanity. Still, the humanity of women, although diminished, has not been destroyed. It has constantly affirmed itself, often in only limited and subversive ways, and it has been touchstone against which we test and criticize all that diminishes us. In the process we experience our larger potential that allows us to begin to imagine a world without sexism.

This principle is hardly new. In fact, the correlation of original, authentic human nature (*imago dei*/Christ) and diminished, fallen humanity provided the basic structure of classical Christian theology. The uniqueness of feminist theology is not the critical principle, full humanity, but the fact that women claim this principle for themselves. Women name themselves as subjects of authentic and full humanity.

The use of this principle in male theology is perceived to have been corrupted by sexism. The naming of males as norms of authentic humanity has caused women to be scapegoated for sin and marginalized in both original and redeemed humanity. This distorts and contradicts the theological paradigm of *imago dei*/Christ. Defined as male humanity against or above women, as ruling-class humanity above servant classes, the *imago dei*/Christ paradigm becomes an instrument of sin rather than a disclosure of the divine and an instrument of grace.

(Taken from Rosemary Radford Ruether, Sexism and God-Talk: Towards a Feminist Theology, *London: SCM Press 1983, pp. 12–20.)*

III.2.6 Linda Woodhead, from 'Spiritualising the Sacred'

Woodhead criticizes the practice of feminist theology as methodologically incoherent, and claims that the failure of its constructive project is a result of this incoherence.

Though this paper is critical of feminist theology, it is not written out of any long-standing or deep-seated antagonism towards the feminist theological enterprise. Indeed, far from growing out of hostility, it grows out of much more positive feelings, out of the high hopes and expectations of feminist theology which I once held. For when I first became aware of feminist theology in the early 1980s it seemed to me, as to many of my fellow students of theology, like water in the desert. It was enormously refreshing to hear women's voices in theology, voices willing to identify themselves as women and to claim their right to do theology. For almost two thousand years, the study and writing of theology had been an almost exclusively male preserve, and the self-conscious and unapologetic emergence of women into this world was truly a momentous thing. So I felt – and I still feel – a debt of gratitude to those pioneering feminist theologians whose courage made me feel a little more courageous and whose presence made me feel a little less like an intruder into a world which was not my own.

Despite this continuing gratitude, my positive feelings about feminist theology have over the years changed to disappointment and frustration. The burden of my complaint is that feminist theology has failed to be sufficiently theological. I believe that this is the result of a failure to engage in any serious and sustained way with the realities of Christian faith and tradition. This failure mars both the critical and the constructive projects of feminist theology: the former is marked by a tendency to ignore the more complex realities of the Christian faith, past and present, and by a preference for a rather simplistic modern construal of Christianity, whilst the latter similarly shuns attentive engagement with Christian tradition, scripture, and community in favour of the higher authority named 'women's experience' or 'women's discourses'. By thus cutting itself off from serious engagement with the central realities of Christianity, I believe that feminist theology has turned itself into just another variant of an individualistic form of modern spirituality which is exemplified in movements such as the New Age. By thus embracing the pervasive idealism of the day, it has abandoned the holy materialism of Christianity and acted against the true interests of women. These are contentious claims. This paper is offered as an attempt to explain and to justify them. It is written in the hope that its critical comments may ultimately prove constructive, and in the belief that feminist theology is important enough to demand nothing less than serious critical engagement.

This critique of feminist theology falls into two parts. In the first I consider the feminist critique of Christianity and in the second the more constructive aspects of feminist theology – the attempts made by 'liberal' or 'reformist' feminist theologians to construct new theologies.

One of the subsidiary arguments of this paper is that, despite other disagreements, the work of feminist theologians of all shades of opinion is in fact less divergent than is usually maintained, and that the conventional distinctions between 'reformist' (or 'liberal') and 'radical' (or 'post-Christian') feminist theologians obscure more fundamental agreement. I will argue that the deep affinity between nearly all feminist theologians lies in their acceptance of the particular construal of Christianity which I outline below, and in their participation in the project of judging Christianity against externally-derived standards. Compared with this very substantial convergence, their divergence over the question of whether all or some of Christianity must be jettisoned seems to me relatively unimportant. Consequently, I believe that it is justifiable to treat the work of different feminist theologians under the blanket heading of 'feminist theology' – providing of course that their differences continue to be acknowledged where relevant.

1. The Feminist Critique of Christianity

From its beginnings in the late nineteenth century, much of the energy of feminist theology has been directed into critiques of traditional Christianity, and by comparison its contribution to constructive theological endeavour has been slight. In the second half of this paper I will discuss this failure at greater length. For the moment I wish only to assess the feminist theological critique of Christianity on its own merits.

The Target of the Feminist Critique – Christianity Misconstrued

The picture of the Christian tradition which emerges from reading feminist critiques is a remarkably consistent one. Whatever their other differences, feminist theologians tend to construe Christianity in very similar ways. In particular they seem to be agreed that in its essence Christianity is *a system of textually encoded beliefs*. The feminist critique construes Christianity as a set of doctrinal formulations or 'dogmas'. The Bible and the creeds are seen as central to this system of belief, with the writings of the great theologians in a secondary and supporting role. On this account, Christianity is a comprehensive metaphysic which explains the nature of God, man and the universe, and Christian ethics is a body of textually encoded laws, a rigid system of 'thou shalts' and (more importantly) 'thou shalt nots'. So Bible and tradition are made up of dogmas and laws, and Christians are those who regard these as literally true rather than as metaphorical or symbolic: Christians treat them as 'absolutes' rather than as provisional or relative truths.

By giving such central emphasis to the textual and the doctrinal nature of

Christianity, the feminist critique relegates the church to a secondary role. Rarely do feminist theologians engage in serious critical analysis of the institution itself, being generally content to dismiss it as a hierarchical organisation run by and for a male priestly caste. It is this clerical caste which is said to shape and control Christianity by deciding what is to count as official dogma and by promulgating this orthodoxy. Priests are viewed by feminist theology as the routinisers of charisma, whether that charisma be viewed as of Christ, of the early church, of the spirit, of ordinary or oppressed people. Priests, aided by theologians, characterise themselves as the sole legitimate guardians of this charisma, and thereby secure their own power. They thereby deprive all lay people, and especially all women, of power, establishing Christianity as a religion which systematically excludes one half of the human race from either heavenly or earthly hierarchies.

In tracing back the authority of Christian belief to the self-interested strategies of patriarchal clerics, the feminist construal of Christianity is of course inherently critical. It undermines Christian dogma's constitutive claim to be true and revelatory and suggests that it is in fact nothing more than what Ruether refers to as 'codified collective experience'.

Lift the veil on scripture and tradition, remove the rhetoric of clerics, and you find only experience. For this reason, feminist theologians argue, it is best to drop mystifying terms like 'dogma' and 'revelation', and speak instead of 'myths', 'symbols', 'models', 'metaphors', and 'parables'. Interestingly, these terms tend to be used almost interchangeably by feminist theologians, usually with little or no attempt at definition or discrimination. Their meaning, it seems, is bestowed simply by the way in which they are used in opposition to the alternative (and similarly undifferentiated) cluster of terms, 'dogma', 'absolute truth', 'revelation'. In other words, it seems that if something is said to be 'mythical' or 'symbolic', it is precisely its refusal to make a claim to absolute truth which is signalised. Not that feminist theologians want to deny the importance and value of religious 'symbols' – rather they want to stress their provisionality and revisability and their subordination to the individual religious 'experience' they inadequately express.

In evaluating the feminist construal of Christianity which I have briefly outlined, the first thing to be said is that it is not entirely new. Indeed, some of its main features may be traced back to the early days of the Enlightenment critique of traditional Christianity.

The feminist construal of Christianity is thus notable not just for what it includes, but for what it leaves out. Feminist theology reduces Christianity to the thin reality of a set of dogmas standing over against the individual. In so doing it ignores the discourses of Christianity itself. It occludes the thick reality of the Trinitarian God and of those communities which are caught up in His life. In the language which is so privileged in the church's self-understanding, the church is the 'body of Christ'. This language shows clearly that God, the believer, the church and its teachings are not separated out from one another as autonomous and wholly independent objects. The church is not an institution which threatens the autonomy of the individual, but the community in which human beings are formed and shaped as faithful and loving creatures. God does not stand over against the church, the latter acting as a barrier between God and the individual. Rather, the church is the place where God, by His grace, is made present to believers, the place where human beings are caught up into God's life in Christ by the Spirit. The church becomes Christ's body on earth, the location where the God become human in Jesus Christ continues to become human in the lives of those animated by His Spirit.

The Basis of the Feminist Critique – Subjecting God to Higher Authority

Even more problematic than the feminist critique's detached intellectualism is, I think, the way in which it often seems by its very nature to prejudge the issue of the value and the truth of Christianity. Clearly no criticism takes place in a vacuum. Criticism implies a set of commitments against which the object of criticism is weighed up. When a critique is labelled 'Marxist' or 'conservative' or 'feminist', a declaration is being made about the nature of these commitments. But when the object of criticism is Christianity, the mere fact of having such commitments may be problematic, for they may compete with the very fundamental commitment which Christians demand from their adherents. As D. Z. Phillips once pointed out, a Christian does not say 'it is more probable than not that my redeemer liveth', but 'I know that my redeemer liveth'. To be a Christian is to have given one's heart to Christ, to have *faith* in him and in the tradition which witnesses to him. Is this compatible with having an alternative set of commitments in the light of which one judges Christianity?

The answer to that question must surely be that it depends both upon the nature and scale of the commitments which underlie one's critical stance towards Christianity, and upon the way in which one holds them. If they are large-scale commitments, commitments to another religion, or quasi-religion, to a 'meta-narrative' or total world-view, then clearly they may be rivals to Christianity. And if, in addition, they are held as basic and foundational, then there is even more reason to think that they may be incompatible with Christianity. In theory, I believe that there is no reason why the feminist critique should be either of these things. It may be less a meta-narrative than an ethical conviction or principle – a belief, for example, in the equal worth of women and men, and a judgement against all beliefs, institutions and practices which violate this. And it may be a commitment which, though deep, is never finally closed to revision or reformulation (as indeed may a believer's commitment to Christianity).

My suspicion, however, is that in practice, many versions of the feminist critique do in fact involve very large-scale commitments, commitments to an entire world-view or spiritual system which is incompatible with Christianity. I shall say more about this in the second half of this article. In addition, it seems that whatever the scale of the feminist commitment, it is common for feminist theologians to hold it as a more basic commitment than their commitment to Christianity, even as their sole incontestable and unrevisable commitment. When this is the case, the feminist critique of Christianity easily ceases to be a creative dialogue between Christianity and feminism and becomes a rather formalistic exercise in weighing up Christianity against an externally imposed, externally derived and unquestionable standard. The radical or post-Christian feminist theologians are those who judge that none of Christianity is acceptable in the light of this standard, the liberal or reform-ist feminist theologians are those who aver that some of it may be. On the nature of the standard both seem to be in agreement, as they are about the propriety of judging the God of Jesus Christ by this higher authority. Their differences concern only the outcome of the judgement.

2. A Critique of the Constructive Enterprise of Feminist Theology

Though relatively rare, some attempts at *constructive* feminist theology have also been made. Such theology is viewed by its proponents as entirely different from traditional theology, and as opening a new era in the theologi-cal enterprise. Generally, feminist theologians explain the distinctiveness of their discipline in terms of its being the expression of women's experience of the divine, in contrast to traditional theology which is castigated as the expression of male experience alone.

The rhetoric surrounding constructive feminist theology stands, however, in marked contrast to the reality of its achievement to date. Not only has feminist theology tended to shy away from construction in favour of critique, its new constructive endeavours are far less original and mould-breaking than we had been led to expect. Not only has feminist theology offered few theological insights, it seems deeply dependent upon existing forms of liberal and post-Christian theology and spirituality.

The failure of feminist theology to produce truly constructive Christian theology is due, in my view, to the incoherence of its project. Christian theology has never been constructed on the basis of 'experience'. Rather, it has been constructed on the basis of encounter with God in Christ, mediated through the Christian tradition. It has more to do with witness than invention. And it has more to do with community and tradition than with the individual. Christian theology is essentially a communal activity, not a private one.

(Taken from Linda Woodhead, 'Spiritualising the Sacred: A Critique of Feminist Theology', Modern Theology 13, 1997, pp. 191–201.)

III.2.7 Emilie Townes, from 'Womanist Theology'

Townes describes the relationship of womanist theology to feminist theology.

TO LOVE OUR NECKS UNNOOSED AND STRAIGHT

Womanist theology challenges the theological presuppositions and assumptions of feminist theology as well. Womanist theology is not purely academic (objective) – it is also personal (subjective). Womanist theology attempts to articulate a theoretical critique of cultural hegemony through a call for the reimaging of the roles of men and women in religious practices and also in secular society. Within a theo-ethical framework, it is inductive and based on praxis. The inductive approach taken by womanist theo-ethical reflection stresses experience as opposed to the deductive approach of classical theological models. Rather than deducing conclusions from principles established out of religious traditions and philosophies, like all theologies of liberation, it begins with lived experience. Within the Christian context, the gospel message is good news to people when it speaks to their needs and proclaims the challenges in a concrete manner.

Ideally, the theoretical constructs of feminist theology (which along with Black theology are the twin academic roots from which womanist theo-ethical reflection emerges) refuse to accept the social location we either allow ourselves to assume due to social mores and strictures or to which we may be assigned by those same forces. The task before feminist theology is to name the particular sin and be able to articulate the universal dimensions of it. Rather, the universal is *manifested* in the particular, but not exhausted by it. Feminist theology, at its best, attempts to be antiracist, antisexist, anticlassist, antiheterosexist – in short, antioppressist.

This movement to live into an antioppression analysis that is truly inclusive has been a part of much of Black and feminist theologies in recent years. This was done through contesting such language as 'blackness/whiteness,' 'oppression/liberation,' 'sisterhood,' 'common oppression,' 'women's experience.' This became crucial as more women of color, women whose religious experience is other than Christian, and women from the spectrum of class differences and sexualities joined the academy under the rubric of feminism and Black liberation. The power of analysis sharpened our ability to name, critique, and strategize against the interstructured nature of oppression. We began, slowly, not only to hear the great diversity of women's experiences and the demands this placed on our methodologies, but we also began to understand the benefits and the costs we all bore. Womanist theology challenged the sexism and classism found in Black theology in its universalization of an uncritical understanding of Black male experience as the norm of all the African American community. We began to realize that the *only* place solidarity comes before work is in the dictionary.

Yet, there is more work to do in forging an inclusive methodology that takes differences seriously and addresses those differences in an integrated and coherent analysis. The emergence of womanist, *mujerista*, Asian women's liberation theology, and liberation theology from African women are indicative that the name, feminism, is problematic. The media have defined it, the church has confined it, academia ignores it, and feminist scholars in religious studies are left to refine it so that it can be an ideology that is broad in the concrete.

We are caught in a major methodological flaw: an incomplete praxis. The action and reflection that are key to any liberatory methodology are impaired. The reflection done in feminist theo-ethical methodologies is not truly inclusive of women's experiences. Women's lives are not a tapestried monolith. The careful consideration of and methodological inclusion of the varying social locations of women are crucial to truly scholarly and rigorous feminist studies in religion. This must take place not only in our scholarship, but also in our day-to-day lives.

This methodological flaw has birthed a postmodern turn in feminist theology that is extremely troubling because of the way it represents a two-headed coin. The postmodern rejection of universal laws, 'objectivity,' linear views of history that legitimate patriarchal notions of subjectivity and social order, science and reason as direct correspondents with objectivity and truth, and totalizing feminisms are welcome additions to theological discourse. In its best sense, postmodern discourse challenges us to rethink master narratives and notions of culture. This side of the coin of postmodern feminist theology continues the project begun within feminist discourse, that to discover, recover, and uncover the fact that women of color, poor women, women from various religious traditions, women of various sexualities were at the table *at the beginning*. Some of us were simply not served, nor were we asked if we were hungry and needed something to eat.

The other side of the coin of postmodern feminist theology is worrisome because of the emerging voice of individualism embedded in this discourse, particularly that which relies heavily if not exclusively on the field of cultural studies. The theoretical and methodological intent of cultural studies is *not* to provide a new rationale for an individualism that serves to relativize experiences in a way that reduces human lives to competing ideologies. However, when cultural studies omits progressive, transformatory political and prophetic dimensions, it *does* serve to do so. This individualism is distinct from referencing the individual. Questions of the self and the self in relation to the community are extremely pertinent for religious reflection. These questions and the exploration of them within feminist reflection have pushed us, both academically and within the lives of religious communities, into a greater faithfulness to live into a fuller humanity.

The individualism that is troubling manifests itself in the privileging of epistemology and aesthetics over ethics and politics. Yet, questions of knowing and taste are interrelated with questions of right action, values, and the ordering of our society. This individualism's understanding of power dynamics and relations is simplistic. It fails to understand that power functions through other than technologies of control and domination. This individualism fails to nuance the value of master or grand narratives. It is true enough that narratives that employ a single standard that is then universalized should be held in deep suspicion and eradicated. Grand narratives, however, often function as powerful tools for identity and solidarity *for* the dispossessed and the marginalized.

General feminist discourse has a new generation of, in bell hooks's words,

> young white privileged women who strive to create a narrative of feminism (not a feminist movement) that recenters the experience of materially privileged white females in ways that deny race and class differences, not solely in relation to the construction of female identity but also in relation to feminist movement.

This impulse has moved within feminist studies in religion as well. When issues of race and class and sexualities challenge their feminist practice, their feminist theological reflection is often found wanting. The danger remains that when far too many feminist scholars in religion weave their vision of a new ordering of creation, women of color, lesbians and transgendered peoples, and poor women are either left out or mere addenda to the analysis. This would not be so troubling if feminist theological reflection was nascent. Youth can be forgiven many things, but feminist theology is a maturing discipline that has faced this challenge of a more broad-based inclusivity, in this generation, since the late 1970s.

Feminist theology that is authentic is more than a vague concept of civil rights within a capitalist and misogynist system. It is more than a further extension of tokenism to include more women in existing social structures. Feminism that is authentic seeks to transform radically the social structures and human relationships within that structure. The agenda of authentic feminism includes relationships between men and women, rich and overly exploited, white and peoples of color, old and young, abled and disabled, student and professor, heterosexual and homosexual, clergy and laity.

It is not enough for feminist scholars of religion to apply the increasingly threadbare apology that they are white, middle-class, and privileged and therefore cannot adequately address the concerns of women who are not from this social location, or fail to see that their experience is not universal and cannot be totalized in such a way that it is inclusive. The essence of our various social locations demands that we understand *how* sociocultural hegemony functions to create that location. There is, in the very construction of race, gender, and class a demand for feminist theology to take these seriously and to explore both the costs and the benefits of our places in the sociocultural order.

(Taken from Emilie M. Townes, 'Womanist Theology', in Roger A. Badham (ed.), Introduction to Christian Theology: Contemporary North American Perspectives, *Louisville, KY: Westminster John Knox Press 1998, pp. 218–21.)*

III.3 Christian theology in a multi-faith world

Introductory essay

At the heart of Christian proclamation lies the conviction that God has acted in Jesus Christ in a way that is both unique and decisive for the redemption of the world. Christian theology, accordingly, is engaged in the investigation and elucidation of this claim. One of its tasks therefore is to consider the coherency of this claim in the face of the vast plurality of alternative views. Although it is sometimes presented as a modern problem, the fact of religious plurality has exercised the minds of Jewish and Christian thinkers throughout the period of biblical history and subsequently in the theological traditions of both faiths. The writers of the Hebrew Scriptures, for instance, claimed that God's dealings with Israel set it apart from other nations and demanded of its people an exclusive allegiance to the God of Abraham and Isaac and a renunciation of all other gods. Similarly in the New Testament, one encounters the conviction that salvation comes through Christ alone, that there is no other name through which humanity might be rescued from its sinful existence and reconciled with the creator of all.

The exclusive nature of these claims is due in large measure to the conviction that God encounters humanity in history, that God has made himself known in particular places and times and supremely so in Jesus Christ. On this account the knowledge of God is not available as a general truth, universally accessible through reason, or mysticism, or through some common feature of human experience. Rather, knowledge of God and reconciliation with him is mediated through God's particular presence in Israel, culminating in the person and work of Jesus of Nazareth. Such claims constitute what is known as the 'scandal of particularity'. They are by their very nature exclusive, but it is a matter of debate whether their exclusivity entails the rejection of all those who, through no fault of their own, remain ignorant of the news that salvation comes through Jesus Christ alone, or of those who being raised within the context of another faith, are devout followers of a path other than that proclaimed by Christianity.

Offence at the suggestion that salvation comes through Christ alone has occasioned numerous attempts throughout the history of theology to evaluate other faiths in a positive light. It is argued by some, for instance, that, the differences between them notwithstanding, all faiths give at least partial access to God and are legitimate means of salvation. That is a view that goes by the name of pluralism, and is discussed in the readings below both by supporters of the view and by its critics. Pluralism is often contrasted with two other approaches to inter-faith relations, namely exclusivism, the view that salvation is available within one faith alone, or inclusivism, which in its Christian form is the view that although there is one saviour, Jesus Christ, his saving influence is effective beyond the boundaries of the Christian church. This threefold typology dominated much of the discussion about inter-faith relations in the last decades of the twentieth century, but the coherence of the typology, and especially of the pluralist position, has been strongly challenged in recent years. The typology, itself, however, remains in use and appears to have considerable appeal at a popular level.

The key question arising for Christian theology in the multi-faith context concerns the person of Jesus Christ. Who is he? Is he the Son of God, the unique mediator through whom God makes himself known and reconciles the world to himself? Is he therefore to be regarded as the one and only saviour of the world, or is he, by contrast, simply one saviour figure among many? Some Christians have felt obliged by their observations of the devout and morally upright adherents of other faiths to affirm the efficacy of those faiths as a means of salvation, and to deny, therefore, the uniqueness of Christ. There are others, however, who continue to affirm the uniqueness of Christ but do not agree that this entails the divine rejection of those of other faiths. It is argued that while some – perhaps many – beyond the bounds of Christian faith may be saved, their salvation too is accomplished through the person and work of Jesus Christ.

Whatever one's view on these questions, it is not difficult to perceive their importance, both at the level of local communities which are increasingly characterized by the plurality of ethnic and religious identities of their members, and at the level of international relations where political, economic and ethical practices are shaped to a significant extent by the religious convictions or underlying religious formation of those who engage in them. The selections below reveal a range of opinion about how the Christian gospel is to be proclaimed within a multi-faith world.

The reading from Athanasius (III.3.1) represents an early Christian polemic against the surrounding religions, all of which are deemed by Athanasius to be forms of idolatry. It is notable that despite being the leading advocate in his time of the unique mediation of Jesus Christ, Athanasius does not offer, in the first instance, a christological argument against the truth of other faiths. He rather supposes that the poverty of their alleged idolatry can be exposed on straightforward rational grounds.

The second reading, by contrast, provides a positive affirmation of the life and faith of one who is not a Christian. Writing to Anzir, King of Mauretania, Pope Gregory VII (III.3.2) praises the king's faith in God, 'though we worship him in diverse forms', and seeks to foster good relations with this man of Muslim faith. The pope appears to be in no doubt that it is the same God who is worshipped in both Islam and Christianity.

A similar generosity of spirit is evident in the reading from John Owen (III.3.3) although, being concerned with intra-ecclesial strife rather than with persons of non-Christian faith, the scope of diversity which Owen considers is more limited than that of Gregory VII. Owen writes in a time of considerable political and ecclesiastical turmoil, and seeks to calm the intolerant and disputatious attitudes of his time. He urges that all people should be treated with toleration, fairness and understanding, and that one should seek to live at peace with all. He also reminds his readers that God alone is finally able to judge the merits or otherwise of the ways and works of others.

Lord Herbert of Cherbury (III.3.4) was a forerunner of the deists and a defender of the popular Enlightenment view that true religion was based upon the rational distillation of innate ideas. Lord Herbert responds to the scandal of particularity simply by rejecting it and by proposing to found religion upon rational truths or innate ideas that are universally accessible. This allows a positive estimation of other faiths which share such ideas, and a corresponding rejection of all ideas in Christianity as well as in other faiths that are not rationally defensible. The universal and rationally accessible ideas of true religion are supposed to include the existence of one supreme God who is worthy of worship, the reality of evil, the virtue of repentance and the surety of final judgment culminating in reward or punishment. This approach is known as 'Natural Religion' and continued to be promoted throughout the seventeenth and eighteenth centuries by such thinkers as Locke, Butler and Rousseau.

It was common in the post-Enlightenment world, when Christian

Europe was increasingly in contact through trade and travel with the religions of other regions, to develop hierarchical and progressive accounts of human religious life. It was typically argued, for example, that the various religions represent more or less primitive expressions of a religious insight which attains its highest form in Christianity. G. W. F. Hegel and Friedrich Schleiermacher, though very different in their approaches, represent two forms of this progressive account of the religions. Schleiermacher (III.3.5) proposes that all forms of 'piety' or 'religious affection' (as he puts it) express the dependence of all finite creatures upon something other than themselves. The 'higher' religions, however, Judaism, Islam and Christianity, are distinguished, from all other (polytheistic) religions by their recognition that there is one God who is creator and sustainer of all. The recognition of the redemption accomplished in Jesus of Nazareth accounts, in Schleierm-acher's view, for the further superiority of Christianity.

Like Schleiermacher, the twentieth-century theologian Karl Rahner (III.3.6) attempts to identify among the religions some common experi-ence which is the basis of their faith. We have already noted in section I.5 of this volume the transcendent anthropology which Rahner espouses. The alleged common experience of a humanity 'open to the transcendent' leads Rahner to the view that while Jesus Christ remains the unique mediator of salvation, devout adherents of other faiths may be accounted as 'anonymous Christians'. While commendable for its attempt to recognize the genuine devotion and integrity of people of other faiths, Rahner's notion of the 'anonymous Christian' has attracted widespread criticism, both from those who dispute the suggestion that salvation can be attained without an explicit confession of faith in Jesus Christ, and from others who accuse Rahner of a patronizing attitude to other faiths.

The reading from Langdon Gilkey (III.3.7) represents a position developed in recent years especially by John Hick, Paul Knitter and Wilfred Cantwell Smith. Impressed in particular by the moral virtue of many of the adherents of non-Christian faiths, these theologians argue that Christianity must renounce its claims to exclusivity and recognize that other faiths provide for their adherents an equally legitimate path to salvation. Such a view, as might be expected, is accompanied by denials of the uniqueness of Jesus Christ. A notable feature of this approach, clearly at odds with the New Testament, is that salvation is thought to be the reward for a person's 'good works'. The observation that non-Christians are eminently capable of living 'good lives' counts, according to such a view, as conclusive evidence of the salvific efficacy of their particular religion. Gilkey thus argues for a 'rough parity' between the religions and proposes that the degree to which they manifest 'love' should be the criterion by which the religions are to be judged.

In contrast to Gilkey, Lesslie Newbigin (III.3.8) is a theologian who upholds the uniqueness of Jesus Christ as the sole mediator of salvation. Rejecting the pluralist thesis on the grounds that it falsely presupposes a dichotomy between facts and values and because it consigns religious faith to opinions about the latter, Newbigin argues for a recovery of confidence in the fact and truth of the gospel. Christian faith is not simply a matter of moral ideals which may be met equally convincingly by people of other faiths; rather it concerns the particular acts of God in creation and redemption which alone form the basis for human salvation. This does not preclude, indeed it encourages, in Newbigin's view, an eager co-operation with people of other faiths, and a readiness to recognize the signs of God's creative and redemptive activity, mediated through Christ, that will also be evident among them.

One of the strongest critiques to emerge in recent years of the pluralist view of religions is that of Gavin D'Costa (III.3.9), once an advocate of the threefold typology that we have outlined above. D'Costa argues that the pluralist position is logically incoherent. While purporting to be inclusive of all religious options and claiming that each is a pathway to truth and salvation, the pluralist position is in fact necessarily exclusive of some religious claims. The pluralist necessarily rejects the view one might take, for instance, that salvation comes through Christ alone. But in rejecting this religious position, to take but one example, the pluralist turns out to be exclusive after all.

MAR

III.3.1 St Athanasius, from *Against the Heathen*

Athanasius here discusses the various religious opinions current in his day.

8. Now the soul of mankind, not satisfied with the devising of evil, began by degrees to venture upon what is worse still. For having experience of diversities of pleasures, and girt about with oblivion of things divine; being pleased moreover and having in view the passions of the body, and nothing but things present and opinions about them, ceased to think that anything existed beyond what is seen, or that anything was good save things temporal and bodily; so turning away and forgetting that she was in the image of the good God, she no longer, by the power which is in her, sees God the Word after whose likeness she is made; but having departed from herself, imagines and feigns what is not. For hiding, by the complications of bodily lusts, the mirror which, as it were, is in her, by which alone she had the power of seeing the Image of the Father, she no longer sees what a soul ought to behold, but is carried about by everything, and only sees the things which come under the senses. Hence, weighted with all fleshly desire, and distracted among the impressions of these things, she imagines that the God Whom her understanding has forgotten is to be found in bodily and sensible things, giving to things seen the name of God, and glorifying only those things which she desires and which are pleasant to her eyes. Accordingly, evil is the cause which brings idolatry in its train; for men, having learned to contrive evil, which is no reality in itself, in like manner feigned for themselves as gods beings that had no real existence. Just, then, as though a man had plunged into the deep, and no longer saw the light, nor what appears by light, because his eyes are turned downwards, and the water is all above him; and, perceiving only the things in the deep, thinks that nothing exists beside them, but that the things he sees are the only true realities; so the men of former time, having lost their reason, and plunged into the lusts and imaginations of carnal things, and forgotten the knowledge and glory of God, their reasoning being dull, or rather following unreason, made gods for themselves of things seen, glorifying the creature rather than the Creator, and deifying the works rather than the Master, God, their Cause and Artificer. But just as, according to the above simile, men who plunge into the deep, the deeper they go down, advance into darker and deeper places, so it is with mankind. For they did not keep to idolatry in a simple form, nor did they abide in that with which they began; but the longer they went on in their first condition, the more new superstitions they invented: and, not satiated with the first evils, they again filled themselves, with others, advancing further in utter shamefulness, and surpassing themselves in impiety. But

to this the divine Scripture testifies when it says, 'When the wicked cometh unto the depth of evils, he despiseth'.

9. For now the understanding of mankind leaped asunder from God; and going lower in their ideas and imaginations, they gave the honour due to God first to the heaven and the sun and moon and the stars, thinking them to be not only gods, but also the causes of the other gods lower than themselves. Then, going yet lower in their dark imaginations, they gave the name of gods to the upper aether and the air and the things in the air. Next, advancing further in evil, they came to celebrate as gods the elements and the principles of which bodies are composed, heat and cold and dryness and wetness. But just as they who have fallen flat creep in the slime like land-snails, so the most impious of mankind, having fallen lower and lower from the idea of God, then set up as gods men, and the forms of men, some still living, others even after their death. Moreover, counselling and imagining worse things still, they transferred the divine and supernatural name of God at last even to stones and stocks, and creeping things both of land and water, and irrational wild beasts, awarding to them every divine honour, and turning from the true and only real God, the Father of Christ. But would that even there the audacity of these foolish men had stopped short, and that they had not gone further yet in impious self-confusion. For to such a depth have some fallen in their understanding, to such darkness of mind, that they have even devised for themselves, and made gods of things that have no existence at all, nor any place among things created. For mixing up the rational with the irrational and combining things unlike in nature, they worship the result as gods, such as the dog-headed and snake-headed and ass-headed gods among the Egyptians, and the ram-headed Ammon among the Libyans. While others, dividing apart the portions of men's bodies, head, shoulder, hand, and foot, have set up each as gods and deified them, as though their religion were not satisfied with the whole body in its integrity. But others, straining impiety to the utmost, have deified the motive of the invention of these things and of their own wickedness, namely, pleasure and lust, and worship them, such as their Eros, and the Aphrodite at Paphos ... According as the wisdom of God testifies beforehand when it says, 'The devising of idols was the beginning of fornication'.

11. But of these and such like inventions of idolatrous madness, Scripture taught us beforehand long ago, when it said, 'The devising of idols was the beginning of fornication, and the invention of them, the corruption of life' ... The beginning and devising of the invention of idols having been, as Scripture witnesses, of such sort, it is now time to shew thee the refutation of it by proofs derived not so much from without as from these men's own opinions about the idols. For to begin at the lowest point, if one were to take

the actions of them they call gods, one would find that they were not only no gods, but had been even of men the most contemptible. For what a thing it is to see the loves and licentious actions of Zeus in the poets! What a thing to hear of him, on the one hand carrying off Ganymede and committing stealthy adulteries, on the other in panic and alarm lest the walls of the Trojans should be destroyed against his intentions! What a thing to see him . . . overcome by pleasures, a slave to women, and for their sakes running adventures in disguises consisting of brute beasts and creeping things and birds; and again, in hiding on account of his father's designs upon him, or Cronos bound by him, or him again mutilating his father! Why, is it fitting to regard as a god one who has perpetrated such deeds, and who stands accused of things which not even the public laws of the Romans allow those to do who are merely men?

13. Again, in worshipping things of wood and stone, they do not see that, while they tread under foot and burn what is in no way different, they call portions of these materials gods. And what they made use of a little while ago, they carve and worship in their folly, not seeing, nor at all considering that they are worshipping, not gods, but the carver's art. For so long as the stone is uncut and the wood unworked, they walk upon the one and make frequent use of the other for their own purposes, even for those which are less honourable. But when the artist has invested them with the proportions of his own skill, and impressed upon the material the form of man or woman, then, thanking the artist, they proceed to worship them as gods, having bought them from the carver at a price. Often, moreover, the image-maker, as though forgetting the work he has done himself, prays to his own productions, and calls gods what just before he was paring and chipping. But it were better, if need to admire these things, to ascribe it to the art of the skilled workman, and not to honour productions in preference to their producer. For it is not the material that has adorned the art, but the art that has adorned and deified the material. Much juster were it, then, for them to worship the artist than his productions, both because his existence was prior to that of the gods produced by art, and because they have come into being in the form he pleased to give them. But as it is, setting justice aside, and dishonouring skill and art, they worship the products of skill and art, and when the man is dead that made them, they honour his works as immortal, whereas if they did not receive daily attention they would certainly in time come to a natural end . . .

14. But better testimony about all this is furnished by Holy Scripture, which tells us beforehand when it says, 'Their idols are silver and gold, the work of men's hands. Eyes have they and will not see; a mouth have they and will not speak; ears have they and will not hear; noses have they and will not smell; hands have they and will not handle; feet have they and will not

walk; they will not speak through their throat. Like unto them be they that make them'.

16. But perhaps, as to all this, the impious will appeal to the peculiar style of poets, saying that it is the peculiarity of poets to feign what is not, and, for the pleasure of their hearers, to tell fictitious tales; and that for this reason they have composed the stories about gods. But this pretext of theirs, even more than any other, will appear to be superficial from what they themselves think and profess about these matters. For if what is said in the poets is fictitious and false, even the nomenclature of Zeus, Cronos, Hera, Ares and the rest must be false. For perhaps, as they say, even the names are fictitious, and, while no such being exists as Zeus, Cronos, or Ares, the poets feign their existence to deceive their hearers. But if the poets feign the existence of unreal beings, how is it that they worship them as though they existed?

19.. . . As to which those who pass for philosophers and men of knowledge among the Greeks, while driven to admit that their visible gods are the forms and figures of men and of irrational objects, say in defence that they have such things to the end that by their means the deity may answer them and be made manifest; because otherwise they could not know the invisible God, save by such statues and rites. While those who profess to give still deeper and more philosophical reasons than these say, that the reason of idols being prepared and fashioned is for the invocation and manifestation of divine angels and powers, that appearing by these means they may teach men concerning the knowledge of God; and that they serve as letters for men, by referring to which they may learn to apprehend God, from the manifestation of the divine angels effected by their means. Such then is their mythology, – for far be it from us to call it a theology. But if one examine the argument with care, he will find that the opinion of these persons also, not less than that of those previously spoken of, is false.

(Taken from the Nicene and Post-Nicene Fathers, series II, vol. 4, ed. Archibald Robertson.)

III.3.2 Pope Gregory VII, from a letter to Anzir

Pope Gregory, writing to a Muslim king, suggests that Christians and Muslims worship the same God, 'although in different ways'.

God, the Creator of all, without whom we cannot do or even think anything that is good, has inspired to your heart this act of kindness. He who enlightens all men coming into this world (*Jn 1.9*) has enlightened your mind for this purpose. Almighty God, who desires all men to be saved (*1 Tim. 2.4*) and none to perish, is well pleased to approve in us most of all that besides loving God men love other men, and do not do to others anything they do not want to be done unto themselves (*cf. Mt. 7.14*). We and you must show in a special way to the other nations an example of this charity, for we believe and confess one God, although in different ways, and praise and worship Him daily as the creator of all ages and the ruler of this world. For as the apostle says: 'He is our peace who has made us both one' (*Eph. 2.14*). Many among the Roman nobility, informed by us of this grace granted to you by God, greatly admire and praise your goodness and virtues. . . . God knows that we love you purely for His honour and that we desire your salvation and glory, both in the present and the future life. And we pray in our hearts and with our lips that God may lead you to the abode of happiness, to the bosom of the holy patriarch Abraham, after long years of life here on earth.

(Taken from J. Neuner and J. Dupuis (eds), **The Christian Faith in the Documents of the Catholic Church,** *Bangalore: Theological Publications in India 1982, pp. 276–7.)*

III.3.3 John Owen, from *Indulgence and Toleration Considered*

Owen argues that toleration is a necessary virtue, which should be extended to all.

The sole question is, Whether God hath authorized and doth warrant any man, of what sort soever, to compel others to worship and serve him contrary to the way and manner that they are in their consciences persuaded that he doth accept and approve. God, indeed, where men are in errors and mistakes about his will and worship, would have them taught and instructed, and sendeth out his own light and truth to guide them, as seemeth good unto him; but to affirm that he hath authorized men to proceed in the way before mentioned is to say that he hath set up an authority *against himself*, and that which may give control to his.

These things being so, – seeing men are bound indispensably not to worship God so as they are convinced and persuaded that he will not be worshipped, and to worship him as he hath appointed and commanded, upon the penalty of answering their neglect and contempt hereof with their everlasting condition at the last day; and seeing God hath not warranted or authorized any man to enforce them to act contrary to their light and that persuasion of his mind and will which he hath given them in their own consciences, nor to punish them for yielding obedience in spiritual things unto the command of God, as his mind is by them apprehended, (if the things themselves, though mistaken, are such as no way interfere with the common light of nature or reason of mankind, the fundamental articles of Christian religion, moral honesty, civil society, and public tranquillity; especially, if the things wherein men acting, as is supposed, according to their own light and conscience, in difference from others, are of small importance, and such as they probably plead are unduly and ungroundedly imposed on their practice, or prohibited unto them), – it remains to be considered whether the grounds and ends proposed in exercise of the severity pleaded for, be agreeable to common rules of prudence, or the state and condition of things in this nation.

The ground which men proceed upon in their resolutions for severity seems to be, that the church and commonwealth may stand upon the same bottom and foundation, that their interest may be every way the same, of the same breadth and length, and to be mutually narrowed or widened by each other.

The interest of the kingdom they would have to stand upon the *bottom of uniformity*, so that the government of it should, as to the beneficial ends of government, comprehend them only whom the church compriseth in its uniformity; and so the kingdom's peace should be extended only unto them unto whom the church's peace is extended. Thus they say that the kingdom and the church, or its present order and establishment, are to be like Hippocrates' twins, – not only to be born together and to die together, but to cry and laugh together, and to be equally affected with their mutual concerns. But these things are evident mistakes in policy, and such as multiplied experience has evidenced so to be.

The true civil interest of this nation, in the policy, government, and laws thereof, with the benefits and advantages of them, and the obedience that is due unto them, *every Englishman is born unto;* he falls into it from the womb; it grows up with him, he is indispensably engaged into it, and holds all his temporal concernments by it. He is able also, by natural reason, to understand it, so far as in point of duty he is concerned; and is not at liberty to dissent from the community. But as for religion, it is the choice of men, and he that chooseth not his religion hath none: for although it is not of necessity that a man formally chooses a religion, or one way in religion in an opposition unto and with the rejection of another, yet it is so that he so chooses in opposition to no religion, and with judgment about it, and approbation of that which he doth embrace; which hath the nature of a voluntary choice.

This being the liberty, this the duty of every man, which is, always hath been, and probably always will be, issued in great variety of persuasions and different apprehensions, to confine the peace and interest of civil societies unto any one of them seems scarce suitable unto that prudence which is requisite for the steerage of the present state of things in the world. For my part, I can see no reason the civil state hath to expose its peace unto all those uncertain events which this principle will lead unto. And it seems very strange, and I am persuaded that, on due consideration, it will seem strange, that any should continue in desire of confining the bottom of the nation's interest in its rule and peace unto that uniformity in religion which, as to a firm foundation in the minds and consciences of men, hath discovered itself to be no more diffused amongst the body of the people than at present it is, and from which such multitudes do, upon grounds to themselves unconquerable, dissent, resolving to continue so doing whatever they suffer for it, who yet otherwise unanimously acquiesce in the civil government, and are willing to contribute to the utmost of their endeavours, in their several places, unto its peace and prosperity.

Whatever, therefore, be the resolution as to a present procedure, I heartily wish that the principle itself might for the future be cast out of the minds of men; that the state and rule of the nation might not, by plausible and specious pretences, suited to the interest of some few men, be rendered obnoxious unto impression from the variety of opinions about things religious, which, as far as I see, is like to be continued in the world.

(Taken from Works, *vol. XIII, pp. 530–4.)*

III.3.4 Edward, Lord Herbert of Cherbury, from *De Veritate*

Lord Herbert believes that certain notions are common to all religions, and proposes that the only proper religion is that which is in accord with these notions and no others.

Before I proceed to discuss revelation, I think that certain assumptions which underlie our notions of revelation ought to be examined. Every religion which proclaims a revelation is not good, nor is every doctrine which is taught under its authority always essential or even valuable. Some doctrines due to revelation may be, some of them ought to be, abandoned. In this connection the teaching of Common Notions is important; indeed, without them it is impossible to establish any standard of discrimination in revelation or even in religion. Theories based upon implicit faith, though widely held not only in our own part of the world but also in the most distant regions, are here irrelevant. Instances of such beliefs are: that human reason must be discarded, to make room for Faith; that the Church, which is infallible, has the right to prescribe the method of divine worship, and in consequence must be obeyed in every detail; that no one ought to place such confidence in his private judgment as to dare to question the sacred authority of priests and preachers of God's word; that their utterances, though they may elude human grasp, contain so much truth that we should rather lay them to heart than debate them; that to God all the things of which they speak and much more are possible. Now these arguments and many other similar ones, according to differences of age and country, may be equally used to establish a false religion as to support a true one. Anything that springs from the productive, not to say seductive seed of Faith will yield a plentiful crop. What pompous charlatan can fail to impress his ragged flock with such ideas? Is there any fantastic cult which may not be proclaimed under such auspices? How can any age escape deception, especially when the cunning authorities declare their inventions to be heaven-born, though in reality they habitually confuse and mix the truth with falsehood? If we do not advance towards truth upon a foundation of Common Notions, assigning every element its true value, how can we hope to reach any but futile conclusions? Indeed, however those who endeavour to base their beliefs upon the disordered and licentious codes of superstition may protest, their behaviour is precisely similar to people who with the purpose of blinding the eyes of the wayfarer with least trouble to themselves offer with singular courtesy to act as guides on the journey. But the actual facts are otherwise. The supreme Judge requires every individual to render an account of his actions in the light, not of another's belief, but of his own. So we must establish the fundamental principles of religion by means of universal wisdom, so that whatever has been added to it by the genuine dictates of Faith may rest on that foundation as a roof is supported on a house. Accordingly we ought not to accept any kind of religion lightly, without first enquiring into the sources of its prestige. And the Reader will find all these considerations depend upon Common Notions. Can anyone, I beg to ask, read the huge mass of books composed with such immense display of learning, without feeling scorn for these age-long impostures and fables, save in so far as they point the way to holiness? What man could yield unquestioning faith to a body which, disguised under the name of the Church, wastes its time over a multitude of rites, ceremonies, and vanities, which fights in so many parts of the world under different banners, if he were not led to perceive, by the aid of conscience, some marks of worship, piety, penance, reward and punishment? Who, finally, would attend to the living voice of the preacher if he did not refer all his deeds and words to the Sovereign Deity? It would take too long to deal with every instance. It is sufficient to make clear that we cannot establish any of them without the Common Notions. I value these so highly that I would say that the book, religion, and prophet which adheres most closely to them is the best. The system of Notions, so far at least as it concerns theology, has been clearly accepted at all times by every normal person, and does not require any further justification. And, first of all, the teaching of Common Notions, or true Catholic Church, which has never erred, nor ever will err and in which alone the glory of Divine Universal Providence is displayed, asserts that

There is a Supreme God.

No general agreement exists concerning the Gods, but there is universal recognition of God. Every religion in the past has acknowledged, every religion in the future will acknowledge, some sovereign deity among the Gods. Thus to the Romans this supreme Power is Optimus Maximus; to the Jews He is YHWH, Jehovah; to the Mahomedans, Allah; to the Indians of the West, Pachama Viracocha, etc. The Eastern Indians have similar names for Him. Accordingly that which is everywhere accepted as the supreme manifestation of deity, by whatever name it may be called, I term God. I pass on to consider His attributes, using the same method. And in the first place I find that He is Blessed. Secondly, He is the end to which all things move. Thirdly, He is the cause of all things, at least in so far as they are good.

This Sovereign Deity ought to be Worshipped.

While there is no general agreement concerning the worship of Gods, sacred beings, saints, and angels, yet the Common Notion or Universal Consent tells us that adoration ought to be reserved for the one God. Hence divine religion – and no race, however savage, has existed without some expression of it – is found established among all nations, not only on account of the benefits which they received from general providence, but also in recognition of their dependence upon Grace, or particular providence. Hence, too, men have been convinced, as I have observed above, that they can not only supplicate that heavenly Power but prevail upon Him, by means of the faculties implanted in every normal man. Hence, finally, what is a more important indication, this Power was consulted by the seers in order to interpret the future and they undertook no important action without referring to it. So far the peoples were surely *guided* by the teaching of Natural Instinct.

The connection of Virtue with Piety, defined in this work as the right conformation of the faculties, is and always has been held to be, the most important part of religious practice.

There is no general agreement concerning rites, ceremonies, traditions, whether written or unwritten, or concerning Revelation; but there is the greatest possible consensus of opinion concerning the right conformation of the faculties. Conscience guided by Common Notions produces virtue combined with piety, from this there springs true hope, from such true hope, faith, from true faith, love, from true love, joy, and from true joy, Blessedness.

The minds of men have always been filled with horror for their wickedness. Their vices and crimes have been obvious to them. They must be expiated by repentance.

There is no general agreement concerning the various rites or mysteries which the priests have devised for the expiation of sin. Among the Romans, ceremonies of purification, cleansing, atonement, among the Greeks, rites of expiation and purging, and in nearly all races, sacrifices, even of human victims, a cruel and abominable device of the priests, were instituted for this purpose. Among the Egyptians and all the heathen races observances of a similar kind prevailed.

But we may pass over such rites, some of which may well appear ridiculous. General agreement among religions, the nature of divine goodness, and above all conscience, tell us that our crimes may be washed away by true penitence, and that we can be restored to new union with God.

There is Reward or Punishment after this life.

The rewards that are eternal have been variously placed in heaven, in the stars, in the Elysian fields, or in contemplation. Punishment has been thought to lie in metempsychosis, in hell (which some describe as filled with fire, but the Chinese imagine pervaded with smoke), or in some infernal regions, or regions of the middle air, or in temporary or everlasting death. But all religion, law, philosophy and, what is more, conscience, teach openly or implicitly that punishment or reward awaits us after this life.

Such, then, are the Common Notions of which the true Catholic or universal church is built. For the church which is built of clay or stone or living rock or even of marble cannot be claimed to be the infallible Church. The true Catholic Church is not supported on the inextricable confusion or oral and written tradition to which men have given their allegiance. Still less is it that which fights beneath any one particular standard, or is comprised in one organisation so as to embrace only a restricted portion of the earth, or a single period of history. The only Catholic and uniform Church is the doctrine of Common Notions which comprehends all places and all men.

(Taken from Meyrick Carré's translation, University of Bristol, undated, pp. 289–303.)

III.3.5 Friedrich Schleiermacher, from *The Christian Faith*

Here Schleiermacher attempts to construct a hierarchical account of religious devotion on which all religions can be given a place.

§7. *The various religious communions which have appeared in history with clearly defined limits are related to each other in two ways: as different of development, and as different kinds.*
. . .

Now in the first place, as regards the different stages of development: the historical appearance is in itself a higher stage, and stands above the mere isolated household worship, just as the civic condition, even in its most incomplete forms, stands above the formless association of the pre-civic condition. But this difference by no means relates only to the form or the compass of the fellowship itself, but also to the constitution of the underlying religious affections, according as they attain to clearness in conscious antithesis to the movements of the sensible self-consciousness. Now this development depends partly on the whole development of the mental powers, so that for that reason alone many a communion cannot continue longer in its own peculiar mode of existence; as, *e.g.*, many forms of idol-worship, even though they might claim a high degree of mechanical skill, are incompatible with even a moderate scientific and artistic education, and perish when confronted by it. Yet it is also partly true that the development takes its own course; and there is no contradiction in saying that, in one and the same whole, the piety may develop to its highest consummation, while other mental functions remain far behind.

But all differences are not to be thus regarded as distinct stages or levels. There are communal religions (Greek and Indian polytheism are good cases in point), of which one might well seem to be at the same point in the scale as the other, but which are yet very definitely different from each other. If, then, several such exist which belong to the same stage or level, the most natural course will be to call them different kinds or species. And indisputably it can be shown, even at the lowest stage, that most religious communions which are geographically separated from each other are also divided by inner differences.
. . .

Our proposition does not assert, but it does tacitly presuppose the possibility, that there are other forms of piety which are related to Christianity as different forms on the same level of development, and thus so far similar. But this does not contradict the conviction, which we assume every Christian to possess, of the exclusive superiority of Christianity . . .

Our proposition excludes only the idea, which indeed is often met with, that the Christian religion (piety) should adopt towards at least most other

forms of piety the attitude of the true towards the false. For if the religions belonging to the same stage as Christianity were entirely false, how could they have so much similarity to Christianity as to make that classification requisite?
. . .

§8. *Those forms of piety in which all religious affections express the dependence of everything finite upon one Supreme and Infinite Being,* i.e. *the monotheistic forms, occupy the highest level; and all others are related to them as subordinate forms, from which men are destined to pass to those higher ones.*

1. As such subordinate stages we set down, generally speaking, Idol-worship proper (also called Fetichism) and Polytheism; of which, again, the first stands far lower than the second. The idol-worshipper may quite well have only one idol, but this does not give such Monolatry any resemblance to Monotheism, for it ascribes to the idol an influence only over a limited field of objects or processes, beyond which its own interest and sympathy do not extend. The addition of several idols is merely an accident, usually caused by the experience of some incapacity in the original one, but not aiming at any kind of completeness. Indeed, the main reason why people remain on this level is that the sense of totality has not yet developed . . . Polytheism proper is present only when the local references quite disappear, and the gods, spiritually defined, form an organized and coherent plurality, which, if not exhibited as a totality, is nevertheless presupposed and striven after as such. The more, then, any single one of these Beings is related to the whole system of them, and this system, in turn, to the whole of existence as it appears in consciousness, the more definitely is the dependence of everything finite, not indeed on a Highest One, but on this highest totality, expressed in the religious self-consciousness. But in this state of religious faith there cannot fail to be here and there at least a presentiment of One Supreme Being behind the plurality of higher Beings; and then Polytheism is already beginning to disappear, and the way to Monotheism is open.

On this highest plane, of Monotheism, history exhibits only three great communions – the Jewish, the Christian, and the Mohammedan; the first being almost in process of extinction, the other two still contending for the mastery of the human race. Judaism, by its limitation of the love of Jehovah to the race of Abraham, betrays a lingering affinity with Fetichism; and the numerous vacillations towards idol-worship prove that during the political heyday of the nation the monotheistic faith had not yet taken fast root, and was not fully and purely developed until after the Babylonian Exile. Islam, on the other hand, with its passionate character, and the strongly sensuous content of its ideas, betrays, in spite of its strict Monotheism, a large measure of that influence of the sensible upon the character of the religious emotions which elsewhere keeps men on the level of Polytheism. Thus Christianity, because it remains free from both these weaknesses, stands higher than either of those other two forms, and takes its place as the purest form of Monotheism which has appeared in history.

. . .

§11. *Christianity is a monotheistic faith, belonging to the ideological type of religion, and is essentially distinguished from other such faiths by the fact that in it everything is related to the redemption accomplished by Jesus of Nazareth.*

The only pertinent way of discovering the peculiar essence of any particular faith and reducing it as far as possible to a formula is by showing the element which remains constant throughout the most diverse religious affections within this same communion, while it is absent from analogous affections within other communions . . .

It is indisputable that all Christians trace back to Christ the communion to which they belong. But here we are also presupposing that the term *Redemption* is one to which they all confess: not only that they all *use* the word, with perhaps different meanings, but that there is some common element of meaning which they all have in mind, even if they differ when they come to a more exact description of it. The term itself is in this realm merely figurative, and signifies in general a passage from an evil condition, which is represented as a state of captivity or constraint, into a better condition – this is the passive side of it. But it also signifies the help given in that process by some other person, and this is the active side of it. Further, the usage of the word does not essentially imply that the worse condition must have been preceded by a better condition, so that the better one which followed would really be only a restoration: that point may at the outset be left quite open. But now apply the word to the realm of religion, and suppose we are dealing with the teleological type of religion. Then the evil condition can only consist in an obstruction or arrest of the vitality of the higher self-consciousness, so that there comes to be little or no union of it with the various determinations of the sensible self-consciousness, and thus little or no religious life. We may give to this condition, in its most extreme form, the name of *Godlessness*, or, better, *God-forgetfulness* . . .

. . .

Thus it could not by any means be said that Christian piety is attributable to every man who in all his religious moments is conscious of being in process of redemption even if he stood in no relation to the person of Jesus or even knew nothing of Him – a case which, of course, will never arise. And no more could it be said that a man's religion is Christian if he traces it to Jesus, even supposing that therein he is not at all conscious of being in process of redemption – a case which also, of course, will never arise. The reference to redemption is in every Christian consciousness simply because the originator of the Christian communion is the Redeemer; and Jesus is

Founder of a religious communion simply in the sense that its members become conscious of redemption through Him . . .

The more detailed elaboration of our proposition, as to how the redemption is effected by Christ and comes to consciousness within the Christian communion, falls to the share of the dogmatic system itself . . .

(Taken from F. D. E. Schleiermacher, The Christian Faith, *ed. H. R. Mackintosh and J. S. Stewart, Edinburgh: T&T Clark 1999, §§7, 8, 11.)*

III.3.6 Karl Rahner, from *Theological Investigations*

Rahner attempts to construct a theological account of other religions, under which their followers can be described as 'anonymous Christians'.

1st Thesis: We must begin with the thesis which follows, because it certainly represents the basis in the Christian faith of the theological understanding of other religions. This thesis states that Christianity understands itself as the absolute religion, intended for all men, which cannot recognize any other religion beside itself as of equal right. This proposition is self-evident and basic for Christianity's understanding of itself. There is no need here to prove it or to develop its meaning.

2nd Thesis: Until the moment when the gospel really enters into the historical situation of an individual, a non-Christian religion (even outside the Mosaic religion) does not merely contain elements of a natural knowledge of God, elements, moreover, mixed up with human depravity which is the result of original sin and later aberrations. It contains also supernatural elements arising out of the grace which is given to men as a gratuitous gift on account of Christ. For this reason a non-Christian religion can be recognized as a *lawful* religion (although only in different degrees) without thereby denying the error and depravity contained in it. This thesis requires a more extensive explanation.

The thesis itself is divided into two parts. It means first of all that it is *a priori* quite possible to suppose that there are supernatural, grace-filled elements in non-Christian religions. Let us first of all deal with this statement.

We are here concerned with dogmatic theology and so can merely repeat the universal and unqualified verdict as to the unlawfulness of the non-Christian religions right from the moment when they came into real and historically powerful contact with Christianity (and at first only thus!). It is clear, however, that this condemnation does not mean to deny the very basic differences within the non-Christian religions especially since the pious, God-pleasing pagan was already a theme of the Old Testament, and especially since this God-pleasing pagan cannot simply be thought of as living absolutely outside the concrete socially constituted religion and constructing his own religion on his native foundations – just as St Paul in his speech on the Areopagus did not simply exclude a positive and basic view of the pagan religion. The decisive reason for the first part of our thesis is basically a theological consideration. This consideration (prescinding from certain more precise qualifications) rests ultimately on the fact that, if we wish to be Christians, we must profess belief in the universal and serious salvific purpose of God towards all men which is true even within the post-paradisean phase of salvation dominated by original sin. We know, to be sure, that this

proposition of faith does not say anything certain about the *individual* salvation of man understood as something which has in fact been reached. But
God desires the salvation of everyone. And this salvation willed by God is
the salvation won by Christ, . . .

Our second thesis goes even further than this, however, and states in its
second part that, from what has been said, the actual religions of 'pre-
Christian' humanity too must not be regarded as simply illegitimate from the
very start, but must be seen as quite capable of having a positive significance.

A lawful religion means here an institutional religion whose 'use' by man
at a certain period can be regarded on the whole as a positive means of
gaining the right relationship to God and thus for the attaining of salvation,
a means which is therefore positively included in God's plan of salvation.
That such a notion and the reality to which it refers can exist even where
such a religion shows many theoretical and practical errors in its concrete
form becomes clear in a theological analysis of the structure of the Old
Covenant.

3rd Thesis: If the second thesis is correct, then Christianity does not simply
confront the member of an extra-Christian religion as a mere non-Christian
but as someone who can and must already be regarded in this or that respect
as an anonymous Christian. It would be wrong to regard the pagan as someone who has not yet been touched in any way by God's grace and truth. If,
however, he has experienced the grace of God – if, in certain circumstances,
he has already accepted this grace as the ultimate, unfathomable entelechy
of his existence by accepting the immeasurableness of his dying existence as
opening out into infinity – then he has already been given revelation in a
true sense even before he has been affected by missionary preaching from
without. For this grace, understood as the *a-priori* horizon of all his spiritual
acts, accompanies his consciousness subjectively, even though it is not known
objectively. And the revelation which comes to him from without is not in
such a case the proclamation of something as yet absolutely unknown,
in the sense in which one tells a child here in Bavaria, for the first time in
school, that there is a continent called Australia. Such a revelation is then
the expression in objective concepts of something which this person has
already attained or could already have attained in the depth of his rational
existence.

But if it is true that a person who becomes the object of the Church's
missionary efforts is or may be already someone on the way towards his
salvation, and someone who in certain circumstances finds it, without being
reached by the proclamation of the Church's message – and if it is at the
same time true that this salvation which reaches him in this way is Christ's
salvation, since there is no other salvation – then it must be possible to be
not only an anonymous theist but also an anonymous Christian. And then
it is quite true that in the last analysis, the proclamation of the gospel does
not simply turn someone absolutely abandoned by God and Christ into a

Christian, but turns an anonymous Christian into someone who now also knows about his Christian belief in the depths of his grace-endowed being by objective reflection and in the profession of faith which is given a social form in the Church.

(Taken from Karl Rahner, Theological Investigations V: Later Writings, *trans. Karl H. Kruger, London: Darton, Longman & Todd 1966, pp. 118–32.)*

III.3.7 Langdon Gilkey, from 'Plurality and its Theological Implications'

Gilkey believes we cannot but accept the equal validity of all religious traditions, and attempts to find a plausible account of unacceptable, because unloving, manifestations of religion.

Plurality, as we have seen, drives in the direction of ecumenical tolerance. Plurality, however, has another face than this, a face fully as terrifying as is the relativity just described. For within the plurality of religions that surround us are forms of the religious that are intolerable, and intolerable because they are demonic. Toleration is here checked by the intolerable; and plurality means *both*.

I bring up the Religious Right, however, to illustrate the complexity and ambiguity of plurality, and to point to the dialectical opposition, even the paradoxes and contradictions, that are latent within diversity. For like the cases of Hitler and Khomenei, the Religious Right represents something we cannot tolerate. I do not mean that we cannot tolerate its fundamentalist theology; we can and have to. I refer rather to its stated goal of theocracy, of establishing a 'Christian America': a national community in which Christianity is the preferred religion, 'Christians' are placed in crucial political roles, a certain sort of religious observance permeates the public sphere (that is, in schools and in public places), fundamentalist doctrine dominates the teaching of science, social science, and history – and in which the supremacy of the nation is identified totally with the will and aims of God. As Jerry Falwell has said: 'It is high time that Christians take back the power to run their own country. . . . The constitution in the hands of Christians is a holy document; in the hands of non-Christians it can be used by the devil to defeat us.' Here religion takes over and uses the public sphere; here religion – and the absolutist politics it spawns – manifests an intolerable face, as the secular religion of Nazism did. Against such religion – traditional or secular – resistance is imperative.

Now the point is that in order to resist – and we must, paradoxically on ecumenical grounds, if for no other reasons – we must ourselves stand somewhere. That is, we must assert some sort of ultimate values – in the face of heaven knows what social, intellectual, moral, and religious pressures – in this case the values of persons and of their rights, and correspondingly, the value of the free, just, and equal community so deeply threatened by this theocratic tyranny. And to assert our ultimate value or values is to assert a 'world,' a view of all of reality. For each affirmed political, moral, or religious value presupposes a certain understanding of humankind, society, and history, and so a certain understanding of the whole in which they exist. Our view of existence as a whole gives locus in reality to the values we defend.

Consequently any practical political action, in resistance to tyranny or in liberation from it, presupposes ultimate values and an ultimate vision of things, an ethic and so a theology. And it presupposes an absolute commitment to this understanding of things. This union of resistance, commitment, and 'world' was made crystal clear by the Barmen confession: to confess our adherence to one Lord is at once to resist the Nazi claim on our allegiance; conversely to resist Nazi ideology, allegiance alone to one Lord and to one Word was required. The necessity of action, liberating action, calls first for the relinquishment of all relativity and secondly for the assertion of some alternative absolute standpoint. Paradoxically, plurality, precisely by its own ambiguity, implies both relativity and absoluteness, a juxtaposition or synthesis of the relative and the absolute that is frustrating intellectually and yet necessary practically.

IV

We have seen the theoretical dilemma that plurality has forced upon us. On the one hand, the inescapable drive toward ecumenical community, toward respect for and recognition of the other as other, and of the religious validity and power he or she embodies, has pushed us toward a relativity that seems to defy intellectual resolution. There seems no consistent theological way to relativize and yet to assert our own symbols – and yet we must do both in dialogue. On the other hand, the shadow side of religious plurality frequently forces us to resist, to stand somewhere, and also to hold some alternative religious position with absolute fidelity, courage, and perseverance. How are we to understand and resolve this contradiction or puzzle dealt us by plurality?
. . .

Perhaps the secret here is like the secret of existence itself – that is, existing with inner strength and outer liberating power: to hold on with infinite passion to both ends of the dialectic of relativity and absoluteness. Perhaps if one keeps these poles together in a synthesis, such a posture for theological reflection may seem possible, as it is already acknowledged to be possible in political action and in dialogue. If such a relativized theology seems, as it certainly will to its cultural critics, a foolish and illogical impossibility, then let them remember that they will face tomorrow the same baffling dialectic as Western consciousness appropriates to itself its own destined travail of relativity. Meanwhile, let us not forget that the present flood of relativity is balanced by the stern demands for liberating praxis and for creative theory.

(Taken from Langdon Gilkey, 'Plurality and its Theological Implications', in John Hick and Paul F. Knitter (eds), The Myth of Christian Uniqueness, *London: SCM Press 1987, pp. 37–50.)*

III.3.8 Lesslie Newbigin, from *The Gospel in a Pluralist Society*

Newbigin attempts to give a theological account of other religious traditions that takes seriously the sole lordship of Jesus Christ.

If, as I have affirmed, we are to reject religious pluralism and acknowledge Jesus Christ as the unique and decisive revelation of God for the salvation of the world, what is the proper attitude which believers in that revelation ought to take toward the adherents of the great world religions?

We must look first at the strictly exclusivist view which holds that all who do not accept Jesus as Lord and Savior are eternally lost. We shall look later at the question whether this is in fact what fidelity to Scripture requires us to hold. There are several reasons which make it difficult for me to believe this. If it were true, then it would be not only permissible but obligatory to use any means available, all the modern techniques of brainwashing included, to rescue others from this appalling fate. And since it is God alone who knows the heart of every person, how are we to judge whether or not another person truly has that faith which is acceptable to him? If we hold this view, it is absolutely necessary to know who is saved and who is not, and we are then led into making the kind of judgments against which Scripture warns us. We are in the business of erecting barriers: Has she been baptized? Has he been confirmed by a bishop in the historic succession? Or has she had a recognizable conversion and can she name the day and the hour when it happened? We are bound to become judges of that which God alone knows. Moreover, every missionary knows that it is impossible to communicate the gospel without acknowledging in practice that there is some continuity between the gospel and the experience of the hearer outside the Christian Church. One cannot preach the gospel without using the word 'God.' If one is talking to a person of a non-Christian religion, one is bound to use one of the words in her language which is used to denote God. But the content of that word has necessarily been formed by his experience outside the Church. By using the word, the preacher is taking the non-Christian experience of the hearer as the starting point. Without this there is no way of communicating. This fact by itself does not refute the position we are considering, but it makes it impossible to affirm a total discontinuity between Christian faith and the religions. And anyone who has had intimate friendship with a devout Hindu or Muslim would find it impossible to believe that the experience of God of which his friend speaks is simply illusion or fraud.

I believe that we must begin with the great reality made known to us in Jesus Christ, that God – the creator and sustainer of all that exists – is in his own triune being an ocean of infinite love overflowing to all his works in all creation and to all human beings. I believe that when we see Jesus eagerly welcoming the signs of faith among men and women outside the house of Israel; when we see him lovingly welcoming those whom others cast out; when we see him on the cross with arms outstretched to embrace the whole world and when we hear his whispered words, 'Father, forgive them; they know not what they do'; we are seeing the most fundamental of all realities, namely a grace and mercy and loving-kindness which reaches out to every creature. I believe that no person, of whatever kind or creed, is without some witness of God's grace in heart and conscience and reason, and none in whom that grace does not evoke some response – however feeble, fitful, and flawed.

The same revelation in Jesus Christ, with its burning center in the agony and death of Calvary, compels me to acknowledge that this world which God made and loves is in a state of alienation, rejection, and rebellion against him. Calvary is the central unveiling of the infinite love of God and at the same time the unmasking of the dark horror of sin. Here not the dregs of humanity, not the scoundrels whom all good people condemn, but the revered leaders in church, state, and culture, combine in one murderous intent to destroy the holy one by whose mercy they exist and were created.

If we are to avoid these two dangers, if we are to live faithfully in this spiritual magnetic field between the amazing grace of God and the appalling sin of the world, how are we to regard the other commitments, faiths, worldviews to which the people around us and with whom we live and move adhere? I believe that the debate about this question has been fatally flawed by the fact that it has been conducted around the question, 'Who can be saved?' It has been taken for granted that the only question was, 'Can the good non-Christian be saved?' and by that question what was meant was not, 'Can the non-Christian live a good and useful life and play a good and useful role in the life of society?' The question was, 'Where will she go when she dies?' I am putting this crudely because I want to make the issue as clear as possible. The quest for truth always requires that we ask the right questions. If we ask the wrong questions we shall get only silence or confusion. In the debate about Christianity and the world's religions it is fair to say that there has been an almost unquestioned assumption that the only question is, 'What happens to the non-Christian after death?' I want to affirm that this is the wrong question and that as long as it remains the central question we shall never come to the truth. And this for three reasons:

a. First, and simply, it is the wrong question because it is a question to which God alone has the right to give the answer. I confess that I am astounded at the arrogance of theologians who seem to think that we are authorized, in our capacity as Christians, to inform the rest of the world about who is to be vindicated and who is to be condemned at the last judgment.

I find this way of thinking among Christians astonishing in view of the emphatic warnings of Jesus against these kinds of judgments which claim to preempt the final judgment of God. Nothing could be more remote from the whole thrust of Jesus' teaching than the idea that we are in a position to know in advance the final judgment of God.

b. The second reason for rejecting this way of putting the question is that it is based on an abstraction. By concentrating on the fate of the individual soul after death, it abstracts the soul from the full reality of the human person as an actor and sufferer in the ongoing history of the world. Being saved has to do with the part we are playing now in God's story and therefore with the question whether we have understood the story rightly. It follows that our dialogue with people of other faiths must be about what is happening in the world now and about how we understand it and take our part in it. It cannot be only, or even mainly, about our destiny as individual souls after death. Insofar as the debate has concentrated on this latter question, it has been flawed.

c. The third reason for rejecting this way of putting the question is the most fundamental: it is that the question starts with the individual and his or her need to be assured of ultimate happiness, and not with God and his glory. All human beings have a longing for ultimate happiness, and the many worldviews, religious or otherwise, have as part of their power some promise of satisfying that longing. We must believe that this longing is something implanted in us by God. He has so made us that we have infinite desires beyond the satisfaction of our biological necessities, desires which only God himself can satisfy. Our hearts are restless till they find rest in him. On our journey he gives us good things which whet our appetite but do not finally satisfy, for they are always corrupted by the selfishness that desires to have them as our own possession. The gospel, the story of the astonishing act of God himself in coming down to be part of our alienated world, to endure the full horror of our rebellion against love, to take the whole burden of our guilt and shame, and to lift us up into communion and fellowship with himself, breaks into this self-centered search for our own happiness, shifts the center from the self and its desires to God and his glory. For anyone who has understood what God did for us all in Jesus Christ, the one question is: 'How shall God be glorified? How shall his amazing grace be known and celebrated and adored? How shall he see of the travail of his soul and be satisfied?'

What are the practical consequences of taking this as the starting point in our relation to people of other faiths? I suggest four immediate implications.

1. The first is this: we shall expect, look for, and welcome all the signs of the grace of God at work in the lives of those who do not know Jesus as Lord. In this, of course, we shall be following the example of Jesus, who was so eager to welcome the evidences of faith in those outside the household of Israel.

2. The second consequence of the approach I suggest is that the Christian will be eager to cooperate with people of all faiths and ideologies in all

projects which are in line with the Christian's understanding of God's purpose in history.

The human story is one which we share with all other human beings – past, present, and to come. We cannot opt out of the story. We cannot take control of the story. It is under the control of the infinitely patient God and Father of our Lord Jesus Christ. Every day of our lives we have to make decisions about the part we will play in the story, decisions which we cannot take without regard to the others who share the story. They may be Christians, Muslims, Hindus, secular humanists, Marxists, or of some other persuasion. They will have different understandings of the meaning and end of the story, but along the way there will be many issues in which we can agree about what should be done. There are struggles for justice and for freedom in which we can and should join hands with those of other faiths and ideologies to achieve specific goals, even though we know that the ultimate goal is Christ and his coming in glory and not what our collaborators imagine.

3. Third, it is precisely in this kind of shared commitment to the business of the world that the context for true dialogue is provided. As we work together with people of other commitments, we shall discover the places where our ways must separate. Here is where real dialogue may begin. It is a real dialogue about real issues. It is not just a sharing of religious experience, though it may include this. At heart it will be a dialogue about the meaning and goal of the human story.

4. Therefore, the essential contribution of the Christian to the dialogue will simply be the telling of the story, the story of Jesus, the story of the Bible. The story is itself, as Paul says, the power of God for salvation. The Christian must tell it, not because she lacks respect for the many excellencies of her companions – many of whom may be better, more godly, more worthy of respect than she is. She tells it simply as one who has been chosen and called by God to be part of the company which is entrusted with the story. It is not her business to convert the others. She will indeed – out of love for them – long that they may come to share the joy that she knows and pray that they may indeed do so. But it is only the Holy Spirit of God who can so touch the hearts and consciences of the others that they are brought to accept the story as true and to put their trust in Jesus. This will always be a mysterious work of the Spirit, often in ways which no third party will ever understand. The Christian will pray that it may be so, and she will seek faithfully both to tell the story and – as part of a Christian congregation – so conduct her life as to embody the truth of the story. But she will not imagine that it is her responsibility to insure that the other is persuaded. That is in God's hands.

(Taken from Lesslie Newbigin, The Gospel in a Pluralist Society, *Grand Rapids, Eerdmans 1989, pp. 171–83.)*

III.3.9 Gavin D'Costa, from 'The Impossibility of a Pluralist View of Religions'

D'Costa argues that genuine pluralism, i.e. the idea that all religious positions are equally valid, is intellectually incoherent.

I am increasingly convinced that the logical impossibility of a pluralist view of religions means that the typology of exclusivism, inclusivism and pluralism as three approaches or paradigms regarding Christianity's view of other religions is untenable. First, I will briefly sketch the genesis of these paradigms.

In 1983 Alan Race coined the threefold typology in his book *Christians and Religious Pluralism*. In 1986 I, amongst others, followed suit and since then the three-fold typology is found in many works dealing with Christian theology and religious pluralism. While these definitions have been employed for examining various Christian attitudes to other religions, they have also been used as logical types to analyse other religions' attitudes to religious pluralism. This indicates that while the typology was developed to analyse Christian attitudes to other religions, it could equally be applied to any Hindu views of Christianity and so on. Hence, my concerns lie with the logical form of the typology. The demarcations between the three positions of exclusivism, pluralism and inclusivism are as follows. On the one extreme of the spectrum there is exclusivism. This type is defined as holding that only one single revelation is true or one single religion is true and all other 'revelations' or 'religions' are false. Here truth, revelation and salvation are tightly and explicitly connected. It will, in its most strict logical form, mean that for example, all those who are not Southern Baptists will be lost to the fires of hell. In various softer versions, it will allow for possibilities such as a post-mortem confrontation with Christ which gives everyone the chance to choose for or against the truth so as to allow to all the possibility of salvation. Or, in Buddhist and Hindu versions, a person in a future life will have the opportunity to come to liberation. Such softer versions still keep the basic exclusivist insight intact: that fundamentally only one single revelation or one single religion is true and all other 'revelations' or religions are false.

On the opposite side of the spectrum of opinions is pluralism. This type is defined as holding that all the major religions have true revelations in part while no single revelation or religion can claim final and definitive truth. Here again truth, revelation and salvation are closely connected. This means that all religions are viewed as more or less equally true and more or less equally valid paths to salvation. The advantage of this position, argue its supporters, is that it renders genuine respect and autonomy to the various different religions. There are no adherents to this position that I know of who imply uncritical endorsement of every phenomenon that might present itself as religious; Jim Jones and his (ex) followers or the more recent Waco incident being cases in point. Pluralists usually criticize exclusivists of their own traditions on two major grounds; that they cannot deny the evidence of good, holy and loving people in other religions; and that exclusivists have incorrect readings of their own sacred texts which misguidedly lead them to exclusivism. The order in which these criticisms are developed is sometimes reversible.

In the middle of the spectrum are those called inclusivists who, as often the case with those in the middle, try and have it both ways. They are committed to claiming that one revelation or religion (sometimes in a specific denomi national form) is the only one true and definitive one, but that truth and therefore salvation can be found in various fragmentary and incomplete forms within other religions and their different claims. It is always the case that such different and sometimes rival claims are judged by the criteria arising from the one true revelation or religion, so that alternative religions and revelations can only be deemed truthful in so much as they do not contradict the normative revelation or religion and in fact must conform to it. The usual implication of this position is that Christianity is regarded as the fulfilment of other religions. Or, if we take a particular form of Hinduism, that Advaita Vedanta is considered the fulfilment of all other religions.

There are important variations within all these types but as I have noted the typology is still employed in much of the discussion in this field. In what follows I want to argue that *pluralism must always logically be a form of exclusivism and that nothing called pluralism really exists.*

Here then are the steps of my argument that will be tested out against two representative pluralists. I want to suggest that there is no such thing as pluralism because all pluralists are committed to holding some form of truth criteria and by virtue of this, anything that falls foul of such criteria is excluded from counting as truth (in doctrine and in practice). Thus, pluralism operates within the same logical structure of exclusivism and in this respect pluralism can never really affirm the genuine autonomous value of religious pluralism for, like exclusivism, it can only do so by tradition specific criteria for truth. If any pluralist were to claim that they did not operate with any such exclusive criteria, they would be unable to distinguish between any two claims to revelation or truth such as that between the claims of the Confessing Church and those of the German Christians following Hitler. Such a pluralism would therefore be entirely unable to distinguish between true and false claims to revelation. It is very difficult to find a pluralist who would go to this extreme, so I shall not consider such a position. Hence, in the use of truth criteria, the pluralist by virtue of the act of exclusion of Jim Jones or the Nazis, can thereby include various other doctrines and practices in so much as they do not contradict their own basic truth claims and in this act of inclusion and exclusion such pluralists are logically no different from exclusivists who simply argue that those who properly relate to the true revelation are included in salvation and those who do not are excluded. In noticing this logical shape, our attention is drawn to the more interesting question as to what precisely are these criteria, how are they justified, and in what fashion do they work? Hence, the real differences between those called pluralists, inclusivists and exclusivists are not, for example, that salvation may be attained by one who is a Muslim in this life (on this they may all agree), or that certain forms of loving one's neighbour are to be valued (on this too they may all agree), but rather they disagree in what counts as normative truth and how it operates:

(Taken from Gavin D'Costa. 'The Impossibility of a Pluralist View of Religions'
Religious Studies *32*, *1996*, pp. *223–32*.)

PART IV

Doing Theology in the University Today

I Does it have a place?

The modern university is a distant descendant of institutions founded towards the end of the Middle Ages to train men to run the church and state. From being a largely clerical institution, it has become secularized, so much so that theology is sometimes made to feel uncomfortable in the place which it once founded. Very different views are held about this. On one extreme is the rather fundamentalist scientist, Richard Dawkins, who thinks that the subject should simply be expelled, while others more moderately wonder whether a system of belief which is widely held to be irrational has a place in an institution dedicated to the pursuit of reason. As we shall see later in this piece, such an assumption begs the question of what counts as rational, and we shall soon explore this at length. Behind it lies the fashionable modern belief, now in retreat, that religious belief is the cause of human division and even war between nations. It is true that religion causes conflict, but so do many other human activities and beliefs, for example economics. The call for its abolition is rarely heard – even though economists are as remarkable for their inability to agree with one another as any other group of academics.

But that is precisely the point we need to realize, for from its very beginning the university has been dedicated to two ends, side by side, with different of them predominating at different times. The first is intellectual: the seeking of truth by disagreement and discussion. A central medieval practice was the *disputatio*, in which a professor would post on the equivalent of the notice board a challenge to a debate, and colleagues would come to join it. The most famous of these challenges was Luther's famous *Ninety-Five Theses*, in which he challenged colleagues to debate what he took to be the scandal of the sale of indulgences, documents claimed to free people from punishment for sin. Today a similar method of enquiry prevails, with public lectures followed by discussion still being at the heart of the life of a modern university.

The second purpose of the modern university, which is being increasingly stressed by modern governments, is practical, and it is the need to train personnel for the complex social and economic structures of the modern world. Of this it must be said that if the aim of education is merely practical, that is a subversion of the way by which universities have at their best performed their functions. History suggests that truth is less likely to emerge when only practical usefulness or profit is sought. Many of the technological advances of recent decades have been the by-products of a quest to discover the ways things in fact are. Until very recently, university education has been directed to the training of minds by way of an enquiry into, for example, the structure of the atom or the credibility of the proofs for the existence of God. Underlying these practices is the notion that students are best prepared for life by being inducted into traditions of scholarship and thought, and it is this approach which has created the distinctive character of universities in the Western world. They have been creators of civilization before – though by no means to the exclusion of – being generators of wealth.

In that respect, we might say that theology has formed a model, because it is often understood as both a theoretical and a practical discipline, the theoretical aspects centring on an enquiry into the meaning and truth of the Christian faith, and so of the world in which we live, the practical on the training of people for ordination in the church or assisting them to find meaning in their lives. Today, relatively fewer students than was the case even a quarter of a century ago will be studying theology as a way into the ordained ministry, a development which has good and bad effects. Certainly, there can be little question that an educated laity strengthens the life of the church, even though it can sometimes be threatening for the clergy. But the loss of orientation to the believing community has not always been to theology's health. Another recent and considerable change is that many students will be studying theology from a position of other than convinced belief, either because they want to see what Christianity teaches, or to learn about its history and sociology, or because they are seeking a religious vision of some kind. Entry to university departments of theology is now open to all who are judged intellectually capable of pursuing the studies, and there are no doctrinal tests.

But that leads us to another question about the respectability of theology in this company. Does not theology rest upon some kind of outside authority, whereas other disciplines are dedicated to absolutely open and free enquiry? (On the other side, some critics have suggested the very opposite, that because modern university theologians under-mine the faith by their critical attitudes they have betrayed their calling – so that at times the same negative assessment of the subject is drawn from opposite starting-points, scarcely a convincing case for abolition.) And do not theologians represent the church, which cannot be trusted not to interfere in free enquiry? (These days, as a matter of fact, some theologians do and some do not represent the church, though few of them are part of the leadership of the church and are more likely simply to be involved in different levels of its life.) Before we turn to our main subject-matter, which is the nature of theology as an intellectual discipline, something must be said about the apparent problem of the restriction on free enquiry which apparently afflicts this subject but not others.

The chief point to be made is that a glance at the spectrum of university subjects will show that there is no such thing as free enquiry in an absolute sense. In many ways, theologians are freer than, for example, scientists to write books which upset the ways things have been done in the subject. In all disciplines there are traditions, some-times quite rigid traditions, about what is and is not acceptable. All academic journals, whether scientific or theological, have editors who act as censors of what is worth publishing, and so often prevent the publication of articles which threaten to upset established ways of thought and experiment. In theology the wide range of journals and publishers representing different approaches to the subject, whether it be traditional Catholic or feminist theology, shows that for all the differences this subject is not very different from others when it comes to patterns of authority and openness.

In one respect, recent social and intellectual changes have made things apparently rather more comfortable. It is now far less easy to claim that there is only one way to the truth and that disciplines which fail to conform to some reigning pattern are to be excluded. Some scientists and apologists for science do still claim that nothing that fails to conform to a particular understanding of scientific method is acceptable in the modern forum, but that is made implausible by the facts. It is widely recognized that even in science there is a wide variety of methods and approaches, and there is even sometimes room for suspicion that scientists are hired to promote the interests of certain commercial or technological interests. Moreover, the evidence demon-strates that scientists can be as mistaken as the rest of us. All of these considerations go to show that a good university flourishes on diversity and debate, and it is only the curmudgeon who would deny theology its place in the conversation of the disciplines. But suppose that rational discussion and debate are the heart of the matter. We still have to ask what place reason plays in theology, how it is related to faith or conviction, and in what kind of intellectual enterprise it involves its exponents. That takes us a long way back into history, for like many disciplines, philosophy especially included, theology has a history that needs to be reviewed if we are to understand what is being done in the present.

II Theology as an intellectual discipline

From the very beginning, theology was a hybrid discipline, the result of the coming together of two rather different worlds. The first is the world of Israel and her Scriptures. Scripture is not a form of enquiry so much as a response to divine speech and action. What we call the Old Testament charts Israel's history as it is understood not simply as a series of human events, but as a story of a people whose life is oriented to God, the creator, ruler and redeemer of all. There are arguments in it, but they are often not arguments as we might understand them, and they are in any case eclipsed by other forms of writing: among them authoritative accounts of the creation, narratives of divine deliverance and judgment, songs of lament and praise, prophecies and laws. They stand in a critical relation to the myths by which surrounding cultures understood themselves, often rejecting them in the name of a more austere and transcendent vision of things. They often simply assert divine revelation against the gods and myths of the pagan nations surrounding them, rather than bothering to criticize them.

The New Testament builds upon this, and many of the forms of literature to be found there have a strong relationship to what its writers called the Scriptures, and what we their successors call the Old Testament. But there are also differences, because their interest is not now focused on hundreds of years of history, but on the life and fate of one man. No attempt is made to demonstrate the truth of the gospel which flows from the impact of this somewhat briefer history. It is proclaimed as gospel, literally good news, but news consisting in the recounting of the way God has acted in Jesus. There is, also, much argument, but argument of a particular kind, argument seeking to convince readers about the meaning of the story of divine action or disputing a point of interpretation or ethics. The New Testament is emphatic that it is making a claim for the truth of what it tells, and it is essentially a truth with a strongly practical bearing. There flows from it a particular form of life – or perhaps more accurately, forms of life, for there is no homogeneity – which is a life in a new community, gathered around Israel's God, but increasingly separate from those Jewish people who did not become Christians. Yet the truth, stated in words, is important for the writers. Doctrine or teaching is important from the very beginning, as is clear from the account in the Acts of the Apostles of the life of the church after the giving of the Spirit at Pentecost (see especially Acts 2.42). But, and this is also important, it is a teaching that they are given, not one that they discover, and that has a strong bearing on what the discipline of theology came to be. The first churches were what one theologian has called 'convictional communities', communities that shaped their life around certain convictions about God and Jesus in particular. Christianity is a faith based upon particular events and particular people.

The second world within which the hybrid discipline called theology took form is that of the Greeks, and particularly their philosophy. Here there is a complication which must be mentioned, for the New Testament especially, but also aspects of the Old, were not untouched by the world about them. There are traces of Greek philosophical teaching in Christian moral teaching, and in the Wisdom literature of the Old Testament. Yet for all that they remain deeply divided worlds. There are two chief differences, and they emerge in the difference in attitude to the ancient myths. Whereas the Hebrews rejected the myths, leaving them as merely bare traces in the language of their Scriptures, the Greeks turned them into philosophy. That is to say, while the Hebrews rejected the ways in which other ancient peoples understood themselves, the Greeks sought to find the rational truths underlying the myths. This difference of approach derives from the fact that the Greeks were for the most part more confident in discovering for themselves the truth of things; and this is because they conceive the human being rather differently. (That is the root of the modern suspicion that theology is not a truly rational discipline.)

The ancient myths were a form of theology in the sense of being ways in which their exponents used them to express an understanding of the human relation to the divine. Yet this does not mean that the theologians rejected the quest for rational understanding and expression. They rather sought and found a new form of intellectual enquiry that was based in and sought to be true to the acts of God to which Scripture bears witness. The outcome is that theology has a great intellectual history because it has in different ways at different times accepted the challenge to think its faith. It was once famously said that the early church outlived, outprayed and outthought the ancient world in which it was set. At its best, theology seeks to do the same with the modern world, not so much to defeat it as to provide a witness to a different conception of truth and life than that which comes naturally to human beings.

It remains the case, however, that early Christian theology had an ambiguous relation to the Greek tradition, and we shall now explore something both of its early history and of what happened to it during later centuries. This will help us to understand some of the complexities of the relation in our time, also, and throw light on the odd situation of a discipline which belongs in a community of belief and yet seeks to be a proper though also properly independent part of the modern university enterprise. And the chief ambiguity is this. On the one hand, some early theologians wished to appeal to the universal human sense of divinity and of the meaning of the creation. In that way, it drew upon aspects of the Greek understanding of reason. This was the attitude taken by the Apologists in the second century – Justin Martyr, for example – and their successors ever since. (It must also be noted that they also argued that the philosophers were incomplete without the gospel. Indeed, they attacked them for inconsistency, arguing that Christianity produced a more true and coherent view of the world than did the platonists and the other Greek schools.)

On the other hand, however, theologians like Tertullian stressed the differences between reason and faith. 'What has Athens to do with Jerusalem?' and 'I believe because it is absurd' are two of the utterances for which he is famed. In that respect, he drew upon aspects of the tradition, stemming from Paul the Apostle, that God saves not by worldly wisdom, but by the absurdity of a crucified saviour (1 Corinthians 1.18–25). Tertullian is the father of those who stress faith *against* reason, at least when reason is understood as the Greeks understood it, although he was, it must be remembered, himself a powerful user of argument, and therefore one who by no means evaded the intellectual task of theology.

His day, however, had not yet come, for the era from Augustine (354–430) to the end of the Middle Ages was a time in which strenuous efforts were made to bring faith and reason into some kind of harmony. The advice of Boethius (c.480–524) as far as possible to combine faith and reason eventually led to what came to be called the medieval synthesis, the era in which philosophy and theology were for the most part treated as parallel and complementary disciplines. Different emphases came to the fore at different times and in different thinkers, but the two chief directions were set in train by Augustine. On the one hand, he was concerned to integrate Christian thought with the Greek (neoplatonist) philosophy which had been for him a stepping stone towards the Christian faith. Yet, on the other, reason was for him to operate within the sphere of faith. He held that 'Unless you believe you will not understand.'

This is important, because it stressed one side of Christian faith that had never been completely absent even in thinkers like Tertullian, and that is the belief that Christian faith is not irrational, but encourages rational thought. One striking feature of the history of Christianity is its production of a long tradition of deeply intellectual thinkers, among whom are included those, like Tertullian and those influenced by him – Luther and Kierkegaard, for example – who have been sceptical about the use of reason as an *independent* faculty. Few Christian thinkers have ever rejected reason in its entirety. What many of them have rejected is reason that operates independently of faith and contaminates faith by imposing upon it ideas which are foreign to it.

The best medieval representative of the second of the two sides of Augustine's thought is Anselm of Canterbury (1033–1109). His most influential work in this respect is what has misleadingly come to be called the ontological argument. It is a proof of the existence of God taken from the idea or 'name' of God. Despite what it became in later eras, this was not for Anselm a piece of pure or independent reason, but of reason operating within the sphere of faith. One title he considered for the work containing this argument was 'Faith seeking understanding', and he himself understands his argument to be a process in which he seeks to understand what he already accepts on faith. In the preface to this work he said that he does not seek to understand in order to believe, but believes in order to understand. Once again, we encounter a theologian whose faith does not avoid but inspires rational thought.

The chief example of the other approach suggested by Augustine – of a determined attempt to understand reason and faith as two parallel faculties – is that of Thomas Aquinas (c.1225–74), who has become the official theologian of the Roman Catholic Church. In distinction from Anselm, he drew more upon Aristotle than Plato, and explicitly contradicts Anselm's view that reason operates within the sphere of faith. For him reason prepares the ground for faith, and it is in this connection that he develops his famous 'Five Ways', or five proofs using the categories of Aristotelian causality, for the existence of God.

These should not be understood as proofs in the modern sense, as primarily concerned to convince unbelievers, of whom there were few in his time. Rather, he was concerned to show that faith had a rational basis in a view of the world that all share – and by all he meant all in the world he knew, whether Jewish, Muslim or Christian. It is important, however, to realize that for him reason was not the sheerly independent faculty it sought to be in some later thinkers. It is only relatively independent, for the whole of Aquinas' thought operates within a broadly religious vision. It is a vision within which reason and faith have their distinct and parallel roles to play.

The conception of reason of the first of the great Reformers, Martin Luther (1483–1546), represented something of a return to the tradition of Tertullian, but, again, has to be understood in its historical context. It was largely determined by his hostility to the dominance of Aristotelian categories in late medieval theology (a hostility which was shared, interestingly, by many of the early modern scientists). Here he was influenced by Nominalist philosophers in the tradition of William of Ockham (c.1285–1347). Ockhamists held that our general concepts – like the platonic forms – did not exist outside the mind, and that therefore general philosophical arguments could not serve as a basis for arguments for the existence of God. God could be known only by faith on the basis of authoritative revelation. But Luther was not an Ockhamist in every respect, for he had additional concerns. Negatively, he objected to a use of reason that appeared to allow or even encourage Christians to merit their own salvation by good works, rather than relying on the free grace of God. Positively, he wanted to encourage a conception of faith as free personal trust in God rather than as consisting in the acceptance of authoritative church teaching. This he believed to be impeded by reliance on a philosophy whose source was external to the faith.

A similar concern marks Calvin's (1509–64) works, though he has other things to say as well. He believed that there was a sense of divinity in everyone, and that the created order everywhere revealed the hand of the Creator. But human sin and blindness, witnessed by our capacity when left to ourselves to create idols and false gods, showed that without Scripture we are unable to bring to understanding what is in front of our eyes. Thus while he appears to take a different position from Luther's, and spent more effort than he did in writing a comprehensive introduction to the Christian faith, their views of the limits of unaided human reason are similar. The one source of our knowledge of God is the Holy Spirit, so that any philosophical source that displaces that is to be rejected. The work of a faithful and obedient Christian theology can take place only in that light.

In that regard, many prominent thinkers in the period that followed the Reformation departed a long way from its insights. Far from accepting the strict limits on reason employed by the Reformers, some of the most influential names in the history of modern thought elevated independent reason to the highest place it had had since the days of the Greeks, often in explicit opposition to Christian teaching. It was a mark of the 'Age of Reason' or Enlightenment that followed the Reformation that it was imbued with a strong confidence in innate human powers, reason among them. The more radical of the thinkers of the next two centuries believed that specific items of Christian faith – the doctrines of the Trinity and of the person and work of Christ, the church and the sacraments – were irrelevant and had to be replaced by a religion of reason that any rational person would discover independently of revelation. These were the deists, whose God is often known as the clockmaker deity, the one who set the universe running and then left it to its own devices. Some Enlightenment thinkers followed this road into a full atheism and demanded a reliance on human reason without any appeal to God. Here faith was effectively replaced by reason; or rather faith came to be placed in reason as the supreme source of human enlightenment.

All Christian thinkers since that time have had to come to grips with the challenge of modern rationalism. Notable among the Enlightenment thinkers who faced the challenge were Locke, Berkeley and Kant. John Locke (1632–1704) belongs somewhere in the tradition of Aquinas, though he developed far in the direction of deism. He believed that reason was sufficient to establish the existence of God, and produced a modernized version of Aquinas' cosmological argument. This had to be supplemented, he argued, by what God provided by miraculous means, especially in connection with Jesus Christ. But this was a narrowing of the Christian content that exacted a heavy penalty. The resultant fashion to defend Christianity by appeal to miracle – the clockmaker intervening to repair the clock – received a savage critique by the Scottish sceptic David Hume (1711–76), who argued that miracles simply could not be established. His critique alongside this of all the traditional arguments for the existence of God has appeared to many since to leave the Christian faith without rational support, and it is this which underlies the scepticism we have met about theology's place in the modern university.

The Irish philosopher Bishop George Berkeley (1685–1753)

attempted to stem the tide of deism in a different way, by a reasoned argument that all of our experience of the world requires explanation in terms of the ceaseless operation of a Creator God. Our experience in perceiving our world is witness to a kind of divine language which God speaks. Berkeley was rarely taken seriously, largely because he was so out of tune with the times, and the crucial word at the end of the Enlightenment was spoken by Immanuel Kant (1724–1804). While Kant sat light to traditional Christianity, his contributions to the debate about faith and reason have been of immense influence. He believed, on the one hand, that reason, though all-powerful in matters to do with this world (science and ethics), was unable to penetrate beyond this world to divine or eternal realities. There could therefore be no argument for the existence of God nor any appeal to historic revelation. Yet his rejection of reason was, he claimed, meant to clear the way for faith, so that, on the other hand, he believed that our moral experience pointed indirectly to God, though not a God who could be truly known. Kant ended up with an odd and finally very sceptical position: religion is a kind of necessity, but gives us nothing that can be called knowledge. In effect, he excluded reason from theology, and turned faith into little more than the handmaid of ethics. Religion was good behaviour with a godly tinge.

To many an observer at the end of the eighteenth century, it appeared that religion was finished. Yet the nineteenth century witnessed a number of brilliant attempts to respond to the challenge represented by Kant. The first was that of F. D. E. Schleiermacher (1768–1834), who argued that feeling – what he called a sense of absolute dependence – not reason, was central not only to religion but to human life as a whole. Drawing on Romanticism's challenge to rationalism, he argued that if human beings did not realize their essential religiousness, they ignored the very heart of what made them human. Building on this, he argued that theology was indeed a rational pursuit, but only as the rational expression of an experience that was fundamentally above reason or 'suprarational'. Reason is to be employed in speaking about what is finally indescribable. Schleiermacher is thus both like and unlike Anselm. He is like him in holding to a kind of faith seeking understanding, yet unlike him in that he does not share Anselm's confidence that religious faith is rational. The chief reason for the difference is that he shared Kant's scepticism about reason in religion, and so tried to find an alternative non-rational focus for it. Schleiermacher remains deeply influential on modern theology.

Against Schleiermacher, about whom he was contemptuous because he thought he was evading the challenge of reason, the second great nineteenth-century thinker, G. W. F. Hegel (1770–1831), attempted to re-establish the complete rationality of the Christian religion. 'I think, therefore I am religious' has been said to be Hegel's slogan, for he believed that all human thought was ultimately God *thinking himself through our thought*. In this way Hegel attempted to combine revelation and reason, arguing that God revealed himself through the processes of reason. Christianity is, according to him, the absolute religion because it is the revealed religion, that is, the religion revealed by reason in and to its deepest depths. Human thought, according to Hegel, took an essentially Christian and trinitarian shape, and his final position, to put it rather crudely, was that the doctrine of the incarnation of God in Christ has to be understood in terms of the realization of the divine in all human thought and culture.

The thought of a third nineteenth-century figure, Søren Kierkegaard (1813–55), is best understood as being in direct opposition to Hegel's. He argued that Hegel's position rationalized away the offence of Christianity by too neatly bringing eternity and time together. Far from being established by reason, real faith was completely abolished by Hegel. Against this, Kierkegaard held, faith is completely resistant to reduction to rational form. Because faith brings together time and eternity, and because time and eternity are opposites, any attempt to think about Christian truth involves paradox or apparent contradiction. For this reason Kierkegaard asserted a position rather like Tertullian's, and argued that Christian faith is resistant to rationalizing. Yet it does not follow that he wishes to be irrational, rather to develop a rational position which does justice to what the Christian faith is. What is objectively paradoxical – the presence of God in Jesus Christ – has to be adopted not by argument, but by the commitment of faith which is passionate and involved, not primarily rational and objective. Once that is accepted, however, Christianity's intrinsic logical shape can be laid out and understood to the limited degree its content allows. From within, faith does make sense although it cannot be fully compassed within our rational categories.

The most influential theologian of the twentieth century, Karl Barth (1886–1968), began the work that made him famous with a Kierkegaard-like protest against most of his nineteenth-century predecessors. He argued that they had domesticated Christianity by reducing it to the rational categories of the time. In his *Epistle to the Romans*, written just after the First World War, he asserted that the Christian faith is 'dialectical' – a combination of time and eternity, divine

Yes and divine No – in the way Kierkegaard had believed, because it resisted all attempts to tie it down to human reason.[1] Later in his life Barth thought very differently, partly as the result of a study he made of the thought of Anselm of Canterbury. This led him to go back beyond the Enlightenment debate to seek again a conception of faith seeking understanding. Taking this from Anselm, he produced a view of the relation of faith and reason that is both in the tradition of Calvin and yet is distinctively modern.

Like Hegel, Barth appealed to an idea of God's self-revelation, but instead of centring it in rational thought as Hegel had done, he based it on Jesus Christ as he is witnessed to in the Bible. Reason's task is to make the best sense it can of this revelation. God proves his reality (an Anselmian note here) by taking human form in Jesus, and it is rational theology's job to 'think after' this – to seek its inner meaning and to find the best language in which to express it. Against Schleiermacher, Barth held that faith is rational, because in revelation God speaks to us in person, so that theology also is rational so long as it focuses on this centre and on that alone. All rational theology must, for Barth, go through the eye of the needle that is the Bible's witness to God in Jesus Christ. This meant that against nearly all of the modern tradition except Kierkegaard he held that independent philosophical reason has no place in theological method, which must *only* be faith seeking understanding. It is on these grounds that he rejected all natural theologies – theologies based on reason alone – as improper ways to speak about the God of faith. They were irrational, he believed, because they sought elsewhere than the place where God actually made himself known. What he did not reject, however, was the use of philosophical language and concepts in the service of faith, so long as they could be shown to be truly usable in such a way.

In the Anglo-Saxon world the challenge to theological rationality took a rather different form. The philosopher A. J. Ayer claimed in *Language, Truth and Logic* (1936) that the only statements with a claim to have any meaning were those that could be verified by the experience of the senses.[2] Excluded, therefore, from the realm of rational thought were not only philosophical speculation about God and religion, but even ethical thought and the arts, which were relegated to the realm of the emotions. According to Ayer, theology was not just wrong; it was meaningless, irrational. This empiricist challenge to faith dominated discussion after the Second World War, but was superseded by the debate about the theological significance of the philosophy of Ludwig Wittgenstein (1889–1951). The interpretation of Wittgenstein's thought is much disputed, but led philosophers of religion to call attention to the actual language of religion rather than to external proofs of the existence of God or to imposed theories of meaning like those of Ayer. According to this view, each object of thought must be looked at in its own right, and not subjected to some external general theory of meaning. In that respect, Wittgenstein's thought has some similarities to Barth's, for it allows attention to be given to the faith as it is expressed rather than bringing outside considerations to bear on it. In the thought of some interpreters, Wittgenstein's philosophy can lead to a theory of religious reason as faith seeking understanding although others reject such an appeal to it as an evasion of the intellectual challenge.

In more recent times, debates about faith and reason have been dominated by the question of 'foundationalism'. Foundationalism is a way of speaking of the Enlightenment's view of reason and the methods of reason. It holds that only those enterprises which conform to the Enlightenment's view of reason can be held to be rational or intellectually respectable. (The view of Ayer mentioned above is a particularly rigid form, holding as it does that only 'science' narrowly understood, can tell us anything worthy of rational belief.) It is now widely held that foundationalism is false. The impact of its rejection has been twofold. First, it has led some to doubt whether anything at all is rational, or whether all beliefs are simply the results of subjective choices. Second, more 'rational' observers have seen in 'antifoundationalism' the possibility not of abolishing the quest for reason, but of seeking a more flexible notion of what it is to be rational. Instead of subjecting everything to the same kind of test, might it not be more reasonable to seek for the rationality that belongs to things as we find them? In other words, might not all intellectual enquiry be a form of 'faith seeking understanding'? That is the view of the scientist and philosopher, Michael Polanyi (1891–1976), who *as a scientist* appealed to the thought of Augustine in explaining what knowledge is about: 'unless you believe, you will not understand.'[3] On this view, reason is that human capacity, which, while allowing things to be themselves, tries to seek their inner meaning, so as to understand them and bring them to expression.

The history of theology shows that there are many conceptions of faith, many of reason. Reason can mean either a God-like faculty by which the mind is able to apprehend divine truths on its own – a view that in its extreme form in some Enlightenment thinkers makes faith or revelation redundant or dispensable; or, at the other end of the spectrum, it can simply refer to the human capacity to think in an orderly manner. In that sense, all the theologians we have met are concerned to use reason positively. Similarly, faith can mean, first, as it tended to mean for medieval thinkers, an acceptance of the teaching of the church; second, as in more recent times, a form of personal relation to God; and third, a general attitude of confidence in the mean-ingfulness of the world that encourages rational enquiry. Or indeed it can mean some combination of all three. In theology, representatives of all these positions may call reason to their assistance, but what makes Christian theology distinctively the enterprise that it is is its basis in worship, revelation, tradition, or teaching which is affirmed to come from God and not from any innate human capacity or unaided discovery.

III Ancient and modern compared

There are two ways in which we can compare the situation of the ancient theologian with the modern who operates in the university. On the one hand, the situation is similar, in some ways remarkably so. Not only is philosophy neutral, or actively hostile to Christian theology, then as now; but theology operates in a world, like the ancient world, when many different religions are competing for attention and acceptance. University theologians are, like their predecessors, offered the chal-lenge of seeking to outthink the now declining philosophies of the modern world – just as their predecessors sought to outthink the tired world of classical culture. It is an exciting time to study theology, as questions claimed to be closed open up again, and the Christian tra-dition appears once again ready to contribute to the great questions of the day, and perhaps especially questions about the nature of the human person in a world apparently threatened with depersonalizing forces.

The differences from the ancient world, however, are also great. Much modern thought and culture have developed in express oppo-sition to Christian thought and institutions. Christian theologians rep-resent their faith in a world which long claimed to be Christian, but has now for the most part rejected its heritage. In that sense, the challenge is greater, for it is almost as though theologians represent a faith against which the world has been inoculated. Moreover, whatever the parallels, the university is a very different place from the churches in which early theology took shape. There will inevitably be differences where worship, even if it takes place, provides less of a focus for the life of the mind than it did classically. It cannot be pretended that Christian theology can ever be fully comfortable in whatever part of the world it is set, university or other institution. In so far as it orients its life and thought to a man executed on a Roman cross, its standards of success and failure will inevitably differ from those of a world in which worldly success necessarily counts for more – a world where intellectual and economic success and their accompanying 'prestige' are the primary ends in view. To teach or study theology in a modern university is to be in some measure 'different', as Jesus is different from all other human beings.

That, however, can be taken not only as a difficulty but as an opportunity of immense promise. Christian theology offers teacher and student alike the opportunity to study a great tradition of thought and literature which not only continues to open up new insights, but also enables the exploration of questions which bear upon the deepest things of human life: of what it is to be human, to be in need of healing and redemption, to live together in family and society with other human beings and on the earth. From the question of the activity and being of God there open up questions of the meaning of everything else that we are and do.

Notes

1 Karl Barth, *The Epistle to the Romans*, trans. E. C. Hoskyns, Oxford: Oxford University Press 1933.
2 A. J. Ayer. *Language, Truth and Logic*, London: Gollancz 1936.
3 Michael Polanyi, *Personal Knowledge. Towards a Post-Critical Philosophy*, London: Routledge, 2nd edition 1962.

Details of Authors and Sources of Documents

1. Councils and documents

Barmen Declaration (1934) The confessional document of the Confessing Church, which was a union of Lutheran and Reformed Christians in Germany united by their opposition to Hitler. It was later influential in South Africa. Written largely by Karl Barth (q.v.).

Chalcedon, Council of (451) The fourth ecumenical council, brought together to oppose various errant conceptions of how Jesus Christ could be both fully human and fully God. The Chalcedonian definition remains influential in christological discussion, but is now also controversial, with some writers suggesting it must be discarded as merely irrelevant to modern ways of thinking, and others insisting it remains a necessary and useful doctrinal standard.

Confession of Dositheus (1672) [also known as the Synod of Jerusalem, or the Synod of Bethlehem]. Dositheus (1641–1707) became the Orthodox Patriarch of Jerusalem in 1669, and called a synod to oppose moves to align Orthodoxy with the Reformed churches. The resulting confession is mostly written by him, and represents the closest approach of Orthodoxy to Tridentine Catholicism.

Constantinople, Council of (381) The second ecumenical council, which settled the Arian controversy in favour of Nicene (q.v.) orthodoxy. The so-called Nicene creed is traditionally believed to have been written by this council, and remains the central doctrinal standard of the Christian churches.

Genevan Confession (1536) Traditionally ascribed to Calvin, now usually considered to have been written by William Farel. Whoever the author was, this is a representative of the confessions that proliferated around the time of the Reformation and afterwards, as new churches sought to define their continuity with the Christian tradition, and their differences from other groups.

Nicaea, Council of (325) The first ecumenical council, called by the recently-converted Emperor Constantine to decide on the Arian controversy. The council's decision eventually triumphed, but not until after several decades of struggle ended by the Council of Constantinople. The creed promulgated by the council, usually known as the 'Creed of Nicaea' is rarely used today, but is reaffirmed by later ecumenical councils such as Constantinople and Chalcedon.

Thirty-Nine Articles (1563) The doctrinal basis of the Church of England, and of other Anglican provinces. Their history is complicated (although the first definitive text was produced in 1563, it owes much to Cranmer's Forty-Two Articles of 1553, and a final revision took place in 1571). They were intended to establish the Church of England as a Reformed church, occupying a middle position between Roman Catholicism and Anabaptism and other radical movements.

Trent, Council of (1545–63) A council called by the Roman Catholic Church in response to the Reformation, which reaffirmed various Catholic teachings and practices as proper in the face of Reformed objections. It met in three stages over an eighteen year period.

Vatican I (First Vatican Council) (1869–70) A council of the Roman Catholic Church which is famous mainly for defining the infallibility of the pope, when making official pronouncements on matters of faith and morals.

Vatican II (Second Vatican Council) (1962–5) A council of the Roman Catholic Church, famous for its reforming of church practice in various areas (e.g., the saying of mass in languages other than Latin). Theologically, the Council issued two 'dogmatic constitutions', one on the nature of the Church and one on divine revelation. The former has widely been interpreted as being more affirming of other Christian denominations than had previously been the case in official Church pronouncements.

2. Individual writers

Anselm of Canterbury, St (c.1033–1109) b. in Italy, he joined the abbey of Bec (in northern France), and became prior there. He later became Archbishop of Canterbury (England). Key writings include two arguments seeking to prove the existence of God, the *Monologion* and the *Proslogion*, and an important discussion of the atonement, *Cur Deus homo*. An influential collection of prayers and meditations has also circulated under his name, although recent scholarship has questioned the authorship of some of these.

Aquinas, St Thomas (c.1225–74) b. in Italy, he became a Dominican friar and went to Paris to study, dividing the rest of his life between there and Italy. Regarded as the greatest medieval theologian, his work grew out of the need to reconcile the newly recovered philosophy of Aristotle with Christian doctrine. The *Summa contra Gentiles* and the *Summa Theologica* were his major writings, but he produced many others, and was an able commentator on Scripture, Aristotle and other writers. The *Summa Theologica* is without doubt a central theological text.

Athanasius, St (c.296–373) from Alexandria, in Egypt, he accompanied the then patriarch to the Council of Nicaea. Soon afterwards he became patriarch himself. Much of his life was spent defending the Nicene doctrine that the Son, Jesus Christ, is of the same substance (*homoousios*) as the Father, i.e. fully divine. The opposing position, denying the deity of Christ, was known as Arianism, and was very popular, forcing Athanasius to endure five exiles. His key writings are *Contra Gentes* ('Against the Pagans'), *Contra Arianos* ('Against the Arians'), and a *Life of St. Antony*, which became a major text in the rise of monasticism. *Letters concerning the Holy Spirit to Serapion* (*Ad Serapion*) is a late work extending the defence of the true deity of the Son to the Holy Spirit.

Augustine of Hippo, St (354–430) b. in North Africa, his early life was spent in a quest for a satisfying philosophy, through which God led him to Christianity, a journey described powerfully in his spiritual auto-biography, the *Confessions*. He became bishop of Hippo (also in N. Africa), and devoted his great intellect to the pressing theological controversies of the day, writing in defence of the goodness of creation against the Manichees, against the idea that human beings are free to save themselves by good works, as suggested by the Pelagians, and in defence of the reception of repentant sinners back into the church against the Donatists. *On the Trinity* is a profound meditation on the triune nature of God that he worked on for decades before releasing it hastily in an unfinished form because 'pirate' copies were circulating. Arguably the most important theologian of the Western church.

Balthasar, Hans Urs von: see von Balthasar, Hans Urs

Barth, Karl (1886–1968) Swiss-German Reformed theologian. He studied under the great teachers of liberal Christianity in Germany, but was profoundly disillusioned when working as a pastor by the failure of that theology to speak to the needs of his people, and by his former teachers' support for militarism as the First World War began. He found in the Bible a 'strange new world', where God spoke a fundamental challenge to all human efforts and constructions from without. He taught for a time in Germany, before being dismissed for refusing to swear allegiance to Hitler. He was the main author of the Barmen Declaration (q.v.), the doctrinal standard of the Confessing Church, set up to oppose National Socialism. Forced to return to Switzerland, he began writing the *Church Dogmatics*, a massive work that, although unfinished, is undoubtedly one of the major texts of the theological tradition. In it, Barth focused on God's revelation of himself in Jesus Christ and, in conversation with the Scriptures and with writers throughout the Christian tradition, sought to understand what that meant for every reality.

Basil of Caesarea, St ('The Great'; c.330–79) Bishop in what is now Turkey. One of the 'Cappadocian Fathers' (the others were St Gregory of Nazianzus (q.v.) and St Gregory of Nyssa), who developed the doctrine of the Trinity which lay behind the decisions taken at the Council of Constantinople (q.v.), and the Nicene Creed. His works include *On the Holy Spirit*, a defence of the claim that the Spirit is divine, and to be worshipped alongside the Father and Son.

Boff, Leonardo (1938–) and *Boff, Clodovis* (1944–) Brazilian brothers, both significant liberation theologians. Leonardo, who is professor of theology at Petrópolis in Brazil, became famous as a result of the Vatican's objections to his *Church, Charism and Power*. Clodovis is professor of theology at São Paulo; his major work thus far is *Theology and Praxis*.

Bultmann, Rudolf (1884–1976) German New Testament scholar who spent much of his life as professor in Marburg. He used existentialist philosophy to interpret the New Testament, and engaged in a process of 'demythologization', i.e., reinterpreting miraculous elements in existentialist terms. His works include a very significant *Theology of the New Testament*.

Butler, Joseph (1692–1752) Anglican clergyman who served as bishop of Bristol and then Durham. His *Analogy of Religion* is an extremely significant work, offering a very sophisticated defence of natural theology against deism.

Calvin, John (1509–64) b. in France, he was converted to the Reformed cause and spent most of his adult life as pastor in Geneva. His writing centred around two foci: biblical commentaries and the *Institutes of the Christian Religion*, in which he collected thematic and controversial material arising from his commentating into an organized structure. The latter went through several editions, the final and definitive version being published in 1559.

Cassian, John (c.360–435) b. in Scythia, he became a monk, first in Bethlehem. He moved around and finally settled in Marseilles, in the process introducing the Western church to Eastern monasticism. His *Institutes* are a classic of spiritual writing; his *Conferences* record conversations with great monastic leaders.

Clement of Alexandria (c.150–c.215) early head of the famous catechetical school in Alexandria in Egypt (where Origen (q.v.) was later to teach), although he was forced to flee from there by persecution. His *Stromata* and other writings are attempts to relate Christianity to the Alexandrian culture of the day, which was heavily influenced by Greek philosophy.

Coleridge, Samuel Taylor (1772–1834) variously a political revolutionary, leading romantic poet, drug addict, literary commentator and Anglican theologian. His theological views were formed by a reading of earlier English platonist-influenced theology, and by an exploration of the German transcendental philosophy which followed Kant. He saw in the Trinity a way of resolving many of the philosophical problems of the day. His works are often fragmentary, but the *Aids to Reflection* became one of the leading devotional manuals of the Victorian era. The *Confessions of an Enquiring Spirit* was a posthumously published work exploring the doctrine of Scripture.

Cone, James Hal (1938–) American pioneer of black theology, an attempt to take seriously the experiences and spirituality of Black Americans in theological work. Of his many books, *God of the Oppressed* is perhaps the clearest exposition of his method.

D'Costa, Gavin (1958–) Roman Catholic theologian who currently teaches at Bristol university. D'Costa has worked extensively on the relationship of theology to other religious traditions.

Dionysius, (Pseudo-) (c.500) a shadowy Syrian mystic whose works were originally thought to be by Paul's convert in Athens (Acts 17), and so to be possessed of apostolic authority. He combines Christianity with Neoplatonism in an influential synthesis. The *Mystical Theology* describes the ascent of the soul to God.

Duns Scotus, John: see Scotus, John Duns

Ebeling, Gerhard (1912–) a German Lutheran theologian, particularly concerned with mediating the theology of Luther and other Reformers to modernity. His works include a major study of *Luther*, a three-volume *Dogmatics of the Christian Faith*, and *The Word of God and Tradition*, a collection of essays attempting to relate Scripture and Christian tradition.

Edwards, Jonathan (1703–58) American Puritan theologian, famous for his involvement in the Great Awakening (the American equivalent of what in Britain is known as the Evangelical Revival) in the eighteenth century. As a result of his experience of sudden conversions during the revival, he wrote several works analysing religious experience, of which *The Religious Affections* is the most famous. His wider theology was a profoundly creative attempt to hold together the Puritan synthesis in the face of new scientific and theological ideas.

Feuerbach, Ludwig Andreas (1804–72) German philosopher, taught by Hegel. *The Essence of Christianity*, his most influential work, denies the existence of any transcendent God, seeing religion instead as a projection outward of human desires and needs. This idea was extremely influential, not least on Marx (q.v.). Feuerbach thought Christian practice could continue, and was valuable, when understood in these terms, but many who have followed him in his critique have disagreed.

Florovsky, Georges (1893–1979) Russian theologian who taught in France and the USA. He played a significant role in the early years of the ecumenical movement. In his theology he called for, and sought to produce, a 'neo-Patristic synthesis'.

Gilkey, Langdon (1919–) American theologian. His work has involved being attentive to other truth claims (from the natural sciences, philosophy and anthropology) and seeking to 'correlate' theology with them. The piece included here, 'The Uniqueness of Christ', represents a desire to get away from conflicting truth claims and evaluate all religions as attempts to approach the divine, the success of which may be gauged by their morality.

Gregory VII, Pope (b. c.1010; pope 1073–85) Most famous for his confrontations with secular rulers, particularly Emperor Henry IV, through which he established the papacy as the pre-eminent power in Christendom. His letters reveal him as a careful and able politician.

Gregory of Nazianzus, St (c.330–c.389) One of the 'Cappadocian Fathers' (the others were St Basil of Caesarea (q.v.) and St Gregory of Nyssa), who developed the doctrine of the Trinity which lay behind the decisions taken at the Council of Constantinople (q.v.), and the Nicene Creed. Gregory's *Theological Orations* were preached in Constantinople before the Council began, and represent a high-point in theological preaching. At the Council itself, he appears to have been a leading figure.

Herbert, Edward Lord, of Cherbury (1583–1648) English philosopher, and forerunner of deism. In his *De Veritate*, he defended the idea that there is a rational religion available to all humanity comprised of various 'common notions', or truths available to all.

Hilary of Poitiers (c.315–67) French theologian. He supported Athanasius (q.v.) in the Arian disputes and was banished to Phrygia, where he became familiar with Eastern theology, which influenced his writing. *On the Trinity* is his major work.

Hubmaier, Balthasar (c.1480–1528) German anabaptist theologian. Hubmaier trained as a Roman Catholic priest, and held a university teaching appointment for a while, but gradually became influenced by the Reformation. By 1523 he had aligned himself with the Reformers, and by 1525 had moved to anabaptism. One of the few anabaptist leaders with formal theological training, he was martyred by burning in 1528.

Irenaeus, St (c.130–c.200) b. in Asia Minor, where he heard the teaching of Polycarp, who in turn had learnt from the apostle John. He became bishop of Lyons (France), and wrote against the various deviations from the 'rule of faith' that he discovered in his major work, *Against the Heresies*. His theology is marked by the doctrine of recapitulation, whereby Christ became a second head of the human race, undoing the failure of Adam, and by a strongly trinitarian account of divine action, particularly in creation.

Jenson, Robert William (1930–) American Lutheran theologian, heavily involved in defending orthodox trinitarian Christianity against all forms of modern accommodation. His recent two-volume *Systematic Theology* summarizes many of the themes of his earlier work, and seems destined to become a major work of late-twentieth-century English language theology.

John of Damascus, St (c.652–c.750) Greek theologian, perhaps best known for his defence of the use of icons in the iconoclastic controversies. His *Exposition of the Orthodox Faith* is a remarkable piece of systematic theology which in many ways summarizes the patristic Greek tradition, at times quoting more-or-less directly from an earlier writer at length.

John of the Cross, St (1542–91) Spanish mystic and monastic reformer, whose mystical writings remain classics. His account of 'the dark night of the soul', the process by which God strips away all helps from a soul that seeks him, remains influential in spiritual writing. The *Ascent of Mt Carmel* is a verse account of the soul's journey to God.

Jüngel, Eberhard (1934–) German theologian who has been influenced by Barth (q.v.) and Bultmann (q.v.). His work stresses the difference the doctrines of the Trinity and incarnation make to the doctrine of God, and the effect of the doctrine of justification on anthropology. His major work so far is *God as the Mystery of the World*.

Kierkegaard, Søren Aabye (1813–55) Danish philosopher/theologian who opposed Hegel's philosophy and reacted against the formal Christianity of his day to stress the need for a radical personal commitment to Christ. Many of his works were written under various pseudonyms, allowing him to work from within different intellectual positions. The *Philosophical Fragments* are ascribed to the pseudonym Johannes Climacus, who is perhaps best regarded as someone examining the logic of Christian faith from without.

Lessing, Gotthold Ephraim (1729–81) German playwright, literary critic and philosopher, who has been called the 'father of German literature'. He published (anonymously) various fragments of a radically sceptical account of the 'historical Jesus' by Reimarus, which have been seen as the beginning of the 'quest of the historical Jesus'. He believed that truth must be universally accessible, and so opposed any particular, historical revelation. This position was explored in *On the Proof of the Spirit and of Power*, and applied to the gospel narratives in *A New Hypothesis . . . .*

Lindbeck, George Arthur (1923–) American theologian (but born in China) who taught at Yale alongside Hans Frei. He developed a 'postliberal' account of *The Nature of Doctrine*, in which he argues that doctrinal formulations are essentially the grammatical rules that govern the discourse of a particular religious tradition.

Locke, John (1632–1704) English philosopher who was extremely influential in a number of fields (such as the development of the concept of liberal democracy). His major work, *An Essay Concerning Human Understanding*, developed an empiricist account of how human beings come to know things, in which he argues that the mind is a blank sheet, which receives sensory impressions, and formulates relationships between them.

Luther, Martin (1483–1546) German theologian and leader of the Reformation. His theology might be considered to be built on three great slogans: faith alone, Christ alone, Scripture alone. The first demands that human beings are not saved from their sins by any merits they accumulate in the sight of God, but only through faith in Christ. The second insists that there is no other mediator between God and the sinner but Christ, and so denies any mediatory role to the church and its priesthood (or to the saints). The third demands that there is no other source of authority for Christian faith than the Bible, although Luther clearly respected the ancient Christian tradition as being faithful to Scripture.

Marx, Karl Heinrich (1818–83) German Jewish economist and social theorist. He gave an account of the inevitable evolution of human societies towards communism, where all things are held in common by the people. He saw religion as a benign and necessary, but ultimately false, force enabling oppressed people to cope in the less developed social structures.

Newbigin, Lesslie (1909–98) British missionary and theologian. Newbigin served for 35 years as a missionary in India, in the process becoming one of the first bishops of the Church of South India and a leading figure in the World Council of Churches. On returning to Britain, he found, famously, that it had turned into a mission field, and he began writing and working to explore a missionary engagement with Western culture.

Newman, John Henry (1801–90) English theologian who was a major figure in the 'Oxford Movement', an attempt to reposition the Church of England, which had generally understood itself to be Reformed, as in continuity with patristic tradition and resisting the errors of both Roman Catholicism and the Reformation. Newman gradually became more convinced that the need for a continuous tradition could only be met within the Roman Church, and finally converted whilst preparing a work that defended the possibility of doctrinal development in the Christian tradition, his *Essay on the Development of Doctrine*, for the press. He died a cardinal, but was never wholly comfortable within Roman Catholicism.

Nietzsche, Friedrich Wilhelm (1844–1900) German philosopher, who thought that Christianity was no longer tenable and sought to envisage a new philosophy and morality which took seriously the 'death of God'. His greatness perhaps lies in his attempt to recognize just how much of Western thought depends on Christian values and concepts, and to look seriously at what a 'de-Christianized' Europe might be. Old concepts like good and evil must go, and the new world will be forged by the 'superman', pursuing his 'will to power' without any scruple or concern for anyone else. Nietzsche's work came to an end due to insanity in 1889.

Origen (c.185–c.254) Egyptian theologian and exegete. He was head of the catechetical school in Alexandria, but later moved to Caesarea and established a school there as a result of a dispute with his bishop. He was arguably the greatest biblical interpreter of the patristic age, working on textual criticism as well as exegesis. *On First Principles* is a systematic account of the Christian faith, which is perhaps too influenced by aspects of the Greek philosophical tradition, but none-theless intellectually outstanding. Many of his teachings were later condemned as heretical.

Otto, Rudolph (1869–1937) German theologian who developed Schlei-ermacher's (q.v.) account of feeling as the essence of all religious practice. He used the concept of the 'holy' or 'numinous' to describe this essential, and irreducible, religious experience, an account which is developed in his major work, *The Idea of the Holy*.

Owen, John (1616–83) English theologian who supported Cromwell during the Civil War and Protectorate, and was for a time vice-chancellor of the University of Oxford. Increasingly recognized as a profound theologian, he is perhaps the outstanding mind of English Puritanism. His voluminous writings cover many areas.

Pannenberg, Wolfhart (1928–) German theologian who studied under (amongst others) Karl Barth (q.v.). He has attempted to take history more seriously than he believes Barth did, seeing God's revelation as mediated through history, and exploring Christology from a historical perspective. In recent years he has also been interested in the inter-action between theology and other academic disciplines, not least the natural sciences. His three-volume *Systematic Theology* is a major work of late-twentieth-century theology.

Pascal, Blaise (1623–62) French mathematician and theologian who became involved in the theological controversies that affected France in the seventeenth century. His *Pensées* are a collection of notes towards a defence of the rationality of Christianity.

Plantinga, Alvin (1932–) American philosopher who has devoted himself to problems within the philosophy of religion, in particular the problem of evil and the question of whether it is rational ('warranted') to believe in the existence of God.

Prosper of Aquitaine, St (c.390–c.463) French monk who supported Augustine's (q.v.) theories concerning predestination and grace by appealing to the authority of the church, and particularly of the pope.

Pseudo-Dionysius: see Dionysius (Pseudo)

Rahner, Karl (1904–84) German Catholic theologian, influential at the Second Vatican Council (q.v.). Influenced by existentialist philosophy, he sought to explain theological meaning by appealing to transcendental experience that is common to all human beings. His major work is the many-volumed *Theological Investigations*, where most of his essays are collected together. *Foundations of Christian Faith* is a summary of his thought.

Ruether, Rosemary Radford (1936–) American feminist theologian. *Sexism and God-Talk*, perhaps her most significant book so far, is one of the major texts of feminist theology thus far.

Schleiermacher, Friedrich Daniel Ernst (1768–1834) German theologian who sought to defend Reformed orthodoxy in the face of post-Kantian philosophy. His *On Religion: Speeches to its Cultured Despisers* was an attempt to find a place for religious experience, defined as a sense of absolute dependence, within the burgeoning Romanticism of his generation. *The Christian Faith* is a classic of Reformed theology, attempting to explore the whole of doctrine from this understanding of what religion is.

Schwöbel, Christoph (1955–) is currently director of the Ecumenical Institute at the University of Heidelberg, having previously taught in London and held a chair in Kiel.

Scotus, John Duns (c. 1265–1308) Scottish Franciscan theologian who taught in Oxford and Paris. He opposed Thomas Aquinas' (q.v.) attempt to harmonize (Aristotelian) philosophy and theology, instead seeking a different philosophical basis for his doctrines. Perhaps the fundamental theological difference, however, is that whereas Aquinas stressed the intellect as basic, Scotus stressed love and will. One result of this is his belief that Christ would have become incarnate even if there had been no fall, since the incarnation is the primary loving action of God.

Soskice, Janet Martin (1951–) currently lectures in theology and ethics in the University of Cambridge.

Tertullian, Quintus Septimius Florens (c.160–c.220) African theologian. Most of his work was polemical, arguing against various heretical teachings. His argumentative style relies on all the rhetorical tricks of his legal training, and is often both entertaining and overwhelming. He saw the attempt to harmonise Christianity with the best pagan thought of the day, Greek philosophy, as the root of many of the errors that he opposed.

Tillich, Paul (1886–1965) German theologian who was forced to emigrate to America in 1933, and decisively influenced American theology. His 'method of correlation' is an attempt to bring together the present perceived needs of human beings and biblical and theological symbols. His three-volume *Systematic Theology* summarizes his thought.

Torrance, Thomas Forsyth (1913–) Scottish theologian who studied under Barth (q.v.). He has been particularly influential with his discussions of the Trinity, his work on the relationships between theology and science, and his writings on theological method. *Theological Science*, perhaps his best-known work, brings together the latter two themes, arguing that theology and natural science each have their own proper method and are each fully rational.

Townes, Emilie M. (1955–) teaches Christian social ethics in Kansas City. She has written a number of books on womanist theology.

Turretin, François (1623–87) Genevan Reformed pastor and theologian. His *Institutes of Elenctic Theology* are one of the masterpieces of Reformed scholasticism.

Vincent of Lérins (dates unknown; probably died before 450) French monk, who wrote two *Commonitoria* with the aim of exposing and opposing every heresy. Chiefly famous for his definition of catholicity as that which is believed 'everywhere, always, by all people'.

von Balthasar, Hans Urs (1905–88) Swiss Roman Catholic theologian. His major work, appearing in three multi-volume parts (*The Glory of the Lord*, the *Theo-Drama*, and the *Theo-logic*), is a massive, erudite and complex attempt to discuss theology in terms of the three classical transcendentals: the beautiful, the good and the true.

Warfield, Benjamin Breckinridge (1851–1921) American Presbyterian theologian most famous for his writings in defence of Calvinism, and promoting the inerrancy of Scripture in the face of challenges from both critical scholarship and scientific work. His thought on the latter point is considerably more subtle than is often assumed.

Watson, Francis B. (1956–) British New Testament scholar, currently professor in Aberdeen. His work on 'biblical theology' in two significant monographs, *Text, Church and World* and *Text and Truth* offers a theologically informed and philosophically acute account of how the Bible is to be read as Christian Scripture.

Woodhead, Linda (1964–) British theologian, currently teaching in Lancaster. Her major work is on understanding spirituality, particularly Christian, in modern society.

Zizioulas, John D. (1931–) Metropolitan Bishop of Pergamum and Greek Orthodox theologian. Zizioulas has been a significant figure in the ecumenical movement, and has sought in his academic work to uncover and reappropriate the thought-world of the Greek Fathers. His major work so far is perhaps *Being as Communion*.

Timeline

Writers born after 1900 are not included

BC 427–347	Plato
BC 348–322	Aristotle
d.c.165 AD	Justin Martyr
c.130–c.200	Irenaeus, Bishop of Lyons: *Against the Heresies*
c.160–c.220	Tertullian of Carthage
c.150–c.215	Clement of Alexandria
204–70	Plotinus, neoplatonist philosopher
c.185–c.254	Origen of Alexandria: *On First Principles*
c.250–336	Arius of Alexandria
c.296–373	Athanasius of Alexandria
c.315–67	Hilary of Poitiers
325	Council of Nicaea. The divinity of Christ
c.330–79	Basil of Caesarea ⎫
c.330–c.389	Gregory of Nazianzus ⎬ 'Cappadocian Fathers'
c.335–94	Gregory of Nyssa ⎭
354–430	Augustine, Bishop of Hippo, Africa
c.360–435	John Cassian
381	Council of Constantinople. The divinity of the Holy Spirit and the doctrine of the Trinity
c.390–c.463	Prosper of Aquitaine
d. before 450	Vincent of Lérins
451	Council of Chalcedon. The doctrine of the person of Christ.
c.480–524	Boethius, philosopher
c.500	Pseudo-Dionysius

c.652–c.750	John of Damascus
c.1010–85	Pope Gregory VII
c.1033–1109	Anselm, Archbishop of Canterbury: *Cur Deus homo*
c.1095–1160	Peter Lombard: *The Sentences*
c.1225–74	Thomas Aquinas: *Summa Theologica*
c.1265–1308	John Duns Scotus
c.1285–1347	William of Ockham
c.1296–1359	Gregory Palamas, Eastern Orthodox theologian
c.1480–1528	Balthasar Hubmaier
1483–1546	Martin Luther
1509–64	John Calvin
1536	Genevan Confession
1542–91	St John of the Cross
1545–63	Council of Trent
1563	Thirty-Nine Articles
1583–1648	Edward, Lord Herbert of Cherbury
1596–1650	René Descartes, 'Father of modern philosophy' – and of the Enlightenment.
1616–83	John Owen
1623–62	Blaise Pascal
1623–87	François Turretin
1632–1704	John Locke, philosopher
1642–1727	Isaac Newton, scientist and theologian
1672	Confession of Dositheus
1685–1753	George Berkeley, philosopher
1692–1752	Joseph Butler
1694–1768	Hermann Samuel Reimarus
1703–58	Jonathan Edwards
1711–76	David Hume, philosopher
1724–1804	Immanuel Kant, philosopher of the Enlightenment.
1729–81	G. E. Lessing
1768–1834	F. D. E. Schleiermacher: *The Christian Faith* (1821–2)

1770–1831	G. W. F. Hegel, philosopher
1772–1834	Samuel Taylor Coleridge
1801–90	John Henry Newman
1804–72	Ludwig Feuerbach
1813–55	Søren Kierkegaard
1818–83	Karl Marx
1844–1900	Friedrich Nietzsche
1851–1921	B. B. Warfield
1869–70	Vatican I
1869–1937	Rudolph Otto
1884–1976	Rudolf Bultmann
1886–1968	Karl Barth: *Church Dogmatics* (1932–67)
1886–1965	Paul Tillich
1893–1979	Georges Florovsky
1934	Barmen Declaration
1962–5	Vatican II

Glossary of Technical Terms

Note: the list below contains only technical theological terms which appear somewhere in this reader. Some of the writers included use some standard English words with which some readers might not be familiar. For these, we refer readers to standard dictionaries. Also, many of the writers use technical terms for which they offer their own definition. Where these terms are restricted to the single extract in which they are defined, they have not been included in the glossary.

affections: roughly, 'emotions'; those ways in which a person is affected by a moving event or message.

anathema: (Gk: 'accursed thing') a formal pronouncement of the church repudiating certain doctrines and those who hold them. The effect is to remove the person anathematized from the fellowship of the church. Traditionally used at the end of formal definitions of doctrines by councils to make explicit the positions which they intended to reject.

Apocrypha, apocryphal: a Protestant term for twelve Old Testament books regarded as Scripture by the Roman Catholic Church (and declared to be such by the Council of Trent), but not included on the earliest lists (e.g., St Athanasius' *Festal Letter* of 367), and rejected by Protestant churches.

apologetics: (Gk *apologia*: 'defence, reason') the attempt to defend the credibility and truth of the Christian gospel against intellectual challenges. From 1 Pet. 3.15 'be ready to give an *apologia* for the hope that is within you'.

apophatic, apophaticism: (Gk *apophasis*: 'negation') apophatic theology takes as its starting-point the idea that God cannot be described by any human categories, and so suggests that negations are more true of God than affirmations. Thus God is best thought of in negative terms, as immortal, invisible, eternal (usually regarded as the negation of time-bound in this tradition), and so on.

apostles, apostolic: whilst there is some discussion over the various uses of the title 'apostle' in the New Testament, in theology it tends to refer to those (including Paul) who received teaching directly from

Jesus Christ, and were sent by him to teach others. Apostolic doctrine is thus true doctrine, and it is a mark of the Church that it is 'apostolic', i.e., in continuity with the apostles and their teachings.

Arian, Arianism: heresy (q.v.) named after Arius, a presbyter from Alexandria, who was denounced at the Council of Nicaea (q.v.). Arianism flourished after the council and was not finally overcome until the Council of Constantinople (q.v.). The essence of Arianism is the belief that the Son who was incarnate in Jesus Christ is somehow less properly divine than the Father. The great Arian slogan, 'there was [a time] when he was not', placed the origin of the Son in time, in contrast to the eternity of the Father. As with many early heresies, it is not entirely clear what Arius himself thought, but the error that bears his name remains a perennially attractive distortion of Christianity, as it avoids the 'scandal of particularity'.

atonement: the reconciling of the world to God through the work of Jesus Christ.

attributes (of God): see perfections

beatific: (Lt *beatus*: 'blessed') an adjective describing those things that pertain to the life of the blessed in heaven. The 'beatific vision' is the sight of God that is the chief joy and reward of the saints.

canon, canonical: (Gk *kanon*: 'rule, measure') (i) 'Canon' is the general term given to an authoritative decree of a council, as in the 'Canons of the Council of Trent'; (ii) 'Canon' also refers to the collection of authoritative books that make up the Scriptures, and 'canonical' describes a scriptural book.

catechumen, catechumenate: A catechumen is one preparing for baptism and reception into the Christian church, and the catechumenate is the order of catechumens. In the patristic period, it was not uncommon for prospective converts to undergo a prolonged period of instruction and preparation before coming to baptism. It appears that the Lenten period was often used for this purpose, with baptisms taking place at Easter.

catholic: (Gk *kath houlou*: 'according to the whole') originally, the term used to describe the oneness and universality of the Christian church.

In the face of divisions and disputes, it became a test of orthodoxy: that which is generally believed by the whole of the church must be true, and local novelties are false. Often now used as a shorthand for 'Roman Catholic', i.e., pertaining to the Roman Catholic Church, as opposed to any other denomination.

charism, charisma, charismatic: (Gk *charisma*: 'gift') a charism, or a charisma, is a gift of the Holy Spirit given for service in the church. Historically, it has usually been used to describe the particular gifts given at ordination, but in the late twentieth century a far wider meaning became current, which recalls the biblical teaching that the Spirit is at work in all members of the church.

Christology, christological: Christology is the branch of theology that deals with the doctrines of who Christ is and, to a lesser extent, what he does. The central christological question in Christian theology is how to acknowledge that Jesus Christ is both truly divine and truly human, and yet undivided.

church militant and triumphant: the church is composed of all who confess the name of Christ, living and dead. The 'church militant' is that part of the church still engaged in 'warfare' or struggle; i.e., those who are still alive. The 'church triumphant' is that part of the church which has triumphed and received God's reward; i.e., those at rest in heaven.

conscience: an inner witness to the morality or otherwise of actions.

covenant: God's commitment of himself to Israel and to all human beings, particularly involving the forming of divine-human relationships. ('They will be my people and I will be their God.')

deism, deist: deism is the belief that God has no continuing involvement with the world beyond its initial creation. A deist is one who holds to this belief.

dialectic: in ancient and medieval usage, simply the art of logical disputation, of constructing an argument well. In modern usage, it refers more to the union of opposites in some manner, as in Hegel's metaphysical dialectics, where thesis and antithesis combine into a synthesis, or Marx's historical dialectic, where the clash of opposing social forces will inevitably finally result in the coming of communism.

doctor, doctors: a teacher, or the teachers, of the church. As with 'saint', there is a formal list of the doctors of the church, defined by the Vatican, but the term is also used more informally to describe someone a particular writer regards as having fulfilled the role.

dogma, dogmatics: (Gk *dogma*: 'teaching') a dogma is an authoritative teaching of the church (e.g., the dogma of the incarnation), or of a particular church (e.g., the dogma of the immaculate conception). Dogmatics is the study of dogma, differing from 'theology' (if at all) by the particular attention paid to authoritative pronouncements.

doxology: an ascription of glory to God, especially during worship.

ecclesiology: the doctrine of the church.

ecumenical, ecumenism: (Gk *oikoumene*: 'world') 'ecumenical' means 'relating to the whole world of God (i.e., church)'; so an 'ecumenical council' is one summoned from the whole church whose pronouncements are binding on the whole church. In recent years, 'ecumenism' has come to mean 'working for the unification of the church', and ecumenical can also relate to this. There is another, related, recent usage where the union desired is not just of the Christian churches, but of all religions.

elenctic: almost unused now, this seventeenth-century term refers to theology done through the consideration of controversial questions.

Enlightenment, enlightened: the Enlightenment was a movement of thought, centred on the eighteenth century, stressing the authority of human reason over tradition or hierarchy.

enthusiasm: in eighteenth-century usage, equivalent to 'fanaticism'.

episcopate, episcopal: (Gk *episcopos*: 'overseer, bishop') 'episcopal' means 'relating to bishops'; the episcopate is the order of bishops.

epistemology: the theory of knowledge.

eschaton, eschatology, eschatological: the 'eschaton' is the end of the world; hence 'eschatology' is the doctrine of the last things – the return of Christ, and so on.

Eucharist: standard theological term for the sacrament variously referred to as holy communion, mass, or the Lord's Supper.

exegesis, exegetical: 'exegesis' is interpretation, usually of Scripture.

foundationalism: an epistemological (q.v.) theory, whereby all knowledge rests upon certain indubitable foundations.

fundamentalism, fundamentalist: originally refers to a commitment to a conservative protestant position on certain disputed questions as spelled out in a series of pamphlets, *The Fundamentals*. It has come to refer to various religious positions characterized by intolerance, anti-intellectualism and conservatism.

generation: a term referring to the relationship of origin of the Son to the Father within the Trinity. Also 'eternal generation'.

glorification: the final perfecting of Christians, usually assumed to occur at the resurrection.

Gnostic, Gnosticism: (Gk *gnosis*: 'knowledge') originally a collection of early quasi-Christian sects that all stressed the need to possess hidden knowledge which only they could reveal. Used more generally in theology of any system which demands elite knowledge, in place of the publicly-declared gospel of what God has done in Christ.

gospel: the good news of what God has done in Jesus Christ, particularly the forgiveness of sins in his death and resurrection.

heresy, heretic: technical terms referring to teachings, and to those who hold to them, which superficially appear to be theologically acceptable, but which have been judged by a church council to be seriously erroneous.

hermeneutics: the study of methods of interpretation.

historical-critical method: an exegetical method which has enjoyed considerable popularity in academic work over the past two centuries.

It asserts that the meaning of a text is the meaning it had in its original historical setting.

icon: a picture, generally of Christ or a saint, painted according to strict rules, which is used as an aid to prayer in Eastern Orthodox churches. In Orthodox theology, icons are understood to be quasi-sacramental.

idol, idolatry: originally a physical object worshipped as a god; used for anything that is worshipped in place of God. Idolatry is the worship of idols.

image of God: that which sets human beings apart from all other animals (see Gen. 1.27–28); there is considerable debate in Christian theology as to what the image of God is.

imago Dei: Lt for 'image of God', q.v.

incarnation: the event of God the Son becoming a human being, the Jewish man Jesus Christ.

justification, justify: to 'justify' is to declare or make righteous; justification is the declaring or making righteous of sinners by the life, death and resurrection of Jesus Christ.

kerygma: (Gk *keryx*: 'herald, preacher') that which is preached; the gospel.

liberal, liberalism: describing a school of nineteenth- and twentieth-century theology which is positive about natural human abilities and sceptical about central Christian miracles (variously, the virgin birth, the resurrection, the incarnation). Liberal theology tends to accept the central positions of the Enlightenment (q.v.).

liturgy, liturgical: 'liturgy' is generally the public worship of God; more specifically it refers to authorized texts for use in worship.

Logos: (Gk: 'word') God the Son, who became incarnate in Jesus Christ (see John 1: 'In the beginning was the Logos, and the Logos was with God, and the Logos was God . . . and the Logos became flesh, and pitched his tent among us.')

magisterium: the official body of the Roman Catholic Church which has authority to define doctrines.

modern, modernist: 'modern' may mean: (i) recent, up-to-date; (ii) relating to a philosophical position deriving from the Enlightenment (q.v.), and committed to foundationalism (q.v.); (iii) relating to a nineteenth-century Roman Catholic theological school holding to similar tenets to liberalism (q.v.).

monotheism: belief in one God.

mystic, mysticism: 'mysticism' refers to a group of religious practices which assume the possibility of direct experience of God, and strive for this experience. A mystic is one who has attained this.

natural theology: theology derived from reasoning about the natural world, without any reference to miracle or revelation.

œcumenical: *see* ecumenical

ontology, ontological: (relating to) the study of being or reality.

pagan: (in theological usage) someone who is not a Christian believer.

pantheism: the teaching that the world is God.

passion: (in theological usage) the opposite of 'action'; 'being done to' (compare 'passive'). Hence, suffering.

patristic: relating to the period of the Church Fathers, c. AD 100–700.

perfections (or 'attributes') of God: descriptions (partial, but accurate) of God, words that adequately complete the sentence 'God is . . .' e.g., good, loving, eternal, omniscient.

piety: Christian commitment and practice. A wholly positive word in the writers represented here.

pontiff: pope.

postmodern: [see chapter III.1]

prolegomena: lit. 'words that come before'; those things that must be said before a discussion can be embarked upon to establish the validity of that discussion.

providence: God's action in sustaining and directing the world he has created. Often used as a circumlocution for 'God' – 'providence has decreed that . . .'.

rationalism: world-view based on reason alone, usually in opposition to all religious belief (and certainly to all ideas of revelation, or of authoritative tradition). Most Christian theologians, however, would claim that true rationality demands belief in God.

Reformation, Reformers: the movement, and its leaders, in the sixteenth century dedicated to restoring the (Western) church to purity, by purging it of certain basic errors. Although it appears that most early Reformers, at any rate, genuinely set out to reform the Roman Catholic Church, not to split from it, the result was the founding of a number of new Christian denominations.

religious: apart from the standard English usage, 'religious' is used as a noun to describe people committed to a monastic lifestyle – monks, nuns, hermits, etc.

sacrament, sacramental: certain rites of the church are defined as sacraments (in Reformed churches, usually only two: baptism and the eucharist; in Roman Catholicism there are traditionally seven, the additional five being: confirmation; holy matrimony; confession and penance; ordination and extreme unction ('the last rites')). The definition varies, but almost always includes a physical sign (water, bread and wine) and a scriptural command and promise linking that sign with God's action. The concept of sacrament, i.e., divine usage of physical realities, has encouraged many theologians to talk about other realities as 'sacramental' – not actual sacraments, but still caught up in that gracing of the created order of which the sacraments are the central signs.

saint: has two distinct theological usages. The more familiar use describes someone whose life has been declared to be of exemplary holiness by an appropriate authority, and who can act as an intercessor for us (St Mary Magdalene; St Augustine; St Thomas Aquinas). This usage is standard in more Catholic churches. The Protestant reaction to this was to insist that all Christians are declared holy by God through Christ's sacrifice (*see* 'justification'), and so to use 'saints' to mean all Christian believers.

scholastic, scholasticism: properly refer simply to 'school' theology, i.e., theology done predominantly and consciously within a particular tradition, devoted to exploring that tradition in detail. Unqualified, these terms refer to the medieval theological tradition exemplified by St Thomas Aquinas; it is becoming increasingly common to talk of 'Protestant scholasticism' in the seventeenth century, recognizing that the work of (e.g.) François Turretin is similar in method, if different in content, to the medieval tradition.

science: carries at least three different senses in the extracts in this reader: (i) the standard English sense, meaning 'natural science', the investigation of the natural world by observation and mathematical approximation; (ii) a medieval sense where 'science' is used to translate Lt *scientia*, which is formally defined as any subject which proceeds by deduction from first principles, and so is exemplified by philosophy (or theology, the 'queen of the sciences' in this sense); (iii) 'science' as a translation of the German *Wissenschaft*, a term which encompasses all traditional university subjects and is perhaps best described as a properly theorized body of knowledge, i.e., one that is attentive to questions of its own validity and status.

secular: non-religious.

simple, simplicity: simplicity is a perfection (q.v.) of God which denies any composition in his essence. Although questioned or discarded in much modern theology, traditionally it is important in insisting that God's love is not something different from his justice, for instance.

sin: a sin is an act contrary to God's law. Sin (or 'original sin') is the vitiation of human nature which means that we are unable to act in ways that are not sinful.

Socinian: one who denies the deity of Christ. Distinguished from Arian and unitarian largely by historical context: Arianism describes the patristic heresy, Socinianism the European Reformation resurgence, and unitarianism the largely British and American enlightened (q.v.) form of the same belief.

theism, theist: the belief that God remains active in the world; one who holds that belief (compare deism, q.v.). Sometimes used to describe the underlying philosophical unity of monotheistic religion (especially Judaism, Christianity and Islam), although this usage is controversial.

theologoumena: a theological statement.

transcend, transcendent: That which is transcendent is beyond the normal realm of experience in some way.

Trinity, trinitarian: the central Christian belief that God is one God existing in three persons, Father, Son and Holy Spirit.

type: typology is a method of exegesis of the Old Testament by which Old Testament events and characters are read as shadowy prefigurements of the coming of Christ. It is based on biblical examples (Noah's escape from the flood as a type of baptism, for instance).